The
Plays of
Christopher
Marlowe

The
Plays of
Christopher
Marlowe

THE
PLAYS OF
CHRISTOPHER
MARLOWE

edited by Leo Kirschbaum

Meridian Books

THE WORLD PUBLISHING COMPANY

Cleveland and New York

LEO KIRSCHBAUM

Leo Kirschbaum was born in Detroit on November 10, 1907. He took his B.A., M.A., and Ph.D. degrees at the University of Michigan, where he also won two major Hopwood prizes. Mr. Kirschbaum is Professor of English at Wayne State University and is widely acknowledged as a leading authority on Elizabethan literature. He is the author of numerous articles and essays, three books—*The True Text of "King Lear," Shakespeare and the Stationers,* and *Clear Writing*—and is the editor of *Edmund Spenser: Selected Poetry.*

AN ORIGINAL MERIDIAN BOOK

Published by The World Publishing Company
2231 West 110 Street, Cleveland 2, Ohio

Published simultaneously in Canada by
Nelson, Foster & Scott Ltd.

First printing April 1962

Library of Congress Catalog Card Number: 61-15746
Printed in the United States of America   CP462

This book is for Aaron Asher, Dr. James W. Johnson, and Dr. Jacques S. Gottlieb.

CONTENTS

PREFACE   7

INTRODUCTION   11

    The Life of Marlowe   11
    Facts   12
    Sequence of Composition   14
    Preliminary Considerations   15
    The Elizabethan Theater   18
    The English Theater Before Marlowe   22
    The Two Machiavellis   24
    Marlowe and Comedy   27
    1 and *2 Tamburlaine*   28
    1 Tamburlaine   35
    2 Tamburlaine   53
    The Elizabethan English History Play   66
    Edward II and Holinshed   71
    Edward II   73
    Doctor Faustus and Its Source   101
    Religious Values in *Doctor Faustus*   101
    Comedy in *Doctor Faustus*   114
    Production of *Doctor Faustus*   122
    The Jew of Malta   130

1 TAMBURLAINE   157

2 TAMBURLAINE   215

EDWARD II   275

DOCTOR FAUSTUS   343

THE JEW OF MALTA   397

TEXTUAL NOTES AND ACT-SCENE COMPARISONS   457

GLOSSARY   469

CONTENTS

PREFACE 7

INTRODUCTION 11

The Life of Marlowe 11
Facts 12
Sequence of Composition 14
Preliminary Considerations 16
The Elizabethan Theater 18
The Earliest Theater-Scene Dialogue 22
The Two Machiavellis 24
Marlowe and Comedy 27
1 and 2 Tamburlaine 29
1 Tamburlaine 31
2 Tamburlaine 33
The Elizabethan English History Play 60
Edward II and Holinshed 71
Edward II 79
Doctor Faustus and Its Source 101
Religious Values in Doctor Faustus 101
Comedy in Doctor Faustus 114
Production of Doctor Faustus 120
The Jew of Malta 130

1 TAMBURLAINE 137

2 TAMBURLAINE 215

EDWARD II 275

DOCTOR FAUSTUS 319

THE JEW OF MALTA 407

TEXTUAL NOTES AND ACT-SCENE COMPARISONS 457
GLOSSARY 480

PREFACE

The last one-volume scholarly edition of the works of Christopher Marlowe was issued a half-century ago in 1910. Since then we have learned much about the integrity of the original Marlowe play editions, but it still can be said, without too much obeisant apology, that even today among scholars and editors the prevalent textual attitude toward the five major plays—*1* and *2 Tamburlaine, The Jew of Malta, Doctor Faustus*, and *Edward II*—is, outside of *Edward II*, one of strong suspicion. I hope the present edition, because of my remarks in the Introduction and Textual Notes, will at last release student and reader from the pressure of erroneous authority, that they will accept my conclusions that for all five major plays we are very fortunate to possess the texts as very close to what Marlowe wrote. The disintegrators of *Doctor Faustus, Tamburlaine*, and *The Jew of Malta*, are, in short, wrong. The text of *Doctor Faustus* which I present should, I believe, be considered both new and authentic.

No one who puts out an edition of Marlowe's dramas can avoid paying his respects to the editions published in the early 1930's under the general editorship of R. H. Case: *Tamburlaine the Great in Two Parts*, ed. U. M. Ellis-Fermor (1930); *Edward II*, ed. H. B. Charlton and R. D. Waller (1933; rev. F. N. Lees, 1955); *The Tragical History of Doctor Faustus*, ed. F. S. Boas (1932); and *The Jew of Malta*, ed. H. S. Bennett (1931).

My texts of the plays are extremely conservative, following

the original first editions closely. For *1* and *2 Tamburlaine*
(1590) and *The Jew of Malta* (1633), I have permission to
use photostats supplied by the Henry E. Huntington Library.
For *Edward II*, I have employed the Malone Society reprint
of the 1594 first edition, prepared under the direction of W. W.
Greg. For *Doctor Faustus*, I have used the reprints of the
1604 and 1616 texts in W. W. Greg (ed.), *Marlowe's Doctor
Faustus, 1604-1616* (Oxford, 1950).

My texts follow Elizabethan usage in not indicating place
before each scene. This is an eighteenth-century innovation,
and can radically disturb our correct conception of the freedom
of the Elizabethan stage, where location is frequently vague,
where the platform stage can at one moment represent *inside
a city's walls,* and the next *outside a city's walls.* Furthermore,
I have been very careful about meter concerning suffixes, as
Marlowe himself was, and as his printers were. When the vowel
of the preterite or past participle is to be pronounced, the spelling is *ed* (e.g., sufficed); when it is not to be pronounced, the
spelling is apostrophe plus *d* (e.g., suffic'd). The general spelling is American rather than British—and hence closer to Elizabethan usage! The line numbering and, frequently, scene division are new. I have employed parentheses to set off asides. It
might be maintained that it is just as important to supply il-
luminating stage directions as it is to get a reading right. Nevertheless, in the following texts my great reliance is on the
original directions themselves. When these are absent, and gross
obscurity is not involved, I allow the action to explain itself,
even when properties are indicated.

For all corrections of the wrong character in speech prefixes
and directions (and in *Doctor Faustus* for all additions from
the 1604 text), pointed brackets are used. For all other corrections, additions, or changes in prefixes, texts, and stage directions, square brackets are employed. Most changes in prefixes
derive from the desire to print the given instead of the geographical name: e.g., [*Orcanes*] for *Natolia,* or the specific instead of the generic name: e.g., [*Bellamira*] for *Courtesan.* In
Edward II, Edmund and *Kent* alternate for the same person
in prefixes and directions; I invariably use the latter for prefixes. There is a similar variation of *Clown* and *Robin* in *Doctor
Faustus;* I use *Robin.*

The Glossary must not be understood as giving *all* the meanings of the defined word—only Elizabethan meanings, when
they are different from ours, or somewhat rare meanings. For
example, *glorious* is glossed as "boastful" (i.e., vainglorious);
its usual modern meanings are omitted. Similarly, words whose
meanings are the same today are **not** included.

Marlowe's geography in the two parts of *Tamburlaine* deserves special notice. As Miss Ethel Seaton showed in "Marlowe's Map," *Essays and Studies by Members of the English Association*, X (1924), Marlowe follows Ortelius' maps closely in the latter's *Theatrum Orbis Terrarum* (1584). In other words, instead of being careless, the playwright was careful. Still, we must realize that Ortelius' knowledge is largely mythical on Africa and Asia, and that Marlowe, somewhat like Milton, is often more interested in an impressionistic effect than he is in precise pointing. I might add that I have received help from another Ortelius volume seemingly unknown to Marlowe scholars: *Synonymia Geographica* (Antwerp, 1578).

I want to add a gentle warning. In some ways, Marlowe's English is closer to Chaucer's than it is to ours. He very often, for example, employs the etymological meanings of words. But more than this, his syntax is often quite grammatically incoherent: and this is due to his refusal to observe subordination—to his customary practice of letting rhetoric rather than grammar dictate what he wants to say. Meaning to Marlowe, in other words, is always paramount to syntax.

My title, perhaps, requires an apology, for two of Marlowe's plays are not included in this volume: (1) *The Tragedie of Dido, Written by Christopher Marlowe and Thomas Nash*, 1594, omitted because Marlowe's share is not clear; and (2) *The Massacre at Paris, Written by Christopher Marlowe*, n.d., omitted because the text is extremely corrupt.

LEO KIRSCHBAUM

December 1961
Wayne State University
Detroit, Michigan

INTRODUCTION

The Life of Marlowe

Christopher Marlowe, poet and playwright, was born in February 1564 in Canterbury. He attended the King's School of the cathedral in 1579 and 1580. In the latter year, at the age of sixteen, he became the recipient of one of Archbishop Parker's scholarships at Corpus Christi, Cambridge, receiving his B.A. in 1584 and his M.A. in 1587. The Privy Council ordered the university to grant him this second degree. He had done some service for the government—what, we do not know. On September 18, 1589, in London, he began a duel with a William Bradley, but Thomas Watson finished it, killing Bradley. Both Watson and Marlowe were eventually released from prison. On May 9, 1592, Constable Nicholls of Shoreditch and Sub-Constable Helliott complained to Sir Owen Hopton, Lieutenant of the Tower, that Marlowe should be bound over to keep the peace. About this time the playwright was sharing a room with Thomas Kyd, author of *The Spanish Tragedy*. There is evidence that at some time in 1593 Marlowe was staying in Scadbury, Kent, at the country house of Thomas Walsingham. In May 1593, two weeks before Marlowe was stabbed to death, the Privy Council ordered him to be brought before them, and he made an appearance. On May 30, 1593, he was killed in a tavern at Deptford by Ingram Frizer. On May 13 Kyd had been arrested, and subsequently claimed that heretical papers found in his room were not his but Marlowe's. (Actually, they had been copied from a book that had appeared in 1549, *The Fall of the Late Arian.*) And around the same time, a Richard Baines made a written accusation of atheism, blasphemy, etc., against our playwright.

Indeed, this is all that contemporary documents yield concerning Christopher Marlowe. All the rest is surmise and interpretation. Assertions about his noble friends, about *their* opinions which he shared, about the poet's temperament, are sheer speculation. Whether he really believed the opinions attributed to him by Kyd and Baines or deliberately set himself to shock others is a query not easy to dismiss. Constant identification of the playwright with his main characters represents, probably, the worst and most continuous example of the so-called personal heresy in English literature. This book will say no more about Marlowe the man. Nor will it concern the translator of Ovid's love poetry and the composer of the unfinished *Hero and Leander.* It will confine itself solely to the playwright, and only to the plays which he wrote alone and and of which "good" texts survive.

Facts

I now give the barest facts concerning the sources, the production, and the printing of the five plays with which this introduction deals. Those who want further scholarly information should consult the section on the dramatist in Volume III of E. K. Chambers, *The Elizabethan Stage* (Oxford, 1923) and the individual prefaces to *The Works of Christopher Marlowe,* under the general editorship of R. H. Case (New York, 1930-3).

1 and *2 Tamburlaine* were entered in the Stationers' Register on August 14, 1590, by their publisher, Richard Jones. They came out the same year. Although Marlowe's name did not appear on the title page, there has never been any question about his authorship. It is probable that Part One was first produced in 1588, possibly not in a regular theater but in an inn-yard. That Marlowe initially wrote the main part for Edward Alleyn seems dubious, but the latter played it subsequently.[1] The Admiral's men produced the First Part on August 30, 1594. It was given fifteen times from that date to

---

[1] Alleyn seems not to have joined the Admiral's company until the winter of 1589: G. L. Hosking, *The Life and Times of Edward Alleyn* (London, 1952), p. 28. But Heywood's *The Prologue to the Stage, At The Cock-Pit* in the 1633 *The Jew of Malta* appears to claim Alleyn as the original actor of the name part in *Tamburlaine.*

November 12, 1595, and the Second Part seven times from
December 19, 1594, to November 13, 1595. "Tamburlaine's
cage, bridle, coat, and breeches were included in the inventories
of the Admiral's men in 1598. . . ." [2] For information on the
great Scythian's career, the dramatist's chief source was
Fortescue's translation, *The Forest* (1571), based on Pedro
Mexia's *Silva*. Nevertheless, Marlowe cast his net wide,
finding as much as he could about his protagonist in various
literary and historical nooks and crannies. Futhermore, for
Part Two he even used a work that was still in manuscript,
Paul Ive's *Practise of Fortification*. The playwright's geography
in both parts is largely as mythical as his classical references,
though it is based definitely on Ortelius' atlas.[3] It is great
fun to trace the campaigns of Parts One and Two on these
maps, but the regions were still more or less completely
unknown territory. To take Marlowe's place-naming and
descriptions seriously, as in any sense "correct" in the modern
sense, is to nominate oneself an academic fool.

It is now generally held that *Doctor Faustus* must have been
written after the appearance in print of *The English Faust-
Book* (1592). The Admiral's men played it twenty-four times
from October 2, 1594, to October 1597. Their 1598 inventory
included "j dragon in fostes." [4] The part of the magician seems
to have been played by Alleyn.[5] For the black magic in the
play, see R. H. West, *The Invisible World: A Study of
Pneumatology in Elizabethan Drama* (University of Georgia
Press, 1939). As a preparative for the play it would not be a
bad idea to look at the various accounts of witches and their
activities in G. T. Matthews (ed.), *News and Rumor in
Renaissance Europe: The Fugger News Letters* (Capricorn
Books, New York, 1959).

Although first entered in 1594 in the Stationers' Register,
The Jew of Malta was not printed until 1633. The 1598 inven-
tory of the Admiral's men included "j cauderm for the
Jewe." [6] Again, Alleyn played the main part.[7] The sources of

[2] *Elizabethan Stage,* III, 422.
[3] Ethel Seaton, "Marlowe's Map," *Essays and Studies by Members
of the English Association,* X (1924), 13-35.
[4] *Elizabethan Stage,* III, 423.
[5] "The gull gets on a surplis/With a crosse upon his breast,/Like
Allen playing Faustus,/In that manner he was drest." S. Rowland,
Knave of Clubs (1609); quoted ibid., II, 297.
[6] Ibid., III, 425.
[7] See note 1 above: Heywood indicates both Barabas and Tamburlaine as Alleyn parts.

The Jew of Malta are popular folklore plus the pseudo-Machiavelli of Gentillet and others. Most of the lineaments of Barabas will be found ready-made in Malcolm Hay, *Europe and the Jews: The Pressure of Christendom on the People of Israel for 1900 Years* (Boston, 1960).[8] Harold Fisch's small book, *The Dual Image* (London, 1959), is a succinct but fresh account of the Jew in English literature. The connection of Barabas with the Vice (or Devil) of medieval mystery and morality plays has been comprehensively treated in Bernard Spivack, *Shakespeare and the Allegory of Evil* (Columbia University Press, 1958). For the old savagely serious farce predating Marlowe, see an extremely fine account in the late A. P. Rossiter's *English Drama from Early Times to the Elizabethans: Its Background, Origins and Developments* (London, 1958).

There apparently was a lost 1593 edition of *Edward II;* the earliest we possess is dated the next year. Its title page indicates performance by Pembroke's men, who may or may not have been an offshoot of the Admiral's company. Its source was the 1587 edition of Holinshed's *Chronicle.*

Sequence of Composition

We surmise that *Tamburlaine* was the first of Marlowe's *popular* plays. But as to the sequence of the other dramas, there is no clear-cut evidence. And so-called internal evidence can be very tricky. Once we grant that Marlowe experimented, then it is very difficult to discover the order of composition, after 1590, of *Doctor Faustus, Edward II,* and *The Jew of Malta.* This is an academic problem anyhow, and I only bring it up to suggest that *The Jew of Malta* in many ways is Marlowe's most theatrically mature play. In *Tamburlaine,* in *Edward II,* and in *Doctor Faustus* we find a recurrent phenomenon of Marlovian drama: a situation or a scene that is very little different, if only in emotional effect or impression, from one that has occurred before. In *The Jew of Malta,* on the contrary, there is progressive novelty in the various scenes. We are constantly being entertained with variety of action and emotion. Furthermore, the artisanship that went into the articulation of the plot seems, on the whole, far superior to that of the three plays just named. In *Edward II* and in *Tamburlaine* one scene

---

[8] The Jew as he *actually* existed in Marlowe's day, not as he *presumably* existed according to anti-Semitic accounts, is well described in Cecil Roth, *The Jews in the Renaissance* (Philadelphia, 1959).

follows another, by and large, in rigid succession. In *Doctor Faustus* one begins to see the technique of a mixed scene—i.e., more than a single element of the plot appears. But in *The Jew of Malta* Marlowe begins to be able to handle a dramatic design which for the individual scene is complex rather than simply additive or simply contrasting. Furthermore, what was so omnipresent in *Tamburlaine* and is perhaps still too discernible in *Edward II*, the long declamatory speech, begins to vanish in *The Jew*. It had already begun to disappear in *Doctor Faustus* in the impetuosity of the dialogue and the action. As a matter of fact, what is found at the beginning of *The Jew of Malta*, the poetic long declamation, which so clearly relates to the previous Marlowe in its lyricism and stasis, is not so much evidence that Marlowe wrote the first part of the play and that somebody else wrote the last: it is evidence rather that the fulfillment of Marlowe's playwriting ability does not appear until the plot hurls Barabas into the actions of restitution, self-protection, and revenge. Thus, what has always been taken as Marlowe's decline is, on the contrary, evidence of his successful progress beyond self-imitation, his invasion of new theatrical territories—experimental progression that undoubtedly was cut short by his untimely death. To trace the working out of the plot of *The Jew of Malta* is to become shocked at the critics' inability to appreciate the progress which Marlowe was able to achieve in the drama in the short time of five years. I want later to exhibit that progress in *The Jew of Malta*. As in my discussions of all the plays except *Doctor Faustus*, I mingle literary discussion with matters of production, etc. This is especially advisable, I believe, in *The Jew*, where costume and make-up, for example, are so inseparable from motive.

Preliminary Considerations

Every history of English drama considers Christopher Marlowe not merely as one of the most formidable of Shakespeare's contemporaries but also as one of the truly great figures of English literature. But much of what has been written about Marlowe as a dramatist is shamefully incomplete and inept. These are strong words, but the critical situation demands them. The main causes of this bad state of criticism are three:

(1) The scholars and critics have not even been sure what the dramatist wrote. There are extant two texts of *Doctor Faustus*, and until recently the good text has been discarded and the bad one reprinted and studied in all anthologies. There is still not one anthology of Elizabethan drama for students

and general readers that contains the only text of *Doctor Faustus* upon which any correct critical opinion can be based. And, as I indicate in my appendix on the texts of the plays, even the modern discovery of the right version of *Doctor Faustus* has led not to clarification but to further unnecessary confusion. A similar state of imperception exists in regard to three others of the five plays with "good" texts which are extant—*Tamburlaine* and *The Jew of Malta*. The first printer of the two parts of *Tamburlaine* claimed that he had "left out some fond and frivolous gestures," with the result that now editorial opinion has refused to believe that what we have in *1* and *2 Tamburlaine* is *all* Marlowe's. An even worse state of affairs exists in regard to *The Jew of Malta*. It would be hard to find one critic today who believes that the play as it stands is the play as it left the dramatist's hands. The consensus of critical opinion is that *The Jew of Malta* is some kind of ruin, Marlowe's hand being clear only in the first two acts. Thus, for four out of the five Marlowe plays on which his reputation rests, greater or less confusion as to what exactly he wrote predominates. (I omit from consideration here *The Tragedy of Dido*, which the original title page attributes to the double authorship of Marlowe and Nashe.) The dramatist has been even more unlucky than this, for a sixth play by him, *The Massacre at Paris*, exists in print only in an extremely corrupt version, in what is called a *bad quarto* or *memorial* reconstruction; one short passage of the play as Marlowe composed it is fortunately, for the sake of comparison, extant in manuscript.[9]

(2) All kinds of a priori notions have constantly misled critics for one hundred and fifty years, critics who instead of writing with fresh investigation and without bias have been content mostly to follow one another in a procession of blindness and prejudice. They assert, either implicitly or explicitly, that Marlowe never wrote humorous scenes, that Marlowe had only one grand style that he applied to all his plays without change, that he had no constant urge to try new kinds of drama different from the ones he had written, and that the difference

---

[9] The reader thinks, perhaps, that I am flogging dead horses in this paragraph? Not so. The most widely used anthology of Elizabethan plays in American colleges prints the wrong version of *Doctor Faustus* and has this in its short preface: "*Dr. Faustus* and *The Jew of Malta* have come down to us in forms worse than the mutilated statues of antiquity, for they have been debased by the adapter's hand. Yet, mangled as they are, they are mangled masterpieces." The same edition declares later on that the prose comic scenes in *1 Tamburlaine* are probably either not by Marlowe or are actors' insertions.

between the early Marlowe and the late Marlowe is not almost as great as the difference between the early Shakespeare and the late Shakespeare.

(3) Today we term the interpretation of literature by biography the *personal heresy*. We should be thankful that no longer do the mass of critics decipher Shakespeare's life by means of his plays and vice versa. Unfortunately, the personal heresy still affects almost every critique of Christopher Marlowe, the dramatist. On the basis of extremely limited documentary evidence concerning the poet's life, the protagonists of Marlowe's plays have been supposed to be speakers of Marlowe's own deepest desires and opinions. For example, the main character of perhaps Marlowe's most famous play, *Doctor Faustus*, has been utterly misconstrued because he has been carelessly studied in terms of a romantic concept of Marlowe himself.

So far I have been more or less negative in indicating what must and should be done if Christopher Marlowe, the dramatist, is to be truly understood and appreciated. I relegate to an appendix textual discussions, merely asserting here that there is little reason to be dubious concerning the extant text of both parts of *Tamburlaine*, the true version of *Doctor Faustus*, the extant text of *Edward II*—which by some luck has escaped the ministrations of the disintegrators—and the extant text of *The Jew of Malta*. With the vexing textual problems out of the way, a fair consideration of Marlowe's dramatic abilities can begin. As for the problem of preconceptions, I insist that we must begin anew, looking at the plays freshly. We then shall be able to see the various facets of Marlowe's genius, whether they be in play construction,[10] characterization, verse, or the other elements of drama. Free of the bias of past criticism, we shall be able to see Marlowe as an inveterate, constant, momentous innovator and experimenter. As for the reading of Marlowe's drama in terms of his own supposed character, I shall escape the problem by refusing to recognize its validity. Let him who wishes find interconnections between Tamburlaine, Doctor Faustus, Barabas, and Edward II, *and* the man who died at Deptford from the dagger of Ingram Frizer. I shall consider the plays in themselves com-

---

[10] An early appreciator of Marlowe's theatrical architectural ability was G. P. Baker, "Dramatic Technique in Marlowe," *Essays and Studies by Members of the English Association*, IV (1913), 172-82. But Baker deals only with the two parts of *Tamburlaine* and *Edward II*. The state of scholarship disenabled him, obviously, from concerning himself with *The Jew of Malta* and *Doctor Faustus*.

pletely apart from Marlowe's supposed spiritual biography.
I shall consider the plays one by one as fully as I can in terms
of their impact on audiences of the early 1590's and also in
terms of their perennial literary worth. But before such
criticism can begin there must be some understanding of the
kind of theater for which the dramatist wrote.

The Elizabethan Theater

Despite a recent loosening of the chains of naturalistic drama,
too many readers, critics, and playgoers still think of the
theater as a place where actual life should be mirrored.[11] This
is unfortunate, for the average audience is quite able, automatically, to accept the conventions of nonnaturalistic drama,
i.e., poetic drama. We have seen that spectators of Thornton
Wilder's *Our Town* do not require sets and properties; that
they can understand and appreciate verse in T. S. Eliot's
Murder in the Cathedral and Christopher Fry's *Venus Observed;* that with no objection they accept the devices of
soliloquy, aside, and direct address to the audience in such
plays as *The Glass Menagerie, Strange Interlude,* and *J.B.*
Also visitors to Antioch, Ohio, and Stratford, Ontario, have
no difficulty in accepting a Shakespeare play more or less as
it was presented in his own day, with few concessions to
realism. The late drama critic of *The New Yorker,* Wolcott
Gibbs, was perverse whenever he reviewed a Shakespeare production, refusing to employ any but realistic criteria, but the
average audience will view a Shakespeare, a Molière, or a
Goldoni drama on a bare stage of a theater-in-the-round with
understanding and delight, accepting spontaneously stock characters, absence of sets, blank verse, and the other conventions
of a nonrealistic theater.

Let us put ourselves then in the place of an Elizabethan
spectator of a Marlowe play.[12] The main features of the
Elizabethan stage are clear, however unsure we must be about
details. We are beginning to realize that, perhaps, *all* Elizabethan theaters were not built alike, that they differed, prob-

[11] May I recommend a superb analysis of naturalistic drama vs.
poetic drama: Raymond Williams, "Film and the Dramatic Tradition," in *Preface to Film* (London, 1954)?
[12] The most trustworthy account of the Elizabethan theater is in
various essays in Allardyce Nicoll (ed.), *Shakespeare Survey XII*
(Cambridge University Press, 1959). I base my discussion of the
Elizabethan theater on this volume. The reader may also consult
F. P. Wilson's small pamphlet, *The Elizabethan Theatre*
(Groningen, 1955).

ably, in many minor and possibly major features.[13] The following description is, however, authentically typical. The stage
itself was a platform, probably from three to six feet high,
on which the actors stood and spoke. It was about forty feet
wide and extended out about twenty to twenty-five feet.
Around it stood the groundlings, those who paid the cheapest
price to enter. Around them, in turn, were three galleries in
which the higher paying spectators sat. On the outer stage were
two pillars, supporting a roof that covered part of the stage:
from this roof could descend heavenly thrones, etc. Some place
on the outer stage was a trap from which devils and ghosts
could ascend. So often are there "sitting scenes" that I suspect
there were permanent seats, perhaps a bench like that in the
Swan drawing, perhaps seats encircling the pillars. (It has been
claimed that there was always a throne at the back of the
stage in the enclosed area. I find no proof for its being a
permanent feature.) At the back there was some kind of an
enclosure which could be curtained off. Above this was the
so-called *tarras,* a second-floor platform of indeterminate width:
this too possessed a trap. (Behind the tarras was a curtained
space which apparently could be employed as an acting space,
a musicians' room, or a spectators' balcony.) Thus, there were
three main playing areas: the outer platform, the curtained
enclosure, and the upper level. The actors made their entrance
through a door or doors. (There is a great deal of doubt about
the number or size of these doors.) Sometimes, it seems, the
actors could also make their entrance from the level at which
the groundlings stood and their departure likewise. It can be
seen that there was an immediacy between the actors and the
audience that we do not have in the normal proscenium
theater of today, where the audience sits in front of the stage
rather than around it. On the Elizabethan stage it was very
easy for soliloquies and asides to be spoken rather than shouted.
All the character had to do to disassociate himself from the
others and to speak directly to the spectators was to move to
the front of the platform. The absence of sets was made up by
appeals in the play itself to the audience's imagination. The
outer stage could be a battlefield, a room in a house, the deck
of a ship, etc. The curtained enclosure could be a study, a cell,
a council chamber, etc. The tarras could be the ramparts of the

---

[13] For example, The Hope did not have the famous pillars of the
typical Elizabethan stage. The contract for its building reads that
"the 'Heavens' [that is, the internal roof over the outer stage] was
to be co-extensive with the stage and be 'borne or carried without
any posts or supports . . . upon the said stage.'" Hosking, *The
Life and Times of Edward Alleyn,* p. 167.

city wall, an observation post, the upper part of a house, etc. But we must not go too far in stressing the bareness of the Elizabethan stage. Upon it were placed beds, trees, thrones, entrances into Hell, etc. But more than anything else, the gorgeousness of the costumes lent color to the Elizabethan stage. In an age when one's rank and profession in society were indicated by one's dress, we can well understand why, sometimes, more money was paid for the main character's costume than was given to the playwright for the play itself! Churchmen, kings, Orientals in the plays wore extremely expensive and colorful robes. We know little about make-up in the Elizabethan theater, but it was probably employed to make the boys who played the parts of young women look as feminine as possible. Adult males, it seems, played the parts of old and comic women. Blood flowed freely, red vinegar in small hidden bags probably being utilized.

There was much music. Where the orchestra played is not completely clear. It may have been used in different places for different plays. It could play music between the acts, e.g., for the jigs, little poetry-dance-dialogues. It played sennets (trumpet calls) for the entrance of kings and for ceremonial occasions. It supplied musical background whenever a song was sung. It played the required music when a dance within the play was performed. Furthermore, all kinds of sound effects from backstage were employed in the Elizabethan theater: a cannon ball was rolled around in a wooden tub to make thunder, guns were shot off to accompany stage battles, alarums (drums and trumpets) signaled sudden arming and incursions.

Repeated references to two-hour performances suggest rapid delivery of lines. And there is no evidence to postulate audience waits during scene changes. One gets the impression of fast onward movement, as the play successively utilizes tarras, as platform, or curtained back recess. But were there intermissions? Were there usually four of these? The evidence seems conflicting, as a study of the extant Marlowe plays will indicate. Furthermore, the problem of five-act structure, act being conceived as an architectonic unit of plot, is not at all the same as the problem of intervals during which the spectators could relax.

There is still much debate about Elizabethan acting style or styles. Marlowe's plays (except, possibly, *Doctor Faustus*) would seem to require the kind of heavily accented, artificial, nonrealistic manner which Shakespeare described in the player who "strutted and bellowed," tearing "a passion to tatters, to

very rags, to split the ears of the groundlings" (*Hamlet*, 3.2).[14]
That is, Marlowe's theatrical abilities do not envisage a subtle
playing style. And the *blocking* (i.e., the arrangement of the
actors in space) in an Elizabethan play was undoubtedly much
more formal in design than that to which we are accustomed,
except in operas and musicals.

In the popular theaters the plays were given in the after-
noon. The audience could be either reverential or bored and
noisy. They chewed nuts and fruit they had bought from
purveyors in the house—and sometimes their nutcracking was
so loud that the actors could not easily be heard. The
spectators were a mixed crowd from all walks and ranks of
London life, and included scholars as well as prostitutes. Only
the Puritans were conspicuousy absent. Sometimes the gentlemen sat on the stage itself. What we must chiefly remember
about the Elizabethan audience was that it was more accustomed to the spoken word than we are: it was made up of
the same people as listened attentively to a hundred-and-
twenty-minute sermon. As to its taste and judgment, it was
remarkably like the average cinema audience of today, relishing
the poor as well as the fine. The one thing it demanded was
that it be entertained for two or three hours. Thus, the
dramatists of the period were tireless in their search for exciting,
sensational, shocking, surprising, or novel effects.

Now that the reader has got this far, I advise him strongly
not to go on with this introduction. *I advise him first to read
the plays.* And then come back and finish.

---

[14] S. L. Bethell, "Shakespeare's Actors," *Review of English
Studies,* New Series, I (1950), 20: "The modern interpretative
acting, in which A's *Hamlet* differs *toto caelo* from B's, is only
one symptom of a general disease. This is an age of virtuosi—or
perhaps of showmen—not of artists. It is an age of orchestral
conductors who impose their meaning upon the work. The
Elizabethans were soaked in music but among them the
conductor was unknown and the composer got his chance. The
theatre, I think, presented a parallel situation. Hence the success
of the boy actor. There is no female Lear, which argues that the
chief male parts demanded something of the modern 'character
actor's' equipment as well as formal excellence, but the existence
of such parts as Lady Macbeth and Cleopatra is surely a final
proof that the acting of the time was fundamentally formal,
however that formality might be shaded by naturalism from time
to time. With such a conception of the actor's function and
method we might be able not only to understand Shakespeare
better, but also to produce him more intelligently."

The English Theater Before Marlowe

The two great influences that acted upon Elizabethan drama-tists were classical drama and native drama. The first can largely be summed up in the names of three Roman dramatists: Plautus and Terence, who wrote comedies, and Seneca, who wrote tragedies. It was they who imposed a form on what had hitherto been largely formless. It was they who taught the English dramatist after roughly 1550 the structure of the five-act play and the technique of verse dialogue. It was they who taught whoever was willing to learn a clear story plot containing clearly defined characters. But it must never be forgotten that what they taught was imposed on native ma-terial. For example, *Gammer Gurton's Needle* (1550-60 *ca.*) is Plautine in its incisive five-act structure, but the story and the characters come from a small, rural English town and engage in a type of horseplay alien to the Plautine theater. Plautus' comedies always have a strong sexual element; *Gam-mer Gurton's Needle* has none—although full of scatological humor. *Gorboduc* (1562) is Senecan in form and speech, but its material is that of the English chronicles. It was the first English play to use blank verse, but the use of the fourteener (seven iambic feet) couplet continued for almost three decades more. We find it, for example, used for farcical elements even in Shakespeare's *The Comedy of Errors*.

The fourteener couplet is by no means graceful, but it can be percussive. And perhaps what should be said about pre-Marlovian drama—popular, court, and school—is that what-ever its literary crudeness it had a tremendous amount of bounce and vitality. This was a carry-over from the still earlier Biblical and medieval drama and from the moralities which, even in their ungainliness, were loud and moving. They were rich in audience-appeal, going easily from the stark tragedy of Christ or of man's life to low, farcical characters and situations. (The well-known morality *Everyman* is an exception to the rule.) Most of the early drama admits, what-ever the main or nominal plot, knockabout farce and low comic characters. The chief of these was the Vice, a descendant of the medieval dramatic cycle devil—troublemaking, parasitic, foul-mouthed, immoral, and amoral. (It was not at all difficult for him to merge with the Plautine Parasite or Intriguing Slave and with the pseudo-Machiavellian regisseur villain, of which more later.) Thus it came about that the double-plot technique was probably an inheritance that enabled later dramatists to shift from high to low within the area of a single play. And

thus it came about that Elizabethan drama has such a bewildering shift of type of fable, of type of character, of mood,
and of attitude.

Marlowe himself in his scorn for "jigging mother wits" probably never fully realized his debt to the past. Before him there
had already been ranting protagonists, before him there had
already been a mixture of comedy and tragedy, and before
him there already had been attempts to limit or coalesce in
emotional significance the wild mixture of clashing moods.
In other words, there is a direct line from *Cambyses* (1570 ca.)
to *Tamburlaine:* both have exclamatory, Oriental despots as
their main characters; both vociferously emphasize bloodshed,
sadism, and torture; both show the rise and eventual fall of
the tyrannical "hero." There is a direct line from the Vice to
pseudo-Machiavellian Barabas, each enjoying, with gusto, cruel
and deadly sport. There is a direct line from *Everyman,* a
morality play, to *Doctor Faustus,* a sophisticated morality play.
There is a direct line from John Bale's *King Johan* (1561, and
before) and *Gorboduc* to *Edward II:* in all three, the problems
of kingship are paramount.

Nevertheless, if one were to seek, and one should not, for
a single omnipresent influence, one must name Seneca. Kyd, in
The Spanish Tragedy, had adapted Seneca's tragedy of blood
and revenge to the popular stage, but his attempts in verse
were jejune in comparison with Marlowe's. The study of classic
poetry taught the Elizabethan dramatists rhetoric, but it was
Seneca who most fully illustrated the various devices of dramatic verse: repetition in a multitude of variations, stichomythia, balanced speeches, high-sounding classical references,
high-sounding mythological and geographical terminology, ex-
plosive end-stopped verse. It was he who taught Marlowe, I am
sure, the way to write the mighty line. But it should never be
forgotten that the language techniques of Marlowe's other plays
are more different from those of *Tamburlaine* than they are
similar to it.

The mixture of comedy and tragedy in *Doctor Faustus,* the
use of the good and bad angels to struggle for the soul of the
protagonist, the emphasis on the charms of the world, the flesh,
and the devil—all these Marlowe owed to past English drama.
But the regularization of these elements in *Doctor Faustus*—
the use of choruses between the acts, for one example—Marlowe
owed to his study of Seneca. But Marlowe did not merely
copy: he absorbed and exploited. We must in no way denigrate
his own great ability. It is astonishing to see how much experi-
mentation Christopher Marlowe was able to do in the five years
he wrote for the popular stage.

I have omitted, so far, extended reference to *The Tragedy of Dido,* which the original title page attributes to Marlowe and Nashe. This probably was not a play for the popular stage. It was apparently, like the plays of Lyly, for court entertainment, but in it we see, significantly, the first use of the hero torn between honor and love; in it we see the hypnotic insistence on death and destruction in Aeneas' recountal to Dido of the fall of Troy, which is based on Book IV of the *Aeneid;* in it we see the Marlovian tremendous line beginning to take shape and form.

The Two Machiavellis

In the sixteenth and seventeenth centuries there were two conceptions of the great Florentine. One was legitimately based on *The Prince* (composed 1513) and *The Discourses* (composed 1512-22).[15] This was the Machiavelli praised by Gabriel Harvey and Sir Philip Sidney and imitated by Sir Walter Raleigh.[16] This was the Machiavelli lying behind *1* and *2 Tamburlaine.*

The other Machiavelli was a heady brew, concocted by emotional rather than cool-headed moral Protestants for public consumption. In it Machiavel was atheistic, murderous, papistic, usurious, revengeful, sadistic, hypocritical, egocentric—no mat-

---

[15] The only modern English one-volume translation that contains both *The Prince* and *Discourses* is the Modern Library (New York, 1950). This is an important bit of information because American and English critics and scholars still are ignorant, by and large, of the *Discorsi.* They base their opinions only on *Il Principe.* There is nothing in *The Prince* which stresses the lust for sovereignty, perhaps the most important single motive in the *Tamburlaine* plays, so much as Book III, Chapter IV of *The Discourses:* "This desire to reign is so powerful that it not only dominates the minds of those born with the expectation of a throne, but also that of those who have no such expectations. This was well illustrated by the wife of Tarquin the younger, daughter of Servius, who, urged on by this mad desire, regardless of all filial piety, stirred up her husband to deprive her father of his life and kingdom; so much more did she value being a queen than being the daughter of a king."

[16] G. C. Moore Smith (ed.), *Gabriel Harvey's Marginalia* (Stratford-upon-Avon, 1913), pp. 94, 96, *passim.* S. A. Pears (ed.), *The Correspondence of Sir Philip Sidney and Hubert Languet, Now First Collected and Translated from the Latin* (London, 1845), pp. 53, 61, *passim.* Philip Edwards, *Sir Walter Raleigh* (London and New York, 1953), p. 138, *passim.*

ter how illogical this monster is! This is the Machiavelli who speaks the prologue to *The Jew of Malta*.

There is still so much debate on what the actual Machiavelli meant, on whether he is immoral or not,[17] that I am going to utilize the best précis available, in the two volumes of Francesco de Sanctis' *History of Italian Literature*, translated by Joan Redfern (New York, 1959).

In his thoroughgoing materialism Machiavelli expresses the spirit of sixteenth-century Italy, which, whatever its emphasis on elegance and culture, was reacting against the asceticism, the scholasticism, the otherworldliness of the Middle Ages. To him truth is only what is experientially effective. Hence imagination, the evader of hard reality, is constantly to be shunned. "The world is what we make it ourselves, and each . . . person is his own Providence and his own fortune" (I, 465-6). The basis of all human achievement, therefore, is individual character. "Every man on this earth has his mission, suited to his abilities" (II, 547). (Cf. Luther's *calling!*) Virtue (or *virtù*) is strength and energy, and the reward of virtue is glory. "Nations, like individuals, have their missions on earth. . . . A nation is great through its virtue or mettle, the energy of body and of mind" (II, 561). History is "the result of the forces put into motion by the opinions, the passions, and the self-interests of man" (II, 550). Patriotism is the highest virtue; all morality is subservient to it. The spirit of man, insatiable for glory, operates in a cruel, logical world. The real hero is he who can govern man and nature—and himself—for his own ends. Once he has determined his purpose, any means he employs are legitimate. "He accepts the terrible, but he does not accept the odious or contemptible" (II, 564). Everything is to be forgiven the successful governor. "The field of politics or the art of government is not an ethical world, determined by the ideal laws of morality, but is the real world of here and now" (II, 550).

Such is the great Florentine to a keen-eyed analyst. And anyone who ponders the above paragraph must, it seems to me, recognize the chief genesis of Marlowe's *Tamburlaine*. But Machiavelli was perhaps not the only sixteenth-century Italian who influenced the playwright. (And this is the best moment to suggest the dramatist need not have *read* any particular Italian writer to absorb the cinquecento *Zeitgeist:* the ideas

---

[17] For Machiavelli, *bad,* see Leo Strauss, *Thoughts on Machiavelli* (Glencoe, Illinois, 1958). For Machiavelli, *good,* see Frederico Chabod, *Machiavelli and the Renaissance* (London, 1958).

were very much in the air.) Guicciardini, also, would have
nothing to do with conventional religion, morality, or politics.
For him every man was for himself, with the aid of some,
against everyone else. And Sadoleto in his *Phaedrus* has one of
his interlocutors preach a self-seeking utilitarian wisdom to be
measured only by the acquisition of authority, wealth, and
glory. *Virtú* is to be understood as the pursuit of power and
riches.[18]

The second conception of Machiavelli, the demonic one, was
largely the creation of Monsieur Gentillet, although from the
start the unco guid had repudiated the realistic Florentine
loudly and piously.[19] Gentillet, a French Huguenot, published
his exposé of the Italian in 1576. It was translated into English
by Simon Patericke, whose *Epistle Dedicatory* is dated 1577,
and hence the work may have circulated in manuscript. Here
is the English title page of the work popularly known as *Contre-
Machiavel:*

> A Discourse upon the Means of Well Governing and Main-
> taining In Good Peace, A Kingdom, Or Other Principality.
> Divided into three parts, namely, the Counsel, the Religion,
> and the Policy, which a Prince ought to hold and follow.
> Against Nicholas Machiavel the Florentine. Translated into
> English by Simon Patericke. London, Printed by Adam Islip,
> 1608.

An excerpt from Gentillet, who knew both *The Prince* and the
Discourses, will immediately indicate the parentage of Marlowe's Machiavelli in *The Jew of Malta*—and of Barabas!

1 Maxim

*A Prince above all things ought to wish and desire to be
esteemed devout, though he be not so indeed.* [Rubric:] *Cap.*
18 of the Prince

This Maxim is a precept, whereby this Atheist *Machiavel*
teacheth the prince to be a true contemner of God and of
Religion . . .

Yet we have cause greatly to deplore the misery and
calamity of the time wherein we are, which is so infected
with Atheists, and contemners of God and of all Religion,
that even they, which have no religion, are best esteemed,
and are called in the court language, People of service:

---

[18] Eugene F. Rice, Jr., *The Renaissance Idea of Wisdom* (Harvard University Press, 1958), pp. 73-7.
[19] See Mario Praz, "The Politic Brain: Machiavelli and the
Elizabethans," in *The Flaming Heart* (Anchor Books, 1958), pp.
93-4.

because being fraughted with all impiety and Atheism, and having well studied their *Machiavel*, which they know upon their fingers, they make no scruple nor conscience at any thing. Command them to slay and massacre, they slay and massacre; command them to rob and spoil good Catholics [i.e., Protestants, true Christians], and Clergymen, they rob and spoil all. They [these papists, Roman Catholics] hold benefices with soldiers' garments and short cloaks, yet exercise no Religion, nor cares, but for the gain thereof. Command them to enterprise the betraying, or impoisoning of this or that person, they make no scruple at it: yea, they themselves excogitate and devise all wickedness and impieties, as the invention of so many imposts [i.e., taxes] upon the poor people, which they destroy and cause to die with hunger, without having any commiseration or compassion upon them, no more than upon brute beasts. . . . Inventors of such novelties, which both by nation [Italy] and religion [Roman Catholicism] are Machiavelists.

Marlowe and Comedy

The great confusion concerning Marlowe's share in the comedy of his extant plays, concerning the validity of comic prose in these texts, concerning the close juxtaposition of such comic prose with serious verse, would probably be dispelled if deniers of Marlovian comedy were to study an Elizabethan half-folio sheet on which is written, on both sides, a different version of what are lines 972-96 in the Malone Society reprint of *The Massacre at Paris* octavo. It is obvious that this fuller version, three to four times longer than the octavo's, is both authentic and "good"—that it is a reproduction, not (as in the octavo) a "bad" memorization, of the original scene. It is also possible that the handwriting is Marlowe's own. The most careful transcription of the leaf is by J. M. Nosworthy, "The Marlowe Manuscript," *Library,* Fourth Series, XXVI (1945), 158-71. The octavo's version and the leaf's can also be found on pp. 228-9 and 254-5, respectively, of H. S. Bennett's edition of *The Jew of Malta,* which includes *The Massacre at Paris.*

The intensely Machiavellian Duke of Guise has discovered that he has been cuckolded by one of Henry III's minions, and he has also been mercilessly jeered at over this by the King. The scene begins—I modernize—with "Enter a soldier with a musket." Guise, it appears, has appointed him to kill the rival. On the bare stage the soldier devotes about a hundred and seventy-five words to commenting in clever semipornographic comic prose on his victim's seduction of the wife. "Enter minion." Obviously the soldier discharges his gun, for "he kills him." The lover is given one line before he dies, "Traitorous Guise, ah, thou hast murdered me!" Now "Enter Guise," who gives money to the soldier and bids him fly. Then the Duke speaks an egomaniacal fifteen-line blank verse soliloquy in which he defies Henry III and vows to destroy him.

The immediate conjunction of the wholly comic, however macabre by inference it be, and the wholly serious is striking. (Furthermore, we must not neglect to notice the presence of spectacle, the shooting of the gun, in the dramatic mixture.) Such a potpourri will be found in more or less degree in both parts of *Tamburlaine*, in *Doctor Faustus*, and in *The Jew of Malta*. And wherever it is present in these plays, this comic material next to the noncomic, it has been pointed to by most critics as prima facie evidence that this part was not written by Christopher Marlowe but by some other hand. And scholars have been by no means lacking to rationalize this disintegration by the employment of supposedly objective analysis. Surely, however, the time has come for unbiased investigation to restore to Marlowe's authorship the comic matter in the extant texts, and so lead to a trust that these texts do reveal the playwright in all his complexity. Even without the evidence of *The Massacre at Paris* leaf, the example of Marlowe's predecessors and contemporaries in the theater should make us chary of refusing to grant him the right to compose comedy and farce in the midst of the serious and the spectacular.

1 and 2 Tamburlaine

When one writes about the two parts of *Tamburlaine*, one must perforce use the hackneyed phrase, *climate of opinion*. This staged account of a monomaniac, sounding off constantly in rodomontade, and then conquering huge chunks of the world's territory, seems almost ridiculous to modern readers and viewers. Perhaps, indeed, the figure that first comes to mind in comparison is Adolf Hitler. But actually this is a very superficial impression, for Tamburlaine rightly interpreted, sensibly acted, is very much a symbol of modern man. One might say that he is a Robert Clive or Cecil Rhodes verbalized.[20] Per-

---

[20] It is astonishing how much Marlowe's hero jibes with his real-life counterparts. See J. W. Pearce (ed.), *Macaulay's Essay on Lord Clive* (New York, 1923), pp. 72-85, 143. R. I. Lovell, *The Struggle for South Africa 1875-1899: A Study in Economic Imperialism* (New York, 1934), pp. 116-20, 167; Stuart Cloete, *Against These Three: A Biography of Paul Kruger, Cecil Rhodes, and Logenbula* (Boston, 1945), pp. 4-5, 85-93. On English

haps he is so loud because he triumphantly indicates and announces the break with the Middle Ages, which definitely began
in Italy in the fourteenth century and which all Europe felt
in the sixteenth century.

In the Middle Ages one was a part of a group, one accepted
without question the rank which birth gave one. One could go
from peasant status to prince *within the church*, but this was
the exception which proved the rule. The world was static,
and the horizon was never more than a couple of miles away.
But the Middle Ages decayed. Beliefs and forms became hollow
shells. It was almost as if the world were waiting for the tremendous explosion of the Renaissance in the fifteenth century
and the Reformation in the sixteenth. From the year 500 to
the year 1400 nothing essentially changed in Europe. But from
1400 on, modern man religiously, culturally, politically began to
find his bearings. *Tamburlaine* is the result of many currents
within the *Zeitgeist*. To understand these currents is to understand the sympathy and enthusiasm and probably fear which
the London spectators had when they viewed the play in 1588.
I shall try to identify and describe these currents so that Marlowe's two-part drama will not quite be the museum piece some
consider it to be.

Tamburlaine is allied to both science fiction and realistic
reporting. Although the sixteenth-century Englishman faced a
new world, it was still largely *terra incognita* to him. He felt
rather than saw what lay before him, welcomed it, rejected it,
and was afraid of it. It both fascinated and repelled him. Consider the wonder and fear in Othello's "travel's history,"
wherein he speaks

> of antres vast and deserts idle,
> Rough quarries, rocks, and hills whose heads touch
>   heaven, . . .
> And of the Cannibals that each other eat,
> The Anthropophagi, and men whose heads
> Do grow beneath their shoulders.

But even the normally physically fashioned human creatures
of the East were utterly abnormal emotionally, ethically, and
religiously to the citizens of Shakespeare's London. The former

---

"superman" imperialism of the nineteenth century, see John
Ruskin's inaugural lecture as Slade Professor at Oxford in
*Lectures on Art Delivered before the University in Hilary Term
1870* (New York, n.d.), pp. 23-4; William Winwood Reade, *The
Martyrdom of Man* [1872] (new American edition, New York,
1937), pp. 417, 448-52, 481-2.

were interesting monsters too, especially in their accouterments, their dress, and their high address.[21] However, when Marlowe chooses a conquering Oriental despot as his hero, he is distancing the play from the contemporary scene and at the same time allowing himself to exploit it. Tamburlaine is some kind of foreign monster, but he is also a monster growing up in the villages and cities of sixteenth-century England. It has been reiterated, monotonously almost, that England at this period was still medieval in thought and attitude, and some scholars argue whether the Renaissance ever occurred at all. Actually it did and it didn't in the sense that the new and the old existed together and the same individual could be very much a figure of the modern world and at the same time decry the destruction of the old. (Henry Ford with his factories and his Greenfield Village is a modern example of the same paradox.) So the largely unknown territories of the East inhabited by the ferocious pagans offer Marlowe a superb means of masking the *here* with the *there*. The morals, spirit, attitudes, acts, desires of Tamburlaine could be looked at from a distance of thousands of miles at the same time that one viewed them twenty feet away in a theater, the members of whose audience felt rather than knew that the spirit of the Scythian was abroad in their own land. So science fiction allowed Marlowe to be realistic. But what was he realistic about?

Most Englishmen of the sixteenth century may not have read Machiavelli or studied Luther. Yet they certainly knew what each chiefly stood for. And Tamburlaine is as neat a synthesis of these two seemingly incompatible figures as can be found. What is often forgotten about the first is that he was by no means an innovator. He himself stressed that his advice on the conduct of a prince derived not from a theory but from actual observation, whether in fifteenth-century Italy or in pagan Rome and Greece. The one thing that Machiavelli stood for was the absolute dependence of the individual ruler on his own abilities. His virtú was to conquer and to hold by means of his own innate abilities. The medieval concept of the

---

[21] The fullest discussion of the Orient as the Englishmen of Marlowe's time understood it is Samuel C. Chew, *The Crescent and the Rose* (Oxford University Press, 1937). We must remember, as Professor Chew warns us (p. 104), that Marlowe and his spectators would make no clear distinction among the various sorts of easterners. That is, the proverbial cruelty of the Turks would be attributed to the other Levantine nations and also to those further east. We must also remember that the Mohammedans were a real, not imaginary, threat to Europe in the sixteenth century.

body politic as the mystical body of Christ was completely
antithetical to Machiavelli's concept of the state. Morality
and immorality were alike beside the point. To conquer and
to hold by means of one's own courage, intelligence, cunning,
glamour were the main criteria of the successful leader. It is
impossible at the present time to understand how thoroughly
uninterested in conventional morality Renaissance Italy was.
A courtesy book like Castiglione's *Il Cortegiano* stresses grace
and fame as the rewards of learning how to be a true gentleman: it says nothing about spirituality and rectitude.[22] Personal glory was the ideal, not hidden sainthood.

Part I of Jacob Burckhardt's magnificent and still irreplacea-
ble *The Civilization of the Renaissance in Italy*[23] is entitled
"The State as a Work of Art." In that title is summed the
whole meaning of what I have just written. Just as a sculptor
takes a rough piece of stone and makes out of it a beautiful
statue, so the *condottieri* of fifteenth-century Italy made themselves splendid city-states. Originally no more than brigands
who hired out their soldiers to the highest bidder, they eventually became conquerors and rulers themselves. Without any
justification in birth, without any moral right to ownership,
such individuals took over cities, small states, and principalities
—and fathered dynasties. Utterly ruthless in achieving and
holding, they yet, almost inconsistently to us, were tremen-
dously interested in beautifying and enhancing their possessions.
That is why your modern viewer of quattrocento masterpieces
is so utterly flabbergasted when he discovers that a beautiful
building or a beautiful painting was commissioned from a
famous artist at a very high cost of money by a prince who
was as famous in his own day for his cultural munificence as
for his treason and murder. The dual role of Tamburlaine, lover
of Zenocrate (i.e., beauty) on the one hand, merciless destroyer
and sadistic conquerer on the other, had its exact counterpart
in the princes of fifteenth-century Italy. (And would it be an
exaggeration to say that Henry VIII also belonged to this
category?) What Machiavelli set down was merely an analysis
and a rule of actual historic performance. So Renaissance Italy
provided an extreme example of unbridled individualism creating glory and renown.

But the individualism of the fifteenth and sixteenth centuries
had sources other than history and theory. Luther in his way

---

[22] See John S. White's remarkable book on Castiglione:
Renaissance Cavalier (Philosophical Library, New York, 1959).
[23] The Harper Torchbooks two-volume edition, 1958, is the best
of modern translations.

was just as much a destroyer as Tamburlaine. And he provided the one ingredient that hitherto the ruthless individualist
had not possessed—religious justification and sanctification. It
was Luther who above all emphasized the matter of *calling*.
God had appointed each Christian to a certain duty in this
world. This was his calling, and he was to pursue it with might
and main.[24] One can easily see that as soon as this justification
was added to economic exploitation, the birth of the modern
robber baron, as full of piety as of predatory energy, would
occur. The Italian despot princes of the fifteenth century paid
lip-service to Christianity. The Protestant merchant of the
sixteenth century worked as hard at his occupation of making
money as he did at praying: both were duties to God.[25] It
is from this concept of *call*, of a special purpose in this world,
defined by God, that the monomania of Tamburlaine probably
derives. He is the scourge of God just as Hamlet is the scourge
and minister of heaven. Each has been given a divine duty to
perform.

Thus Tamburlaine's titanic belief in himself had its roots in
Machiavellian virtú and Protestant ethic. But a third force
was operating in sixteenth-century England and must not be
minimized. Its horrible aspect has been symbolized by Shakespeare in Edmund of *King Lear*, who was born illegitimate and
as a second son but almost becomes king of England. Edmund
represents the new order, the new men, those who without
birth, unrestrained by the medieval restrictions, by means of
force of character and intelligence, and looking out for the
main opportunity, rise to the top. Sixteenth-century England
was beginning to produce such individuals in profusion.[26]
Edmund represents them darkly, but in the novels of Thomas
Deloney one sees the middle-class dream enshrined in semi-
historical fiction in which the man of no birth by means of
capitalistic endeavor becomes not only wealthy but also mayor
of London.[27] In short, the medieval class system was breaking

---

[24] See Max Weber, *The Protestant Ethic and the Spirit of
Capitalism* (New York, 1958), pp. 79-86, *passim*.

[25] See Louis B. Wright, *Religion and Empire: The Alliance
between Piety and Commerce in English Expansion 1558-1625*
(The University of North Carolina Press, 1943).

[26] See L. C. Knights, *Drama and Society in the Age of Jonson*
(London, 1937).

[27] See L. B. Wright, *Middle-Class Culture in Elizabethan
England* (Folger Shakespeare Library, Cornell University Press,
1958); M. E. Lawlis (ed.), *The Novels of Thomas Deloney*
(Indiana University Press, 1961).

down.[28] The old feudal nobility of England had been almost destroyed in the War of the Roses. Henry VII gave titles to the men around him who would be completely faithful to his new regime. His son, Henry VIII, brought into being—by means of rewards in land and money from confiscation of the monasteries—a whole new class of nobles whose loyalty was founded securely on economic grounds. In the small towns of England a peasant could become a master craftsman; the master craftsman could buy land in the country and become gentry; the gentry could invest in mines and factories and through the good will of their sovereign become barons. Although nominally the old classes still remained, actually the strong walls between them were cracking because of the new era of capitalism, and it is interesting to see how the new nobles and gentry were taking every opportunity in this new economic era to make wealth. The noble Sir Philip Sidney, for example, was interested in tin mines, and so was Sir Walter Raleigh.[29] But what allies Tamburlaine even more closely with the economic aggrandizer of sixteenth-century England is foreign trade and foreign plunder. Drake's voyage around the world gave the incredible return of 4,700 per cent to his investors.[30] In India and the Spice Islands, in Mexico and Peru, were untold millions which could without too much trouble be stolen from the Spanish or bargained for with the natives. Tamburlaine, looking out for new worlds to conquer, is much like the Elizabethan merchant adventurer looking abroad outside the boundaries of England for an increase of his wealth. For each there seems no limit to the amount of gold or territory to be won. And it is no accident that in Professor Mattingly's *The Armada* there is a paragraph which fits the Scythian hero almost exactly:

> From the lay preacher, Edmund Drake, Francis learned a simple Puritan faith. Everything that happened, happened by God's will. One thing God certainly willed was the ultimate destruction of the bishop of Rome and all his works. Therefore steadfast hostility to the church of Rome and its adherents was a sure sign that a man was on God's side,

---

[28] For a succinct summary on the scholarship of social mobility in the Elizabethan age, see Paul N. Siegel, *Shakespearean Tragedy and the Elizabethan Compromise* (New York University Press, 1957), pp. 3-40. Do not omit Prof. Siegel's rich notes.

[29] See Chapter IV, "The New Wealth: Economic Advance," in A. L. Rowse, *The England of Elizabeth, The Structure of Society* (London, 1951).

[30] See "Sir Francis Drake and British Enterprise," pp. 98-108, in A. L. Rowse, *An Elizabethan Garland* (London, 1954).

was one of His elect. Consequently Francis Drake was never shaken in his confidence that, as he waged war against the king of Spain, he was spoiling the idolaters, like an Old Testament hero, under the highest auspices.[31]

To be a great man, then, did not require high birth. To get possessions one needed only one's own abilities. Conventional morality was not so important as one's calling, a divine dispensation to accumulate worldly goods.

One must not forget that Oriental subject matter was of tremendous interest in the sixteenth century, when the Turks almost took Vienna. Before *Tamburlaine* we had had *Cambyses*, which poor drama as it is, still shows an Oriental despot enflamed with love and utterly ruthless in cruelty.[32] But there never is one single source in literature. Various strands come together. Behind Tamburlaine lies the Senecan hero or villain-hero, half-mad in his wild fervent declamation. Behind Tamburlaine lie the amoral epic heroes of the *Iliad* and the *Aeneid*, whose chivalry is as remarkable as their primitive bloodthirstiness. The particular quality of brutality-in-civilization which is found in the classic epics is also found in *Tamburlaine*. The thirst for glory that one finds in them one also finds in Cicero, Petrarch, Pico della Mirandola, and Castiglione.[33] And just as in Ariosto and Tasso and Spenser there is an attempt to acclimatize the classical epic to the sixteenth-century spirit and beliefs, so in *Tamburlaine* there is an attempt to put on the stage a dramatic equivalent of the epic material and mode of the *Iliad* and the *Aeneid*.

Thus just as Shakespeare's contemporary spectators could half-consciously perceive in Shylock the money-lending merchant in the next London street over, or perceive in Edmund the younger brother who is learning how to sidestep primogeniture in a new economic atmosphere, so the Elizabethan spectator could see in Tamburlaine not merely a figure who appalled and frightened them but also a figure who in fifteenth-century Italy, sixteenth-century England, contemporary events, contemporary religion, and contemporary economic and trade conditions was unconsciously or consciously familiar to them.

---

[31] Garrett Mattingly, *The Armada* (Boston, 1959), pp. 82-3.

[32] *Cambyses* (1570 *ca.*) is in various anthologies, conveniently as a reprint of the sixteenth-century edition in Vol. II of J. M. Manly (ed.), *Specimens of Pre-Shakespearean Drama* (Boston and London, 1897).

[33] See Gordon Worth O'Brien, *Renaissance Poetics and the Problem of Power*, (Institute of Elizabethan Studies, Chicago, 1956).

1 Tamburlaine

In contrast with most critical opinion, I myself consider
2 Tamburlaine superior to *1 Tamburlaine*. Speaking metaphorically, one sees Part One as tending to duplicate the same
event in different parts of the field. The Second Part, I think,
is full of variety—and the possibilty of rich, conflicting response. There is a geometric progress of the hero in the First
Part, which has been beautifully demonstrated by the late
Professor Brereton in one of the best pieces of Marlowe criticism extant.[34] The essay is also very significant in showing
Marlowe's use of the real Machiavelli, not the spurious one he
used for *The Jew of Malta*. Values are seen to create dramatic
structure in Brereton's analysis:

> Marlowe secures his climax by his characterization of the
> hero's opponents, beginning with the weak Mycetes and end-
> ing with the formidable Souldan, and to each of them he
> devotes an act. The motives and events are so intertwined
> that the actions and interests of the successive antagonists
> are not necessarily confined in each example to a single act,
> or the result would certainly be a series of short plays; but
> the fate of Mycetes is decided in the first act, though he
> dies in the second, which exhibits the fall of Cosroe, whose
> rise we have witnessed in the first. The third act is devoted
> to the ruin of Bajazeth, who does not commit suicide until
> the fifth. The Souldan's mustering of forces is the theme of
> the fourth; and the fifth shows us Tamburlaine victorious
> and willing to proclaim a truce with all the world. One might,
> then, head the several acts with the names of Mycetes,
> Cosroe, Bajazeth, the Souldan and Tamburlaine. And if you
> read the piece with full consciousness of this, you will realize
> what a magnificent crescendo is provided.
>
>   To Marlowe, daring and ambitious, the Machiavellian phi-
> losophy was fascinating, and the hero of his first play is a
> colossal embodiment of his idea of the Machiavellian man of
> virtue, with such additions and modifications as were sug-
> gested by his own predilections. Tamburlaine is the youth
> who sees opportunities where others would see only dis-
> couragement, and mounts by the ladder provided by Fortune.
> The advantage of birth he scorns, and bases his power on

---

[34] J. Le Gay Brereton, "Marlowe's Dramatic Art Studied in His
Tamburlaine," in *Writings on Elizabethan Drama* (Melbourne
University Press, 1948), pp. 67-80.

virtue alone. When he bestows titles of royalty on his followers, he warns them:

> Deserve these tytles I endow you with,
> By valour and by magnanimity—

by manly worth and by greatness of soul, courage and intellectual capacity. And he adds:

> Your byrthes shall be no blemish to your fame,
> For vertue is the fount whence honor springs
> And they are worthy she investeth kings.

Hereditary honour in itself, unsupported by real kingliness, is
a shadow, and the true sovereignty belongs to him who merits
it, for

> vertue solely is the sum of glorie,
> And fashions men with true nobility.

Lordship cannot exist without worthy action. "I am a Lord,"
he assures Zenocrate, "for so my deeds shall prove." And
so successful is he, that it seems as though Fortune were
thoroughly subdued to his unfettered will,

> And well his merits show him to be made
> His Fortunes maister and the king of men.

So says Cosroe, and Theridamas at a later stage (*II Tamburlaine* III. iv) is even more emphatic, when he describes
Tamburlaine as the man

> That treadeth Fortune underneath his feete,
> And makes the mighty God of armes his slave.

He is the lion, royal of aspect and rushing on his prey
directly; there is in him very little of the fox. We do not find
him making sly plots and trusting to a mean diplomacy.
He can turn on one who has been his ally; but he will not
"steale upon him cowardly," but gives him warning, and the
plan does not occur to him until the immediate cause for
alliance is past. He is thoroughly Machiavellian in his out-
spoken pride, and his swift unsparing resentment of injury;
he has no trace of that humility and sufferance that charac-
terize the philosophy of Jesus. He is generous and affable to
his supporters, as Machiavelli recommends, and establishes
himself by removing all cause of jealousy; it is part of his
policy. To traitors and to those who persist in opposition he
is horribly stern, but behaves with clemency where there is

anything to be gained thereby. He is never unprepared, but always ready to take the field against his ever-gathering enemies.

Marlowe shows him, as we have seen, in conflict with a series of adversaries, contrasting thus the man of virtue with the pretenders to virtue—little men, or, at best, men who fall short of his standard. First there is Mycetes, who has no initial difficulties to overcome, for he is the heir of a royal line; and, to quote the words of Machiavelli, "hereditary states, accustomed to the family of their prince, are carried on with far less trouble than new states . . . so that if an hereditary prince have ordinary ability, he will always maintain his position as ruler, unless deprived of it by some extraordinary and irresistible force." But Mycetes has not ordinary ability, but is feeble in intellect and quite without dignity. He is a peevish and ridiculous weakling, taking the posture of a tyrant. He knows that he is deficient in intellect, and that he cannot express his feelings in adequate words, and yet he feels bound to attempt a style befitting his rank, and his speech of metrical prose is grotesque with mangled and distorted imagery. Insult rouses him to a show of resentment, unsupported by action. He is plaintive, after the fashion of a spoiled infant. And this whining creature is met by "some extraordinary and irresistible force." He himself has no sense of proportion. Tamburlaine he regards as a "paltry Scythian" thief, yet he despatches a thousand horse, under command of a leading nobleman, to apprehend him. He has no imagination, and consequently no perception of realities. To him, " 'tis a prety toy to be a Poet"; but Tamburlaine is a poet as well as a soldier, and, if he were not a poet, his ambition would be mean and his success quite insignificant. And just as Mycetes underrates the power of the imagination, so he shrinks from the exercise of military power. War is the very element in which Tamburlaine lives—the one activity that he feels worthy of his gigantic desires: Mycetes, who has no practical experience, feels very differently:

> Accurst be he that first invented war!
> They knew not, ah, they knew not, simple men,
> How those were hit by pelting Cannon shot
> Stand staggering like a quivering Aspen leafe
> Fearing the force of Boreas boistrous blasts.
> His light is suddenly swallowed up in darkness.

His brother Cosroe, his rival, is a fellow of good intentions and vigorous action. Insistently Fortune, as Menaphon tells

him, gives him opportunity "to gaine the tytle of a Con-
querour." The disaffected nobles place the imperial crown
upon his head, and, had he been sufficiently politic to see
where the real danger lay, and sufficiently self-confident to
trust solely to his own strength, he might have been safe.
But he relies on the aid of a warrior more dominating than
himself, and thinks to satisfy Tamburlaine by giving him
the regency of Persia. His want of judgment brings him to his
end. When he forms his alliance with the Scythian, he defers
to him, and accepts his opinion "as from assured oracle."
"Thy words assure me of kind successe," he says with satisfaction. He makes it evident that he counts upon Tamburlaine
to win the victory, and gives him the honour of making the
first assault. He talks, too, of the sovereignty that is to be
his own, in terms that excite the imagination of the real victor
to dreams of glory. Beside Mycetes, he is a sterling but not
extraordinary man. Compared with Tamburlaine, he is seen
to fall far short of virtue; and soon he, too, is eclipsed. He
humbly accepts his two imperial crowns from the hand of
the man whom he looks upon as a useful vassal, but whom
he is to recognize too late as "that fiery thirster after
Soveraigntie," the "bloody and insatiate Tamburlain." The
hand that has set him up casts him down again with equal
ease.

No sooner has his soul made flight to Hell on the last
breath that he can shape into a curse, than Bajazeth, the
Emperor of the Turks, appears, in all the prestige of military
achievements. He is "the greatest Potentate of Africa," and
his army is reputed invincible. He is skilled in warlike arti-
fices, but his strength really lies in numbers, and he arrogantly
ascribes to his own greatness the ruin wrought by his host.
He is subject to a fault against which Machiavelli warns the
prince who would be safe. "One error," Machiavelli writes,
"to which princes are liable, unless they are very prudent or
very lucky in choosing their friends, is of such importance,
that I must not omit to mention it. I mean the danger of
flatterers." Bajazeth is surrounded by petty kings, and
acquiesces, with sublime self-satisfaction, in their most extravagant praises of his magnificence. He is certainly not,
as Cosroe was, distrustful of himself; but he has to learn
that marching multitudes are of no avail against an army
led by a man of men.

With every victory the power of Tamburlaine increases,
and now he has to meet an opponent worthy of his steel—the
Souldan, whose words are resonant and whose heart is un-
afraid.

> Villain, I tell thee, were that Tamburlaine
> As monstrous as Gorgon prince of Hell,
> The Souldan would not start a foot from him.

His cause is good, his rage high and his valour and wisdom are his guides. He does not underrate the strength and ability of "the rogue of Volga," though he is angered by his whole-sale atrocities:

> The slave usurps the glorious name of war.

He arrives too late to raise the siege of Damascus, but swoops on the army of the victor. There is a brief struggle, and he finds himself the captive of a friend and would-be son-in-law, who restores his kingdom and increases the strength of his dominions. And above a blood-stained world shines in cold calm the star of Tamburlaine.

The whole play is an artistic unity, the characterization and plot being together an exposition of the Machiavellian ideal.

There is one passage in *1 Tamburlaine* which seems to indi-cate that Marlowe early in his dramatic career deliberately eschewed a kind of drama which he could have written and which Shakespeare after him extensively exploited—the drama of psychological subtleties. Though occasionally a Marlowe character is capable of internal conflict—specifically, Faustus—on the whole his personages are drawn in heavy outline with strong primary colors: there is no delicate shading. He obvi-ously chooses the character technique of the epic, or of farce, or of melodrama, or of the morality play—in all of which, motive must be obvious and untempered.

But there is evidence that Marlowe need not have limited himself to this intensive simplicity. In dealing with Tambur-laine's relationship to Zenocrate, the dramatist anticipates by almost twenty years the love vs. honor conflict of *Antony and Cleopatra*. Let us look at the Scythian's famous passage on beauty in 5.1, which commentary has tended to dismiss as nondramatic and inconsistent, as being the poet's own paean. Tamburlaine has commanded Techelles to destroy the citizens of Damascus, who have dared to refuse his early offers of sur-render plus mercy. He then in soliloquy turns to the subject of Zenocrate. Her beloved, Tamburlaine, and her father, the Soldan of Egypt, are about to engage in battle: she is woe-fully beautiful, as beautifully woeful.

> Rain'st on the earth resolved pearl in showers,
> And sprinklest sapphires on thy shining face,

Where Beauty, mother to the Muses, sits
And comments volumes with her ivory pen,
Taking instruction from thy flowing eyes. . . .
There angels in their crystal armors fight
A doubtful battle with my tempted thoughts
For Egypt's freedom and the Soldan's life. . . .

Note, he is "tempted." Her sorrows "Lay . . . siege unto [his] soul." No enemy has hitherto

Troubled my senses with conceit of foil
So much by much as doth Zenocrate.

It is interesting that his adoration of the Soldan's daughter is not Platonic. It is a matter of acute sensual and sensuous attraction, which threatens to thwart his martial hopes and ambitions. So far the conflict has been clear, although the sudden *internalizing* of Tamburlaine's love does come as somewhat of a surprise to the spectator or reader. It gives the protagonist a humanity that his hyperbole and posturing throughout the play have not hitherto suggested.

Then comes the famous passage, "What is beauty, saith my sufferings, then?" etc. What are these sufferings? They are not merely the conflict between his love for Zenocrate and his imperial drive. The sufferings come from the inexplicable, the irrational, the wondrous in a woman's loveliness that defeats both ascertainment and description. This is not the customary Tamburlaine dealing in thoughts as if they were hewn out of mensurable marble. This is a man enmeshed importantly by the mystery of feminine attractiveness—the mystery that we see and feel in the wonderful, debasing, also spiritualizing affair of Shakespeare's Queen of Egypt and her Roman paramour. But both Marlowe and his hero reject this ascent into psychological complexity:

But how unseemly is it for my sex,
My discipline of arms and chivalry,
My nature, and the terror of my name,
To harbor thoughts effeminate and faint?

To be extremely sensitive is to be *effeminate*. *Faint* is a pun: (a) not clear, precise, strong, (b) leading to emasculation, weak. Rather, he, Tamburlaine, will "give the world to note": "That virtue solely is the sum of glory,/And fashions men with true nobility!" Not the archaic *virtue*, but virtú.

For *1 Tamburlaine,* the first drama of sole Marlovian authorship on record, I think it would be unwise to divide discussion of the various dramatic aspects into separate assayals. Characterization, costume, spectacle, and thunderous speech so coalesce as to make a physically palpable unity, behind which lies almost unrestrained power but little subtlety of either meaning or effect. This is not to fall into the usual trap of literary critics of either not recognizing or denigrating that which is obviously efficient in catching and holding the spectator's interest. On the whole *Tamburlaine* is a kick in the stomach rather than an equivocal whisper in the ear. Nevertheless, as I have indicated, its appeals to the Elizabethan audience are multiple, the protagonist exhibiting many of the spiritual and moral gestures by which the Renaissance, the Reformation, and the new political and economic impulses were throwing off the bonds of the Middle Ages. That is why the play is such a peculiar mixture of beauty, of poetry, of love and respect on the one hand and of horror, of farce, of cruelty and vanity on the other. *1 Tamburlaine* is as sleek and murderous as a wild beast in the cage of the theater. The Scythian is astonishing in his sweeping power, which is regardless of the New Testament dicta of man and God, and hence is also frightening, perhaps, even menacing if, as I suggested above, he stands for the "new" man. And I would even agree with those critics who regard both parts of *Tamburlaine* as a *Fortune's Wheel* piece in which the tyrant falls, as all of us must, at the hands of mightier death. In his attempts to escape his humanity, Tamburlaine is indeed from one point of view ludicrous, but he is no more ludicrous than any great man who is abnormally successful. The worm waits for him too, and the audience knows it. Thus the play satisfies in us our unconscious desire for complete domination, for infantile amoral power which knows no stop. At the same time it has a poster-thin quality in its screaming color which makes of it a nightmare from which one wants to awaken. The audience brings to *Tamburlaine* a knowledge of the facts of life against which all the main character's boasts break like brittle china. The play is a fairy tale of leaders and soldiers. And just as Barabas is to Tamburlaine, so Tamburlaine is to the spectator who after the circus goes home. Thus it is unnecessary to argue with Battenhouse that both parts of the drama are a moral lesson concerning man's arrogance.[35] Of course, they are. But they are also satisfying demonstrations of every man's immoral but unconscious hunger for power and fame. Tamberlaine is like the Hollywood male star who bears the double distinction

---

[35] Roy W. Battenhouse, *Marlowe's "Tamburlaine": A Study in Renaissance Moral Philosophy* (Vanderbilt University Press, 1941). Incidentally, this fine book is the best treatment of the sources.

of being one of the most famous men in the land and a fool
whose extravagance and amorous adventures fill the cheap
columns of newspapers.

The first scene of the First Part of *Tamburlaine*—in that it
definitely possesses comedy which is inextractable from the
plot—should long ago have warned critics who prate of Marlowe's refusal or inability to write comedy. Mycetes, the
weak and foolish king of Persia, is a farcical figure: and
his foolishness in 1.1 is inseparable from his witlessness
in 2.3, in which he meets Tamburlaine. These scenes are
organically related to the rest of the play. Thus instead of
a Marlowe who never wrote comedy, at the very beginning of
his career we meet a playwright who utilized it extensively and
effectively for the particular effects he wanted. The contrast
between the silly initial king of Persia, Mycetes, and the later
gigantic king of Persia, Tamburlaine, is splendid theatrical stuff.
There is similar if not so glaring comedy in the fall of Bajazeth.
To have the Scythian conqueror use the former mighty Turkish
ruler as a footstool, to have him kept in a cage and fed
through the bars, to have him forced to commit suicide by
dashing his head against the bars of his prison—all this is
grotesque comedy too. And this viewpoint enables us to receive the boasting of Tamburlaine's foes, even of himself perhaps, as not only impressive but ridiculous—especially in the
case of Bajazeth, who boasts continuously even when he is
powerless. As we go over the play, I shall point out other
scenes where a kind of comedy which is not so much that of
farce as of the grotesque exhibits itself. This is not at all surprising in view of the lineage of early English drama where
laughter and shock jostle each other so closely as on occasion
to be indistinguishable emotions.

1.1

Mycetes, in a way, indicates what the weapon for success
must be in this drama: "a great and thund'ring speech." He
does not possess it, and it is rather interesting to see Marlowe,
whose blank verse line in *1 Tamburlaine* announced unequivo-
cally the coming era of great Elizabethan drama, giving this
weak king of Persia rhymed couplets and quatrains on occasion.
For example,

Thou shalt be leader of this thousand horse *ff.* (1.1.62-8).

Mycetes is indeed farcical in his pretense at wit, and he even
draws from his brother a rough humor that recalls the interludes:

Myc. Well, here I swear by this my royal seat—
Cos. (You may do well to kiss it, then.) [*Aside*.]

Bradbrook and others have taught us the great symbolic significance of stage properties of Elizabethan drama, such as the crown, the possession of which does not merely *indicate* sovereignty but *is* sovereignty; and we must be very careful in watching this play to see what use Marlowe makes of these golden ringlets in Tamburlaine's progress. Cosroe here is crowned by Ortygius and Ceneus. "Sound up the trumpets then! God save the King!"

And this talk of properties leads us to a topic that is of the utmost importance in the production of these two plays— costume.[36] We know very little about what the actors in the play wore, and we can be pretty sure that their dress was not historically correct. But splendid, even glaring, it must be, Oriental in the fullest common meaning of the adjective. For these are creatures of the legendary East, strange and mysterious to the Elizabethans. Tamburlaine himself must have a number of costumes, as we shall see, but what must be enforced on the producer is that his leading actor must give the visual impression of tremendous power and height. High cork shoes and high turban can and must make of him a figure that draws gasps. He must as visually rule the stage and the theater as he must orally. And so potent properties, astonishing robes, and thunderous speech must all go together to make a percussive effect on the audience—a strong one that will almost rob them of conventional judgment. We will see the exemplification of what I have just written even better in the next scene.

1.2

Tamburlaine dressed as a shepherd enters leading Zenocrate. He is accompanied by his two lieutenants, Techelles and Usumcasane, and soldiers laden with bags of treasure. (These bags will be later open to view to entice Theridamas' troops.) I think that Tamburlaine's shepherd's dress should be accompanied by a deliberate attempt on the part of the actor not to stand out at the moment, so that when he throws off his disguise and we see his huge height encased in gleaming armor, the effect is electrifying. At line 40 the true Tamburlaine reveals himself and begins his mighty utterance. And I would be the last to deny that the ear in this play does more in creating magnificence than do cloth and buttons. Nay, the

---

[36] An inventory of the Admiral's men in 1598 included Tamburlaine's coat with copper lace and his breeches of crimson velvet.

hyperbolic vocabulary is really the truest vesture of everybody and everything. For example, the soldier announces that
"A thousand Persian horsemen are at hand." We are told that

> Their plumed helms are wrought with beaten gold,
> Their swords enamell'd, and about their necks
> Hangs massy chains of gold, down to the waist:
> In every part exceeding brave and rich.

These are the real enterers, not Theridamas with a few soldiers
who come in a few lines later. I cannot enforce this point
enough—that treasure, victory, great battle, tremendous emotion are the word in this play and that if we do not un-
sparingly and uncritically react to this word, we should stay at
home.[37] Theridamas, himself, understands this after Tamburlaine's great appeal to him to forsake Persia and join the
Scythian:

> *Ther.* Not Hermes, prolocutor to the gods,
> Could use persuasions more pathetical. . . .
> —Won with thy words, and conquered with thy looks,
> I yield myself, my men, and horse to thee. . . .

Let us get just a taste of what words are constantly doing in
this loud drama. Theridamas sees Tamburlaine for the first
time:

> Tamburlaine! A Scythian shepherd so embellished *ff.* (1.2.
>   154-61).

---

[37] Queerly enough, although there are many general statements,
there is not one adequate particular analysis of Marlowe's verse in
Tamburlaine. It is rhetorical, with all the rhetorical tricks, and
behind it I am sure lies Seneca the dramatist. The best edition
of the latter is the Loeb Library's, trans. F. J. Miller (London
and New York, 1927), two volumes, Latin on one side, English
on the other. T. S. Eliot's "Seneca in Elizabethan Translation,"
Selected Essays 1917-1932 (London, 1932) is too general for our
purpose. Tucker Brooke, "Marlowe's Versification and Style,"
Studies in Philology, XIX (1922), 186-205, is narrowly metrical.
The reader will get some valuable suggestions from rhetorical
studies of Marlowe's contemporary: Sister Miriam Joseph, *Shakespeare's Use of the Arts of Language* (Columbia University Press,
1947); Gladys D. Willcock, *Language and Poetry in Shakespeare's
Early Plays* (Annual Shakespeare Lecture of the British Academy,
1954). If only one could find an extensive study of *repetition* in
Marlowe's verse in *1* and *2 Tamburlaine*! One begins to feel that
not even an adequate beginning has been made in Marlowe
studies!

Here is part of the Scythian's appeal to the Persian:

If thou wilt stay with me, renowned man, *ff*. (1.2.188-201).

Watch Zenocrate as she changes from fear and almost loath-
ing of Tamburlaine to love and admiration—even to ardent
defense against Bajazeth's queen—and ultimately to conflict
between love for the Scythian and love for her father. Watch
too what happens to Agydas, the lord who accompanied her.

2.1

Menaphon's description to Cosroe of Tamburlaine is, again,
meant to be the spectacles through which we view the former
shepherd:

Of stature tall, and straightly fashioned, *ff*. (2.1.7-30).

Note that Cosroe is crowned. He now is going to join with
Theridamas and the latter's new lord against Mycetes.

2.2

Mycetes' wrath is ludicrous, and his mock-epic utterances
contrast effectively with the boastful terms of his general,
Meander. The latter's description of Tamburlaine's troops:

Yet being void of martial discipline,
All running headlong after greedy spoils,
And more regarding gain than victory—

should indirectly tell us that the stage position of the Scythian's
followers should always be rigid and hard in design—these
characteristics to enforce the Scythian's iron discipline and his
cohorts' iron discipline. Mycetes' chatter about the poet,

Myc. Was there such brethren, sweet Meander, say,
That sprung of teeth of dragons venomous?
Mean. So poets say, my lord.
Myc. And 'tis a pretty toy to be a poet.
Well, well, Meander, thou art deeply read:
And having thee, I have a jewel sure.
Go on my lord, and give your charge, I say.
Thy wit will make us conquerors today.

is partly a joke on Marlowe's part against himself and partly
the very opposite of a joke: Marlowe's understanding of his
most potent dramatic weapon.

2.3

After Tamburlaine makes to Cosroe one of his typical
thunderous statements concerning the partisanship of heaven,

the uncountable number of soldiers he will muster, and the
Olympian character and destructiveness of his weapons,
Theridamas says:

> You see, my lord, what working words he hath.
> But when you see his actions top his speech,
> Your speech will stay. . . .

This is the methodology of the two *Tamburlaine* plays regarding battles. By and large most of the martial action occurs off
stage and is prepared for *before* and commented on *after* it
occurs by means of Marlowe's mighty line. I think I rather
differ from those critics who would get too specific about exact
meaning in either one of these plays. If rhetoric means, as the
ancients thought, persuasion by whatever methods, then Marlowe's poetry in the two parts of *Tamburlaine* is rhetorical
poetry. Its effect is to be measured not so much by meaning as
by volume and pitch. That is, one gets so used to the hyperbole
that it is the hyperbole itself rather than its sense that effects
Marlowe's purpose. One grows astonished ultimately that Marlowe can get so much variety in what is essentially the same
high vaunt.

A Messenger enters to tell the approach of Mycetes' army,
and the huge Scythian draws his curtle-ax and goes forth to
battle. Now ensues one of the most obviously comic passages
in the two parts. The cowardly Mycetes comes out alone with
his crown in his hand trying to find a place where to hide it.
Like many stage idiots, he is proud of his wit:

> In what a lamentable case were I
> If nature had not given me wisdom's lore,
> For kings are clouts that every man shoots at,
> Our crown the pin that thousands seek to cleave.
> Therefore in policy I think it good
> To hide it close. A goodly stratagem!
> —And far from any man that is a fool.
> So shall not I be known. Or if I be,
> They cannot take away my crown from me.
> Here will I hide it in this simple hole.

The confrontation of Tamburlaine and the Persian king is
ridiculous:

> *Tamb.* Is this your crown?
> *Myc.* Ay, didst thou ever see a fairer? [*Hands Tamburlaine*
> *crown.*]
>
> *Tamb.* You will not sell it, will ye?

Myc. Such another word, and I will have thee executed.
   Come, give it me!
Tamb. No, I took it prisoner.
Myc. You lie, I gave it you.
Tamb. Then 'tis mine.
Myc. No, I mean I let you keep it.

When Mycetes discovers that it is the Scythian to whom he
has been talking, he swiftly runs in.

2.4

After the victory, Tamburlaine enters with the crown. Thus
Cosroe is wearing one crown, and is offered the other. Cosroe
returns it and makes the Scythian regent of Persia. "And now,"
cries Cosroe, "we will to fair Persepolis." Cosroe tells Tamburlaine to follow him "to fair Persepolis," and Menaphon tells
Cosroe that he "shall shortly have your wish,/And ride in
triumph through Persepolis." This, after Cosroe and his party
leave, gives the theme to Tamburlaine:

And ride in triumph through Persepolis!
Is it not brave to be a king, Techelles,
Usumcasane, and Theridamas?
Is it not passing brave to be a king,
And ride in triumph through Persepolis?

It is kingship with its pomp and its glory that Tamburlaine
and his three henchmen will pursue from now on. First, Persia,
and then the rest of the world:

   Tamb. Why then, Theridamas, I'll first assay
To get the Persian kingdom to myself.
Then thou for Parthia. They for Scythia and Media.
And if I prosper, all shall be as sure
As if the Turk, the Pope, Afric and Greece
Came creeping to us with their crowns apace.

2.5

Of course Cosroe is defeated, and dies on-stage. He is the
first visible example in the play of the appalling results of Tamburlaine's insatiable ambition. Later on, we shall see that
coupled with this ambition and valor are bloodthirstiness,
vengeance, and sadism. The Elizabethan audience could understand the struggle for regality: but cruelty for cruelty's sake,
probably ultimately derivable from Seneca, was to flourish in
Elizabethan drama until finally it emanated into the horrors of
Jacobean shock melodrama—which modern critics sweat to

portray as meaningful tragedy. Of course, Tamburlaine takes the crown from the dead Cosroe and puts it on his head. This is his first great victory.

3.1

One of the more peculiar aspects of the *Tamburlaine* plays is that everybody sounds like everybody else. Tamburlaine and his opponents use the same degree of exaggeration. Hence, a certain kind of confusion may or may not result because, as I have indicated, words are really the armies and the weapons in these plays. Nevertheless, a kind of rejection by the audience of the boast ultimately results too. The plays convey the truism that words without deeds are ineffective. And thus a kind of paradox ultimately derives from the *Tamburlaine* dramas— the contrast between verbal intention and accomplished act. This is irony. And it is this irony that pervades the Second Part, where there is an even further dislocation between verbal potency and accomplishment. Tamburlaine never ceases to speak like Tamburlaine, but he dies. And it is this irony that we encounter in this initial scene of Act III. The story of Bajazeth was well-known, and the Elizabethan audience knew that soon the Turkish emperor's vainglory, of boast and numeration, would be utterly smashed.

3.2

But before the Bajazeth material can be completely exploited, Zenocrate has to become to Tamburlaine as Zabina is to Bajazeth. This relationship of Tamburlaine and Zenocrate is once and for all established in the present scene. And it should be remarked how interestingly from the dramaturgic viewpoint Marlowe accomplishes his end. Agydas tries to persuade Zenocrate from her love for her conqueror. This leads to her declaration:

> Ah, life and soul still hover in his breast,
> And leave *my* body senseless as the earth!
> —Or else unite you to his life and soul,
> That I may live and die with Tamburlaine!

While they are talking, the silent Tamburlaine enters behind and hears both Agydas' dissuasion and Zenocrate's praise. Thus we have an extremely fine preparation for the action in which the silent Scythian "goes to her and takes her away lovingly by the hand looking wrathfully on Agydas and says nothing." When Techelles enters with a naked dagger for the traitor, the latter stabs himself on-stage and Techelles and Usumcasane carry his body off.

3.3

The meeting of Bajazeth with his cohorts and Zabina, and
Tamburlaine with his cohorts and Zenocrate, prepares us for
the climax of the play in which the Scythian defeats the Turk.
There is an unusual amount of parallelism, as one would expect
given the initial situation. For example, three of Bajazeth's
kings speak individually; then the great Turk comments. This
is followed by Tamburlaine's three henchmen speaking individually, and Tamburlaine's comments. Bajazeth speaks, Zabina praises him. Tamburlaine speaks, Zenocrate praises him.
And so it goes, almost like a dance between opposing groups.

This readies us for the flyting which takes place between the
two women—each of whom has been given her beloved's crown,
while he is engaging in battle off-stage. Not only do Zenocrate
and Zabina insult each other, but their maids too are brought
into the dance of boast and denial. Zenocrate prays for Tamburlaine's victory, and Zabina prays for Bajazeth's victory, and
the verbal battle goes on till the tremendous stage direction:
"Bajazeth flies, and he pursues him. The battle short, and they
enter: Bajazeth is overcome." What this means is that Tamburlaine at last catches and defeats Bajazeth in single combat on-
stage, and this symbolizes the overwhelming of the Turkish
army.

Now we see why Marlowe invented the bit where the two
opponents give their crowns to their ladies. Bajazeth being
defeated, Tamburlaine takes the crown away from Zabina and
gives it to Zenocrate. In such a superb visual manner, therefore,
does the Scythian not only indicate his great victory but also his
great love for his mistress. The binding of the Turkish emperor
on-stage is another spectacular effect.

4.1

We now meet Zenocrate's father who, of course, intends to
rescue his daughter. The Soldan stresses what can easily be
forgotten in the deluge of language that constitutes the play.
Tamburlaine is of base parentage: the would-be conqueror
of the world is very much a self-made man. Listen to the
Soldan:

> Merciless villain! Peasant ignorant
> Of lawful arms or martial discipline!
> Pillage and murder are his usual trades.
> The slave usurps the glorious name of war.

4.2

This is one of the most spectacular scenes in the entire play.
For one thing it is the first scene in which Tamburlaine's
procedure of white, red, and black—mercy, death, and utter
destruction—is utilized. So Tamburlaine is to be dressed in
white. This, of course, contrasts with the coal blackness of
the two Moors pulling Bajazeth in his cage. Possibly, Zenocrate
has changed her costume to indicate Tamburlaine's glory, but
more probably Zabina now is dressed in rags. Probably, too,
Bajazeth's appearance has been robbed of its color and gold.

Even today this initial direction of the Scythian, his cohorts, Zenocrate and Anippe, two Moors drawing Bajazeth in
his cage, and his wife following him—even today in the mind's
eye, this is a tremendous visual metaphor of the Scythian's un-
believable progress. When they take Bajazeth out of his cage
and Tamburlaine steps on the Turkish emperor's back to climb
on to his throne, one still thrills.

4.3

This next scene is mainly here to tell us that ultimately
there will be a martial meeting of Zenocrate's father and
Zenocrate's lover; between Zenocrate's former lover, the
Arabian king, and her present lover, the Scythian leader.

4.4

There is a banquet on the stage. To it comes Tamburlaine,
all in scarlet now before Damascus. He is followed by his
three great henchmen, and servants pulling Bajazeth in his
cage. Perhaps Marlowe showed the progressive deterioration of
the former Turkish emperor by means of make-up and torn
garments. The degradation of Bajazeth is inevitably to be
compared with, on the one hand, the terror promised Zenocrate's city, Damascus, and, on the other hand, the fact of
feasting by the great Scythian and his lieutenants. As a matter
of fact, there is probably no other scene in Elizabethan drama
that so astringently contrasts the rewards and facts of victory
with the powerlessness and facts of defeat:

> *Tamb.* Now hang our bloody colors by Damascus,
> Reflexing hues of blood upon their heads,
> While they walk quivering on their city walls,
> Half dead for fear before they feel my wrath!
> Then let us freely banquet and carouse
> Full bowls of wine unto the god of war—
> That means to fill your helmets full of gold
> And make Damascus spoils as rich to you

As was to Jason Colchos golden fleece.
—And now, Bajazeth, hast thou any stomach?
   Baj. Ay, such a stomach, cruel Tamburlaine, as I could
willingly feed upon thy blood-raw heart.

While Zenocrate and the others eat, Bajazeth and Zabina
curse them. And it is strange to observe Zenocrate unmoved at
their woes, inciting her master to heap fresh indignities upon
them. Using vulgar prose, Tamburlaine and his men savagely
tease the starving Egyptian, laugh when he irefully throws
meat upon the ground, and when he flings the water away.
When, suddenly, in a shift that is really not so much shocking to
our human nature as to our sense of decorum, Tamburlaine
tenderly turns to Zenocrate, she tenderly begs for her city's
protection, and asks a truce with her father. The boastful
Tamburlaine asks whether she really wants him to forego his
great honor for such a price. And Zenocrate has not much of a
reply:

   Zeno. Honor still wait on happy Tamburlaine!

We have had enough, apparently, of a man's love for a
woman, of a citizen's love for her city, of a daughter's love for
her father, for the speeches swiftly turn again to making fun
of the starving royal prisoner and his wife. But, again, there
is a shocking change of mood! A trencher with three gold
crowns is brought in, and Tamburlaine presents them with
pomp to his three generals.

   How is one to respond to these broken-glass transitions? How
is one to correlate the lover and the destroyer? Are we supposed
to possess the unity that comprises not merely the laughter at a
dying slave but the sense of grandeur for world conquerors? I
suspect that modern psychology has a better defense for this
shocking scene than neoclassic criticism.

5.1

Enter above (?) the Governor of Damascus and some
citizens. Enter below, probably, four virgins with branches
of laurel in their hands. The Governor tells us that Tamburlaine's color is now the fateful black, which we know portends
complete destruction. Then enter Tamburlaine "all in black
and very melancholy." Despite the plea of the young girls,
asking for pity for the inhabitants, Tamburlaine somberly but
firmly refuses—and orders the virgins to be taken away and be
slain by his horsemen's spears. Techelles re-enters to say that
this has been done. The Scythian orders his lieutenants to
put the rest of the inhabitants to the sword. They leave,

and for Tamburlaine's soliloquy we have another one of those astonishing shifts in which Marlowe and Elizabethan drama abound. Tamburlaine now grieves for Zenocrate's pain over the destruction of her city and over her fear for her father, the Soldan's, safety. But Tamburlaine is adamant—and again there is another startling shift in mood!—this time to the horrible humor of the baiting of Bajazeth. Tamburlaine asks, "Hath Bajazeth been fed today?" And he orders him to be brought forth. But before the cage is brought in, Techelles re-enters to announce the destruction and spoil of the town and the arrival of the Soldan and the Arabian King's army. Bajazeth and Zabina are left on the stage while the battle takes place.

The two curse their torturers. Bajazeth is hopeless. Both he and his wife complain equally of hunger and despair. After she goes out to get him water, he curses his great enemy in a Senecan outburst and then "brains himself against the cage." I suspect that the Elizabethan producer was quite liberal with the accouterments of dashed-out brains. Zabina counterpoints the fine spectacle we have just witnessed by going mad at the sight and raving in insane prose. Then she follows her lord's lead, and brains herself against the cage, with, I assume, similar vermilion results.

Now enter Zenocrate and Anippe, her maid. In her speech Zenocrate comes as close to being human as anyone in the two parts of *Tamburlaine:*

Zeno. Wretched Zenocrate, that livest to see *ff.* (5.1.320-44).

Is it possible that a conventional moral is going to be twisted out of this horrendous, Oriental, epical-romantic drama? Zenocrate speaks,

Those that are proud of fickle empery *ff.* (5.1.353-72).

But such sensitive and thoughtful reaction to the horrors exhibited is a transitory breath. Zenocrate is not really in conflict. Despite her hopes for a truce and for the preservation of her betrothed Arabian King's life, it is obvious that she is Tamburlaine's creature. In short, there is no real tension in her soul-conflict.

Battle is joined. Tamburlaine enjoys the victory. Arabia enters wounded and dies on the stage before his beloved, then enter Tamburlaine leading the Soldan. Truce is declared. And with high ceremony, Zenocrate is crowned Queen of Persia. After promising rewards for her father, "Tamburlaine takes truce with all the world!" The play probably ends in a

colorful procession, in which the body of the Arabian King is
carried off with muted drums and solemn clarion calls.

2 Tamburlaine

I have already indicated my preference for the Second Part.
The reader, before I discuss the play, may welcome two
different critical analyses. The first is by Professor Clifford
Leech; the second, by Professor G. I. Duthie:

> The Prologue to *2 Tamburlaine* frankly announces that
> Part as an addition:

> > The general welcomes Tamburlaine receiv'd,
> > When he arrived last upon our stage,
> > Hath made our poet pen his second part.

There are, indeed, many signs that Marlowe had thought
to stop at the end of Part I. In the continuation he suffered
from a shortage of material, and had to go back to his source
and incorporate into Part II some of the incidents that belonged to the historical accounts of Tamburlaine's rise. He
made the Sigismund episode out of the events that led up
to the battle of Varna in 1544; he invented the death of
Zenocrate and the unheroic behaviour of Calyphas; he
conflated stories from Ariosto and Belleforest's *Cosmographia*
to produce the Olympia episode. A first glance at Part II
suggests indeed a man labouring to fill out a play that
popular demand rather than an inner impulsion had led
him to. C. F. Tucker Brooke suggested that Part I bears
the marks of being written for an inn-yard stage, while
Part II "with its relatively more detailed stage devices"
seems to belong to the fully developed stage. But we may
find it more likely that Marlowe in Part II looked more
carefully at his staging, getting from it a variety of effect
that the simpler impulse of Part I hardly called for. The
common view is that Part II shows a falling-off in dramatic
quality, and that it is marked by a critical temper that is
not in Part I. Speaking of the other characters' attitude to
the hero, Miss Ellis-Fermor says: "No man, in the first
part of the tale, criticizes; all are sunk in a profound
mesmeric adoration"; but in Part II Tamburlaine faces the
critical Calyphas, and there are continual hints that the
dream of glory has grown tarnished. It is, however, an
over-simplification to see Part I as a mere glorification of
the hero and Part II as a predominantly critical presentation
of the same character. There is indeed no doubt that in the

sequel we find a generally colder view of the subject:
Tamburlaine is placed in a larger context, he is absent from
the stage while we watch events in the Eastern Empire and
in Egypt, he is less immediately active when his subordinate
generals bring him reports of their far-extending triumphs,
and his straining for a satisfactory demonstration of his
powers becomes more obviously grotesque than it was in
Part I. Yet the critical view is inherent in much of the
earlier play; Bajazeth's cage is a first design for the chariot
drawn by kings; the idea of ambition's ultimate vanity is
just kept below the surface in the account of Tamburlaine's
rise. Although we have every reason to believe Marlowe's
statement that Part II was not in his original plan, we can
see it as bringing to full expression much that was un-
obtrusively present in the thought of Part I.[38]

I should summarize the essentials of the plot of Part II
as follows. Tamburlaine continues his career of conquest,
still loving and inspired by Zenocrate, but still resolved to
resist any attempt by her to influence him excessively, as
he sees it, in the direction of gentleness. Early in the play
he shows that he is conscious that he will grow old and that
he will die: and so he concerns himself to prepare his sons
to be worthy successors to him (i.e. he prepares to win a
victory over Death). He encourages and trains them. One
is unworthy (both as a son of Tamburlaine and as a son of
Zenocrate): the other two he finds satisfactory. Meanwhile
Death attacks Tamburlaine in the first instance through
Zenocrate, and she dies. Her restraining influence is now
removed. Tamburlaine tries to keep her encouraging influence alive by carrying her body and her picture with him
on his martial journeys; but it is gone too, and Tamburlaine
becomes, instead of a type of inspired courage and mental
fire, a type of fury and savage rage. Death has won this
initial bout. Then Death attacks Tamburlaine directly. At
first Tamburlaine attempts resistance (foolishly, of course),
but then he acquiesces, and his death, a defeat in one sense,
is a triumph in another, since his two surviving sons, his own
flesh containing his own spirit, will continue his work on
earth while he himself steps on to a higher plane of being.
All this is surely a well-conceived dramatic design.[39]

[38] Clifford Leech, "The Two-Part Play: Marlowe and the Early
Shakespeare," *Shakespeare Jahrbuch*, XCIV (1958), 90-2.
[39] G. I. Duthie, "The Dramatic Structure of Marlowe's *Tamburlaine the Great,* Parts I and II," *Essays and Studies Collected for
the English Association,* New Series, I (1948), 126-7.

The Second Part of *Tamburlaine* is, I conceive, more strident, and perhaps more intellectually evocative than the First Part, but it is no less spectacular. I think special credit should be given to Marlowe for this successful sequel, for he had the dramatic task of continuing the characterizations and themes of the original play, and yet being constantly inventive and new. As far as spectacle goes, it is no less colorful. As far as character, that of Tamburlaine appears even more brutal: he reiterates that he is the Scourge of God, a kind of destructive half-deity whose element is war and blood, whose purpose is egocentric annihilation and aggrandizement. Counterpointing the entire action is the death of Zenocrate and the coming death of Tamburlaine. The play is a kind of *memento mori,* as though the Middle Ages were at last laughing at the human pretensions of the Renaissance. The protagonist is quite as successful as he was in the First Part, his opponents are flattened just as effectively, but now his hyperbolic verbiage is played against the intermittent but insistent fact of physiological failure. Tamburlaine in this Second Part is dreadfully comic, for the proud man, however potent he has been, however he glories in his sons who will succeed him, will be laid in wormy ground. Marlowe and his audience know this.

1.1

Before Orcanes, King of Natolia, and his cohorts meet Tamburlaine, they must encounter Sigismund, the Christian ruler of Hungary. The pagans decide to make a truce. It is indicative of Marlowe's excellent feeling for theater that on his entrance Sigismund extends his sword to Orcanes, saying:

> I here present thee with a naked sword:
> Wilt thou have war, then shake this blade at me;
> If peace, restore it to my hands again,
> And I will sheath it to confirm the same!

And Orcanes returns it:

>   if Sigismund
> Speak as a friend, and stand not upon terms,
> Here is his sword! . . .
>   *Sig.* Then here I sheathe it. . . .

Two scrolls stating the truce—sworn by Mahomet on one side, sworn by Christ on the other—are to be inscribed. That of Orcanes will soon figure in the action.

1.2

Almeda, the keeper of Callapine, is a semicomic figure, and

hence speaks in prose. (Later on his stupid cowardice will make
him farcical.)

> *Call.* By Cairo runs—.
> *Alm.* No talk of running, I tell you, sir!

> *Alm.* . . . But tell me, my lord, if I should let you go,
> would you be as good as your word? Shall I be made a king
> for my labor?

Hence Callapine's promises to him of a crown, of a thousand
galleys "Fraughted with gold of rich America," of "Grecian
virgins," of riding in a chariot on Turkish carpets, of having
a hundred mounted bassoes to attend on him, of progressing
under "a golden canopy/Enchas'd with precious stones"—these
promises of tremendous sensuous beauty contrasted with
Almeda's servant appearance, gestures, and speech make for
snickering.

So Callapine leaves, "farewell cursed Tamburlaine!/Now go
I to revenge my father's death!"

1.3

In this scene, awaiting the encounter of the Natolian and the
Scythian forces, we observe Tamburlaine's three sons for the
first time. Amyras and Celebinus are stamps of their father,
but Calyphas must be portrayed as an effeminate, unmartial
creature—somewhat like the foppish, cowardly courtier who
is the not infrequent butt of Shakespeare and Jonson later on.
He should awaken derisive laughter in the audience, especially
by contrast with the battle-enamored, blood-bathed creatures
surrounding him. After the company enters with drums and
trumpets, Zenocrate appeals to her lord:

> Sweet Tamburlaine, when wilt thou leave these arms
> And save thy sacred person free from scathe
> And dangerous chances of the wrathful war?

We need not repeat the Scythian's reply. We can anticipate it.
But nevertheless it should be noted that what we have here
parallels the First Part, where Tamburlaine also rejects the
softness which Zenocrate represents. (Cf. Lady Percy and
Hotspur in *1 Henry IV*.) And so Tamburlaine looks upon his
sons, caustically and severely, thinking them too like their dam:

> Their fingers made to quaver on a lute,
> Their arms to hang about a lady's neck,
> Their legs to dance and caper in the air. . . .

But the young men now imitate their sire in rodomontade and satisfy him—except Calyphas:

> But while my brothers follow arms, my lord,
> Let me accompany my gracious mother.
> They are enough to conquer all the world,
> And you have won enough for me to keep.

Tamburlaine responds to this Mycetes-like speech as we should expect: rather, he that wishes to sit in the royal seat of Persia "Must armed wade up to the chin in blood!" Such talk pleases Celebinus and Amyras, but Calyphas answers his father's request to cleave the pericranium of the Turkish deputy with a ludicrous reply: "If any man will hold him, I will strike!" Definitely, this third son of Tamburlaine is a ridiculous figure.

Now enter the three viceroys of Tamburlaine—Theridamas, Techelles, and Usumcasane: the first by himself, the last two together. Such simple variation shows Marlowe's awareness of the dangers of too rigid design and the necessity of variety. (Nevertheless, the youthful playwright is as yet unable to introduce much differentiation in his voices. One can be amazed at the modulations, one should be, but they are mostly all of the same note!) (1) Theridamas enters, offers his crown to his overlord, and enumerates his great powers. Tamburlaine returns the crown to the King of Argier. (2) and (3) Techelles, King of Morocco, and Usumcasane, King of Fez enter; the former announces his "hundred thousand expert soldiers" and presents his crown. The Scythian returns it. The King of Fez presents his crown and "millions" of coal-black Moors. Tamburlaine returns the crown. Simple but effective spectacle, these three bits!

Usumcasane now lists his victories. Techelles follows suit. Theridamas does the same. And so all exeunt to a banquet.

2.1

Spectacle, it should be reiterated in dramatic criticism, must not be confined merely to unusual stage effect, visual or aural. It was not understanding this that led the Jacobean dramatists astray in their feverish invention of new on-stage horrors. And it was, and is, not appreciating this that eventually led, or leads, to a nonrecognition or minimizing of Shakespeare's superb sense of theater. Search and you will see that every scene Shakespeare wrote contains a *something* that immediately, not esoterically, appeals to the audience. Ultimately, of course, there is only one failure in the theater—losing the audience's attention. Marlowe knew this as well as Ibsen.

And so the present scene in which Sigismund breaks his
Christian oath to Orcanes is *per se* a spectacular one—it is
wrong to assert that Marlowe is being deliberately anti-
Christian. Rather, the Elizabethan audience would understand,
this is the kind of faithlessness characteristic of the papists.

2.2

Again, critically, we require the wider sense of spectacle.
I am not calling attention to the minor matter of Natolia tearing the scroll to pieces. No, here we have the amazing action
of a Mohammedan praying to the Christian God:

Thou Christ that art esteem'd omnipotent,
If thou wilt prove thyself a perfect God,
Worthy the worship of all faithful hearts,
Be now reveng'd upon this traitor's soul.

—And the prayer is granted! Orcane's minor forces defeat
the Hungarian hosts—"Sigismund comes out wounded" and
dies before our eyes. How can critics continue to talk of
Marlowe's constant atheism in his plays when we hear the
King of Natolia assert Christ's power and justice shown?

. . . in my thoughts shall Christ be honored,
Not doing Mahomet an injury,
Whose power had share in this our victory.

2.3

"The arras is drawn, and Zenocrate lies in her bed of state,
Tamburlaine sitting by her: Physicians about her bed tempering potions. Theridamas, Techelles, Usumcasane and the three
sons." Without a word, this is potent visual attraction.
Tamburlaine utters his threnody in which the motif "To
entertain divine Zenocrate" is constantly repeated. Her
answer to her master's query anticipates the last scene of all
of this strange, eventful history (i.e., Tamburlaine's death) and
sets into macabre relief the yet ensuing bloody, sadistic glory
which the Scythian achieves.

Zeno. I fare, my lord, as other emperesses,
That, when this frail and transitory flesh
Hath suck'd the measure of that vital air
That feeds the body with his dated health,
Wanes with enforc'd and necessary change.

She is dying, and Tamburlaine wants to die with her. This
gesture, is it not characteristic of his regard for her from the
start? And yet how uncharacteristic of the brutal Titan! So

Marlowe makes of Tamburlaine somebody recognizable as a
human being, despite his unnatural appearance and vaunts.
And suddenly, unexpectedly, astonishingly, the mighty line
becomes muted,

> Live still, my lord! O, *let* my sovereign live!
> And sooner *let* the fiery element
> Dissolve. . . .
> But *let* me die, my love, yet *let* me die—
> With love and patience *let* your true love die!
> Your grief and fury hurts my second life.
> Yet *let* me kiss my lord before I die,
> And *let* me die with kissing of my lord.
> But since my life is lengthened yet awhile,
> *Let* me take leave of these my loving sons. . . .

There is much pathos in this repeated imperative, *let*, which
veers helplessly, like the cry of a sick person, from heaven to
husband. And after a typical Scythian outburst, amidst music,
she dies. And her master rages! He orders the town where
she had her end to be burnt—and the arras closes.

3.1
This act begins with grand spectacle. "Enter the Kings of
Trebizon and Soria, one bringing a sword, & another a scepter.
Next, Natolia [Orcanes] and Jerusalem with the imperial
crown. After, Callapine; and after him, other lords: Orcanes
and Jerusalem crown him, and the other give him the scepter."
After his investiture, Bajazeth's son promises vengeance in high
astounding terms on Tamburlaine. Each of the tributary kings
vows thousands of soldiers. The scene ends with a bit of
comedy. Callapine repeats his promise to make Almeda king,
and the latter clownishly replies in prose, "That's no matter,
sir, for being a king; for Tamburlaine came up of nothing."

3.2
Enter "Tamburlaine with Usumcasane, and his three sons;
four bearing the hearse of Zenocrate; and the drums sounding
a doleful march; the town burning." Was burning hemp in
dishes strewn over the tarras? The sons and the father, individually, place memorials to Zenocrate about the stage.
Then their father teaches them how to attack and defend a
fort:

> When this is done, then are ye soldiers
> And worthy sons of Tamburlaine the Great.

Cal. My lord, but this is dangerous to be done—
We may be slain or wounded ere we learn!

So bitter comedy intrudes, and Tamburlaine castigates his worthless offspring. In order to teach the latter bravery, the Scythian lances his arm *coram populo*, and we can be sure that much stage blood poured from the aperture!

Come, boys, and with your fingers search my wound,
And in my blood wash all your hands at once. . . .

While his sons dip their hands in his blood, the great Scythian smiles. (Did Shakespeare remember this scene in the writing of *Julius Caesar*, where the conspirators bathe their arms in Caesar's blood [3.1.106 *ff.*]?) And the march toward Theridamas and Techelles, who have been sent before against Callapine, begins. Drum and trumpets, now, of course!

3.3

Techelles and Theridamas have set down before Belsira, Soria's chief fort. The latter orders the drum to sound a parley. "Summon the battle. Captain with his wife and son": they appear on the city walls above, the tarras of course. The Captain refuses to yield and defies the two kings. And he and his family leave.

Tech. Trumpets and drums, alarum presently!
And, soldiers, play the men, the holds is yours!

Enter, on the platform this time, the Captain, wife, and son: for "in" has become *out;* we are supposed to be within the city, which Tamburlaine's forces have taken. The Captain has been wounded and dies, probably with plenty of gore showing. Olympia, his wife, stabs her son *coram populo*— Marlowe is inventive of new theatrical horror. (Though the deed goes back to Seneca's *Medea*.) She then casts both bodies into the open trap, from which flames and smoke emerge. Theridamas, Techelles, and their train enter—and after describing the great Scythian in typical fashion ("greater than Mahomet," "treadeth fortune underneath his feet," "brains of slaughtered men," etc.), Theridamas announces he loves her. They march toward Tamburlaine and Natolia. As can be observed, this relatively short scene contains many novelties.

3.4

The four kings—Orcanes, Trebizon, Jerusalem, and Soria— announce to Callapine their horrendous hosts ready to face the Scythian. Now enter Tamburlaine, his three sons, and

Usumcasane. See the balance: Callapine, crowned, and his four crowned kings: Tamburlaine crowned, Usumcasane crowned, and possibly the three sons wear small golden roundlets too. Each side rails at the other, but the Egyptians stress the hero's base birth. He replies,

Villain! the shepherd's issue (at whose birth *ff*. (3.4.79-89).

(So Marlowe never lets us forget one of the main motifs of this two-part drama—the mean birth of the great protagonist.)

The Callapine-Almeda material seems bound to thrust in comedy. For example, listen to Tamburlaine in prose: "Sirrah Callapine, I'll hang a clog about your neck for running away again. You shall not trouble me thus to come and fetch you." (And then he gets into blank verse again, promising the three opposing tributary kings that they shall be "harness'd like my horses." Marlowe, of course, is already thinking of the famous succeeding scenes where the kings will draw his chariot on the stage.) Then Celebinus points to Almeda, who, I suppose, so far has been trying to make himself inconspicuous behind Callapine! Tamburlaine bursts forth, and again we see the phenomenon of the comic Almeda (and he is truly laughable here as he asks his former master's permission to take the crown!) forcing the medium to become prose. To Almeda,

> *Tamb*. Villain! Traitor! Damned fugitive!
> I'll make thee wish the earth had swallowed thee. . . .

Almeda quakes, and Callapine reassures him:

> *Call*. Well, in despite of thee he shall be king.
> Come, Almeda, receive this crown of me.
> I here invest thee King of Ariadan,
> Bordering on Mare Roso, near to Mecca.

But Almeda is reluctant:

> *Orc*. What! Take it, man.
> *Alm*. Good, my lord, let me take it. [*to Tamburlaine!*]
> *Call*. Dost thou ask him leave? Here, take it.
> *Tamb*. Go to, sirrah, take your crown, and make up the half dozen [Callapine plus the four kings = five crowns]. So, sirrah, now you are a king, you must give arms.
> *Orc*. So he shall, and wear thy head in his scutcheon!
> *Tamb*. No, let him hang a bunch of keys on his standard to put him in remembrance he was a jailor—that when I take him, I may knock out his brains with them, and lock *you* in the stable when you shall come sweating from my chariot!

Treb. Away, let us to the field that the villain may be slain!

Tamb. Sirrah [*to a servant*], prepare whips and bring my chariot to my tent, for as soon as the battle is done I'll ride in triumph through my camp!

After Theridamas and Techelles enter, Almeda is once more a figure of prose fun—and note, particularly, the reference to Mycetes. The Scythian points to him:

> See ye this rout, and know ye this same king?
>
> *Ther.* Ay, my lord, he was Callapine's keeper.
>
> *Tamb.* Well, now, you see he is a king! [Does Almeda wear his crown askew? Surely he must look a silly figure.] Look to him, Theridamas, when we are fighting lest he hide his crown as the foolish King of Persia did!

4.1

And so the battle is joined off-stage, with the sound of cries, arms-clashing, drums, and trumpets—alarums, in short. The curtains at the back open, and Amyras and Celebinus issue out—but Calyphas sits asleep in a chair. They awaken him, but he refuses to join the fight:

> I know, sir, what it is to kill a man.
> It works remorse of conscience in me.
> I take no pleasure to be murderous,
> Nor care for blood when wine will quench my thirst.

Thus, Almeda is not the only comic figure in this particular part of the play. So is the mighty Scythian's cowardly son. The other two sons rush to battle, while he plays cards on-stage with his servant, Perdicas. One must imagine the scene: the martial uproar off-stage, while these two calmly play with billets in the tent:

> They say I am a coward, Perdicas, and I fear as little their tarantantaras . . . as I do a naked woman in a net of gold. . . .

How silly he is:

> What a coil they keep! I believe there will be some hurt done among them.

I suppose that when the coward sees his victorious father and brothers enter, leading the Turkish kings, he hurriedly closes the arras, but Tamburlaine goes to the tent and pulls him out. All beg the Scythian to forgive Calyphas, but he stabs the shrinking coward to death before our eyes!

Orcanes and Jerusalem rebuke him for his barbarism, but he announces his "war's justice," "To scourge the pride of such as heaven abhors," for he is "The Scourge of God, and Terror of the World!" Who resists him resists "The power of heaven's eternal majesty!" He threatens the four kings and their lands with terrible cruelty and destruction:

> And till by vision or by speech I hear
> Immortal Jove say, "Cease my Tamburlaine!"
> I will persist a terror to the world. . . .

And so this mixed, this awful and funny and awful, scene ends.

4.2

The trick by which Olympia gets the enamored Theridamas to stab her, announcing that her annointed throat is proof against any weapon, is simple-minded indeed. But that does not mean that it would not be highly effective on the stage. And so this "queen of chastity" dies, carried off lovingly by her unwilling executioner. The scene also provides a nice break between the end of the battle and the entrance of the bridled kings.

4.3

"Tamburlaine drawn in his chariot by Trebizon and Soria with bits in their mouths, reins in his left hand, in his right hand a whip with which he scourgeth them. Techelles, Theridamas, Usumcasane, Amyras, Celebinus. Natolia [Orcanes] and Jerusalm led by . . . five or six common soldiers." (I suspect that the four captured kings still wear crowns: this would increase the spectacle mightily!)

> *Tamb*. Holla, ye pamper'd jades of Asia!
> What can ye draw but twenty miles a day,
> And have so proud a chariot at your heels,
> And such a coachman as great Tamburlaine?

No wonder this stage picture and this speech became famous, and parodied, in Elizabethan drama. Its, in a way, innocent wondrousness could still draw shouts from today's groundlings, or cheers from men-or-children. Like Bajazeth and Zabina, the prisoners curse: and are answered cruelly and tauntingly. Amyras and Celebinus, Tamburlaine's two fierce sons, join in the fun.

Now Marlowe, sugaring the frosting, devises another spectacle. He orders the Turkish concubines to be brought in, the soldiers joy in anticipation, and "They run away with the ladies." This bit should be played farcically, I believe.

Boasting in his accustomed fashion, the Scythian directs the chariot drawn by the royal tandem off the stage, toward Babylon, with drum and trumpet, followed by his splendiferous sons and generals.

5.1

Here, then, is the last act of the *Tamburlaine* plays. We have seen that the brilliant young playwright's stage inventiveness has not faltered, despite the sequel: and it does not in this act, which contains new surprises.

"Enter the Governor of Babylon upon the walls, with others." They are, of course, *above*, on the tarras. The citizens beg him to submit to Tamburlaine, who is besieging the city, but, full of high rectitude, he refuses. Now enter below the Scythian's chief lieutenants, Theridamas and Techelles, who also, in their way, request him to yield before the city and its inhabitants are slaughtered.

Then there is an alarum, "and they scale the walls." This, a frequent device in Elizabethan drama, especially that of the 1590's, means that soldiers put ladders against the back wall, fight with the defenders on the tarras, and overcome them.

"Enter Tamburlaine [in black, in his chariot] with Usumcasane, Amyras, and Celebinus; with others; the two spare kings." Hence, through the main back entrance, at the rear, comes Tamburlaine—in dismal black: in his chariot drawn by the captive kings of Trebizon and Soria, he wields his whip with shouts, amidst the glorious sound of victory, played by drums and trumpets. He is followed in procession by his two sons and his third general. He announces, in his usual resounding verse, the fall of Babylon; and enter his other two leaders, Theridamas and Techelles, "bringing the Governor of Babylon," who is still full of stubborn resistance. But— remember what has been said about the necessary width of the definition of *spectacle*—when the Scythian announces his doom, the Governor caves in before our eyes: and promises treasure if his life be saved! But he is taken out to be hung alive on the walls by chains. Tamburlaine then orders Soria and Trebizon to be unharnessed and hung off-stage and the two fresh kings to be put in their place. "They bridle them." Then the Governor is hung by the armpits from the tarras—imagine his fear and gestures—and Theridamas shoots at him—with blank bullets of course. "They shoot." And he drops, limp. But the visual spectacle is not over. Tamburlaine orders Mohammedan books to be brought on-stage, they are flung into the open trap, and a fire is lighted. Tamburlaine speaks a speech that must have sent shivers down the backs of the spectators, for all of us are superstitious, are we not?

Now, Mahomet, if thou have any power, *ff*. (5.1.185-200).

This is superb in its infantile religious defiance—and capitulation! No wonder Marlowe can win all but the most stiff-necked to his dramas. It is a very clever artist who can satisfy the libido and super ego at the same time.

Then, the first note of dissolution!

> *Tamb.* Let it be so. About it, soldiers.
> —But stay, I feel myself distempered suddenly.
> *Tech.* What is it dares distemper Tamburlaine?
> *Tamb.* Something, Techelles, but I know not what . . .

What is happening? Then with a renewed buoyance the great leader roars:

> But forth, ye vassals, whatsoe'er it be,
> Sickness or death can never conquer me!

And he whips and shouts his chariot off the stage.

5.2

Callapine and his forces are going to march against their great enemy. There is the significant prescient note:

> Yet when the pride of Cynthia is at full,
> She wanes again, and so shall his, I hope.

But not even Tamburlaine's foes seem to know, really, who his greatest foe now is!

5.3

It would be superogatory for Marlowe to do much in this last scene besides record the death of the tremendous protagonist. His three henchmen, whom we have known from the beginning of his ascent, verbally assault the heavens:

> But if he die, your glories are disgrac'd,
> Earth droops and says that hell in heaven is plac'd!

> So honor, heaven (till heaven dissolved be),
> His birth, his life, his health, and majesty!

> For if he die, thy glory is disgrac'd,
> Earth droops and says that hell in heaven is plac'd!

Thus, Marlowe's operatic technique functions.

Tamburlaine enters in his man-drawn regal chariot, with physicians. He is ill, and dying. And threats the heavens, seeing his invisible enemy, Death. There is an alarum, and a Messenger announces Callapine's forces. Tamburlaine momentarily rises to his former height, rides off the stage. "Alarm. Tamburlaine goes in, and comes out again with all the rest." The sound of battle between his exit and return denotes victory. He comes on again with his human chariot and asks for a map, detailing his world conquests. To Amyras and Celebinus, watching his finger, are left the rest of the globe to conquer. To the latter he gives his whip, the crown he gives to Theridamas (?), as he asks his sons to take his place in the chariot. He is carried from it, put against a stage post, and they sit in the glorious vehicle. Theridamas (?) crowns Amyras. The trumpets bray.

Gasping, the great Scythian, supported by Techelles and Usumcasane, leans against a pillar. He orders Zenocrate's hearse to be brought in. It is, she lying there in all her glaring color as though she were alive. The astounding leader then dies. Amyras delivers his encomium. Borne by soldiers (or by Theridamas, Usumcasane, Techelles, and Celebinus?) Tamburlaine's body is carried from the stage amidst martial sounds, in procession: the chariot with the two sons; Theridamas, Techelles, Usumcasane—bearing standards?; the hearse carried by slaves; and soldiers filling the rear. And so the Second Part of *Tamburlaine* ends.

The Elizabethan English History Play

Most modern criticism of the Elizabethan English history play assumes that it is rigidly doctrinaire in its Tudor interpretation of history—i.e., however bad the king is, rebellion against him is forbidden by God: if such rebellion does occur, evil consequences *must* follow.[40] This modern conception is based largely (1) on the repeated lessons of two official homilies, *An Exhortation to Obedience* and *An Homily Against Disobedience and Wilful Rebellion,* which were to be read in church on

---

[40] Lily B. Campbell, *Shakespeare's "Histories," Mirrors of Elizabethan Policy* (San Marino, 1947). E. M. W. Tillyard, *Shakespeare's History Plays* (London, 1956). Irving Ribner, *The English History Play in the Age of Shakespeare* (Princeton University Press, 1957).

Sundays,[41] and (2) on Edward Hall's *The Union of the Two Noble and Illustre Families of Lancaster and York* (1548), wherein the usurpation of Henry IV (Bolingbroke) is deemed the cause of the ensuing national misfortunes till Henry VII (of Lancaster) solved the breach by marrying Elizabeth of York, and so founded the Tudor lineage. Yet those who read Shakespeare's *Richard II* in this light forget that it was not the first but the fifth of his history plays dealing with the last century; that it was preceded by *1, 2, 3 Henry VI* and *Richard III;* and that it was the first of a second tetralogy, which included *Richard II, 1 Henry IV, 2 Henry IV,* and *Henry V.* (Furthermore, there is the probability that there was a lapse of two years between the composition of *Richard III* and *Richard II.*) But even in the second tetralogy the effects of Bolingbroke's crime are personal guilt rather than national misadventure. On the contrary, Henry IV defeats his self-seeking opponents, Hotspur, Glendower, and Mortimer, who want to cut up England like a large cheese. And his great son, Henry V, wins imperishable glory in France. (It is significant that Henry V begs God's forgiveness not for the usurpation but for Richard's murder: "the fault/My father made in compassing the crown" consists, apparently, in the "forced drops of blood" of the deposed king. *Henry V* 4.1.310-22.)

England instead of suffering from the reigns of the two Lancasters is ultimately benefited by order and prosperity. The dire prophecies of Richard and the Bishop of Carlisle in *Richard II* are not accomplished, surely, within the circumscription of the second tetralogy. Shakespeare meant them to point to the reign of Henry VI, which he had dealt with in his first tetralogy. But the application of Edward Hall's doom to this first tetralogy is a second thought, a thought which does not seem to have been in Shakespeare's mind when he wrote these first four plays.

I would certainly agree that Shakespeare was endeavoring to create a huge drama of nemesis beginning in Richard II's reign and ending in Henry VII's. Unfortunately, the facts don't neatly fit Shakespeare's later hypothesis. In *1, 2, 3 Henry VI* and *Richard III* no character ever claims that the misfortunes of England, internal and external, proceed from Bolingbroke's crime. There is not a single reference to his usurpation as a

---

[41] Reprinted in *Certain Sermons or Homilies Appointed to be Read in Churches in the Time of Queen Elizabeth of Famous Memory* (S.P.C.K., 1843). See Alfred Hart, *Shakespeare and the Homilies* (Melbourne University Press, 1934).

sin against God that must be paid for. No, it is the incompetence
and weakness of Henry VI as ruler; the bickering, the non-
co-operativeness, and downright enmity for one another of his
nobles; the Machiavellian ambitions of York—which lead to
the loss of possessions in France and the splitting of England
into the internecine factions of the War of the Roses. I would
not deny for a minute that the hero of both tetralogies is,
ultimately, England itself. What must be denied vehemently is
that the first tetralogy fits the Procrustean theory of modern
critics and scholars.

But even in the second tetralogy there is an important
debate going on that weakens the official Tudor premise. Given
God's threat of reprisal, is it nevertheless better to have a
weak, profligate, destructive monarch whose claim is that
of primogeniture, or a strong usurper from whose strength
and cunning the country obviously benefits? The second
tetralogy certainly gives no clear-cut answer to this problem.

As a matter of fact, despite his later and occasional surface
adherence to the official line, Shakespeare is always being quite
as surprisingly nonreverential as his fellow dramatists in his
portrayal of English kings. The character and actions of
Richard II, with his sycophants and cronies and his complete
lack of true care for his good lords and his good people, in the
anonymous manuscript play *Woodstock* (1592 *ca.*), are shocking.[42] And the unknown author seems implicitly to be justifying
the rebellion of the nobles and commons against him. The fact
is that *Woodstock*, Marlowe's *Edward II*, and Shakespeare's
1, 2, 3 Henry VI—all three written probably between 1590 and
1592—present appalling portraits of past English kings, against
each of whom armed rebellion seems almost necessary for the
good of England. This cannot be denied.

The modern critical theory of dramatic compliance with
official doctrine has come about not because of the content of
the above plays but in spite of it! Perhaps this theory has
gained acceptance precisely because scholars *do* recognize the
truth of what I have written above and have considered it
unthinkable that in an era when Elizabeth was threatened from
abroad and at home by Catholic enemies the government should
have allowed the popular stage to denigrate English royalty, to
show scenes of regicide, and more or less to justify rebellion.
What is the answer to this paradox? I think it lies in the power
of contrast. Elizabeth was such a popular, careful, patriotic

---

[42] A. P. Rossiter (ed.), *"Woodstock," A Moral History* (London,
1946).

monarch that no harm could come from seeing the opposite type of ruler in the theater. This is a guess, unsupported by documentary evidence. But at least it is a guess that does not run counter to the evidence of the plays themselves.

One further point should be made. The official Tudor doctrine concerning unswerving loyalty to the king, whatever his faults, was merely one theory among many conflicting ones in Europe. In Calvin, for example, the English Protestants could certainly find rebellion by the magistrates (i.e., the estate of the nobles) clearly supported.[43] I advise readers of the Elizabethan history plays either to base their determination of the inherent political values on the plays themselves or to read (a) Otto Gierke's *Political Theories of the Middle Ages* (Beacon Paperback, 1958); (b) J. W. Allen's *A History of Political Thought in the Sixteenth Century* (London, 1928); and (c) J. H. M. Salmon's *The French Religious Wars in English Political Thought* (Oxford, 1959) as a preparative. In this way they will be protected from letting a priori notions of the "correct" contents of these early plays of the 1590's obscure their own appraisals.

The source of *Edward II* is the second edition of Holinshed's *Chronicle* (1587). Like Shakespeare and the *Woodstock* playwright, Marlowe feels free to invent and employ his imagination, even to the extent of denying the historical fact. These plays are as far from being truly "historical" in our sense, or even in the Elizabethan sense in so far as the given data of available chronicles controlled, as possible. It almost seems as though only the main facts of birth and death of the leading characters are retained—and even here one cannot be sure! In short, Marlowe's Gaveston, Kent, and Young Mortimer are about as true to Holinshed as Falstaff is. And he is purely a theatrical invention!

The Elizabethan playwrights were very much concerned with the man behind the political *persona* (or mask). In play after play, for example, from *Richard III* through *Julius Caesar* and *Macbeth* to *Antony and Cleopatra*, Shakespeare showed the divergence between public role and private person. Both he and Marlowe, within the space of a few years, the former in *Richard II*, the latter in *Edward II*, queried: What kind of

---

[43] John T. McNeill, *John Calvin on God and Political Duty* (New York, 1950), p. xviii. See also Merritt Y. Hughes' summary of sixteenth-century defenses of deposition and regicide in *The Seventeenth Century: Studies in the History of English Thought and Literature . . . by R. F. Jones and Others* (Stanford University Press, 1951), pp. 247-63.

creature behind his royal robes and gestures is this king? [44]
Now this may give us a clue as how to interpret Marlowe's
historical play. Not only the King, but the Queen, and the
leader of the nobles, Young Mortimer, ultimately reveal themselves—say, after the beginning of Scene 3 of Act 4. It is not
that they have been hypocritical hitherto in their public functions. It is, rather, that their dramatic roles at first as King,
Queen, and Lord are symbolic. Marlowe is showing that the
King is a poor monarch because, not recognizing birth and rank,
he prefers base sycophants to the lords' estate. He infuriates
both priest and peer, with whom he should to some extent
share power, or from whom, at least, he should ask and accept
advice, by insisting on his total right of choice, however irrational or politically disintegrative it may be. His great disorder
is illustrated by a choice of a male favorite, Gaveston, to share
his throne and bed instead of Isabella, his royal consort. Marlowe uses Gaveston and the Spencers not so much for their own
dramatic interest as for their relationship to the blindly wilful
King. Thus, Isabella is not so much for the first two thirds of
the play an identifiable, particular woman as a forsaken queen.
Young Mortimer for most of the play acts and talks in no way
differently from Warwick and Lancaster, for each represents
the same political stratum. The Bishop of Coventry is not a
person (say, like Shakespeare's Winchester in *2 Henry VI*)
but the church which Edward violates and pillages for the
sake of his minion, Gaveston. In the last part of the play
Edward, Isabella, and Young Mortimer are personalized: the
first, as a pathetic, suffering man; the second, as a treacherous,
unfaithful wife; and the third, as a Machiavellian individualist,
villainous in his plans, uninterested in the good of the state,
avid only for power. But I must not be understood as imply-
ing their later manifestations are more psychologically viable
than their earlier. The psychology of this play is never more
than skin-deep. But what does happen is that characters who
are functions in a political arena become characters who are
individual people. The exception to this illustrates the rule.
Kent never forsakes his function of chorus, *that* in the play
which is meant to regulate our reactions and emotions.

---

[44] Cf. L. C. Knights, *Shakespeare's Politics: With Some Reflections on the Nature of Tradition* (Annual Shakespeare Lecture of
the British Academy, 1957).

Edward II and Holinshed

By and large Marlowe regarded the 1587 Holinshed account of
the reign of Edward II as inchoate material and freely invented.
The main facts of the opposition to Gaveston and the Spencers,
the insurrection of the nobles, and Edward's defeat by the
Queen's forces are in the chronicle. But this is just an outline
on which the dramatist imposed his own interpretation and
invention. For example, the fondness of the king for Gaveston
is in Holinshed's pages, but there is no hint that it is homosexual. Readers of the play have probably wondered why
Lancaster and Warwick are sent to death, whereas Young
Mortimer is merely committed to the Tower. This is because
the latter begins to become a main character in the chronicle
only after the Queen arrives in France. Thus, in Holinshed,
it is the Bishop of Hereford, not Mortimer, who orders the
King's death in the riddling Latin sentence. And it is not until
shortly before the end of the section on Edward II that we
hear that "without him [Mortimer] the queen did nothing."
It is only in the next reign, that of Edward III, that we are
told they are lovers. So Mortimer as chief of the nobles and
the Queen's paramour is largely the playwright's invention.
Nevertheless, there is at least one point where history seems
to have tripped up the dramatist. The whole business of
Gaveston's relationship to the Earl of Gloucester's niece is
very confusing in the play. (In Holinshed, Young Spencer and
Baldock are not connected with her.) This is what the
chronicle has:

> About the thirteenth day of October [1308], a parliament
> was holden at Northampton. . . . [in which] a marriage
> was concluded betwixt the earl of Cornwall Peers de Gaves-
> ton, and the daughter of Gilbert de Clare earl of Gloucester
> . . . , which marriage was solemnized on All Hallows Day
> next ensuing.

But in the drama where our attention is on the unnaturalness
of the King's affection for his favorite, the introduction of the
Gaveston-Niece love affair is most bewildering.

In the following passages the reader can see what in the
chronicle gave Marlowe his basic conceptions. The first is from
the reign of the King's father:

> In the three and thirtieth year of his reign [1304], king
> Edward [I] put his son prince Edward in prison, because

that he had riotously broken the park of Walter Langston bishop of Chester; and because the prince had done this deed by the procurement of a lewd and wanton person, one Peers Gaveston, an esquire of Gascoigne, the king banished him the realm, lest the prince, who delighted much in his company, might by his evil and wanton counsel fall to evil and naughty rule.

[Edward II began his reign July 7, 1307.] Within three days after, when the lord treasurer Walter de Langston bishop of Coventry and Lichfield (through whose complaint Peers de Gaveston had been banished the land) was going towards Westminster, to make preparation for the same burial [of Edward I], he was upon commandment from the new king arrested, committed to prison, and after delivered to the hands of the said Peers, being then returned into the realm, who sent him from castle to castle as prisoner. His lands and tenements were seized to the king's use, but his movables were given to the foresaid Peers.

But now concerning the demeanor of the new king, whose disordered manner brought himself and many others unto destruction; we find that in the beginning of his government, though he was of nature given to lightness, yet being restrained with the prudent advertisements of certain of his councillors, to the end he might show some likelihood of good proof, he counterfeited a kind of gravity, virtue and modesty, but yet he could not thoroughly be so bridled, but that forthwith he began to play divers wanton and light parts, at the first not outrageously, but little by little, and that covertly. For having revoked again into England his old mate the said Peers de Gaveston, he received him into most high favor, creating him earl of Cornwall, and lord of Man, his principal secretary, and lord chamberlain of the realm, through whose company and society he was suddenly so corrupted, that he burst out into most heinous vices; for then using the said Peers as a procurer of his disordered doings, he began to have his nobles in no regard, to set nothing by their instructions, and to take small heed to the good government of the commonwealth, so that within a while, he gave himself to wantoness, passing his time in voluptuous pleasure, and riotous excess: and to help them forward in that kind of life, the foresaid Peers, who (as it may be thought, he had sworn to make the king to forget himself, and the state, to the which he was called) furnished his court with companies of jesters, ruffians, flattering parasites, musicians, and other vile and naughty ribalds, that the king might spend both days and nights in jesting, playing, banquetting, and in such other filthy and dishonorable exercises: and moreover, desirous to advance those that were like to himself, he procured for them honorable offices. . . .

Edward II

1.1

The first speech of Gaveston might be considered as exculpating him from sycophancy merely for the sake of personal advantage in power and wealth. For does he not truly love the King for himself alone, as the sensuality of the first nine lines indicates? But Marlowe is really making a quite different point. Edward has written Gaveston "to share the kingdom," and the latter, joying in his return to London, exclaims:

The sight of London to my exil'd eyes
Is as Elysium to a new-come soul.
—Not that I love the city or the men
But that it harbors him I hold so dear,
The King—upon whose bosom let me lie,
And with the world be still at enmity!

Gaveston sneers at "the lordly peers" and "the multitude" in their "poverty." Thus, he whom the King has chosen to share the rule, as it were, hates the estates of England, the nobles and the commons. Neither Edward II nor his favorite, apparently, cares tuppence for the welfare of the country. They are engrossed only in themselves. (Has anyone ever considered that the seed of *Edward II* might have led to the flowering which is *Antony and Cleopatra*?) Marlowe, therefore, very quickly, in a few lines at the beginning of his play, sets forth the wretched political condition of England.

"Enter three Poor men," representing, obviously, the commons. Gaveston at first cruelly taunts them, but then, hypocritically, promises his future favor. They don't fit into his plans. He "must have" wanton music, poetry, and entertainment which will "draw the pliant King which way I please"— a statement that is both sexual and political. When the King and the peers enter, Gaveston draws aside. He stays, unknown, in the background until the lords leave.

The immediate subject of argument between ruler and ruled is Gaveston. In an aside, Edward II speaks like an angry infant, "I'll have my will!" But putting the problem in the terms Marlowe has already set, the Elder Mortimer says, "If you love us, my lord, hate Gaveston!" And to reinforce his major point, Marlowe indicates in Young Mortimer's speech

that the present King's father, Edward I, also wanted Gaveston
out of the realm. Marlowe now shows that Young Mortimer
at first merely threatens to deny aid to his feudal superior: it is
the King's uncompromising attitude that drives the former to
a declaration of rebellion. Who, exclaims Edward, dare "contradict [the] King?" And he threatens the elder statesman
Lancaster with disgraceful death if the latter refuses to bend
to his wishes concerning his favorite.

Lancaster now puts the nobles' position succinctly. Why
should Edward prefer the "base and obscure Gaveston"—who
neither by birth nor rank should have a strong voice in the
realm—to the "peers/That *naturally* would love and honor
you." The King, in short, is being *unnatural*. Again and again
the play indicates that the centrality of the nobles' opposition
to Gaveston is that he is an ignoble upstart who has usurped
the political relationship to the King which the nobles should
rightfully possess. So outrageous is Edward's position that
Lancaster promises to sell his four earldoms to keep Gaveston—
and, of course, his influence—out of England.

Now before we interpret Kent's reaction to the lords' stand
against their sovereign, let us remember that the doctrine of
unquestioning obedience to the monarch has to be stated at
least once categorically and vehemently at the beginning of
the play if we are to measure the forces generated by Edward
and Gaveston's political immaturity which undermine this
doctrine. Those, says Kent, who oppose their King, must be
immediately and completely put down—beheaded.

Young Mortimer cannot restrain himself, breaks to the front,
threatens rather to have Gaveston beheaded. Now he refers
to Edward II as "brain-sick" and promises armed revolution.
His father, Warwick, and Lancaster join with him and speak
irony:

> *E. Mor.* Wiltshire hath men enough to save our heads.
> *War.* All Warwickshire will love him for my sake.
> *Lan.* And northward Gaveston hath many friends.
> Adieu, my lord. And either change your mind,
> Or look to see the throne where you should sit
> To float in blood and at thy wanton head
> The glozing head of thy base minion thrown!

The four voices are one. And the peers exeunt.

Edward is furious. "Am I a king, and must be overrul'd?" His
minion is all-important to him. He will fight with the nobles
"And either die—or live with Gaveston." The latter now comes
forward, and they throw themselves in each other's arms. And

as though to spite the lords who rebuked the King because he
had so elevated the obscurely born favorite, Edward cries:

> I here create thee Lord High-Chamberlain,
> Chief Secretary to the state and me,
> Earl of Cornwall, King and Lord of Man.

(Again, the last line is a sexual pun.) Now Kent, our chorus,
confronts and corrects the King, echoing the objection of the
nobles:

> Brother, the least of these may well suffice
> For one of greater birth than Gaveston.

But Edward can no more listen to his own brother than he
could to the peers of the realm: "Cease, brother, for I cannot
brook these words." (Remember that he is also disobeying his
father in favoring Gaveston.) His kingship is but a means of
pleasing his beloved: "but to honor thee/Is Edward pleas'd
with kingly regiment." It is not merely that they will share the
sovereignty—Gaveston can actually act in the King's stead:

> Would'st thou be lov'd and fear'd? Receive my seal,
> Save or condemn, and in our name command
> Whatso thy mind affects or fancy likes.

Now the King and his favorite, having already antagonized
the estate of the nobility, desecrate the honor of the church too
in the person of the Bishop of Coventry. Kent is shocked:

> Ah, brother, lay not violent hands on him,
> For he'll complain unto the see of Rome.

Thus, by the end of the scene Marlowe has shown us how
King Edward II has alienated the three great estates of the
realm: the commons, the lords, and the church. And Kent, who
at first was defensive of the doctrine of total obedience, has
already begun to waver, in realization of his brother's lack of
regal sagacity.

1.2

Close to the surface in the second scene of the play is the
political doctrine held by some in the sixteenth century that if
the sovereign refused the advice of the three estates, the latter
could rebel and supplant him. Even the Archbishop of Canterbury does not quite voice the Tudor doctrine that God demands
absolute obedience to the monarch. When asked whether he
will "take arms against the King," he is evasive with "God

himself is up in arms." (Contrast this with the King's statement concerning the rebels in Shakespeare's *Richard II*:

> God for his Richard hath in heavenly pay
> A glorious angel. Then, if angels fight,
> Weak men must fall, for heaven still guards the right.
>
> 3.2.60-2.)

But the Archbishop does agree to "join" with the "peers" to
"banish or behead that Gaveston." Young Mortimer threatens
that unless the favorite is exiled, "The King shall lose his
crown"—and the last word can mean *head* as well as golden
ringlet. Now the priest intervenes: "But yet lift not your
swords against the King." But Warwick and Lancaster declare
that war is the only means to get rid of Gaveston. Queen
Isabella, however, would rather her rival stay than "civil
mutinies" against her lord occur. Thus, we have seen a kind of
debate taking place concerning the right and wrong of armed
rebellion and the limits to which it can go. The next three
speeches are extremely important in this debate:

> *Archb. of Cant.* My lords, to ease all this, but hear me
>   speak:
> We and the rest that are his counsellors
> Will meet, and with a general consent
> Confirm his [Gaveston's] banishment with our hands and
>   seals.
> *Lan.* What we confirm the King will frustrate.
> *Y. Mor.* Then may we lawfully revolt from him.

Note, especially, the phrase "his counsellors." These are, or
rather should be, the lords plus the higher hierarchy of the
church. They are, in short, the magistrates who, Calvin averred,
might lawfully revolt against a bad king.

The loyal Queen has been supplanted in the King's favor by
Gaveston. It is not accidental on Marlowe's part that the ap-
position of Edward to his consort, to the church, and to the
nobility should dramatically coalesce in this scene. Isabella's
farewell to Young Mortimer asking him not "to levy arms
against the King," but addressing him as "sweet," begins the
dramatic relationship between the two. Her two lines to him are
prescient.

The emphasis on Gaveston's Gallic extraction in "peevish
Frenchman" and "sly inveigling Frenchman" not only stresses
the foreign country which Marlowe's xenophobic audience especially detested (cf. similar treatment of the French in Shake-

speare's *1 Henry VI*) but also may indicate the minion's foppish and effeminate manner and attire.

1.3

This short dialogue between Gaveston and Kent is a bridge
scene, allowing an interval to occur before the next conflict
of the King and his opponents. The scene does show Gaveston
speaking familiarly to the King's brother, too familiarly, using
the latter's given name. Probably Kent's face is noncommital
as the favorite speaks scornfully and disparagingly of the
nobles.

1.4

This scene consists of five movements, each of which, except
for the final one, causes the next. The peers and the Archbishop,
representing two of the three estates, enter and subscribe to
a document banishing Gaveston, "that base peasant." Then the
King, Gaveston, and Kent make their entrance. Edward seats
the favorite by his side and to the nobles' anger at this un-
kingly act heedlessly declares, "It is our pleasure, we will have
it so!" To the Elder Mortimer the sight of the "scornful . . .
peasant" sharing the throne is offensive to any "man of
noble birth." To the nobility Gaveston is a "creeping ant,"
an "Ignoble vassal," who—forgetting his real social status—
now endeavors to "overpeer" them all. Edward calls Young
Mortimer a traitor, and the latter responds with the same term
for Gaveston. Kent again raises the problem of obedience: "Is
this the duty that you owe your King?" But Warwick makes
the answer that many scholars made in the Middle Ages, that
if the country owes duties to the monarch, the monarch owes
duties to the country; there is, implicit, a contractual relationship: "We know our duties, let him know his peers." The
nobles try to hustle Gaveston away, and the King utters the
kind of empty threat which Shakespeare's Richard II so often
employs: "Stay, or ye shall die!" The Elder Mortimer promptly
indicates the emptiness of this promise. Gaveston's "Were I a
king" causes a rejoinder in Young Mortimer that is the
essence of the nobles' objection to the minion. He is a villain
—a *villein*, a peasant, as well as a wicked creature, "hardly
. . . a gentleman by birth!" Edward II's response is meant by
Marlowe to show that it is the King who is really the innovator
—in Elizabethan terms, the overthrower of honorable tradition:
"Were he a peasant, being my minion,/I'll make the proudest
of you stoop to him." This is a tremendous affront, that an
earl should bow to a serf!

Lancaster immediately cries out, "You may not thus disparage us!" and orders the attendants to remove "hateful

Gaveston"; and the Elder Mortimer includes Kent "that favors him." Edward is refulgent with dramatic irony as he offers his kingship to Mortimer, Warwick, and Lancaster in turn. It is as though it is impossible for Edward to rule by himself. "Was ever king thus over-rul'd as I?" he asks. The nobles tell him why they have not been obedient. He must learn to rule better: he has miscalculated the concern of the nobility for the state's condition, and he has not realized the implications for the nobles of his maintaining "this upstart pride," Gaveston. When the furious King declares that he can no longer speak, the Archbishop tells him to control himself and to look over the document banishing his minion. The Archbishop's phrase "your counsellors" indicates that the two estates of the church and the nobility mean to save Edward from himself. But the King utters a fretful rodomontade, which, incidentally, contains the point that Gaveston is more important to him than England itself.

Now "the counsellors" play their trump card. The Archbishop indirectly threatens the papal interdict unless the King, too, puts his signature to Gaveston's official exile. Young Mortimer is more direct. If the King refuses, an episcopal curse will make it possible for "the counsellors" to "Depose him and elect another king!" But the King is obdurate, and the Archbishop threatens to discharge the lords from their obedience. In an aside Edward realizes that he is caught. (Whatever the feelings of the Elizabethan audience against Rome, at the present juncture of the play they would probably accept the Archbishop not so much as the representative of the Scarlet Whore as of the English church.) The obsessed King promises all kinds of offices to the lords, even to the giving up of the kingdom itself, if they will let him "frolic with my dearest Gaveston." The King apparently does not realize the implications of his statement that Gaveston loves him "more than all the world"—England included! When Edward says that the "noble-born" should pity his minion, Warwick replies, "You that are princely-born should shake him off./For shame, subscribe, and let the lown depart." His descriptive term "the lown" is extremely astringent. And the King knowing that he must bend or lose all subscribes to the banishment. The nobles immediately go into action to carry out their consuming desire, and Pembroke adds a significant statement, "This will be good news to the common sort." As I have indicated *all* the estates of the realm want Edward to put away his favorite.

Now begins the second movement of this scene. The King, alone on the stage, sounds like a parody of Tamburlaine or Barabas in his threats against the clergy and the peers. "Enter

Gaveston." The King gives him the inescapable alternatives:
either "thou must hence, or I shall be depos'd." Each grieves
at the parting like heterosexual lovers. They exchange pictures
—one is reminded of Romeo's parting from Juliet—and Edward
makes Gaveston Governor of Ireland.

Now with the entrance of Queen Isabella the third movement
of the scene begins. The King takes his grief and anger out on
her, bidding the "French strumpet" be gone. And with feline
nastiness—but, unwittingly, with ironic prescience—the King's
favorite suggests that Isabella and Young Mortimer are having
an affair. Edward echoes his minion and accuses the Queen
of being the cause of Gaveston's banishment. Then he says

> But I would wish thee reconcile the lords—
> Or thou shalt ne'er be reconcil'd to me.

Isabella and Gaveston confront each other like two lovers
quarreling over the same woman—with the difference that the
King is definitely on the side of the favorite. After Edward
and Gaveston leave, the Queen declares her impossible position:

> I must entreat him, I must speak him fair,
> And be a means to call home Gaveston—
> And yet he'll ever dote on Gaveston!
> And so am I for ever miserable!

Now ensues the fourth movement. When the lords return, the
Queen indicates her dilemma to them and begs Young Mortimer
to take her plea to the peers for the repeal of Gaveston, and
she draws him aside to reason with him. After their pantomime
discussion, Young Mortimer makes clear that she has won him
over:

> 'Tis not for his [Gaveston's] sake but for our avail—
> Nay, for the realm's behoof and for the King's.

But the audience's surprise at Young Mortimer's shift is allayed
by his further explanation:

> But were he [Gaveston] here, detested as he is,
> How easily might some base slave be suborn'd
> To greet his lordship with a poniard—
> And none so much as blame the murderer
> But rather praise him for that brave attempt
> And in the chronicle enroll his name
> For purging of the realm of such a plague!

It is to be noted that Isabella utters no word of objection to
this murderous solution of their problem. Furthermore, says

Young Mortimer, Gaveston will now know their power "And fear to offend the meanest nobleman." But if he do not,

> Then may we with some color rise in arms.
> For howsoever we have borne it out,
> 'Tis treason to be up against the King.
> So shall we have the people of our side,
> Which for his father's sake lean to the King
> But cannot brook a night-grown mushroom,
> Such a one as my lord of Cornwall is,
> Should bear us down of the nobility.
> And when the commons and the nobles join,
> 'Tis not the King can buckler Gaveston!

Note how this implicitly continues the debate on the justification of rebellion and deposition. It *is* treason to oppose the King, who holds his realm by primogeniture; but if all the estates are against Gaveston, his overthrow is both logically and morally inevitable. Isabella promises never to forget Young Mortimer's "favor." The King re-enters mourning,

> And could my crown's revénue bring him back,
> I would freely give it to his enemies—
> And think I gain'd, having bought so dear a friend!

This suggests Edward's unconcern for the finances of his realm. When the Queen addresses him, he again suggests her involvement with Young Mortimer. But when she reveals that Gaveston is repealed, he is beside himself with joy and is fulsome in his regard for her and the nobles. He reveals that he is going to marry his favorite to the daughter of the Duke of Gloucester. The word "heir" applied to his niece, with its suggestion of land and gold, may reveal his purpose.

After this reconciliation all leave the stage except the Mortimers. And this is the last movement of the scene. The Elder indicates that homosexual love is very common in history. And as though to reinforce the point that I have tried to make that it is not Gaveston's sexual but his political relationship which is so disturbing to the lords, Young Mortimer says,

> Uncle, his wanton humor grieves not me.
> But this I scorn, that one so basely born
> Should by his sovereign's favor grow so pert
> And riot it with the treasure of the realm
> While soldiers mutiny for want of pay—.

It is the fact that the all-powerful Gaveston, base-born, not a peer of the realm, should have more potent influence with

the King than any one of the three estates—this it is that
inflames Young Mortimer's anger. And so the scene ends.

2.1

At the beginning of this act we meet Young Spencer and
Baldock. They have been retainers of the Earl of Gloucester
who has recently died and seem at present to be marking time
with King Edward's niece, the dead Earl's daughter. The conversation of these two would-be court-climbers is semicomic,
and provides an interlude between two scenes that are not
only very serious but also rather repetitive. Young Spencer
and Baldock are somewhat Machiavellian in their attitude
toward success in court. And the two, though separate, represent a dramatic promise and a parallel: that although Gaveston
disappear from the action, there will be others to take a
similar role with the King. I also believe that the absence here
of any sign of homosexuality or effeminacy is Marlowe's indication of what we have already surmised, that it is the political
aspect of the *arriviste* Gaveston that is of concern to the
estates of the realm and not his sexual relationship with Edward. Baldock and Young Spencer intend to become followers
of the Gascon, who implicitly promises, because of his success
with the King, success for themselves.

The present-day reader and spectator may well be confused
by the bond between the Lady (Gloucester's heir and Edward's niece) and the King's minion. We have heard nothing
of it from the Frenchman and are somewhat surprised, first,
by Edward's backing of the marriage in the last scene of Act
One and, second, by Young Spencer's insistence that she still
loves Gaveston. The King's plan in the marriage, one has no
difficulty in assuming, is the hope of advancing his favorite by
a step which will ally him socially with royalty. What Gaveston's attitude toward the match is we never find out except
for his epistolary assertion of eternal love, although the two
confront each other at the end of the next scene when the
dramatic focus must perforce be on the war that has broken
out. Marlowe's insertion of the Gaveston-Lady material seems
somewhat unfinished; nevertheless, any expansion of it would
surely have interfered with the progress of the main plot as
Marlowe envisages it. Again, Marlowe may be deliberately
puzzling us to seek an answer, just as he does with the Young
Mortimer-Isabella relationship.

At any rate the niece takes Young Spencer with her to the
court at the end of the scene, promising him reward for his
services.

2.2

Edward is shown as very much on edge for the return of his favorite. And by a subtle, dramatic touch Marlowe has the later close alliance of the Queen and the rebels suggested in Isabella's remark on the King's present passion to Lancaster. Young Mortimer is angry at the King's impatience for Gaveston's return, and again it is not the personal relationship but the political significance that is underlined. While the King is stewing about his minion, "matters of more weight" are being forgotten: "The King of France sets foot in Normandy." Edward considers the invasion as "A trifle!" (Later, this *trifle* of the Normandy incident will lead step by step to Edward's downfall, for it will put Isabella in France, where she will ultimately receive the military aid necessary to defeat her husband.)

The King has decreed a "stately triumph" for his favorite's delight. At the King's questioning, Young Mortimer and Lancaster reveal that their shield devices symbolically castigate the upstart. Kent angrily comments on their rancor, but the angry King answers the lords' threats with his own. "They love me not that hate my Gaveston." Enter Gaveston. He and Edward embrace and joy in their reunion. Then the King turns to the lords, "Will none of you salute my Gaveston?" Lancaster, Young Mortimer, Warwick, and Pembroke mockingly greet the arrival with his new titles. And Kent again points out how insulting to the sovereign the peers are. The King encourages Gaveston to return the taunts at his base birth. Gaveston with his typical Frenchman's attitude toward supposed English dullness cries out:

Base, leaden earls that glory in your birth—
Go sit at home and eat your tenant's beef—
And come not here to scoff at Gaveston—
Whose mounting thoughts did never creep so low
As to bestow a look on such as you!

Lancaster draws his sword in the presence of his monarch, and the latter bawls "Treason!" Gaveston probably draws his own sword, and Young Mortimer thrusts at him. After Gaveston is removed, because of the King's fear that he is in real danger, Edward expels Young Mortimer from the court. The latter braves his sovereign and refuses to leave. Each side now threatens the other, and Warwick is blunt. "Look to your own crown, if you back him thus." Once more Kent admonishes the nobility because of its defiance of the ruler. And now it is the King that threatens military action, " 'Tis war that must abate

these barons' pride!" After Edward, Isabella and Kent leave
the stage, the nobles swear not to cease until Gaveston, that
"abject villain," is dead. Young Mortimer is open in hoping
that the King "perish in his wrath." And Lancaster wants
heralds to be sent out to get the commons on their side.

Just at this moment Young Mortimer is informed by a
Messenger that his uncle, the Elder Mortimer, whom we have
met, has been taken prisoner by the Scots—who demand a
ransom of five thousand pounds. Young Mortimer points out
that since his uncle was fighting the King's wars, the King
should furnish the money for his release. After Warwick and
Pembroke leave to carry out their military plans in "secrecy,"
Mortimer and Lancaster set out to see Edward about the
ransom, but a guard bars their way. Edward enters, sees who
is awaiting him, and starts to leave. Young Mortimer tells him
the news about his uncle, but the King scornfully answers,
"Then ransom him." Young Mortimer is furious. Kent again
rebukes the nobleman who is threatening his Sovereign, but
the King sneers at Young Mortimer by telling him that he shall
have a beggar's warrant to collect monies for his uncle throughout the realm. At this insult Young Mortimer strikes his sword
and says this is the prayer that the proud Mortimers will use.

And now comes an itemized account of Edward's poor rule:

> *Y. Mor.* The idle triumphs, masks, lascivious shows, *ff.*
> (2.2.157-95).

It should be noted that the emphasis is very definitely beginning to shift from the political disparagement of his minion
to disparagement of the King himself. (And as I have tried to
point out again and again, Gaveston is more a political symbol
in the play than merely a homosexual beloved. The nobles hate
him because he represents as a person the King's failure as a
true prince of his realm.) After Mortimer and Lancaster leave,
Edward reveals to Kent that though he has been so often
"baited by these peers," he has been afraid to retaliate because
"their power is great." Yet now he will take tyrannous revenge. At this announcement, the choral Kent indicates that
Gaveston is not worth the wars that his retention will cause.
He rebukes the King because of this ruinous love, and the King
angrily sends him to stand with the nobles.

> *Kent.* No marvel though thou scorn thy noble peers
> When I thy brother am rejected thus—. *Exit* [*Kent*].

Truly Edward is losing the whole world for his love. He will
not admit his faults or responsibilities.

As the Queen enters with his niece, Gaveston, Baldock, and

Young Spencer, the King infantilely accuses her of being the cause of all his troubles, but a Gaveston aside tells him to play the hypocrite and "speak her fair"; so Edward begs forgiveness, which is quickly got. Now the King turns to the barons' wars. The last six words of the following quotation are extremely important:

> *Gav.* Why do you not commit him [Young Mortimer] to the Tower?
> *K. Edw.* I dare not, *for the people love him well.*

The King and his favorite talk about a private murder of their enemies. (In both *Edward II* and *Richard II* our reaction to the misery of the fallen ruler, however compassionate, can never wholly avoid remembrance of his own cruelty when in power.)

Edward turns to Baldock and Spencer. He promises his favors to the former despite his lack of noble birth (cf. Gaveston). And when Gaveston praises Spencer, the King indicates that Spencer will climb high because of his minion's recommendation. The scene ends with Edward's easy verbal victory over his opponents:

> The headstrong barons shall not limit me!
> He that I list to favor shall be great.
> Come, let's away! And when the marriage ends,
> Have at the rebels, and their 'complices!

2.3

This scene marks the opening of the lords' armed rebellion against Edward, but the issue as to whether this warfare will lead to the deposition of the King is deliberately still left ambiguous by the dramatist. Lancaster's speech,

> None be so hardy as to touch the King—
> But neither spare you Gaveston nor his friends.

is meant to show the state of mind of the King's opponents at this particular time. It is interesting to see Marlowe's dramaturgic technique here. The falling-away of the choral Kent should surely go in the direction of redeeming the peers' martial behavior toward their ruler. Instead, Marlowe, by the speech of Lancaster which has just been quoted, shows the nobles more discriminating between the King and his favorite than they have hitherto been. Note again the playwright's insistence on the political interpretation of the King-Gaveston relationship. Kent is leaving his brother because "of love to this our native land" and "the realm's behoof" and joining with the lords in their "quarrel."

2.4

After drums and alarums, the King and Young Spencer enter from different directions. Marlowe immediately emphasizes the pathological attachment of Edward to his favorite. In spite of the fact that his kingdom and perhaps his very life are in danger, the King can think only of Gaveston. When the latter enters with the Queen and his betrothed, Edward sends the favorite away by boat and prepares to leave by land himself. He says farewell to his minion and to his niece, but thrusts the Queen aside with a sneer at her love for Mortimer. (It should be noted that the King is almost forcing her to make a reality of his unfounded suspicions.) The Queen's soliloquy on the bare stage witnesses her true love for her husband.

More alarums, and the armed lords enter searching, whether for Gaveston or his master is deliberately not made clear. It is instructive that no animosity is shown toward Isabella, who indicates that she shares their feelings about "wicked Gaveston." There is a nice distinction, perhaps, between what Mortimer intends in this rebellion and what Lancaster intends. At Young Mortimer's query about Edward's whereabouts, the Queen asks, "What would you with the King? Is't him you seek?" Lancaster, whether speaking for himself or not we do not know, replies:

No, madam, but that cursed Gaveston.
Far be it from the thought of Lancaster
To offer violence to his sovereign!
We would but rid the realm of Gaveston:

Now Marlowe indicates the Queen's deeper involvement in the fight against her master. She informs the nobles where Gaveston is gone. "Pursue him quickly and he cannot scape." The affair between Queen Isabella and Young Mortimer is slowly taking on bulk and credence:

Q. Isab. You know the King is so suspicious
As if he hear I have but talk'd with you
Mine honor will be call'd in question
And therefore, gentle Mortimer, be gone.
    Y. Mor. Madam, I cannot stay to answer you.
But think of Mortimer as he deserves!
                                        [Exeunt all but Queen.]
    Q. Isab. So well hast thou deserv'd, sweet Mortimer,
As Isabel could live with thee for ever.
In vain I look for love at Edward's hand,
Whose eyes are fix'd on none but Gaveston.

Yet the Queen is not yet ready to give up her husband. She will
"importune" him; if he does not pay attention to her prayers,
she will go to France with her son and complain to her brother
the King.

2.5

Gaveston enters hurriedly, trying to escape his pursuers, and
again the deep love between him and his master is stressed.
The counterpoint of the situation is that although Gaveston and
the King to themselves are lover and beloved, to the nobles they
are ruler and base parasite. But Mortimer and the rest come in
and take Gaveston prisoner. They scorn him.

> Corrupter of thy King, cause of these broils,
> Base flatterer, yield!

Mortimer indicates his contempt for the minion's social rank
by refusing to engage in combat with him. Lancaster compares
him to Helen of Troy who caused the Trojan War. And Warwick calls him a "slave" whom they intend to hang. He will
be executed not like a baron but like a common thief. Arundel
enters to ask for temporary custody of the favorite so the
King may see him before he dies, but the nobles refuse. Listen
to Warwick:

> Arundel, no! We wot,
> He that the care of his realm remits,
> And drives his nobles to these exigents
> For Gaveston, will if he seize him once
> Violate any promise to possess him.

And Mortimer, with the insistent motif of Gaveston's low
birth, calls the prisoner "base groom, robber of king's renown!" However, Pembroke decides to give in to the King's
request and upon his honor promises to return Gaveston to
the lords. They reluctantly agree, but Warwick in an aside tells
us that Gaveston will never reach the King.

3.1

Warwick enters to take Gaveston from Pembroke's men.
Though the latter try to retain Gaveston, Warwick insists that
he be given up. When James, Pembroke's retainer, tells Warwick that he is making James' lord break his oath, Warwick
replies, "it is my country's cause I follow." And so Gaveston
goes to his death.

3.2

In this scene Marlowe soon makes his dramatic purpose
clear. The conflict between the lords and the King is apparently

unresolvable in that the King on the one hand obviously must
always rule with the aid of one or two base-born parasites,
whereas, on the other hand, the lords will constantly insist on
their hereditary rights as advisers of the sovereign. The audience, knowing that Gaveston is dead, immediately sees in 3.2
that his place has been taken by Young Spencer and Baldock.
We saw in 2.1 and 2.2 how the role in such a scene as the present
of these two "flatterers" was being dramatically prepared for.
Included in Edward's first lines in this scene,

> I shall never see
> My lovely Pierce, my Gaveston again!
> The barons overbear me with their pride.

are, as I say, the essence of the political situation. The King
dotes on his lowly born sycophants, *now* Spencer and Baldock,
and the lords in their pride will be in rebellion. Young Spencer's
advice, together with Baldock's, however, shows a subtle shift
from the Gaveston position and attitude. The relationship of
these parasites and their King is not one of sexual love but one
of overflattering praise and obeisance.

Young Spencer wants the King to "Strike off their heads,
and let them preach on poles!" Thus, the nobles will "learn
obedience to their lawful King!" The King admits that he has
been "too mild"—and, of course, Marlowe is indicating here
and elsewhere the dichotomy between Edward's bombastic
verbiage and his actual ineffective power. Baldock pours more
oil on the fire by implicitly denying the necessity of political
relationship between the King and the peers of the realm. He
advises Edward II

> Not to be tied to their affection
> As though Your Highness were a schoolboy still:
> And must be aw'd and govern'd like a child.

Hence, the dramatist in definite fashion is pointing out that
continued exacerbation and rebellion between the nobles and
their ruler are inevitable. Edward's soldiers have already entered with drums and fifes. Now enter the Elder Spencer with
his faithful followers. (Of course, Marlowe implicitly wants us
to compare the roles of the rebelling, nobly born Mortimers with
those of the Gaveston substitutes, Young and Elder Spencer.)
And just as Edward threw title after title on the unworthy
shoulders of Gaveston, so here Edward makes Young Spencer
the Earl of Wiltshire and promises him large territories.

"Enter the Queen and her son and Levune, a Frenchman."
Together with the King's incompetent handling of the question
of the Queen; of the rights of the peers; of the advice of his

own brother, Kent, we have heard of Edward's unsuccessful attempts upon the marauding Scots. Now we learn of his carelessness in important dealings with his brother-in-law, the King of France. Because Edward has been "slack in homage," Valois "Hath seized Normandy into his hands." Edward's reply to Isabella is, as usual, fatuous:

> Tush Sib, if this be all,
> Valois and I will soon be friends again.
> —But to my Gaveston! Shall I never see,
> Never behold thee now?—Madam, in this matter
> We will employ you and your little son:
> You shall go parley with the King of France.

The childish term *Sib* and the intrusion of Gaveston into his thoughts show how uncomprehensive of his royal duties Edward is.

Arundel enters and reports Gaveston's death. Young Spencer, taking over Gaveston's relationship completely, urges on Edward continued and stronger martial efforts against the "Proud recreants!" In rodomontade, Edward—kneeling—swears:

> I will have heads and lives for him as many *ff*. (3.1.135-45).

And to make matters absolutely clear to the audience, the King cries that in "this place of [Gaveston's] honor and of trust,"

> Spencer, sweet Spencer, I adopt thee here:
> And merely of our love we do create thee
> Earl of Gloucester and Lord Chamberlain,
> Despite of times, despite of enemies.

What I have already indicated is brought out bluntly by the nobles' emissary. Their Messenger announces:

> The barons up in arms by me salute
> Your Highness with long life and happiness—
> And bid me say, as plainer to your grace,
> That if without effusion of blood
> You will this grief have ease and remedy
> That from your princely person you remove
> This Spencer as a putrifying branch
> That deads the royal vine, whose golden leaves
> Empale your princely head, your diadem,
> Whose brightness such pernicious upstarts dim—
> Say they, and lovingly advise Your Grace
> To cherish virtue and nobility
> And have old servitors in high esteem

And shake off smooth dissembling flatterers:
This granted, they, their honors, and their lives
Are to Your Highness vow'd and consecrate.

Like his predecessor Young Spencer points at the barons'
"pride." And not having learned a single thing, Edward in reply
embraces Spencer openly. And so the internecine war continues.

Battle is joined. "Alarums, excursions, a great fight, and a
retreat." Edward, like Richard II, still acts as though he is
God's viceroy:

Why do we sound retreat? Upon them, lords!
This day I shall pour vengeance with my sword
On those proud rebels that are up in arms
And do confront and countermand their King.

And Young Spencer backs him up in this stubborn opinion: "I
doubt it not, my lord, right will prevail." Now the rebel lords
enter and there is recriminatory stichomythia. Young Mortimer
points to Edward "Among his flatterers." A few lines later he
again refers to "thy flatterers." Pembroke calls Young Spencer
"base upstart." Young Mortimer refers to Edward's entourage
as "that pernicious company." But Edward, as usual, is in-
fatuated with his own will:

Ay, traitors all, rather than thus be brav'd,
Make England's civil towns huge heaps of stones,
And ploughs to go about our palace-gates.

He will destroy his country rather than give up one grain of
self-reverence. Warwick makes the inevitable political reply:

A desperate and unnatural resolution!
Alarum to the fight!
St. George for England, and the barons' right!
    K. Edw. Saint George for England, and King Edward's
right!

The barons are defeated and the King, because of Gaveston's
death, vows to take wholesale revenge. Kent points out that the
lords' actions were not personal but political:

Brother, in regard of thee, and of thy land,
Did they remove that flatterer from thy throne.

However, as a reward for his careful advice, the King banishes
Kent the presence. Before they leave to be beheaded, Warwick
and Lancaster utter their position. The King is a "Tyrant" and
it is better to die "Than live in infamy under such a King."

Before the scene ends, certan motifs begin to take on bulk

and pressure. (1) Young Mortimer, though about to be imprisoned, declares in what must be an aside:

> What, Mortimer, can ragged stony walls
> Immure thy virtue that aspires to Heaven?

Mortimer's *virtue* appears to be turning into *virtú*. (2) Young
Spencer suborns Levune, the King of France's messenger, to
bribe the lords of France so that no help will come to Isabella
in her "plaints" against her husband. In such a way, the subject
of Isabella's embassage to Valois is beginning to shift—from a
request of aid *for* her husband to aid *against* her husband.

4.1

When Kent enters, we remember that in the preceding scene
the King had dismissed his brother because the latter had dared
to state that the lords' rebellion was due to their regard for
the ruler-plus-realm and to their hatred of the influence and
machinations of Gaveston. Kent's role in the present scene
continues to be functional. He is going to France "for England's good," for his "country's cause." His brother is a
"butcher of thy friends." This word *friends* is extremely important. It indicates that the others know better than the King
what is good for him. Kent will go to France to reveal what
Edward II's "looseness" is:

> Unnatural King, to slaughter noblemen
> And cherish flatterers!

But before he goes, he enables Mortimer to escape from the
Tower. And both leave the stage for the other side, where we
know the Queen already is.

4.2

Enter the Queen and her son. We immediately discover that
the King of France has refused to aid his sister. Marlowe
stresses, as it were, in the Prince's first speech, the vagueness
of the Queen's motives in leaving England: Let them return
and win Edward's love and then he will reject his sycophants,
the Spencers. The Queen's speech indicates that no longer is
she in France to get aid for her husband: rather it is in opposition to Edward. She and the King can no longer "be tun'd
together./No, no, we jar too far." Sir John of Hainault enters
to offer aid. Again the Prince indicates his basic antagonism
in the promise that when he is older he will "have at the
proudest Spencer's head!" This implies war against the flatterers. And so Marlowe is indicating how politically confused
at the present moment of the play motivations are—for how
can opposition to the Spencers be other than opposition to his

father? At this moment the Queen subtly introduces further addition to Edward II's ill-doing: she "moans" the "wrongs" that the Prince is enduring, "Yet [I] triumph in the hope of thee, my joy!" The dramatist is preparing for the Queen and Mortimer's tyranny under the guise of supporting the heir to the realm. (Yet a new dramatic "twist" will occur when we discover that the faithless Isabella truly loves her son!)

Now enter Kent and Young Mortimer. Mortimer tells the Prince that he "lives t' advance your standard, good my lord." Young Edward gets *the* point, so that the audience may understand that there no longer can be what was at best an illusory distinction between the King and his flatterers:

> How mean you? and the King, my father, lives?
> No, my Lord Mortimer, not I, I trow!

But his mother silences his objections. Mortimer now asserts that the rebelling faction has friends in England who

> Would cast up caps and clap their hands for joy
> To see us there appointed for our foes.

This surely refers to the adhesion of the commons to the lords' and Queen's cause. Again the unclarity of motive as to the action against the King is indicated in two contiguous speeches:

> *Kent.* Would all were well, and Edward well reclaim'd—
> For England's honor, peace, and quietness.
> *Y. Mor.* But by the sword, my lord, it must be deserv'd.
> The King will ne'er forsake his flatterers.

Kent consistently appears to act for England's honor. Mortimer's purposes by comparison are clouded. Sir John of Hainault promises "comfort, money, men, and friends" to face the English King. Again the Prince indicates admiration of his father in "I think King Edward will outrun us all," but the Queen argues that he "must not discourage/Your friends that are so forward in your aid."

4.3

We return to England where Edward and his friends—specifically Young Spencer, now the Earl of Gloucester—are triumphing in their victory. They delight in all the executions that are being done throughout the country. And now we discover that the King, too, is in the plot to bribe the French so that Isabella will get no aid. But a Messenger enters with a letter from Levune to tell them that the Queen, Edmund, Mortimer, and others will soon arrive to give him battle. The King prays, vaingloriously, that the time be short till he meet

them in the field. The dubious role of the Prince in the altercation is indicated, again, in Edward's speech:

> Ah, nothing grieves me but my little boy
> Is thus misled to countenance their ills.

4.4

At their arrival in England Isabella addresses her group with
an explanation of their purpose:

> Our kindest friends in Belgia have we left, *ff*. (4.4.3-14).

Mortimer interrupts her declaration with the statement that
they are there "in this Prince's right":

> Here for our country's cause swear we to him
> All homage, fealty, and forwardness. *ff*. (4.4.19-27).

What exactly will be done with the King if the rebels win is still
not made clear, but the choric Kent's last line is ominous, "I
would he never had been flatter'd more!"

4.5

The King's forces are defeated. We do not quite know how
to react to the King's speech:

> What, was I born to fly and run away,
> And leave the Mortimers conquerors behind?
> Give me my horse, and let's re'nforce our troops:
> And in this bed of honor die with fame.

Are we to regard it as flamboyant verbiage or royal resolution?
Probably the former, for the King has always been both im-
perceptive and a user of big words. After the King leaves,
Kent enters with a speech that is extremely directive as to
his and others' *present* motives:

> This way he fled, but I am come too late. *ff*. (4.5.10-27).

Thus to Kent Edward is still the "lawful King," and Mortimer
is a "Proud traitor." God must punish—and here we listen to
the official Tudor doctrine—those who have unnaturally taken
arms against their sovereign. Mortimer and Isabella have become lovers who intend to rule England with force and blood.
Their hypocrisy must be met with hypocrisy.

After this important soliloquy, the leaders enter. Contra-
puntally, Isabella gives thanks to God for their victory because *they* fought with right on their side. And single-handedly
—and surprisingly!—she verbally deposes Edward II and ap-
points her son "Lord Warden of the realm." What is to be
done with the former King is a problem which she turns over

to the lords. When Kent, however, tries to find out what *exactly* is to be done, Mortimer hypocritically says that this is not a question for them now:

> But as the realm and parliament shall please:
> So shall your brother be disposed of.

His aside to the Queen indicates that Edmund and his "relenting mood" may be adverse to their plans: he must be looked to.

Now Rice ap Howell brings in the Elder Spencer prisoner.

> Spencer, the father to that wanton Spencer,
> That like the lawless Catiline of Rome
> Revell'd in England's wealth and treasury!

The ensuing dialogue again brings up the problem of the disposal of the King: the love of the son for his father, the concern of Kent, Isabella's hypocrisy hiding ruthlessness, and Mortimer's blunt assumption of power.

4.6

The fleeing King with Baldock and Young Spencer enter in disguise. For the first time in the play, but not for the last, Marlowe casts the defeated King in a pathetic role. Edward begs the Abbot not to betray him. He refers to the inevitable turning of Fortune's wheel. Young Spencer's incidental remark, "all the land . . . is up in arms," reveals that all the estates (except, perhaps, the church represented by the Abbot?) have turned against their legal sovereign. Rice ap Howell and Leicester now enter to take the King and his cohorts prisoner. A sympathetic aside of Leicester again points not only to the Isabella-Mortimer assumption of power, but also to the King's sorrowful downfall. Yet even now when he, Spencer, and Baldock are prisoners, and Leicester shows clearly that he makes a distinction between the flatterers, whom he hates and whom he will not designate with their new titles, and Edward, whom he still honors, Edward still clings strongly to his "friends":

> For friends hath Edward none but these and these,
> And these must die under a tyrant's sword. . . .
> Sweet Spencer, gentle Baldock, part we must.

After the King leaves with Leicester, Baldock and Young Spencer vehemently mourn their enforced separation from "noble Edward," and then grow philosophical about their coming death. But Rice ap Howell brings them and us down to earth: "You and such as you are have made wise work in England."

5.1

We see the King as the prisoner of the gentle Leicester. Edward still feels his kingship, and the opposition between him and the "ambitious Mortimer." Now we know his statements about Mortimer and Isabella being lovers are no longer the feline insults of a homosexual King: they are the truth. The prisoned ruler feels both anger and frustration, but he now knows his "regiment is gone" and that his "nobles rule." Nevertheless, he surmises that it is Mortimer who has deposed him and taken his place. (And thus we are being prepared by Marlowe for an ending in which the nobles themselves and the King's heir, Edward III, will supplant the usurper, once the leader of the peers but *not* of the peers who join with the new King to take vengeance on the usurper.) However, that the deposition *at the moment* has the consent of the entire realm and its estates is indicated by the Bishop of Winchester requiring Edward II's crown:

> It is for England's good
> And princely Edward's right we crave the crown.

For the first—and perhaps last—time in the play Edward thinks deeply and sincerely of his son. (However, we might remember his complaint in 4.3 when the Queen and Prince Edward are still in France: "Ah, nothing grieves me but my little boy/Is thus misled to countenance their ills.") Mortimer has seized the power and the heir apparent is

> a lamb, encompassed by wolves
> Which in a moment will abridge his life.

That Mortimer will inherit his power is one of the King's strongest feelings against giving up the royal crown. Nevertheless, for a moment he is resigned: "But what the heavens appoint, I must obey"—and removes the crown. Still, yearningly, he asks that time not move, "That Edward may be still fair England's King . . ." But suddenly with passion he puts the crown on again and berates those around him—and, again, in a moment despairs. Trussel's statement

> My lord, the parliament must have present news.
> And therefore say, will you resign or no?

enforces what I have said a moment ago, that entire England is behind the deposition. The original stage direction, *"The King rageth,"* represents a startlingly clear transition between the Edward whom we see in the first part of the play using his power indiscriminately and the powerless Edward in this part

of the play using his passions indiscriminately. It is the same
figure, but the first is that of a king and the second is that of
an hysterical failure. Nevertheless, so skillful is Marlowe's
dramaturgy that the second, because of our empathy, is pathetic; whereas the first, because of his power, not only dis-
gusted but frightened us.

> *K. Edw.* I'll not resign! But whilst I live—.
> Traitors, be gone! Join you with Mortimer!
> Elect, conspire, install, do what you will!
> Their blood and yours shall seal these treacheries!

Leicester's plea for the young Prince appears to bring Edward
to his senses and he takes off the crown—but he does not immediately give it—

> No, these *innocent* hands of mine
> Shall not be guilty of so foul a crime—.

So Marlowe shows us one whom, despite our deep feeling for
his agony, we can never admire because he is neither willing nor
able to discern the faults that have put him in his present
position. Subtly the dramatist is saying that Edward II was
a bad king, and would continue to be one if he retained the
kingship. Instead of confessing his sins as sovereign, Edward
pleads for pity and rages at Mortimer and Isabella. Then in
a sudden decision he acts the part of the cloistered saint. Whatever our feelings toward him in this scene are—and as I have
indicated, surely much pathos is engendered—the spectators
cannot respect this hysterical creature of many moods, except
the important one of self-guilt. For a moment, such is Marlowe's complexity of response, we *do* find Edward about to
understand himself, but the mood passes as quickly as it comes:

> Commend me to my son, and bid him rule
> Better than I.—Yet how have I transgress'd
> Unless it be with too much clemency?

Now Berkeley enters telling Leicester to give up his prisoner.
And, of course, the document is signed by Mortimer! Edward
full of thoughts of death leaves the stage.

5.2

Here we see Queen Isabella and Young Mortimer at the top
of Fortune's wheel. All they need is the King's official deposition
and Mortimer made protector of the heir, and they will have
all that they desire—except the old King's death. And this
they are beginning to plan. What is interesting is Isabella's
real and unsimulated devotion to her son:

And therefore—so the Prince my son be safe,
Whom I esteem as dear as these mine eyes—
Conclude against his father what thou wilt!
—And I myself will willingly subscribe.

When a Messenger from Killingworth tells her that her husband
is "In health, madam, but full of pensiveness," the Queen
indulges her hypocrisy to the full. The Bishop of Winchester
enters with the crown, and surely he is the cousin of his name-
part in Shakespeare's *2 Henry VI*, for he reveals that the
King's brother, Kent, has laid a plot to free his brother. And
the Bishop is sadistic too: Berkeley is as kind to the King as
Leicester was before him. The implication is that Winchester
wants Edward not to be saved from bad usage and pain. Mortimer promises to rectify the situation—and remember that
Isabella is present throughout. She openly suggests to her
lover that the former King be murdered. When Matrevis and
Gurney enter, Young Mortimer tells the latter:

As thou intend'st to rise by Mortimer—
Who now makes Fortune's wheel turn as he please!—
Seek all the means thou canst to make him droop,
And neither give him kind word nor good look. . . .
Speak curstly to him, and in any case
Let no man comfort him. If he chance to weep
But amplify his grief with bitter words.

Isabella, who has been standing aside, now hypocritically tells
the two to bear her love and grief to the former majesty.

Enter the Prince and Kent whispering together. Isabella and
Mortimer like all tyrants are suspicious, but she tells her
lover to simulate friendship. Kent, however, recognizes their
hypocrisy. For a moment or two, both sides feint.

Y. Mor. Thou being his uncle and the next of blood,
Do look to be protector over the Prince?
Kent. Not I, my lord. Who should protect the son
But she that gave him life? I mean the Queen.

Hypocrisy against hypocrisy! Young Edward wants to see his
father. Kent backs him up, and Isabella is now forced to come
somewhat in the open.

Q. Isab. Brother, you know it is impossible.
P. Edw. Why is he dead?
Q. Isab. No, God forbid!

At this Kent breaks the calm and they all hurl accusations at
one another. The Prince refuses to go with Mortimer, but the

latter takes him away by force. Kent resolves to rescue the
"aged Edward from his foes." (Note how Marlowe makes Edward to grow old and his son the Prince to grow up within the
span of his play.)

5.3

Enter Matrevis, Gurney, soldiers with torches, and Edward.
Conceive of Edward in ragged robes now, uncrowned, and with
a ragged beard. Depressed, he is becoming bent and stumbling
due to his incarceration and sufferings. Matrevis' hypocritical
friendship falls without much effect on Edward. He is too engrossed in his grief. Part of Marlowe's psychological acuteness
here is Edward's fixation on Mortimer as the *sole* cause of his
troubles:

> When will his heart be satisfied with blood?
> If mine will serve, unbowel straight this breast
> And give my heart to Isabel and him!
> It is the chiefest mark they level at!

Thus even in his misery the King is avoiding responsibility for
what has happened to him. Never for a moment does the
thought of England at large or even of his young son cross his
mind:

> Thus lives old Edward, not reliev'd by any—
> And so must die, though pitied by many!

Still, he is a pathetic figure. And the degradation of having his
beard removed with puddle water is not wholly understandable
to a modern generation which does not recognize how symbolic
in Shakespeare's day a beard was of reverent age and dignity.
Edward still appeals to the heavens to avenge his wrongs.

> Immortal powers! that knows the painful cares
> That waits upon my poor distressed soul,
> O, level all your looks upon these daring men,
> That wrongs their liege and sovereign, England's King!

But his prayer *now* is evidence not so much of vanity but of
weakness. In the Machiavellian atmosphere of this last act
where a hypocritical tyrant and his paramour are doing what
they will, this appeal sounds almost foolish—yet, and this is an
important condition, it must be remembered by those who want
to get a total view of the "philosophy" of the play that at
length Mortimer *is* beheaded, the dead King *does get* his
vengeance indirectly, and the rightful King *does take* his
place as the head of the state.

What I have said above about the King still refusing to
recognize the true causes of his downfall is borne out by his
apostrophe to his dead sycophants:

> O Gaveston, it is for thee that I am wrong'd,
> For me both thou and both the Spencers died!
> And for your sakes a thousand wrongs I'll take!
> The Spencers' ghosts wherever they remain
> Wish well to mine. Then hush, for them I'll die.

When Kent and his cohorts enter to rescue Edward, the
stichomythia indicates how thoroughly Mortimer has a grip
on the political power. Gurney, his man, orders Kent, who
is after all the legitimate King's brother, to desist. And Matrevis
makes the point explicit, "The court is where Lord Mortimer
remains."

5.4

Here we see the Mortimer who has become completely the
Machiavellian usurper and tyrant, ruling without the lords and
the commons, not even any longer taking the advice of Isabella
but rather giving it. He has decided that the King must die
in order that he, Mortimer, retain his high position. His
tyranny is reflected in the statement that "The commons now
begin to pity him." Like all true Elizabethan Machiavellian
villains, Mortimer intends to achieve Edward's death cunningly
and indirectly. He himself is to bear no open responsibility. His
lieutenant for the deed, Lightborn, is a typical Italianate villain
—and like Pendringano in *The Spanish Tragedy* will be got
rid of when Mortimer's immediate purpose is accomplished.
(Note how easily murder comes to these Machiavellian creatures.) After Lightborn leaves, we find through Mortimer's
soliloquy more about what he is and what he is doing. The
line, "The proudest lords salute me as I pass," along with the
previous reference to the murmuring of the commons, another
line, "The Prince I rule, the Queen do I command," indicate
that all power is within his single grasp. And like the noted
Florentine prince, however others think of him, he intends to
retain his ruthless political grip:

> Fear'd am I more than lov'd—let me be fear'd
> And when I frown make all the court look pale.
> I view the Prince with Aristarchus' eyes
> Whose looks were as a breeching to a boy.

Again, according to the advice of the Florentine, he plays the
hypocrite consummately:

While at the council-table, grave enough,
And not unlike a bashful Puritan,
First I complain of imbecility,
Saying it is *onus quam gravissimum*—
Till, being interrupted by my friends,
Suscepi that *provinciam* as they term it.
And to conclude, I am Protector now!

But like other Elizabethan dramatic tyrants his very assumption of total power will end in his ruin:

And that this be the coronation-day,
It pleaseth me, and Isabel the Queen.

The young King will soon show Mortimer who is master! Mortimer shows his power first by having Young Edward crowned, and then overruling the young King in the matter of Kent's life. Mortimer's use of power, we feel, is so egregious that it must bring, and soon, an antidote. It is to be noted in this scene how compliant to Mortimer Isabella is, even though the evidence still reveals that she truly loves her young son.

5.5

There is a curious mixture of sadism and sympathy in the attitude of Matrevis and Gurney, the King's keepers, for his present suffering. There is some admiration in the following passage:

Mat. He hath a body able to endure
More than we can inflict. And therefore now
Let us assail his mind another while.
Gur. Send for him out thence, and I will anger him.

And we too, perhaps, are beginning to have more and more sympathy for the poor down-thrown creature. The flashy Lightborn enters and instructs the other two what he will need. The curtains at the back part and we see Edward in his dungeon. Edward recognizes Lightborn as a murderer, but so in need of comfort is he that he must tell even this obvious homicide his present sufferings:

And there in mire and puddle have I stood *ff*. (5.5.61-72).

There is intended pathos, on Marlowe's part, in Edward's memory of the wooing of his Queen. The former King knows what Lightborn's purpose there is. He tries to believe the latter's lies. But his fear almost overcomes his hope.

> Know that I am a king! O, at that name
> I feel a hell of grief! Where is my crown?
> Gone, gone, and do I remain alive?

He is naught but a king of shadows and sorrows now. He is too feeble to resist and is murdered easily. Lightborn's own death just as he begins to brave over his accomplishment ends the sordid scene with a sordid note.

5.6

Enter Young Mortimer and Matrevis. The latter now is conscience-stricken, and Mortimer's hardness in the face of this decency is threatening. And like the pride that cometh before a fall, he boasts just before he is sent off-stage to his death. Queen Isabella tells us that the young King is raging at the news of his father's death, but what is very important is to see that the new King is assuming his powers in a regular and legal fashion:

> Into the council-chamber he is gone
> To crave the aid and succor of his peers:
> Ay me, see where he comes, and they with him!
> Now, Mortimer, begins our tragedy.

In other words, Edward III is not a king who is going to rule according to his own willfulness. He and the lords will make up the power. He disposes of Mortimer scornfully and quickly:

> Why stays he here?
> Bring him unto a hurdle, drag him forth;
> Hang him, I say, and set his quarters up:
> But bring his head back presently to me.

However, Marlowe has not finished. Mortimer dies a very brave man.

> Base Fortune, now I see, that in thy wheel *ff*. (5.6.59-66).

With the advice of his lords the new King commits his mother to the Tower. When the first Lord enters with the head of Young Mortimer, Edward III orders the attendants to bring in the coffin in which his father is lying. Upon the body he places the head of the corpse's enemy:

> Sweet father, here unto thy murder'd ghost
> I offer up this wicked traitor's head.
> And let these tears, distilling from mine eyes,
> Be witness of my grief and innocency.

Exeunt in procession.

Doctor Faustus and Its Source

The English Faust-Book was the basic source of Marlowe's play. For example, Chapters 29 and 30 were the origin of 4.1, in which Emperor Charles sees Alexander and Darius, etc., and in which Doctor Faustus puts horns on Benvolio: in other words, two actions are conflated by Marlowe. Here is the horns on the knight episode as it appears in *EFB:*

> *How Doctor Faustus in the sight of the Emperor conjured a*
> *pair of Hart's horns upon a Knight's head that*
> *slept out of a casement. Chap. 30.*

When Doctor Faustus had accomplished the Emperor's desire in all things as he was requested, he went forth into a gallery, and leaning over a rail to look into the privy garden, he saw many of the Emperor's Courtiers walking and talking together, and casting his eyes now this way, now that way, he espied a Knight leaning out at a window of the great hall; who was fast asleep (for in those days it was hot) but the person shall be nameless that slept, for that he was a Knight, although it was done to a little disgrace of the Gentleman: it pleased Doctor Faustus, through the help of his Spirit Mephostophiles, to firm upon his head as he slept, an huge pair of Hart's horns, and as the Knight awaked thinking to pull his head, he hit his horns against the glass that the panes thereof flew about his ears. Think here how this good Gentleman was vexed, for he could neither get backward nor forward: which when the Emperor heard all the Courtiers laugh, and came forth to see what was happened, the Emperor also when he beheld the Knight with so fair a head, laughed heartily thereat, and was therewithal well pleased: at last Faustus made him quit of his horns again, but the Knight perceived how they came. . . .[45]

Religious Values in Doctor Faustus

Marlowe's Faustus has so often been described by modern critics as a superman, reaching out for infinite knowledge and ineffable beauty, as an individual whom we ought proudly to esteem as representative of aspiring humanity, that one almost hesitates to disagree with this well-nigh universal opinion. Yet, surprisingly, it is unsupported by the play itself. One surmises that

---

[45] H. Logeman (ed.), *The English Faust-Book of 1592* (Gand and Amsterdam, 1900). There is also a modernized edition in the Broadway Translations, ed. William Rose [1925?].

such a view of Faustus is a fiction derived ultimately from reactions against medievalism, against Christianity, and against
past assertions of man's fundamental weakness and limits. The
nineteenth and early twentieth centuries, with their faith in
science and progress, and with their concept of man's yet
unrealized potentialities, tended to reject any view, be it
religion or philosophy, which denied this faith and this
concept. Thus it has come about that Marlowe's protagonist
has been chosen as a symbol of the "new" man. Critics, frankly,
have been unable to see the drama in its own terms, have
persisted in seeing it in the light of our own *Zeitgeist*.

Only recently has the literary tide begun to turn. Indulgent
empathy for Marlowe's magician is slowly being supplanted by
a more objective appraisal. Rid of present-day preconceptions,
whether they be borrowed from the critics or supplied by
ourselves, we are beginning to perceive that the late sixteenth
century drama *Doctor Faustus* is wholly conventional in its
Christian values and is in no sense iconoclastic. St. Thomas
Aquinas would have approved of its innate doctrine. And
Richard Hooker could have used it as an exemplum to teach
the correct Christian path to God. Nor would Luther, Calvin,
or Knox—the founders of European Protestantism—have found
anything inflammatory in it. Marlowe's play is in no way
destructive of the basic tenets of Christianity. On the contrary,
it enforces and illuminates those very tenets.

There is no more obvious Christian document in all Elizabethan drama than the play under discussion. Let the reader or
spectator forget about the paganism of the Renaissance or the
sectism of the Reformation. Let us see the play in the terms
of the basic Christian values it preaches, for it is, we must
recognize, a morality play. Let us examine the play Marlowe
wrote—which is not the play most critics think he wrote,
not the play some critics want him to have written.

In the theater watching *Doctor Faustus,* or in the study
reading it, we must, for the nonce, either accept its values or
choose some other drama more congenial to our beliefs and
tastes. We must accept, for the occasion, that man's most
precious possession is his immortal soul and that what he
does on earth will determine whether he goes to Heaven or
Hell, whether after his worldly life he will enjoy perpetual
bliss with God or perpetual pain with the Devil. (We need
not get mired here in debate about the Calvinistic doctrine of
the elect: those who are chosen reveal their future sanctity
by their earthly conduct.) The premises of basic Christianity
are inherent in every line of *Doctor Faustus*. The doctrine of
damnation pervades it.

In the play the Devil and Hell are omnipresent, potent, dangerous, and terrifying realities. But the protagonist makes a bargain with Evil, and for the sake of earthly learning, earthly power, earthly satisfaction goes down to horrible and everlasting perdition. As we shall observe, it is actually a poor bargain, for the gains of knowledge and power are largely offset by egocentric self-satisfaction. Marlowe portrays his "hero" as a wretched creature who for lower values gives up higher ones. Thus, the drama is a morality play in which Heaven combats with Hell for the soul of a Renaissance Everyman and, due to the latter's psychological and moral weaknesses, loses.

Faustus' apostrophe to Helen of Troy in the last act has again and again been presented as a pagan paean to beauty, Marlowe's own sensuous declaration of sensual delight, a declaration of Renaissance man's newfound freedom:

Was this the face that launch'd a thousand ships *ff*. (5.1.92-111).

Here, say the critics, Marlowe celebrates the program of modern man, who has at last fully escaped the contempt of the world and the flesh which the Middle Ages taught. But before we reread this passage, let us see it in the context of the play. I believe that we will find that the passage signals the protagonist's final defeat by the powers of darkness.

I think I should stress here that the viable eschatology of the play is so rigid that ambivalence in interpretation is ruled out. If the modern mind, for example, sees Marlowe's main character as the noble victim of a tyrannical Deity, it is simply being blind. On the contrary, God is exceedingly good in his gifts to the "hero," until the latter becomes the victim of his own insatiable desires—and even then God is willing to forgive if the magician repents. But Faustus willfully refuses all aid—and so goes down to damnation. No, there is no ambiguity on the main issues in the play. But there is much irony, which Marlowe skillfully employs.

The dramatist establishes the viable values of his drama by various means: by the Choruses; by Faustus' own recognition; by the Good Angel; by Mephostophilis, interestingly enough; by the Old Man—and, of course, by the action itself. I am not thinking merely of the macabre ending. As an example of the pervasive Christian viewpoint, there is, for example, the cumulative coarsening of the magician's character and his indulgence in cheap, sadistic fun: this is due to *habitude*, constant indulgence in sin.

The Prologue, or First Chorus, sets Faustus, his character and his doom, before us in clear, emphatic terms:

> So much he profits in divinity
> That shortly he was grac'd with doctor's name,
> Excelling all, and sweetly can dispute
> In th' heavenly matters of theology—
> Till swoll'n with cunning, of a self-conceit,
> His waxen wings did mount above his reach
> And melting, Heavens conspir'd his over-throw!
> For falling to a devilish exercise
> And glutted now with learning's golden gifts
> He surfeits upon cursed necromancy:
> Nothing so sweet as magic is to him
> Which he prefers before his chiefest bliss . . .
> And this the man that in his study sits.

We must trust Marlowe's *ex cathedra* description of his protagonist—a man who, swollen with pride in his attainments, comes to a deserved end because he has preferred forbidden pursuits to "his chiefest bliss." (Certainly Marlowe guides us deftly by the analogy with Icarus—who, of course, equates with Lucifer.) The Faustus whom Marlowe gives us in the ensuing action is both more complex and less radiant than the utterances of most critics would lead us to expect.

At the very beginning of Faustus' temptation, the Good Angel —the voice of God, the expounder of things as they are, the opponent of the Bad Angel, who is the emissary of Satan— declares:

> O, Faustus, lay that damned book aside
> And gaze not on it lest it tempt thy soul
> And heap God's heavy wrath upon thy head!
> Read, read the Scriptures—that is blasphemy!

But Faustus hearkens to the Bad Angel. And note what he expects as a reward for practicing the forbidden black magic. Before the Good Angel enters, he gloats:

> O, what a world of profit and delight,
> Of power, of honor, and omnipotence
> Is promis'd to the studious artisan!

He not only will get knowledge and power: his mind also dwells longingly on satisfaction of material appetite. The spirits will bring him "gold," "orient pearl," "pleasant fruits," "princely delicates," and "silk."

Faustus has intellectual pride to an odious degree, but he is also avid for more vainglory:

> And I, that have with subtle syllogisms
> Gravell'd the pastors of the German church
> And made the flow'ring pride of Wittenberg
> (Swarm) to my problems, as th' infernal spirits
> On sweet Musaeus when he came to Hell,
> Will be as cunning as Agrippa was,
> Whose shadows made all Europe honor him.

Faustus is wholly egocentric. To himself, he is either the greatest of men, or the greatest of abject sinners. He underrates his opponents, and relishes his inflated sense of his own abilities. Thus, after Mephostophilis has left the stage at the behest of the magician that he reappear in the more pleasant guise of a Franciscan (Marlowe is indeed subtle: Faustus will not and cannot accept things as they are: the truth must be side-stepped some way, the bitter pill must be coated with sugar), Faustus wallows in a delusion of self-importance:

> How pliant is this Mephostophilis,
> Full of obedience and humility,
> Such is the force of magic and my spells!

But Mephostophilis quickly disillusions him:

> *Faust.* Did not my conjuring raise thee? Speak.
> *Meph.* That was the cause, but yet *per accidens:*
> For when we hear one rack the name of God,
> Abjure the Scriptures and his Savior Christ,
> We fly in hope to get his glorious soul.
> Nor will we come unless he use such means
> Whereby he is in danger to be damn'd.
> Therefore the shortest cut for conjuring
> Is stoutly to abjure all godliness
> And pray devoutly to the Prince of Hell.

Faustus agrees to worship Belzebub:

> This word *damnation* terrifies not me
> For I confound hell in Elysium:
> My ghost be with the old philosophers!
> But, leaving these vain trifles of men's souls,
> Tell me, what is that Lucifer thy lord?

But note how Marlowe immediately shows up the vanity and foolhardiness of this last speech. In order to set forth that damnation and soul are not mere trifles, the playwright has the enemy of man strip Faustus of those very delusions which the enemy of man wants Faustus to possess in order that the enemy of man may destroy Faustus. The enemy of the truth supports the truth so that the audience will be absolutely clear as to what the truth is. And mark that Mephostophilis foreshadows Faustus' fall in Lucifer's, and that insolence and pride are the instigators in both cases:

Faust. Was not that Lucifer an angel once? *ff.* (1.3.61-79).

But the foolhardy Faustus, having been warned by the Devil himself, reprimands the latter for cowardliness! He boasts:

What, is great Mephostophilis so passionate
For being deprived of the joys of Heaven?
Learn thou of Faustus manly fortitude
And scorn those joys thou never shalt possess.

How can any one read the scene and call the self-deluded, foolishly boastful Faustus a superman?

Note carefully what Faustus wants in return for selling his soul to the Devil:

Say, he surrenders up to him his soul
So he will spare him four and twenty years,
Letting him live in all voluptuousness,
Having thee ever to attend on me,
To give me whatsoever I shall ask,
To tell me whatsoever I demand,
To slay mine enemies and to aid my friends
And always be obedient to my will.

Utter satisfaction of the will and utter satisfaction of the senses are what Faustus desires. And how he prates—who a little later will be quaking!

Had I as many souls as there be stars,
I'd give them all for Mephostophilis!

The next time we see Faustus, midnight of the same day, his emotional and intellectual instability is fully revealed. He veers between God and the Devil. At first he is conscience-stricken. All his cocky effrontery is gone. But in a moment he is once more the user of egocentric hyperbole:

Now, Faustus, must thou needs be damn'd, canst thou not be say'd *ff.* (2.1.1-12).

A weakling, he must cover his fears with megalomaniacal fantasy. Two points should be made. We must understand that Faustus' conclusion as to the impossibility of God's mercy is the mark of a diseased ego—a lack of humility. And also, we must particularly remark Faustus' self-recognition of his driving passion: "The god thou serv'st is thine own appetite."

The struggle between Faustus' uncontrolled appetite and the powers of Heaven continues:

> *Enter the two Angels.*
> *Bad Ang.* Go forward, Faustus, in that famous art.
> *Good Ang.* Sweet Faustus, leave that execrable art. *ff.*
> (2.1.13-25).

He thus deludes himself: "What power can hurt me?" But again Faustus is warned by the emissary of Hell what awaits him if he sells his soul to the Devil:

> *Faust.* Stay, Mephostophilis, and tell me
> What good my soul will do thy lord?
> *Meph.* Enlarge his kingdom.
> *Faust.* Is that the reason why he tempts us thus?
> *Meph. Solamen miseris socios habuisse doloris.*
> *Faust.* Why, have you any pain that torture other?
> *Meph.* As great as have the human souls of men.

And that Faustus has free will, free choice, ability to affirm or deny God if he so wishes; that he cannot (as he does later) blame anyone but himself for his act and its consequences, Faustus himself makes clear when, after his blood has congealed so that he cannot sign the document and give his soul to Hell, he says:

> Why streams it not that I may write afresh:
> "Faustus gives to thee his soul?" O there it stay'd . . .
> Why shouldst thou not? Is not thy soul thine own?
> Then write again: "Faustus gives to thee his soul."

Marlowe's powers of compressed dramatic irony can be tremendous. As soon as Faustus has signed, he says *"Consummatum est,"* the last words of Christ on earth according to St. John. What an insight into the twisted mind of the magician! And what blasphemy! Jesus died that Faustus' soul might live; Faustus flings away this priceless gift for a mess of earthly pottage! But the words are also true in a more literal sense: the good life, the possibility of reaching Heaven, are indeed being finished for Faustus.

When, immediately afterward, God's warning *"Homo fuge!"* appears on Faustus' arm, he—characteristically—affirms the God whom he has just denied and gets into a turmoil of conflicting impulses:

> *Homo fuge!* Whither should I fly?
> If unto Heav'n, He'll throw me down to Hell.
> —My senses are deceiv'd, here's nothing writ.
> —O yes, I see it plain! Even here is writ
> *Homo fuge!* Yet shall not Faustus fly!

Hence, Faustus consciously and deliberately sets his will against God's. But as he is in this state, Mephostophilis, knowing his victim, says in an aside, "I'll fetch him somewhat to delight his mind." And then to the voluptuary *"Enter Devils, giving crowns and rich apparel to Faustus. They dance and then depart."*

Thus, Mephostophilis deliberately offers Faustus sensual satisfaction in order to distract his mind from spiritual concern —which might, of course, lead to repentance. This pattern is a basic one in the play, and an understanding of it will eventually enable us to interpret truly the Helen of Troy apostrophe. Whenever there is danger, from the Devil's viewpoint, that Faustus will turn to God's mercy, the powers of Hell will deaden their victim's conscience by providing him with some great satisfaction of the senses. But sometimes Faustus will ask for the opiate himself.

In the same scene, Faustus receives a true description of his condition, but cheaply flaunts his disbelief—as though one should deny gravity! Once more it is Mephostophilis who forcefully establishes the values:

> *Faust.* I think Hell's a fable.
> *Meph.* Ay, think so still—till experience change thy mind!
> *ff.* (2.1.124-35).

And here, again, Marlowe shows the constitution of Faustus' mind. As soon as Mephostophilis has stated that Hell with its tortures and damnation do exist, Faustus asks for his customary anodyne for uncomfortable conscience:

> *Faust.* Nay, and this be Hell, I'll willingly be damn'd—
> What, sleeping, eating, walking, and disputing? But leaving this, let me have a wife, the fairest maid in Germany, for I am wanton and lascivious and cannot live without a wife.
> *ff.* (2.1.135-50).

See again Marlowe's compressed irony—Faustus shall have his appetite satisfied by women as beautiful "As was bright Lucifer before his fall."

In the next scene (2.2), the Devil's agent and Faustus are again together. Faustus is going through another of his struggles between repentance and nonrepentance. He blames

Mephostophilis for his misery, but the latter points out that the magician made his choice of his own free will: " 'Twas thine own seeking Faustus, thank thyself." When Faustus says that he "will renounce this magic and repent," he himself in a lucid moment recognizes that repentance is still possible. And the Good Angel at once announces also that a true act of contrition followed by God's forgiveness can still occur. But continued exercise in sin is robbing Faustus of volition—"My heart is harden'd, I cannot repent." However, this too must be taken as an egocentric conclusion. No sooner does he think of holy things than all kinds of instruments for self-destruction are placed before him. But in self-revelation he gives us another sharp insight into his essential make-up:

> And long ere this I should have done the deed
> Had not sweet pleasure conquer'd deep despair.

As I have pointed out, sensuous pleasure is always Faustus' remedy for spiritual despair. He has had Homer and Orpheus sing for him. And now the very thought of former pleasure drugs his conscience:

> Why should I die then or basely despair?—
> I am resolv'd Faustus shall not repent!

It is instructive to compare Macbeth with Faustus. The former is tremendous in his spiritual agony. But the Faustus who, here and elsewhere, goes through such rapid mental and emotional gyrations is surely conceived of by his creator as of infinitely smaller dimension.

In the latter part of the same scene there is almost a replica of the pattern of the first part. Mephostophilis tells Faustus: "Thou art damn'd. Think thou of Hell!" And the magician once more characteristically blames Lucifer's servant for his plight: " 'Tis thou hast damn'd distressed Faustus' soul." And so again the protagonist is in spiritual distress. The Good Angel tells him there is still time to repent. But the Bad Angel threatens, "If thou repent, devils will tear thee in pieces." (We must remember that the obverse of love of pleasure is fear of pain.) Just as Faustus calls upon his Savior for help, Lucifer, Belzebub, and Mephostophilis enter. Lucifer appears menacing and frightening:

> *Faust.* O, what art thou that look'st so terribly?

And after a few lines of prodding, the wretchedly irresolute hedonist once more veers and vows "never to look to Heaven!" Again the Devil gets Faustus out of his melancholy by providing him with some satisfaction of the senses—the show of the Seven Deadly Sins. Note again Marlowe's dramatic irony:

> That sight will be as pleasant to me, as Paradise was to Adam the first day of his creation.

And after the show, the deluded magician in unconscious irony says, "O, how this sight doth delight my soul!"

In 3.1 at the beginning of the anti-papal scene, we have another statement by Faustus of his motivating passion:

> Sweet Mephostophilis, thou pleasest me.
> Whilst I am here on earth, let me be cloy'd
> With all the things that delight the heart of man.
> My four and twenty years of liberty
> I'll spend in pleasure and in dalliance. . . .

And in 4.3, the Horse-Courser scene, Marlowe shows the protagonist still tormented—but still capable of rapid self-delusion:

> What art thou, Faustus, but a man condemn'd to die?
> Thy fatal time draws to a final end . . .
> Despair doth drive distrust into my thoughts.
> Confound these passions with a quiet sleep.
> Tush, Christ did call the thief upon the cross!
> Then rest thee Faustus, quiet in conceit.

In the last act, Marlowe once more returns us forcefully to the serious business of his play. At the very beginning Wagner is struck by the inconsistency of his master's character. The latter has made his will and hence "means to die shortly." But, says the puzzled servant, "If death were nigh, he would not frolic thus. He's now at supper with the scholars, where there's such belly-cheer as Wagner in his life ne'er saw the like!" Thus, through the mouth of another character, the playwright shows us Faustus as still the incorrigible hedonist. The scholars wish him to show them Helen of Troy. Mephostophilis brings in the peerless dame, and the scholars are ravished. The latter leave—and *"Enter an Old Man."* The latter movingly begs Faustus to give up his wicked life. Here we have explicit statement that Faustus is still a man (and not a spirit); that he still has "an amiable soul"; that he is still capable of repentance; that if he does not change his wicked ways, his nature will become incapable of contrition; and that by "checking [his] body" he "may amend [his] soul." Faustus' reaction to the Old Man's speech is typical. He utterly despairs, is positive of his damnation, and is about to kill himself with a dagger which Mephostophilis provides. Thus, in the reverse kind of egotism in which Faustus indulges when he is conscience-stricken, he completely misses the burden of the Old Man's message: no man's sins are too great for God to forgive. But the Old Man cries out for him to stop, tells him that "precious grace" waits only upon prayer for mercy. Faustus thanks the Old Man for words that "comfort my distressed soul" and asks to be left alone to ponder his sins. But the Old Man knows how weak the magician is:

> Faustus, I leave thee; but with grief of heart,
> Fearing the enemy of thy hapless soul.

We immediately see that the Old Man was right in his apprehensions. Faustus is now in the toils:

> Accursed Faustus! Wretch, what hast thou done!
> I do repent, and yet I do despair:
> Hell strives with grace for conquest in my breast!
> What shall I do to shun the snares of death?

Hell strives against Heaven: despair against repentance. But as soon as Mephostophilis arrests him for disobedience, commands him to deny God, threatens physical pain—"or I'll in piecemeal tear thy flesh"—the weak-willed voluptuary caves in. He "repents" (*sic!*) that he has offended Lucifer, offers of his own volition to confirm with blood his former vow, and—characteristically blaming another for his treason—brutally begs Mephostophilis to torture the Old Man "With greatest torment that our [*sic!*] Hell affords." Is this the superman whom devotees of the Renaissance describe?

Once more we see the familiar pattern operating. Faustus requests the moly which will deaden his spiritual apprehension:

> One thing, good servant, let me crave of thee
> To glut the longing of my heart's desire:
> That I may have unto my paramour
> That heavenly Helen which I saw of late,
> Whose sweet embraces may extinguish clear
> Those thoughts that do dissuade me from my vow,
> And keep [the] ⟨oath⟩ I made to Lucifer.

Helen appears. Faustus delivers the famous apostrophe, "Was this the face . . ." and leaves the stage with her.

How are we to take these lines? For the sake of bodily pleasure, Faustus has given up the last possibility of redemption and embraced Hell. Surely we do not even have to recognize that Helen is a succuba, the Devil in female guise, to recognize Marlowe's point!

The next scene is that of Faustus' going down to Hell. The comment of Mephostophilis at its beginning is sharply descriptive:

> Fond worldling, now his heart blood dries with grief,
> His conscience kills it, and his laboring brain
> Begets a world of idle fantasies
> To overreach the Devil—but all in vain:
> His store of pleasures must be sauc'd with pain!

And note how admirably Marlowe shows us the kernel of this unstable, foolish worldling. The Second Scholar has asked him to repent, "mercy is infinite." Faustus replies:

> But Faustus' offense can ne'er be pardoned. The serpent that tempted Eve may be saved, but not Faustus! O, gentlemen, hear with patience and tremble not at my speeches. Though my heart pant and quiver to remember that I have been a student here these thirty years, O, would I had never seen Wittenberg, never read book.—And what wonders I have done, all Germany can witness, yea all the world!—For which Faustus hath lost both Germany and the world, yea, Heaven itself—Heaven, the seat of God, the throne of the blessed, the kingdom of joy—and must remain in Hell forever! Hell, O Hell forever! Sweet friends, what shall become of Faustus being in Hell forever?

One should not pass over lightly the exceedingly dramatic nature of this speech. The quaking Faustus is still the blatant egotist. He knows that God cannot pardon him! And in the midst of his self-reproach, lo! the basic vanity leaps forth—"And what wonders I have done, all Germany can witness, yea all the world!"

Faustus sums up his situation succinctly: "For the vain pleasure of four and twenty years hath Faustus lost eternal joy and felicity." He gave up higher values for lower. And the burden of the Good and Bad Angels who enter now is that for small pleasure the voluptuary has given up great pleasures, for small pleasures he must now endure all the horrible sensory tortures of Hell. The Bad Angel concludes, "He that loves pleasure must for pleasure fall." Such is the ironic outcome.

But the most trenchant stroke of Marlowe's pervading irony is in the famous last soliloquy. Faustus, too late, begs for time to repent, and in his agony cries out, *"O lente lente currite noctis equi!"* This is Ovid, *Amores*, I. xiii. 40. Habituated to sensual pleasure, Faustus—begging now for time to save his soul—must perforce use the words of Ovid in his mistress's arms!

I hope I have shown that the Helen of Troy speech is hardly what some critics take it, an unencumbered pagan apostrophe; that in the pattern of the play Helen is a temporary pleasure who costs the protagonist eternal pain. It is worthwhile to examine the lines to Helen more carefully, for they are fraught with dramatic irony. Faustus himself points out the danger in Helen's beauty. It caused the great Trojan war—and the destruction of man's greatest edifices. Faustus' request, "Sweet Helen, make me immortal with a kiss," is, of course, blasphemous. On the contrary, it will mean eternal torment; and it will rob him of immortal joy. When he says, "Her lips suck forth my soul," he is being literally true. And as he once more kisses her, what an ironic confusion of values there is!

> Here will I dwell, for Heaven is in these lips
> And all is dross that is not Helena.

Rather, Hell lies in her lips—for the sake of which he has given up Heaven; and Helen is the "dross" for which he is giving up the "all." In the rest of the passage, Marlowe's irony persists—but not so near the surface. There is still a reversal of the normal. Faustus will be Paris (who was defeated) and fight "weak Menelaus" (who was stronger, actually). Furthermore, Faustus will be like the violator of order (Paris), whereas his opponent (the husband, the symbol of order) will be weak; but at Troy order wins—and it is bound to win in the play, too. Faustus will wear the colors of Hell on his crest. He will ignominiously fight a weak opponent—and he will wound another in his foot! Helen's beauty is like the night and stars. One remembers:

> Had I as many souls as there be stars
> I'd give them all for Mephostophilis! (1.3.99-100).

and

> as beautiful
> As was bright Lucifer before his fall. (2.1.149-50).

"Brighter art thou than flaming Jupiter" suggests the ever-burning flames of Hell—of which we hear much in the next scene. And note the proportion—Helen: Jupiter: Faustus: "hapless Semele." Helen indeed overcomes the hapless Faustus. And note the next proportion—Helen: Jupiter: Faustus: "wanton Arethusa." Wanton Faustus!

Comedy in Doctor Faustus

As I have indicated, the whole question of comedy in Marlowe's
plays represents one of the greatest failures in the criticism of
Elizabethan drama. Misunderstanding of the purpose of comedy
in such drama not only led Coleridge to be oblivious of the
dramatic appropriateness of the Porter scene in *Macbeth* but
has also led many other critics to be uncognizant of the role
of double plot, paying attention only to the so-called serious
parts of the play and sometimes omitting even mention of the
comic or farcical parts. But often, as I have again indicated,
in a medieval drama, such as *Secunda Pastorum,* the comic
and the serious interact: in this piece the mystery of the
incarnation at the end becomes something as real as the
sheep stolen on the English moor. Not that the intrusion of
the comic was always meaningful or functional—and definitely
not that the kind we find in the moralities, in the interludes, in
the Plautine imitations of the schools, and in the popular plays
for town performance did not contain a comedy which was
usually merely rough-and-tumble for its own sake.

There are flashes of farce in *Tamburlaine.* More often what is
there is something closely related to comic, the grotesque or
the sardonic. On the other hand, *The Jew of Malta* is, as T. S.
Eliot has indicated, farce that goes directly back to the
melodrama of the mysteries and the Vices of the moralities.
In *Doctor Faustus,* however, Marlowe uses comedy not merely
as relief and contrast but also as an architectonic device to
show the corruption and degradation of the protagonist.[46] At
the beginning of the play we have the sequence of a serious
scene of Faustus and Mephostophilis; *then* a comic scene
utilizing the clowns, Robin and Dick. But by the end of the
play, Doctor Faustus has descended to cheap, clownish tricks
himself—such as losing a false head or a false leg—and has
intertwined himself so much with the low comics that he
seems part of them. Let us, however, cease being general
and go over the play scene by scene to show Marlowe's great
mastery of the double plot form which mixed farce and
tragedy.

One further caveat. As I have warned, the Marlowe critic,
textual or dramatic, must not go in a circle. To assume
that the dramatist did not write comedy and then proceed to

---

[46] For a preliminary, but excellent, correlation of the comic
and serious in *Doctor Faustus,* see R. Ornstein, "The Comic
Synthesis in *Doctor Faustus,*" ELH, XXII (1955), 165-72. Unfortunately, the author uses the 1604 text as his norm.

the plays and rationalize that the comic parts are non-Marlo-vian is unallowable. In *Doctor Faustus* there is verse, such as in the papal scenes, that does not look like typical Marlovian thunderous utterance: some of it is in rhyme. To take it for granted that Marlowe did not or could not write such passages is to fall into the same error as critics have fallen into with the rhymed Talbot scenes of *1 Henry VI*. Shakespeare was experimenting here, and we must allow Marlowe the same privilege. That we find what does not seem his does not at all mean that it is not his. He may have been trying new modes and new effects. One might just as well say that there is no comedy in *An Enemy of the People* and *A Doll's House* just because Ibsen is generally an extremely serious playwright. Using the same principle, one would take *Ethan Frome* from Mrs. Wharton just because she never either before or again ever wrote anything like it. And there are stylistic portions of *A Farewell to Arms* that read more like the usual James Joyce, with his stream-of-consciousness technique, than they read like Hemingway with his usual staccato, objective technique. Coming down to Elizabethan literature, one finds at least three different styles employed by John Donne in his poetry. Thus, I stress again that what seems unusual verse for Marlowe in *Doctor Faustus* is not necessarily un-Marlovian. This is similar to the dilemma that critics have created for themselves because the dramatic technique of *The Jew of Malta* is different from that of *Tamburlaine* or that of *Edward II*.

And another warning. Our aesthetics is often not subtle enough to discriminate significantly among the *comic*, the *farcical*, and the *grotesque*. And the usual definition of *comedy* is often much too blunt when we try to apply it to a particular play. I myself think the distinction between *low comedy* and *high comedy*, for example, constantly breaks down completely. Beatrice and Benedick in *Much Ado About Nothing* are always referred to as the progenitors of a long line of witty ladies and witty gentlemen who are engaged in the war of love. But the tricks by which they are caught are about as farcical as can be imagined. And nearly always in the drama that comes after them, although the wit continues to be verbal, the witty persons and plots continue to be farcical—that is, resulting in a loud mix-up and a belly-laugh reaction. Ben Jonson's *Epicene, or The Silent Woman,* is an excellent example of what I am talking about. Thus, *comedy* is a foggy term, and I myself am tempted to use it in a general sense to apply to the whole of Marlowe's *Doctor Faustus* in which, typically, a would-be wit gets fooled and defeated. (In this sense *Oedipus the King* is also both tragedy and comedy.) But more than

this, the constant appearance of the grotesque devils, the
emphasis on such spectacle as the Seven Deadly Sins, the
appearance of Alexander and Darius, the crossing over the
stage from the audience and into the audience of the
apparition of Helen of Troy—all these are so intense in their
eye appeal that they make of the play somewhat of a musical
comedy, with a series of reactions moving all the way between
fear and delight. Furthermore, we must not forget that aspect
of *Doctor Faustus* which allies the play with the magic tricks
of a professional magician, making of it at times a species of
vaudeville act. This is the same dramatic region which
Shakespeare exploited in *A Midsummer Night's Dream* and
The Tempest; and Greene and Peele, respectively, in *Friar
Bacon and Friar Bungay* and *The Old Wive's Tale.*

1.1

If one defines irony as belonging to comedy, one is never
far away from comedy in *Doctor Faustus.* When Faustus says
"A sound magician is a demi-god," and a moment later the
Good Angel tells him that he is incurring "God's heavy wrath,"
and then Faustus says that he can "Perform what *desperate*
enterprise I will," we are in the presence of irony. But so
pervasive is this quality and so intertwined with the religious
values of the play that I will allow my above discussion of
these values to stand for its critical appreciation in this drama.

1.2

In some ways the comedy in this scene is subtle. Wagner,
Faustus' servant, is semicomic only in this scene and in
1.4. He does not reappear in the play until 4.3, where his role
is merely that of a messenger. Examine Wagner carefully in 1.2
and you will see that he has become inflated with Doctor
Faustus' pride. He triumphs over the two scholars with
verbal trickery and boasts that they must not "come within
forty foot of the place of execution"—that is, the place
where magic is about to occur. He is, in other words, unduly
proud that his master is within at dinner with Valdes and
Cornelius. His cheap aping of Faustus' superiority is contrasted
too with the humility of the two scholars, who are troubled
that their friend, Faustus, has "fall'n into that damned art,
/For which they two [Cornelius and Valdes] are infamous
through the world."

1.3

The joke in this scene is cosmic. Like hungry animals,
Lucifer and the four devils above watch Doctor Faustus invoke
their agent, Mephostophilis, who tells the doctor bluntly that

he has no power but that they cherish his soul, and watch
grimly while he makes fun of Hell. Their silence as Faustus
boasts and swells is a terrible comment on the ludicrousness
of his pride.

1.4

In this scene, Marlowe parodies the horrible bargain for the
things of this world which Wagner's master is making with the
powers of Hell. Wagner with his guilders buying the Clown
parallels Mephostophilis' buying Faustus' eternal soul for the
guilders of power and glory. In other words, Robin the Clown
in his ludicrousness and greediness definitely parallels the
haughty magician. Furthermore, Wagner's puffed vanity is
meant to parallel Doctor Faustus', and the ease with which
he calls the two demons, Banio and Belcher, is meant to
illustrate the self-deception of Doctor Faustus in thinking it
was difficult to call the powers of darkness. The Clown's
request of Wagner to "teach me this conjuring occupation" and
to be "A dog or a cat or a mouse or a rat? O brave Wagner!"
directly echoes Faustus' request from Mephostophilis for
power and his admiration of the Devil's agent. Furthermore,
the cheapness of the request suggests the magician's mundane
stupidity, and Wagner's orders to Robin to follow at his
heel prognosticate the career and end of Wagner's master.

2.1

The present conflict of Faustus between the two spiritual
forces within him, Good and Evil, show his earlier strength
of mind to be almost comically thin. His verbal threats to
"build an altar and a church" to the Devil "And offer lukewarm
blood of newborn babes!" support our notion of a small man
comically trying to surmount his ultimate nonentity. The easy
triumph which Mephostophilis wins over the magician after
the latter has signed the bill of sale of his soul and has a
strong reaction of religious fear is emphasized in the simplicity
of what the devils give him "to delight his mind." Some
crowns, some rich apparel, and a dance seem much too little,
economically speaking, to offset the terrible price · for them
that Faustus is paying.

When Faustus tells Mephostophilis, "I think Hell's a
fable," one sees the human tendency to fool oneself at its
most tragic, or comic, worth. The woman-devil, ugly and
deformed, whom Mephostophilis fetches in when the Doctor
says he wants a wife, is an early presage of the famous Helen
of Troy appearance, for the latter is merely a succuba, despite
her lovely appearance, merely a hideous demon from the
underworld.

2.2

Again Faustus is in the spiritual toils but decides he will not repent. Throughout the play, Doctor Faustus' refusal to ask God's aid and constantly to seek instead that of the Devil is part of his inane stupidity. We remember that the Fool-in-Christ is smart enough to recognize his own weakness and to beg aid from the Almighty. But the great sinner sometimes has so much inverse pride in his vice that he believes himself incapable of God's forgiveness. To refuse God's grace and mercy is truly the non-act of a truly great fool. I must comment on the irony of Mephostophilis' giving Faustus in this scene scholarly information which the latter could have got out of any contemporary treatise. That Mephostophilis refuses to answer the really difficult question of God's creation of the world stresses the poor bargain which Faustus has made. We have often heard that Marlowe's protagonist is a superman of unusual knowledge, but Marlowe's play shows that what he mostly gets for his so-called spiritual bravery is various travel trips and the ability to do low-class conjuring.

Again Faustus in a spiritual agony caves in when the devils ascend from Hell and is again assuaged by the pastime of the Seven Deadly Sins. This is a kind of vaudeville show in which Pride, Covetousness, Envy, Wrath, Gluttony, Sloth, and Lechery act out overemphatically, to the laughter of the audience, their proclivities.

2.3

Again a clown scene parallels the main action. Robin tells Dick that now he has stolen one of Faustus' books he can get for them whatever they want. The cheapness of their request parallels the wages Doctor Faustus is receiving for his contract:

> Do but speak what thou't have me to do, and I'll do't.
> If thou't dance naked, put off thy clothes, and I'll conjure
> thee about presently. Or if thou't go but to the tavern with
> me, I'll give thee white wine, red wine, claret wine, sack,
> muscadine, malmesey, and whippincrust—hold-belly-hold.
> And we'll not pay one penny for it!

Interestingly, the fact that Robin can scarcely read and yet believes he can call on the powers of darkness to accomplish his ends undercuts Faustus' belief that his intelligence and wisdom had anything to do with the first arrival of Mephostophilis.

3.1 and 3.2

From now on the comic and the tragic, or if you wish the serious, in this play are going to be so intertwined that they are inextricable. But surely Marlowe means to stress the magician's continuing degradation by showing him first playing his tricks with the spiritual head of all Roman Catholic Christendom and then ultimately declining, to play them with the clowns: Robin, Dick, the Carter, and the Horse-Courser, who are drunk, and the poor Hostess who wants money for the beer she has fetched. Is it accidental that Faustus' victims are first the Pope; second, the courtier, Benvolio; third, the Horse-Courser; and fourth, the Carter—steadily downhill in dignity and social prominence? The victim becomes less and less intelligent and less and less powerful, and the conjurer becomes less and less discriminating in his jackanapes. All this, I assume, is meant on Marlowe's part.

Part of what I am saying is that in the papal scene Marlowe is still giving dignity to the magician by having him save the rival Pope, Bruno, who is meant apparently to be some kind of representative of anti-Catholic feeling in sixteenth-century Europe. In other words, the Doctor is allied, for the nonce, with the great powers of Protestantism, which are opposing the splendor, vanity, and overweening pride of Rome. From this point of view, Faustus' tricks of acting like a cardinal, of snatching dishes from the Pope at the banquet, of striking the great prelate when he superstitiously crosses himself have a kind of *Zeitgeist* excuse of great significance. That he and Mephostophilis throw fireworks among the friars engaging in one of their superstitious ceremonies couples them with the age-old anticlericalism of the *fabliaux*.

3.3

The first part of this is an old burlesque routine. As the Vintner's boy searches one clown, the latter gives the cup to the other clown, and so on. It may be that Marlowe took advantage of a theatrical opportunity and had Robin throw the goblet finally into the audience, where there would be much laughter and a wild scramble, just like what happens when a baseball goes into the crowd today at a major league game. Robin's making a magic circle, calling for Mephostophilis, and the Vintner's boy rushing off frightened when the latter appears are Keystone comedy stuff, but Mephostophilis' anger at being called by these clowns has, I believe, its purpose in the design of the play. These creatures are garbage to him. Doctor Faustus too is garbage, but he has a valuable possession

—his immortal soul, which the Devil is willing to adopt temporary mildness and subservience to get. Dick's acting like an ape and Robin's acting like a dog and the one's crawling off the stage with the other on top of him perhaps not only give us cheap fun but promise the ultimate transformation of the magician, for Mephostophilis says, I "fly amain/Unto my Faustus."

4.1

Benvolio's being above and smart-cracking just before the great dumb show of Darius and Alexander is a great stroke on Marlowe's part in showing the coming together of Doctor Faustus as a great magician and as a crude conjurer. The fact that Benvolio's horns must be put on him while this dumb show is occurring enforces the point I have just made.

4.2

That in this scene the magician overcomes the three courtiers by means of the trick of the false head shows a declination from the Faustus who opposed the Catholic potentate of the world. The present scene is a bridge between the magic invisibility of the papal scene and the farcicality of the Horse-Courser scene. Perhaps too the courtiers' scorning the false head has some sort of symbolic significance. At any rate, it is pretty cheap humor. Perhaps, too, we should comment on the extreme revenge that Faustus takes on Martino, Frederick, and Benvolio. That they are left with horns seems bullying of an egregious sort on the part of the magician, and however offensive and dangerous they have tried to be they are surely weak victims against the Doctor's magic wiles, as are the soldiers who are bedazzled by the moving trees and among whom fireworks are thrown.

4.3

In the correlation of comic and serious, this little scene is in some ways the most significant that we have hitherto examined. The tricking of the Horse-Courser occupies what can be called the first fourth and the third fourth of this scene. The buyer is warned not to put the horse into the water (is there not a bit of pathos in the magician's taking advantage of this boor?) but, of course, he does, off-stage; returns wet—note this farcical effect!—pulls off the Doctor's leg; and runs off screaming. "Ha, ha, ha!" laughs the conjurer, "Faustus hath his leg again, and the horse-courser a bundle of hay for his forty dollars." The degradation of him who at the beginning of the play sought through magic the answers of the universe has obviously reached a very low point. But what is remarkable here in Marlowe's dramatic technique is that for the first time extremely important tragic material is inserted right within the farce. In the second fourth of the scene, that is, between the Horse-Courser's first appearance and his second appearance, comes one of the most relevant soliloquies of the play:

> *Faust.* What are thou, Faustus, but a man condemn'd to
> die?
> Thy fatal time draws to a final end . . .
> Despair doth drive distrust into my thoughts.
> Confound these passions with a quiet sleep.
> Tush, Christ did call the thief upon the cross!
> Then rest thee Faustus, quiet in conceit.

In the last fourth of the scene, Wagner enters to extend the Duke of Vanholt's invitation. Faustus' low diction that the Duke is "one to whom I must be no *niggard* of my *cunning*" seems to augment the mood of this part of the play.

4.4

All are clowns here, including the Hostess. (Parts like the Nurse in *Romeo and Juliet* and Dame Quickly were taken on the Elizabethan stage by older men, who would stress the burlesque costume, make-up, speech, and actions of their parts.) It is significant that although this is a low comedy scene with such a line as the following: "What ho, hostess! Where be these whores?", its content is made up of accounts of Faustus' individual actions against the clowns. In other words, instead of correlation between comic and serious, the two are merged into what must be esteemed a loss of the latter—with conscious or unconscious reactions on the part of the audience to the magician's increasing spiritual cheapness. Two points: The bit where Robin hides behind the others because he owes the Hostess money can be made quite funny. And, two, although there is no stage direction, beer must be brought at least once to these creatures.

4.5

This is the climax of Faustus' relations with the clowns. After this they do not appear. There surely is some kind of dramaturgic relationship between the come-down in the magician's necromancy and the appearance of the low comics. Instead of an Emperor, we have a Duke; and, instead of the appearance of magical Darius and Alexander, we have a magical bunch of grapes. The appearance of the pregnant Duchess, a boy playing the part with a couple of pillows tied around his middle, may also lend its share to the commonness of this scene. The drunken clowns "bounce at the gate within." "They knock again and call out to talk with Faustus." Their calling off-stage for Faustus and their intrusions into the Duke's presence symbolically represent a great decline in the magician's prestige and values. Their acting as though the place is an inn, Faustus' bowing to the Carter, the Hostess' entering with drink, and the charming dumb of each of them makes of the great "superman" the equivalent of a razzle-dazzle artist in a country fair.

5.1 and 5.2

Is there any comedy in this concluding act of the tragedy of the eminent necromancer of Wittenberg? It depends on how one defines the term. As I explained in my above analysis of the religious values, there is much, much irony in these last two scenes. The fact that Faustus gives up all hope of Heaven in order to lie with a succuba is surely savage comedy of some kind. And Faustus' boasting of his accomplishments to the scholars in the very midst of his despair is surely ludicrous too. That Faustus' limbs are tossed out by the devils after he descends into Hell for his eternal damnation cannot but remind us of the various comic occasions in the preceding play in which false body parts were utilized. The limbs are not funny now!

Production of Doctor Faustus

The reader should constantly understand for the paragraphs under this topic what, perhaps, I should baldly state whenever I write on Elizabethan production in this Introduction: that my descriptions of staging are almost always inferences.

Act 1

Apparently the Chorus in Elizabethan drama wore a particular kind of cloak.

1.1

After the Chorus finishes his last line, "And this the man that in his study sits," the curtains of the enclosure at the back of the stage are opened and we see Doctor Faustus, probably standing, at a desk on which many books lie. Possibly Marlowe meant to make a distinction between the doctor as scholar and the doctor as magician by means of the particular kind of robe the player wore. (A magician's robe was conventional on the Elizabethan stage; cf. Prospero in *The Tempest*.) Here in this scene, 1.1, Faustus is probably wearing a doctor's academic gown. He opens book after book and discounts each, but stops finally and praises that on magic. He calls his servant, Wagner, and tells him to request two famous magicians, Valdes and Cornelius, to visit him. After the servant exits, Faustus continues to read in the magic book. As his head is bent over it, enter the two Angels. Probably throughout the play, each took the same place on the stage. The Good Angel was probably conventionally dressed in white, with wings. The Bad Angel would be costumed in black, for contrast, and may have been a demon in appearance. At no time in the play is Faustus supposed to have cognizance of their presence. Expressionistically, they represent separate voices within him. As they leave the stage, Doctor Faustus lifts his head and commends magic. Thus, dramatically speaking, there already had been a debate for the soul of Doctor Faustus in which the Devil has won. Enter Valdes and Cornelius with books under their arms. They are dressed probably in magician robes, which automatically contrast, of course, with the scholar's garb that Faustus is wearing. Valdes gives him magic books, and they leave the stage.

1.2

Enter two scholars. They are wearing academic robes in order to show group identity at the present moment with Doctor Faustus. This grouping Doctor Faustus' becoming an addict and practicer of necromancy will break, and that is why his assumption of a magician's cloak when we next see him is visually important.

1.3

There is a great noise of thunder and Lucifer and four devils enter, probably above on the tarras. Doctor Faustus turns toward them but does not see them. Throughout the scene, they watch him intently. Lucifer's appearance and costume as the leader of the hosts of Hell are probably very distinctive. Faustus, as I have said, is wearing the magician's garb and with more thunder he begins his incantations, asking Mephostophilis to arise. At the end of his invocation, the trap opens and a dragon's head appears. (Possibly smoke is coming from its nostrils.) Doctor Faustus shows revulsion at its appearance and orders it to return as "an old Franciscan friar." A moment later from the back enters Mephostophilis, dressed according to command. (Perhaps it is Goethe's *Faust* that has made us accustomed to a youthful Mephistophilis, but even then it is difficult to envisage Marlowe's figure as old. There is a possibility that "old" here is Elizabethan diction for "customary.")

1.4

Enter Wagner and Robin the Clown. The latter undoubtedly wears high make-up and a typical clown's costume. It may be motley; it may be peasant's dress. He may or may not have a coxcomb cap and a coxcomb stick. At any rate, he is not clean-shaven but has a pointed beard. After Wagner has given him money, the former makes magical gestures and two devils, probably hideous, enter. The Clown runs about the stage rapidly and awkwardly to get away from the demons, who may or may not menace him. Wagner orders the spirits away and the Clown follows him off the stage, in step with him.

Act 2

There is a probability that a Chorus is meant to enter to introduce this act. There is none in the extant texts.

2.1

The curtains open at the back and Faustus is again discovered in his study. As he is in the toils of conflict between God and the Devil, the two Angels enter and take their customary places. Here there is a rather interesting bit of action: *we* hear the Angels but Faustus is hearkening to inner voices; and so his replies to these voices are not made to the Angels but to us, the audience. The Angels leave and Faustus calls for Mephostophilis. He enters still dressed as the friar, and probably this is the robe that he wears for the rest of the play. Faustus takes a knife, cuts his arm, dips a pen in the blood that is supposed to be flowing, and writes a bill at his desk. When he cries that the blood stops, Mephostophilis brings in a chafer of fire, probably stones painted vermilion to indicate great heat. That Faustus holds his arm over this without flinching is part of the spectacle of the scene. As he raises his head from writing, he seems to see words on his arm (probably he has pulled back one sleeve of his robe to get at his blood). The words he sees on his arm are probably to be imagined by the spectators. As Faustus is again in a spiritual conflict, Mephostophilis fetches him "somewhat to delight his mind." "Enter devils giving crowns and rich apparel to Faustus. They dance and then depart." (We must remember that devils were coal-black in Shakespeare's day.) Probably the devils heap the crowns and the apparel in Faustus' arms and then do a devil dance around him. After Doctor Faustus reads the bill aloud, he indicates that he wants a wife. And Mephostophilis brings in a hideous female devil who probably goes through lascivious gyrations. She leaves and Mephostophilis takes a book from under his robe and gives it to Doctor Faustus, who hugs it. Exeunt.

At this point in the play, there must have occurred a comic scene which is now lost. Who was in it, what they did, we shall never know. But such a scene is necessary to divide 2.1 and 2.2.

2.2

Although Mephostophilis is present, Faustus is again in conflict, and the two Angels enter to their customary positions. They speak to him and he answers as before. Exeunt Angels. After much dialogue with Mephostophilis, Faustus again falls into despair. Mephostophilis angrily leaves and enter the two Angels again. They leave after four lines, but this time the Good Angel has deeply affected the protagonist. As he probably falls to his knees praying to Christ, enter Lucifer, Belzebub, and Mephostophilis (from the trap?) and Faustus recoils in terror. That he so quickly gets used to the terrible appearances of Mephostophilis' companions is some indication of his increasing degradation. The show of the Seven Deadly Sins which Lucifer puts on for the Doctor's enjoyment is one of the high points of spectacle in the play. They are led by a piper, who is undoubtedly a devil. Since they are allegorical figures, their actions and costumes must represent their identity. Pride is probably a foppish courtier. Covetousness probably looks like an old, writhen, conventional miser. Envy may have had a robe with snakes' tongues upon it, for that is how the Elizabethans often conceived of this sin. Wrath probably is like raging Herod in the mysteries, red hair and possibly violently red costume. Gluttony is a fat figure with pillows inside his dress, moving lethargically. Sloth is possibly dressed in a flower costume and yawns frequently. Lechery is a highly made-up woman wearing the loose gown that Elizabethan whores affected. Just as the piper piped them on, so he pipes them off. That the stage direction reads "Exeunt omnes several ways" possibly means that the magician left through a conventional entrance, whereas the devils descended into the trap.

2.3

Robin the Clown enters with a book and calls off-stage to Dick to look to the horses. When Dick enters, Robin is spelling out letter by letter a passage in his book of magic, and both leave exultant at what they will accomplish through necromancy in the future.

Act 3

Enter the Chorus.

3.1

Enter Faustus and Mephistophilis, whom we are now to imagine in Rome. The Pope enters in brilliant procession with cardinals and bishops wearing their miters, some bearing crosses, some maces. Monks and friars are chanting. The Pope is accompanied by the King of Hungary wearing a crown and "Bruno led in chains." (There is a strong possibility that Bruno's costume duplicates the Pope's.) Bruno kneels and the Pope steps on him in order to get into his throne, for which the curtains at the back have just been opened. After Bruno rises, the Pope sends two cardinals off the stage. Faustus and Mephostophilis are watching this at the side or at the front of the stage. While the Pope talks to the King of Hungary, Faustus sends Mephostophilis off the stage after the two cardinals and leaves with him. After the colloquy between the Pope and Bruno, Faustus and Mephostophilis enter in the two cardinals' costumes and play the latters' parts. The Pope removes the tiara from Bruno and gives it to Faustus. Exit Faustus, carrying Bruno's crown, along with Mephostophilis and Bruno. The Pope orders a banquet to be brought in and all his party leave the stage.

3.2

There is a sennet of trumpets and attendants bring in a table and chairs. Faustus and Mephostophilis re-enter in their own costumes, and Mephostophilis makes the magician invisible by giving him a magic girdle. Thus in the ensuing scene when the Doctor interferes in the banquet, it is presumed by the audience that no one on the stage can see him. The Pope's procession enters again and the chief dignitaries seat themselves at the table. At this moment, the two cardinals enter in their own robes again and there is a bit of comedy as, expostulating, they are violently removed a few lines later. Faustus insults the Pope verbally but no one knows from whence the voice is coming, and the friars busily look about in wonderment and fear. As the Pope presents a dish to the King of Hungary, Faustus snatches it. He does the same thing to a dish for the Archbishop of Rheims. When wine is served and the Pope is about to drink, Faustus grabs the goblet from his hands. The Pope begins to cross himself, and Faustus strikes him. The former and his train leave in confusion. Now the friars enter with bell, book, and candle and begin to sing a dirge. When one of the friars curses him who struck the Pope, Faustus strikes him. Then Faustus and Mephostophilis, it doesn't matter whether they are considered to be invisible or not now, beat the friars and fling fireworks among them.

3.3

This scene continues an old, farcical routine which I have
seen used in burlesque, vaudeville, and the movies. Just before
Robin tells the Vintner's boy to search him, he hands the cup
to Dick. And just before Dick says the same thing, he hands
the cup to Robin. And just before the Vintner's boy searches
both of them at one time, Robin flings the cup away—perhaps
into the audience! Aside, Robin tells Dick to make a circle. They
both stand within it. Robin utters an invocation. Mephostophilis suddenly appears (from the trap?), probably with
smoke, and the Vintner's boy, frightened, rushes off the stage.
When Mephostophilis tells Dick he is transformed to an ape,
probably the latter grimaces and acts like a monkey. When
Mephostophilis tells Robin that he is a dog, probably the latter
gets down on all fours. Dick probably leaves the stage on
Robin's back. Mephostophilis descends through the trap with
smoke coming out again(?).

Act 4

Enter Chorus.

4.1

We are now told of Charles V's court. Martino and Frederick,
two of the Emperor's courtiers, enter. There is a window,
either right or left of the tarras, at which they shout for
Benvolio to appear. "Enter Benvolio above at a window, in
his night-cap, buttoning." He sticks his head out to watch what
is going on below. Martino and Frederick leave to return immediately in the Emperor's retinue. There is a sennet and
Charles V, Bruno wearing the Pope's robe and the triple crown,
the Duke of Saxony, Faustus, Frederick, Martino, and attendants enter. The Emperor seats himself. Mephostophilis,
too, has entered but there is a strong probability that he is
made to appear invisible. (This convention is very simple to
create on the stage. All that the other players have to do is to
act as though they don't see the invisible being.) Whenever
Benvolio speaks from above, there is probably a pantomime
of talk and kneeling on the stage below. Aside, Faustus sends
Mephostophilis away. Now when Benvolio speaks, Faustus
looks up and promises him something will happen. There is a
sound of trumpets and a dumb show enters, quite elaborate.
Alexander, Darius, and the great conqueror's beloved must be
dressed very sumptuously. "Sennet. Enter at one [door] the
Emperor Alexander, at the other Darius. They meet. Darius is
thrown down. Alexander kills him, takes off his crown, and
offering to go out, his Paramour meets him. He embraceth her

and sets Darius' crown upon her head, and coming back both salute the Emperor; who leaving his state offers to embrace them, which Faustus seeing suddenly stays him. Then trumpets cease and music sounds." While this show has been going on, Benvolio has put his head on his arms and fallen asleep so that his head is extended outside the window. While the audience's attention is on the show, he must have horns attached to his head. I assume that Marlowe gives this task to Mephostophilis, who continues to stand, unknown, behind the unfortunate courtier until he has to remove the appendage. After the show exits, the Emperor awakens Benvolio, who tries to pull his head in, but the width of the horns prevents him. He puts his hands to his head in pain and continually tries to pull off the horns. When Faustus tells Mephostophilis to remove them, he does, and Benvolio exits from the window. So the scene ends.

4.2

Benvolio, Martino, Frederick, and the soldiers enter. Soon Frederick leaves with the soldiers, to put them in ambush, and then returns. "Enter Faustus with the false head." This *the* is extremely interesting, for it indicates that a customary stage property is being used. First Benvolio strikes him with the sword. Faustus falls to his knees and Benvolio cuts off the false head. The magician falls flat. Frederick and Martino kick the head around on the floor(?) and Benvolio lifts it by the hair. Without a head, Faustus rises: and the three courtiers are frightened out of their wits. Then Faustus puts his own head out and orders Mephostophilis and the other devils to appear. Behemoth clasps Frederick, Asteroth clasps Martino, Mephostophilis clasps Benvolio, and they drag them off the stage. The soldiers enter to face Doctor Faustus. At this moment, a line of trees which has been standing on the stage moves (by means of a rope, I suppose) between the soldiers and the magician. Then "Faustus strikes the door, and enter a devil playing on a drum, after him another bearing an ensign, and divers with weapons: Mephostophilis with fireworks: they set upon the soldiers and drive them out." Then "Enter at several doors Benvolio, Frederick, and Martino, their heads and faces bloody and besmeared with mud and dirt, all having horns on their heads." And they finally exeunt.

4.3

All the low characters in this play are more or less clowns. And the Horse-Courser is probably to be depicted as a coarse peasant. In the present routine, Faustus is probably sitting against the back of the stage from which a false leg can be put under his robe. The entrance of the Horse-Courser with actual water upon him is a fine effect, which Shakespeare later duplicated in the first scene of *The Tempest*. The Horse-Courser, trying to wake the magician, pulls out the false leg and runs with it shrieking from the stage. Then Faustus stands up on his own two legs, and leaves the stage with Wagner.

4.4

The Hostess, also, is a comic figure. During this scene Robin, Dick, the Horse-Courser, and the Carter are served with beer by the Hostess or nameless attendants and drink it. They leave the stage somewhat drunk.

4.5

Enter the Duke of Vanholt, his Duchess who is to be portrayed as pregnant, Faustus, Mephostophilis, and servants. Again it is quite probable that Mephostophilis is to be taken as invisible. Faustus asides to him and tells him to bring in grapes. He re-enters, gives them to the magician, and the latter gives them to the Duchess. "The Clowns [Robin, Dick, the Carter, and the Horse-Courser, who are all drunk] bounce at the gate within." "They knock again and call out to talk with Faustus." In other words, they ad-lib. A servant is sent to question them and they talk off-stage. Then they all enter. Faustus makes a gesture to have beer brought to them. When the Carter questions him about his leg, Doctor Faustus bows. Then enter the Hostess with drink. It is possible that Mephostophilis, invisible, brings her in. Now Faustus opens his robe to show that he has two legs. As the Carter advances on him, the magician waves his hands and the Carter becomes dumb, ditto Dick, ditto Horse-Courser, ditto Robin, ditto Hostess. And so ends the scene.

Act 5

5.1

"Thunder and lightning. Enter devils with covered dishes: Mephostophilis leads them into Faustus' study. Then enter Wagner." After Wagner leaves the stage, enter Faustus and three scholars—together with Mephostophilis, who again, I presume, is invisible. Faustus motions to Mephostophilis, there is music, and Mephostophilis brings in Helen of Troy. "She passeth over the stage" probably means that she comes in from the audience and exits through the audience. After the scholars leave, enter an Old Man. He begs Faustus to repent. Mephostophilis, I would guess, is invisible now, even to Doctor Faustus, and hands him a dagger. As he is about to use it, the Old Man restrains him. After the latter leaves the stage,

Mephostophilis reveals himself and threatens Doctor Faustus. When the latter requests Helen's reappearance, Mephostophilis waves and she comes in the same way from the audience, but this time between two Cupids. Faustus utters an apostrophe to her, kisses her, embraces her, and leaves the stage with her.

5.2

This is the catastrophe. There is thunder and enter Lucifer, Belzebub, and Mephostophilis. Perhaps they enter from the trap and then go above, or perhaps they enter above immediately. At any rate, through the ensuing action of this scene, they watch. Then enter Faustus and Wagner. Wagner presumably exits and then enter the three scholars. After the scholars leave, Mephostophilis apparently descends to the stage and, after laughing at Faustus, exits. Enter the Good Angel and the Bad Angel at several doors, taking their usual places. A throne descends from the Heavens (i.e., the stage roof). And, very graphically, the Good Angel for the first time leaves the stage to the Bad Angel alone. "Hell is discovered," perhaps in the trap from which smoke ascends, perhaps in the back of the stage, and the Bad Angel tells Faustus to look within it. After the Bad Angel tortures him with the sight of horrors, he leaves and Faustus is alone on the stage. Thrice the clock strikes, and it is twelve o'clock. There is thunder and lightning and the devils enter to drag Faustus through the trap. The devils above exeunt. Faustus is heard shrieking and his limbs are thrown from the trap, which closes.

5.3

Enter the scholars, lamenting, pick up Faustus' limbs, and leave the stage.

Enter the final Chorus.

The Jew of Malta

So intertwined are character, action, and stage technique in this superb melodrama that I have included particular production points within the critical analysis of the play. I think it may be hazarded that the spectator of *The Jew of Malta* tends not to separate, as he can do to some extent in the other Marlowe plays, costume, gesture, and theatrical effect from the story line. But this is an impalpable point and need not be stressed except that it is characteristic of melodrama to have this peculiarly theatrical unity: and that if critics had paid more

attention to this phenomenon in *The Jew* they would not have
fragmented it as they have done—seeing the verse, for example,
as dramatically divisible from the Judas wig.

1.1

As soon as we see Barabas, with his red mop of hair, his
elongated nose, his yellow gabardine with distinctive badge,
his extravagant gestures, we are prepared for the traditional
stock responses to this traditional monster of a Jew-Devil-Vice.
We are prepared, by the direction of the Gentillet-Machiavel
of the Prologue, for an egocentric, criminal, sadistic, avaricious,
and revengeful enemy of conventional moral Christian society.
We are prepared for a doer, not a prater, in the ensuing *farce*,
"the farce of the Old English humour . . . terrbily serious, even
savage[ly] comic." [47] But perhaps there is even more than this.
"If we detach the elements of incredible evil from Barabas
(those elements which come from his medieval background)
we see him as an essentially modern figure, a symbol of the
new industrial and political power which was to emerge in the
course of the next two centuries in Western Europe and
America." [48] The internationally wealthy Hebrew has become
a king-without-title in his power and influence, suggests Marlowe's bogy (1.1.130-36).

Here he is now, at the beginning, in his counting-house, heaps
of gold before him, as unreal but as frightening as a fairy-tale
ogre. His ships have ventured the globe: Spain, Greece, Asia
Minor, Morocco, Arabia, Persia, and India. And like a typical
successful Renaissance merchant-prince, he has amassed vast
amounts of silver, gold, and precious jewels.

And thus methinks should men of judgment frame
Their means of traffic from the vulgar trade.

When a Merchant enters to say that the Jew's Egyptian fleet
has just arrived, Barabas sends "threescore camels, thirty
mules,/And twenty wagons to bring up the ware." (One observes that the hyperbolic Jew with his hyperbolic enumeration
is a Tamburlaine figure, not of warfare but of finance, which, of
course, is a kind of warfare too!) The Merchant wonders why
Barabas, who is apprehensive about his Alexandrian argosy,
"durst with so much wealth/Trust such a crazed vessel, and

---

[47] T. S. Eliot, "Christopher Marlowe," in *Selected Essays, 1917-
1932* (London, 1932), p. 123.
[48] Harold Fisch, *The Dual Image: A Study of the Jew in English
Literature* (London, 1959), p. 28. See also Edgar Rosenberg, *From
Shylock to Svengali, Jewish Stereotypes in English Fiction*
(Stanford University Press, 1960), pp. 21-38.

so far." This is a trenchant touch. Barabas *is* a miser, who, in order to squeeze every penny out of a venture, will employ leaky, overladen boats—oblivious to the possible loss of human life. As a matter of fact, Barabas' entire attitude to the Merchant is of one who scorns his underlings.

Marlowe's *weaving* in this play is sometimes unobtrusive. The Second Merchant, reporting the arrival of the Alexandrian ship, says,

> Sir, we were wafted by a Spanish fleet
> That never left us till within a league,
> That had the galleys of the Turk in chase.

We soon find out that Malta owes much tribute money to the Turks, but the above suggests that the latter are not all-powerful and that the Spanish represent a potent enemy. Later, in 2.2, the Spanish Vice-Admiral, Del Bosco, will advise Ferneze, Governor of Malta, to break his truce with the Turks—and from this decision comes the material of 3.5 and the entire last act. Furthermore, Del Bosco has come to Malta to sell the Turkish prisoners he has just taken as slaves—and one of these is Ithamore.

Again, in soliloquy, Barabas gloats over his winnings. These are the blessings promised to Abraham!

> What more may Heaven do for earthly man
> Than thus to pour out plenty in their laps,
> Ripping the bowels of the earth for them,
> Making the seas their servants, and the winds
> To drive their substance with successful blasts?

Thus, brilliantly, Marlowe joins the stock Jewish financier of folklore—and, also, to some extent, of actual history—to the "new" economic man of the Renaissance period, gaining incredible wealth directly or indirectly from the mines of Peru and from extended voyages over the surface of the entire globe. Nature is losing her status as man's severe mistress: she, too, is becoming his underling!

To Barabas, the man of today, *honor* is *wealth*. To be a hated, isolated rich man is better than to be a "Christian" poor man. (Besides, the Christians are hypocrites anyhow!) *Conscience* is silly. So Barabas defines a Jew, and takes pride in his lineage. Christian "faith" brings no monetary rewards. (Just as the dramatist has a dual depiction here—from Barabas' viewpoint, admittedly, but the rest of the play bears out the bifurcation—of the Christians as moral but immoral too, so in a moment he is going to present us with a dual delineation of the Jew: Barabas, the individualist, vs. the Three Jews, representing the long-suffering, patient race.) Now Barabas mentions his sole heir, Abigail, "whom I hold as dear/As Agamemnon did his Iphigen." This, of course, is Marlowe's prophetic irony. The Greek, too, sacrificed his daughter to his own interests.

Enter three Jews to tell Barabas that Turkish vessels have arrived in the harbor: and the Maltese leaders are entertaining the embassy. Now Marlowe begins to utilize a dramatic device that he employs skillfully in this play for Barabas, the aside, by means of which the latter can reveal to the audience his real, as opposed to his ostensible, intentions. Sometimes the aside is spoken to his daughter, Abigail; but more often it is addressed directly to the spectators. (Traditionally, of course, the soliloquy and the aside are meant to tell the truth about the speaker: it is not until *Hamlet* that this hitherto absolute convention begins to be psychologized, and hence no longer choral and trustworthy.)

> (—Nay, let 'em combat, conquer, and kill all,
> So they spare me, my daughter, and my wealth!)

This aside cuts Barabas off not only from the Maltese and Turks but also from his own race. The Jews have been called to the Senate House. The three visitors do not know what is happening, and Barabas plays along with them. But as soon as they leave, he tells us that, unlike these "silly men," he *knows* why the Turks have come: to collect tribute. Let them take the town as long as he doesn't lose! Thus Marlowe finishes this scene with the soliloquy of a man who has no loyalties except to himself.

1.2

We are in the Senate House where Christian faces Turk. (It is not accidental that Marlowe presents Ferneze as churlish at first and the Mohammedan as courteous. Elizabethan drama must never forget that the playwrights did their best to satisfy the audience's expectations that a Roman Catholic priest or temporal dignitary would be vicious.) Calymath demands of the Governor of Malta the ten years' tribute due. When Ferneze avers that time is needed to collect it, a basso objects. Calymath rebukes him,

> What, Callipine, a little courtesy!
> Let's know their time, perhaps it is not long:
> And 'tis more kingly to obtain by peace
> Than to enforce conditions by constraint.

After he grants a month's delay, he politely takes his leave: "Farewell, great governors and brave Knights of Malta."

We now can guess why the Jews have been summoned. They enter. Barabas deliberately acts the part of a simpleton. Let

Malta pay its debt to Turkey and "keep your quiet still." When Ferneze indicates that the money is not available, Barabas continues his role as innocent: he and his fellows are no soldiers. It is indicative that when the knight demands "thy money," probably referring to all the Hebrews, Barabas answers him with the outraged gasp: "How, my lord, *my* money?" The First Jew claims that "most of us are poor!" (It is permissible to infer that in both dress and make-up the three Jews are different from the caricature, Barabas: they, probably, are to be presented with a certain amount of dignity, at least without a melodramatic, villainous aura.) As in *The Merchant of Venice* the fact that Jews are aliens, both metaphorically and legally, is stressed:

> *Bar.* Are strangers with your tribute to be tax'd?
> *2 Knight.* Have strangers leave with us to get their wealth?
> Then let them with us contribute.

The point is that the Jew is considered a parasite.

Now Barabas outsmarts himself, just as he outsmarts himself at the end of the play. (He overrates himself and underrates his enemies, just as Shylock is to do.) The three Jews are willing to pay one half of their estates to escape total confiscation, followed by forced baptism; but Barabas strongly demurs. Finally he sees the trap he is in, but it is too late. The decree has already gone out to seize his property. When Barabas angrily sneers,

> Will you, then, steal my goods?
> Is theft the ground of your religion?

Marlowe puts into Ferneze's mouth a choric speech that harks back to the Middle Ages in its insistence on community good as opposed to individualism:

> No, Jew, we take particularly thine
> To save the ruin of a multitude:
> And better one want for a common good
> Than many perish for a private man!

(That such a figure as Ferneze is given this approvable dictum is merely another example of the complex reaction Elizabethan drama often demands. Ferneze's being a Christian does not mean that he is really good: Barabas' not being a Christian means that he is totally bad: his religious compatriots' not being Christian does not mean that they are to be automatically esteemed evil.) The First Knight invokes the "curse," the "inherent sin" under which all Jews labor. Why, says Barabas in an extremely Marlovian ironic speech, make me representative of my tribe: *I* am good? I think Marlowe wants us to see Barabas here as somewhat out of control. For a moment he drops his holy mask and cries, "Some Jews are wicked, as all Christians are," which is the statement of an angry villain, not of a clever one. "The man that dealeth righteously shall live" signals his return to the role of the persecuted saint, a pretense that is truly calculated to make the spectator's gorge rise.

The Maltese determine to turn Barabas' mansion into a nunnery. Officers return saying they have seized his goods. With a curse, he throws off his hypocrisy and shouts, "Take it to you, i' th' Devil's name." I suspect that in this scene Marlowe wants us to see fake matched by fake: the Christians' smug defense of their rape is as bad as Barabas' sanctimoniousness.

The stage is left to Barabas and the three Jews. Correctly he diagnoses the Christians' professions as not simple but politic. They are not as innocent as they have tried to appear. (*Politic* is strictly a Machiavellian term in Elizabethan literature.) It is illustrative of Barabas that first he curses his tormentors with the plagues of Egypt, a Biblical reference, and then uses the periphrasis *Primus Motor* for God. Actually he is substituting for the Hebrew deity a Renaissance dynamism, which is his true worship. Although his coreligionists repeatedly preach patience, Barabas rages: he can think only of his own deprivation, not of theirs. *They* are responsible for his plight because of not opposing the Christians. His loss is worse than Job's! The other Jews comment on his "ireful mood," "ecstasy," "affliction"—and leave.

As soon as he is alone, Barabas goes through a sudden transformation. In soliloquy he is once more the cold, cocksure Machiavellian, whom we met at the beginning of the play. The other Jews are "base slaves," who consider him "a senseless lump of clay."

> No, Barabas is born to better chance
> And fram'd of finer mold than common men
> That measure naught but by the present time!
> A reaching thought will search his deepest wits
> And cast with cunning for the time to come:

How has he been able to abate his "ecstasy" so quickly? What do the above words mean? As soon as Abigail enters, we get the answers. She rages, but he (now!) advocates silence and patience. Time may bring them an occasion for revenge. Her father foresaw the future and hid a great fortune in their house. When Abigail tells him it is now a nunnery and he cannot get admission, Barabas explodes into recriminations against the stars. Characteristically in his egoism he conceives of the result of self-destruction as "vanish[ing] . . . in air,' leaving no memory that he once existed. But the vain Machiavellian suddenly flares forth again:

No, I will live! Nor loathe I this my life!
And since you leave me in the ocean thus
To sink or swim, and put me to my shifts,
I'll rouse my senses. . . .

And he conceives of the plan of his daughter's turning Christian only to get within their former dwelling.

This allows him to talk of religion hiding mischief, of the preference of momentary dissembling to constant hypocrisy. (The Elizabethan dramatists, including Shakespeare, loved *sententiae* as much as G. B. Shaw loved epigrams!) He even manages to take a swipe at the precisianists (i.e., Puritans). Once Abigail is in the house, she will find the treasure underneath an upstairs plank. As they see the friars and nuns coming their way (do the former enter from the audience?), father and daughter retire to the back of the stage. Friar Jacomo and Friar Barnardine are undoubtedly greasy, corpulent creatures. Abigail comes forward and begs to be a novice,

Fearing the afflictions which my father feels
Proceed from sin, or want of faith in us. . . .

Unctuously, the friars, no doubt ogling the beautiful Jewess, make *double-entendre* remarks. The Abbess admits her. Meanwhile, Barabas smirks at the audience and speaks an aside. Now he comes forward, berates her for apostasy, but manages to whisper how the plank is marked and when he will be at the door. It is brilliant theatrics, this combination of righteous grief and anger—appalling both dissembling Abigail and the fooled religious—and the sudden darting aside. Just as all are leaving, Mathias enters.

He sees the Jew's lovely daughter and falls in love with her. On Mathias' description his friend Lodowick also finds himself deeply attracted to her. And in what is perhaps an aside, he promises intense rivalry. And so the conflict, which Barabas will later expedite, is being prepared for. And so Marlowe has already introduced us to his friars, who will have a large place in the plot later on. And so he has used in wholesale fashion the conventions of soliloquy, aside, and sudden love. How could Barabas function except on an obviously nonnaturalistic stage?

The next act—with Barabas' recovery of his fortune; Ferneze's decision to break his truce with the Turks; the Jew's machinations to embroil Ferneze's son, Lodowick, and Mathias over Abigail, with the introduction of Ithamore—is a superb preparation for the fast-moving scenes of the rest of the play. Marlowe's mastery of stage speech—the intermixture of soliloquy, relatively long and short passages, stichomythia, aside—continues to astonish by its ease and maturity.

2.1

"Enter Barabas with a light." Hence we are to accept that all is in darkness. The introductory soliloquy, after the Jew has come forward, is undoubtedly one of those speeches which have led critics to believe that the latter part of the play is un-Marlovian, for this particular speech *seems* dignified and moving in its setting forth of Barabas' despair and anxiety:

Thus, like the sad presaging raven that tolls *ff*. (2.1.1-19).

Actually, the speech is mock-epic, and the effect should be ludicrous. For one thing, deflation of a bully is always welcome to an audience: and the Jew's appeal to pity was probably met with Elizabethan hoots. For another, how can one take seriously this comic ghoul who probably after line 6 runs to the back of the stage, shakes his fist at what we are to take as the nunnery, and then runs forward to continue to the audience his obscene plea for sympathy? What is he mourning but the loss of— for once, the cliché is exact—his ill-gotten gains? "The incertain pleasures of swift-footed time" fit Hector's parting from Andromache, not a miser whom we saw pawing his piles of gold. The reference to a "soldier's scar" recalls the reply to Ferneze, "*Bar*. Alas, my lord, we are no soldiers!" This mis-apropos allusion is to remind us that the Jew creates his wealth not by patriotic endeavor but by parasitism on the public. The appeal to the God who led Israel out of Egypt, and the echo of Job ("Let the day perish," etc.) are meant to emphasize Barabas' hypocrisy and selfishness, for hitherto he has repudiated both his race and Jehovah. In short, the whole speech should be taken as unserious—as farcical.

Now "Enter Abigail above," uncognizant that her father is below. She has the wealth with her. Probably the dramatist intended a laugh—she on the tarras, he sitting on the platform, each oblivious of the other. Probably, too, Barabas' comparison of himself to a ghost haunting "the place where treasure hath been hid" drew laughter, too, because of his obviously non-human appearance. Abigail's hope that her parent were there continues the joke, and so do her poetical references to him. Suddenly he sees her, and she "throws down bags," which Barabas "hugs." "O girl! O gold! O beauty! O my bliss!" His choice of greater affection is indicative. As they part, he kisses his fingers to her, then addresses his fortune as though it were a bride:

> Now, Phoebus, ope the eye-lids of the day,
> And, for the raven, wake the morning lark,
> That I may hover with her in the air—
> Singing o'er these, as she does o'er her young!

One's laughter is mixed with revulsion at the sight of this monster crooning to his beloved!

2.2

The purpose of this scene is (a) to set the Turkish siege in Act 5 and (b) to account for the sale of the Turkish slave, Ithamore, in 2.3. Del Bosco, Vice-Admiral of the Spanish navy, wants to sell in Malta the Turks whom he has defeated in a recent sea-fight. Ferneze says that he cannot give consent because of his "tributary league" with the Mohammedans. However, when Del Bosco asserts that the King of Spain intends soon to take over the isle and will give aid, and that the Maltese should keep their gold, Ferneze capitulates:

> On this condition shall thy Turks be sold:
> Go, officers and set them straight in show.
> Bosco, thou shalt be Malta's general.

Knowing what we know of the popular reputation of Spanish vessels in England, we can surmise that Del Bosco is somewhat of a puffy braggart. (Is it accidental that though present he has only one single line speech in the entire fifth act?) As a matter of fact his description of the defeat of the "creeping galleys" seems to indicate the agile Spanish ships were far more maneuverable than the lumbering Turkish ones. We must also note that the Maltese Catholics are breaking their word here and justifying their act on religious grounds, just as their correligionists do in *2 Tamburlaine*. Only now does the Governor see the overlords as "barbarous misbelieving Turks."

2.3

For construction, the present scene is my favorite, in a play which throughout exhibits a remarkable dramaturgic ability to advance a complex plot.

Some place on the stage, the officers put the slaves who are for sale. On each back is a placard announcing price. Ithamore must stand out from the rest. Since he definitely is the comic servant (i.e., a stock type), I suspect that he wears clownish make-up and exaggerated Oriental dress.

Barabas enters and talks directly to the audience. Now that he has regained his wealth and his daughter, he can think upon revenge against the Governor, Ferneze, "whose heart I'll have—/Ay, and his son's too." Again he disassociates himself from the patient, long-suffering Jews:

> I am not of the tribe of Levi, I,
> That can so soon forget an injury.

No, he belongs to the traditional venomous anti-Semitic tradition:

> We Jews can fawn like spaniels when we please:
> And when we grin we bite: yet are our looks
> As innocent and harmless as a lamb's . . .

Of course, as he says this, our stage Hebrew looks as capable of innocent guise as a hungry demon! He smiles frighteningly at *grin,* and his teeth click together at *bite!* Where did he learn to be such a hypocritical sadist? In Florence, Machiavelli's town! Menacingly he announces,

> Here comes Don Lodowick, the Governor's son,
> One that I love for his good father's sake.

I suggest that at the word *love,* the Jew grimaces—and spits on the floor; then rubs his hands together for the pleasant task he has ahead concerning "the good father."

Lodowick enters, a fresh young gallant. He wishes to pay court to the Jew's beautiful daughter. Barabas, not yet revealing his presence, in an aside promises the audience knavery. The gallant spies him, "Now for fair Abigail." In another aside, the Jew ironically promises, "she's at your command." (From this time on, the Jew must always assert utter dominance of the stage.) Lodowick announces his parentage. Barabas replies sweetly but ambiguously—and then asides viciously on the lad's smooth cheeks. (I propose that this means that the protagonist is also red-*bearded.*) We are to feel that a lion is readying itself to gobble a doe. So virulent does Barabas now feel, that he openly insults the Governor's son: he doesn't, with a facial wrench, like to breathe the same air as a Christian. I take it that he regards Lodowick as a complete fool who doesn't have enough intelligence to understand a nasty remark. It is a striking contrast, this, between perfumed springal and savage, witty monster!

Characteristic of the fool is his belief that he can outsmart others. Lodowick, plotting to get a sight of the young Jewess, informs her father he is interested in purchasing a diamond. Now ensues a dialogue in which the youthful aspirant talks about a jewel, and his cunning enemy, wholly awake to the gallant's scheme, first answers him directly and then asides with threats of horrible revenge or with explanations of his double meaning. The effect needed is, as I have indicated, the Jew's complete control of the situation and the lad's complete obtuseness. Barabas promises to give his precious possession to the other, but so little does the Jew think of his victim that he makes the following speech:

Your father has deserv'd it at my hands *ff.* (2.3.74-81).

But there is a kind of prescience of what will happen in the last act. The Jew underrates Lodowick *too* much, and goes *too* far in his irony concerning the religious: "The prayers of those nuns/And holy friars . . . /Are wondrous."

And seeing they are not idle but still doing,
'Tis likely they in time may reap some fruit,
I mean in fullness of perfection.

Every Elizabethan knew that "doing" meant coitus; hence, "fullness of perfection" means pregnancy. (Of course, we must sympathetically relish the enjoyment of the average Elizabethan theatergoer at such anti-Roman Catholic jokes.)

Lod. Good Barabas, glance not at our holy nuns.

No, replies the Jew, he is sincere: but promises in an aside to fire the nunnery. He invites the Governor's son to his house to see "the diamond"—Abigail, of course. Then an aside, "It shall go hard but I will see your death." Thus, Barabas' overweening superiority continues to exhibit itself, until—as I have indi-cated—it defeats itself in the last act. Now the young man and the old one move to "the market-place," which is probably at the back of the stage where Del Bosco's prisoners have been standing.

We must envisage the Jew examining each of the merchan-dise carefully, as though he were about to buy a mule—making him open his mouth to show his teeth, pinching his ribs to see whether he eats too much, pondering the price quoted on his back. After some farcical, cynical byplay with one of the other slaves, Barabas comes to Ithamore. That the Jew must choose him has been theatrically clear from the beginning of the scene: both are completely nonnaturalistic in physiognomy and manner. Immediately Barabas promises the audience that Ithamore "by my help shall do much villainy." They are two of a kind.

As Barabas begins his farewell to Lodowick, inviting him to his house to receive the diamond—"All that I have shall be at your command"—Mathias and his mother, Katherine, enter. In an aside the former is immediately suspicious of the closeness of the Jew and Lodowick: "I fear me 'tis about fair Abigail." Barabas tells Lodowick that he is going to frustrate the mutual love of Mathias and Abigail. Before Lodowick exits, surely both he and Katherine's son have been bitterly glaring at each other.

As Mathias and his mother look over the slaves, Barabas— Katherine being some distance away—tells Mathias to come to his house: "Think of me as thy father. Son, farewell." Into the Jew's purpose will go all who fit his plans, and it is not hard to see that is he going to destroy Lodowick and Mathias through the jealousy engendered by Abigail and fomented by himself. Lodowick will die because he is the Governor's son: that is revenge. Mathias will die too, but what of that? He is a despicable creature, a Christian, by definition! As Katherine turns her attention to her son and the Jew together, the latter is ready with a pious remark. She warns her offspring against such an acquaintance, and both leave the stage.

Now there occurs one of the most famous, but one of the most misunderstood passages in the play. Ithamore and Barabas are alone on the stage, and the Jew tests his tawdry human purchase as to his capacity for villainy. He tells lies about his own criminality, but, true, they are falsehoods not too far from the truth. Nevertheless, what most critics have not recognized is that in the play proper the Jew's actions are always purposive, whether for further wealth, revenge, or self-protection —never, as in this list, primarily for enjoyment. This mythical past is to fathom the depth of Ithamore's potential criminality, and Barabas gets the response he wants.

Bar. As for myself, I walk abroad a-nights *ff.* (2.3.180-218).

The slave's outrageous reply pleases his master,

We are villains both!
—Both circumsised, we hate Christians both!

Lodowick re-enters, and Barabas leads him to the back of the stage, the door to his new mansion. Enter Abigail, bringing her father commercial letters. The Jew, pretending to be engrossed in them, encourages her to entertain the Governor's son, but in an aside orders her to dissemble. Abigail welcomes Lodowick, and Barabas again asides to her that she must "Kiss him. Speak him fair . . . like a cunning Jew": the point is that

she must by wiles entangle him to love her. But here is a
plot development: Abigail now whispers to her father—we can
imagine Lodowick standing aside and admiring the beauty he
thinks he is about to win—that she really is in love with
Mathias. Nevertheless, the Jew insists on her continuing hypocrisy to the Governor's son. At last he raises his head from his
epistles, and tells Abigail and her would-be lover to enter his
home.

Much critical confusion has arisen from regarding Barabas
merely as a money-worshipper. That he sometimes prefers revenge to gold (like his co-mate, Shylock) is definitely made
clear by his speech when the young people have left. The Jew
tells us that a monetary loss described in one of his letters
matters less to him than satisfying vengeance on the two
Maltese, Lodowick, the Governor's son, and Mathias, whose
father was Barabas' "chiefest enemy." The word *account* in his
speech is superbly placed:

> The account is made, for Lodowick dies!
> My factor sends me word a merchant's fled
> That owes me for a hundred tun of wine.

Enter Mathias, and hypocritically Barabas promises his
daughter to him. *But*, he tells the already excited youngster,
Lodowick is pursuing her hard.

> *Math.* O treacherous Lodowick!

He draws his sword, but, as the Jewess and the Governor's son
enter, Barabas persuades the angry gallant to leave. Lodowick
sees his rival exit, and Barabas tells him that Mathias "hath
sworn your death." Now, despite Abigail's open unwillingness
to us, Lodowick gets the Jew's consent to a marriage. But in a
long aside to his daughter the Hebrew scorns "This gentle
maggot," Lodowick, the adjective being a pun, standing for
"gentile" as well as "weak." Barabas is now even hypocritical
to his own daughter,

> But keep thy heart till Don Mathias comes,

seeming to respect her real feelings. (Thus Marlowe prepares
us for the time when the Jew casts off and murders his own
daughter to gain his ends.)

Barabas now turns to the young man, lying that he has got
her to consent to a betrothal. The two young people probably
clasp hands; Lodowick attempts to kiss her, she turns her
head aside to tell us once more of her devotion to Mathias;
and Barabas, eupeptic, tells the audience he, too, will soon get

that—revenge!—for which his "soul hath long'd." Lodowick
is struck by the Jewess' sudden silence, but Barabas explains
this is Hebrew custom, "She is thy wife, and thou shalt be my
heir."

At the sight of Mathias, Lodowick probably draws his
sword, but Barabas dissuades him too. The point is, as the
Jew himself makes clear, he doesn't want to "Be made an
accessory of your deeds." In other words, he is open in his
looking out for himself. But Mathias can, if he wish, "Revenge
it on him when you meet him next." Now, after having a
short time before given his daughter to Lodowick, the Jew
formally gives her to Mathias! Moreover, he works to inflame
the latter even more. Lodowick, Barabas avers, has gone to
Katherine, Mathias' mother (whom we have seen to be
violently anti-Semitic) "to cross your love." And Mathias
rushes off.

Abigail wants to know why her father has "incens'd them
both"; she'll make them friends again. Barabas sneers at her,
and orders Ithamore to push her in. He asks the comic slave
how he likes his scheme for revenge, which the slave has
understood. Ithamore applauds, and wants to share in the
promised entertainment. The Jew gives him a counterfeit
letter for Mathias, "And tell him that it comes from Lodowick."
Ithamore, gleefully: "Tis poison'd, is it not?" No, it is a
feigned challenge. The Jew joys in his servant's enthusiasm, and
tells the audience his work now lies in Lodowick's direction,
"Till I have set 'em both at enmity!" And the scene ends.

The plotting of the next act, the third, as of the entire play,
is admirable. Remember that Barabas is responsible for the
demise of Lodowick and Mathias, using Ithamore to carry
the feigned challenge. After Ithamore tells Abigail, there
are three persons, therefore, who know of the Jew's machi-
nation: himself, his daughter, his servant. When Abigail turns
against her father, she becomes a potential danger who must
be destroyed. (And as is usual with the Jew, the particular
victim always brings others along to their deaths, for Barabas
is unscrupulous in his plans, unfeelingly sacrificing the
unhated or undangerous in order to get rid of the hated or
dangerous.) Thus, Barabas poisons the whole nunnery to kill
his daughter, employing Ithamore for this purpose. But
before she dies, Abigail confesses her father's plot in the
gallants' deaths to Friar Barnardine, who automatically,
therefore, becomes a candidate for extinction. (This will be
the material of the first half of Act 4. It will be observed that

the promoted enmity of the two Friars parallels the promoted
enmity of Abigail's two lovers: the Jew knows how to play
on the basic passions of love and greed to secure his ends.)
After the Friars are got rid of, only Ithamore will know
of his master's crimes. Hence, Barabas will have to take
action against his servant when the latter threatens him with
exposure. So Ithamore, Bellamira, and Pilia-Borza, who now
know too, must be poisoned. (Ithamore's affair with Bellamira
and its consequences constitutes the last half of Act 4.) But
in Act 5, before she dies, the courtesan reveals the truth. And
so, at the beginning of Act 3, in Bellamira's appearance and
Ithamore's attraction to her, we already have preparation on
Marlowe's part for action to come much later.

3.1

Bellamira is a bedizened meretrix. (That Ithamore admires
her correlates with his own spectacular appearance.) Her
pimp, Pilia-Borza, is graphically described in 4.3:

> . . . a shaggy totter'd staring slave,
> That when he speaks draws out his grisly beard
> And winds it twice or thrice about his ear;
> Whose face has been a grindstone for men's swords;
> His hands are hack'd, some fingers cut quite off;
> Who, when he speaks, grunts like a hog and looks
> Like one that is employ'd in catzerie
> And crossbiting—such a rogue
> As is the husband to a hundred whores.

He has stolen a bag of money from the Jew. Now enter
Ithamore on his way to deliver the challenge and falls in
love with the courtesan. How admirable is Marlowe's plotting!
Ithamore is on his way, as it were, to have one part of the
play completed and Marlowe, by means of the stealing of the
Jew's gold and the amorous confrontation of Ithamore and
Bellamira, is preparing for scenes that will not occur for
another act.

3.2

Mathias and Lodowick enter, immediately draw their swords,
and slash at each other, Barabas above enjoying the encounter.
They kill each other, and Barabas leaves with great pleasure.
The entrance of Ferneze and Katherine to lament their sons
is to indicate to the audience that it is highly important for
Barabas to keep his role in the two deaths from becoming
known. The Governor is intensely anxious to discover "the
causers of our smarts."

3.3

Ithamore enters gloating over the cunning of himself and his master and in his euphoria reveals to Abigail the plot which has ended in the death of her beloved, Mathias. Without revealing to the servant what her intentions are, she sends him off for one of the Friars—and, of course, the comic villain has to get in a bawdy remark about the religious.

Her blank verse soliloquy, following the prose of the above colloquy, contains within it a significant warning for careless critics of this play:

Hard-hearted father, unkind Barabas! *ff.* (3.3.41-53).

This is as careful an analysis of Barabas' motivation as can be found within the drama. His drive toward vengeance is so strong that innocent victims who get in the way of his egotism are destroyed too, without great thought or compunction. The acting of the boy who plays Abigail has to be quite powerful here. Hitherto, the Jewess has been only the tool of her father, displaying altruistic emotion only in relation to Mathias. However, now, her loss of her lover and her father's guilt and character drive her to a change of spirit and countenance. The contrast between her real grief and contrition and her father's melodramatic criminality should be pronounced. Thus, the cheap trick of the rice-poisoning must not take away from the audience's reaction that the Jew has murdered not merely his own flesh and blood but a creature whom the play, to some extent, has showed growing into a tragic young woman and also one who, though she hates what her father has done, still refuses *by contrast* to be *his* enemy: "O Barabas,/Though thou deservest hardly at my hands,/Yet never shall these lips bewray thy life!" The contrast between her dignity and the comic Friar Jacomo is also part of Marlowe's dramaturgy here.

3.4

Barabas' decision to sweep his daughter away takes few words:

I fear she knows ('tis so!) of my device
In Don Mathias' and Lodovico's deaths.
If so, 'tis time that it be seen into!

To Ithamore, however, he puts on an act of some reluctance for her destruction:

Bar. O unhappy day!
False, credulous, inconstant Abigail! *ff.* (3.4.26-38).

Of course, Ithamore capitulates completely to the Jew's plans. Hypocritically, Barabas calls him "my friend"; "mine only heir"; offers him the keys to his treasure, but draws his hand back immediately; orders him to buy "garments," but immediately rescinds his command. All this is to show the Jew handling this poor creature as he once handled his daughter. The Jew's comment, after Ithamore leaves the stage for the pot of rice, indicates his real attitude toward his tawdry servant accomplice. The poisoning of the pot of rice, along with Ithamore's hunger for it, stresses absolutely the melodramatic nature of this play—its insistence, by and large, on broad, grotesque effects that are closer to farce than they are to serious theater. Barabas' last line in this scene, "I'll pay thee with a vengeance, Ithamore," shows essentially what he is and what will eventually happen. (We might remember that it is customary in Elizabethan drama—in Marlowe, Kyd, and Shakespeare—for the big villain to destroy the small villain after he has utilized him.)

3.5

The purpose of this scene is to announce the Turkish siege of Malta, which will be the material of the last act.

3.6

The two Friars enter with news that all the nuns are ill. Friar Jacomo's reference to "fair Maria" undoubtedly is supposed to bring a lewd grin to the spectator. After Jacomo leaves, the dying Abigail's confession to Barnardine and her giving him the document which contains her father's guilt are, of course, Marlowe's preparations for the continuing action in which the Friars will confront the Jew and he will have to get rid of them. Marlowe, at this point, gets much humor out of Roman Catholicism: (1) Barnardine, according to his priesthood is not supposed to tell what he hears in confession, but does, almost immediately; (2) he regrets the loss of a desirable piece of flesh:

Death seizeth on my heart. Ah, gentle friar,
Convert my father that he may be sav'd.
And witness that I die a Christian!
    Friar Barn. Ay, and a virgin too; that grieves me most.
But I must to the Jew, and exclaim on him,
And make him stand in fear of me.

He tells Jacomo in general, but not in particular, what he is about, "to exclaim against the Jew."

Friar Jac. Why? What has he done?
Friar Barn. A thing that makes me tremble to unfold.
Friar Jac. What, has he crucified a child?

The reference to the murder of a child reinforces, of course, the traditional figure of the Jew as villain, of which Barabas is the quintessence.

4.1

Enter Barabas and Ithamore. "Bells within." The portrait of the savage Jew has been slowly highlighted—the prominent, grotesque features coming more and more into prominence. His wickedness is becoming more and more outrageous and his enjoyment of it more and more open and melodramatic. Now, as he hears the bells tolling the multiple deaths in the nunnery, he comments on "How sweet the bells ring now the nuns are dead" and manages to make another joke about their frequent pregnancies. Ithamore, too, joys in his master's accomplishment:

> *Itha.* That's brave, master, but think you it will not be
>   known?
> *Bar.* How can it if we two be secret?
> *Itha.* For my part fear you not.
> *Bar.* I'd cut thy throat if I did.
> *Itha.* And reason too.
> But here's a royal monastery hard by.
> Good master, let me poison all the monks?

The Jew is happy, too, at his own daughter's demise. "Enter the two friars." Now ensues one of the most theatrically powerful bits of dialogue in the play. Each Friar interrupts the other to get the Jew's attention, but he manages with extreme rapidity to lead the point away from his recent criminality. When, however, they reveal that they know about the false challenge, Barabas realizes that his daughter has confessed. With great and immediate cunning, he immediately disengages the Friars' attention from his former plots and, stressing his wealth, asks to be converted:

> All this I'll give to some religious house.
> So I may be baptiz'd, and live therein!

He could not have chosen a better method, not only of obscuring his crime but of getting the Friars into an altercation. In other words, he is using somewhat of the same technique for the destruction of his present enemies as he used with the two gallants. As he encourages one Friar, then the other,

they get more and more heated and, at length, engage in a
fist fight, which is exactly what the Jew wanted. He sends
Ithamore to the back of the stage with Friar Barnardine and
tells Jacomo to come that evening. He rubs his hands together:

> Now I have such a plot for both their lives
> As never Jew nor Christian knew the like!
> One turn'd my daughter, therefore he shall die:
> The other knows enough to have my life,
> Therefore 'tis not requisite he should live.

He walks towards the back of the stage as the curtains open.
Friar Barnardine is seen sitting asleep in a chair. Barabas takes
off the monk's girdle, and he and Ithamore strangle him.
The Jew's handiwork is brilliant: " 'Tis neatly done, sir,
here's no print at all." Now Ithamore gets the inspiration
of standing the dead body against the wall, held up by the
Friar's staff. The curtains close—and perhaps the Jew and his
servant peek out to await the other Friar's arrival. Jacomo,
jealous of his opponent, enters, sees him, cries out, grabs
the staff, and strikes—and, of course, the body falls to the
floor. Now Barabas and Ithamore come forward, hold the
confused, supposed murderer, and prepare to turn him over to
the law. Marlowe's neat stagecraft is shown in the last couplet:

> Take in the staff too, for that must be shown:
> Law wills that each particular be known.

Of course, the property must not be left on the stage.

4.2

Now Marlowe finds plot use for the character of the
courtesan whom he had introduced much earlier. Bellamira is
going to extract money from Ithamore. (And since we know
that he is attracted to her, perforce he is going to squeeze
the Jew. And the Jew, of course, in fear of Ithamore's possible
revelations and his constant protection of his own wealth,
is going to take action against his servant, Bellamira
herself, and the highly-colored procurator and thief, Pilia-
Borza.) She has sent a letter by hand of her pimp to the
comic servant. (Pilia, by the way, is amusing in his own egotism.
Horrible-looking and threatening, as is frequently stressed,
he believes himself to be "a tall man," possessing a "terrible
countenance.") Ithamore enters to them, after Friar Jacomo's
hanging, comically commenting on her adoring letter to him and
her man's sweeping bow:

> I wonder what the reason is. It may be she sees more
> in me than I can find in myself: for she writes
> further that she loves me ever since she saw me!

That Ithamore, the farcical villain, should now be shy of an acknowledged whore is very funny, and he responds to Pilia's address of "Gentleman" with an attempt to leave. Bellamira's parody of love-making:

> Though woman's modesty should hale me back, I can
> withhold no longer. Welcome, sweet love!

and Ithamore's decision to improve his appearance:

> I'll go steal some money from my master to make me
> handsome.

advance the action. Pilia and Bellamira, old-timers in their craft, know how to get at the Jew's money:

> But you know some secrets of the Jew
> Which if they were reveal'd would do him harm?
>   *Itha.* Ay, and such as—. Go to, no more! I'll make him send
> me half he has, and glad he scapes so too . . . I'll write unto
> him. We'll have money straight!

And Pilia exits with Ithamore's financial request to Barabas. Marlowe continues, by means of obvious parody, to make us laugh at this love affair between the cheap servant and the cheap prostitute. Pilia-Borza almost immediately re-enters and instead of the three hundred crowns puts down ten. Of course, Ithamore asks for "a ream of paper." He will now request "a kingdom of gold." (What we discover, however, in the next scene is that the Jew has sent three hundred crowns and the pimp must have kept two hundred and ninety for himself and his lady!) Ithamore writes again for six hundred crowns, one hundred for the bearer of the letter. He acts the freehanded gallant, while Bellamira professes that it is not his gold but himself she wants. They kiss and leave the stage.

4.3

Barabas enters reading the first letter that Ithamore sent, but before he is finished commenting on the appearance of Pilia, who brought the letter, the latter enters again with a further request. Pilia is very threatening. Unlike others, he is not interested in the Jew's hypocritical promises and demands the money. After he leaves, the "tormented" Jew

resolves that he must kill them all, otherwise his crimes will
become known. And he leaves the stage promising us that
the next time we see him he will be in disguise.

4.4

Ithamore holds a goblet, into which Bellamira constantly
pours wine. He is very drunk and in his drunkenness, as the
Jew suspected, tells all about the gallants', the nuns', and the
Friar's deaths.

> *Pilia.* (This shall with me unto the Governor.)
>   [*Aside to Bellamira.*]
> *Bell.* (And fit it should! But first let's ha' more gold—.)
>   [*Aside to Pilia-Borza.*]

That Pilia and his woman are going to reveal the Jew's
murders to the Governor does not indicate their patriotism, but
merely their hatred of and distrust for the malevolent
Hebrew. (Or merely of that Elizabethan plot technique that
refuses tacitly to explain motive!) Barabas enters, disguised
as a French musician, with a lute and a posy in his hat. Part
of the audience's fun is that though his disguise fools his
victims, it no more fools us than the wolf disguised as Red
Riding Hood's grandmother! His French talk is typical stage
convention. And, as he speaks and postures, he tunes his
instrument. He tosses his nosegay to Bellamira, they
all smell it, and we are not surprised by the melodramatic,
Machiavellian aside: "The scent thereof was death. I poison'd
it." Barabas plays music and the drunken Ithamore tells him
how much he scorns his master. It is amusing to see the egocentric Barabas highly offended and irritated by the inebriated
Ithamore's lies about the Jew's parsimony. Barabas leaves the
stage, and we await the coming death of those he leaves behind,
who, unbeknownst of their fate, are planning actions on him
who has already avenged himself on them.

5.1

Malta is being besieged, and it appears that the Turks are
about ready to make an assault. At this moment enter
Bellamira and Pilia-Borza who are sick unto death but
yet reveal to Ferneze the Jew's crimes. Ferneze wants
proof and the officers bring in Barabas and Ithamore. The
latter also dying backs up the word of the courtesan and her
man. Barabas meanwhile in an aside is regretting that he failed
to use enough poison for the immediate demise of his accusers.
Echoing Shylock, he asks for "law," and is promised law.
The Jew and his accusers are removed. An officer enters to

report the deaths of the latter—and also that of the Jew! The improbable action goes so fast here that, as is not uncommon in the Elizabethan drama, before we have time to question the cause, our interest is being held by the result. For example, Del Bosco says, "This sudden death of his is very strange." But Ferneze brushes aside our surprise with, "Wonder not at it, sir, the heavens are just."

How the business of Barabas being thrown over the walls was managed on the Elizabethan stage is very difficult to figure. All we get in the original text are Ferneze's command that this be done, the Maltese leave, and Barabas rises. (There is a possibility that the officers carried Barabas' body off-stage, appeared with it on the tarras, and then dropped it on the stage proper.) As is customary in Elizabethan drama, the platform easily shifts in the imagination from being the inside of the city to the outside. The Jew in typical fashion promises retribution, in which both his sadism and cupidity will be satisfied:

> Bar. [rising.] What, all alone? Well fare, sleepy drink!
> I'll be reveng'd on this accursed town
> For by my means Calymath shall enter in:
> I'll help to slay their children and their wives!
> To fire the churches! pull their houses down!
> Take my goods too, and seize upon my lands!
> I hope to see the Governor a slave,
> And rowing in a galley whipt to death!

Calymath promises to make him governor for his good deed. Probably what happens is that the Jew leads some of the Turks down through the trap, which is to be construed as a secret tunnel into the city, while the others assault the walls.

5.2

Then after alarums, the Turks, the Maltese, and Barabas enter, and we are to understand that the city has fallen. Barabas is made governor, Ferneze mourns:

> O fatal day, to fall into the hands
> Of such a traitor and unhallow'd Jew!
> What greater misery could Heaven inflict?

Barabas sends him and the other Maltese to prison, and alone on the stage delivers what is almost a chapter—e.g., XIX— from The Prince:

> Thus hast thou gotten by thy policy ff. (5.2.28-47).

Now he sends for Ferneze. In front of the Janizaries who are
guarding the former, he blusters his authority; but as soon
as the guard exeunts, Barabas becomes businesslike and unfolds
his plan to the former Governor. Is it somewhat subtle psychology on Marlowe's part to have Barabas forget revenge and
take advantage of occasion for gain?

But first the Jew questions the Maltese on what he expects
him, the Jew, to do. Ferneze replies with "Malta's wrack" and
"extreme cruelty." Barabas answers him in a passage that is
remarkable in its honesty except for its last two lines:

> Governor, good words, be not so furious. *ff.* (5.2.62-74).

The sincere avarice of this communication is one of the most
remarkable things in this remarkable play.

Barabas gets down to business:

> What will you give me if I render you
> The life of Calymath, surprise his men,
> And in an out-house of the city shut
> His soldiers, till I have consum'd 'em all with fire?
> What will you give him that procureth this?

Ferneze, of course, promises a huge sum of money. Again,
the mixture of apparent friendship but true rapaciousness is
skillfully delineated in Barabas' reaction:

> Nay, do thou this, Ferneze, and be free!
> Governor, I enlarge thee. Live with me.
> Go walk about the city, see thy friends.
> —Tush, send not letters to 'em, go thyself,
> And let me see what money thou canst make.

For the money, Barabas will free Malta forever by a trick
against Calymath. Ferneze is to be present to do something
"that I'll impart to thee." After the Governor exits, Barabas
once more identifies himself:

> Thus, loving neither, will I live with both,
> Making a profit of my policy:
> And he from whom my most advantage comes
> Shall be my friend.
> This is the life we Jews are us'd to lead—
> And reason too, for Christians do the like.

5.3

After Calymath enters, a Messenger brings him the Jew's
invitation to a feast and Calymath happily consents.

5.4

Marlowe's dramaturgy is very sharp in this last act. Remember that although we have been told that a stratagem will be used against Calymath, we have not been told what it is. Our suspense is increased in the present scene by Ferneze's directions to his countrymen:

Have special care that no man sally forth
Till you shall hear a culverin discharg'd
By him that bears the linstock, kindled thus;
Then issue out and come to rescue me,
For happily I shall be in distress,
Or you released of this servitude.

What will follow the discharge of the cannon we still do not know. Furthermore, there is a hint in the next-to-the-last line that, perhaps, Ferneze is hatching a counterplan to the Jew's plan. What will it be?

5.5

Barabas enters above on the tarras "with hammer, very busy." Below are carpenters to whom he addresses queries about cranes and pullies and hinges. After they leave, we get a typical pronouncement, "For, so I live, perish may all the world!" The Messenger brings word that the great Turk is coming and has also commanded his men to go feast in the citadel, where Barabas' second plan is to operate. Ferneze enters below with a bag of gold for the Jew. (It is interesting to see how stage technique affects characterization. That Barabas wants the Governor satisfied first with the success of his plot seems on reflection strange. But the fact that he is above and the Governor below really explains what seems this unusal quirk of sincerity.) Now Barabas reveals his plans. The soldiers will be blown up in the monastery where they have gone. And as for Calymath, Barabas intends to have him on this gallery (i.e., the tarras) over a trap which will open when a rope is cut. He gives the knife to Ferneze and tells him to use it when a cannon is shot off in the tower. (Note how completely Marlowe is using his stage: platform, tarras, trap in the tarras, tower.)

Barabas glows with appreciation of his own cunning. Calymath and his bassoes enter. Barabas invites him up. Ferneze, who has been concealed, comes forward and stays the Turk. A cannon is shot off, Ferneze cuts the cord, the Jew falls through the trap. And as he does so, the curtains at the back open and we see the cauldron into which the Jew has fallen. (Now

enter the Maltese?) Barabas screams for help—presumably
the cauldron is filled with boiling oil. He dies cursing. Calymath
wants to leave. Ferneze reveals, however, that he is prisoner
and that his soldiers have been destroyed in the monastery.
And so the play ends with the Maltese palpable victors over
the Turks on the platform.

Much, much of this Introduction is tentative. If it can induce
the reader to look attentively at a great Elizabethan playwright,
it will have served its purpose.

[1 TAMBURLAINE]

Tamburlaine the Great.

Who, from a Scythian shepherd, by his rare and wonderful conquests, became a most puissant and mighty monarch. And, for his tyranny and tenor in war, was termed The Scourge of God. Divided into two tragical discourses.

THE FIRST PART

[Speaking Characters

MYCETES
COSROE
ORTYGIUS
CENEUS
MEANDER
MENAPHON
THERIDAMAS
TAMBURLAINE
ZENOCRATE
TECHELLES
USUMCASANE
AGYDAS
SOLDIER
SPY
MAGNETES
MESSENGER
BAJAZETH
KING OF FEZ
KING OF MOROCCO
KING OF ARGIER
ANIPPE
BASSO
ZABINA
EBEA
SOLDAN OF EGYPT
KING OF ARABIA
CAPOLIN
GOVERNOR OF DAMASCUS
1 VIRGIN OF DAMASCUS
2 VIRGIN OF DAMASCUS
VIRGINS OF DAMASCUS
PHILEMUS

Mute Characters

LORDS, BASSOES, SOLDIERS, MOORS]

THE PROLOGUE

From jigging veins of rhyming mother wits,
And such conceits as clownage keeps in pay,
We'll lead you to the stately tent of war,
Where you shall hear the Scythian Tamburlaine
Threat'ning the world with high astounding terms,
And scourging kingdoms with his conquering sword.
View but his picture in this tragic glass,
And then applaud his fortunes as you please.

ACTUS. 1.

SCAENA. 1.

[Enter] *Mycetes* [crowned], *Cosroe, Meander, Theridamas,
Ortygius, Ceneus,* [*Menaphon,*] *with others.*

Myc. Brother Cosroe, I find myself aggriev'd,
Yet insufficient to express the same,
For it requires a great and thund'ring speech:
Good brother, tell the cause unto my lords.
I know you have a better wit than I.

Cos. Unhappy Persia, that in former age
Hast been the seat of mighty conquerors,
That in their prowess and their policies
Have triumph'd over Afric and the bounds
Of Europe, where the sun dares scarce appear
For freezing meteors and congealed cold:

10

Now to be rul'd and governed by a man,
At whose birthday Cynthia with Saturn join'd,
And Jove, the Sun, and Mercury denied
To shed [their] influence in his fickle brain!
Now Turks and Tartars shake their swords at thee,
Meaning to mangle all thy provinces.

   Myc. Brother, I see your meaning well enough,
And through your planets I perceive you think
I am not wise enough to be a king.   20
But I refer me to my noblemen
That know my wit, and can be witnesses.
I might command you to be slain for this:
Meander, might I not

   Meand. Not for so small a fault, my sovereign lord.

   Myc. I mean it not, but yet I know I might:
Yet live, yea live, Mycetes wills it so.
Meander, thou, my faithful counsellor,
Declare the cause of my conceived grief
Which is (God knows) about that Tamburlaine,   30
That like a fox in midst of harvest time
Doth prey upon my flocks of passengers;
And, as I hear, doth mean to pull my plumes.
Therefore 'tis good and meet for to be wise.

   Meand. Oft have I heard Your Majesty complain
Of Tamburlaine, that sturdy Scythian thief,
That robs your merchants of Persepolis
Treading by land unto the Western Isles,
And in your confines with his lawless train
Daily commits incivil outrages—   40
Hoping (misled by dreaming prophecies)
To reign in Asia, and with barbarous arms
To make himself the Monarch of the East!
But ere he march in Asia or display
His vagrant ensign in the Persian fields,
Your Grace hath taken order by Theridamas,
Charg'd with a thousand horse, to apprehend
And bring him captive to Your Highness' throne.

   Myc. Full true thou speak'st, and like thyself, my lord:
Whom I may term a Damon for thy love.   50
Therefore 'tis best, if so it like you all,
To send my thousand horse incontinent
To apprehend that paltry Scythian.
How like you this, my honorable lords?
Is't not a kingly resolution?

   Cos. It cannot choose, because it comes from you!

   Myc. Then hear thy charge, valiant Theridamas,

The chiefest captain of Mycetes' host,
The hope of Persia, and the very legs
Whereon our state doth lean as on a staff   60
That holds us up and foils our neighbor foes:
Thou shalt be leader of this thousand horse
Whose foaming gall with rage and high disdain
Have sworn the death of wicked Tamburlaine.
Go frowning forth. But come thou smiling home,
As did Sir Paris with the Grecian dame.
Return with speed—time passeth swift away;
Our life is frail, and we may die today.
      Ther. Before the moon renew her borrowed light,
Doubt not, my lord and gracious sovereign,   70
But Tamburlaine and that Tartarian rout
Shall either perish by our warlike hands
Or plead for mercy at Your Highness' feet.
      Myc. Go, stout Theridamas, thy words are swords!
And with thy looks thou conquerest all thy foes!
I long to see thee back return from thence,
That I may view these milk-white steeds of mine
All loaden with the heads of killed men,
And from their knees e'en to their hoofs below
Besmear'd with blood: *that* makes a dainty show!   80
      Ther. Then now, my lord, I humbly take my leave.
      Myc. Theridamas, farewell, ten thousand times!

                                                    Exit.

Ah, Menaphon, why stay'st thou thus behind
When other men press forward for renown?
Go, Menaphon, go into Scythia
And foot by foot follow Theridamas.
      Cos. Nay, pray you let him stay. A greater [task]
Fits Menaphon than warring with a thief!
Create him Prorex of all Africa,
That he may win the Babylonians' hearts   90
Which will revolt from Persian government,
Unless they have a wiser king than you.
      Myc. "Unless they have a wiser king than you."
These are his words—Meander, set them down.
      Cos. And add this to them—that all Asia
Lament to see the folly of their king.
      Myc. Well, here I swear by this my royal seat—
      Cos. (You may do well to kiss it then.) [*Aside.*]
      Myc. Emboss'd with silk as best beseems my state,
To be reveng'd for these contemptuous words.   100
Oh, where is duty and allegiance now?
Fled to the Caspian or the Ocean main?

What, shall I call thee brother—No, a foe,
Monster of nature! Shame unto thy stock,
That dar'st presume thy sovereign for to mock!
Meander, come, I am abus'd, Meander.

> *Exit. Manent Cosroe and Menaphon.*

Men. How now, my lord? What, mated and amaz'd
To hear the King thus threaten like himself?

Cos. Ah, Menaphon, I pass not for his threats.
The plot is laid by Persian noblemen   110
And captains of the Median garrisons
To crown me Emperor of Asia.
But this it is that doth excruciate
The very substance of my vexed soul—
To see our neighbors that were wont to quake
And tremble at the Persian monarch's name,
Now sits and laughs our regiment to scorn;
And that which might resolve me into tears—
Men from the farthest equinoctial line
Have swarm'd in troops into the Eastern India,   120
Lading their ships with gold and precious stones,
And made their spoils from all our provinces.

Men. This should entreat Your Highness to rejoice,
Since fortune gives you opportunity
To gain the title of a conqueror
By curing of this maimed empery.
Afric and Europe bordering on your land,
And continent to your dominions,
How easily may you with a mighty host
Pass into Græcia, as did Cyrus once,   130
And cause them to withdraw their forces home,
Lest you subdue the pride of Christendom?

> [*Trumpets sound within.*]

Cos. But, Menaphon, what means this trumpet's sound?

Men. Behold, my Lord Ortygius and the rest
Bringing the crown to make you Emperor!

Enter Ortygius and Ceneus bearing a crown, with others.

Orty. Magnificent and mighty Prince Cosroe,
We, in the name of other Persian states
And commons of the mighty monarchy,
Present thee with the imperial diadem!

Cen. The warlike soldiers and the gentlemen,   140
That heretofore have fill'd Persepolis
With Afric captains taken in the field
(Whose ransom made them march in coats of gold,
With costly jewels hanging at their ears,

And shining stones upon their lofty crests),
Now living idle in the walled towns—
Wanting both pay and martial discipline—
Begin in troops to threaten civil war,
And openly exclaim against the King.
Therefore, to stop all sudden mutinies, 150
We will invest Your Highness, Emperor—
Whereat the soldiers will conceive more joy
Than did the Macedonians at the spoil
Of great Darius and his wealthy host.

    Cos. Well, since I see the state of Persia droop
And languish in my brother's government,
I willingly receive th' imperial crown,
And vow to wear it for my country's good,
In spite of them shall malice my estate.

    Orty. And in assurance of desir'd success, 160
We here do crown thee Monarch of the East!   [*Crowns him.*]
Emperor of Asia and of Persia!
Great Lord of Media and Armenia!
Duke of Africa and Albania!
Mesopotamia and of Parthia!
East India and the late-discovered isles!
Chief Lord of all the wide, vast Euxine sea,
And of the ever-raging Caspian lake!
Long live Cosroe, mighty Emperor!

    Cos. And Jove may never let me longer live 170
Than I may seek to gratify your love
And cause the soldiers that thus honor me
To triumph over many provinces!
By whose desires of discipline in arms
I doubt not shortly but to reign sole king,
And with the army of Theridamas
(Whither we presently will fly, my lords)
To rest secure against my brother's force.

    Orty. We knew, my lord, before we brought the crown,
Intending your investion so near 180
The residence of your despised brother,
The lord[s] would not be too exasperate
To injure or suppress your worthy title.
—Or if they would, there are in readiness
Ten thousand horse to carry you from hence
In spite of all suspected enemies.

    Cos. I know it well, my lord, and thank you all.

    Orty. Sound up the trumpets then! God save the King!
                           [*Trumpets sound.*]
                                   Exeunt.

ACTUS. 1.

SCAENA. 2.

[*Enter*] *Tamburlaine* [*in a shepherd's robe*] *leading Zenocrate* [*followed by Magnetes and Agydas*], [*then*] *Techelles, Usumcasane, other lords, and soldiers loaden with treasure.*

Tamb. Come, lady, let not this appal your thoughts.
The jewels and the treasure we have ta'en
Shall be reserv'd, and you in better state
Than if you were arriv'd in Syria,
Even in the circle of your father's arms,
The mighty Soldan of Ægyptia.
  Zeno. Ah, shepherd, pity my distressed plight!
—If, as thou seem'st, thou art so mean a man.
And seek not to enrich thy followers
By lawless rapine from a silly maid,   10
Who travelling with these Median lords
To Memphis, from my uncle's country of Media,
Where all my youth I have been governed,
Have pass'd the army of the mighty Turk,
Bearing his privy signet and his hand
To safe-conduct us thorough Africa.
  Mag. And since we have arriv'd in Scythia,
Besides rich presents from the puissant Cham,
We have His Highness' letters to command
Aid and assistance if we stand in need.   20
  Tamb. But now you see these letters and commands
Are countermanded by a greater man:
And through my provinces you must expect
Letters of conduct from *my* mightiness
If you intend to keep your treasure safe.
But since I love to live at liberty,
As easily may you get the Soldan's crown
As any prizes out of my precinct:
For they are friends that help to wean my state
Till men and kingdoms help to strengthen it,   30
And must maintain my life exempt from servitude.
But, tell me, madam, is Your Grace betroth'd?
  Zeno. I am, *my lord*—for so you do import.
  Tamb. I am a lord, for so my deeds shall prove!
—And yet a shepherd by my parentage.
But, lady, this fair face and heavenly hue
Must grace his bed that conquers Asia
And means to be a terror to the world,
Measuring the limits of his empery

By east and west, as Phœbus doth his course! 40
    [*Removes shepherd's robe and is revealed in armor,*
                          sword at his side.]
Lie here ye weeds that I disdain to wear!
This complete armor and this curtle-axe
Are adjuncts more beseeming Tamburlaine.
And, madam, whatsoever you esteem
Of this success and loss unvalued,
Both may invest you Empress of the East;
And these that seem but silly country swains
May have the leading of so great an host
As with their weight shall make the mountains quake,
Even as when windy exhalations 50
Fighting for passage, tilt within the earth.
  Tech. As princely lions when they rouse themselves,
Stretching their paws and threat'ning herds of beasts,
So in his armor looketh Tamburlaine.
Methinks I see kings kneeling at his feet,
And he with frowning brows and fiery looks,
Spurning their crowns from off their captive heads.
  Usum. And making thee and me, Techelles, kings,
That even to death will follow Tamburlaine.
  Tamb. Nobly resolv'd, sweet friends and followers! 60
These lords, perhaps, do scorn our estimates,
And think we prattle with distempered spirits:
But since they measure our deserts so mean,
That in conceit bear empires on our spears,
Affecting thoughts coequal with the clouds,
They shall be kept our forced followers,
Till with their eyes they view us emperors.
  Zeno. The gods, defenders of the innocent,
Will never prosper your intended drifts,
That thus oppress poor friendless passengers. 70
Therefore at least admit us liberty,
Even as thou hop'st to be eternized
By living Asia's mighty Emperor.
  Agyd. I hope our ladies' treasure and our own,
May serve for ransom to our liberties:
Return our mules and empty camels back,
That we may travel into Syria,
Where her betrothed, Lord Alcidamus,
Expects th' arrival of Her Highness' person.
  Mag. And wheresoever we repose ourselves, 80
We will report but well of Tamburlaine.
  Tamb. Disdains Zenocrate to live with me?
Or you, my lords, to be my followers?

Think you I weigh this treasure more than you?
Not all the gold in India's wealthy arms
Shall buy the meanest soldier in my train!
—Zenocrate, lovelier than the love of Jove!
Brighter than is the silver [Rhodope]!
Fairer than whitest snow on Scythian hills!
Thy person is more worth to Tamburlaine   90
Than the possession of the Persian crown
Which gracious stars have promis'd at my birth.
A hundred Tartars shall attend on thee,
Mounted on steeds swifter than Pegasus;
Thy garments shall be made of Median silk,
Enchas'd with precious jewels of mine own,
—More rich and valurous than Zenocrate's:
With milk-white harts upon an ivory sled,
Thou shalt be drawn amidst the frozen pools,
And scale the icy mountains' lofty tops   100
—Which with thy beauty will be soon resolv'd:
My martial prizes with five hundred men,
Won on the fifty-headed Volga's waves,
Shall all we offer to Zenocrate—
And then myself to fair Zenocrate.
     Tech. What now? In love?
     Tamb. (Techelles, women must be flattered.   [*Aside to*
But this *is* she with whom I am in love.)   *Techelles.*]

                    Enter a Soldier.

     Sold. News! News!
     Tamb. How now, what's the matter?   110
     Sold. A thousand Persian horsemen are at hand,
Sent from the King to overcome us all!
     Tamb. How now, my lords of Egypt and Zenocrate!
Now must your jewels be restor'd again?
And I, that triumph'd so, be overcome?
How say you, lordings, is not this your hope?
     Agyd. We hope yourself will willingly restore them.
     Tamb. Such hope, such fortune, have the thousand horse!
Soft ye, my lords, and sweet Zenocrate:
You must be forced from me ere you go.   120
A thousand horsemen? We five hundred foot?
An odds too great for us to stand against?
But are they rich? And is their armor good?
     Sold. Their plumed helms are wrought with beaten gold,
Their swords enamell'd, and about their necks
Hangs massy chains of gold down to the waist:
In every part exceeding brave and rich.

Tamb. Then shall we fight courageously with them,
Or look you I should play the orator?

Tech. No, cowards and faint-hearted runaways   130
Look for orations when the foe is near.
Our swords shall play the orators for us.

Usum. Come, let us meet them at the mountain foot
And with a sudden and a hot alarm
Drive all their horses headlong down the hill!

Tech. Come, let us march!

Tamb. Stay, Techelles, ask a parley first. [*Trumpet sounds
a parley.*]
The soldiers enter.

Open the mails, yet guard the treasure sure:
Lay out our golden wedges to the view,
That their reflections may amaze the Persians.   140
And look we friendly on them when they come.
But if they offer word or violence,
We'll fight five hundred men-at-arms to one,
Before we part with our possession!
And 'gainst the General we will lift our swords—
And either lanch his greedy thirsting throat;
Or take him prisoner, and his chain shall serve
For manacles, till he be ransom'd home. [*Trumpets sound
Tech. I hear them come. Shall we encounter them? *within.*]
Tam. Keep all your standings and not stir a foot,   150
Myself will bide the danger of the brunt.

Enter Theridamas and others.

Ther. Where is this Scythian Tamburlaine?
Tamb. Whom seek'st thou, Persian? I am Tamburlaine.
Ther. Tamburlaine! [*Aside to audience:*]
(A Scythian shepherd so embellished
With nature's pride and richest furniture!
His looks do menace heaven and dare the gods;
His fiery eyes are fix'd upon the earth
As if he now devis'd some stratagem
Or meant to pierce Avernus' darksome vaults   160
To pull the triple-headed dog from hell!)
Tamb. Noble and mild this Persian seems to be,
If outward habit judge the inward man.
Tech. His deep affections make him passionate.
Tamb. With what a majesty he rears his looks!—
In thee, thou valiant man of Persia,
I see the folly of thy emperor.
Art thou but captain of a thousand horse,

That by characters graven in thy brows,
And by thy martial face and stout aspect,   170
Deserv'st to have the leading of a host?
Forsake thy king, and do but join with me,
And we will triumph over all the world!
I hold the Fates bound fast in iron chains,
And with my hand turn Fortune's wheel about:
And sooner shall the sun fall from his sphere
Than Tamburlaine be slain or overcome.
Draw forth thy sword, thou mighty man-at-arms,
Intending but to raze my charmed skin,
And Jove himself will stretch his hand from heaven   180
To ward the blow and shield me safe from harm!
See how he rains down heaps of gold in showers [*Soldiers open*
As if he meant to give my soldiers pay!   *bags and gold*
And as a sure and grounded argument   *pours out.*]
That I shall be the Monarch of the East,
He sends this Soldan's daughter rich and brave
To be my Queen and portly Emperess.
If thou wilt stay with me, renowed man,
And lead thy thousand horse with my conduct,
Besides thy share of this Egyptian prize,   190
Those thousand horse shall sweat with martial spoil
Of conquered kingdoms and of cities sack'd.
Both we will walk upon the lofty clifts
And Christian merchants, that with Russian stems
Plough up huge furrows in the Caspian sea,
Shall vail to us as lords of all the lake.
Both we will reign as consuls of the earth,
And mighty kings shall be our senators.
Jove sometimes masked in a shepherd's weed:
And by those steps that he hath scal'd the heavens   200
May we become immortal like the gods!
Join with me now in this my mean estate
(I call it mean because being yet obscure
The nations far remov'd admire me not),
And when my name and honor shall be spread
As far as Boreas claps his brazen wings,
Or fair Boötes sends his cheerful light,
Then shalt thou be competitor with me,
And sit with Tamburlaine in all his majesty!

    Ther. Not Hermes, prolocutor to the gods,   210
Could use persuasions more pathetical.

    Tamb. Nor are Apollo's oracles more true
Than thou shalt find my vaunts substantial.

    Tech. We are his friends, and if the Persian king

Should offer present dukedoms to our state,
We think it loss to make exchange for that
We are assured of by our friend's success.
   Usum. And kingdoms at the least we all expect.
—Besides the honor in assured conquests
Where kings shall crouch unto our conquering swords   220
And hosts of soldiers stand amaz'd at us—
When with their fearful tongues they shall confess:
These are the men that all the world admires!
   Ther. What strong enchantments tice my yielding soul?
Are these resolved, noble Scythians?
But shall I prove a traitor to my king?
   Tamb. No, but the trusty friend of Tamburlaine.
   Ther. —Won with thy words, and conquered with thy looks,
I yield myself, my men, and horse to thee,
To be partaker of thy good or ill,   230
As long as life maintains Theridamas!
   Tamb. Theridamas, my friend, take here my hand,
Which is as much as if I swore by heaven,
And call'd the gods to witness of my vow.   [*They clasp hands.*]
Thus shall my heart be still combin'd with thine,
Until our bodies turn to elements,
And both our souls aspire celestial thrones.
Techelles and Casane, welcome him!
   Tech. Welcome, renowned Persian, to us all!
   Usum. Long may Theridamas remain with us!   240
   Tamb. These are my friends in whom I more rejoice
Than doth the King of Persia in his crown.
And by the love of Pylades and Orestes,
Whose [statues] we adore in Scythia,
Thyself and them shall never part from me
Before I crown you kings in Asia.
Make much of them, gentle Theridamas,
And they will never leave thee till the death.
   Ther. Nor thee, nor them, thrice noble Tamburlaine,
Shall want my heart to be with gladness pierc'd   250
To do you honor and security!
   Tamb. A thousand thanks, worthy Theridamas!
And now, fair madam and my noble lords,
If you will willingly remain with me,
You shall have honors as your merits be:
Or else you shall be forc'd with slavery.
   Agyd. We yield unto thee, happy Tamburlaine.
   Tamb. For you then, madam, I am out of doubt.
   Zeno. I must be pleas'd perforce. Wretched Zenocrate!
                                    Exeunt.

ACTUS. 2.

SCAENA. 1.

[Enter] Cosroe, Menaphon, Ortygius, Ceneus, with other soldiers.

Cos. Thus far are we towards Theridamas,
And valiant Tamburlaine, the man of fame,
The man that in the forehead of his fortune.
Bears figures of renown and miracle.
But tell me, that has seen him, Menaphon,
What stature wields he, and what personage?
    Men. Of stature tall, and straightly fashioned,
Like his desire, lift upward and divine:
So large of limbs, his joints so strongly knit,
Such breadth of shoulders as might mainly bear   10
Old Atlas' burthen: 'twixt his manly pitch
A pearl more worth than all the world is plac'd,
Wherein by curious sovereignty of art
Are fix'd his piercing instruments of sight,
Whose fiery circles bear encompassed
A heaven of heavenly bodies in their spheres,
That guides his steps and actions to the throne
Where honor sits invested royally:
Pale of complexion, wrought in him with passion,
Thirsting with sovereignty, with love of arms: 20
His lofty brows in folds do figure death,
And in their smoothness amity and life:
About them hangs a knot of amber hair,
Wrapped in curls, as fierce Achilles' was,
On which the breath of heaven delights to play,
Making it dance with wanton majesty:
His arms and fingers, long, and [sinewy],
Betokening valor and excess of strength—
In every part proportioned like the man
Should make the world subdued to Tamburlaine.   30
    Cos. Well has thou portray'd in thy terms of life
The face and personage of a wondrous man.
Nature doth strive with Fortune and his stars
To make him famous in accomplish'd worth.
And well his merits show him to be made
His fortune's master and the king of men,
That could persuade at such a sudden pinch,
With reasons of his valor and his life,
A thousand sworn and overmatching foes.

Then, when our powers in points of swords are join'd   40
And clos'd in compass of the killing bullet,
Though strait the passage and the port be made
That leads to palace of my brother's life,
Proud is his fortune if we pierce it not.
And when the princely Persian diadem
Shall overweigh his weary witless head
And fall like mellowed fruit, with shakes of death,
In fair Persia noble Tamburlaine
Shall be my regent and remain as king.

    Orty. In happy hour we have set the crown   50
Upon your kingly head that seeks our honor
In joining with the man ordain'd by heaven
To further every action to the best.

    Cen. He that with shepherds and a little spoil
Durst in disdain of wrong and tyranny
Defend his freedom 'gainst a monarchy,
What will he do supported by a king,
Leading a troop of gentlemen and lords,
And stuff'd with treasure for his highest thoughts?

    Cos. And such shall wait on worthy Tamburlaine.   60
Our army will be forty thousand strong
When Tamburlaine and brave Theridamas
Have met us by the river Araris—
And all conjoin'd to meet the witless king,
That now is marching near to Parthia
(And with unwilling soldiers faintly arm'd)
To seek revenge on me and Tamburlaine.
—To whom, sweet Menaphon, direct me straight.

    Men. I will, my lord.   *Exeunt.*

ACTUS. 2.

SCAENA. 2

[Enter] Mycetes, Meander, with other lords and soldiers.

    Myc. Come, my Meander, let us to this gear.
I tell you true, my heart is swoln with wrath
On this same thievish villain, Tamburlaine,
And on that false Cosroe, my traitorous brother.
Would it not grieve a king to be so abus'd
And have a thousand horsemen ta'en away?
And, which is worst, to have his diadem
Sought for by such scald knaves as love him not?
I think it would! Well then, by heavens I swear,
Aurora shall not peep out of her doors   10

But I will have Cosroe by the head
And kill proud Tamburlaine with point of sword!
Tell you the rest, Meander—I have said.

    Meand. Then having passed Armenian deserts now
And pitch'd our tents under the Georgian hills
Whose tops are covered with Tartarian thieves
That lie in ambush, waiting for a prey,
What should we do but bid them battle straight
And rid the world of those detested troops?
—Lest, if we let them linger here awhile,   20
They gather strength by power of fresh supplies.
This country swarms with vile outrageous men
That live by rapine and by lawless spoil,
Fit soldiers for the wicked Tamburlaine:
And he that could with gifts and promises
Inveigle him that led a thousand horse,
And make him false his faith unto his king,
Will quickly win such as be like himself.
Therefore cheer up your minds, prepare to fight!
He that can take or slaughter Tamburlaine   30
Shall rule the province of Albania:
Who brings that traitor's head, Theridamas,
Shall have a government in Media,
Beside the spoil of him and all his train:
But if Cosroe (as our spials say,
And as we know) remains with Tamburlaine,
His Highness' pleasure is that he should live,
And be reclaim'd with princely lenity.

    A Spy. A hundred horsemen of my company
Scouting abroad upon these champion plains   40
Have view'd the army of the Scythians,
Which make reports it far exceeds the King's.

    Meand. Suppose they be in number infinite.
Yet being void of martial discipline,
All running headlong after greedy spoils,
And more regarding gain than victory—
Like to the cruel brothers of the earth,
Sprung of the teeth of dragons venomous,
Their careless swords shall lanch their fellows' throats
And make us triumph in their overthrow.   50

    Myc. Was there such brethren, sweet Meander, say,
That sprung of teeth of dragons venomous?

    Meand. So poets say, my lord.

    Myc. And 'tis a pretty toy to be a poet.
Well, well, Meander, thou art deeply read:
And having thee, I have a jewel sure.

Go on, my lord, and give your charge, I say.
Thy wit will make us conquerors today.
    Meand. Then, noble soldiers, to entrap these thieves,
That live confounded in disordered troops,   60
If wealth or riches may prevail with them,
We have our camels laden all with gold,
Which you that be but common soldiers
Shall fling in every corner of the field:
And while the base-born Tartars take it up,
You, fighting more for honor than for gold,
Shall massacre those greedy-minded slaves:
And when their scattered army is subdu'd,
And you march on their slaughtered carcasses,
Share equally the gold that bought their lives   70
And live like gentlemen in Persia!
Strike up the drum and march courageously!
Fortune herself doth sit upon our crests.
    Myc. He tells you true, my masters, so he does.
Drums, why sound ye not when Meander speaks?
                          Exeunt [drums sounding].

ACTUS. 2.

SCAENA. 3.

[Enter] Cosroe, Tamburlaine, Theridamas, Techelles, Usumca-
sane, Ortygius, with others.

    Cos. Now, worthy Tamburlaine, have I repos'd
In thy approved fortunes all my hope.
What think'st thou, man, shall come of our attempts?
For even as from assured oracle,
I take thy doom for satisfaction.
    Tamb. And so mistake you not a whit, my lord—
For fates and oracles, heaven have sworn
To royalise the deeds of Tamburlaine,
And make them blest that share in his attempts.
And doubt you not but if you favor me   10
And let my fortunes and my valor sway
To some direction in your martial deeds,
The world will strive with hosts of men-at-arms
To swarm unto the ensign I support.
The host of Xerxes, which by fame is said
To drink the mighty Parthian Araris,
Was but a handful to that we will have.
Our quivering lances shaking in the air
And bullets like Jove's dreadful thunderbolts,

Enroll'd in flames and fiery smoldering mists,   20
Shall threat the gods more than Cyclopian wars.
And with our sun-bright armor as we march,
We'll chase the stars from heaven and dim their eyes
That stand and muse at our admired arms.
    Ther. You see, my lord, what working words he hath.
But when you see his actions stop his speech,
Your speech will stay, or so extol his worth,
As I shall be commended and excus'd
For turning my poor charge to his direction.
And these his two renowned friends, my lord,   30
Would make one thrust and strive to be retain'd
In such a great degree of amity.
    Tech. With duty [and] with amity we yield
Our utmost service to the fair Cosroe!
    Cos. —Which I esteem as portion of my crown.
Usumcasane and Techelles both,
When She that rules in Rhamnis golden gates
And makes a passage for all prosperous arms
Shall make me solely Emperor of Asia,
Then shall your meeds and valors be advanc'd   40
To rooms of honor and nobility.
    Tamb. Then haste, Cosroe, to be king alone,
That I with these my friends and all my men
May triumph in our long-expected fate.
The king, your brother, is now hard at hand.
Meet with the fool, and rid your royal shoulders
Of such a burthen as outweighs the sands
And all the craggy rocks of Caspia.

                    [*Enter a Messenger.*]

    Mes. My lord, we have discovered the enemy
Ready to charge you with a mighty army.   50
    Cos. Come, Tamburlaine, now whet thy winged sword,
And lift thy lofty arm into the clouds
That it may reach the King of Persia's crown
And set it safe on my victorious head!
    Tamb. See where it is, the keenest curtle-axe   [*Points to his
That e'er made passage thorough Persian arms.   sword.*]
These are the wings shall make it fly as swift   [*Points to his
As doth the lightning or the breath of heaven,   arms.*]
And kill as sure as it swiftly flies.
    Cos. Thy words assure me of kind success.   60
Go, valiant soldier, go before and charge
The fainting army of that foolish king.
    Tamb. Usumcasane and Techelles, come:

We are enow to scare the enemy,
And more than needs to make an emperor!

[*Drums and trumpets sound within.*] *To the battle, and
Mycetes comes out alone with his crown in his hand, offering
to hide it.*

Myc. Accurs'd be he that first invented war!
They knew not, ah, they knew not, simple men,
How those were hit by pelting cannon shot
Stand staggering like a quivering aspen leaf
Fearing the force of Boreas' boist'rous blasts.   70
In what a lamentable case were I
If nature had not given me wisdom's lore,
For kings are clouts that every man shoots at,
Our crown the pin that thousands seek to cleave.
Therefore in policy I think it good
To hide it close. A goodly stratagem!
—And far from any man that is a fool.
So shall I not be known. Of if I be,
They cannot take away my crown from me.
Here will I hide it in this simple hole.   80

Enter Tamburlaine.

Tamb. What, fearful coward, straggling from the camp
When kings themselves are present in the field?
Myc. Thou liest.
Tamb. Base villain, darest give the lie?
Myc. Away, I am the King, go, touch me not.
Thou break'st the law of arms unless thou kneel
And cry me "Mercy, noble king!"
Tamb. Are you the witty King of Persia?
Myc. Ay, marry am I. Have you any suit to me?
Tamb. I would entreat you speak but three wise words.   90
Myc. So I can, when I see my time.
Tamb. Is this your crown?
Myc. Ay, didst thou ever see a fairer?   [*Hands Tamburlaine
Tamb.* You will not sell it, will ye?   *crown.*]
Myc. Such another word and I will have thee executed.
       Come, give it me!
Tamb. No, I took it prisoner.
Myc. You lie, I gave it you.
Tamb. Then, 'tis mine.
Myc. No, I mean I let you keep it.   100
Tamb. Well, I mean you shall have it again.
Here, take it for a while: I lend it thee,
Till I may see thee hemm'd with armed men.

Then shalt thou see me pull it from thy head.
Thou art no match for mighty Tamburlaine.

[Exit Tamburlaine.]

Myc. O gods, is this Tamburlaine the thief?
I marvel much he stole it not away.

Sound trumpets to the battle, and he runs in.

ACTUS. 2.

SCAENA. 4.

[*Enter*] *Cosroe* [*crowned*], *Tamburlaine, Theridamas, Menaphon, Meander, Ortygius, Techelles, Usumcasane, with others.*

Tamb. Hold thee, Cosroe. Wear two imperial crowns!   [*Gives
Think thee invested now as royally   Cosroe a crown.*]
Even by the mighty hand of Tamburlaine
As if as many kings as could encompass thee
With greatest pomp had crown'd thee Emperor!

Cos. So do I, thrice renowned man-at-arms!   [*Hands him
And none shall keep the crown but Tamburlaine!   back the
Thee do I make my regent of Persia,   crown.*]
And general lieutenant of my armies.

Meander, you, that were our brother's guide,   10
And chiefest counsellor in all his acts,
Since he is yielded to the stroke of war,
On your submission we with thanks excuse,
And give you equal place in our affairs.

Meand. Most happy Emperor, in humblest terms,
I vow my service to Your Majesty,
With utmost virtue of my faith and duty.

Cos. Thanks, good Meander. Then Cosroe reign
And govern Persia in her former pomp!
Now send embassage to thy neighbor kings,   20
And let them know the Persian king is chang'd
From one that knew not what a king should do
To one that can command what 'longs thereto.
And now we will to fair Persepolis
With twenty thousand expert soldiers.
The lords and captains of my brother's camp
With little slaughter take Meander's course,
And gladly yield them to my gracious rule.
Ortygius and Menaphon, my trusty friends,
Now will I gratify your former good,   30
And grace your calling with a greater sway.

Orty. And as we ever [aim'd] at your behoof,
And sought your state all honor it deserv'd,

So will we with our powers and our lives
Endeavor to preserve and prosper it!
   Cos. I will not thank thee, sweet Ortygius:
Better replies shall prove my purposes.
And now, Lord Tamburlaine, my brother's camp
I leave to thee and to Theridamas,
To follow me to fair Persepolis.   40
Then will we march to all those Indian mines,
My witless brother to the Christians lost,
And ransom them with fame and usury.
And till thou overtake me, Tamburlaine
(Staying to order all the scattered troops),
Farewell, lord regent and his happy friends!
I long to sit upon my brother's throne.
   Mena. Your Majesty shall shortly have your wish,
And ride in triumph through Persepolis.

   [Exeunt.] Manent Tamburlaine, Techelles, Theridamas, Usum-
                          casane.

   Tamb. And ride in triumph through Persepolis!   50
Is it not brave to be a king, Techelles,
Usumcasane, and Theridamas?
Is it not passing brave to be a king,
And ride in triumph through Persepolis?
   Tech. O, my lord, 'tis sweet and full of pomp!
   Usum. To be a king is half to be a god!
   Ther. A god is not so glorious as a king!
I think the pleasure they enjoy in heaven
Cannot compare with kingly joys in earth.
To wear a crown enchas'd with pearl and gold,   60
Whose virtues carry with it life and death:
To ask and have, command and be obeyed:
When looks breed love, with looks to gain the prize,
Such power attractive shines in princes' eyes!
   Tamb. Why say, Theridamas, wilt thou be a king?
   Ther. Nay, though I praise it, I can live without it.
   Tamb. What says my other friends, will you be kings?
   Tech. Ay, if I could, with all my heart, my lord.
   Tamb. Why, that's well said, Techelles. So would I.
And so would you, my masters, would you not?   70
   Usum. What then, my lord?
   Tamb. Why then, Casane, shall we wish for aught
The world affords in greatest novelty
And rest attemptless, faint, and destitute?
Methinks we should not. I am strongly mov'd
That if I should desire the Persian crown

I could attain it with a wondrous ease.
And would not all our soldiers soon consent
If we should aim at such a dignity?

    Ther. I know they would with our persuasions.   80
    Tamb. Why then, Theridamas, I'll first assay
To get the Persian kingdom to myself.
Then thou for Parthia. They for Scythia and Media.
And if I prosper, all shall be as sure
As if the Turk, the Pope, Afric and Greece
Came creeping to us with their crowns apace.

    Tech. Then shall we send to this triumphing king
And bid him battle for his novel crown?

    Usum. Nay, quickly then, before his room be hot.

    Tamb. 'Twill prove a pretty jest, in faith, my friends.   90
    Ther. A jest to charge on twenty thousand men?
I judge the purchase more important far.

    Tamb. Judge by thyself, Theridamas, not me!
For presently Techelles here shall haste
To bid him battle ere he pass too far
And lose more labor than the game will quit.
Then shalt thou see this Scythian Tamburlaine
Make but a jest to win the Persian crown.
Techelles, take a thousand horse with thee,
And bid him turn him back to war with us   100
That only made him king to make us sport.
We will not steal upon him cowardly
But give him warning and more warriors.
Haste thee, Techelles, we will follow thee.
What saith Theridamas?

    Ther. Go on for me.   *Exeunt.*

ACTUS. 2.

SCAENA. [5].

[*Enter*] *Cosroe, Meander, Ortygius, Menaphon, with other
soldiers.*

    Cos. What means this devilish shepherd to aspire
With such a giantly presumption
To cast up hills against the face of heaven
And dare the force of angry Jupiter?
But as he thrust them underneath the hills
And press'd out fire from their burning jaws,
So will I send this monstrous slave to hell,
Where flames shall ever feed upon his soul!

    Meand. Some powers divine, or else infernal, mix'd

Their angry seeds at his conception: 10
For he was never sprung of human race,
Since with the spirit of his fearful pride
He dare so doubtlessly resolve of rule
And by profession be ambitious.
    Orty. What god, or fiend, or spirit of the earth,
Or monster turned to a manly shape,
Or of what mold or mettle he be made,
What star or fate soever govern him,
Let us put on our meet encount'ring minds:
And in detesting such a devilish thief,   20
In love of honor and defense of right,
Be arm'd against the hate of such a foe,
Whether from earth, or hell, or heaven, he grow.
    Cos. Nobly resolv'd, my good Ortygius!
And since we all have a suck'd one wholesome air
And with the same proportion of elements
Resolve, I hope we are resembled,
Vowing our loves to equal death and life.
Let's cheer our soldiers to encounter him—
That grievous image of ingratitude,   30
That fiery thirster after sovereignty—
And burn him in the fury of that flame
That none can quench but blood and empery!
Resolve, my lords and loving soliders, now
To save your king and country from decay.
Then strike up, drum! And all the stars that make
The loathsome circle of my dated life,
Direct my weapon to his barbarous heart
That thus opposeth him against the gods
And scorns the powers that govern Persia!   40

Enter to the battle; and after the battle, enter Cosroe wounded,
Theridamas, Tamburlaine, Techelles, Usumcasane, with others.

    Cos. Barbarous and bloody Tamburlaine,
Thus to deprive me of my crown and life!
Treacherous and false Theridamas,
Even at the morning of my happy state,
Scarce being seated in my royal throne,
To work my downfall and untimely end!
An uncouth pain torments my grieved soul,
And death arrests the organ of my voice,
Who, entering at the breach thy sword hath made,
Saks every vein and artier of my heart!   50
Bloody and insatiate Tamburlaine!
    Tamb. The thirst of reign and sweetness of a crown

That caus'd the eldest son of heavenly Ops
To thrust his doting father from his chair
And place himself in the empyreal heaven,
Mov'd me to manage arms against thy state.
What better precedent than mighty Jove?
Nature that fram'd us of four elements,
Warring within our breasts for regiment,
Doth teach us all to have aspiring minds: 60
Our souls, whose faculties can comprehend
The wondrous architecture of the world,
And measure every wandering planet's course,
Still climbing after knowledge infinite,
And always moving as the restless spheres,
Wills us to wear ourselves, and never rest,
Until we reach the ripest fruit of all,
That perfect bliss and sole felicity—
The sweet fruition of an earthly crown.

    Ther. And that made me to join with **Tamburlaine**:   70
For he is gross and like the massy earth
That moves not upwards, nor by princely deeds
Doth mean to soar above the highest sort.

    Tech. And that made us the friends of Tamburlaine
To lift our swords against the Persian king.

    Usum. For as when Jove did thrust old Saturn down,
Neptune and Dis gain'd each of them a crown,
So do we hope to reign in Asia,
If Tamburlaine be plac'd in Persia.

    Cos. The strangest men that ever nature made!   80
I know not how to take their tyrannies.
My bloodless body waxeth chill and cold,
And with my blood my life slides through my wound.
My soul begins to take her flight to hell
And summons all my senses to depart.
The heat and moisture which did feed each other
For want of nourishment to feed them both
Is dry and cold and now doth ghastly death
With greedy talons gripe my bleeding heart
And like a harpy tires on my life.   90
Theridamas and Tamburlaine, I die!
And fearful vengeance light upon you both!

[*Cosroe dies. Tamburlaine*] *takes the crown and puts it on.*

    Tamb. Not all the curses which the furies breathe
Shall make me leave so rich a prize as this!
Theridamas, Techelles, and the rest,
Who think you now is King of Persia?

All. Tamburlaine! Tamburlaine!

Tamb. Though Mars himself, the angry god of arms,
And all the earthly potentates conspire
To disposess me of this diadem,   100
Yet will I wear it in despite of them
As great commander of this eastern world,
If you but say that Tamburlaine shall reign.

All. Long live Tamburlaine and reign in Asia!

Tamb. So now it is more surer on my head,
Than if the gods had held a parliament
And all pronounc'd me King of Persia!

[*Exeunt.*]

ACTUS. 3.

SCAENA. 1.

[*Enter*] *Bajazeth, the Kings of Fez, Morocco, and Argier,*
[*Basso,*] *with others, in great pomp.*

Baj. Great kings of Barbary and my portly bassoes,
We hear the Tartars and the eastern thieves—
Under the conduct of one, Tamburlaine—
Presume a bickering with your Emperor,
And thinks to rouse us from our dreadful siege
Of the famous Grecian Constantinople.
You know our army is invincible:
As many circumcised Turks we have
And warlike bands of Christians renied
As hath the ocean or the Terrene Sea   10
Small drops of water when the moon begins
To join in one her semicircled horns.
Yet would we not be brav'd with foreign power,
Nor raise our siege before the Grecians yield,
Or breathless lie before the city walls.

Fez. Renowned Emperor and mighty General,
What if you sent the bassoes of your guard
To charge him to remain in Asia,
Or else to threaten death and deadly arms
As from the mouth of mighty Bajazeth?   20

Baj. Hie thee, my Basso, fast to Persia.
Tell him thy Lord, the Turkish Emperor,
Dread Lord of Afric, Europe, and Asia,
Great King and conqueror of Græcia,
The ocean, Terrene, and the Coal-Black Sea,
The high and highest monarch of the world,
Wills and commands (for say not I entreat)

Not once to set his foot in Africa
Or spread his colors in Græcia
Lest he incur the fury of my wrath!   30
Tell him I am content to take a truce
Because I hear he bears a valiant mind.
But if presuming on his silly power,
He be so mad to manage arms with me,
Then stay thou with him. Say, I bid thee so.
And if before the sun have measured heaven
With triple circuit, thou regreet us not,
We mean to take his morning's next arise
For messenger he will not be reclaim'd,
And mean to fetch thee in despite of him.   40

   Bas. Most great and puissant monarch of the earth,
Your Basso will accomplish your behest
And show your pleasure to the Persian
As fits the legate of the stately Turk.   *Exit Basso.*

   Arg. They say he is the King of Persia.
But if he dare attempt to stir your siege,
'Twere requisite he should be ten times more
For all flesh quakes at your magnificence.

   Baj. True, Argier, and tremble at my looks.

   Mor. The spring is hind'red by your smothering host,   50
For neither rain can fall upon the earth,
Nor sun reflex his virtuous beams thereon,
The ground is mantled with such multitudes.

   Baj. All this is true as holy Mahomet,
And all the trees are blasted with our breaths.

   Fez. What thinks Your Greatness best to be achiev'd
In pursuit of the city's overthrow?

   Baj. I will the captive pioners of Argier
Cut off the water that by leaden pipes
Runs to the city from the mountain Carnon.   60
Two thousand horse shall forage up and down
That no relief or succor come by land,
And all the sea my galleys countermand.
Then shall our footmen lie within the trench,
And with their cannons mouth'd like Orcus' gulf
Batter the walls, and we will enter in.
And thus the Grecians shall be conquered!   *Exeunt.*

ACTUS. 3.

SCAENA. 2.

[Enter] Agydas, Zenocrate, Anippe, with others.

Agyd. Madam Zenocrate, may I presume
To know the cause of these unquiet fits
That work such trouble to your wonted rest?
'Tis more than pity such a heavenly face
Should by heart's sorrow wax so wan and pale,
When your offensive rape by Tamburlaine
(Which of your whole displeasures should be most)
Hath seem'd to be digested long ago.

Zeno. Although it be digested long ago,
As his exceeding favors have deserv'd   10
(And might content the Queen of Heaven, as well
As it hath changed my first conceiv'd disdain),
Yet, since, a farther passion feeds my thoughts
With ceaseless and disconsolate conceits,
Which dyes my looks so lifeless as they are,
And might, if my extremes had full events,
Make me the ghastly counterfeit of death.

Agyd. Eternal heaven sooner be dissolv'd,
And all that pierceth Phœbe's silver eye,
Before such hap fall to Zenocrate!   20

Zeno. Ah, life and soul, still hover in his breast
And leave *my* body senseless as the earth!
—Or else unite you to his life and soul,
That I may live and die with Tamburlaine!

Enter Tamburlaine with Techelles and others. [They stand apart.]

Agyd. With Tamburlaine? Ah, fair Zenocrate,
Let not a man so vile and barbarous,
That holds you from your father in despite,
And keeps you from the honors of a queen—
Being suppos'd his worthless concubine!—
Be honored with your love but for necessity!   30
So now the mighty Soldan hears of you,
Your Highness needs not doubt but in short time
He will with Tamburlaine's destruction
Redeem you from this deadly servitude.

Zeno. Leave to wound me with these words,
And speak of Tamburlaine as he deserves!

The entertainment we have had of him
Is far from villainy or servitude,
And might in noble minds be counted princely.

    Agyd. How can you fancy one that looks so fierce,   40
Only disposed to martial stratagems?
—Who when he shall embrace you in his arms,
Will tell you how many thousand men he slew:
And when you look for amorous discourse,
Will rattle forth his facts of war and blood!
Too harsh a subject for your dainty ears!

    Zeno. As looks the Sun through Nilus flowing stream,
Or when the Morning holds him in her arms,
So looks my lordly love, fair Tamburlaine!
—His talk much sweeter than the Muses' song   50
They sung for honor 'gainst Pierides;
Or when Minerva did with Neptune strive:
And higher would I rear my estimate
Than Juno, sister to the highest god,
If I were match'd with mighty Tamburlaine.

    Agyd. Yet be not so inconstant in your love,
But let the young Arabian live in hope
After your rescue to enjoy his choice.
You see, though first the King of Persia
(Being a shepherd) seem'd to love you much,   60
Now in his majesty he leaves those looks,
Those words of favor, and those comfortings,
And gives no more than common courtesies.

    Zeno. Thence rise the tears that so distain my cheeks,
Fearing his love through my unworthiness.

*Tamburlaine goes to her and takes her away lovingly by the
hand, looking wrathfully on Agydas, and says nothing.* [*Exeunt
all but Agydas.*]

    Agyd. Betray'd by fortune and suspicious love,
Threat'ned with frowning wrath and jealousy,
Surpris'd with fear of hideous revenge,
I stand aghast!—but most astonied
To see his choler shut in secret thoughts,   70
And wrapt in silence of his angry soul.
Upon his brows was portray'd ugly death,
And in his eyes the furies of his heart
That shine as comets, menacing revenge,
And cast a pale complexion on his cheeks.
As when the seaman sees the Hyades
Gather an army of Cimmerian clouds

(Auster and Aquilon with winged steeds,
All sweating, tilt about the watery heavens,
With shivering spears enforcing thunder claps,   80
And from their shields strike flames of lightning)
All-fearful folds his sails and sounds the main,
Lifting his prayers to the heavens for aid
Against the terror of the winds and waves,
So fares Agydas for the late-felt frowns
That sent a tempest to my daunted thoughts
And makes my soul divine her overthrow.

Enter Techelles with a naked dagger [followed by Usumcasane].

Tech. See you, Agydas, how the King salutes you.
He bids you prophesy what it imports.
Agyd. I prophesied before, and now I prove   90
The killing frowns of jealousy and love.
He needed not with words confirm my fear,
For words are vain where working tools present
The naked action of my threat'ned end.
It says, "Agydas, thou shalt surely die,
And of extremities elect the least:
More honor and less pain it may procure
To die by this resolved hand of thine
Than stay the torments he and heaven have sworn!"
Then haste, Agydas, and prevent the plagues   100
Which thy prolonged fates may draw on thee.
Go wander free from fear of tyrant's rage,
Removed from the torments and the hell
Wherewith he may excruciate thy soul!
And let Agydas by Agydas die,   *[Takes dagger and*
And with this stab slumber eternally.   *stabs himself.]*
Tech. Usumcasane, see, how right the man
Hath hit the meaning of my lord, the King.
Usum. Faith, and Techelles, it was manly done.
And since he was so wise and honorable,   110
Let us afford him now the bearing hence
And crave his triple-worthy burial.
Tech. Agreed, Casane. We will honor him.
                              [Exeunt bearing out the body.]

ACTUS. 3.

SCAENA. 3.

[*Enter*] *Tamburlaine, Techelles, Usumcasane, Theridamas,*
Basso, Zenocrate, [*Anippe,*] *with others.*

Tamb. Basso, by this thy lord and master knows
I mean to meet him in Bithynia.
See how he comes! Tush, Turks are full of brags,
And menace more than they can well perform.
He meet me in the field and fetch thee hence?
Alas, poor Turk, his fortune is too weak
T' encounter with the strength of Tamburlaine.
View well my camp and speak indifferently:
Do not my captains and my soldiers look
As if they meant to conquer Africa?   10
  Bas. Your men are valiant, but their number few,
And cannot terrify his mighty host.
My lord, the great commander of the world,
Besides fifteen contributory kings,
Hath now in arms ten thousand Janizaries,
Mounted on lusty Mauritanian steeds,
Brought to the war by men of Tripoli;
Two hundred thousand footmen that have serv'd
In two set battles fought in Græcia;
And for the expedition of this war,   20
If he think good, can from his garrisons
Withdraw as many more to follow him!
  Tech. The more he brings the greater is the spoil:
For when they perish by our warlike hands,
We mean to set our footmen on their steeds
And rifle all those stately Janizars!
  Tamb. But will those kings accompany your lord?
  Bas. Such as His Highness please—but some must stay
To rule the provinces he late subdu'd.
  Tamb. Then fight courageously! Their crowns are yours!   30
This hand shall set them on your conquering heads
That made me Emperor of Asia!
  Usum. Let him bring millions infinite of men,
Unpeopling Western Africa and Greece,
Yet we assure us of the victory.
  Ther. Even he that in a trice vanquish'd two kings,
More mighty than the Turkish Emperor,
Shall rouse him out of Europe, and pursue
His scattered army till they yield or die.

Tamb. Well said, Theridamas! Speak in that mood!   40
For *Will* and *Shall* best fitteth Tamburlaine,
Whose smiling stars gives him assured hope
Of martial triumph ere he meet his foes.
I that am term'd the scourge and wrath of God,
The only fear and terror of the world,
Will first subdue the Turk, and then enlarge
Those Christian captives which you keep as slaves
(Burdening their bodies with your heavy chains,
And feeding them with thin and slender fare)
That naked row about the Terrene Sea,   50
And when they chance to rest or breathe a space
Are punish'd with bastones so grievously
That they lie panting on the galley's side
And strive for life at every stroke they give.
These are the cruel pirates of Argier,
That damned train, the scum of Africa,
Inhabited with straggling runagates,
That make quick havoc of the Christian blood!
But as I live that town shall curse the time
That Tamburlaine set foot in Africa.   60

Enter Bajazeth with his bassoes, and contributory Kings [of
Fez, Morocco, and Argier, Zabina and Ebea].

Baj. Bassoes and Janizaries of my guard,
Attend upon the person of your lord,
The greatest potentate of Africa.
    Tamb. Techelles, and the rest, prepare your swords.
I mean to encounter with that Bajazeth.
    Baj. Kings of Fez, Moroccus, and Argier,
He calls me Bajazeth, whom you call lord!
Note the presumption of this Scythian slave!
I tell thee, villain, those that lead my horse
Have to their names titles of dignity—   70
And dar'st thou bluntly call me Bajazeth?
    Tamb. And know, thou Turk, that those which lead my
      horse
Shall lead thee captive thorough Africa—
And dar'st thou bluntly call me Tamburlaine?
    Baj. By Mahomet my kinsman's sepulcher,
And by the holy Alcoran I swear:
He shall be made a chaste and lustless eunuch,
And in my sarell tend my concubines!
And all his captains that thus stoutly stand
Shall draw the chariot of my Emperess,   80
Whom I have brought to see their overthrow!

Tamb. By this my sword, that conquer'd Persia,
Thy fall shall make me famous through the world!
I will not tell thee how I'll handle thee,
But every common soldier of my camp
Shall smile to see thy miserable state.
    Fez. What means the mighty Turkish Emperor
To talk with one so base as Tamburlaine?
    Mor. Ye Moors and valiant men of Barbary,
How can ye suffer these indignities?   90
    Arg. Leave words, and let them feel your lances' points,
Which glided through the bowels of the Greeks.
    Baj. Well said, my stout contributory kings!
Your threefold army and my hugy host
Shall swallow up these base-born Persians!
    Tech. Puissant, renown'd, and mighty Tamburlaine,
Why stay we thus prolonging all their lives?
    Ther. I long to see those crowns won by our swords,
That we may rule as kings of Africa.
    Usum. What coward would not fight for such a prize?   100
    Tamb. Fight all courageously, and be you kings!
I speak it, and my words are oracles.
    Baj. Zabina, mother of three braver boys
Than Hercules, that in his infancy
Did pash the jaws of serpents venomous:
Whose hands are made to gripe a warlike lance;
Their shoulders broad, for complete armor fit;
Their limbs more large and of a bigger size
Than all the brats ysprung from Typhon's loins;
Who, when they come unto their father's age,   110
Will batter turrets with their manly fists—
Sit here upon this royal chair of state
And on thy head wear my imperial crown
Until I bring this sturdy Tamburlaine
And all his captains bound in captive chains!
    Zab. Such good successs happen to Bajazeth!   *[Zabina sits*
    Tamb. Zenocrate, the loveliest maid alive,   *and wears the*
Fairer than rocks of pearl and precious stone,   *crown.]*
The only paragon of Tamburlaine,
Whose eyes are brighter than the lamps of heaven,   120
And speech more pleasant than sweet harmony,
That with thy looks canst clear the darkened sky
And calm the rage of thund'ring Jupiter—
Sit down by her, adorned with my crown,
As if thou wert the Empress of the World!
Stir not, Zenocrate, until thou see
Me march victoriously with all my men,

Triumphing over him and these his kings—
Which I will bring as vassals to thy feet;
Till then, take thou my crown, vaunt of my worth,   130
And manage words with her as we will arms.

   Zeno. And may my love, the King of Persia,
Return with victory and free from wound!   [*Zenocrate sits and*
   Baj. Now shalt thou feel the force of Turkish arms,   *wears*
Which lately made all Europe quake for fear.   *the crown.*]
I have of Turks, Arabians, Moors, and Jews
Enough to cover all Bithynia.
Let thousands die: their slaughtered carcasses
Shall serve for walls and bulwarks to the rest:
And as the heads of Hydra, so my power,   140
Subdued, shall stand as mighty as before.
If they should yield their necks unto the sword,
Thy soldiers' arms could not endure to strike
So many blows as I have heads for thee.
Thou knowest not—foolish, hardy Tamburlaine!—
What 'tis to meet me in the open field,
That leave no ground for thee to march upon.

   Tamb. Our conquering swords shall marshal us the way
We use to march upon the slaughtered foe,
Trampling their bowels with our horses' hoofs—   150
Brave horses, bred on the white Tartarian hills.
My camp is like to Julius Cæsar's host,
That never fought but had the victory:
Nor in Pharsalia was there such hot war
As these, my followers, willingly would have.
Legions of spirits fleeting in the air
Direct our bullets and our weapons' points
And make [your] strokes to wound the senseless [air]:
And when she sees our bloody colors spread,
Then Victory begins to take her flight,   160
Resting herself upon my milk-white tent.
But come, my lords, to weapons let us fall:
The field is ours, the Turk, his wife, and all!
                              Exit with his followers.

   Baj. Come, kings and bassoes, let us glut our swords,
That thirst to drink the feeble Persians' blood!
                              Exit with his followers.

   Zab. Base concubine, must thou be plac'd by me,
That am the Empress of the mighty Turk?

   Zeno. Disdainful Turkess and unreverend boss!
Call'st thou *me* concubine that am betroth'd
Unto the great and mighty Tamburlaine?   170

   Zab. To Tamburlaine, the great Tartarian thief!

    Zeno. Thou wilt repent these lavish words of thine,
When thy great basso-master and thyself
Must plead for mercy at his kingly feet,
And sue to me to be your advocates.
    Zab. And sue to thee? I tell thee, shameless girl,
Thou shalt be laundress to my waiting maid.
How lik'st thou her, Ebea, will she serve?
    Ebea. Madam, she thinks perhaps she is too fine,
But I shall turn her into other weeds,   180
And make her dainty fingers fall to work.
    Zeno. Hear'st thou, Anippe, how thy drudge doth talk?
And how my slave, her mistress, menaceth?
Both for their sauciness shall be employed
To dress the common soldiers' meat and drink—
For we will scorn they should come near ourselves!
    Anip. Yet sometimes let Your Highness send for them
To do the work my chambermaid disdains.
                 They sound the battle within and stay.
    Zeno. Ye gods and powers that govern Persia,
And made my lordly love her worthy King,   190
Now strengthen him against the Turkish Bajazeth!
And let his foes, like flocks of fearful roes
Pursu'd by hunters, fly his angry looks,
That I may see him issue conqueror!
    Zab. Now, Mahomet, solicit God himself!
And make him rain down murdering shot from heaven
To dash the Scythians' brains—and strike them dead
That dare to manage arms with him
That offered jewels to thy sacred shrine
When first he warr'd against the Christians!   200

                 To the battle again.

    Zeno. By this the Turks lie welt'ring in their blood,
And Tamburlaine is Lord of Africa.
    Zab. Thou art deceiv'd. I heard the trumpets sound
As when my Emperor overthrew the Greeks
And led them captive into Africa.
Straight will I use thee as thy pride deserves:
Prepare thyself to live and die my slave!
    Zeno. If Mahomet should come from heaven and swear
My royal lord is slain or conquered,
Yet should he not persuade me otherwise   210
But that he lives and will be conqueror!

*Bajazeth flies, and he pursues him [offstage]. The battle shout
    [within], and they enter: Bajazeth is overcome.*

Tamb. Now, king of bassoes, who is conqueror?
Baj. Thou, by the fortune of this damned [foil.]
Tamb. Where are your stout contributory kings?

Enter Techelles, Theridamas, Usumcasane [, each carrying a crown].

Tech. We have their crowns—their bodies strow the field.
Tamb. Each man a crown? Why kingly fought i' faith.
Deliver them into my treasury.
Zeno. Now let me offer to my gracious lord
His royal crown again so highly won.
Tamb. Nay, take the crown from her, Zenocrate,   220
And crown me Emperor of Africa.
Zab. No, Tamburlaine! Though now thou gat the best,
Thou shalt not yet be lord of Africa.
Ther. Give her the crown, Turkess, you were best.

He takes it from her and gives it to Zenocrate.

Zab. Injurious villains, thieves, runagates!
How dare you thus abuse my majesty?
Ther. Here, madam, you are Empress. She is none.
Tamb. Not now, Theridamas, her time is past.
The pillars that have bolstered up those terms
Are fall'n in clusters at my conquering feet.   230
Zab. Though he be prisoner, he may be ransomed?
Tamb. Not all the world shall ransom Bajazeth!
Baj. Ah, fair Zabina, we have lost the field.
And never had the Turkish Emperor
So great a foil by any foreign foe.
Now will the Christian miscreants be glad,
Ringing with joy their superstitious bells,
And making bonfires for my overthrow.
But ere I die, those foul idolaters
Shall make me bonfires with their filthy bones!   240
For though the glory of this day be lost,
Afric and Greece have garrisons enough
To make me sovereign of the earth again.
Tamb. Those walled garrisons will I subdue—
And write myself great Lord of Africa!
So from the East unto the furthest West
Shall Tamburlaine extend his puissant arm!
The galleys and those pilling brigandines,
That yearly sail to the Venetian gulf
And hover in the Straits for Christians' wrack   250
Shall lie at anchor in the Isle Asant,
Until the Persian fleet and men of war,

Sailing along the oriental sea,
Have fetch'd about the Indian continent,
Even from Persepolis to Mexico,
And thence unto the Straits of Jubalter,
Where they shall meet and join their force in one,
Keeping in awe the Bay of Portingale
And all the ocean by the British shore—
And by this means I'll win the world at last!   260
    Baj. Yet set a ransom on me, Tamburlaine.
    Tamb. What, think'st thou Tamburlaine esteems thy gold?
I'll make the kings of India ere I die
Offer their mines to sue for peace to me,
And dig for treasure to appease my wrath.
Come, bind them both, and one lead in the Turk.
The Turkess let my love's maid lead away.

They bind them.

    Baj. Ah, villains, dare you touch my sacred arms?
O Mahomet! O sleepy Mahomet!
    Zab. O cursed Mahomet that makest us thus   270
The slaves to Scythians rude and barbarous!
    Tamb. Come, bring them in. And for this happy conquest,
Triumph and solemnize a martial feast.   *Exeunt.*

ACTUS. 4.

SCAENA. 1.

*[Enter] Soldan of Egypt with three or four lords, Capolin
[, Messenger].*

    Sold. Awake, ye men of Memphis! Hear the clang
Of Scythian trumpets! Hear the basilisks
That, roaring, shake Damascus turrets down!
The rogue of Volga holds Zenocrate,
The Soldan's daughter, for his concubine,
And with a troop of thieves and vagabonds,
Hath spread his colors to our high disgrace!
—While you, faint-hearted, base Egyptians
Lie slumbering on the flowery banks of Nile
As crocodiles that unaffrighted rest   10
While thund'ring cannons rattle on their skins—.
    Mess. Nay, mighty Soldan, did your greatness see
The frowning looks of fiery Tamburlaine
That with his terror and imperious eyes

Commands the hearts of his associates,
It might amaze Your Royal Majesty.
 Sold. Villain, I tell thee, were that Tamburlaine
As monstrous as Gorgon, Prince of Hell,
The Soldan would not start a foot from him.
But speak, what power hath he?   20
 Mess. Mighty lord,
Three hundred thousand men in armor clad
Upon their prancing steeds, disdainfully
With wanton paces trampling on the ground:
Five hundred thousand footmen threat'ning shot,
Shaking their swords, their spears, and iron bills,
Environing their standard round, that stood
As bristle-pointed as a thorny wood:
Their warlike engines and munition
Exceed the forces of their martial men.   30
 Sold. Nay, could their numbers countervail the stars,
Or ever-drizzling drops of April showers,
Or withered leaves that autumn shaketh down,
Yet would the Soldan by his conquering power
So scatter and consume them in his rage
That not a man should live to rue their fall!
 Capo. So might Your Highness, had you time to sort
Your fighting men, and raise your royal host:
But Tamburlaine by expedition
Advantage takes of your unreadiness.   40
 Sold. Let him take all th' advantages he can.
Were all the world conspir'd to fight for him,
Nay, were he devil, as he is no man,
Yet in revenge of fair Zenocrate,
Whom he detaineth in despite of us,
This arm should send him down to Erebus
To shroud his shame in darkness of the night.
 Mess. Pleaseth your mightiness to understand,
His resolution far exceedeth all:
The first day when he pitcheth down his tents, 50
White is their hue; and on his silver crest
A snowy feather spangled white he bears
To signify the mildness of his mind
That satiate with spoil refuseth blood.
But when Aurora mounts the second time
As red as scarlet is his furniture;
Then must his kindled wrath be quench'd with blood,
Not sparing any that can manage arms!
But if these threats move not submission,
Black are his colors, black pavilion;   60

His spear, his shield, his horse, his armor, plumes,
And jetty feathers menace death and hell!
—Without respect of sex, degree, or age,
He razeth all his foes with fire and sword.
  Sold. Merciless villain! Peasant ignorant
Of lawful arms or martial discipline!
Pillage and murder are his usual trades.
The slave usurps the glorious name of war.
See, Capolin, the fair Arabian king
(That hath been disappointed by this slave   70
Of my fair daughter, and his princely love)
May have fresh warning to go war with us,
And be reveng'd for her disparagement.   [*Exeunt*.]

ACTUS. 4.

SCAENA. 2.

[*Enter*] *Tamburlaine* [*in white*], *Techelles, Theridamas, Usumcasane, Zenocrate, Anippe, two moors drawing Bajazeth in his cage, and his wife following him.*

  Tamb. Bring out my footstool.

              They take him out of the cage.

  Baj. Ye holy priests of heavenly Mahomet—
That, sacrificing, slice and cut your flesh,
Staining his altars with your purple blood—
Make heaven to frown and every fixed star
To suck up poison from the moorish fens
And pour it in this glorious tyrant's throat!
  Tamb. The chiefest God, first mover of that sphere,
Enchas'd with thousands ever-shining lamps,
Will sooner burn the glorious frame of heaven   10
Than it should so conspire my overthrow.
But, villain, thou that wishest this to me,
Fall prostrate on the low disdainful earth
And be the footstool of great Tamburlaine
That I may rise into my royal throne!
  Baj. First shalt thou rip my bowels with thy sword
And sacrifice my soul to death and hell
Before I yield to such a slavery!
  Tamb. Base villain, vassal, slave to Tamburlaine!
Unworthy to embrace or touch the ground   20
That bears the honor of my royal weight!
Stoop, villain, stoop!—Stoop! for so he bids
That may command thee piecemeal to be torn

Or scattered like the lofty cedar trees
Struck with the voice of thundering Jupiter.
  Baj. Then, as I look down to the damned fiends,
Fiends look on me! And thou, dread god of hell,
With ebon scepter strike this hateful earth
And make it swallow both of us at once!

He gets up upon him to his chair.

  Tamb. Now clear the triple region of the air,   30
And let the majesty of heaven behold
Their scourge and terror tread on emperors.
Smile stars, that reign'd at my nativity,
And dim the brightness of their neighbor lamps!
Disdain to borrow light of Cynthia,
For I, the chiefest lamp of all the earth,
First rising in the East with mild aspect,
But fixed now in the meridian line,
Will send up fire to your turning spheres,
And cause the sun to borrow light of you!   40
My sword struck fire from his coat of steel,
Even in Bithynia, when I took this Turk—
As when a fiery exhalation
Wrapt in the bowels of a freezing cloud,
Fighting for passage, make the welkin crack,
And casts a flash of lightning to the earth.
But ere I march to wealthy Persia,
Or leave Damascus and th' Egyptian fields,
As was the fame of [Clymene's] brain-sick son,
That almost brent the axle-tree of heaven,   50
So shall our swords, our lances, and our shot
Fill all the air with fiery meteors:
Then when the sky shall wax as red as blood,
It shall be said I made it red myself,
To make me think of nought but blood and war.
  Zab. Unworthy king, that by thy cruelty
Unlawfully usurpest the Persian seat,
Dar'st thou that never saw an emperor
Before thou met my husband in the field,
Being thy captive, thus abuse his state,   60
Keeping his kingly body in a cage,
That roofs of gold and sun-bright palaces
Should have prepar'd to entertain His Grace?
And treading him beneath thy loathsome feet—
Whose feet the kings of Africa have kiss'd!
  Tech. You must devise some torment worse, my lord,
To make these captives rein their lavish tongues.

    Tamb. Zenocrate, look better to your slave.

    Zeno. She is my handmaid's slave, and she shall look
That these abuses flow not from her tongue.   70
Chide her, Anippe!

    Anip. Let these be warnings for you then, my slave,
How you abuse the person of the King:
Or else I swear to have you whipt stark-nak'd.

    Baj. Great Tamburlaine, great in my overthrow,
Ambitious pride shall make thee fall as low:
For treading on the back of Bajazeth
That should be horsed on four mighty kings—.

    Tamb. Thy names and titles and thy dignities
Are fled from Bajazeth and remain with me,   80
That will maintain it against a world of kings!
Put him in again.   *[They put him in the cage.]*

    Baj. Is this a place for mighty Bajazeth?
Confusion light on him that helps thee thus!

    Tamb. There, whiles he lives, shall Bajazeth be kept,
And where I go be thus in triumph drawn:
And thou, his wife, shalt feed him with the scraps
My servitors shall bring thee from my board;
For he that gives him other food than this
Shall sit by him and starve to death himself: 90
This is my mind and I will have it so.
Not all the kings and emperors of the earth,
If they would lay their crowns before my feet,
Shall ransom him, or take him from his cage.
The ages that shall talk of Tamburlaine,
Even from this day to Plato's wondrous year,
Shall talk how I have handled Bajazeth:
These Moors, that drew him from Bithynia
To fair Damascus where we now remain
Shall lead him with us wheresoe'er we go.   100
—Techelles, and my loving followers,
Now may we see Damascus' lofty towers,
Like to the shadows of Pyramides,
That with their beauties grac'd the Memphian fields:
The golden statue of their feathered bird
That spreads her wings upon the city walls
Shall not defend it from our battering shot:
The townsmen mask in silk and cloth of gold,
And every house is as a treasury:
The men, the treasure, and the town is ours.   110

    Ther. Your tents of white now pitch'd before the gates,
And gentle flags of amity display'd,
I doubt not but the Governor will yield,

Offering Damascus to Your Majesty.

   Tamb. So shall he have his life and all the rest.
But if he stay until the bloody flag
Be once advanc'd on my vermilion tent,
He dies, and those that kept us out so long.
And when they see me march in black array,
With mournful streamers hanging down their heads,   120
Were in that city all the world contain'd,
Not one should scape, but perish by our swords.

   Zeno. Yet would you have some pity for my sake,
Because it is my country's and my father's.

   Tamb. Not for the world, Zenocrate, if I have sworn.
Come, bring in the Turk.   *Exeunt.*

ACTUS. 4.

SCAENA. 3.

*[Enter] Soldan, Arabia, Capolin, with st[r]eaming colors, and
soldiers.*

   Sold. Methinks we march as Meleager did,
Environed with brave Argolian knights,
To chase the savage Calydonian boar;
Or Cephalus with lusty Theban youths
Against the wolf that angry Themis sent
To waste and spoil the sweet Aonian fields,
A monster of five hundred thousand heads,
Compact of rapine, piracy, and spoil.
The scum of men, the hate and scourge of God,
Raves in Ægyptia and annoyeth us.   10
My lord, it is the bloody Tamburlaine,
A sturdy felon and a base-bred thief,
By murder raised to the Persian crown,
That dares control us in our territories.
To tame the pride of this presumptuous beast,
Join your Arabians with the Soldan's power:
Let us unite our royal bands in one
And hasten to remove Damascus' siege.
It is a blemish to the majesty
And high estate of mighty emperors   20
That such a base usurping vagabond
Should brave a king, or wear a princely crown.

   Arab. Renowned Soldan, have you lately heard
The overthrow of mighty Bajazeth
About the confines of Bithynia?
—The slavery wherewith he persecutes

The noble Turk and his great Emperess?

Sold. I have, and sorrow for his bad success.
But noble lord of great Arabia,
Be so persuaded that the Soldan is   30
No more dismay'd with tidings of his fall
Than in the haven when the pilot stands
And views a stranger's ship rent in the winds
And shivered against a craggy rock.
Yet in compassion of his wretched state,
A sacred vow to heaven and him I make,
Confirming it with Ibis' holy name:
That Tamburlaine shall rue the day, the hour,
Wherein he wrought such ignominious wrong
Unto the hallowed person of a prince,   40
Or kept the fair Zenocrate so long
As concubine, I fear, to feed his lust.

Arab. Let grief and fury hasten on revenge!
Let Tamburlaine for his offenses feel
Such plagues as we and heaven can pour on him!
I long to break my spear upon his crest,
And prove the weight of his victorious arm;
For Fame, I fear, hath been too prodigal
In sounding through the world his partial praise.

Sold. Capolin, hast thou survey'd our powers?   50

Capo. Great Emperors of Egypt and Arabia,
The number of your hosts united is
A hundred and fifty thousand horse,
Two hundred thousand foot—brave men-at-arms,
Courageous and full of hardiness,
As frolic as the hunters in the chase
Of savage beasts amid the desert woods.

Arab. My mind presageth fortunate success.
And Tamburlaine, my spirit doth foresee
The utter ruin of thy men and thee.   60

Sold. Then rear your standards, let your sounding drums
Direct our soldiers to Damascus walls!
Now, Tamburlaine, the mighty Soldan comes
And leads with him the great Arabian King
To dim thy baseness and obscurity,
Famous for nothing but for theft and spoil:
To raze and scatter thy inglorious crew
Of Scythians and slavish Persians.   *Exeunt.*

ACTUS. 4.

SCAENA. [4].

The banquet, and to it cometh Tamburlaine all in scarlet,
Theridamas, Techelles, Usumcasane, the Turk [in his cage,
Zenocrate, Zabina], with others.

Tamb. Now hang our bloody colors by Damascus,
Reflexing hues of blood upon their heads,
While they walk quivering on their city walls,
Half dead for fear before they feel my wrath!
Then let us freely banquet and carouse
Full bowls of wine unto the god of war—
That means to fill your helmets full of gold
And make Damascus spoils as rich to you
As was to Jason Colchos' golden fleece.
—And now, Bajazeth, hast thou any stomach?   10
Baj. Ay, such a stomach, cruel Tamburlaine, as I could will-
ingly feed upon thy blood-raw heart.
Tamb. Nay thine own is easier to come by. Pluck out that
and 'twill serve thee and thy wife—. Well, Zenocrate, Techelles,
and the rest, fall to your victuals.
Baj. Fall to, and never may your meat digest!
Ye furies that can mask invisible,
Dive to the bottom of Avernus' pool
And in your hands bring hellish poison up
And squeeze it in the cup of Tamburlaine!   20
Or winged snakes of Lerna, cast your stings,
And leave your venoms in this tyrant's dish!
Zab. And may this banquet prove as ominous
As Progne's to th' adulterous Thracian king,
That fed upon the substance of his child.
Zeno. My lord, how can you tamely suffer these outrageous
curses by these slaves of yours?
Tamb. To let them see, divine Zenocrate,
I glory in the curses of my foes,
Having the power from the imperial heaven   30
To turn them all upon their proper heads.
Tech. I pray you give them leave, madam. This speech is a
goodly refreshing to them.
Ther. But if His Highness would let them be fed, it would
do them more good.
Tamb. Sirrah, why fall you not to? Are you so daintily
brought up, you cannot eat your own flesh?

Baj. First legions of devils shall tear thee in pieces!

Usum. Villain, know'st thou to whom thou speakest?

Tamb. O, let him alone. Here eat, sir! Take it from　　40
my sword's point, or I'll thrust it to thy heart.

　　　　　　　　　　　　He takes it and stamps upon it.

Ther. He stamps it under his feet, my lord.

Tamb. Take it up, villain, and eat it—or I will make thee
slice the brawns of thy arms into carbonadoes and eat them.

Usum. Nay, 'twere better he kill'd his wife, and then she
shall be sure not to be starv'd, and he be provided for a
month's victual beforehand!

Tamb. Here is my dagger. Despatch her while she is fat,
for if she live but a while longer, she will fall into a consumption with fretting, and then she will not be worth the eating.　50

Ther. Dost thou think that Mahomet will suffer this?

Tech. 'Tis like he will when he cannot let it.

Tamb. Go to, fall to your meat.—What, not a bit? Belike
he hath not been watered today. Give him some drink.

They give him water to drink, and he flings it on the ground.

Tamb. Fast, and welcome, sir, while hunger make you eat.
—How now, Zenocrate, doth not the Turk and his wife make
a goodly show at a banquet?

Zeno. Yes, my lord.

Ther. Methinks, 'tis a great deal better than a consort of
music.

Tamb. Yet music would do well to cheer up Zenocrate. Pray
thee, tell why thou art so sad?—If thou wilt have a song, the
Turk shall strain his voice. But why is it?

Zeno. My lord, to see my father's town besieg'd,
The country wasted where myself was born—
How can it but afflict my very soul?
If any love remain in you, my lord,
Or if my love unto Your Majesty
May merit favor at Your Highness' hands,
Then raise your siege from fair Damascus walls　　70
And with my father take a friendly truce.

Tamb. Zenocrate, were Egypt Jove's own land,
Yet would I with my sword make Jove to stoop!
I will confute those blind geographers
That make a triple region in the world,
Excluding regions which I mean to trace,
And with this pen reduce them to a map,　　[*Points to his*
Calling the provinces, cities, and towns　　*sword.*]
After my name and thine, Zenocrate.

Here at Damascus will I make the point   80
That shall begin the perpendicular.
—And would'st thou have me buy thy father's love
With such a loss? Tell me, Zenocrate.

   Zeno. Honor still wait on happy Tamburlaine!
Yet give me leave to plead for him, my lord.

   Tamb. Content thyself! His person shall be safe
And all the friends of fair Zenocrate,
If with their lives they may be pleas'd to yield
Or may be forc'd to make me Emperor:
For Egypt and Arabia must be mine!   90
—Feed, you slave! Thou may'st think thyself happy to be fed
from my trencher.

   Baj. My empty stomach, full of idle heat,
Draws bloody humors from my feeble parts,
Preserving life by hasting cruel death.
My veins are pale, my sinews hard and dry,
My joints benumb'd. Unless I eat, I die.

   Zab. Eat, Bajazeth! Let us live in spite of them, looking some
happy power will pity and enlarge us.

              [Bajazeth eats ravenously.]

   Tamb. Here, Turk, wilt thou have a clean trencher?   100
   Baj. Ay, tyrant, and more meat.
   Tamb. Soft, sir, you must be dieted: too much eating will
make you surfeit.

   Ther. So it would, my lord, specially having so small a walk
and so little exercise.

           Enter a second course of crowns.

   Tamb. Theridamas, Techelles, and Casane, here are the cates
you desire to finger, are they not?

   Ther. Ay, my lord—but none save kings must feed with these.

   Tech. 'Tis enough for us to see them, and for Tamburlaine
only to enjoy them.   110

   Tamb. Well, here is now to the Soldan of Egypt, the King of
Arabia, and the Governor of Damascus. Now take these three
crowns, and pledge me, my contributory kings. *[Each takes a
crown.]* I crown you here, Theridamas, King of Argier;
Techelles, King of Fez; and Usumcasane, King of Moroccus.
[Each puts his crown on.] How say you to this, Turk? These
are not your contributory kings.

   Baj. Nor shall they long be thine, I warrant them.

   Tamb. Kings of Argier, Moroccus, and of Fez,
You that have march'd with happy Tamburlaine   120

As far as from the frozen place of heaven
Unto the watery morning's ruddy bower,
And thence by land unto the torrid zone—
Deserve these titles I endow you with,
By valor and by magnanimity.
Your births shall be no blemish to your fame,
For virtue is the fount whence honor springs,
And they are worthy she investeth kings.

    Ther. And since Your Highness hath so well vouchsaf'd:
If we deserve them not with higher meeds   130
Than erst our states and actions have retain'd,
Take them away again and make us slaves.

    Tamb. Well said, Theridamas. When holy fates
Shall stablish me in strong Ægyptia,
We mean to travel to th' antarctic pole,
Conquering the people underneath our feet,
And be renown'd as never emperors were.
Zenocrate, I will not crown thee yet,
Until with greater honors I be grac'd.   [*Exeunt*.]

ACTUS. 5.

SCAENA. 1.

[*Enter*] *the Governor of Damasco, with three or four citizens,
and four virgins with branches of laurel in their hands.*

    Gov. Still doth this man, or rather god of war,
Batter our walls and beat our turrets down;
And to resist with longer stubbornness
Or hope of rescue from the Soldan's power
Were but to bring our wilful overthrow,
And make us desperate of our threat'ned lives.
We see his tents have now been altered
With terrors to the last and cruellest hue.
His coal-black colors everywhere advanc'd
Threaten our city with a general spoil.   10
And if we should with common rites of arms
Offer our safeties to his clemency,
I fear the custom proper to his sword,
Which he observes as parcel of his fame—
Intending so to terrify the world—
By any innovation or remorse
Will never be dispens'd with till our deaths.
Therefore, for these our harmless virgins' sakes,

Whose honors and whose lives rely on him,
Let us have hope that their unspotted prayers,   20
Their blubbered cheeks, and hearty, humble moans,
Will melt his fury into some remorse,
And use us like a loving conqueror.
   [1] *Virg.* If humble suits or imprecations
(Uttered with tears of wretchedness and blood
Shed from the heads and hearts of all our sex—
Some made your wives and some your children)
Might have entreated your obdurate breasts
To entertain some care of our securities
Whiles only danger beat upon our walls,   30
These more than dangerous warrants of our death   [*Points to*
Had never been erected as they be,   *black banners.*]
Nor you depend on such weak helps as we.
   Gov. Well, lovely virgins, think our country's care,
Our love of honor, loath to be inthrall'd
To foreign powers and rough imperious yokes,
Would not with too much cowardice or fear
(Before all hope of rescue were denied)
Submit yourselves and us to servitude.
Therefore in that your safeties and our own,   40
Your honors, liberties, and lives were weigh'd
In equal care and balance with our own,
Endure as we the malice of our stars,
The wrath of Tamburlaine, and power of wars—
Or be the means the overweighing heavens
Have kept to qualify these hot extremes,
And bring us pardon in your cheerful looks!
   2 *Virg.* Then here before the majesty of heaven
And holy patrons of Ægyptia,
With knees and hearts submissive we entreat   50
Grace to our words and pity to our looks
That this device may prove propitious,
And through the eyes and ears of Tamburlaine
Convey events of mercy to his heart:
Grant that these signs of victory we yield
May bind the temples of his conquering head
To hide the folded furrows of his brows
And shadow his displeased countenance
With happy looks of ruth and lenity!
Leave us, my lord, and loving countrymen;   60
What simple virgins may persuade, we will.
   Gov. Farewell, sweet virgins, on whose safe return
Depends our city, liberty, and lives.   *Exeunt.*

[*Enter*] *Tamburlaine, Techelles, Theridamas, Usumcasane, with*
others; Tamburlaine all in black and very melancholy.

Tamb. What, are the turtles fray'd out of their nests?
Alas, poor fools, must you be first shall feel
The sworn destruction of Damascus?
They know my custom. Could they not as well
Have sent ye out when first my milk-white flags,
Through which sweet mercy threw her gentle beams,
Reflexing them on your disdainful eyes,   70
As now, when fury and incensed hate
Flings slaughtering terror from my coal-black tents
And tells for truth submission comes too late?

1 *Virg.* Most happy King and Emperor of the Earth,
Image of honor and nobility,
For whom the powers divine have made the world,
And on whose throne the holy graces sit;
In whose sweet person is compris'd the sum
Of nature's skill and heavenly majesty—
Pity our plights! O pity poor Damascus!   80
Pity old age, within whose silver hairs
Honor and reverence evermore have reign'd!
Pity the marriage bed, where many a lord
In prime and glory of his loving joy
Embraceth now with tears of ruth and blood
The jealous body of his fearful wife—
Whose cheeks and hearts so punish'd with conceit
To think thy puissant, never-stayed arm
Will part their bodies and prevent their souls
From heavens of comfort yet their age might bear—   90
Now wax all pale and withered to the death,
As well for grief our ruthless Governor
Hath thus refus'd the mercy of thy hand
(Whose scepter angels kiss and furies dread),
As for their liberties, their loves, or lives!
O then for these, and such as we ourselves,
For us, for infants, and for all our bloods,
That never nourish'd thought against thy rule,
Pity, O pity, sacred Emperor,
The prostrate service of this wretched town,   100
And take in sign thereof this gilded wreath
Whereto each man of rule hath given his hand
And wish'd, as worthy subjects, happy means
To be investers of thy royal brows
Even with the true Egyptian diadem!

Tamb. Virgins, in vain you labor to prevent

That which mine honor swears shall be perform'd.
Behold my sword! What see you at the point?
   [1] *Virg.* Nothing but fear and fatal steel, my lord.
   Tamb. Your fearful minds are thick and misty then: 110
For there sits Death, there sits imperious Death
Keeping his circuit by the slicing edge.
But I am pleas'd you shall not see him there:
He now is seated on my horsemen's spears,
And on their points his fleshless body feeds.
Techelles, straight go charge a few of them
To charge these dames, and show my servant, Death,
Sitting in scarlet on their armed spears.
   Virgins. O pity us!
   Tamb. Away with them, I say, and show them Death!   120
                        They take them away.
I will not spare these proud Egyptians,
Nor change my martial observations
For all the wealth of Gihon's golden waves,
Or for the love of Venus, would she leave
The angry god of arms and lie with me.
They have refus'd the offer of their lives,
And know my customs are as peremptory
As wrathful planets, death, or destiny.

Enter Techelles.

What, have your horsemen shown the virgins Death?
   Tech. They have, my lord, and on Damascus walls   130
Have hoisted up their slaughtered carcasses.
   Tamb. A sight as baneful to their souls, I think,
As are Thessalian drugs or mithridate.
But go, my lords, put the rest to the sword.
                 Exeunt [*all except Tamburlaine*].
Ah, fair Zenocrate, divine Zenocrate!
Fair is too foul an epithet for thee,
That in thy passion for thy country's love
And fear to see thy kingly father's harm
With hair dishevell'd wip'st thy watery cheeks:
And like to Flora in her morning pride,   140
Shaking her silver tresses in the air,
Rain'st on the earth resolved pearl in showers,
And sprinklest sapphires on thy shining face,
Where Beauty, mother to the Muses, sits
And comments volumes with her ivory pen,
Taking instructions from thy flowing eyes—
Eyes when that Ebena steps to heaven,
In silence of thy solemn evening's walk,

Making the mantle of the richest night,
The moon, the planets, and the meteors, light—   150
There angels in their crystal armors fight
A doubtful battle with my tempted thoughts
For Egypt's freedom, and the Soldan's life—
His life that so consumes Zenocrate,
Whose sorrows lay more siege unto my soul,
Than all my army to Damascus walls:
And neither Persians' sovereign, nor the Turk
Troubled my senses with conceit of foil
So much by much as doth Zenocrate . . .
What is beauty, saith my sufferings, then?   160
If all the pens that ever poets held
Had fed the feeling of their masters' thoughts,
And every sweetness that inspir'd their hearts,
Their minds and muses on admired themes:
If all the heavenly quintessence they still
From their immortal flowers of poesy,
Wherein, as in a mirror, we perceive
The highest reaches of a human wit:
If these had made one poem's period,
And all combin'd in beauty's worthiness,   170
Yet should there hover in their restless heads
One thought, one grace, one wonder at the least,
Which into words no virtue can digest!
But how unseemly is it for my sex,
My discipline of arms and chivalry,
My nature, and the terror of my name,
To harbor thoughts effeminate and faint?
—Save only that in beauty's just applause,
With whose instinct the soul of man is touch'd:
And every warrior that is rapt with love   180
Of fame, of valor, and of victory,
Must needs have beauty beat on his conceits.
I thus conceiving and subduing both
That which hath stopp'd the tempest of the gods,
Even from the fiery-spangled veil of heaven
To feel the lowly warmth of shepherds' flames
And march in cottages of strowed reeds,
Shall give the world to note for all my birth
That virtue solely is the sum of glory,
And fashions men with true nobility!   190
—Who's within there?

Enter two or three.

Hath Bajazeth been fed today?

Atten. Ay, my lord.

Tamb. Bring him forth. And let us know if the town be
ransack'd.   [*Exeunt.*]

Enter Techelles, Theridamas, Usumcasane, and others.

Tech. The town is ours, my lord, and fresh supply
Of conquest and of spoil is offered us.

Tamb. That's well, Techelles. What's the news?

Tech. The Soldan and the Arabian king together
March on us with such eager violence   200
As if there were no way but one with us.

Tamb. No more there is not, I warrant thee, Techelles.

They bring in the Turk [in his cage and Zabina].

Ther. We know the victory is ours, my lord,
But let us save the reverend Soldan's life
For fair Zenocrate that so laments his state.

Tamb. That will we chiefly see unto, Theridamas,
For sweet Zenocrate, whose worthiness
Deserves a conquest over every heart.
—And now, my footstool, if I lose the field,
You hope of liberty and restitution?   210
Here let him stay, my masters, from the tents,
Till we have made us ready for the field.
Pray for us, Bajazeth! We are going.   *Exeunt.*

Baj. Go, never to return with victory.
Millions of men encompass thee about
And gore thy body with as many wounds!
Sharp, forked arrows light upon thy horse!
Furies from the black Cocytus lake
Break up the earth and with their firebrands
Enforce thee run upon the baneful pikes!   220
Volleys of shot pierce through thy charmed skin,
And every bullet dipp'd in poisoned drugs!
Or roaring cannons sever all thy joints,
Making thee mount as high as eagles soar!

Zab. Let all the swords and lances in the field
Stick in his breast as in their proper rooms!
At every pore let blood come dropping forth
That ling'ring pains may massacre his heart
And madness send his damned soul to hell!

Baj. Ah, fair Zabina, we may curse his power,   230

The heavens may frown, the earth for anger quake,
But such a star hath influence on his sword
As rules the skies and countermands the gods
More than Cimmerian Styx or destiny!
And then shall we in this detested guise,
With shame, with hunger, and with horror aye
Griping our bowels with retorqued thoughts—
And have no hope to end our ecstasies.
 Zab. Then is there left no Mahomet, no God,
No fiend, no fortune, nor no hope of end   240
To our infamous monstrous slaveries.
Gape earth, and let the fiends infernal view
[A] hell as hopeless and as full of fear
As are the blasted banks of Erebus
Where shaking ghosts with ever-howling groans
Hover about the ugly ferryman
To get a passage to Elysium!
Why should we live? O, wretches, beggars, slaves!
Why live we, Bajazeth, and build up nests
So high within the region of the air   250
By living long in this oppression
That all the world will see and laugh to scorn
The former triumphs of our mightiness
In this obscure infernal servitude?
 Baj. O life, more loathsome to my vexed thoughts
Than noisome parbreak of the Stygian snakes
Which fills the nooks of hell with standing air,
Infecting all the ghosts with cureless griefs!
O dreary engines of my loathed sight
That sees my crown, my honor, and my name   260
Thrust under yoke and thraldom of a thief,
Why feed ye still on day's accursed beams
And sink not quite into my tortur'd soul?
You see my wife, my Queen, and Emperess,
Bought up and propped by the hand of fame,
Queen of fifteen contributory queens,
Now thrown to rooms of black abjection,
Smear'd with blots of basest drudgery,
And villeiness to shame, disdain, and misery!
Accursed Bajazeth!—Whose words of ruth,   270
That would with pity cheer Zabina's heart
And make our souls resolve in ceaseless tears—
Sharp hunger bites upon and gripes the root
From whence the issues of my thoughts do break.
O poor Zabina! O my Queen, my Queen,
Fetch me some water for my burning breast

To cool and comfort me with longer date
That in the shorten'd sequel of my life
I may pour forth my soul into thine arms
With words of love, whose moaning intercourse   280
Hath hitherto been stay'd with wrath and hate
Of our expressless bann'd inflictions!
   Zab. Sweet Bajazeth, I will prolong thy life
As long as any blood or spark of breath
Can quench or cool the torments of my grief.

She goes out.

   Baj. Now, Bajazeth, abridge thy baneful days,
And beat thy brains out of thy conquer'd head!
—Since other means are all forbidden me
That may be ministers of my decay!
O, highest lamp of ever-living Jove,   290
Accursed day, infected with my griefs,
Hide now thy stained face in endless night
And shut the windows of the lightsome heavens!
Let ugly Darkness with her rusty coach,
Engirt with tempests wrapt in pitchy clouds,
Smother the earth with never-fading mists!
And let her horses from their nostrils breathe
Rebellious winds and dreadful thunder-claps
That in this terror Tamburlaine may live,
And my pin'd soul, resolv'd in liquid air,   300
May still excruciate his tormented thoughts!
Then let the stony dart of senseless cold
Pierce through the center of my withered heart
And make a passage for my loathed life!

He brains himself against the cage.

Enter Zabina.

   Zab. What do mine eyes behold? My husband dead?
His skull all riven in twain, his brains dash'd out?
The brains of Bajazeth, my lord and sovereign?
O Bajazeth, my husband and my lord!
O Bajazeth! O Turk! O Emperor!

[She raves.]

Give him his liquor? Not I! Bring milk and fire, and   310
my blood I bring him again. Tear me in pieces. Give me the
sword with a ball of wild-fire upon it. Down with him! Down
with him! Go to my child! Away! Away! Away! Ah, save
that infant, save him, save him! I, even I, speak to her. The
sun was down. Streamers. White. Red. Black. Here, here, here!
Fling the meat in his face! Tamburlaine! Tamburlaine! Let

the soldiers be buried. Hell! Death! Tamburlaine! Hell! Make
ready my coach, my chair, my jewels. I come, I come,
I come!

She runs against the cage and brains herself.

[Enter] Zenocrate with Anippe.

Zeno. Wretched Zenocrate, that livest to see   320
Damascus walls dy'd with Egyptian blood,
Thy father's subjects and thy countrymen!
—The streets strowed with dissevered joints of men
And wounded bodies gasping yet for life!
—But most accurs'd, to see the sun-bright troop
Of heavenly virgins and unspotted maids
(Whose looks might make the angry god of arms
To break his sword and mildly treat of love)
On horsemen's lances to be hoisted up
And guiltlessly endure a cruel death: 330
For every fell and stout Tartarian steed
(That stamped on others with their thund'ring hoofs
When all their riders charg'd their quivering spears)
Began to check the ground and rein themselves,
Gazing upon the beauty of their looks!
Ah, Tamburlaine, wert thou the cause of this
That term'st Zenocrate thy dearest love,
Whose lives were dearer to Zenocrate
Than her own life, or aught save thine own love?
But see another bloody spectacle!   340
Ah, wretched eyes, the enemies of my heart,
How are ye glutted with these grievous objects,
And tell my soul more tales of bleeding ruth!
See, see, Anippe, if they breathe or no.
Anippe. No breath, nor sense, nor motion in them both.
Ah, madam, this their slavery hath enforc'd,
And ruthless cruelty of Tamburlaine.
Zeno. Earth, cast up fountains from thy entrails,
And wet thy cheeks for their untimely deaths!
Shake with their weight in sign of fear and grief!   350
Blush heaven, that gave them honor at their birth
And let them die a death so barbarous!
Those that are proud of fickle empery
And place their chiefest good in earthly pomp,
Behold the Turk and his great Emperess!
Ah, Tamburlaine, my love, sweet Tamburlaine,
That fight'st for scepters and for slippery crowns,
Behold the Turk and his great Emperess!
Thou that in conduct of thy happy stars

Sleep'st every night with conquests on thy brows,   360
And yet would'st shun the wavering turns of war,
In fear and feeling of the like distress,
Behold the Turk and his great Emperess!
Ah, mighty Jove and holy Mahomet,
Pardon my love, O pardon his contempt
Of earthly fortune and respect of pity—
And let not conquest, ruthlessly pursu'd,
Be equally against his life incens'd
In this great Turk and hapless Emperess!
And pardon me that was not mov'd with ruth   370
To see them live so long in misery!
Ah, what may chance to *thee*, Zenocrate?

   Anippe. Madam, content yourself, and be resolv'd
Your love hath Fortune so at his command
That she shall stay and turn her wheel no more
As long as life maintains his mighty arm,
That fights for honor to adorn your head!

                Enter [Philemus,] a Messenger.

   Zeno. What other heavy news now brings Philemus?
   Phil. Madam, your father, and th' Arabian king,
The first affecter of your excellence,   380
Comes now, as Turnus 'gainst Æneas did,
Armed with lance into the Egyptian fields,
Ready for battle 'gainst my lord the King.
   Zeno. Now shame and duty, love and fear presents
A thousand sorrows to my martyred soul.
Whom should I wish the fatal victory
When my poor pleasures are divided thus
And rack'd by duty from my cursed heart?
My father and my first betrothed love
Must fight against my life and present love,   390
Wherein the change I use condemns my faith
And makes my deeds infamous through the world.
But as the gods to end the Trojans' toil
Prevented Turnus of Lavinia
And fatally enrich'd Æneas' love,
So for a final issue to my griefs,
To pacify my country and my love
Must Tamburlaine by their resistless powers
With virtue of a gentle victory
Conclude a league of honor to my hope: 400
Then as the powers divine have preordain'd,
With happy safety of my father's life
Send like defense of fair Arabia.

They sound to the battle. And Tamburlaine enjoys the victory.
After, Arabia enters wounded.

   Arab. What cursed power guides the murdering hands
Of this infamous tyrant's soldiers
That no escape may save their enemies
Nor fortune keep themselves from victory?
Lie down, Arabia, wounded to the death,
And let Zenocrate's fair eyes behold
That, as for her thou bear'st these wretched arms,   410
Even so for her thou diest in these arms,
Leaving thy blood for witness of thy love.
   Zeno. Too dear a witness for such love, my lord.
Behold Zenocrate, the cursed object
Whose fortunes never mastered her griefs!
Behold her wounded in conceit for thee,
As much as thy fair body is for me!
   Arab. Then shall I die with full, contented heart,
Having beheld divine Zenocrate,
Whose sight with joy would take away my life   420
As now it bringeth sweetness to my wound,
If I had not been wounded as I am!
Ah, that the deadly pangs I suffer now
Would lend an hour's license to my tongue
To make discourse of some sweet accidents
Have chanc'd thy merits in this worthless bondage,
And that I might be privy to the state
Of thy deserv'd contentment and thy love.
But making now a virtue of thy sight
To drive all sorrow from my fainting soul,   430
Since death denies me farther cause of joy,
Depriv'd of care, my heart with comfort dies
Since thy desired hand shall close mine eyes.   *[Dies.]*
Enter Tamburlaine leading the Soldan, Techelles, Theridamas,
Usumcasane, with others.
   Tamb. Come, happy father of Zenocrate,
A title higher than thy Soldan's name!
Though my right hand have thus enthralled thee,
Thy princely daughter here shall set thee free.
—She that hath calm'd the fury of my sword,
Which had ere this been bath'd in streams of blood
As vast and deep as Euphrates or Nile.   440
   Zeno. O sight thrice welcome to my joyful soul,
To see the King my father issue safe
From dangerous battle of my conquering love!
   Sold. Well met, my only dear Zenocrate,
Though with the loss of Egypt and my crown.

Tamb. 'Twas I, my lord, that gat the victory,
And therefore grieve not at your overthrow,
Since I shall render all into your hands,
And add more strength to your dominions
Than ever yet confirm'd th' Egyptian crown.   450
The god of war resigns his room to me,
Meaning to make me general of the world:
Jove, viewing me in arms, looks pale and wan,
Fearing my power should pull him from his throne:
Where'er I come the Fatal Sisters sweat,
And grisly Death, by running to and fro
To do their ceaseless homage to my sword:
And here in Afric, where it seldom rains,
Since I arriv'd with my triumphant host,
Have swelling clouds, drawn from wide gasping-wounds,   460
Been oft resolv'd in bloody purple showers,
A meteor that might terrify the earth
And make it quake at every drop it drinks:
Millions of souls sit on the banks of Styx
Waiting the back return of Charon's boat;
Hell and Elysium swarm with ghosts of men,
That I have sent from sundry foughten fields,
To spread my fame through hell and up to heaven.
And see, my lord, a sight of strange import,
Emperors and kings lie breathless at my feet: 470
The Turk and his great Emperess, as it seems,
Left to themselves while we were at the fight,
Have desperately despatch'd their slavish lives:
With them Arabia, too, hath left his life:
All sights of power to grace my victory!
And such are objects fit for Tamburlaine!
—Wherein, as in a mirror, may be seen
His honor, that consists in shedding blood
When men presume to manage arms with him.
    Sold. Mighty hath God and Mahomet made thy hand,   480
Renowned Tamburlaine, to whom all kings
Of force must yield their crowns and emperies!
And I am pleas'd with this my overthrow
If as beseems a person of thy state
Thou hast with honor used Zenocrate.
    Tamb. Her state and person want no pomp, you see.
And for all blot of foul inchastity,
I record heaven, her heavenly self is clear.
Then let me find no further time to grace
Her princely temples with the Persian crown.   490
But here these Kings that on my fortunes wait,

And have been crown'd for proved worthiness,
Even by this hand that shall establish them,
Shall now, adjoining all their hands with mine,
Invest her here the Queen of Persia.
What saith the noble Soldan and Zenocrate?
   Sold. I yield with thanks and protestations
Of endless honor to thee for her love.
   Tamb. Then doubt I not but fair Zenocrate
Will soon consent to satisfy us both.   500
   Zeno. Else should I much forget myself, my lord.
   Ther. Then let us set the crown upon her head,
That long hath ling'red for so high a seat.
   Tech. My hand is ready to perform the deed:
For now her marriage time shall work us rest.
   Usum. And here's the crown, my lord. Help set it on.
   Tamb. Then sit thou down, divine Zenocrate,
And here we crown thee Queen of Persia,
And all the kingdoms and dominions
That late the power of Tamburlaine subdued.   510
                        [She sits and is crowned.]
As Juno, when the giants were suppress'd
That darted mountains at her brother Jove,
So looks my love, shadowing in her brows
Triumphs and trophies for my victories:
Or as Latona's daughter bent to arms,
Adding more courage to my conquering mind.
To gratify the sweet Zenocrate,
Egyptians, Moors, and men of Asia,
From Barbary unto the western Inde,
Shall pay a yearly tribute to thy sire;   520
And from the bounds of Afric to the banks
Of Ganges shall his mighty arm extend.
And now, my lords and loving followers,
That purchas'd kingdoms by your martial deeds,
Cast off your armor, put on scarlet robes,
Mount up your royal places of estate,
Environed with troops of noble men,
And there make laws to rule your provinces.
Hang up your weapons on Alcides' post,
For Tamburlaine takes truce with all the world!   530
Thy first betrothed love, Arabia,
Shall we with honor, as beseems, entomb
With this great Turk and his fair Emperess.
Then after all these solemn exequies,
We will our rites of marriage solemnize.
                        [Exeunt with great pomp.]

[2 TAMBURLAINE]

The second part of the bloody conquests of mighty Tamburlaine. With his impassionate fury for the death of his lady and love, Zenocrate. His form and exhortation of discipline to his three sons. And the manner of his own death.

[*Speaking Characters*

ORCANES
GAZELLUS
URIBASSA
SIGISMUND
FREDERICK
BALDWIN
CALLAPINE
ALMEDA
TAMBURLAINE
ZENOCRATE
CALYPHAS
AMYRAS
CELEBINUS
THERIDAMAS
TECHELLES
USUMCASANE
MESSENGER
PHYSICIAN
KING OF JERUSALEM
KING OF TREBIZON
KING OF SORIA
SOLDIER
CAPTAIN OF BALSERA
OLYMPIA
SON
PIONER
PERDICAS
TURKISH LADY
GOVERNOR OF BABYLON
MAXIMUS
CITIZEN OF BABYLON
ANOTHER CITIZEN OF BABYLON
CAPTAIN
KING OF AMASIA

Mute Characters

SOLDIERS, PHYSICIANS, TURKISH CONCUBINES]

THE PROLOGUE

The general welcomes Tamburlaine receiv'd
When he arrived last upon the stage
Hath made our poet pen his second part,
Where death cuts off the progress of his pomp,
And murd'rous fates throws all his triumphs down.
But what became of fair Zenocrate,
And with how many cities' sacrifice
He celebrated her said funeral,
Himself in presence shall unfold at large.

ACTUS. 1.

SCAENA. 1.

[Enter] Orcanes, King of Natolia, Gazellus, Viceroy of Byron,
    Uribassa, and their train, with drums and trumpets.

Orc. Egregious viceroys of these eastern parts,
Plac'd by the issue of great Bajazeth,
And sacred lord, the mighty Callapine,
Who lives in Egypt, prisoner to that slave
Which kept his father in an iron cage—
Now have we march'd from fair Natolia
Two hundred leagues, and on Danubius banks
Our warlike host, in complete armor, rest,
Where Sigismund, the King of Hungary,

Should meet our person to conclude a truce.   10
What, shall we parle with the Christian?
Or cross the stream and meet him in the field?
    Byr. King of Natolia, let us treat of peace.
We are all glutted with the Christians' blood,
And have a greater foe to fight against—
Proud Tamburlaine, that now in Asia
Near Guyron's head doth set his conquering feet,
And means to fire Turkey as he goes.
'Gainst him, my lord, you must address your power!
    Uri. Besides, King Sigismund hath brought from
        Christendom,   20
More than his camp of stout Hungarians:
Sclavonians, Almains, rutters, [Russ], and Danes,
That with the halberd, lance, and murdering axe
Will hazard that we might with surety hold.
    ⟨*Orc.*⟩ Though from the shortest northern parallel,
Vast Gruntland compass'd with the frozen sea
(Inhabited with tall and sturdy men,
Giants as big as hugy Polypheme),
Millions of soldiers cut the arctic line,
Bringing the strength of Europe to these arms,   30
Our Turkey blades shall glide through all their throats,
And make this champion mead a bloody fen!
Danubius stream, that runs to Trebizon,
Shall carry wrapt within his scarlet waves
As martial presents to our friends at home
The slaughtered bodies of these Christians!
The Terrene Main, wherein Danubius falls,
Shall by this battle be the Bloody Sea!
The wand'ring sailors of proud Italy
Shall meet those Christians fleeting with the tide,   40
Beating in heaps against their argosies,
And make fair Europe, mounted on her bull,
Trapp'd with the wealth and riches of the world,
Alight, and wear a woful mourning weed!
    [*Gaz.*] Yet, stout Orcanes, Prorex of the world,
Since Tamburlaine hath must'red all his men,
Marching from Cairon northward with his camp,
To Alexandria and the frontier towns,
Meaning to make a conquest óf our land,
'Tis requisite to parle for a peace   50
With Sigismund the King of Hungary,
And save our forces for the hot assaults
Proud Tamburlaine intends Natolia.
    Orc. Viceroy of Byron, wisely hast thou said.

My realm, the center of our empery,
Once lost, all Turkey would be overthrown:
And for that cause the Christians shall have peace.
Sclavonians, Almain rutters, [Russ], and Danes
Fear not Orcanes, but great Tamburlaine . . .
Nor he but Fortune that hath made him great . . .   60
We have revolted Grecians, Albanese,
Sicilians, Jews, Arabians, Turks, and Moors,
Natolians, Sorians, black Egyptians,
Illyrians, Thracians, and Bithynians,
Enough to swallow forceless Sigismund,
Yet scarce enough t' encounter Tamburlaine!
He brings a world of people to the field!
From Scythia to the oriental plage
Of India, where raging Lantchidol
Beats on the regions with his boisterous blows,   70
That never seaman yet discovered—
All Asia is in arms with Tamburlaine:
Even from the midst of fiery Cancer's tropic
To Amazonia under Capricorn,
And thence as far as Archipelago—
All Afric is in arms with Tamburlaine.
Therefore, viceroys, the Christians must have peace.

[*Enter*] *Sigismund, Frederick, Baldwin, and their train, with
drums and trumpets.*

     Sig. Orcanes, as our legates promis'd thee,
We with our peers have crossed Danubius stream
To treat of friendly peace or deadly war.   80
Take which thou wilt, for as the Romans us'd,
I here present thee with a naked sword:
Wilt thou have war, then shake this blade at me;
If peace, restore it to my hands again,
And I will sheathe it to confirm the same!   [*Presents sword.*]
     Orc. Stay, Sigismund. Forget'st thou, I am he
That with the cannon shook Vienna walls
And made it dance upon the continent,
As when the massy substance of the earth
Quiver about the axle-tree of heaven?   90
Forget'st thou, that I sent a shower of darts,
Mingled with powdered shot and feathered steel,
So thick upon the blink-ey'd burghers' heads
That thou thyself, then County Palatine,
The King of Boheme, and the Austric Duke,
Sent heralds out which basely on their knees
In all your names desir'd a truce of me?

Forget'st thou, that to have me raise my siege
Wagons of gold were set before my tents,
Stamp'd with the princely fowl that in her wings   100
Carries the fearful thunderbolts of Jove?
How canst thou think of this and offer war?

   Sig. Vienna was besieg'd, and I was there,
Then County Palatine, but now a king—
And what we did was in extremity.
But now, Orcanes, view my royal host
That hides these plains and seems as vast and wide
As doth the desert of Arabia
To those that stand on Bagdeth's lofty tower:
Or as the ocean to the traveller   110
That rests upon the snowy Apennines.
And tell me whether I should stoop so low,
Or treat of peace with the Natolian king?

   [*Gaz.*] Kings of Natolia and of Hungary,
We came from Turkey to confirm a league,
And not to dare each other to the field.
A friendly parle might become ye both.

   Fred. And we from Europe to the same intent,
Which if your General refuse or scorn,
Our tents are pitch'd, our men stand in array,   120
Ready to charge you ere you stir your feet.

   [*Orc.*] So prest are we.—But yet if Sigismund
Speak as a friend, and stand not upon terms,
Here is his sword! Let peace be ratified   [*Takes sword, and*
On these conditions, specified before,   *returns it.*]
Drawn with advice of our ambassadors.

   Sig. Then here I sheathe it, and give thee my hand, [*Sheathes*
Never to draw it out, or manage arms   *sword and*
Against thyself or thy confederates,   *extends hand.*]
But whilst I live will be at truce with thee.   130

   [*Orc.*] But, Sigismund, confirm it with an oath,
And swear in sight of Heaven and by thy Christ.

   Sig. By Him that made the world and sav'd my soul,
The Son of God and issue of a maid,
Sweet Jesus Christ, I solemnly protest
And vow to keep this peace inviolable!

   [*Orc.*] By sacred Mahomet, the friend of God,
Whose holy Alcoran remains with us,
Whose glorious body, when he left the world,
Clos'd in a coffin mounted up the air,   140
And hung on stately Mecca's temple-roof,
I swear to keep this truce inviolable!
—Of whose conditions and our solemn oaths,

Sign'd with our hands, each shall retain a scroll
As memorable witness of our league.
Now, Sigismund, if any Christian king
Encroach upon the confines of thy realm,
Send word Orcanes of Natolia
Confirm'd this league beyond Danubius stream,
And they will trembling sound a quick retreat—   150
So am I fear'd among all nations.
   Sig. If any heathen potentate or king
Invade Natolia, Sigismund will send
A hundred thousand horse train'd to the war,
And back'd by stout lanceres of Germany,
The strength and sinews of the imperial seat.
   [*Orc.*] I thank thee, Sigismund—but when I war,
All Asia Minor, Africa, and Greece
Follow my standard and my thund'ring drums.
Come, let us go and banquet in our tents.   160
I will despatch chief of my army hence
To fair Natolia and to Trebizon
To stay my coming 'gainst proud Tamburlaine.
Friend Sigismund, and peers of Hungary,
Come, banquet and carouse with us a while,
And then depart we to our territories.   *Exeunt.*

ACTUS. 1.

SCAENA. [2].

[Enter] Callapine with Almeda, his keeper.

   Call. Sweet Almeda, pity the ruthful plight
Of Callapine, the son of Bajazeth,
Born to be monarch of the western world,
Yet here detain'd by cruel Tamburlaine.
   Alm. My lord, I pity it, and with all my heart
Wish you release: but he whose wrath is death,
My sovereign lord, renowned Tamburlaine,
Forbids you farther liberty than this.
   Call. Ah, were I now but half so eloquent
To paint in words what I'll perform in deeds,   10
I know thou would'st depart from hence with me.
   Alm. Not for all Afric! Therefore, move me not.
   Call. Yet hear me speak, my gentle Almeda.
   Alm. No speech to that end, by your favor, sir!
   Call. By Cairo runs—.
   Alm. No talk of running, I tell you, sir!
   Call. A little farther, gentle Almeda.

Alm. Well, sir, what of this?

Call. By Cairo runs to Alexandria bay
Darote's streams, wherein at anchor lies   20
A Turkish galley of my royal fleet,
Waiting my coming to the river side,
Hoping by some means I shall be releas'd,
Which when I come aboard will hoist up sail
And soon put forth into the Terrene Sea,
Where 'twixt the isles of Cyprus and of Crete
We quickly may in Turkish seas arrive.
Then shalt thou see a hundred kings and more,
Upon their knees, all bid me welcome home.
Amongst so many crowns of burnish'd gold,   30
Choose which thou wilt, all are at thy command!
A thousand galleys mann'd with Christian slaves
I freely give thee, which shall cut the Straits,
And bring armadoes from the coasts of Spain
Fraughted with gold of rich America!
The Grecian virgins shall attend on thee,
Skilful in music and in amorous lays,
As fair as was Pygmalion's ivory girl,
Or lovely Io metamorphosed!
With naked Negroes shall thy coach be drawn,   40
And as thou rid'st in triumph through the streets,
The pavement underneath thy chariot wheels
With Turkey carpets shall be covered—
And cloth of Arras hung about the walls—
Fit objects for thy princely eye to pierce!
A hundred bassoes cloth'd in crimson silk
Shall ride before thee on Barbarian steeds!
And when thou goest, a golden canopy
Enchas'd with precious stones, which shine as bright
As that fair veil that covers all the world   50
When Phœbus, leaping from his hemisphere,
Descendeth downward to th' Antipodes . . .
And more than this, for all I cannot tell.

Alm. How far hence lies the galley, say you?

Call. Sweet Almeda, scarce half a league from hence.

Alm. But need we not be spied going aboard?

Call. Betwixt the hollow hanging of a hill
And crooked bending of a craggy rock,
The sails wrapt up, the mast and tacklings down,
She lies so close that none can find her out.   60

Alm. I like that well. But tell me, my lord, if I should
let you go, would you be as good as your word? Shall I be
made a king for my labor?

Call. As I am Callapine the Emperor,
And by the hand of Mahomet I swear
Thou shalt be crown'd a king and be my mate!
Alm. Then here I swear, as I am Almeda
Your keeper under Tamburlaine the Great
(For that's the style and title I have yet)
Although he sent a thousand armed men   70
To intercept this haughty enterprise,
Yet would I venture to conduct Your Grace,
And die before I brought you back again!
Call. Thanks, gentle Almeda. Then let us haste,
Lest time be past, and ling'ring let us both.
Alm. When you will, my lord. I am ready.
Call. Even straight. And farewell, cursed Tamburlaine!
Now go I to revenge my father's death!   *Exeunt.*

ACTUS. 1.

SCAENA. [3].

[*Enter*] *Tamburlaine with Zenocrate, and his three sons:
Calyphas, Amyras, and Celebinus, with drums and trumpets.*

Tamb. Now, bright Zenocrate, the world's fair eye,
Whose beams illuminate the lamps of heaven,
Whose cheerful looks do clear the cloudy air
And clothe it in a crystal livery,
Now rest thee here on fair Larissa plains,
Where Egypt and the Turkish empire parts,
Between thy sons that shall be emperors
And every one commander of a world.

[*She sits.*]

Zeno. Sweet Tamburlaine, when wilt thou leave these arms
And save thy sacred person free from scathe   10
And dangerous chances of the wrathful war?
Tamb. When heaven shall cease to move on both the poles,
And when the ground whereon my soldiers march
Shall rise aloft and touch the horned moon—
And not before, my sweet Zenocrate!
Sit up and rest thee like a lovely queen.
So, now she sits in pomp and majesty
When these, my sons, more precious in mine eyes
Than all the wealthy kingdoms I subdued,
Plac'd by her side, look on their mother's face.   20
But yet methinks their looks are amorous,
Not martial as the sons of Tamburlaine:

Water and air, being symboliz'd in one,
Argue their want of courage and of wit:
Their hair as white as milk and soft as down
(Which should be like the quills of porcupines,
As black as jet and hard as iron or steel)
Bewrays they are too dainty for the wars:
Their fingers made to quaver on a lute,
Their arms to hang about a lady's neck,   30
Their legs to dance and caper in the air
Would make me think them bastards not my sons,
But that I know they issued from thy womb
That never look'd on man but Tamburlaine.
    Zeno. My gracious lord, they have their mother's looks;
But when they list their conquering father's heart.
This lovely boy, the youngest of the three,
Not long ago bestrid a Scythian steed,
Trotting the ring, and tilting at a glove,
Which when he tainted with his slender rod,   40
He rein'd him straight and made him so curvet,
As I cried out for fear he should have fall'n!
    Tamb. Well done, my boy! Thou shalt have shield and
        lance,
Armor of proof, horse, helm, and curtle-axe.
And I will teach thee how to charge thy foe
And harmless run among the deadly pikes.
If thou wilt love the wars and follow me,
Thou shalt be made a king and reign with me,
Keeping in iron cages emperors.
If thou exceed thy elder brothers' worth   50
And shine in complete virtue more than they,
Thou shalt be king before them, and thy seed
Shall issue crowned from their mother's womb.
    Cel. Yes, father, you shall see me if I live
Have under me as many kings as you—
And march with such a multitude of men
As all the world shall tremble at their view!
    Tamb. These words assure me, boy, thou art my son!
When I am old and cannot manage arms,
Be *thou* the scourge and terror of the world.   60
    Amy. Why may not I, my lord, as well as he,
Be term'd the scourge and terror of the world?
    Tamb. Be all a scourge and terror to the world.
Or else you are not sons of Tamburlaine!
    Cal. But while my brothers follow arms, my lord,
Let me accompany my gracious mother.

They are enough to conquer all the world,
And you have won enough for me to keep.
   Tamb. Bastardly boy, sprung from some coward's loins,
And not the issue of great Tamburlaine!   70
Of all the provinces I have subdued,
Thou shalt not have a foot unless thou bear
A mind courageous and invincible.
For he shall wear the crown of Persia
Whose head hath deepest scars, whose breast most wounds,
Which being wroth sends lightning from his eyes,
And in the furrows of his frowning brows
Harbors revenge, war, death, and cruelty:
For in a field, whose [superficies]
Is covered with a liquid purple veil   80
And sprinkled with the brains of slaughtered men,
My royal chair of state shall be advanc'd:
And he that means to place himself therein
Must armed wade up to the chin in blood!
   Zeno. My lord, such speeches to our princely sons
Dismays their minds before they come to prove
The wounding troubles angry war affords.
   Cel. No, madam, these are speeches fit for us:
For if his chair were in a sea of blood
I would prepare a ship and sail to it   90
Ere I would lose the title of a king!
   Amy. And I would strive to swim through pools of blood
Or make a bridge of murdered carcasses,
Whose arches should be fram'd with bones of Turks,
Ere I would lose the title of a king!
   Tamb. Well, lovely boys, ye shall be emperors both,
Stretching your conquering arms from east to west.
And, sirrah, if you mean to wear a crown,
When we shall meet the Turkish deputy
And all his viceroys, snatch it from his head,   100
And cleave his pericranium with thy sword.
   Cal. If any man will hold him, I will strike,
And cleave him to the channel with my sword.
   Tamb. Hold him, and cleave him too, or I'll cleave thee—
For we will march against them presently.
Theridamas, Techelles, and Casane
Promis'd to meet me on Larissa plains
With hosts apiece against this Turkish crew:
For I have sworn by sacred Mahomet
To make it parcel of my empery.   110
The trumpets sound. Zenocrate, they come!   [*Trumpets*.]

Enter Theridamas and his train, with drums and trumpets.

Tamb. Welcome, Theridamas, King of Argier.
Ther. My lord, the great and mighty Tamburlaine,
Arch-monarch of the world, I offer here
My crown, myself, and all the power I have
In all affection at thy kingly feet.

[*Kneels and presents crown.*]

Tamb. Thanks, good Theridamas.
Ther. Under my colors march ten thousand Greeks;
And of Argier and Afric's frontier towns
Twice twenty thousand valiant men-at-arms,   120
All which have sworn to sack Natolia;
Five hundred brigandines are under sail,
Meet for your service on the sea, my lord,
That launching from Argier to Tripoli
Will quickly ride before Natolia
And batter down the castles on the shore.
Tamb. Well said, Argier. Receive thy crown again.

Enter Techelles and Usumcasane together.

Tamb. Kings of Moroccus and of Fez, welcome.
Usum. Magnificent and peerless Tamburlaine,
I and my neighbor King of Fez have brought   130
To aid thee in this Turkish expedition
A hundred thousand expert soldiers;
From Azamor to Tunis near the sea
Is Barbary unpeopled for thy sake,
And all the men in armor under me,
Which with my crown I gladly offer thee.

[*Kneels and presents crown.*]

Tamb. Thanks, King of Moroccus, take your crown again.
Tech. And, mighty Tamburlaine, our earthly god,
Whose looks make this inferior world to quake,
I here present thee with the crown of Fez,   140
And with an host of Moors train'd to the war,
Whose coal-black faces make their foes retire
And quake for fear, as if infernal Jove
Meaning to aid thee in these Turkish arms
Should pierce the black circumference of hell
With ugly furies bearing fiery flags
And millions of his strong tormenting spirits.
From strong Tesella unto Biledull
All Barbary is unpeopled for thy sake.

[*Kneels and presents crown.*]

Tamb. Thanks, King of Fez; take here thy crown again. 150
Your presence, loving friends, and fellow kings,
Makes me to surfeit in conceiving joy.
If all the crystal gates of Jove's high court
Were opened wide, and I might enter in
To see the state and majesty of heaven,
It could not more delight me than your sight!
Now will we banquet on these plains awhile,
And after march to Turkey with our camp,
In number more than are the drops that fall
When Boreas rents a thousand swelling clouds.   160
And proud Orcanes of Natolia
With all his viceroys shall be so afraid,
That though the stones, as at Deucalion's flood,
Were turn'd to men, he should be overcome.
Such lavish will I make of Turkish blood
That Jove shall send his winged messenger
To bid me sheath my sword and leave the field:
The sun, unable to sustain the sight,
Shall hide his head in Thetis' watery lap,
And leave his steeds to fair Boötes' charge—   170
For half the world shall perish in this fight!
But now, my friends, let me examine ye.
How have ye spent your absent time from me?

Usum. My lord, our men of Barbary have march'd
Four hundred miles with armor on their backs,
And lain in leaguer fifteen months and more:
For since we left you at the Soldan's court,
We have subdu'd the southern Guallatia,
And all the land unto the coast of Spain;
We kept the narrow Strait of Gibraltar   180
And made Canarea call us kings and lords.
—Yet never did they recreate themselves
Or cease one day from war and hot alarms:
And therefore let them rest awhile, my lord.

Tamb. They shall, Casane, and 'tis time, i' faith.

Tech. And I have march'd along the river Nile
To Machda, where the mighty Christian priest,
Called John the Great, sits in a milk-white robe—
Whose triple mitre I did take by force,
And made him swear obedience to my crown;   190
From thence unto Cazates did I march,
Where Amazonians met me in the field,
With whom, being women, I vouchsaf'd a league,
And with my power did march to Zanzibar,

The western part of Afric, where I view'd
The Ethiopian sea, rivers and lakes,
But neither man nor child in all the land;
Therefore I took my course to Manico,
Where unresisted, I remov'd my camp;
And by the coast of Byather, at last   200
I came to Cubar, where the Negroes dwell,
And conquering that, made haste to Nubia;
There, having sack'd Borno the kingly seat,
I took the king and led him bound in chains
Unto Damasco, where I stay'd before.
  Tamb. Well done, Techelles. What saith Theridamas?
  Ther. I left the confines and the bounds of Afric,
And made a voyage into Europe,
Where by the river Tyras I subdu'd
Stoka, Podolia, and Codemia;   210
Thence cross'd the sea and came to Oblia
And Nigra Silva, where the devils dance,
Which in despite of them I set on fire;
From thence I cross'd the gulf call'd by the name
Mare Majore of th' inhabitants.
—Yet shall my soldiers make no period,
Until Natolia kneel before your feet.
  Tamb. Then will we triumph, banquet, and carouse.
Cooks shall have pensions to provide us cates
And glut us with the dainties of the world.   220
Lachryma Christi and Calabrian wines
Shall common soldiers drink in quaffing bowls,
Ay, liquid gold (when we have conquer'd him)
Mingled with coral and with oriental pearl.
Come, let us banquet and carouse the whiles!   *Exeunt.*

ACTUS. 2.

SCAENA. 1.

[Enter] Sigismund, Frederick, Baldwin, with their train.

  Sig. Now say, my lords of Buda and Bohemia,
What motion is it that inflames your thoughts
And stirs your valors to such sudden arms?
  Fred. Your Majesty remembers, I am sure,
What cruel slaughter of our Christian bloods
These heath'nish Turks and pagans lately made
Betwixt the city Zula and Danubius—
How through the midst of Verna and Bulgaria,
And almost to the very walls of Rome,

They have not long since massacred our camp.   10
It resteth now, then, that Your Majesty
Take all advantages of time and power
And work revenge upon these infidels.
Your Highness knows, for Tamburlaine's repair,
That strikes a terror to all Turkish hearts,
Natolia hath dismiss'd the greatest part
Of all his army pitch'd against our power
Betwixt Cutheia and Orminius mount,
And sent them marching up to Belgasar,
Acantha, Antioch, and Cæsarea   20
To aid the Kings of Soria and Jerusalem.
Now then, my lord, advantage take hereof,
And issue suddenly upon the rest—
That in the fortune of their overthrow
We may discourage all the pagan troop
That dare attempt to war with Christians.
    Sig. But calls not then Your Grace to memory
The league we lately made with King Orcanes,
Confirm'd by oath and articles of peace,
And calling Christ for record of our truths?   30
This should be treachery and violence
Against the grace of our profession.
    Bald. No whit, my lord, for with such infidels,
In whom no faith nor true religion rests,
We are not bound to those accomplishments
The holy laws of Christendom enjoin:
But as the faith, which they profanely plight,
Is not by necessary policy
To be esteem'd assurance for ourselves,
So what we vow to them should not infringe   40
Our liberty of arms or victory.
    Sig. Though I confess the oaths they undertake
Breed little strength to our security,
Yet those infirmities that thus defame
Their faiths, their honors, and their religion
Should not give us presumption to the like.
Our faiths are sound, and must be [consummate]—
Religious, righteous, and inviolate.
    Fred. Assure Your Grace 'tis superstition
To stand so strictly on dispensive faith.   50
And should we lose the opportunity
That God hath given to venge our Christians' death
And scourge their foul blasphemous paganism,
As fell to Saul, to Balaam, and the rest
That would not kill and curse at God's command,

So surely will the vengeance of the Highest
And jealous anger of His fearful arm
Be pour'd with rigor on our sinful heads
If we neglect this offered victory!

    Sig. Then arm, my lords, and issue suddenly,   60
Giving commandment to our general host
With expedition to assail the pagan,
And take the victory our God hath given!   *Exeunt.*

ACTUS. 2.

SCAENA. 2.

[Enter] Orcanes, Gazellus, and Uribassa, with their train.

    Orc. Gazellus, Uribassa, and the rest,
Now will we march from proud Orminius mount
To fair Natolia, where our neighbor kings
Expect our power and our royal presence,
T' encounter with the cruel Tamburlaine,
That nigh Larissa sways a mighty host,
And with the thunder of his martial tools
Makes earthquakes in the hearts of men and heaven.

    Gaz. And now come we to make his sinews shake
With greater power than erst his pride hath felt: 10
An hundred kings by scores will bid him arms,
And hundred thousands subjects to each score,
Which, if a shower of wounding thunderbolts
Should break out of the bowels of the clouds
And fall as thick as hail upon our heads
In partial aid of that proud Scythian,
Yet should our courages and steeled crests
And numbers more than infinite of men
Be able to withstand and conquer him!

    Uri. Methinks I see how glad the Christian King   20
Is made for joy of your admitted truce,
That could not but before be terrified
With unacquainted power of our host.

Enter a Messenger.

    Mess. Arm, dread sovereign and my noble lords!
The treacherous army of the Christians,
Taking advantage of your slender power,
Comes marching on us, and determines straight
To bid us battle for our dearest lives.

    Orc. Traitors! Villains! Damned Christians!
Have I not here the articles of peace,   30

And solemn covenants we have both confirm'd,
He by his Christ, and I by Mahomet?

    Gaz. Hell and confusion light upon their heads
That with such treason seek our overthrow
And cares so little for their prophet, Christ!

    Orc. Can there be such deceit in Christians,
Or treason in the fleshly heart of man
Whose shape is figure of the highest God?
Then if there be a Christ, as Christians say,
But in their deeds deny him for their Christ: 40
If he be son to everliving Jove,
And hath the power of his outstretched arm:
If he be jealous of his name and honor
(As is our holy prophet, Mahomet),
Take here these papers as our sacrifice
And witness of Thy servant's perjury!   [*He tears the papers.*]
Open, thou shining veil of Cynthia,
And make a passage from the empyreal Heaven
That He that sits on high and never sleeps,
Nor in one place is circumscriptible,   50
But everywhere fills every continent
With strange infusion of His sacred vigor,
May in His endless power and purity
Behold and venge this traitor's perjury!
Thou Christ, that art esteem'd omnipotent,
If thou wilt prove thyself a perfect God,
Worthy the worship of all faithful hearts,
Be now reveng'd upon this traitor's soul—
And make the power I have left behind
(Too little to defend our guiltless lives)   60
Sufficient to discomfort and confound
The trustless force of those false Christians.
To arms, my lords! On Christ still let us cry!
If there be Christ, we shall have victory! [*They exeunt, crying
Christ! Christ!*]

    Sound to the battle, and Sigismund comes out wounded.

    Sig. Discomfited is all the Christian host!
And God hath thundered vengeance from on high
For my accurs'd and hateful perjury.
O, just and dreadful punisher of sin,
Let the dishonor of the pains I feel
In this my mortal well-deserved wound   70
End all my penance in my sudden death:
And let this death wherein to sin I die
Conceive a second life in endless mercy!   [*Dies.*]

Enter Orcanes, Gazellus, Uribassa with others.

Orc. Now lie the Christians bathing in their bloods,
And Christ or Mahomet hath been my friend.

Gaz. See here the perjur'd traitor, Hungary,
Bloody and breathless for his villainy.

Orc. Now shall his barbarous body be a prey
To beasts and fowls, and all the winds shall breathe
Through shady leaves of every senseless tree   80
Murmurs and hisses for his heinous sin.
Now scalds his soul in the Tartarean streams
And feeds upon the baneful tree of hell,
That Zoacum, that fruit of bitterness,
That in the midst of fire is ingraff'd,
Yet flourisheth as Flora in her pride,
With apples like the heads of damned fiends.
The devils there, in chains of quenchless flame
Shall lead his soul through Orcus' burning gulf
From pain to pain, whose change shall never end.   90
What say'st thou yet, Gazellus, to his foil
Which we referr'd to justice of his Christ
And to His power, which here appears as full
As rays of Cynthia to the clearest sight?

Gaz. 'Tis but the fortune of the wars, my lord,
Whose power is often prov'd a miracle.

Orc. Yet in my thoughts shall Christ be honored,
Not doing Mahomet an injury,
Whose power had share in this our victory.
And since this miscreant hath disgrac'd his faith,   100
And died a traitor both to heaven and earth,
We will both watch and ward shall keep his trunk
Amidst these plains for fowls to prey upon.
Go, Uribassa, give it straight in charge.

Uri. I will, my lord.   *Exit Uri.*

Orc. And now, Gazellus, let us haste and meet
Our army, and our brother of Jerusalem,
Of Soria, Trebizon, and Amasia.
And happily, with full Natolian bowls
Of Greekish wine, now let us celebrate   110
Our happy conquest and *his* angry fate.   *Exeunt.*

ACTUS. 2.

SCAENA ULTIMA [3].

The arras is drawn, and Zenocrate lies in her bed of state,
Tamburlaine sitting by her: three physicians about her bed
tempering potions. Theridamas, Techelles, Usumcasane, and
the three sons.

    Tamb. Black is the beauty of the brightest day:
The golden ball of heaven's eternal fire,
That danc'd with glory on the silver waves,
Now wants the fuel that inflam'd his beams—
And all with faintness, and for foul disgrace,
He binds his temples with a frowning cloud,
Ready to darken earth with endless night.
Zenocrate, that gave him light and life,
Whose eyes shot fire from their ivory bowers,
And tempered every soul with lively heat,   10
Now by the malice of the angry skies,
Whose jealousy admits no second mate,
Draws in the comfort of her latest breath,
All dazzled with the hellish mists of death.
—Now walk the angels on the walls of heaven,
As sentinels to warn th' immortal souls
To entertain divine Zenocrate.
—Apollo, Cynthia, and the ceaseless lamps
That gently look'd upon this loathsome earth,
Shine downward now no more, but deck the heavens   20
To entertain divine Zenocrate.
—The crystal springs, whose taste illuminates
Refined eyes with an eternal sight,
Like tried silver runs through Paradise
To entertain divine Zenocrate.
—The cherubins and holy seraphins,
That sing and play before the King of Kings,
Use all their voices and their instruments
To entertain divine Zenocrate.
—And in this sweet and curious harmony,   30
The god that tunes this music to our souls
Holds out his hand in highest majesty
To entertain divine Zenocrate.
Then let some holy trance convey my thoughts
Up to the palace of th' imperial Heaven,

That this my life may be as short to me
As are the days of sweet Zenocrate.
—Physicians, will no physic do her good?
   Phys. My lord, Your Majesty shall soon perceive:
And if she pass this fit, the worst is past.   40
    Tamb. Tell me, how fares my fair Zenocrate?
    Zeno. I fare, my lord, as other emperesses,
That, when this frail and transitory flesh
Hath suck'd the measure of that vital air
That feeds the body with his dated health,
Wanes with enforc'd and necessary change.
    Tamb. May never such a change transform my love,
In whose sweet being I repose my life!
—Whose heavenly presence, beautified with health,
Gives light to Phœbus and the fixed stars!   50
Whose absence makes the sun and moon as dark
As when, oppos'd in one diameter,
Their spheres are mounted on the serpent's head,
Or else descended to his winding train!
Live still, my love, and so conserve my life,
Or, dying, be the anchor of my death!
    Zeno. Live still, my lord! O, let my sovereign live!
And sooner let the fiery element
Dissolve and make your kingdom in the sky
Than this base earth should shroud your majesty!   60
—For should I but suspect your death by mine,
The comfort of my future happiness
And hope to meet Your Highness in the heavens,
Turn'd to despair, would break my wretched breast,
And fury would confound my present rest.
But let me die, my love, yet let me die—
With love and patience let your true love die!
Your grief and fury hurts my second life.
Yet let me kiss my lord before I die,
And let me die with kissing of my lord.   70
But since my life is lengthened yet a while,
Let me take leave of these my loving sons,
And of my lords, whose true nobility
Have merited my latest memory.
Sweet sons, farewell! In death resemble me,
And in your lives your father's excellency.
Some music, and my fit will cease, my lord.

                They call music.

Tamb. Proud fury and intolerable fit
That dares torment the body of my love
And scourge the scourge of the immortal God!   80
Now are those spheres where Cupid us'd to sit,
Wounding the world with wonder and with love,
Sadly supplied with pale and ghastly death,
Whose darts do pierce the center of my soul.
Her sacred beauty hath enchanted heaven!
And had she liv'd before the siege of Troy,
Helen, whose beauty summon'd Greece to arms
And drew a thousand ships to Tenedos,
Had not been nam'd in Homer's *Iliads:*
Her name had been in every line he wrote!   90
Or had those wanton poets, for whose birth
Old Rome was proud, but gaz'd a while on her,
Nor Lesbia nor Corinna had been nam'd:
Zenocrate had been the argument
Of every epigram or elegy!

                The music sounds and she dies.

What, is she dead? Techelles, draw thy sword
And wound the earth that it may cleave in twain
And we descend into th' infernal vaults
To hale the Fatal Sisters by the hair
And throw them in the triple moat of hell   100
For taking hence my fair Zenocrate!
Casane and Theridamas, to arms!
Raise cavalieros higher than the clouds,
And with the cannon break the frame of heaven:
Batter the shining palace of the sun
And shiver all the starry firmament—
For amorous Jove hath snatch'd my love from hence,
Meaning to make her stately Queen of Heaven!
What god soever holds thee in his arms,
Giving thee nectar and ambrosia,   110
Behold me here, divine Zenocrate,
Raving, impatient, desperate, and mad,
Breaking my steeled lance, with which I burst
The rusty beams of Janus' temple-doors,
Letting out death and tyrannizing war,
To march with me under this bloody flag!
And if thou pitiest Tamburlaine the Great,
Come down from heaven, and live with me again!

Ther. Ah, good my lord, be patient! She is dead!
And all this raging cannot make her live!   120
If words might serve, our voice hath rent the air:
If tears, our eyes have watered all the earth:
If grief, our murdered hearts have strain'd forth blood.
Nothing prevails, for she is dead, my lord.
   Tamb. "For she is dead!" Thy words do pierce my soul!
Ah, sweet Theridamas, say so no more!
Though she be dead, yet let me think she lives,
And feed my mind that dies for want of her.
Where'er her soul be, thou shalt stay with me,
Embalm'd with cassia, ambergris, and myrrh,   130
Not lapp'd in lead but in a sheet of gold,
And till I die thou shalt not be interr'd.
Then in as rich a tomb as Mausolus
We both will rest and have one epitaph
Writ in as many several languages
As I have conquered kingdoms with my sword.
This cursed town will I consume with fire
Because this place bereft me of my love:
The houses, burnt, will look as if they mourn'd.
And here will I set up her statue,   140
And march about it with my mourning camp,
Drooping and pining for Zenocrate!

The arras is drawn.

ACTUS. 3.

SCAENA. 1.

[*Enter*] *the Kings of Trebizon and Soria, one bringing a*
sword, and another a scepter. Next, Natolia and Jerusalem
with the imperial crown. After, Callapine; and after him, other
lords. Orcanes and Jerusalem crown [*Callapine*], *and the other*
give him the scepter.

   Orc. Callapinus Cyricelibes, otherwise Cybelius, son and
successive heir to the late mighty Emperor, Bajazeth, by the
aid of God and his friend Mahomet, Emperor of Natolia,
Jerusalem, Trebizon, Soria, Amasia, Thracia, Illyria, Carmonia,
and all the hundred and thirty kingdoms late contributory to
his mighty father. Long live Callapinus, Emperor of Turkey!
   Call. Thrice worthy kings of Natolia and the rest,
I will requite your royal gratitudes
With all the benefits my empire yields.

And were the sinews of th' imperial seat   10
So knit and strength'ned as when Bajazeth
My royal lord and father fill'd the throne,
Whose cursed fate hath so dismemb'red it,
Then should you see this thief of Scythia,
This proud, usurping King of Persia,
Do us such honor and supremacy,
Bearing the vengeance of our father's wrongs,
As all the world should blot our dignities
Out of the book of base-born infamies.
And now I doubt not but your royal cares   20
Have so provided for this cursed foe
That, since the heir of mighty Bajazeth
(An emperor so honored for his virtues)
Revives the spirits of true Turkish hearts,
In grievous memory of his father's shame,
We shall not need to nourish any doubt
But that proud Fortune who hath followed long
The martial sword of mighty Tamburlaine
Will now retain her old inconstancy
And raise our honors to as high a pitch   30
In this our strong and fortunate encounter:
For so hath heaven provided my escape
From all the cruelty my soul sustain'd,
By this my friendly keeper's happy means,
That Jove, surcharg'd with pity of our wrongs,
Will pour it down in showers on our heads,
Scourging the pride of cursed Tamburlaine.
    Orc. I have a hundred thousand men in arms;
Some that in conquest of the perjur'd Christian,
Being a handful to a mighty host,   40
Think them in number yet sufficient
To drink the river Nile or Euphrates
And for their power enow to win the world!
    Jer. And I as many from Jerusalem,
Judæa, Gaza, and Scalonian's bounds,
That on Mount Sinai with their ensigns spread
Look like the parti-colored clouds of heaven
That show fair weather to the neighbor morn.
    Treb. And I as many bring from Trebizon,
Chio, Famastro, and Amasia,   50
All bord'ring on the Mare Major sea,
Riso, Sancina, and the bordering towns
That touch the end of famous Euphrates,
Whose courages are kindled with the flames

The cursed Scythian sets on all their towns,
And vow to burn the villain's cruel heart.

Sor. From Soria with seventy thousand strong
Ta'en from Aleppo, Soldino, Tripoli,
And so on to my city of Damasco,
I march to meet and aid my neighbor kings—   60
All which will join against this Tamburlaine,
And bring him captive to Your Highness' feet.

Orc. Our battle then in martial manner pitch'd
According to our ancient use, shall bear
The figure of the semicircled moon—
Whose horns shall sprinkle through the tainted air
The poisoned brains of this proud Scythian.

Call. Well then, my noble lords, for this my friend
That freed me from the bondage of my foe,
I think it requisite and honorable   70
To keep my promise and to make him king—
That is a gentleman, I know, at least.

Alm. That's no matter, sir, for being a king; for
Tamburlaine came up of nothing.

Jer. Your Majesty may choose some 'pointed time
Performing all your promise to the full:
'Tis nought for Your Majesty to give a kingdom.

Call. Then will I shortly keep my promise, Almeda.

Alm. Why, I thank Your Majesty.   *Exeunt.*

ACTUS. 3.

SCAENA. 2.

[*Enter*] *Tamburlaine with Usumcasane, and his three sons;
four bearing the hearse of Zenocrate; and the drums sounding a
doleful march; the town burning.*

Tamb. So burn the turrets of this cursed town!
Flame to the highest region of the air,
And kindle heaps of exhalations,
That being fiery meteors may presage
Death and destruction to th' inhabitants!
Over my zenith hang a blazing star,
That may endure till heaven be dissolv'd,
Fed with the fresh supply of earthly dregs,
Threat'ning a death and famine to this land!
Flying dragons, lightning, fearful thunderclaps,   10
Singe these fair plains, and make them seem as black
As is the island where the furies mask,
Compass'd with Lethe, Styx, and Phlegethon—

Because my dear Zenocrate is dead.

   Cal. This pillar plac'd in memory of her,   [*As each speaks,*
Where in Arabian, Hebrew, Greek, is writ: *he places the*
This town being burnt by Tamburlaine the Great   *property*
Forbids the world to build it up again.   *against a part*

   Amy. And here this mournful streamer shall be plac'd,   *of the*
Wrought with the Persian and Egyptian arms,   *stage.*]   20
To signify she was a princess born
And wife unto the Monarch of the East.

   Cel. And here this table as a register
Of all her virtues and perfections.

   Tamb. And here the picture of Zenocrate,
To show her beauty which the world admir'd—
Sweet picture of divine Zenocrate
That, hanging here, will draw the gods from heaven,
And cause the stars fix'd in the southern arc
(Whose lovely faces never any viewed   30
That have not pass'd the center's latitude)
As pilgrims travel to our hemisphere
Only to gaze upon Zenocrate.
Thou shalt not beautify Larissa plains,
But keep within the circle of mine arms.
At every town and castle I besiege,
Thou shalt be set upon my royal tent:
And when I meet an army in the field,
Those looks will shed such influence in my camp
As if Bellona, goddess of the war,   40
Threw naked swords and sulphur-balls of fire
Upon the heads of all our enemies.
—And now, my lords, advance your spears again!
Sorrow no more, my sweet Casane, now.
Boys, leave to mourn. This town shall ever mourn,
Being burnt to cinders for your mother's death.

   Cal. If I had wept a sea of tears for her,
It would not ease the sorrow I sustain.

   Amy. As is that town, so is my heart consum'd
With grief and sorrow for my mother's death.   50

   Cel. My mother's death hath mortified my mind,
And sorrow stops the passage of my speech.

   Tamb. But now, my boys, leave off and list to me
That mean to teach you rudiments of war.
I'll have you learn to sleep upon the ground;
March in your armor through watery fens;
Sustain the scorching heat and freezing cold,
Hunger and cold, right adjuncts of the war;
And after this to scale a castle wall,

Besiege a fort, to undermine a town,   60
And make whole cities caper in the air;
Then next the way to fortify your men;
In champion grounds, what figure serves you best,
For [which] the quinque-angle form is meet,
Because the corners there may fall more flat
Whereas the fort may fittest be assail'd
And sharpest where th' assault is desperate—
The ditches must be deep, the counterscarps
Narrow and steep, the walls made high and broad,
The bulwarks and the rampiers large and strong,   70
With cavalieros and thick counterforts,
And room within to lodge six thousand men;
It must have privy ditches, countermines,
And secret issuings to defend the ditch;
It must have high argins and covered ways
To keep the bulwark fronts from battery,
And parapets to hide the musketers,
Casemates to place the great artillery
And store of ordinance, that from every flank
May scour the outward curtains of the fort,   80
Dismount the cannon of the adverse part,
Murder the foe, and save the walls from breach.
When this is learn'd for service on the land,
By plain and easy demonstration
I'll teach you how to make the water mount
That you may dry-foot march through lakes and pools,
Deep rivers, havens, creeks, and little seas,
And make a fortress in the raging waves,
Fenc'd with the concave of monstrous rock,
Invincible by nature of the place.   90
When this is done, then are ye soldiers
And worthy sons of Tamburlaine the Great.
   Cal. My lord, but this is dangerous to be done—
We may be slain or wounded ere we learn!
   Tamb. Villain! Art thou the son of Tamburlaine,
And fear'st to die, or with a curtle-axe
To hew thy flesh and make a gaping wound?
Hast thou beheld a peal of ordinance strike
A ring of pikes, mingled with shot and horse,
Whose shatter'd limbs, being toss'd as high as heaven, 100
Hang in the air as thick as sunny motes,
And canst thou, coward, stand in fear of death?
Hast thou not seen my horsemen charge the foe,
Shot through the arms, cut overthwart the hands,
Dyeing their lances with their streaming blood,

And yet at night carouse within my tent,
Filling their empty veins with airy wine,
That being concocted turns to crimson blood,
And wilt thou shun the field for fear of wounds?
View me, thy father, that hath conquered kings,   110
And, with his host march round about the earth,
Quite void of scars, and clear from any wound,
That by the wars lost not a dram of blood,
And see him lance his flesh to teach you all.   *He cuts his arm.*
A wound is nothing, be it ne'er so deep.
Blood is the god of war's rich livery!
Now look I like a soldier, and this wound
As great a grace and majesty to me
As if a chair of gold, enamelled,
Enchas'd with diamonds, sapphires, rubies,   120
And fairest pearl of wealthy India,
Were mounted here under a canopy,
And I sat down cloth'd with the massy robe
That late adorn'd the Afric potentate
Whom I brought bound unto Damascus walls.
Come, boys, and with your fingers search my wound,
And in my blood wash all your hands at once,
While I sit smiling to behold the sight.   [*Each son touches*
Now, my boys, what think ye of a wound?   *the wound.*]
    Cal. I know not what I should think of it; methinks 'tis
        a pitiful sight.   130
    Cel. 'Tis nothing! Give me a wound, father!
    Amy. And me another, my lord!
    Tamb. Come, sirrah, give me your arm.
    Cel. Here, father, cut it bravely, as you did your own.
    Tamb. It shall suffice thou darest abide a wound.
My boy, thou shalt not lose a drop of blood
Before we meet the army of the Turk:
But then run desperate through the thickest throngs,
Dreadless of blows, of bloody wounds, and death;
And let the burning of Larissa walls,   140
My speech of war, and this my wound you see
Teach you, my boys, to bear courageous minds
Fit for the followers of great Tamburlaine!
Usumcasane, now come let us march
Towards Techelles and Theridamas
That we have sent before to fire the towns,
The towers, and cities of these hateful Turks,
—And hunt that coward, faint-heart runaway,
With that accursed traitor, Almeda,
Till fire and sword have found them at a bay.   150

Usum. I long to pierce his bowels with my sword
That hath betrayed my gracious sovereign—
That curs'd and damned traitor, Almeda.

   Tamb. Then let us see if coward Callapine
Dare levy arms against our puissance,
That we may tread upon his captive neck
And treble all his father's slaveries!   *Exeunt.*

ACTUS. 3.

SCAENA. 3.

[Enter] Techelles, Theridamas, and their train.

   Ther. Thus have we march'd northward from Tamburlaine,
Unto the frontier point of Soria;
And this is Balsera, their chiefest hold,
Wherein is all the treasure of the land.

   Tech. Then let us bring our light artillery,
Minions, falc'nets, and sakers to the trench,
Filling the ditches with the walls' wide breach,
And enter in to seize upon the gold.
How say you, soldiers? shall we not?

   Sold. Yes, my lord, yes, come, let's about it.   10

   Ther. But stay awhile, summon a parle, drum.
It may be they will yield it quietly,
Knowing two kings, the friend[s] to Tamburlaine,
Stand at the walls with such a mighty power.

Summon the battle. Captain with his wife and son [above].

   Capt. What require you, my masters?

   Ther. Captain, that thou yield up thy hold to us.

   Capt. To you! Why, do you think me weary of it?

   Tech. Nay, captain, thou art weary of thy life
If thou withstand the friends of Tamburlaine.

   Ther. These pioners of Argier in Africa,   20
Even in the cannon's face, shall raise a hill
Of earth and faggots higher than the fort,
And over thy argins and covered ways
Shall play upon the bulwarks of thy hold
Volleys of ordinance, till the breach be made
That with his ruin fills up all the trench:
And when we enter in, not heaven itself
Shall ransom thee, thy wife, and family!

   Tech. Captain, these Moors shall cut the leaden pipes
That bring fresh water to thy men and thee,   30
And lie in trench before thy castle walls

That no supply of victual shall come in,
Nor issue forth but they shall die:
And, therefore, captain, yield it quietly.
   Capt. Were you, that are the friends of Tamburlaine,
Brothers of holy Mahomet himself,
I would not yield it. Therefore do your worst!
Raise mounts, batter, intrench, and undermine,
Cut off the water, all convoys that can,
Yet I am resolute, and so farewell.   [*Exeunt above.*]   40
   Ther. Pioners, away, and where I stuck the stake,
Intrench with those dimensions I prescribed.
Cast up the earth towards the castle wall,
Which, till it may defend you, labor low,
And few or none shall perish by their shot.
   Pio. We will, my lord.   *Exeunt*
   Tech. A hundred horse shall scout about the plains
To spy what force comes to relieve the hold.
Both we, Theridamas, will entrench our men,
And with the Jacob's staff measure the height   50
And distance of the castle from the trench
That we may know if our artillery
Will carry full point-blank unto their walls.
   Ther. Then see the bringing of our ordinance
Along the trench into the battery,
Where we will have [gabions] of six feet broad
To save our cannoneers from musket shot:
Betwixt which shall our ordinance thunder forth,
And with the breach's fall, smoke, fire, and dust,
The crack, the echo, and the soldier's cry,   60
Make deaf the air and dim the crystal sky.
   Tech. Trumpets and drums, alarum presently!
And, soldiers, play the men, the holds is yours!   [*Exeunt.*]

[*Alarms.*] Enter [*below*] the Captain, with his wife [*Olympia*]
and son.

   Olymp. Come, good my lord, and let us haste from hence
Along the cave that leads beyond the foe:
No hope is left to save this conquered hold.
   Capt. A deadly bullet gliding through my side
Lies heavy on my heart. I cannot live.
I feel my liver pierc'd, and all my veins,
That there begin and nourish every part,   70
Mangled and torn, and all my entrails bath'd
In blood that straineth from their orifex.
Farewell, sweet wife! sweet son, farewell! I die.   [*Dies.*]
   Olymp. Death, whither art thou gone that both we live?

Come back again, sweet Death, and strike us both!
One minute end our days! And one sepulcher
Contain our bodies! Death, why com'st thou not?
Well, this must be the messenger for thee:
Now, ugly Death, stretch out thy sable wings,
And carry both our souls where his remains.   80
Tell me, sweet boy, art thou content to die?
These barbarous Scythians, full of cruelty,
And Moors, in whom was never pity found,
Will hew us piecemeal, put us to the wheel,
Or else invent some torture worse than that;
Therefore die by thy loving mother's hand,
Who gently now will lance thy ivory throat,
And quickly rid thee both of pain and life.
    Son. Mother, despatch me, or I'll kill myself;
For think you I can live and see him dead?   90
Give me your knife, good mother, or strike home:
The Scythians shall not tyrannize on me:
Sweet mother, strike, that I may meet my father.

She stabs him.

    Olymp. Ah, sacred Mahomet, if this be sin,
Entreat a pardon of the God of Heaven,
And purge my soul before it come to thee.
[*She pushes bodies into open trap. Smoke rises.*]

Enter Theridamas, Techelles, and all their train.

    Ther. How now, madam, what are you doing?
    Olymp. Killing myself, as I have done my son,
Whose body, with his father's, I have burnt,
Lest cruel Scythians should dismember him.   100
    Tech. 'Twas bravely done and like a soldier's wife!
Thou shalt with us to Tamburlaine the Great,
Who, when he hears how resolute thou wert,
Will match thee with a viceroy or a king.
    Olymp. My lord deceas'd was dearer unto me
Than any viceroy, king, or emperor—
And for his sake here will I end my days.
    Ther. But, lady, go with us to Tamburlaine,
And thou shalt see a man greater than Mahomet,
In whose high looks is much more majesty   110
Than from the concave superficies
Of Jove's vast palace, the empyreal orb,
Unto the shining bower where Cynthia sits,
Like lovely Thetis, in a crystal robe;
That treadeth fortune underneath his feet,

And makes the mighty god of arms his slave;
On whom Death and the Fatal Sisters wait
With naked swords and scarlet liveries;
Before whom, mounted on a lion's back,
Rhamnusia bears a helmet full of blood   120
And strews the way with brains of slaughtered men;
By whose proud side the ugly furies run,
Hearkening when he shall bid them plague the world;
Over whose zenith, cloth'd in windy air,
And eagle's wings join'd to her feathered breast,
Fame hovereth, sounding of her golden trump—
That to the adverse poles of that straight line,
Which measureth the glorious frame of heaven,
The name of mighty Tamburlaine is spread!
And him, fair lady, shall thy eyes behold.   130
Come!

   Olymp. Take pity of a lady's ruthful tears,
That humbly craves upon her knees to stay
And cast her body in the burning flame
That feeds upon her son's and husband's flesh.

   Tech. Madam, sooner shall fire consume us both
Than scorch a face so beautiful as this,
In frame of which nature hath showed more skill
Than when she gave eternal chaos form,
Drawing from it the shining lamps of heaven.   140

   Ther. Madam, I am so far in love with you
That you must go with us—no remedy.

   Olymp. Then carry me, I care not, where you will,
And let the end of this my fatal journey
Be likewise end to my accursed life.

   Tech. No, madam, but the beginning of your joy.
Come willingly therefore.

   Ther. Soldiers, now let us meet the General,
Who by this time is at Natolia,
Ready to charge the army of the Turk.   150
The gold and silver and the pearl ye got,
Rifling this fort, divide in equal shares:
This lady shall have twice so much again
Out of the coffers of our treasury.   *Exeunt*

ACTUS. 3.

SCAENA. 4.

[*Enter*] *Callapine, Orcanes, Jerusalem, Trebizon, Soria, Almeda,
with their train* [*and Messenger*].

  Mess. Renowned emperor, mighty Callapine,
God's great lieutenant over all the world,
Here at Aleppo, with an host of men,
Lies Tamburlaine, this King of Persia,
In number more than are the quivering leaves
Of Ida's forest, where Your Highness' hounds
With open cry pursues the wounded stag—
Who means to girt Natolia's walls with siege,
Fire the town, and overrun the land.
  Call. My royal army is as great as his,   10
That, from the bounds of Phrygia to the sea
Which washeth Cyprus with his brinish waves,
Covers the hills, the valleys, and the plains.
Viceroys and peers of Turkey, play the men—
Whet all your swords to mangle Tamburlaine,
His sons, his captains, and his followers!
By Mahomet, not one of them shall live!
The field wherein this battle shall be fought
For ever term the Persian's sepulcher,
In memory of this our victory!   20
  Orc. Now, he that calls himself the Scourge of Jove,
The Emperor of the World, and Earthly God
Shall end the warlike progress he intends
And travel headlong to the lake of hell
Where legions of devils, knowing he must die
Here in Natolia by Your Highness' hands,
All brandishing their brands of quenchless fire,
Stretching their monstrous paws, grin with their teeth
And guard the gates to entertain his soul!
  Call. Tell me, viceroys, the number of your men,   30
And what our army royal is esteem'd.
  Jer. From Palestina and Jerusalem,
Of Hebrews threescore thousand fighting men
Are come since last we showed Your Majesty.
  Orc. So from Arabia Desert, and the bounds
Of that sweet land whose brave metropolis
Re-edified the fair Semiramis,
Came forty thousand warlike foot and horse
Since last we numb'red to Your Majesty.

Treb. From Trebizon in Asia the Less,   40
Naturalized Turks and stout Bithynians
Came to my bands full fifty thousand more
That, fighting, knows not what retreat doth mean,
Nor e'er return but with the victory,
Since last we numb'red to Your Majesty.

Sor. Of Sorians from Halla is repair'd,
And neighbor cities of Your Highness' land,
Ten thousand horse and thirty thousand foot
Since last we numb'red to Your Majesty—
So that the royal army is esteem'd   50
Six hundred thousand valiant fighting men.

Call. Then welcome, Tamburlaine, unto thy death.
Come, puissant viceroys, let us to the field,
The Persians' sepulcher, and sacrifice
Mountains of breathless men to Mahomet,
Who now with Jove opens the firmament
To see the slaughter of our enemies.

[Enter] Tamburlaine with his three sons, Usumcasane with
other.

Tamb. How now, Casane? See a knot of kings,
Sitting as if they were a-telling riddles.

Usum. My lord, your presence makes them pale and wan. 60
Poor souls, they look as if their death were near . . .

Tamb. And so he is, Casane. I am here.
But yet I'll save their lives, and make them slaves.
Ye petty kings of Turkey, I am come,
As Hector did into the Grecian camp,
To overdare the pride of Græcia
And set his warlike person to the view
Of fierce Achilles, rival of his fame.
I do you honor in the simile:
For if I should, as Hector did Achilles   70
(The worthiest knight that ever brandish'd sword)
Challenge in combat any of you all,
I see how fearfully ye would refuse
And fly my glove as from a scorpion!

Orc. Now thou art fearful of thy army's strength,
Thou would'st with overmatch of person fight.
But, shepherd's issue, base-born Tamburlaine,
Think of thy end! This sword shall lance thy throat!

Tamb. Villain! the shepherd's issue (at whose birth
Heaven did afford a gracious aspect   80
And join'd those stars that shall be opposite
Even till the dissolution of the world,

And never meant to make a conqueror
So famous as is mighty Tamburlaine)
Shall so torment thee and that Callapine—
That like a roguish runaway suborn'd
That villain there, that slave, that Turkish dog,
To false his service to his sovereign—
As ye shall curse the birth of Tamburlaine!

  Call. Rail not, proud Scythian! I shall now revenge   90
My father's vile abuses, and mine own.

  Jer. By Mahomet, he shall be tied in chains,
Rowing with Christians in a brigandine
About the Grecian isles to rob and spoil,
And turn him to his ancient trade again!
Methinks the slave should make a lusty thief!

  Call. Nay, when the battle ends, all we will meet,
And sit in council to invent some pain
That most may vex his body and his soul.

  Tamb. Sirrah Callapine, I'll hang a clog about your   100
neck for running away again! You shall not trouble me thus to
come and fetch you.
But as for you, viceroy, you shall have bits,
And harness'd like my horses draw my coach:
And when ye stay, be lash'd with whips of wire:
I'll have you learn to feed on provender
And in a stable lie upon the planks.

  Orc. But, Tamburlaine, first thou shalt kneel to us
And humbly crave a pardon for thy life!

  Treb. The common soldiers of our mighty host   110
Shall bring thee bound unto the General's tent.

  Sor. And all have jointly sworn thy cruel death,
Or bind thee in eternal torments' wrath.

  Tamb. Well, sirs, diet yourselves, you know I shall have
occasion shortly to journey you.

  Cel. See, father, how
Almeda the jailor looks upon us.

  Tamb. Villain! Traitor! Damned fugitive!
I'll make thee wish the earth had swallowed thee!
See'st thou not death within my wrathful looks?   120
Go, villain, cast thee headlong from a rock,
Or rip thy bowels and rend out thy heart
T' appease my wrath, or else I'll torture thee,
Searing thy hateful flesh with burning irons
And drops of scalding lead, while all thy joints
Be rack'd and beat asunder with the wheel:
For if thou liv'st, not any element

Shall shroud thee from the wrath of Tamberlaine.

Call. Well, in despite of thee he shall be king.

Come, Almeda, receive this crown of me.   130
I here invest thee King of Ariadan
Bordering on Mare Roso, near to Mecca.   [*Tenders him*

    Orc. What! Take it, man.   *a crown.*]

    Alm. Good my lord, let me take it.

    Call. Dost thou ask him leave? Here, take it.

    Tamb. Go to, sirrah, take your crown, and make up the
half dozen. So, sirrah, now you are a king, you must give
arms.

    Orc. So he shall, and wear thy head in his scutcheon.

    Tamb. No, let him hang a bunch of keys on his standard   140
to put him in remembrance he was a jailor—that when I
take him, I may knock out his brains with them, and lock
you in the stable when you shall come sweating from my
chariot!

    Treb. Away, let us to the field that the villain may be
slain!

    Tamb. Sirrah, prepare whips and bring my chariot to my
tent, for as soon as the battle is done I'll ride in triumph
through the camp.

    Enter Theridamas, Techelles, and their train.

How now, ye petty kings! Lo, here are bugs   150
Will make the hair stand upright on your heads
And cast your crowns in slavery at their feet!
Welcome, Theridamas and Techelles, both!
See ye this rout, and know ye this same king?

    Ther. Ay, my lord, he was Callapine's keeper.

    Tamb. Well, now ye see he is a king. Look to him,
Theridamas, when we are fighting, lest he hide his crown as the
foolish King of Persia did.

    Sor. No, Tamberlaine, he shall not be put to that exigent, I
warrant thee.   160

    Tamb. You know not, sir!
But now, my followers and my loving friends,
Fight as you ever did, like conquerors.
The glory of this happy day is yours.
My stern aspect shall make fair victory
Hovering betwixt our armies light on me,
Loaden with laurel wreaths to crown us all.

    Tech. I smile to think how, when this field is fought
And rich Natolia ours, our men shall sweat
With carrying pearl and treasure on their backs   170

Tamb. You shall be princes all, immediately.
Come, fight ye Turks, or yield us victory!
    Orc. No, we will meet thee, slavish Tamburlaine!

                                  Exeunt.

ACTUS. 4.

SCAENA. 1.

*Alarm. Amyras and Celebinus issues from the tent where
Calyphas sits asleep.*

[*Amy.*] Now in their glories shine the golden crowns
Of these proud Turks, much like so many suns
That half dismay the majesty of heaven.
Now, brother, follow we our father's sword
That flies with fury swifter than our thoughts
And cuts down armies with his conquering's wings.
    Cel. Call forth our lazy brother from the tent,
For if my father miss him in the field,
Wrath kindled in the furnace of his breast
Will send a deadly lightning to his heart.   10
    Amy. Brother, ho! What, given so much to sleep
You cannot leave it when our enemies' drums
And rattling cannons thunder in our ears
Our proper ruin and our father's foil?
    Cal. Away, ye fools, my father needs not me.
—Nor you, in faith, but that you will be thought
More childish-valorous than manly-wise.
If half our camp should sit and sleep with me,
My father were enough to scare the foe.
You do dishonor to his majesty   20
To think our helps will do him any good.
    Amy. What, dar'st thou then be absent from the field,
Knowing my father hates thy cowardice,
And oft hath warn'd thee to be still in field
(When he himself amidst the thickest troops
Beats down our foes) to flesh our taintless swords?
    Cal. I know, sir, what it is to kill a man.
It works remorse of conscience in me.
I take no pleasure to be murderous,
Nor care for blood when wine will quench my thirst.   30
    Cel. O cowardly boy! Fie! For shame, come forth!
Thou dost dishonor manhood and thy house.
    Cal. Go, go, tall stripling, fight you for us both,

And take my other toward brother here,
For person like to prove a second Mars.
'Twill please my mind as well to hear both you
Have won a heap of honor in the field
And left your slender carcasses behind
As if I lay with you for company!

Amy. You will not go then? 40

Cal. You say true.

Amy. Were all the lofty mounts of Zona Mundi
That fill the midst of farthest Tartary
Turn'd into pearl and proffered for my stay,
I would not bide the fury of my father,
When, made a victor in these haughty arms,
He comes and finds his sons have had no shares
In all the honors he propos'd for us.

Cal. Take you the honor, I will take my ease.
My wisdom shall excuse my cowardice. 50
—*I* go into the field before I need?

Alarm, and Amyras and Celebinus run in.

The bullets fly at random where they list.
And should I go and kill a thousand men
I were as soon rewarded with a shot,
And sooner far than he that never fights;
And should I go and do nor harm nor good,
I might have harm which all the good I have,
Join'd with my father's crown, would never cure.
I'll to cards. Perdicas!

[Enter Perdicas.]

Perd. Here, my lord. 60

Cal. Come, thou and I will go to cards to drive away the time.

Perd. Content, my lord, but what shall we play for?

Cal. Who shall kiss the fairest of the Turks' concubines first when my father hath conquered them.

Perd. Agreed, i' faith. *They play.*

Cal. They say I am a coward, Perdicas, and I fear as little their taratantaras, their swords, or their cannons as I do a naked lady in a net of gold, and, for fear I should be afraid, would put it off and come to bed with me. 70

Perd. Such a fear, my lord, would never make ye retire.

Cal. I would my father would let me be put in the front of such a battle once to try my valor. *Alarm.*
What a coil they keep! I believe there will be some hurt done anon amongst them.

Enter Tamburlaine, Theridamas, Techelles, Usumcasane,
Amyras, Celebinus, leading the Turkish Kings.

Tamb. See now, ye slaves, my children stoops your pride,
And leads your bodies sheeplike to the sword.
Bring them, my boys, and tell me if the wars
Be not a life that may illustrate gods,
And tickle not your spirits with desire   80
Still to be train'd in arms and chivalry?

Amy. Shall we let go these kings again, my lord,
To gather greater numbers 'gainst our power,
That they may say it is not chance doth this
But matchless strength and magnanimity?

Tamb. No, no, Amyras tempt not fortune so:
Cherish thy valor still with fresh supplies,
And glut it not with stale and daunted foes.
But where's this coward villain, not my son,
But traitor to my name and majesty?   90

                    He goes in and brings [Calyphas] out.

Image of sloth and picture of a slave!
The obloquy and scorn of my renown!
How may my heart, thus fired with mine eyes,
Wounded with shame and kill'd with discontent,
Shroud any thought may hold my striving hands
From martial justice on thy wretched soul?

Ther. Yet pardon him, I pray Your Majesty!

Tech. and Usum. Let all of us entreat Your Highness'
          pardon!   [*They kneel.*]

Tamb. Stand up, ye base, unworthy soldiers!
Know ye not yet the argument of arms?   100

Amy. Good my lord, let him be forgiven for once,
And we will force him to the field hereafter.   [*Sons kneel.*]

Tamb. Stand up, my boys, and I will teach ye arms,
And what the jealousy of wars must do.
O Samarcanda, where I breathed first
And joy'd the fire of this martial flesh,
Blush, blush, fair city, at thine honor's foil!
And shame of nature, which Jaertis stream
Embracing thee with deepest of his love
Can never wash from thy distained brows!   110
Here, Jove, receive his fainting soul again—
A form not meet to give that subject essence
Whose matter is the flesh of Tamburlaine!
—Wherein an incorporeal spirit moves,
Made of the mold whereof thyself consists,
Which makes me valiant, proud, ambitious,

Ready to levy power against thy throne,
That I might move the turning spheres of heaven:
For earth and all this airy region
Cannot contain the state of Tamburlaine.   120
By Mahomet, thy mighty friend, I swear,
In sending to my issue such a soul,
Created of the massy dregs of earth,
The scum and tartar of the elements,
Wherein was neither courage, strength, or wit,
But folly, sloth, and damned idleness,
Thou hast procur'd a greater enemy
Than he that darted mountains at thy head,
Shaking the burden mighty Atlas bears;
Whereat thou trembling hid'st thee in the air,   130
Cloth'd with a pitchy cloud for being seen.
And now, ye cank'red curs of Asia,
That will not see the strength of Tamburlaine
Although it shine as brightly as the sun,
Now you shall feel the strength of Tamburlaine,
And by the state of his supremacy   [*Stabs Calyphas.*]
Approve the difference 'twixt himself and you!
    Orc. Thou show'st the difference 'twixt ourselves and thee,
In this thy barbarous damned tyranny.
    Jer. Thy victories are grown so violent   140
That shortly heaven fill'd with the meteors
Of blood and fire thy tyrannies have made
Will pour down blood and fire on thy head,
Whose scalding drops will pierce thy seething brains
And with our bloods revenge our bloods on thee!
    Tamb. Villains, these terrors and these tyrannies
(If tyrannies war's justice ye repute)
I execute, enjoin'd me from above
To scourge the pride of such as heaven abhors.
Nor am I made arch-monarch of the world,   150
Crown'd and invested by the hand of Jove
For deeds of bounty or nobility:
But since I exercise a greater name,
The Scourge of God, and Terror of the World,
I must apply myself to fit those terms,
In war, in blood, in death, in cruelty,
And plague such peasants as resisting me,
The power of heaven's eternal majesty.
Theridamas, Techelles, and Casane,
Ransack the tents and the pavilions   160
Of these proud Turks, and take their concubines,
Making them bury this effeminate brat,

For not a common soldier shall defile
His manly fingers with so faint a boy.
Then bring those Turkish harlots to my tent,
And I'll dispose them as it likes me best.
Meanwhile, take him in.

   Sold. We will, my lord.

                       [Exeunt with Calyphas' body.]

   Jer. O damned monster! Nay, a fiend of hell,
Whose cruelties are not so harsh as thine   170
Nor yet impos'd with such a bitter hate!

   Orc. Revenge it, Rhadamanth and Æacus,
And let your hates extended in his pains
Expel the hate wherewith he pains our souls!

   Treb. May never day give virtue to his eyes
Whose sight compos'd of fury and of fire
Doth send such stern affections to his heart!

   Sor. May never spirit, vein, or artier, feed
The cursed substance of that cruel heart!
But, wanting moisture and remorseful blood,   180
Dry up with anger and consume with heat!

   Tamb. Well, bark, ye dogs! I'll bridle all your tongues,
And bind them close with bits of burnish'd steel
Down to the channels of your hateful throats;
And, with the pains my rigor shall inflict,
I'll make ye roar, that earth may echo forth
The far-resounding torments ye sustain—
As when an herd of lusty Cymbrian bulls
Run mourning round about the females' miss
And stung with fury of their following   190
Fill all the air with troublous bellowing!
I will with engines never exercis'd
Conquer, sack, and utterly consume
Your cities and your golden palaces;
And with the flames that beat against the clouds,
Incense the heavens and make the stars to melt,
As if they were the tears of Mahomet,
For hot consumption of his country's pride.
And till by vision or by speech I hear
Immortal Jove say "Cease, my Tamburlaine!"   200
I will persist a terror to the world,
Making the meteors that like armed men
Are seen to march upon the towers of heaven
Run tilting round about the firmament
And break their burning lances in the air
For honor of my wondrous victories!
Come, bring them in to our pavilion.   *Exeunt.*

ACTUS. 4.

SCAENA. [2].

Olympia alone.

[*Olymp.*] Distress'd Olympia, whose weeping eyes
Since thy arrival here behold no sun,
But clos'd within the compass of a tent
Hath stain'd thy cheeks and made thee look like death,
Devise some means to rid thee of thy life
Rather than yield to his detested suit
Whose drift is only to dishonor thee:
And since this earth, dew'd with thy brinish tears,
Affords no herbs whose taste may poison thee,
Nor yet this air, beat often with thy sighs,   10
Contagious smells and vapors to infect thee,
Nor thy close cave a sword to murder thee,
Let this invention be the instrument.

Enter Theridamas.

Ther. Well met, Olympia. I sought thee in my tent,
But when I saw the place obscure and dark
Which with thy beauty thou was't wont to light,
Enrag'd, I ran about the fields for thee,
Supposing amorous Jove had sent his son,
The winged Hermes, to convey thee hence!
But now I find thee, and that fear is past.   20
Tell me, Olympia, wilt thou grant my suit?
   Olymp. My lord and husband's death, with my sweet son's
(With whom I buried all affections
Save grief and sorrow, which torment my heart)
Forbids my mind to entertain a thought
That tends to love, but meditate on death,
A fitter subject for a pensive soul.
   Ther. Olympia, pity him, in whom thy looks
Have greater operation and more force
Than Cynthia's in the watery wilderness,   30
For with thy view my joys are at the full,
And ebb again as thou departest from me.
   Olymp. Ah, pity me, my lord, and draw your sword,
Making a passage for my troubled soul,
Which beats against this prison to get out
And meet my husband and my loving son!
   Ther. Nothing but still thy husband and thy son!
Leave this, my love, and listen more to me.

Thou shalt be stately Queen of fair Argier:
And cloth'd in costly cloth of massy gold,   40
Upon the marble turrets of my court
Sit like to Venus in her chair of state,
Commanding all thy princely eye desires;
And I will cast off arms to sit with thee,
Spending my life in sweet discourse of love.
    Olymp. No such discourse is pleasant in mine ears,
But that where every period ends with death,
And every line begins with death again.
I cannot love, to be an emperess.
    Ther. Nay, lady, then, if nothing will prevail,   50
I'll use some other means to make you yield:
Such is the sudden fury of my love,
I must and will be pleas'd, and you shall yield!
Come to the tent again.
    Olymp. Stay, good my lord: and will you save my honor,
I'll give Your Grace a present of such price
As all the world cannot afford the like.
    Ther. What is it?
    Olymp. An ointment which a cunning alchemist
Distilled from the purest balsamum   60
And simplest extracts of all minerals,
In which the essential form of marble stone,
Tempered by science metaphysical
And spells of magic from the mouths of spirits,
With which if you but 'noint your tender skin,
Nor pistol, sword, nor lance can pierce your flesh.
    Ther. Why, madam, think you to mock me thus palpably?
    Olymp. To prove it, I will 'noint my naked throat,
Which, when you stab, look on your weapon's point,
And you shall see't rebated with the blow.   70
    Ther. Why gave you not your husband some of it
If you loved him and it so precious?
    Olymp. My purpose was, my lord, to spend it so,
But was prevented by his sudden end
And for a present easy proof thereof,
That I dissemble not, try it on me.
    Ther. I will, Olympia, and will keep it for
The richest present of this eastern world.

                    She anoints her throat.

    Olymp. Now stab, my lord, and mark your weapon's point,
That will be blunted if the blow be great.   80
    Ther. Here then, Olympia.   [*Stabs her. She dies.*]
What, have I slain her? Villain, stab thyself!

Cut off this arm that murdered thy love,
In whom the learned rabbis of this age
Might find as many wondrous miracles
As in the theoria of the world!
Now hell is fairer than Elysium!
A greater lamp than that bright eye of heaven,
From whence the stars do borrow all their light,
Wanders about the black circumference: 90
And now the damned souls are free from pain,
For every fury gazeth on her looks;
Infernal Dis is courting of my love,
Inventing masks and stately shows for her,
Opening the doors of his rich treasury
To entertain this queen of chastity.
—Whose body shall be tomb'd with all the pomp
The treasure of my kingdom may afford.

Exit, taking her away.

ACTUS. 4.

SCAENA. [3].

*[Enter] Tamburlaine, drawn in his chariot by Trebizon and
Soria with bits in their mouths: reins in his left hand, in his
right hand a whip with which he scourgeth them. Techelles,
Theridamas, Usumcasane, Amyras, Celebinus. Natolia and
Jerusalem led by with five or six common soldiers.*

Tamb. Holla, ye pampered jades of Asia!
What, can ye draw but twenty miles a day,
And have so proud a chariot at your heels,
And such a coachman as great Tamburlaine?
—But from Asphaltis, where I conquer'd you,
To Byron here, where thus I honor you?
The horse that guide the golden eye of heaven,
And blow the morning from their nosterils,
Making their fiery gait above the clouds,
Are not so honored in their governor   10
As you, ye slaves, in mighty Tamburlaine.
The headstrong jades of Thrace Alcides tam'd,
That King Egeus fed with human flesh
And made so wanton that they knew their strengths,
Were not subdu'd with valor more divine
Than you by this unconquered arm of mine.
To make you fierce and fit my appetite,
You shall be fed with flesh as raw as blood
And drink in pails the strongest muscadel.

If you can live with it, then live, and draw   20
My chariot swifter than the racking clouds:
If not, then die like beasts, and fit for naught
But perches for the black and fatal ravens!
Thus am I right the Scourge of Highest Jove—
And see the figure of my dignity
By which I hold my name and majesty!
  Amy. Let me have coach, my lord, that I may ride,
And thus be drawn with these two idle kings.
  Tamb. Thy youth forbids such ease, my kingly boy.
They shall tomorrow draw my chariot,   30
While these their fellow-kings may be refresh'd.
  Orc. O thou that sway'st the region under earth,
And art a king as absolute as Jove,
Come as thou didst in fruitful Sicily,
Surveying all the glories of the land,
And as thou took'st the fair Proserpina
Joying the fruit of Ceres' garden-plot,
For love, for honor, and to make her queen,
So for just hate, for shame, and to subdue
This proud contemner of thy dreadful power,   40
Come once in fury and survey his pride,
Haling him headlong to the lowest hell!
  Ther. Your Majesty must get some bits for these,
To bridle their contemptuous cursing tongues
That like unruly, never-broken jades
Break through the hedges of their hateful mouths
And pass their fixed bounds exceedingly.
  Tech. Nay, we will break the hedges of their mouths
And pull their kicking colts out of their pastures.
  Usum. Your Majesty already hath devis'd   50
A mean as fit as may be to restrain
These coltish coach-horse tongues from blasphemy.
  Cel. How like you that, Sir King? Why speak you not?
  Jer. Ah, cruel brat, sprung from a tyrant's loins!
How like his cursed father he begins
To practice taunts and bitter tyrannies!
  Tamb. Ay, Turk, I tell thee, this same boy is he
That must (advanc'd in higher pomp than this)
Rifle the kingdoms I shall leave unsack'd,
If Jove, esteeming me too good for earth,   60
Raise me to match the fair Aldeboran,
Above the threefold astracism of heaven,
Before I conquer all the triple world.
Now, fetch me out the Turkish concubines;

I will prefer them for the funeral
They have bestowed on my abortive son.

The concubines are brought in.

Where are my common soldiers, now, that fought
So lion-like upon Asphaltis plains?
    Sold. Here, my lord.
    Tamb. Hold ye, tall soldiers, take ye queens apiece: 70
I mean such queens as were kings' concubines:
Take them, divide them, and their jewels too,
And let them equally serve all your turns.
    Sold. We thank Your Majesty!
    Tamb. Brawl not, I warn you, for your lechery:
For every man that so offends shall die.
    Orc. Injurious tyrant, wilt thou so defame
The hateful fortunes of thy victory,
To exercise upon such guiltless dames
The violence of thy common soldiers' lust?   80
    Tamb. Live continent then, ye slaves, and meet not me
With troops of harlots at your slothful heels.
    Lady. O pity us, my lord, and save our honors.
    Tamb. Are ye not gone, ye villains, with your spoils

They run away with the ladies.

    Jer. O merciless, infernal cruelty!
    Tamb. "Save your honors!" 'Twere but time indeed,
Lost long before ye knew what honor meant.
    Ther. It seems they meant to conquer us, my lord,
And make us jesting pageants for their trulls.
    Tamb. And now themselves shall make our pageant,   90
And common soldiers jest with all their trulls.
Let them take pleasure soundly in their spoils
Till we prepare our march to Babylon,
Whither we next make expedition.
    Tech. Let us not be idle then, my lord,
But presently be prest to conquer it.
    Tamb. We will, Techelles. Forward then, ye jades!
Now crouch, ye kings of greatest Asia,
And tremble when ye hear this Scourge will come
That whips down cities and controlleth crowns,   100
Adding their wealth and treasure to my store.
The Euxine sea, north to Natolia;
The Terrene, west; the Caspian, north-north-east;
And on the south, Sinus Arabicus
Shall all be loaden with the martial spoils

We will convey with us to Persia.
Then shall my native city, Samarcanda,
And crystal waves of fresh Jaertis stream,
The pride and beauty of her princely seat,
Be famous through the furthest continents,   110
For there my palace royal shall be plac'd,
Whose shining turrets shall dismay the heavens,
And cast the fame of Ilion's tower to hell.
Thorough the streets with troops of conquered kings,
I'll ride in golden armor like the sun;
And in my helm a triple plume shall spring,
Spangled with diamonds, dancing in the air,
To note me emperor of the threefold world—
Like to an almond tree ymounted high
Upon the lofty and celestial mount   120
Of ever-green Selinus quaintly deck'd
With blooms more white than Erycina's brows,
Whose tender blossoms tremble every one
At every little breath thorough heaven is blown.
Then in my coach, like Saturn's royal son
Mounted, his shining chariot gilt with fire,
And drawn with princely eagles through the path
Pav'd with bright crystal and enchas'd with stars,
When all the gods stand gazing at his pomp,
So will I ride through Samarcanda streets,   130
Until my soul, dissevered from this flesh,
Shall mount the milk-white way, and meet Him there.
To Babylon, my lords, to Babylon!   *Exeunt.*

ACTUS. 5.

SCAENA. 1.

Enter the Governor of Babylon upon the walls, with others.

    Gov. What saith Maximus?
    Max. My lord, the breach the enemy hath made
Gives such assurance of our overthrow
That little hope is left to save our lives
Or hold our city from the conqueror's hands.
Then hang out flags, my lord, of humble truce,
And satisfy the people's general prayers,
That Tamburlaine's intolerable wrath
May be suppress'd by our submission.
    Gov. Villain, respects thou more thy slavish life   10
Than honor of thy country or thy name?

Are not my life and state as dear to me,
The city and my native country's weal,
As anything of price with thy conceit?
Have we not hope, for all our battered walls,
To live secure and keep his forces out,
When this our famous lake of Limnasphaltis
Makes walls afresh with everything that falls
Into the liquid substance of his stream,
More strong than are the gates of death or hell?   20
What faintness should dismay our courages
When we are thus defenc'd against our foe
And have no terror but his threatening looks?

    Enter [above] another, kneeling to the Governor.

    [*Cit.*] My lord, if ever you did deed of ruth,
And now will work a refuge to our lives,
Offer submission, hang up flags of truce,
That Tamburlaine may pity our distress
And use us like a loving conqueror.
Though this be held his last day's dreadful siege,
Wherein he spareth neither man nor child,   30
Yet are there Christians of Georgia here,
Whose state he ever pitied and reliev'd,
Will get his pardon if Your Grace would send.
    Gov. How is my soul environed,
And this eterniz'd city, Babylon,
Fill'd with a pack of faint-heart fugitives
That thus entreat their shame and servitude!
    Another. My lord, if ever you will win our hearts,
Yield up the town, save our wives and children:
For I will cast myself from off these walls   40
Or die some death of quickest violence
Before I bide the wrath of Tamburlaine!
    Gov. Villains, cowards, traitors to our state!
Fall to the earth and pierce the pit of hell,
That legions of tormenting spirits may vex
Your slavish bosoms with continual pains!
I care not, nor the town will never yield
As long as any life is in my breast.

Enter Theridamas and Techelles [below] with other soldiers.

    [*Ther.*] Thou desperate Governor of Babylon,
To save thy life, and us a little labor,   50
Yield speedily the city to our hands,
Or else be sure thou shalt be forc'd with pains

More exquisite than ever traitor felt.

Gov. Tyrant, I turn the traitor in thy throat,
And will defend it in despite of thee!
Call up the soldiers to defend these walls!

Tech. Yield, foolish Governor! We offer more
Than ever yet we did to such proud slaves
As durst resist us till our third day's siege.
Thou seest us prest to give the last assault,   60
And that shall bide no more regard of parley.

Gov. Assault and spare not! We will never yield! [*Exeunt
above.*]

Alarm, and they scale the walls.

*Enter Tamburlaine [in black, in his chariot] with Usumcasane,
Amyras, and Celebinus; with others; the two spare Kings.*

Tamb. The stately buildings of fair Babylon,
Whose lofty pillars higher than the clouds
Were wont to guide the seaman in the deep,
Being carried thither by the cannon's force
Now fill the mouth of Limnasphaltis lake
And make a bridge unto the battered walls.
Where Belus, Ninus, and great Alexander
Have rode in triumph, triumphs Tamburlaine!   70
—Whose chariot wheels have burst th' Assyrians' bones,
Drawn with these kings on heaps of carcasses.
Now in the place where fair Semiramis,
Courted by kings and peers of Asia,
Hath trod the measures, do my soldiers march:
And in the streets, where brave Assyrian dames
Have rid in pomp like rich Saturnia,
With furious words and frowning visages
My horsemen brandish their unruly blades.

*Enter Theridamas and Techelles, bringing the Governor of
Babylon.*

Who have ye there, my lords?   80

Ther. The sturdy Governor of Babylon,
That made us all the labor for the town,
And us'd such slender reck'ning of Your Majesty.

Tamb. Go, bind the villain! He shall hang in chains
Upon the ruins of this conquered town.
Sirrah, the view of our vermilion tents—
Which threat'ned more than if the region
Next underneath the element of fire
Were full of comets and of blazing stars

Whose flaming trains should reach down to the earth—   90
Could not affright you. No, nor I myself,
The wrathful messenger of mighty Jove,
That with his sword hath quail'd all earthly kings,
Could not persuade you to submission,
But still the ports were shut. Villain, I say,
Should I but touch the rusty gates of hell,
The triple-headed Cerberus would howl
And make black Jove to crouch and kneel to me!
But I have sent volleys of shot to you,
Yet could not enter till the breach was made.   100

 Gov. Nor, if my body could have stopt the breach,
Should'st thou have ent'red, cruel Tamburlaine.
'Tis not thy bloody tents can make me yield,
Nor yet thyself, the Anger of the Highest,
For though thy cannon shook the city walls,
My heart did never quake or courage faint.

 Tamb. Well, now I'll make it quake! Go draw him up,
Hang him in chains upon the city walls,
And let my soldiers shoot the slave to death.

 Gov. Vile monster, born of some infernal hag,   110
And sent from hell to tyrannize on earth,
Do all thy worst! Nor death, nor Tamburlaine,
Torture or pain can daunt my dreadless mind!

 Tamb. Up with him, then! his body shall be scarr'd.

 Gov. But, Tamburlaine, in Limnasphaltis lake
There lies more gold than Babylon is worth,
Which when the city was besieg'd I hid.
Save but my life and I will give it thee.

 Tamb. Then for all your valor you would save your life?
Whereabout lies it?   120

 Gov. Under a hollow bank, right opposite
Against the western gate of Babylon.

 Tamb. Go thither, some of you, and take his gold. [*Exeunt.*]
The rest forward with execution!
Away with him hence, let him speak no more.
I think I make your courage something quail.   [*Exeunt.*]
When this is done, we'll march from Babylon,
And make our greatest haste to Persia.
These jades are broken-winded and half-tir'd,
Unharness them, and let me have fresh horse.   130
So, now their best is done to honor me,
Take them and hang them both up presently.

 Treb. Vile tyrant! Barbarous, bloody Tamburlaine!

 Tamb. Take them away, Theridamas. See them despatch'd.

 Ther. I will, my lord.   [*Exeunt.*]

Tamb. Come, Asian viceroys: to your tasks awhile,
And take such fortune as your fellows felt.

Orc. First let thy Scythian horse tear both our limbs,
Rather than we should draw thy chariot,
And like base slaves abject our princely minds   140
To vile and ignominious servitude.

Jer. Rather lend me thy weapon, Tamburlaine,
That I may sheathe it in this breast of mine.
A thousand deaths could not torment our hearts
More than the thought of this doth vex our souls.

Amy. They will talk still, my lord, if you do not bridle them.

Tamb. Bridle them, and let me to my coach.

*They bridle them. [They hang up the Governor. Theridamas
enters.]*

Amy. See now, my lord, how brave the captain hangs.

Tamb. 'Tis brave indeed, my boy, well done.
Shoot first, my lord, and then the rest shall follow.   150

Ther. Then have at him to begin withal.

Theridamas shoots.

Gov. Yet save my life, and let this wound appease
The mortal fury of great Tamburlaine.

Tamb. No, though Asphaltis lake were liquid gold
And offer'd me as ransom for thy life,
Yet should'st thou die. Shoot at him all at once!

They shoot.

So now he hangs like Bagdeth's Governor,
Having as many bullets in his flesh
As there be breaches in her battered wall.
Go now, and bind the burghers hand and foot,   160
And cast them headlong in the city's lake.
Tartars and Persians shall inhabit there,
And to command the city I will build
A citadel that all Africa
Which hath been subject to the Persian king
Shall pay me tribute for in Babylon.

Tech. What shall be done with their wives and children, my
lord?

Tamb. Techelles, drown them all, man, woman, and child.
Leave not a Babylonian in the town.

Tech. I will about it straight. Come, soldiers.   *Exit.* 170

Tamb. Now, Casane, where's the Turkish Alcoran
And all the heaps of superstitious books
Found in the temples of that Mahomet,

Whom I have thought a god? They shall be burnt.
  Usum. Here they are, my lord.
  Tamb. Well said; let there be a fire presently.

          [They light a fire.]

In vain, I see, men worship Mahomet:
My sword hath sent millions of Turks to hell,
Slew all his priests, his kinsmen, and his friends,
And yet I live untouch'd by Mahomet.   180
There is a God, full of revenging wrath,
From whom the thunder and the lightning breaks,
Whose Scourge I am, and Him will I obey!
So, Casane, fling them in the fire!
Now, Mahomet, if thou have any power,
Come down thyself and work a miracle:
Thou art not worthy to be worshipped
That suffers flame of fire to burn the writ
Wherein the sum of thy religion rests.
Why send'st thou not a furious whirlwind down   190
To blow thy Alcoran up to thy throne,
Where men report thou sit'st by God himself?
—Or vengeance on the head of Tamburlaine
That shakes his sword against thy majesty,
And spurns the abstracts of thy foolish laws?
Well, soldiers, Mahomet remains in hell;
He cannot hear the voice of Tamburlaine.
Seek out another Godhead to adore,
The God that sits in Heaven, if any God:
For He is God alone, and none but He!   200

          [Enter Techelles.]

  Tech. I have fulfill'd Your Highness' will, my lord.
Thousands of men, drown'd in Asphaltis lake,
Have make the waters swell above the banks,
And fishes, fed by human carcasses,
Amaz'd, swim up and down upon the waves,
As when they swallow asafetida
Which makes them fleet aloft and gape for air.
  Tamb. Well then, my friendly lords, what now remains
But that we leave sufficient garrison
And presently depart to Persia   210
To triumph after all our victories?
  Ther. Ay, good my lord, let us in haste to Persia.
And let this captain be remov'd the walls
To some high hill about the city here.
  Tamb. Let it be so. About it, soldiers.

—But stay, I feel myself distempered suddenly . . .

    Tech. What is it dares distemper Tamburlaine?

    Tamb. Something, Techelles, but I know not what . . .
But forth, ye vassals, whatsoe'er it be,
Sickness or death can never conquer me!   *Exeunt.*   220

ACTUS. 5.

SCAENA. [2].

Enter Callapine, Amasia, [Captain,] with drums and trumpets.

    Call. King of Amasia, now our mighty host
Marcheth in Asia Major where the streams
Of Euphrates and Tigris swiftly runs.
And here may we behold great Babylon
Circled about with Limnasphaltis lake
Where Tamburlaine with all his army lies,
Which being faint and weary with the siege,
We may lie ready to encounter him
Before his host be full from Babylon—
And so revenge our latest grievous loss,   10
If God or Mahomet send any aid.

    Ama. Doubt not, my lord, but we shall conquer him.
The monster that hath drunk a sea of blood
And yet gapes still for more to quench his thirst,
Our Turkish swords shall headlong send to hell!
And that vile carcass drawn by warlike kings
The fowls shall eat! For never sepulcher
Shall grace this base-born tyrant Tamburlaine!

    Call. When I record my parents' slavish life,
Their cruel death, mine own captivity,   20
My viceroys' bondage under Tamburlaine,
Methinks I could sustain a thousand deaths
To be reveng'd of all his villany!
Ah, sacred Mahomet, thou that hast seen
Millions of Turks perish by Tamburlaine,
Kingdoms made waste, brave cities sack'd and burnt,
And but one host is left to honor thee,
Aid thy obedient servant, Callapine,
And make him after all these overthrows
To triumph over cursed Tamburlaine!   30

    Ama. Fear not, my lord, I see great Mahomet
Clothed in purple clouds, and on his head
A chaplet brighter than Apollo's crown,
Marching about the air with armed men

To join with you against this Tamburlaine!
　[*Capt.*] Renowned General, mighty Callapine,
Though God himself and holy Mahomet
Should come in person to resist your power,
Yet might your mighty host encounter all
And pull proud Tamburlaine upon his knees　　　　　40
To sue for mercy at Your Highness' feet!
　Call. Captain, the force of Tamburlaine is great,
His fortune greater, and the victories
Wherewith he hath so sore dismay'd the world
Are greatest to discourage all our drifts.
Yet when the pride of Cynthia is at full,
She wanes again, and so shall his, I hope:
For we have here the chief selected men
Of twenty several kingdoms at the least:
Nor ploughman, priest, nor merchant stays at home:　　　50
All Turkey is in arms with Callapine:
And never will we sunder camps and arms
Before himself or his be conquered.
This is the time that must eternize me
For conquering the tyrant of the world!
Come, soldiers, let us lie in wait for him,
And if we find him absent from his camp,
Or that it be rejoin'd again at full,
Assail it and be sure of victory!　　　　　*Exeunt.*

ACTUS. 5.

SCAENA. [3].

[Enter] Theridamas, Techelles, Usumcasane.

　Ther. Weep, heavens, and vanish into liquid tears!
Fall stars that govern his nativity,
And summon all the shining lamps of heaven
To cast their bootless fires to the earth
And shed their feeble influence in the air—
Muffle your beauties with eternal clouds!
For Hell and Darkness pitch their pitchy tents,
And Death with armies of Cimmerian spirits
Gives battle 'gainst the heart of Tamburlaine!
Now in defiance of that wonted love　　　　　10
Your sacred virtues pour'd upon his throne
And made his state an honor to the heavens,
These cowards invisible assail his soul
And threaten conquest on our sovereign.

But if he die your glories are disgrac'd,
Earth droops and says that hell in heaven is plac'd!

Tech. O then, ye powers that sway eternal seats
And guide this massy substance of the earth,
If you retain desert of holiness
As your supreme estates instruct our thoughts,   20
Be not inconstant, careless of your fame.
Bear not the burden of your enemies' joys
Triumphing in his fall whom you advanc'd—
But as his birth, life, health, and majesty
Were strangely blest and governed by heaven,
So honor, heaven (till heaven dissolved be)
His birth, his life, his health, and majesty!

Usum. Blush, heaven, to lose the honor of thy name!
To see thy footstool set upon thy head!
And let no baseness in thy haughty breast   30
Sustain a shame of such inexcellence:
To see the devils mount in angels' thrones,
And angels dive into the pools of hell!
And though they think their painful date is out,
And that their power is puissant as Jove's,
Which makes them manage arms against thy state,
Yet make them feel the strength of Tamburlaine
(Thy Instrument and Note of Majesty)
Is greater far than they can thus subdue:
For if he die thy glory is disgrac'd,   40
Earth droops and says that hell in heaven is plac'd!

[*Enter Tamburlaine drawn in his chariot as before; Amyras,*
Celebinus, and Physicians.]

Tamb. What daring god torments my body thus,
And seeks to conquer mighty Tamburlaine?
Shall sickness prove me now to be a man,
That have been term'd the Terror of the World?
Techelles and the rest, come, take your swords,
And threaten him whose hand afflicts my soul!
Come, let us march against the powers of heaven,
And set black streamers in the firmament
To signify the slaughter of the gods!   50
Ah, friends, what shall I do? I cannot stand.
Come carry me to war against the gods
That thus envy the health of Tamburlaine.

Ther. Ah, good my lord, leave these impatient words
Which add much danger to your malady.

Tamb. Why, shall I sit and languish in this pain?

No, strike the drums, and in revenge of this,
Come, let us charge our spears and pierce his breast
Whose shoulders bear the axis of the world—
That if I perish, heaven and earth may fade!   60
Theridamas, haste to the court of Jove,
Will him to send Apollo hither straight,
To cure me, or I'll fetch him down myself!
    Tech. Sit still, my gracious lord; this grief will cease,
And cannot last, it is so violent.
    Tamb. Not last, Techelles? No, for I shall die?
See, where my slave, the ugly monster, Death,
Shaking and quivering, pale and wan for fear,
Stands aiming at me with his murdering dart,
Who flies away at every glance I give,   70
And, when I look away, comes stealing on.
Villain, away, and hie thee to the field!
I and mine army come to load thy bark
With souls of thousand mangled carcasses.
Look, where he goes. But see, he comes again
Because I stay. Techelles, let us march
And weary Death with bearing souls to hell.
    Phy. Pleaseth Your Majesty to drink this potion
Which will abate the fury of your fit
And cause some milder spirits govern you.   80
    Tamb. Tell me, what think you of my sickness now?
    Phy. I view'd your urine, and the [hypostasis]
Thick and obscure doth make your danger great;
Your veins are full of accidental heat,
Whereby the moisture of your blood is dried.
The humidum and calor, which some hold
Is not a parcel of the elements
But of a substance more divine and pure,
Is almost clean extinguished and spent;
Which, being the cause of life, imports your death.   90
Besides, my lord, this day is critical,
Dangerous to those whose crisis is as yours:
Your artiers which alongst the veins convey
The lively spirits which the heart engenders,
Are parch'd and void of spirits, that the soul
Wanting those organons by which it moves,
Cannot endure, by argument of art.
Yet, if Your Majesty may escape this day,
No doubt but you shall soon recover all.
    Tamb. Then will I comfort all my vital parts,   100
And live, in spite of death, above a day.   *Alarm within.*

[Enter Messenger.]

Mes. My lord, young Callapine, that lately fled from Your
Majesty, hath now gather'd a fresh army, and hearing your
absence in the field, offers to set upon us presently.

Tamb. See, my physicians now, how Jove hath sent
A present medicine to recure my pain.
My looks shall make them fly, and might I follow,
There should not one of all the villain's power
Live to give offer of another fight.

Usum. I joy, my lord, Your Highness is so strong,　　　110
That can endure so well your royal presence,
Which only will dismay the enemy.

Tamb. I know it will, Casane. Draw, you slaves!
In spite of death, I will go show my face.

*Alarm. Tamburlaine goes in, and comes out again with all
the rest.*

Tamb. Thus are the villain cowards fled for fear,
Like summer's vapors vanish'd by the sun;
And could I but awhile pursue the field,
That Callapine should be my slave again.
But I perceive my martial strength is spent:
In vain I strive and rail against those powers　　　120
That mean t' invest me in a higher throne,
As much too high for this disdainful earth.
Give me a map. Then let me see how much
Is left for me to conquer all the world
That these, my boys, may finish all my wants.

One brings a map.

Here I began to march towards Persia,
Along Armenia and the Caspian Sea,
And thence unto Bithynia, where I took
The Turk and his great Empress prisoners.
Then march'd I into Egypt and Arabia,　　　130
And here, not far from Alexandria,
Whereas the Terrene and the Red Sea meet,
Being distant less than full a hundred leagues,
I meant to cut a channel to them both
That men might quickly sail to India.
From thence to Nubia near Borno lake,
And so along the Ethiopian sea,
Cutting the Tropic line of Capricorn,
I conquered all as far as Zanzibar.

Then, by the northern part of Africa,   140
I came at last to Græcia, and from thence
To Asia, where I stay against my will
—Which is from Scythia, where I first began,
Backwards and forwards near five thousand leagues.
Look here, my boys, see what a world of ground
Lies westward from the midst of Cancer's line
Unto the rising of this earthly globe
Whereas the sun, declining from our sight,
Begins the day with our Antipodes.
And shall I die, and this unconquered?   150
Lo, here, my sons, are all the golden mines,
Inestimable drugs and precious stones,
More worth than Asia and the world beside.
And from th' Antarctic Pole eastward behold
As much more land, which never was descried,
Wherein are rocks of pearl that shine as bright
As all the lamps that beautify the sky.
And shall I die, and this unconquered?
Here, lovely boys, what death forbids my life,
That let your lives command in spite of death.   160
    Amy. Alas, my lord, how should our bleeding hearts,
Wounded and broken with Your Highness' grief,
Retain a thought of joy or spark of life?
Your soul gives essence to our wretched subjects,
Whose matter is incorporate in your flesh.
    Cel. Your pains do pierce our souls. No hope survives,
For by your life we entertain our lives.
    Tamb. But, sons, this subject, not of force enough
To hold the fiery spirit it contains,
Must part, imparting his impressions   170
By equal portions into both your breasts:
My flesh, divided in your precious shapes,
Shall still retain my spirit, though I die,
And live in all your seeds immortally.
Then now remove me, that I may resign
My place and proper title to my son.
First, take my scourge and my imperial crown,
And mount my royal chariot of estate,
That I may see thee crown'd before I die.
Help me, my lords, to make my last remove.   180
    Ther. A woeful change, my lord, that daunts our thoughts,
More than the ruin of our proper souls!
    Tamb. Sit up, my son, and let me see how well
Thou wilt become thy father's majesty.

They crown him.

Amy. With what a flinty bosom should I joy
The breath of life and burden of my soul
If not resolv'd into resolved pains
My body's mortified lineaments
Should exercise the motions of my heart
Pierc'd with the joy of any dignity?   190
O father, if the unrelenting ears
Of death and hell be shut against my prayers,
And that the spiteful influence of heaven
Deny my soul fruition of her joy,
How should I step or stir my hateful feet
Against the inward powers of my heart,
Leading a life that only strives to die,
And plead in vain unpleasing sovereignty?
    Tamb. Let not thy love exceed thine honor, son,
Nor bar thy mind that magnanimity   200
That nobly must admit necessity.
Sit up, my boy, and with those silken reins
Bridle the steeled stomachs of those jades.
    Ther. My lord, you must obey His Majesty,
Since fate commands and proud necessity.
    Amy. Heavens witness me with what a broken heart
And damned spirit I ascend this seat,
And send my soul, before my father die,
His anguish and his burning agony!
    Tamb. Now fetch the hearse of fair Zenocrate.   210
Let it be plac'd by this my fatal chair,
And serve as parcel of my funeral.
    Cas. Then feels Your Majesty no sovereign ease?
Nor may our hearts, all drown'd in tears of blood,
Joy any hope of your recovery?
    Tamb. Casane, no. The monarch of the earth,
And eyeless monster that torments my soul,
Cannot behold the tears ye shed for me,
And therefore still augments his cruelty.
    Tech. Then let some god oppose his holy power   220
Against the wrath and tyranny of Death,
That his tear-thirsty and unquenched hate
May be upon himself reverberate!

They bring in the hearse.

    Tamb. Now eyes enjoy your latest benefit,
And when my soul hath virtue of your sight,

Pierce through the coffin and the sheet of gold,
And glut your longings with a heaven of joy.
So reign, my son. Scourge and control those slaves,
Guiding thy chariot with thy father's hand.
As precious is the charge thou undertak'st   230
As that which Clymene's brain-sick son did guide,
When wandering Phœbe's ivory cheeks were scorch'd,
And all the earth, like Ætna, breathing fire.
Be warn'd by him. Then learn with awful eye
To sway a throne as dangerous as his,
For if thy body thrive not full of thoughts
As pure and fiery as Phyteus' beams,
The nature of these proud rebelling jades
Will take occasion by the slenderest hair
And draw thee piecemeal like Hippolytus   240
Through rocks more steep and sharp than Caspian clifts.
The nature of thy chariot will not bear
A guide of baser temper than myself,
More than heaven's coach the pride of Phaeton.
Farewell, my boys; my dearest friends, farewell!
My body feels, my soul doth weep to see,
Your sweet desires depriv'd my company,
For Tamburlaine, the Scourge of God, must die!
   Amy. Meet heaven and earth, and here let all things end,
For earth hath spent the pride of all her fruit,   250
And heaven consum'd his choicest living fire:
Let earth and heaven his timeless death deplore,
For both their worths will equal him no more.   [*Exeunt.*]

[EDWARD II]

The troublesome reign and lamentable death of Edward the Second, King of England. With the tragical fall of proud Mortimer.

[*Speaking Characters*

GAVESTON
1 POOR MAN
2 POOR MAN
3 POOR MAN
EDWARD II
LANCASTER
MORTIMER THE ELDER
MORTIMER THE YOUNGER, *his nephew*
EDMUND, EARL OF KENT
WARWICK
BISHOP OF COVENTRY
ARCHBISHOP OF CANTERBURY
QUEEN ISABELLA
PEMBROKE
BEAUMONT
SPENCER THE YOUNGER
BALDOCK
KING'S NIECE
1 MESSENGER
GUARD
ARUNDEL
JAMES, *servant to Pembroke*
SPENCER THE ELDER, *father of* YOUNGER
LEVUNE
2 MESSENGER
PRINCE EDWARD
JOHN OF HAINAULT
3 MESSENGER
RICE AP HOWELL
ABBOT
MONKS
LEICESTER
MOWER
BISHOP OF WINCHESTER
TRUSSEL
BERKELEY
4 MESSENGER
MATREVIS
GURNEY
LIGHTBORN
CHAMPION
SOLDIER
1 LORD
2 LORD

Mute Characters
MAYOR OF BRISTOL, LADIES, SOLDIERS, ATTENDANTS]

Enter Gaveston reading on a letter that was brought him from the King.

Gav. "My father is deceas'd. Come, Gaveston,
And share the kingdom with thy dearest friend."
Ah, words that make me surfeit with delight!
What greater bliss can hap to Gaveston
Than live and be the favorite of a king?
Sweet prince, I come! These, these thy amorous lines
Might have enforc'd me to have swum from France
And, like Leander, gasp'd upon the sand
So thou would'st smile and take me in thine arms!
The sight of London to my exil'd eyes   10
Is as Elysium to a new-come soul.
—Not that I love the city or the men
But that it harbors him I hold so dear,
The King—upon whose bosom let me die,
And with the world be still at enmity!
What need the arctic people love starlight,
To whom the sun shines both by day and night?
Farewell base stooping to the lordly peers,
My knee shall bow to none but to the King.
As for the multitude that are but sparks   20
Rak'd up in embers of their poverty,
Tanti: I'll fawn first on the wind
That glanceth at my lips, and flieth away.
But how now, what are these?

Enter three Poor Men.

Poor Men. [Poor men,] such as desire your worship's service.

Gav. [*to 1 Poor Man.*] What canst thou do?

1 *P. Man.* I can ride.

Gav. But I have no horses. [*To 2 Poor Man.*] What art thou?

2 *P. Man.* A traveler.

Gav. Let me see: Thou would'st do well 30
To wait at my trencher and tell me lies at dinnertime—
And as I like your discoursing, I'll have you.
[*To 3 Poor Man.*] And what art thou?

3 *P. Man.* A soldier, that hath serv'd against the Scot.

Gav. Why, there are hospitals for such as you.
I have no war, and therefore, sir, begone!

3 *P. Man.* Farewell, and perish by a soldier's hand,
That would'st reward them with an hospital!

Gav. [*aside.*] (Ay, ay, these words of his move me as much
As if a goose would play the porpentine 40
And dart her plumes, thinking to pierce my breast.
But yet it is no pain to speak men fair.
I'll flatter these and make them live in hope.)
—You know that I came lately out of France,
And yet I have not view'd my lord the King;
If I speed well, I'll entertain you all.

All. We thank your worship.

Gav. I have some business, leave me to myself.

All. We will wait here about the court. *Exeunt.*

Gav. Do. These are not men for me. 50
I must have wanton poets, pleasant wits,
Musicians that with touching of a string
May draw the pliant King which way I please.
Music and poetry is his delight.
Therefore I'll have Italian masks by night,
Sweet speeches, comedies, and pleasing shows;
And in the day when he shall walk abroad,
Like sylvan nymphs my pages shall be clad:
My men, like satyrs grazing on the lawns,
Shall with their goat feet dance an antic hay: 60
Sometime a lovely boy in Dian's shape,
With hair that gilds the water as it glides,
Crownets of pearl about his naked arms—
And in his sportful hands an olive-tree
To hide those parts which men delight to see—
Shall bathe him in a spring: and there hard by,
One like Actæon peeping through the grove,
Shall by the angry goddess be transform'd:
And running in the likeness of an hart
By yelping hounds pull'd down, and seem to die. 70

Such things as these best please His Majesty,
My lord!—Here comes the King and the nobles
From the parliament.—I'll stand aside.

*Enter the King, Lancaster, Mortimer Senior, Mortimer Junior,
Edmund Earl of Kent, Guy Earl of Warwick, etc.*

    K. Edw. Lancaster!
    Lan. My lord!
    Gav. [*aside.*] (That Earl of Lancaster do I abhor.)
    K. Edw. Will you not grant me this? [*aside*]—(In spite of
      them
I'll have my will! And these two Mortimers
That cross me thus, shall know I am displeas'd!)
    E. Mor. If you love us, my lord, hate Gaveston!   80
    Gav. [*aside.*] (That villain Mortimer, I'll be his death!)
    Y. Mor. Mine uncle here, this earl, and I myself
Were sworn to your father at his death,
That he should ne'er return into the realm.
And know, my lord, ere I will break my oath,
This sword of mine, that should offend your foes,
Shall sleep within the scabbard at thy need,
And underneath thy banners march who will,
For Mortimer will hang his armor up.
    Gav. [*aside.*] (*Mort Dieu!*)   90
    K. Edw. Well, Mortimer, I'll make thee rue these words!
Beseems it thee to contradict thy King?
Frown'st thou thereat, aspiring Lancaster?
The sword shall plane the furrows of thy brows
And hew these knees that now are grown so stiff!
I will have Gaveston—and you shall know
What danger 'tis to stand against your King!
    Gav. [*aside.*] (Well done, Ned!)
    Lan. My lord, why do you thus incense your peers
That naturally would love and honor you   100
But for that base and obscure Gaveston?
Four earldoms have I, besides Lancaster—
Derby, Salisbury, Lincoln, Leicester—
These will I sell to give my soldiers pay
Ere Gaveston shall stay within the realm!
Therefore if he be come, expel him straight!
    Kent. Barons and earls, your pride hath made me mute,
But now I'll speak, and to the proof, I hope.
I do remember in my father's days
Lord Percy of the north being highly mov'd   110
Brav'd Mowbray in presence of the King:
For which, had not His Highness lov'd him well,

He should have lost his head: but with his look
Th' undaunted spirit of Percy was appeas'd
And Moubray and he were reconcil'd.
Yet dare you brave the King unto his face?
Brother, revenge it, and let these their heads
Preach upon poles for trespass of their tongues!
   War. O, our heads!
   K. Edw. Ay, yours. And therefore I would wish you
     grant—   120
   War. Bridle thy anger, gentle Mortimer.
   Y. Mor. I cannot, nor I will not. I must speak.
Cousin, our hands I hope shall fence our heads
And strike off his that makes you threaten us.
Come, uncle, let us leave the brain-sick King,
And henceforth parle with our naked swords.
   E. Mor. Wiltshire hath men enough to save our heads.
   War. All Warwickshire will love him for my sake.
   Lan. And northward Gaveston hath many friends.
Adieu, my lord. And either change your mind,   130
Or look to see the throne where you should sit
To float in blood and at thy wanton head,
The glozing head of thy base minion thrown!

Exeunt nobles.

   K. Edw. I cannot brook these haughty menaces.
Am I a king, and must be overrul'd?
Brother, display my ensigns in the field!
I'll bandy with the barons and the earls,
And either die—or live with Gaveston.
   Gav. I can no longer keep me from my lord.

                       [Comes forward.]
   K. Edw. What, Gaveston! Welcome! Kiss not my
     hand—   140
Embrace me, Gaveston as I do thee.
Why should'st thou kneel? knowest thou not who I am?
—Thy friend, thyself, another Gaveston!
Not Hylas was more mourn'd of Hercules
Than thou hast been of me since thy exile.
   Gav. And since I went from hence, no soul in Hell
Hath felt more torment than poor Gaveston.
   K. Edw. I know it. Brother, welcome home my friend.
Now let the treacherous Mortimers conspire,
And that high-minded Earl of Lancaster.   150
I have my wish in that I joy thy sight!
And sooner shall the sea o'erwhelm my land,
Than bear the ship that shall transport thee hence!

I here create thee Lord High Chamberlain,
Chief Secretary to the state and me,
Earl of Cornwall, King and Lord of Man.
    Gav. My lord, these titles far exceed my worth.
    Kent. Brother, the least of these may well suffice
For one of greater birth than Gaveston.
    K. Edw. Cease, brother, for I cannot brook these words. 160
Thy worth, sweet friend, is far above my gifts.
Therefore, to equal it, receive my heart!
If for these dignities thou be envied,
I'll give thee more, for but to honor thee
Is Edward pleas'd with kingly regiment.
Fear'st thou thy person? Thou shalt have a guard.
Want'st thou gold? Go to my treasury.
Would'st thou be lov'd and fear'd? Receive my seal,
Save or condemn, and in our name command
Whatso thy mind affects or fancy likes. 170
    Gav. It shall suffice me to enjoy your love,
Which whiles I have, I think myself as great
As Cæsar riding in the Roman street,
With captive kings at his triumphant car.

Enter the Bishop of Coventry.

    K. Edw. Whither goes my lord of Coventry so fast?
    B. of Cov. To celebrate your father's exequies.
—But is that wicked Gaveston return'd?
    K. Edw. Ay, priest, and lives to be reveng'd on thee
That wert the only cause of his exile.
    Gav. 'Tis true! And but for reverence of these robes, 180
Thou should'st not plod one foot beyond this place.
    B. of Cov. I did no more than I was bound to do.
And, Gaveston, unless thou be reclaim'd,
As then I did incense the parliament,
So will I now, and thou shalt back to France.
    Gav. Saving your reverence, you must pardon me.
                          [Bows ironically.]
    K. Edw. Throw off his golden miter, rend his stole,
                          [Grasps Bishop.]
And in the channel christen him anew.
    Kent. Ah, brother, lay not violent hands on him,
For he'll complain unto the see of Rome. 190
    Gav. Let him complain unto the see of Hell!
I'll be reveng'd on him for my exile.   *[Roughs Bishop.]*
    K. Edw. No, spare his life, but seize upon his goods.
Be thou lord bishop and receive his rents—
And make him serve thee as thy chaplain.

I give him thee. Here, use him as thou wilt.
                    [*Pushes Bishop toward Gaveston.*]
   Gav. He shall to prison, and there die in bolts.
   K. Edw. Ay, to the Tower, the Fleet, or where thou wilt.
   B. of Cov. For this offense, be thou accurst of God!
   K. Edw. Who's there? [*Calls off-stage. Attendants appear.*]
      Convey this priest to the Tower.   200
   B. of Cov. True, true.   [*Attendants remove Bishop.*]
   K. Edw. But in the meantime, Gaveston, away,
And take possession of his house and goods.
Come, follow me, and thou shalt have my guard
To see it done, and bring thee safe again.
   Gav. What should a priest do with so fair a house?
A prison may best beseem his holiness.   [*Exeunt.*]

[1.2]   *Enter both the Mortimers, Warwick, and Lancaster.*

   War. 'Tis true, the bishop is in the Tower,
And goods and body given to Gaveston.
   Lan. What, will they tyrannize upon the church?
Ah, wicked King! Accursed Gaveston!
This ground which is corrupted with their steps
Shall be their timeless sepulcher or mine.
   Y. Mor. Well, let that peevish Frenchman guard him sure—
Unless his breast be sword-proof he shall die.
   E. Mor. How now, why droops the Earl of Lancaster?
   Y. Mor. Wherefore is Guy of Warwick discontent?   10
   Lan. That villain Gaveston is made an earl.
   E. Mor. An earl!
   War. Ay, and besides Lord Chamberlain of the realm,
And Secretary too, and Lord of Man.
   E. Mor. We may not, nor we will not suffer this!
   Y. Mor. Why post we not from hence to levy men?
   Lan. "My Lord of Cornwall," now at every word!
And happy is the man whom he vouchsafes,
For vailing of his bonnet, one good look.
Thus, arm in arm, the King and he doth march—   20
Nay more, the guard upon his lordship waits,
And all the court begins to flatter him.
   War. Thus leaning on the shoulder of the King,   [*Leans on*
He nods and scorns and smiles at those that pass.   *Lancaster.*]
   E. Mor. Doth no man take exceptions at the slave?
   Lan. All stomach him, but none dare speak a word.
   Y. Mor. Ah, that bewrays their baseness, Lancaster!
Were all the earls and barons of my mind,
We'll hale him from the bosom of the King
And at the court-gate hang the peasant up: 30

Who swoln with venom of ambitious pride
Will be the ruin of the realm and us.
   War. Here comes my lord of Canterbury's grace.
   Lan. His countenance bewrays he is displeas'd.

Enter the [Arch]bishop of Canterbury [and an Attendant].

   A. of Cant. First were his sacred garments rent and torn,
Then laid they violent hands upon him next;
Himself imprisoned, and his goods asseiz'd:
This certify the Pope. Away, take horse.   *[Exit Attendant.]*
   Lan. My lord, will you take arms against the King?
   A. of Cant. What need I? God himself is up in arms   40
When violence is offer'd to the church.
   Y. Mor. Then will you join with us that be his peers
To banish or behead that Gaveston?
   A. of Cant. What else, my lords? For it concerns me near:
The bishopric of Coventry is his.

Enter the Queen.

   Y. Mor. Madam, whither walks Your Majesty so fast?
   Q. Isab. Unto the forest, gentle Mortimer,
To live in grief and baleful discontent,
For now my lord the King regards me not,
But dotes upon the love of Gaveston—   50
He claps his cheeks, and hangs about his neck,
Smiles in his face, and whispers in his ears—
And when I come he frowns, as who should say,
"Go whither thou wilt seeing I have Gaveston!"
   E. Mor. Is it not strange that he is thus bewitch'd?
   Y. Mor. Madam, return unto the court again.
That sly inveigling Frenchman we'll exile,
Or lose our lives. And yet, ere that day come,
The King shall lose his crown, for we have power,
And courage too, to be reveng'd at full.   60
   A. of Cant. But yet lift not your swords against the King.
   Lan. No but we'll lift Gaveston from hence.
   War. And war must be the means, or he'll stay still.
   Q. Isab. Then let him stay. For rather than my lord
Shall be oppress'd by civil mutinies,
I will endure a melancholy life.
—And let him frolic with his minion.
   A. of Cant. My lords, to ease all this, but hear me speak:
We and the rest that are his counsellors
Will meet, and with a general consent   70
Confirm his banishment with our hands and seals.
   Lan. What we confirm the King will frustrate.

Y. Mor. Then may we lawfully revolt from him.

War. But say, my lord, where shall this meeting be?

A. of Cant. At the New Temple.

Y. Mor. Content.

[*A. of Cant.*] And, in the meantime, I'll entreat you all
To cross to Lambeth, and there stay with me.

Lan. Come then, let's away.

Y. Mor. Madam, farewell!   80

Q. Isab. Farewell, sweet Mortimer; and for my sake
Forbear to levy arms against the King.

Y. Mor. Ay, if words will serve; if not, I must.   [*Exeunt.*]

[1.3]   *Enter Gaveston and the Earl of Kent.*

Gav. [*familiarly.*] Edmund, the mighty Prince of Lancaster
(That hath more earldoms than an ass can bear!)
And both the Mortimers (two goodly men!)
With Guy of Warwick (that redoubted knight!)
Are gone toward Lambeth. There let them remain.   *Exeunt.*

[1.4] *Enter nobles* [*: Lancaster with document, Warwick, Pembroke, Elder Mortimer, Younger Mortimer, the Archbishop of
Canterbury, and attendants*].

Lan. Here is the form of Gaveston's exile.
May it please your lordship to subscribe your name.

A. of Cant. Give me the paper.

                              [*Subscribes, as do the rest.*]

Lan. Quick, quick, my lord, I long to write my name.

War. But I long more to see him banish'd hence.

Y. Mor. The name of Mortimer shall fright the King,
Unless he be declin'd from that base peasant.

Enter the King and Gaveston [*and Kent. Edward seats
Gaveston by him on the throne*].

K. Edw. What, are you mov'd that Gaveston sits here?
It is our pleasure, we will have it so!

Lan. Your Grace doth well to place him by your side,   10
For nowhere else the new earl is so safe.

E. Mor. What man of noble birth can brook this sight?
Quam male conveniunt!
See what a scornful look the peasant casts!

Pem. Can kingly lions fawn on creeping ants?

War. Ignoble vassal, that like Phaeton
Aspir'st unto the guidance of the sun!

Y. Mor. Their downfall is at hand, their forces down—
We will not thus be fac'd and over-peer'd.

K. Edw. Lay hands on that traitor Mortimer!   20

E. Mor. Lay hands on that traitor Gaveston!

[*Attendants hold Gaveston.*]

Kent. Is this the duty that you owe your King?

War. We know our duties, let him know his peers.

K. Edw. Whither will you bear him? Stay, or ye shall die!

E. Mor. We are no traitors: therefore threaten not.

Gav. No, threaten not, my lord, but pay them home.
Were I a king——.

Y. Mor. Thou villain, wherefore talk'st thou of a king
That hardly art a gentleman by birth!

K. Edw. Were he a peasant, being my minion,   30
I'll make the proudest of you stoop to him.

Lan. My lord, you may not thus disparage us!
Away, I say, with hateful Gaveston!

E. Mor. And with the Earl of Kent that favors him.

[*Attendants remove Kent and Gaveston.*]

K. Edw. Nay, then, lay violent hands upon your King.
Here, Mortimer, sit thou in Edward's throne.
Warwick and Lancaster, wear you my crown.
Was ever king thus over-rul'd as I?

Lan. Learn then to rule us better, and the realm.

Y. Mor. What we have done, our heart blood shall main-
          tain.   40

War. Think you that we can brook this upstart pride?

K. Edw. Anger and wrathful fury stops my speech.

A. of Cant. Why are you mov'd? Be patient, my lord,
And see what we your counsellors have done. [*Gives him docu-*

Y. Mor. My lords, now let us all be resolute: *ment exiling*
And either have our wills, or lose our lives.   *Gaveston.*]

K. Edw. Meet you for this, proud over-daring peers?
Ere my sweet Gaveston shall part from me,
This isle shall fleet upon the ocean
And wander to the unfrequented Inde.   50

A. of Cant. You know that I am legate to the Pope.
On your allegiance to the see of Rome,
Subscribe as we have done to his exile.

Y. Mor. Curse him, if he refuse; and then may we
Depose him and elect another king!

K. Edw. Ay, there it goes! But yet I will not yield.
Curse me, depose me, do the worst you can!

Lan. Then linger not, my lord, but do it straight.

A. of Cant. Remember how the bishop was abus'd.
Either banish him that was the cause thereof,   60
Or I will presently discharge these lords
Of duty and allegiance due to thee.

K. Edw. [*aside.*] (It boots me not to threat. I must speak fair.

The legate of the Pope will be obey'd.)
—My lord, [*to Archbishop*] you shall be Chancellor of the
    realm;
Thou, Lancaster, High Admiral of our fleet;
Young Mortimer and his uncle shall be earls;
And you, Lord Warwick, President of the North;
And thou [*to Pembroke*] of Wales. If this content you not,
Make several kingdoms of this monarchy   70
And share it equally amongst you all—
So I may have some nook or corner left
To frolic with my dearest Gaveston.
    A. of Cant. Nothing shall alter us. We are resolv'd.
    Lan. Come, come, subscribe.
    Y. Mor. Why should you love him whom the world hates so?
    K. Edw. Because he loves me more than all the world!
Ah, none but rude and savage-minded men
Would seek the ruin of my Gaveston!
You that be noble-born should pity him.   80
    War. You that are princely-born should shake him off.
For shame subscribe, and let the lown depart.
    E. Mor. Urge him, my lord.
    A. of Cant. Are you content to banish him the realm?
    K. Edw. I see I must, and therefore am content.
Instead of ink I'll write it with my tears.   [*Subscribes.*]
    Y. Mor. The King is love-sick for his minion.
    K. Edw. 'Tis done—and now, accursed hand, fall off!
    Lan. Give it me. I'll have it publish'd in the streets.
    Y. Mor. I'll see him presently dispatch'd away.   90
    A. of Cant. Now is my heart at ease.
    War. And so is mine.
    Pem. This will be good news to the common sort.
    E. Mor. Be it or no, he shall not linger here.
                            Exeunt nobles.
    K. Edw. How fast they run to banish him I love!
They would not stir, were it to do me good.
Why should a king be subject to a priest?
Proud Rome, that hatchest such imperial grooms,
For these thy superstitious taper-lights,
Wherewith thy antichristian churches blaze,   100
I'll fire thy crazed buildings and enforce
The papal towers to kiss the lowly ground!
With slaughter'd priests may Tiber's channel swell,
And banks rais'd higher with their sepulchers!
As for the peers that back the clergy thus,
If I be King, not one of them shall live.

Enter Gaveston.

Gav. My lord, I hear it whisper'd everywhere
That I am banish'd and must fly the land.

K. Edw. 'Tis true, sweet Gaveston.—O! were it false!
The legate of the Pope will have it so—   110
And thou must hence, or I shall be depos'd.
But I will reign to be reveng'd of them!
And therefore, sweet friend, take it patiently.
Live where thou wilt, I'll send thee gold enough;
And long thou shalt not stay; or if thou dost,
I'll come to thee. My love shall ne'er decline!

Gav. Is all my hope turn'd to this hell of grief?

K. Edw. Rend not my heart with thy too-piercing words—
Thou from this land, I from myself am banish'd.

Gav. To go from hence grieves not poor Gaveston—   120
But to forsake you, in whose gracious looks
The blessedness of Gaveston remains:
For nowhere else seeks he felicity.

K. Edw. And only this torments my wretched soul
That, whether I will or no, thou must depart.
Be governor of Ireland in my stead,
And there abide till fortune call thee home.
Here, take my picture, and let me wear thine.
                    [*They exchange pictures and embrace.*]
O, might I keep thee here as I do this,
Happy were I, but now most miserable!   130

Gav. 'Tis something to be pitied of a king.

K. Edw. Thou shalt not hence—I'll hide thee, Gaveston.

Gav. I shall be found, and then 'twill grieve me more.

K. Edw. Kind words and mutual talk makes our grief
            greater:
Therefore, with dumb embracement, let us part.
Stay, Gaveston, I cannot leave thee thus.

Gav. For every look, my lord drops down a tear.
Seeing I must go, do not renew my sorrow.

K. Edw. The time is little that thou hast to stay,
And, therefore, give me leave to look my fill.   140
But come, sweet friend, I'll bear thee on thy way.

Gav. The peers will frown.

K. Edw. I pass not for their anger. Come, let's go.
O that we might as well return as go!

Enter Queen Isabella.

Q. Isab. Whither goes my lord?

K. Edw. Fawn not on me, French strumpet! Get thee gone!

Q. Isab. On whom but on my husband should I fawn?

Gav. On Mortimer, with whom, ungentle Queen—
I say no more. Judge you the rest, my lord.

Q. Isab. In saying this, thou wrong'st me, Gaveston.   150
Is't not enough that thou corrupt'st my lord,
And art a bawd to his affections,
But thou must call mine honor thus in question?

Gav. I mean not so. Your Grace must pardon me.

K. Edw. Thou art too familiar with that Mortimer:
And by thy means is Gaveston exil'd.
But I would wish thee reconcile the lords—
Or thou shalt ne'er be reconcil'd to me.

Q. Isab. Your Highness knows, it lies not in my power.

K. Edw. Away then! touch me not, come, Gaveston.   160

Q. Isab. Villain, 'tis thou that robb'st me of my lord!

Gav. Madam, 'tis you that rob me of my lord!

K. Edw. Speak not unto her, let her droop and pine.

Q. Isab. Wherein, my lord, have I deserv'd these words?
Witness the tears that Isabella sheds;
Witness this heart that sighing for thee breaks,
How dear my lord is to poor Isabel!

K. Edw. And witness Heaven how dear thou art to me!
There weep. For till my Gaveston be repeal'd,
Assure thyself thou com'st not in my sight.   170

        Exeunt Edward and Gaveston.

Q. Isab. O miserable and distressed Queen!
Would when I left sweet France and was embark'd
That charming Circes walking on the waves
Had chang'd my shape, or at the marriage-day
The cup of Hymen had been full of poison!
Or with those arms that twin'd about my neck
I had been stifled, and not liv'd to see
The King my lord thus to abandon me!
Like frantic Juno will I fill the earth
With ghastly murmur of my sighs and cries,   180
For never doted Jove on Ganymede
So much as he on cursed Gaveston.
But that will more exasperate his wrath.
I must entreat him, I must speak him fair,
And be a means to call home Gaveston—
And yet he'll ever dote on Gaveston!
And so am I for ever miserable!

*Enter the nobles [Lancaster, Warwick, Pembroke, Elder
  Mortimer, and Younger Mortimer] to the Queen.*

Lan. Look where the sister of the King of France

Sits wringing of her hands and beats her breast.

 War. The King, I fear, hath ill-entreated her.   190

 Pem. Hard is the heart that injures such a saint.

 Y. Mor. I know 'tis 'long of Gaveston she weeps.

 E. Mor. Why? He is gone.

 Y. Mor. Madam, how fares Your Grace?

 Q. Isab. Ah, Mortimer! now breaks the King's hate forth,
And he confesseth that he loves me not.

 Y. Mor. Cry quittance, madam, then, and love not him.

 Q. Isab. No, rather will I die a thousand deaths.
And yet I love in vain, he'll ne'er love me.

 Lan. Fear ye not, madam. Now his minion's gone, 200
His wanton humor will be quickly left.

 Q. Isab. O never, Lancaster! I am enjoin'd
To sue upon you all for his repeal.
This wills my lord, and this must I perform,
Or else be banish'd from His Highness' presence!

 Lan. For his repeal, madam? He comes not back,
Unless the sea cast up his shipwrack body.

 War. And to behold so sweet a sight as that
There's none here but would run his horse to death!

 Y. Mor. But, madam, would you have us call him home? 210

 Q. Isab. Ay, Mortimer, for till he be restor'd,
The angry King hath banish'd me the court.
And, therefore, as thou lov'st and tender'st me,
Be thou my advocate unto these peers.

 Y. Mor. What! Would ye have me plead for Gaveston?

 E. Mor. Plead for him that will, I am resolv'd.

 Lan. And so am I, my lord. Dissuade the Queen.

 Q. Isab. O Lancaster, let him dissuade the King,
For 'tis against my will he should return.

 War. Then speak not for him, let the peasant go. 220

 Q. Isab. 'Tis for myself I speak, and not for him.

 Pem. No speaking will prevail, and therefore cease.

 Y. Mor. Fair Queen, forbear to angle for the fish
Which being caught strikes him that takes it dead:
I mean that vile torpedo, Gaveston,
That now, I hope, floats on the Irish seas!

 Q. Isab. Sweet Mortimer, sit down by me awhile,
And I will tell thee reasons of such weight
As thou wilt soon subscribe to his repeal.

 Y. Mor. It is impossible, but speak your mind. [*They sit.*] 230

 Q. Isab. Then thus.—But none shall hear it but ourselves.
            [*They whisper apart.*]

 Lan. My lords, albeit the Queen win Mortimer,
Will you be resolute, and hold with me?

E. Mor. Not I, against my nephew.

Pem. Fear not. The Queen's words cannot alter him.

War. No? Do but mark how earnestly she pleads.

Lan. And see how coldly his looks make denial.

War. She smiles. Now for my life his mind is chang'd!

Lan. I'll rather lose his friendship, I, than grant.   [*Young Mortimer and Queen rise.*]

Y. Mor. Well, of necessity it must be so.   [*Aloud.*]   240
My lords, that I abhor base Gaveston   [*He turns to them.*]
I hope your honors make no question.
And therefore though I plead for his repeal,
'Tis not for his sake but for our avail—
Nay for the realm's behoof and for the King's.

Lan. Fie, Mortimer! Dishonor not thyself!
Can this be true, 'twas good to banish him?
And is this true, to call him home again?
Such reasons make white black, and dark night day.

Y. Mor. My lord of Lancaster, mark the respect—   250

Lan. In no respect can contraries be true.

Q. Isab. Yet, good my lord, hear what he can allege.

War. All that he speaks is nothing. We are resolv'd!

Y. Mor. Do you not wish that Gaveston were dead?

Pem. I would he were!

Y. Mor. Why then, my lord, give me but leave to speak.

E. Mor. But, nephew, do not play the sophister.

Y. Mor. This which I urge is of a burning zeal
To mend the King, and do our country good.
Know you not Gaveston hath store of gold   260
Which may in Ireland purchase him such friends
As he will front the mightiest of us all?
And whereas he shall live and be belov'd,
'Tis hard for us to work his overthrow?

War. Mark you but that, my lord of Lancaster.

Y. Mor. But were he here, detested as he is,
How easily might some base slave be suborn'd
To greet his lordship with a poniard—
And none so much as blame the murderer
But rather praise him for that brave attempt   270
And in the chronicle enroll his name
For purging of the realm of such a plague!

Pem. He saith true.

Lan. Ay, but how chance this was not done before?

Y. Mor. Because, my lords, it was not thought upon.
Nay, more, when he shall know it lies in us
To banish him, and then to call him home,
'Twill make him vail the top-flag of his pride,

And fear to offend the meanest nobleman.
    E. Mor. But how if he do not, nephew?   280
    Y. Mor. Then may we with some color rise in arms.
For howsoever we have borne it out,
'Tis treason to be up against the King.
So we shall have the people of our side,
Which for his father's sake lean to the King
But cannot brook a night-grown mushroom,
Such a one as my lord of Cornwall is,
Should bear us down of the nobility.
And when the commons and the nobles join,
'Tis not the King can buckler Gaveston: 290
We'll pull him from the strongest hold he hath.
My lords, if to perform this I be slack,
Think me as base a groom as Gaveston.
    Lan. On that condition, Lancaster will grant.
    War. And so will Pembroke and I.
    E. Mor. And I.
    Y. Mor. In this I count me highly gratified,
And Mortimer will rest at your command.
    Q. Isab. And when this favor Isabel forgets,
Then let her live abandon'd and forlorn.   300
But see, in happy time, my lord the King,
Having brought the Earl of Cornwall on his way,
Is new return'd. This news will glad him much,
Yet not so much as me—I love him more
Than he can Gaveston. Would he lov'd me
But half so much. Then were I treble-bless'd!

    Enter King Edward mourning [,Beaumont, attendants].

    K. Edw. He's gone, and for his absence thus I mourn.
Did never sorrow go so near my heart
As doth the want of my sweet Gaveston!
And could my crown's revénue bring him back,   310
I would freely give it to his enemies—
And think I gain'd, having bought so dear a friend!
    Q. Isab. Hark, how he harps upon his minion!
    K. Edw. My heart is as an anvil unto sorrow,
Which beats upon it like the Cyclops' hammers
And with the noise turns up my giddy brain
And makes me frantic for my Gaveston!
Ah, had some bloodless fury rose from Hell,
And with my kingly scepter struck me dead
When I was forc'd to leave my Gaveston!   320
    Lan. Diablo, what passions call you these?
    Q. Isab. My gracious lord, I come to bring you news.

K. Edw.—That you have parled with your Mortimer?

Q. Isab.—That Gaveston, my lord, shall be repeal'd.

K. Edw. Repeal'd! The news is too sweet to be true.

Q. Isab. But will you love me, if you find it so?

K. Edw. If it be so, what will not Edward do?

Q. Isab. For Gaveston, but not for Isabel—.

K. Edw. For thee, fair Queen, if thou lov'st Gaveston!
I'll hang a golden tongue about thy neck,   330
Seeing thou hast pleaded with so good success.

   Q. Isab. No other jewels hang about my neck
                            [Puts his arms around her.]
Than these, my lord! Nor let me have more wealth
Than I may fetch from this rich treasury.   *[Kisses him.]*
O how a kiss revives poor Isabel!

   K. Edw. Once more receive my hand, and let this be
A second marriage 'twixt thyself and me.

   Q. Isab. And may it prove more happy than the first!
My gentle lord, bespeak these nobles fair
That wait attendance for a gracious look   340
And on their knees salute Your Majesty.   *[Nobles kneel.]*

   K. Edw. Courageous Lancaster, embrace thy King.
And as gross vapors perish by the sun,
Even so let hatred with thy sovereign's smile.
Live thou with me as my companion.

   Lan. This salutation overjoys my heart.

   K. Edw. Warwick shall be my chiefest counsellor.
These silver hairs will more adorn my court
Than gaudy silks, or rich embroidery.
Chide me, sweet Warwick, if I go astray.   350

   War. Slay me, my lord, when I offend Your Grace.

   K. Edw. In solemn triumphs and in public shows
Pembroke shall bear the sword before the King.

   Pem. And with this sword Pembroke will fight for you.

   K. Edw. But wherefore walks young Mortimer aside?
Be thou commander of our royal fleet.
Or, if that lofty office like thee not,
I make thee here Lord Marshal of the realm.

   Y. Mor. My lord, I'll marshal so your enemies
As England shall be quiet and you safe.   360

   K. Edw. And as for you, Lord Mortimer of Chirke,
Whose great achievements in our foreign war
Deserves no common place nor mean reward,
Be you the general of the levied troops,
That now are ready to assail the Scots.

   E. Mor. In this Your Grace hath highly honor'd me,
For with my nature war doth best agree.

Q. Isab. Now is the King of England rich and strong,
Having the love of his renowned peers.
    K. Edw. Ay, Isabel, ne'er was my heart so light.   370
Clerk of the crown, direct our warrant forth   [*To one of the
                                                        attendants.*]
For Gaveston to Ireland.—Beaumont, fly
As fast as Iris or Jove's Mercury!
    Bea. It shall be done, my gracious lord.   [*Exeunt Beaumont
                                                    and attendant.*]
    K. Edw. Lord Mortimer, we leave you to your charge.
Now let us in and feast it royally
Against our friend the Earl of Cornwall comes.
We'll have a general tilt and tournament;
And then his marriage shall be solemniz'd.
For wot you not that I have made him sure   380
Unto our cousin, the Earl of Gloucester's heir?
    Lan. Such news we hear, my lord.
    K. Edw. That day, if not for him, yet for my sake,
Who in the triumph will be challenger,
Spare for no cost, we will requite your love.
    War. In this or aught Your Highness shall command us.
    K. Edw. Thanks, gentle Warwick. Come, let's in and revel.
                                    Exeunt. Manent Mortimers.
    E. Mor. Nephew, I must to Scotland. Thou stay'st here.
Leave now to oppose thyself against the King.
Thou seest by nature he is mild and calm.   390
And seeing his mind so dotes on Gaveston,
Let him without controlment have his will:
The mightiest kings have had their minions—
Great Alexander lov'd Hephestion;
The conquering Hector for Hylas wept;
And for Patroclus stern Achilles droop'd.
And not kings only, but the wisest men—
The Roman Tully lov'd Octavius;
Grave Socrates, wild Alcibiades.
Then let His Grace, whose youth is flexible   400
And promiseth as much as we can wish,
Freely enjoy that vain, light-headed earl,
For riper years will wean him from such toys.
    Y. Mor. Uncle, his wanton humor grieves not me.
But this I scorn, that one so basely born
Should by his sovereign's favor grow so pert
And riot it with the treasure of the realm
While soldiers mutiny for want of pay—.
He wears a lord's revénue on his back,
And Midas-like he jets it in the court   410

With base outlandish cullions at his heels
Whose proud fantastic liveries make such show
As if that Proteus, god of shapes, appear'd!
I have not seen a dapper Jack so brisk:
He wears a short Italian hooded cloak,
Larded with pearl, and in his Tuscan cap
A jewel of more value than the crown.
While others walk below, the King and he
From out a window laugh at such as we,
And flout our train, and jest at our attire—.   420
Uncle, 'tis this makes me impatient.

    E. Mor. But, nephew, now you see the King is chang'd.

    Y. Mor. Then so am I, and live to do him service.
But whiles I have a sword, a hand, a heart,
I will not yield to any such upstart!
You know my mind. Come, uncle, let's away.   *Exeunt.*

[2.1] *Enter [Younger] Spencer, and Baldock [in academic robes].*

    Bald. Spencer,
Seeing that our lord th' Earl of Gloucester's dead,
Which of the nobles dost thou mean to serve?

    Y. Spen. Not Mortimer, nor any of his side,
Because the King and he are enemies.
Baldock, learn this of me: a factious lord
Shall hardly do himself good, much less us;
But he that hath the favor of a king
May with one word advance us while we live.
The liberal Earl of Cornwall is the man   10
On whose good fortune Spencer's hope depends.

    Bald. What, mean you then to be his follower?

    Y. Spen. No, his companion, for he loves me well,
And would have once preferr'd me to the King.

    Bald. But he is banish'd, there's small hope of him.

    Y. Spen. Ay, for a while—but, Baldock, mark the end:
A friend of mine told me in secrecy
That he's repeal'd and sent for back again.
And even now a post came from the court
With letters to our lady from the King: 20
And as she read she smil'd, which makes me think
It is about her lover Gaveston.

    Bald. 'Tis like enough, for since he was exil'd
She neither walks abroad nor comes in sight.

—But I had thought the match had been broke off,
And that his banishment had chang'd her mind.

   Y. Spen. Our lady's first love is not wavering;
My life for thine, she will have Gaveston.

   Bald. Then hope I by her means to be preferr'd,
Having read unto her since she was a child.   30

   Y. Spen. Then, Baldock, you must cast the scholar off
And learn to court it like a gentleman!
'Tis not a black coat and a little band,
A velvet-caped coat (faced before with serge),
And smelling to a nosegay all the day—
Or holding of a napkin in your hand—
Or saying a long grace at a table's end—
Or making low legs to a nobleman—
Or looking downward with your eyelids close
And saying, "Truly, an't may please your honor,"   40
Can get you any favor with great men.
You must be proud, bold, pleasant, resolute:
And now and then stab as occasion serves.

   Bald. Spencer, thou know'st I hate such formal toys,
And use them but of mere hypocrisy.
Mine old lord whiles he liv'd was so precise
That he would take exceptions at my buttons,
And, being like pin's heads, blame me for the bigness—
Which made me curate-like in mine attire,
Though inwardly licentious enough   50
And apt for any kind of villainy!
I am none of these common pedants, I,
That cannot speak without *propterea quod*.

   Y. Spen. But one of those that saith *quandoquidem*
And hath a special gift to form a verb.

   Bald. Leave off this jesting, here my lady comes.

Enter the Lady.

   [*Niece.*] The grief for his exile was not so much,
As is the joy of his returning home.
This letter came from my sweet Gaveston—
What need'st thou, love, thus to excuse thyself?   60
I know thou could'st not come and visit me.
"I will not long be from thee, though I die."   [*Reads.*]
This argues the entire love of my lord.
"When I forsake thee, death seize on my heart!"   [*Reads.*]
But stay thee here where Gaveston shall sleep.
                        [*Puts letter in bosom.*]
Now to the letter of my lord the King.
He wills me to repair unto the court

And meet my Gaveston! Why do I stay,
Seeing that he talks thus of my marriage day?
Who's there? Baldock,   70
See that my coach be ready, I must hence.
   Bald. It shall be done, madam.
   [*Niece.*] And meet me at the park-pale presently.
                                    Exit [*Baldock*].
Spencer, stay you and bear me company,
For I have joyful news to tell thee of:
My lord of Cornwall is acoming over,
And will be at the court as soon as we.
   Y. Spen. I knew the King would have him home again.
   [*Niece.*] If all things sort out as I hope they will,
Thy service, Spencer, shall be thought upon.   80
   Y. Spen. I humbly thank your ladyship.
   [*Niece.*] Come, lead the way.—I long till I am there.
                                          [Exeunt.]

[2.2] *Enter Edward, the Queen, Lancaster, [Younger] Morti-*
     mer, Warwick, Pembroke, Kent, attendants.

   K. Edw. The wind is good, I wonder why he stays,
I fear me he is wrack'd upon the sea.
   Q. Isab. Look, Lancaster, how passionate he is,
And still his mind runs on his minion!
   Lan. My lord—.
   K. Edw. How now, what news, is Gaveston arriv'd?
   Y. Mor. Nothing but Gaveston! What means Your Grace?
You have matters of more weight to think upon:
The King of France sets foot in Normandy.
   K. Edw. A trifle, we'll expel him when we please.   10
But tell me, Mortimer, what's thy device
Against the stately triumph we decreed?
   Y. Mor. A homely one, my lord, not worth the telling.
   K. Edw. Prithee, let me know it.
   Y. Mor. But seeing you are so desirous, thus it is:
A lofty cedar tree fair flourishing
On whose top branches kingly eagles perch,
And by the bark a canker creeps me up
And gets into the highest bough of all:
The motto, *Æque tandem.*   20
   K. Edw. And what is yours, my lord of Lancaster?
   Lan. My lord, mine's more obscure than Mortimer's.
Pliny reports there is a flying fish
Which all the other fishes deadly hate,
And therefore being pursu'd it takes the air;
No sooner is it up, but there's a fowl

That seizeth it. This fish, my lord, I bear:
The motto this, *Undique mors est.*

    Kent. Proud Mortimer! Ungentle Lancaster!
Is this the love you bear your sovereign?   30
Is this the fruit your reconcilement bears?
Can you in words make show of amity
And in your shields display your rancorous minds?
What call you this but private libelling
Against the Earl of Cornwall and my brother?

    Q. Isab. Sweet husband, be content, they all love you.

    K. Edw. They love me not that hate my Gaveston.
I am that cedar—shake me not too much!
And you, the eagles, soar ye ne'er so high—
I have the jesses that will pull you down!   40
And *Æque tandem* shall that canker cry
Unto the proudest peer of Britainy!
Though thou compar'st him to a flying fish
And threat'nest death whether he rise or fall,
'Tis not the hugest monster of the sea,
Nor foulest harpy, that shall swallow him.

    Y. Mor. If in his absence thus he favors him,
What will he do whenas he shall be present?

    Lan. That shall we see. Look where his lordship comes!

Enter Gaveston.

    K. Edw. My Gaveston!   50
Welcome to Tynemouth! Welcome to thy friend!
Thy absence made me droop and pine away;
For as the lovers of fair Danae
When she was lock'd up in a brazen tower
Desir'd her more and wax'd outrageous,
So did it sure with me! And now thy sight
Is sweeter far than was thy parting hence
Bitter and irksome to my sobbing heart.

    Gav. Sweet lord and King, your speech preventeth mine,
Yet have I words left to express my joy: 60
The shepherd nipp'd with biting winter's rage
Frolics not more to see the painted spring,
Than I do to behold Your Majesty!

    K. Edw. Will none of you salute my Gaveston?

    Lan. Salute him! Yes! Welcome, Lord Chamberlain!

    Y. Mor. Welcome is the good Earl of Cornwall!

    War. Welcome, Lord Governor of the Isle of Man!

    Pem. Welcome, Master Secretary!

    Kent. Brother, do you hear them?

    K. Edw. Still will these earls and barons use me thus.   70

Gav. My lord, I cannot brook these injuries.

Q. Isab. (Ay me, poor soul, when these begin to jar.) [*Aside.*]

K. Edw. Return it to their throats, I'll be thy warrant.

Gav. Base, leaden earls, that glory in your birth—
Go sit at home and eat your tenant's beef—
And come not here to scoff at Gaveston—
Whose mounting thoughts did never creep so low
As to bestow a look on such as you!

Lan. Yet I disdain not to do this for you!
                    [*Draws his sword and offers to stab Gaveston.*]

K. Edw. Treason! Treason! Where's the traitor?   80

Pem. Here! Here!   [*Points to Gaveston.*]

K. Edw. Convey hence Gaveston! They'll murder him!

Gav. [*draws his sword.*] The life of thee shall salve this foul
        disgrace.   [*To Lancaster.*]

Y. Mor. Villain, thy life, unless I miss mine aim!
                                        [*Stabs at Gaveston.*]

Q. Isab. Ah, furious Mortimer, what hast thou done?

Y. Mor. No more than I would answer, were he slain.
                        [*Exit Gaveston with attendants.*]

K. Edw. Yes, more than thou canst answer, though he live.
Dear shall you both abide this riotous deed!
Out of my presence, come not near the court!

Y. Mor. I'll not be barr'd the court for Gaveston.   90

Lan. We'll hale him by the ears unto the block.

K. Edw. Look to your own heads, his is sure enough.

War. Look to your own crown, if you back him thus.

Kent. Warwick, these words do ill beseem thy years.

K. Edw. Nay, all of them conspire to cross me thus.
But if I live, I'll tread upon their heads
That think with high looks thus to tread me down!
Come, Edmund, let's away and levy men.
'Tis war that must abate these barons' pride!

Exit the King [*, Queen, and Kent*].

War. Let's to our castles, for the King is mov'd.   100

Y. Mor. Mov'd may he be, and perish in his wrath!

Lan. Cousin, it is no dealing with him now.
He means to make us stoop by force of arms.
And therefore let us jointly here protest
To prosecute that Gaveston to the death.

Y. Mor. By Heaven, the abject villain shall not live!

War. I'll have his blood, or die in seeking it!

Pem. The like oath Pembroke takes!

Lan. And so doth Lancaster!
                        [*They all put right hands together.*]

Now send our heralds to defy the King   110
And make the people swear to put him down.

Enter [*1 Messenger*].

Y. Mor. Letters, from whence?
Mess. From Scotland, my lord.
                    [*Giving letters to Mortimer.*]
Lan. Why, how now, cousin, how fares all our friends?
Y. Mor. My uncle's taken prisoner by the Scots.   [*Reads.*]
Lan. We'll have him ransom'd, man. Be of good cheer!
Y. Mor. They rate his ransom at five thousand pound.
Who should defray the money but the King,
Seeing he is taken prisoner in his wars?
I'll to the King.   120
Lan. Do, cousin, and I'll bear thee company.
War. Meantime, my lord of Pembroke and myself
Will to Newcastle here and gather head.
Y. Mor. About it then, and we will follow you.
Lan. Be resolute and full of secrecy.
War. I warrant you.   [*Exeunt Warwick and Pembroke.*]
Y. Mor. Cousin, an if he will not ransom him,
I'll thunder such a peal into his ears,
As never subject did unto his King.
Lan. Content, I'll bear my part. Holla, who's there?   130
                    [*Calls within.*]

[*Enter Guard.*]

Y. Mor. Ay, marry, such a guard as this doth well.
Lan. Lead on the way.
Guard. Whither will your lordships?
Y. Mor. Whither else but to the King.
Guard. His Highness is dispos'd to be alone.
Lan. Why, so he may—but we will speak to him.
Guard. You may not in, my lord.
Y. Mor. May we not?

[*Enter King Edward and Kent.*]

K. Edw. How now!
What noise is this? who have we there? is' you? [*Going.*]   140
Y. Mor. Nay, stay, my lord, I come to bring you news:
Mine uncle's taken prisoner by the Scots.
K. Edw. Then ransom him.
Lan. 'Twas in your wars. *You* should ransom him.
Y. Mor. And *you* shall ransom him, or else——.

[*Kent.*] What, Mortimer, you will not threaten him?

K. Edw. Quiet yourself. . . . You shall have the broad seal
To gather for him thoroughout the realm.

Lan. Your minion Gaveston hath taught you this!

Y. Mor. My lord, the family of the Mortimers   150
Are not so poor, but would they sell their land
'Twould levy men enough to anger you:
We never beg, but use such prayers as these.   [*Draws sword.*]

K. Edw. Shall I still be haunted thus?

Y. Mor. Nay, now you are here alone, I'll speak my mind.

Lan. And so will I, and then, my lord, farewell.

Y. Mor. The idle triumphs, masks, lascivious shows,
And prodigal gifts bestow'd on Gaveston,
Have drawn thy treasury dry and made thee weak,
The murmuring commons overstretched hath.   160

Lan. Look for rebellion, look to be depos'd;
Thy garrisons are beaten out of France,
And lame and poor lie groaning at the gates;
The wild O'Neil with swarms of Irish kerns
Lives uncontroll'd within the English pale;
Unto the walls of York the Scots made road,
And unresisted drave away rich spoils—

Y. Mor. The haughty Dane commands the narrow seas
While in the harbor ride thy ships unrigg'd.

Lan. What foreign prince sends thee ambassadors?   170

Y. Mor. Who loves thee but a sort of flatterers?

Lan. Thy gentle Queen, sole sister to Valois,
Complains that thou hast left her all forlorn.

Y. Mor. Thy court is naked, being bereft of those
That make a king seem glorious to the world,
I mean the peers, whom thou should'st dearly love—
Libels are cast again thee in the street,
Ballads and rhymes made of thy overthrow.

Lan. The Northern borderers, seeing their houses burnt,
Their wives and children slain, run up and down   180
Cursing the name of thee and Gaveston.

Y. Mor. When wert thou in the field with banner spread,
But once? and then thy soldiers march'd like players—
With garish robes, not armor; and thyself,
Bedaub'd with gold, rode laughing at the rest,
Nodding and shaking of thy spangl'd crest,
Where women's favors hung like labels down.

Lan. And therefore came it, that the fleering Scots,
To England's high disgrace, have made this jig:
        Maids of England, sore may you mourn   190
        For your lemans you have lost at Bannocksbourn,

With a heave and a ho!
What weeneth the King of England,
So soon to have won Scotland,
   With a rombelow!
Y. Mor. Wigmore shall fly to set my uncle free.
Lan. And when 'tis gone, our swords shall purchase more.
If ye be mov'd, revenge it as you can!
Look next to see us with our ensigns spread!

Exeunt nobles.

K. Edw. My swelling heart for very anger breaks!   200
How oft have I been baited by these peers,
And dare not be reveng'd, for their power is great.
Yet, shall the crowing of these cockerels
Affright a lion? Edward, unfold thy paws
And let their lives' blood slake thy fury's hunger!
If I be cruel and grow tyrannous,
Now let them thank themselves and rue too late!
Kent. My lord, I see your love to Gaveston
Will be the ruin of the realm and you,
For now the wrathful nobles threaten wars.   210
And therefore, brother, banish him forever.
K. Edw. Art thou an enemy to my Gaveston?
Kent. Ay, and it grieves me that I favor'd him!
K. Edw. Traitor, begone, whine thou with Mortimer!
Kent. So will I, rather than with Gaveston.
K. Edw. Out of my sight, and trouble me no more!
Kent. No marvel though thou scorn thy noble peers
When I thy brother am rejected thus—.
K. Edw. Away!   *Exit [Kent].*
Poor Gaveston, that has no friend but me.   220
Do what they can, we'll live in Tynemouth here.
And so I walk with him about the walls,
What care I though the earls begirt us round?
Here cometh she that's cause of all these jars.

Enter the Queen, Ladies 3 [one of whom is King's Niece],
   Baldock, and [Younger] Spencer [and Gaveston].

Q. Isab. My lord, 'tis thought the earls are up in arms.
K. Edw. Ay, and 'tis likewise thought you favor him.
Q. Isab. Thus do you still suspect me without cause.
[Niece.] Sweet uncle, speak more kindly to the Queen.
Gav. (My lord, dissemble with her, speak her fair.) *[Aside to*
K. Edw. Pardon me, sweet, I forgot myself: *King.]*   230
Q. Isab. Your pardon is quickly got of Isabel.
K. Edw. The younger Mortimer is grown so brave
That to my face he threatens civil wars.

Gav. Why do you not commit him to the Tower?

K. Edw. I dare not, for the people love him well.

Gav. Why, then we'll have him privily made away.

K. Edw. Would Lancaster and he had both carous'd
A bowl of poison to each other's health!
But let them go, and tell me what are these.

                 [*Baldock and Younger Spencer bow deeply.*]

[*Niece.*] Two of my father's servants whilst he liv'd.   240
May't please Your Grace to entertain them now.

K. Edw. Tell me, where wast thou born? What is thine arms?

Bald. My name is Baldock and my gentry
I fetch from Oxford, not from heraldry.

K. Edw. The fitter art thou, Baldock, for my turn.
Wait on me and I'll see thou shall not want.

Bald. I humbly thank Your Majesty.

K. Edw. Knowest thou him, Gaveston   [*Points to Younger*
Gav. Ay, my lord;   *Spencer.*]
His name is Spencer. He is well allied.   250
For my sake let him wait upon Your Grace,
Scarce shall you find a man of more desert.

K. Edw. Then, Spencer, wait upon me for his sake.
I'll grace thee with a higher style ere long.

Y. Spen. No greater titles happen unto me,
Than to be favor'd of Your Majesty.

K. Edw. Cousin, this day shall be your marriage feast—
And, Gaveston, think that I love thee well,
To wed thee to our niece, the only heir
Unto the Earl of Gloucester late deceas'd.   260

Gav. I know, my lord, many will stomach me—
But I respect neither their love nor hate.

K. Edw. The headstrong barons shall not limit me!
He that I list to favor shall be great.
Come, let's away! And when the marriage ends,
Have at the rebels and their complices!   *Exeunt omnes.*

[2.3] *Enter Lancaster, [Younger] Mortimer, Warwick, Pembroke, Kent [before the walls of Tynemouth Castle].*

Kent. My lords, of love to this our native land
I come to join with you and leave the King:
And in your quarrel and the realm's behoof
Will be the first that shall adventure life.

Lan. I fear me you are sent of policy
To undermine us with a show of love.

War. He is your brother, therefore have we cause
To cast the worst and doubt of your revolt.

Kent. Mine honor shall be hostage of my truth.

If that will not suffice, farewell my lords! [*Makes as though* 10
  Y. Mor. Stay, Edmund! Never was Plantagenet *to go.*]
False of his word, and therefore trust we thee.
  Pem. But what's the reason you should leave him now?
  Kent. I have inform'd the Earl of Lancaster.
  Lan. And it sufficeth. Now, my lords, know this,
That Gaveston is secretly arriv'd,
And here in Tynemouth frolics with the King.
Let us with these our followers scale the walls,
And suddenly surprise them unawares.
  Y. Mor. I'll give the onset.   20
  War. And I'll follow thee.
  Y. Mor. This tottered ensign of my ancestors,
Which swept the desert shore of that Dead Sea
Whereof we got the name of Mortimer,
Will I advance upon this castle['s] walls,
Drums, strike alarum, raise them from their sport,
And ring aloud the knell of Gaveston!
  Lan. None be so hardy as to touch the King—
But neither spare you Gaveston nor his friends. *Exeunt.*

[2.4] [*Drums and trumpets sound within.*] *Enter the King and* [*Younger*] *Spencer, to them Gaveston,* [*Niece, Queen,*] *etc.*

  K. Edw. O tell me, Spencer, where is Gaveston?
  Spen. I fear me he is slain, my gracious lord.
  K. Edw. No, here he comes. Now let them spoil and kill.
Fly, fly, my lords! The earls have got the hold.
Take shipping and away to Scarborough.
Spencer and I will post away by land.
  Gav. O stay, my lord, they will not injure you.
  K. Edw. I will not trust them. Gaveston, away!
  Gav. Farewell, my lord.
  K. Edw. Lady, farewell.   10
  [*Niece.*] Farewell, sweet uncle, till we meet again.
  K. Edw. Farewell, sweet Gaveston, and farewell, niece.
  Q. Isab. No farewell to poor Isabel thy Queen?
  K. Edw. Yes, yes, for Mortimer your lover's sake!
  Q. Isab. Heaven can witness I love none but you!

       Exeunt omnes, manet Isabella.

From my embracements thus he breaks away.
O that mine arms could close this isle about
That I might pull him to me where I would—
Or that these tears that drizzle from mine eyes
Had power to mollify his stony heart—   20
That when I had him we might never part!

Enter the barons [*Lancaster, Warwick, Younger Mortimer.*]
Alarums [*within*].

  Lan. I wonder how he scap'd.
  Y. Mor. Who's this? the Queen!
  Q. Isab. Ay, Mortimer, the miserable Queen,
Whose pining heart her inward sighs have blasted,
And body with continual mourning wasted.
These hands are tir'd with haling of my lord
From Gaveston, from wicked Gaveston!
—And all in vain! For when I speak him fair,
He turns away and smiles upon his minion!   30
  Y. Mor. Cease to lament, and tell us where's the King?
  Q. Isab. What would you with the King? Is't him you seek?
  Lan. No, madam, but that cursed Gaveston.
Far be it from the thought of Lancaster
To offer violence to his sovereign!
We would but rid the realm of Gaveston:
Tell us where he remains, and he shall die!
  Q. Isab. He's gone by water unto Scarborough.
Pursue him quickly and he cannot scape:
The King hath left him and his train is small.   40
  War. Foreslow no time, sweet Lancaster. Let's march.
  Y. Mor. How comes it that the King and he is parted?
  Q. Isab. That thus your army going several ways
Might be of lesser force, and with the power
That he intendeth presently to raise,
Be easily suppress'd. And therefore be gone!
  Y. Mor. Here in the river rides a Flemish hoy.
Let's all aboard and follow him amain!
  Lan. The wind that bears him hence will fill our sails.
Come, come aboard! 'Tis but an hour's sailing.   50
  Y. Mor. Madam, stay you within this castle here?
  Q. Isab. No, Mortimer, I'll to my lord the King.
  Y. Mor. Nay, rather sail with us to Scarborough.
  Q. Isab. You know the King is so suspicious
As if he hear I have but talk'd with you
Mine honor will be call'd in question
And therefore, gentle Mortimer, be gone.
  Y. Mor. Madam, I cannot stay to answer you.
But think of Mortimer as he deserves!
                        [*Exeunt all but Queen.*]
  Q. Isab. So well hast thou deserv'd, sweet Mortimer,   60
As Isabel could live with thee forever.
In vain I look for love at Edward's hand,
Whose eyes are fix'd on none but Gaveston:

Yet once more I'll importune him with prayers;
If he be strange and not regard my words,
My son and I will over into France
And to the King my brother there complain
How Gaveston hath robb'd me of his love.
But yet I hope my sorrows will have end,
And Gaveston this blessed day be slain!   *Exit.*   70

[2.5]   *Enter Gaveston, pursued.*

  Gav. Yet, lusty lords, I have escap'd your hands,
Your threats, your 'larums, and your hot pursuits;
And though divorced from King Edward's eyes,
Yet liveth Pierce of Gaveston unsurpris'd,
Breathing, in hope—malgrado all your beards,
That muster rebels thus against your King—
To see his royal sovereign once again.

*Enter the nobles [Warwick, Lancaster, Pembroke, Younger
Mortimer, soldiers, James, Horse-Boy, Pembroke's servants].*

  War. Upon him, soldiers! Take away his weapons.
  Y. Mor. Thou proud disturber of thy country's peace,
Corrupter of thy King, cause of these broils,   10
Base flatterer, yield! And were it not for shame,
Shame and dishonor to a soldier's name,
Upon my weapon's point here should'st thou fall
And welter in thy gore!
  Lan. Monster of men
That (like the Greekish strumpet!) train'd to arms
And bloody wars so many valiant knights,
Look for no other fortune, wretch, than death!
Kind Edward is not here to buckler thee.
  War. Lancaster, why talk'st thou to the slave?—   20
Go, soldiers, take him hence, for, by my sword,
His head shall off. Gaveston, short warning
Shall serve thy turn: it is our country's cause,
That here severely we will execute
Upon thy person.—Hang him at a bough!
  Gav. My lord—.
  War. Soldiers, have him away—
But for thou wert the favorite of a king,
Thou shalt have so much honor at our hands.
           [Warwick uses hands to imitate head-chopping.]
  Gav. I thank you all, my lords: then I perceive,   30
That heading is one and hanging is the other,
And death is all. . . .

Enter Earl of Arundel.

Lan. How now, my lord of Arundel?

Arun. My lords, King Edward greets you all by me.

War. Arundel, say your message.

Arun. His Majesty,
Hearing that you had taken Gaveston,
Entreateth you by me, yet but he may
See him before he dies. For why, he says,
And sends you word, he knows that die he shall: 40
And if you gratify His Grace so far,
He will be mindful of the courtesy.

War. How now!

Gav. Renowned Edward, how thy name
Revives poor Gaveston!

War. No, it needeth not.
Arundel, we will gratify the King
In other matters, he must pardon us in this.
Soldiers, away with him!

Gav. Why, my lord of Warwick,   50
Will not these delays beget my hopes?   [*Sarcastically.*]
I know it, lords, it is this life you aim at,
Yet grant King Edward this.

Y. Mor. Shalt thou appoint
What we shall grant? Soldiers, away with him!
Thus we'll gratify the King—
We'll send his head by thee. Let him bestow
His tears on that, for that is all he gets
Of Gaveston, or else his senseless trunk.

Lan. Not so, my lords, lest he bestow more cost   60
In burying him than he hath ever earn'd.

Arun. My lords, it is His Majesty's request
And in the honor of a king he swears,
He will but talk with him, and send him back.

War. When, can you tell? Arundel, no. We wot,
He that the care of his realm remits
And drives his nobles to these exigents
For Gaveston, will if he seize him once
Violate any promise to possess him.

Arun. Then if you will not trust His Grace in keep,   70
My lords, I will be pledge for his return.

Y. Mor. It is honorable in thee to offer this.
But for we know thou art a noble gentleman,
We will not wrong thee so, to make away
A true man for a thief.

Gav. How mean'st thou, Mortimer? That is over-base!

Y. Mor. Away, base groom, robber of king's renown!
Question with thy companions and mates.

    Pem. My Lord Mortimer, and you, my lords, each one,
To gratify the King's request therein,   80
Touching the sending of this Gaveston,
Because His Majesty so earnestly
Desires to see the man before his death,
I will upon mine honor undertake
To carry him and bring him back again—
Provided this, that you my lord of Arundel
Will join with me.

    War. Pembroke, what wilt thou do?
Cause yet more bloodshed? Is it not enough
That we have taken him, but must we now   90
Leave him on *had-I-wist* and let him go?

    Pem. My lords, I will not over-woo your honors.
But if you dare trust Pembroke with the prisoner,
Upon mine oath, I will return him back.

    Arun. My lord of Lancaster, what say you in this?

    Lan. Why, I say, let him go on Pembroke's word.

    Pem. And you, Lord Mortimer?

    Y. Mor. How say you, my lord of Warwick?

    War. Nay, do your pleasures, I know how 'twill prove.

    Pem. Then give him me.   100

    Gav. Sweet sovereign, yet I come
To see thee ere I die!

    War. [*aside.*] (Yet not perhaps,
If Warwick's wit and policy prevail.)

    Y. Mor. My lord of Pembroke, we deliver him you.
Return him on your honor. Sound, away!

    [*Trumpet sounds.*] *Exeunt. Manent Pembroke,* ⟨*Arundel,*⟩
        Gaveston, and Pembroke's men, four soldiers.

    Pem. My lord, you shall go with me.
My house is not far hence, out of the way
A little, but our men shall go along.
We that have pretty wenches to our wives,   110
Sir, must not come so near to balk their lips.

    ⟨*Arun.*⟩ 'Tis very kindly spoke, my lord of Pembroke:
Your honor hath an adamant of power
To draw a prince.

    Pem. So, my lord. Come hither, James:
I do commit this Gaveston to thee.
Be thou this night his keeper. In the morning
We will discharge thee of thy charge. Be gone.

    Gav. Unhappy Gaveston, whither goest thou now?

[*Exeunt Gaveston, James, and some of Pembroke's men.*]
Horse-Boy. My lord, we'll quickly be at Cobham.   120
                                                              Exeunt.

[3.1] [*Alarum. Enter Warwick and his men pursuing Gaveston.
Exeunt.*] *Enter Gaveston mourning and the Earl of Pembroke's
      men.* [*They are in disorder and fleeing from Warwick.*]

Gav. O treacherous Warwick, thus to wrong thy friend!
James. I see it is your life these arms pursue.
Gav. Weaponless must I fall, and die in bands?
O, must this day be period of my life?
Center of all my bliss? An ye be men,
Speed to the King.

                Enter Warwick and his company.

War. My lord of Pembroke's men,
Strive you no longer. I will have that Gaveston!
James. Your lordship does dishonor to yourself,
And wrong our lord, your honorable friend.   10
War. No, James, it is my country's cause I follow.
Go, take the villain! Soldiers, come away!
We'll make quick work. Commend me to your master,
My friend, and tell him that I watch'd it well.
—Come, let thy shadow parley with King Edward.
Gav. Treacherous earl, shall I not see the King?
War. The King of Heaven perhaps—no other king.
Away!   *Exeunt Warwick and his men with Gaveston.*
James. Come fellows, it booted not for us to strive.
We will in haste go certify our lord.   *Exeunt.*   20

[3.2] *Enter King Edward and* [*Younger*] *Spencer,* [*Baldock,
      and soldiers*] *with drums and fifes.*

K. Edw. I long to hear an answer from the barons
Touching my friend, my dearest Gaveston.
Ah, Spencer, not the riches of my realm
Can ransom him! Ah, he is mark'd to die!
I know the malice of the younger Mortimer,
Warwick I know is rough, and Lancaster
Inexorable—and I shall never see
My lovely Pierce, my Gaveston again!
The barons overbear me with their pride.—
    Y. Spen. Were I King Edward, England's sovereign,   10
Son to the lovely Eleanor of Spain,
Great Edward Longshanks' issue, would I bear

These braves, this rage, and suffer uncontroll'd
These barons thus to beard me in my land,
In mine own realm? My lord, pardon my speech—
Did you retain your father's magnanimity,
Did you regard the honor of your name,
You would not suffer thus Your Majesty
Be counterbuft of your nobility—
Strike off their heads, and let them preach on poles!   20
No doubt, such lessons they will teach the rest
As by their preachments they will profit much
And learn obedience to their lawful King!
   K. Edw. Yea, gentle Spencer, we have been too mild,
Too kind to them—but now have drawn our sword!
And if they send me not my Gaveston,
We'll steel it on their crest and poll their tops!
   Bald. This haught resolve becomes Your Majesty,
Not to be tied to their affection
As though Your Highness were a schoolboy still: 30
And must be aw'd and govern'd like a child.

*Enter Hugh Spencer, an old man, father to the young Spencer,
with his truncheon, and soldiers.*

   E. Spen. Long live my sovereign, the noble Edward—
In peace triumphant, fortunate in wars!
   K. Edw. Welcome, old man! Com'st thou in Edward's aid?
Then tell thy prince of whence and what thou art.
   E. Spen. Lo, with a band of bowmen and of pikes,
Brown bills and targeteers, four hundred strong,
Sworn to defend King Edward's royal right,
I come in person to Your Majesty—
Spencer, the father of Hugh Spencer there,   40
Bound to Your Highness everlastingly
For favors done in him unto us all.
   K. Edw. Thy father, Spencer?
   Y. Spen. True, an it like Your Grace—
That pours in lieu of all your goodness shown
His life, my lord, before your princely feet.
   K. Edw. Welcome ten thousand times, old man, again!
Spencer, this love, this kindness to thy King,
Argues thy noble mind and disposition.
Spencer, I here create thee Earl of Wiltshire   50
And daily will enrich thee with our favor,
That as the sunshine shall reflect o'er thee.
Beside, the more to manifest our love,
Because we hear Lord Bruce doth sell his land
And that the Mortimers are in hand withal,

Thou shalt have crowns of us t' outbid the barons:
And, Spencer, spare them not but lay it on!
Soldiers, a largess, and thrice welcome all!
   Y. Spen. My lord, here comes the Queen.

Enter the Queen and her son and Levune, a Frenchman.

   K. Edw. Madam, what news?   60
   Q. Isab. News of dishonor, lord, and discontent.
Our friend Levune, faithful and full of trust,
Informeth us by letters and by words
That Lord Valois our brother, King of France,
Because Your Highness hath been slack in homage
Hath seized Normandy into his hands.
These be the letters, this the messenger.
   K. Edw. Welcome, Levune. Tush Sib, if this be all,
Valois and I will soon be friends again.
—But to my Gaveston! Shall I never see,   70
Never behold thee now?—Madam, in this matter
We will employ you and your little son:
You shall go parley with the King of France.
Boy, see you bear you bravely to the King,
And do your message with a majesty.
   P. Edw. Commit not to my youth things of more weight
Than fits a Prince so young as I to bear.
And fear not, lord and father, Heaven's great beams
On Atlas's shoulder shall not lie more safe
Than shall your charge committed to my trust.   80
   Q. Isab. Ah, boy, this towardness makes thy mother fear
Thou art not mark'd to many days on earth.
   K. Edw. Madam, we will that you with speed be shipp'd,
And this our son. Levune shall follow you
With all the haste we can despatch him hence.
Choose of our lords to bear you company,
And go in peace: Leave us in wars at home.
   Q. Isab. Unnatural wars, where subjects brave their King—
God end them once! My lord, I take my leave
To make my preparation for France.   [*Exeunt.*] 90

Enter ⟨Arundel⟩.

   K. Edw. What, Lord ⟨Arundel⟩, dost thou come alone?
   ⟨*Arun.*⟩ Yea, my good lord, for Gaveston is dead!
   K. Edw. Ah, traitors, have they put my friend to death?
—Tell me, ⟨Arundel,⟩ died he ere thou cam'st?
Or didst thou see my friend to take his death?
   ⟨*Arun.*⟩ Neither, my lord; for as he was surpris'd,

Begirt with weapons and with enemies round,
I did Your Highness' message to them all,
Demanding him of them—entreating rather,
And said, upon the honor of my name,   100
That I would undertake to carry him
Unto Your Highness, and to bring him back.
   K. Edw. And tell me, would the rebels deny me that?
   Y. Spen. Proud recreants!
   K. Edw. Yea, Spencer, traitors all.
   ⟨*Arun.*⟩ I found them at the first inexorable.
The Earl of Warwick would not bide the hearing,
Mortimer hardly, Pembroke and Lancaster
Spake least; and when they flatly had denied,
Refusing to receive me pledge for him,   110
The Earl of Pembroke mildly thus bespake:
"My lords, because our sovereign sends for him
And promiseth he shall be safe return'd,
I will this undertake, to have him hence
And see him re-delivered to your hands."
   K. Edw. Well, and how fortunes that he came not?
   Y. Spen. Some treason or some villainy was cause.
   ⟨*Arun.*⟩ The Earl of Warwick seiz'd him on his way.
For being deliver'd unto Pembroke's men,
Their lord rode home thinking his prisoner safe.   120
But ere he came, Warwick in ambush lay
And bare him to his death: and in a trench
Strake off his head—and march'd unto the camp.
   Y. Spen. A bloody part, flatly against law of arms!
   K. Edw. O shall I speak, or shall I sigh and die?
   Y. Spen. My lord, refer your vengeance to the sword
Upon these barons. Hearten up your men.
Let them not unreveng'd murder your friends!
Advance your standard, Edward, in the field,
And march to fire them from their starting holes!   130
   K. Edw. kneels. By earth, the common mother of us all,
By Heaven and all the moving orbs thereof,
By this right hand, and by my father's sword,
And all the honors 'longing to my crown,
I will have heads and lives for him as many
As I have manors, castles, towns, and towers!
Treacherous Warwick! Traitorous Mortimer!
If I be England's King, in lakes of gore
Your headless trunks, your bodies will I trail
That you may drink your fill and quaff in blood   140
And stain my royal standard with the same

—That so my bloody colors may suggest
Remembrance of revenge immortally
On your accursed traitorous progeny!
You villains that have slain my Gaveston!
And in this place of honor and of trust,
Spencer, sweet Spencer, I adopt thee here:
And merely of our love we do create thee
Earl of Gloucester and Lord Chamberlain,
Despite of times, despite of enemies.   150
    Y. Spen. My lord, here is a messenger from the barons
Desires access unto Your Majesty.
    K. Edw. Admit him near.

Enter [2 Messenger] from the barons with his coat of arms.

    Mess. Long live King Edward, England's lawful lord!
    K. Edw. So wish not they, I wis, that sent thee hither.
Thou com'st from Mortimer and his complices.
A ranker rout of rebels never was!
Well, say thy message.
    Mess. The barons up in arms by me salute
Your Highness with long life and happiness—   160
And bid me say, as plainer to Your Grace,
That if without effusion of blood
You will this grief have ease and remedy
That from your princely person you remove
This Spencer as a putrifying branch
That deads the royal vine, whose golden leaves
Empale your princely head, your diadem,
Whose brightness such pernicious upstarts dim—
Say they, and lovingly advise Your Grace
To cherish virtue and nobility   170
And have old servitors in high esteem
And shake off smooth dissembling flatterers:
This granted, they, their honors, and their lives
Are to Your Highness vow'd and consecrate.
    Y. Spen. Ah, traitors, will they still display their pride?
    K. Edw. Away, tarry no answer but be gone!
Rebels, will they appoint their sovereign
His sports, his pleasures, and his company?
Yet, ere thou go, see how I do divorce   *Embrace Spencer.*
Spencer from me.—Now get thee to thy lords   180
And tell them I will come to chastise them
For murdering Gaveston. Hie thee, get thee gone!
Edward with fire and sword follows at thy heels.
                          [Exit 2 Messenger.]

My lord, perceive you how these rebels swell?
Soldiers, good hearts, defend your sovereign's right,
For now, even now, we march to make them stoop!
Away!

*Exeunt. Alarums, excursions, a great fight, and a retreat
[sounded]. Enter the King, Spencer the father, Spencer the
son, and the noblemen of the King's side.*

K. Edw. Why do we sound retreat? Upon them, lords!
This day I shall pour vengeance with my sword
On those proud rebels that are up in arms   190
And do confront and countermand their King.
  Y. Spen. I doubt it not, my lord, right will prevail.
  E. Spen. 'Tis not amiss, my liege, for either part
To breathe awhile. Our men with sweat and dust
All chok'd well near, begin to faint for heat:
And this retire refresheth horse and man.
  Y. Spen. Here come the rebels.

*Enter the barons: [Younger] Mortimer, Lancaster, Warwick,
Pembroke, cum caeteris [with Kent, a silent watcher].*

  Y. Mor. Look, Lancaster, yonder is Edward
Among his flatterers.
  Lan. And there let him be   200
Till he pay dearly for their company.
  War. And shall, or Warwick's sword shall smite in vain.
  K. Edw. What, rebels, do you shrink and sound retreat?
  Y. Mor. No, Edward, no, thy flatterers faint and fly.
  Lan. They'd best betimes forsake thee, and their trains,
For they'll betray thee, traitors as they are!
  Y. Spen. Traitor on thy face, rebellious Lancaster!
  Pem. Away, base upstart, brav'st thou nobles thus?
  E. Spen. A noble attempt, and honorable deed,
Is it not, trow ye, to assemble aid,   210
And levy arms against your lawful King!
  K. Edw. For which ere long their heads shall satisfy
To appease the wrath of their offended King.
  Y. Mor. Then, Edward, thou wilt fight it to the last,
And rather bathe thy sword in subjects' blood
Than banish that pernicious company?
  K. Edw. Ay, traitors all, rather than thus be brav'd,
Make England's civil towns huge heaps of stones,
And ploughs to go about our palace gates.
  War. A desperate and unnatural resolution!   220
Alarum to the fight!
St. George for England, and the barons' right!

K. Edw. Saint George for England, and King Edward's
     right.

[*Alarums. Exeunt the two parties severally.*] *Enter Edward,*
[the Bishop of Winchester, and soldiers] with the barons [and
     Kent] captives.

K. Edw. Now, lusty lords, now, not by chance of war
But justice of the quarrel and the cause,
Vail'd is your pride! Methinks you hang the heads—
But we'll advance them, traitors! Now 'tis time
To be aveng'd on you for all your braves,
And for the murder of my dearest friend,
To whom right well you knew our soul was knit,   230
Good Pierce of Gaveston, my sweet favorite.
Ah, rebels, recreants, you made him away!
     Kent. Brother, in regard of thee, and of thy land,
Did they remove that flatterer from thy throne.
     K. Edw. So, sir, you have spoke: Away, avoid our presence!
                                                    [*Exit Kent.*]
Accursed wretches, was't in regard of us,
When we had sent our messenger to request
He might be spar'd to come to speak with us,
And Pembroke undertook for his return,
That thou, proud Warwick, [snatch'd] the prisoner,   240
Poor Pierce, and headed him against law of arms?
For which *thy* head shall overlook the rest
As much as thou in rage outwent'st the rest!
     War. Tyrant, I scorn thy threats and menaces.
It is but temporal that thou canst inflict.
     Lan. The worst is death. And better die to live
Than live in infamy under such a King.
     K. Edw. Away with them, my lord of Winchester!
These lusty leaders, Warwick and Lancaster,
I charge you roundly, off with both their heads!   250
Away!
     War. Farewell, vain world!
     Lan. Sweet Mortimer, farewell.
     Y. Mor. England, unkind to thy nobility,
Groan for this grief. Behold how thou art maim'd!
     K. Edw. Go, take that haughty Mortimer to the Tower.
There see him safe bestow'd. And for the rest,
Do speedy execution on them all.
Be gone!
     Y. Mor. [*aside.*] (What, Mortimer, can ragged stony   260
          walls
Immure thy virtue that aspires to Heaven?
No, Edward, England's scourge, it may not be—

Mortimer's hope surmounts his fortune far.)

> [*The captive barons are led off.*]

  K. Edw. Sound drums and trumpets! March with me, my
friends,
Edward this day hath crown'd him King anew.

> *Exit. Manent Spencer filius, Levune, and Baldock.*

  Y. Spen. Levune, the trust that we repose in thee,
Begets the quiet of King Edward's land:
Therefore be gone in haste and with advice
Bestow that treasure on the lords of France
That therewith all enchanted like the guard   270
That suffer'd Jove to pass in showers of gold
To Danaë, all aid may be denied
To Isabel the Queen, that now in France
Makes friends: to cross the seas with her young son
And step into his father's regiment.—
  Levune. That's it these barons and the subtle Queen
Long [leveled] at.
  Bald. Yea, but, Levune, thou seest,
These barons lay their heads on blocks together.
What they intend, the hangman frustrates clean.   280
  Levune. Have you no doubt, my lords, I'll clap [so] close
Among the lords of France with England's gold
That Isabel shall make her plaints in vain
And France shall be obdurate with her tears.
  Y. Spen. Then make for France, amain. Levune, away!
Proclaim King Edward's wars and victories.   *Exeunt omnes.*

[4.1]   *Enter Edmund [Earl of Kent].*

  Kent. Fair blows the wind for France. Blow gentle gale,
Till Edmund be arriv'd for England's good.
Nature, yield to my country's cause in this.
A brother? No, a butcher of thy friends!
Proud Edward, dost thou banish me thy presence?
But I'll to France, and cheer the wronged Queen,
And certify what Edward's looseness is.
Unnatural King, to slaughter noblemen
And cherish flatterers! Mortimer, I stay
Thy sweet escape. Stand gracious, gloomy night,   10
To his device!

> *Enter Mortimer, disguised.*

  Y. Mor. Holla! Who walketh there?
Is't you, my lord?

Kent. Mortimer, 'tis I.
But hath thy potion wrought so happily?
Y. Mor. It hath, my lord. The warders all asleep,
I thank them, gave me leave to pass in peace.
But hath your grace got shipping unto France?
Kent. Fear it not.   *Exeunt.*

[4.2]   *Enter the Queen and [Prince Edward,] her son.*

Q. Isab. Ah, boy, our friends do fail us all in France.
The lords are cruel, and the King unkind.
What shall we do?
P. Edw. Madam, return to England,
And please my father well. And then a fig
For all my uncle's friendship here in France.
I warrant you, I'll win His Highness quickly.
A loves me better than a thousand Spencers.
Q. Isab. Ah, boy, thou art deceiv'd at least in this,
To think that we can yet be tun'd together.   10
No, no, we jar too far.—Unkind Valois!
Unhappy Isabel, when France rejects!
Whither, O, whither dost thou bend thy steps?

Enter Sir John of Hainault.

Sir J. Madam, what cheer?
Q. Isab. Ah, good Sir John of Hainault,
Never so cheerless nor so far distress'd.
Sir J. I hear, sweet lady, of the King's unkindness.
But droop not, madam. Noble minds contemn
Despair. Will Your Grace with me to Hainault?
—And there stay time's advantage with your son?   20
How say you, my lord, will you go with your friends
And shake off all our fortunes equally?
P. Edw. So pleaseth the Queen, my mother, me it likes.
The King of England nor the court of France
Shall have me from my gracious mother's side—
Till I be strong enough to break a staff—
And then have at the proudest Spencer's head!
Sir J. Well said, my lord!
Q. Isab. O, my sweet heart, how do I moan thy wrongs—
Yet triumph in the hope of thee, my joy!   30
Ah sweet Sir John, even to the utmost verge
Of Europe, or the shore of Tanais,
We will with thee to Hainault, so we will.
The marquis is a noble gentleman:
His grace, I dare presume, will welcome me.
But who are these?

Enter Edmund [Earl of Kent] and Mortimer.

Kent. Madam, long may you live,
Much happier than your friends in England do!
   Q. Isab. Lord Edmund and Lord Mortimer alive!
Welcome to France! The news was here, my lord,   40
That you were dead or very near your death.
   Y. Mor. Lady, the last was truest of the twain.
But Mortimer, reserv'd for better hap,
Hath shaken off the thraldom of the Tower
And lives t' advance your standard, good my lord.
   P. Edw. How mean you and the King my father lives?
No, my Lord Mortimer, not I, I trow!
   Q. Isab. Not, son? Why *not?* I would it were no worse!
—But, gentle lords, friendless we are in France.
   Y. Mor. Monsieur le Grand, a noble friend of yours,   50
Told us at our arrival all the news:
How hard the nobles, how unkind the King
Hath show'd himself. But, madam, right makes room
Where weapons want. And though a many friends
Are made away (as Warwick, Lancaster,
And others of our party and faction),
Yet have we friends, assure Your Grace, in England
Would cast up caps and clap their hands for joy
To see us there appointed for our foes.
   Kent. Would all were well, and Edward well reclaim'd—   60
For England's honor, peace and quietness.
   Y. Mor. But by the sword, my lord, it must be deserv'd.
The King will ne'er forsake his flatterers.
   Sir J. My lords of England, sith th' ungentle King
Of France refuseth to give aid of arms
To this distressed Queen his sister here,
Go you with her to Hainault. Doubt ye not
We will find comfort, money, men, and friends
Ere long to bid the English King a base.
How say'st, young Prince what think you of the match?   70
   P. Edw. I think King Edward will outrun us all.
   Q. Isab. Nay, son, not so. And you must not discourage
Your friends that are so forward in your aid.
   Kent. Sir John of Hainault, pardon us, I pray.
These comforts that you give our woeful Queen
Bind us in kindness all at your command.
   Q. Isab. Yea, gentle brother. And the God of Heaven
Prosper your happy motion, good Sir John!
   Y. Mor. This noble gentleman, forward in arms,
Was born, I see, to be our anchor-hold.   80

Sir John of Hainault, be it thy renown
That England's Queen and nobles in distress
Have been by thee restor'd and comforted.

   Sir J. Madam, along, and you my lord, with me
That England's peers may Hainault's welcome see.   [*Exeunt.*]

[4.3] *Enter the King, ⟨Arundel⟩, the two Spencers with others.*

   K. Edw. Thus after many threats of wrathful war,
Triumpheth England's Edward with his friends—
And triumph, Edward, with his friends uncontroll'd!
My lord of Gloucester, do you hear the news?

   Y. Spen. What news, my lord?

   K. Edw. Why, man, they say there is great execution
Done through the realm. My Lord of Arundel,
You have the note, have you not?

   ⟨*Arun.*⟩ From the Lieutenant of the Tower, my lord.

   K. Edw. I pray let us see it. What have we there?   10
Read it, Spencer.   *Spencer reads their names.*

   [*Y. Spen.* "The Lord William Tuchet, the Lord William fitz
William, the Lord Warren de Lisle, the Lord Henry Bradborne,
and the Lord William Chenie—barons—with John Page, an
esquire, were drawn and hanged at Pomfret. . . .

   "And then shortly after, Roger Lord Clifford, John Lord
Mowbray, and Sir Gosein d'Eevill—barons—were drawn and
hanged at York.

   "At Bristow in like manner were executed Sir Henry de
Willington and Sir Henry Montford, baronets.   20

   "And at Gloucester, the Lord John Gifford and Sir William
Elmebridge, knight.

   "And at London, the Lord Henry Teies, baron.

   "At Winchelsea, Sir Thomas Culpepper, knight.

   "At Windsor, the Lord Francis de Aldham, baron.

   "And at Canterbury, the Lord Bartholomew de Badelismere
and the Lord Bartholomew de Ashbornham, barons.

   "Also at Cardiff, in Wales, Sir William Fleming, knight was
executed.

   Divers were executed in their counties, as Sir Thomas   30
Mandit and others."]

   K. Edw. Why, so: they bark'd apace a month ago.
Now, on my life, they'll neither bark nor bite!
Now, sirs, the news from France? Gloucester, I trow
The lords of France love England's gold so well
As Isabella gets no aid from thence.
What now remains? Have you proclaim'd, my lord,
Reward for them can bring in Mortimer?

   Y. Spen. My lord, we have. And if he be in England,

A will be had ere long, I doubt it not.   40
   K. Edw. If, dost thou say? Spencer, as true as death,
He is in England's ground. Our portmasters
Are not so careless of their King's command.

Enter [3 Messenger].

How now, what news with thee? From whence come these?
   Post. Letters, my lord, and tidings forth of France.
To you, my lord of Gloucester, from Levune.
[Gives letter to Younger Spencer.]
   K. Edw. Read.
Y. Spen. reads the letter.
   "My duty to your honor promised, &c., I have, according
to instructions in that behalf, dealt with the King of France his
lords and effected that the Queen, all discontented and dis-   50
comforted, is gone. Whither? If you ask, with Sir John of Hai-
nault, brother to the marquis, into Flanders. With them are gone
Lord Edmund and the Lord Mortimer, having in their company
divers of your nation, and others. And as constant report goeth,
they intend to give King Edward battle in England sooner than
he can look for them. This is all the news of import.
Your honor's in all service, Levune."
   K. Edw. Ah, villains, hath that Mortimer escap'd?
With him is Edmund gone associate?
And will Sir John of Hainault lead the round?   60
Welcome, a God's name, madam, and your son:
England shall welcome you and all your rout!
Gallop apace, bright Phœbus, through the sky,
And dusky night in rusty iron car,
Between you both shorten the time, I pray,
That I may see that most desired day
When we may meet these traitors in the field!
Ah, nothing grieves me but my little boy
Is thus misled to countenance their ills.
Come, friends, to Bristow, there to make us strong.   70
And, winds, as equal be to bring them in,
As you injurious were to bear them forth!   *[Exeunt.]*

[4.4] *Enter the Queen, her son, Edmund [Earl of Kent], Mor-*
timer, and Sir John [and soldiers].

   Q. Isab. Now, lords, our loving friends and countrymen,
Welcome to England all, with prosperous winds!
Our kindest friends in Belgia have we left,
To cope with friends at home—a heavy case
When force to force is knit, and sword and glaive
In civil broils make kin and countrymen

Slaughter themselves in others, and their sides
With their own weapons gor'd. But what's the help?
Misgovern'd kings are cause of all this wreck.
And Edward, thou art one among them all   10
Whose looseness hath betray'd thy land to spoil
And made the channels overflow with blood
Of thine own people. Patron shouldst thou be,
But thou——.

   Y. Mor. Nay, madam, if you be a warrior,
You must not grow so passionate in speeches.
Lords, sith that we are by sufferance of Heaven
Arriv'd and armed in this Prince's right,
Here for our country's cause swear we to him
All homage, fealty, and forwardness.   20
And for the open wrongs and injuries
Edward hath done to us, his Queen, and land,
We come in arms to wreak it with the sword—
That England's Queen in peace may repossess
Her dignities and honors, and withal
We may remove these flatterers from the King,
That havocs England's wealth and treasury.

   Sir J. Sound trumpets, my lord, and forward let us march.
Edward will think we come to flatter him.

   Kent. I would he never had been flatter'd more!   30
                      [Trumpets sound. Exeunt.]

[4.5] [*Alarms and excursions.*] *Enter the King, Baldock, and*
       Spencer the son, flying about the stage.

   Y. Spen. Fly, fly, my lord! the Queen is over-strong!
Her friends do multiply, and yours do fail.
Shape we our course to Ireland, there to breathe.

   K. Edw. What, was I born to fly and run away,
And leave the Mortimers conquerors behind?
Give me my horse, and let's re'nforce our troops:
And in this bed of honor die with fame.

   Bald. O no, my lord, this princely resolution
Fits not the time, away, we are pursu'd!   *[Exeunt.]*

   [*Enter*] *Edmund alone with a sword and target.*

   Kent. This way he fled, but I am come too late.   10
Edward, alas, my heart relents for thee!
Proud traitor, Mortimer, why dost thou chase
Thy lawful King, thy sovereign, with thy sword?
—Vilde wretch, and why hast *thou*, of all unkind,
Borne arms against thy brother and thy King?
Rain showers of vengeance on my cursed head,

Thou God, to whom in justice it belongs
To punish this unnatural revolt!
Edward, this Mortimer aims at thy life.
O fly him, then!—But, Edmund, calm this rage. 20
Dissemble or thou diest, for Mortimer
And Isabel do kiss, while they conspire:
And yet she bears a face of love forsooth!
Fie on that love that hatcheth death and hate!
Edmund, away! Bristow to Longshanks' blood
Is false. Be not found single for suspect.
Proud Mortimer pries near unto thy walks.

Enter the Queen, Mortimer, the young Prince, and Sir John of Hainault [, with soldiers].

 Q. Isab. Successful battle gives the God of kings
To them that fight in right and fear His wrath.
Since, then, successfully we have prevail'd, 30
Thanks be Heaven's great architect, and you!
Ere farther we proceed, my noble lords,
We here create our well-beloved son,
Of love and care unto his royal person,
Lord Warden of the realm, and sith the fates
Have made his father so infortunate,
Deal you, my lords, in this, my loving lords,
As to your wisdoms fittest seems in all.
 Kent. Madam, without offense, if I may ask,
How will you deal with Edward in his fall? 40
 P. Edw. Tell me, good uncle, what Edward do you mean?
 Kent. Nephew, your father—I dare not call him King.
 Y. Mor. My lord of Kent, what needs these questions?
'Tis not in her controlment, nor in ours,
But as the realm and parliament shall please:
So shall your brother be disposed of.
 —(I like not this relenting mood in Edmund. [*Aside to Queen.*]
Madam, 'tis good to look to him betimes.)
 Q. Isab. (My lord, the Mayor of Bristow knows our mind.)
             [*Aside to Mortimer.*]
 Y. Mor. (Yea, madam, and they scape not easily 50
That fled the field.)   [*Aside.*]
 Q. Isab. Baldock is with the King.
A goodly chancellor, is he not, my lord?
 Sir J. So are the Spencers, the father and the son.
 Kent. (This, Edward, is the ruin of [thy] realm!) [*Aside, despairingly.*]

*Enter Rice ap Howell and the Mayor of Bristow with Spencer
the father [prisoner].*

Rice. God save Queen Isabel and her princely son!
Madam, the mayor and citizens of Bristow,   [*Points to the*
In sign of love and duty to this presence,   *Mayor.*]
Present by me this traitor to the state,
Spencer, the father to that wanton Spencer,   60
That like the lawless Catiline of Rome
Revell'd in England's wealth and treasury!

   Q. Isab. We thank you all.

   Y. Mor. Your loving care in this
Deserveth princely favors and rewards.
But where's the King and the other Spencer fled?

   Rice. Spencer the son, created Earl of Gloucester,
Is with that smooth-tongu'd scholar Baldock gone
And shipp'd but late for Ireland with the King.

   Y. Mor. (Some whirlwind fetch them back or sink them
      all!—)   [*Aside.*]   70
They shall be started thence, I doubt it not.

   P. Edw. Shall I not see the King my father yet?

   Kent. (Unhappy Edward, chas'd from England's bounds.)
                                                      [*Aside.*]

   Sir J. Madam, what resteth? Why stand you in a muse?

   Q. Isab. I rue my lord's ill-fortune, but alas,
Care of my country call'd me to this war.

   Y. Mor. Madam, have done with care and sad complaint.
Your King hath wrong'd your country and himself,
And we must seek to right it as we may.—
Meanwhile have hence this rebel to the block: 80
Your lordship cannot privilege your head!   [*Sarcastically.*]

   E. Spen. Rebel is he that fights against his prince!
So fought not they that fought in Edward's right.

   Y. Mor. Take him away, he prates.
                        [*Exeunt soldiers with Elder Spencer.*]
                                        You, Rice ap Howell,
Shall do good service to Her Majesty,
Being of countenance in your country here,
To follow these rebellious runagates.
We in meanwhile, madam, must take advice
How Baldock, Spencer, and their complices
May in their fall be follow'd to their end. *Exeunt omnes.*   90

[4.6] *Enter the Abbot, Monks, [King] Edward, [Younger]
Spencer, and Baldock [the last three disguised].*

   Abbot. Have you no doubt, my lord, have you no fear:

321 ACT 4 SCENE 6

As silent and as careful we will be
To keep your royal person safe with us,
Free from suspect and fell invasion
Of such as have Your Majesty in chase—
Yourself, and those your chosen company—
As danger of this stormy time requires.

    K. Edw. Father, thy face should harbor no deceit.
O, hadst thou ever been a king, thy heart,
Pierc'd deeply with a sense of my distress,   10
Could not but take compassion of my state.
Stately and proud, in riches and in train,
Whilom I was, powerful and full of pomp—
But what is he whom rule and empery
Have not in life or death made miserable?
Come Spencer, come Baldock, come, sit down by me,
Make trial now of that philosophy
That in our famous nurseries of arts
Thou sucked'st from Plato and from Aristotle.
Father, this life contemplative is heaven.   20
O, that I might this life in quiet lead!
But we, alas, are chas'd—and you, my friends,
Your lives and my dishonor they pursue!
Yet, gentle monks, for treasure, gold nor fee,
Do you betray us and our company.

    Monks. Your Grace may sit secure, if none but we
Do wot of your abode.

    Y. Spen. Not one alive. But shrewdly I suspect
A gloomy fellow in a mead below.
A gave a long look after us, my lord: 30
And all the land I know is up in arms,
Arms that pursue our lives with deadly hate.

    Bald. We were embark'd for Ireland—wretched we
With awkward winds and sore tempests driven
To fall on shore and here to pine in fear
Of Mortimer and his confederates!

    K. Edw. Mortimer, who talks of Mortimer?
Who wounds me with the name of Mortimer,
That bloody man?—Good father, on thy lap   [*Kneels.*]
Lay I this head, laden with mickle care.   40
O, might I never open these eyes again,
Never again lift up this drooping head,
O never more lift up this dying heart!

    Y. Spen. Look up, my lord. Baldock, this drowsiness
Betides no good. Here even we are betray'd!

Enter, with Welsh hooks, Rice ap Howell, a Mower, and the Earl of Leicester.

Mow. Upon my life, those be the men ye seek.   [*Points.*]

Rice. Fellow, enough.—My lord, I pray be short. [*To Leices-*

A fair commission warrants what we do.   *ter.*]

Leices. The Queen's commission, urged by Mortimer.—

(What cannot gallant Mortimer with the Queen? [*Paren-* 50

Alas, see where he sits and hopes unseen   *thesis is spoken as*

T'escape their hands that seek to reave his life!   *an aside.*]

Too true it is: *Quem dies vidit veniens superbum,*

Hunc dies vidit fugiens jacentem.

But, Leicester, leave to grow so passionate . . .)

Spencer and Baldock, by no other names,

I do arrest you of high treason here.

Stand not on titles, but obey th' arrest;

'Tis in the name of Isabel the Queen.

My lord, why droop you thus?   60

K. Edw. O day the last of all my bliss on earth,

Center of all misfortune! O my stars,

Why do you lour unkindly on a King?

Comes Leicester then in Isabella's name

To take my life, my company from me?

Here, man, rip up this panting breast of mine

And take my heart, in rescue of my friends!

Rice. Away with them!

Y. Spen. It may become thee yet

To let us take our farewell of His Grace.   70

Abbot. (My heart with pity earns to see this sight—

A king to bear these words and proud commands!)   [*Aside.*]

K. Edw. Spencer, ah sweet Spencer, thus then must we part?

Y. Spen. We must, my lord! So will the angry heavens.

K. Edw. Nay, so will Hell and cruel Mortimer!

The gentle heavens have not to do in this.

Bald. My lord, it is in vain to grieve or storm.

Here humbly of Your Grace we take our leaves;

Our lots are cast, I fear me so is thine.

K. Edw. In Heaven we may, in earth ne'er shall we meet. 80

And, Leicester, say, what shall become of us?

Leices. Your Majesty must go to Killingworth.

K. Edw. Must! 'Tis somewhat hard when kings *must* go.

Leices. Here is a litter ready for Your Grace,

That waits your pleasure—and the day grows old.

Rice. As good be gone as stay and be benighted.

K. Edw. A litter hast thou? Lay me in a hearse

And to the gates of Hell convey me hence!

Let Pluto's bells ring out my fatal knell
And hags howl for my death at Charon's shore   90
For friends hath Edward none but these,
And these must die under a tyrant's sword.

   Rice. My lord, be going. Care not for these,
For we shall see them shorter by the heads.

   K. Edw. Well, that shall be, shall be. Part we must.
Sweet Spencer, gentle Baldock, part we must.
Hence feigned weeds, unfeigned are my woes!

                          [*Throws off his disguise.*]
Father, farewell! Leicester, thou stay'st for me
And go I must. Life, farewell, with my friends!

               Exeunt [*King*] *Edward and Leicester.*

   Y. Spen. O is he gone? Is noble Edward gone?   100
Parted from hence? never to see us more?
Rent sphere of heaven, and, fire, forsake thy orb!
Earth, melt to air! Gone is my sovereign,
Gone, gone, alas, never to make return!

   Bald. Spencer, I see our souls are fleeted hence.
We are depriv'd the sunshine of our life.
Make for a new life, man. Throw up thy eyes
And heart and hand to Heaven's immortal throne!
Pay nature's debt with cheerful countenance.
Reduce we all our lessons unto this: 110
To die, sweet Spencer, therefore live we all.
Spencer, all live to die, and rise to fall.

   Rice. Come, come, keep these preachments till you come to
the place appointed. You and such as you are have made wise
work in England.—Will your lordships away?   [*Ironically.*]

   Mow. Your lordship I trust will remember me?

   Rice. Remember thee, fellow! What else? Follow me to the
town.   [*Exeunt.*]

[5.1] *Enter the King, Leicester, with* [*the*] *Bishop* [*of Win-*
       chester and Trussel] *for the crown.*

   Leices. Be patient, good my lord, cease to lament,
Imagine Killingworth Castle were your court,
And that you lay for pleasure here a space,
Not of compulsion or necessity.

   K. Edw. Leicester, if gentle words might comfort me,
Thy speeches long ago had eas'd my sorrows:
For kind and loving hast thou always been.
The griefs of private men are soon allay'd,
But not of kings. The forest deer being struck

Runs to an herb that closeth up the wounds.   10
But when the imperial lion's flesh is gor'd,
He rends and tears it with his wrathful paw!
—Highly scorning that the lowly earth
Should drink his blood, mounts up into the air!
And so it fares with me whose dauntless mind
Th' ambitious Mortimer would seek to curb,
And that unnatural Queen, false Isabel,
That thus hath pent and mew'd me in a prison—
For such outrageous passions cloy my soul
As with the wings of rancor and disdain   20
Full often am I soaring up to heaven
To plain me to the gods against them both!
—But when I call to mind I am a King,
Methinks I should revenge me of my wrongs,
That Mortimer and Isabel have done. . . .
But what are kings when regiment is gone
But perfect shadows in a sunshine day?
My nobles rule: I bear the name of King;
I wear the crown: but am controll'd by them—
By Mortimer and my unconstant Queen   30
Who spots my nuptial bed with infamy!
—Whilst I am lodg'd within this cave of care
Where sorrow at my elbow still attends,
To company my heart with sad laments
That bleeds within me for this strange exchange.
But tell me, must I now resign my crown
To make usurping Mortimer a king?

    B. of Win. Your Grace mistakes. It is for England's good
And princely Edward's right we crave the crown.

    K. Edw. No, 'tis for Mortimer, not Edward's head!   40
For he's a lamb, encompassed by wolves
Which in a moment will abridge his life.
But if proud Mortimer do wear this crown,
Heavens turn it to a blaze of quenchless fire!
Or like the snaky wreath of Tisiphon,
Engirt the temples of his hateful head!
So shall not England's vines be perished,
But Edward's name survives, though Edward dies.

    Leices. My lord, why waste you thus the time away?
They stay your answer. Will you yield your crown?   50

    K. Edw. Ah, Leicester, weigh how hardly I can brook
To lose my crown and kingdom without cause:
To give ambitious Mortimer my right,
That like a mountain overwhelms my bliss—
In which extreme my mind here murder'd is!

But what the Heavens appoint, I must obey.
Here, take my crown—the life of Edward too.

                                [Takes off crown.]

Two Kings in England cannot reign at once.
But stay a while! Let me be King till night
That I may gaze upon this glittering crown: 60
So shall my eyes receive their last content;
My head, the latest honor due to it;
And jointly both yield up their wished right.
Continue ever thou celestial sun—
Let never silent night possess this clime!
Stand still you watches of the element!
All times and seasons, rest you at a stay!
—That Edward may be still fair England's King. . . .
But day's bright beams doth vanish fast away,
And needs I must resign my wished crown.   70
Inhuman creatures nurs'd with tiger's milk,
Why gape you for your sovereign's overthrow?
My diadem I mean, and guiltless life—
See, monsters, see, I'll wear my crown again!

                                  [Puts on crown.]

What, fear you not the fury of your King?
—But, hapless Edward, thou art fondly led,
They pass not for thy frowns as late they did,
But seeks to make a new-elected King—
Which fills my mind with strange despairing thoughts,
Which thoughts are martyred with endless torments,   80
And in this torment comfort find I none
But that I feel the crown upon my head!
And therefore let me wear it yet awhile. . . .

    Trus. My lord, the parliament must have present news.
And therefore say, will you resign or no?

                                The King rageth.

    K. Edw. I'll not resign! But whilst I live—.
Traitors, be gone! And join you with Mortimer!
Elect, conspire, install, do what you will!
Their blood and yours shall seal these treacheries!

    B. of Win. This answer we'll return, and so farewell.   90

                                [Going with Trussel.]

    Leices. Call them again, my lord, and speak them fair:
For if they go, the Prince shall lose his right.

    K. Edw. Call thou them back, I have no power to speak.

    Leices. My lord, the King is willing to resign.

    B. of Win. If he be not, let him choose.

    K. Edw. O would I might! But heavens and earth conspire
To make me miserable! Here, receive my crown.

Receive it? No, these innocent hands of mine
Shall not be guilty of so foul a crime—
He of you all that most desires my blood   100
And will be called the murderer of a king,
Take it. What, are you mov'd? Pity you me?
Then send for unrelenting Mortimer
And Isabel, whose eyes being turn'd to steel
Will sooner sparkle fire than shed a tear.
Yet stay, for rather than I'll look on them,
Here, here!   [*Gives crown.*]
           Now, sweet God of Heaven,
Make me despise this transitory pomp,
And sit for aye enthronized in Heaven!
Come, death, and with thy fingers close my eyes!   110
Or if I live, let me forget myself.
(B. of Win.) My lord—
   K. Edw. Call me not lord! Away, out of my sight!
—Ah, pardon me, grief makes me lunatic.
Let not that Mortimer protect my son;
More safety there is in a tiger's jaws,
Than his embracements! Bear this to the Queen,
Wet with my tears and dried again with sighs—
                              [*Gives handkerchief.*]
If with the sight thereof she be not moved,
Return it back and dip it in my blood!   120
Commend me to my son, and bid him rule
Better than I.—Yet how have I transgress'd
Unless it be with too much clemency?
   Trus. And thus most humbly do we take our leave.
   K. Edw. Farewell.
                       [*Exeunt Bishop and Trussel with crown.*]
             I know the next news that they bring
Will be my death. And welcome shall it be!
To wretched men death is felicity.
   Leices. Another post, what news brings he?

             [*Enter Berkeley, who gives a paper to Leicester.*]

   K. Edw. Such news as I expect. Come, Berkeley, come,
And tell thy message to my naked breast.   130
   Berk. My lord, think not a thought so villainous
Can harbor in a man of noble birth.
To do Your Highness service and devoir
And save you from your foes, Berkeley would die.
   Leices. My lord, the council of the Queen commands
That I resign my charge.
   K. Edw. And who must keep me now? Must you, my lord?

Berk. Ay, my most gracious lord, so 'tis decreed.

K. Edw. [*takes the paper.*]—By Mortimer, whose name is
written here!

Well may I rent his name that rends my heart! 140

[*Tears it.*]

This poor revenge has something eas'd my mind—

So may his limbs be torn as is this paper!

Hear me, immortal Jove, and grant it too!

Berk. Your Grace must hence with me to Berkeley straight.

K. Edw. Whither you will. All places are alike.

And every earth is fit for burial.

Leices. Favor him, my lord, as much as lieth in you.

Berk. Even so betide my soul as I use him!

K. Edw. Mine enemy hath pitied my estate,

And that's the cause that I am now remov'd. 150

Berk. And thinks Your Grace that Berkeley will be cruel?

K. Edw. I know not. But of this am I assured—

That death ends all, and I can die but once.

Leicester, farewell.

Leices. Not yet, my lord, I'll bear you on your way.

Exeunt omnes.

[5.2]   *Enter Mortimer and Queen Isabella.*

Y. Mor. Fair Isabel, now have we our desire:

The proud corrupters of the light-brain'd King

Have done their homage to the lofty gallows,

And he himself lies in captivity.

Be rul'd by me, and we will rule the realm.

In any case, take heed of childish fear—

For now we hold an old wolf by the ears,

That if he slip will seize upon us both

And gripe the sorer being grip'd himself.

Think therefore, madam, that imports us much 10

To erect your son with all the speed we may

And that I be protector over him.

For our behoof will bear the greater sway

Whenas a king's name shall be underwrit.

Q. Isab. Sweet Mortimer, the life of Isabel!

Be thou persuaded that I love thee well.

And therefore—so the Prince my son be safe,

Whom I esteem as dear as these mine eyes—

Conclude against his father what thou wilt!

—And I myself will willingly subscribe. 20

Y. Mor. First would I hear news he were depos'd:

And then let me alone to handle him.

Enter [4] Messenger.

Letters, from whence?

Mess. From Killingworth, my lord.

Q. Isab. How fares my lord the King?

Mess. In health, madam, but full of pensiveness.

Q. Isab. Alas, poor soul, would I could ease his grief!

[*Enter the Bishop of Winchester. He bows deeply.*]

Thanks, gentle Winchester. [*To the Messenger.*] Sirrah, be gone.

[*Exit Messenger.*]

B. of Win. The King hath willingly resign'd his crown.

Q. Isab. O happy news! Send for the Prince, my son!   30

B. of Win. [*pointing to letter in Queen's hand.*] Further, ere
    this letter was seal'd, Lord Berkeley came

So that he now is gone from Killingworth.

And we have heard that Edmund laid a plot

To set his brother free. No more but so.

The lord of Berkeley is so pitiful

As Leicester that had charge of him before.

Q. Isab. Then let some other be his guardian.

Y. Mor. Let me alone. *Here* is the privy seal!   [*Points to
                                                            himself.*]

[*Exit the Bishop of Winchester.*]

Who's there? Call hither Gurney and Matrevis.

To dash the heavy-headed Edmund's drift,   40

Berkeley shall be discharg'd, the King remov'd,

And none but we shall know where[as] he lieth.

Q. Isab. But, Mortimer, as long as he survives,

What safety rests for us or for my son?

Y. Mor. Speak, shall he presently be despatch'd and die?

Q. Isab. I would he were, so 'twere not by my means!

Enter Matrevis and Gurney. [*The Queen steps aside.*]

Y. Mor. Enough—.

Matrevis, write a letter presently

Unto the lord of Berkeley from ourself

That he resign the King to thee and Gurney.   50

And when 'tis done, we will subscribe our name.

Mat. It shall be done, my lord.   [*Writes.*]

Y. Mor. Gurney!

Gur. My lord.

Y. Mor. As thou intend'st to rise by Mortimer—

Who now makes Fortune's wheel turn as he please!—

Seek all the means thou canst to make him droop,

And neither give him kind word nor good look.

Gur. I warrant you, my lord.

Y. Mor. And this above the rest. Because we hear   60
That Edmund casts to work his liberty,
Remove him still from place to place by night
And at the last [be]come to Killingworth—
And then from thence to Berkeley back again!
And by the way to make him fret the more,
Speak curstly to him, and in any case
Let no man comfort him. If he chance to weep
But amplify his grief with bitter words.

Mat. Fear not, my lord! We'll do as you command.

Y. Mor. So now away! [*The Queen steps forward.*] Post
    thitherwards amain!   70

Q. Isab. Whither goes this letter? to my lord the King?
Commend me humbly to His Majesty,
And tell him that I labor all in vain
To ease his grief and work his liberty.
And bear him this as witness of my love.   [*Gives a jewel.*]

Mat. I will, madam.   *Exeunt Matrevis and Gurney.*

Y. Mor. Finely dissembled! Do so still, sweet Queen.
Here comes the young Prince with the Earl of Kent.

Q. Isab. Something he whispers in his childish ears.

Y. Mor. If he have such access unto the Prince,   80
Our plots and stratagems will soon be dash'd.

Q. Isab. Use Edmund friendly as if all were well.

Enter the young Prince and the Earl of Kent talking with him.

Y. Mor. How fares my honorable lord of Kent?

Kent. In health, sweet Mortimer. How fares Your Grace?

Q. Isab. Well, if my lord your brother were enlarg'd.

Kent. I hear of late he hath depos'd himself.

Q. Isab. The more my grief.

Y. Mor. And mine.

Kent. (Ah, they do dissemble!)   [*Aside.*]

Q. Isab. Sweet son, come hither, I must talk with thee.   90

Y. Mor. Thou being his uncle and the next of blood,
Do look to be protector over the Prince?

Kent. Not I, my lord. Who should protect the son
But she that gave him life? I mean the Queen.

P. Edw. Mother, persuade me not to wear the crown.
Let him be King! I am too young to reign.

Q. Isab. But be content, seeing it is His Highness' pleasure.

P. Edw. Let me but see him first, and then I will.

Kent. Ay, do, sweet nephew!

Q. Isab. Brother, you know it is impossible.   100

P. Edw. Why, is he dead?

Q. Isab. No, God forbid!

Kent. I would those words proceeded from your heart!

Y. Mor. Inconstant Edmund, dost thou favor him
That wast a cause of his imprisonment?

Kent. The more cause have I now to make amends!

Y. Mor. I tell thee, 'tis not meet that one so false
Should come about the person of a Prince.
My lord, he hath betrayed the King his brother,
And therefore trust him not.   110

P. Edw. But he repents and sorrows for it now.

Q. Isab. Come son, and go with this gentle lord and me.

P. Edw. With you I will, but not with Mortimer.

Y. Mor. Why, youngling, 'sdain'st thou so of Mortimer?
Then I will carry thee by force away.

P. Edw. Help, uncle Kent! Mortimer will wrong me!

[*Mortimer grasps the Prince. Kent tries to intervene.*]

Q. Isab. Brother Edmund, strive not. We are his friends.
Isabel is nearer than the Earl of Kent.

Kent. Sister, Edward is my charge, redeem him.

Q. Isab. Edward is my son, and I will keep him.   120

Kent. [*aside.*] (Mortimer shall know that he hath wrong'd me.
Hence will I haste to Killingworth Castle
And rescue aged Edward from his foes
To be reveng'd on Mortimer and thee!)   *Exeunt omnes.*

[5.3] *Enter Matrevis and Gurney* [*and soldiers*] *with the King.*

Mat. My lord, be not pensive. We are your friends.
Men are ordain'd to live in misery.
Therefore come, dalliance dangereth our lives.

K. Edw. Friends, whither must unhappy Edward go?
Will hateful Mortimer appoint no rest?
Must I be vexed like the nightly bird
Whose sight is loathsome to all winged fowls?
When will the fury of his mind assuage?
When will his heart be satisfied with blood?
If mine will serve, unbowel straight this breast   10
And give my heart to Isabel and him!
It is the chiefest mark they level at!

Gur. Not so, my liege. The Queen hath given this charge
To keep Your Grace in safety.
Your passions make your dolors to increase.

K. Edw. This usage makes my misery increase.
But can my air of life continue long
When all my senses are annoy'd with stench?
Within a dungeon England's King is kept
Where I am starv'd for want of sustenance—   20

My daily diet is heart-breaking sobs
That almost rents the closet of my heart!
Thus lives old Edward, not reliev'd by any—
And so must die, though pitied by many!
O, water, gentle friends, to cool my thirst
And clear my body from foul excrements.

  Mat. Here's channel water, as our charge is given.
Sit down, for we'll be barbers to Your Grace.

  K. Edw. Traitors, away, what, will you murder me?
Or choke your sovereign with puddle water? 30

  Gur. No, but wash your face, and shave away your beard,
Lest you be known and so be rescued.

  Mat. Why strive you thus? Your labor is in vain.

  K. Edw. The wren may strive against the lion's strength!
But all in vain, so vainly do I strive
To seek for mercy at a tyrant's hand. *They wash him with*
                     puddle water and shave his beard away.
Immortal powers! that knows the painful cares
That wait upon my poor distressed soul,
O level all your looks upon these daring men,
That wrongs their liege and sovereign, England's King! 40
O Gaveston, it is for thee that I am wrong'd,
For me both thou and both the Spencers died!
And for your sakes a thousand wrongs I'll take!
The Spencers' ghosts wherever they remain
Wish well to mine. Then [hush], for them I'll die.

  Mat. 'Twixt theirs and yours shall be no enmity.
Come, come away! Now put the torches out:
We'll enter in by darkness to Killingworth.

Enter Edmund.

  Gur. How now, who comes there?

  Mat. Guard the King sure! It is the Earl of Kent! 50

  K. Edw. O gentle brother, help to rescue me!

  Mat. Keep them asunder! Thrust in the King!

  Kent. Soldiers, let me but talk to him one word.

  Gur. Lay hands upon the earl for his assault!
                                [*Soldiers hold Kent.*]

  Kent. Lay down your weapons! Traitors, yield the King!

  Mat. Edmund, yield thou thyself, or thou shalt die.

  Kent. Base villains, wherefore do you gripe me thus?

  Gur. Bind him and so convey him to the court.

  Kent. Where is the court but here? Here is the King
And I will visit him! Why stay you me? 60

  Mat. The court is where Lord Mortimer remains.
Thither shall your honor go; and so farewell.

Exeunt Matrevis and Gurney with the King.
Manent Edmund and the soldiers.

Kent. O miserable is that commonweal
Where lords keep courts and kings are lock'd in prison!

Sol. Wherefore stay we? On, sirs, to the court!

Kent. Ay, lead me whither you will, even to my death,
Seeing that my brother cannot be releas'd!   *Exeunt.*

[5.4]   *Enter Mortimer alone.*

Y. Mor. The King must die, or Mortimer goes down.
The commons now begin to pity him.
Yet he that is the cause of Edward's death,
Is sure to pay for it when his son is of age:
And therefore will I do it cunningly.
This letter, written by a friend of ours,
Contains his death, yet bids them save his life: [*Reads.*]
Edwardum occidere nolite timere, bonum est—
"Fear not to kill the King, 'tis good he die."
But read it thus and that's another sense: 10
Edwardum occidere nolite, timere bonum est—
"Kill not the King, 'tis good to fear the worst."
Unpointed as it is, thus shall it go.
—That being dead, if it chance to be found,
Matrevis and the rest may bear the blame
And we be quit that caus'd it to be done!
Within this room is lock'd the messenger
That shall convey it and perform the rest.
And by a secret token that he bears
Shall he be murder'd when the deed is done!   20
—Lightborn, come forth!

[*Enter Lightborn.*]

Art thou so resolute as thou wast?

Light. What else, my lord? and far more resolute!

Y. Mor. And hast thou cast how to accomplish it?

Light. Ay, ay, and none shall know which way he died!

Y. Mor. But at his looks, Lightborn, thou wilt relent?

Light. Relent, ha, ha! I use much to relent!

Y. Mor. Well, do it bravely, and be secret.

Light. You shall not need to give instructions.
'Tis not the first time I have kill'd a man: 30
I learn'd in Naples how to poison flowers,
To strangle with a lawn thrust through the throat,
To pierce the windpipe with a needle's point,
Or whilst one is asleep, to take a quill
And blow a little powder in his ears,

Or open his mouth and pour quicksilver down.
And yet I have a braver way than these.
 Y. Mor. What's that?
 Light. Nay, you shall pardon me. None shall know my tricks.
 Y. Mor. I care not how it is, so it be not spi'd.   **40**
Deliver this to Gurney and Matrevis.   [*Gives letter.*]
At every ten mile end thou hast a horse.
Take this. [*Gives money.*] Away and never see me more!
 Light. No?
 Y. Mor. No—
Unless thou bring me news of Edward's death.
 Light. That will I quickly do. Farewell, my lord.
               [*Exit.*]
 Y. Mor. The Prince I rule, the Queen do I command,
And with a lowly congé to the ground,
The proudest lords salute me as I pass.   **50**
I seal, I cancel, I do what I will.
Fear'd am I more than lov'd—let me be fear'd
And when I frown make all the court look pale.
I view the Prince with Aristarchus' eyes
Whose looks were as a breeching to a boy.
They thrust upon me the Protectorship
And sue to me for that that I desire.
While at the council-table, grave enough,
And not unlike a bashful Puritan,
First I complain of imbecility,   **60**
Saying it is *onus quam gravissimum*—
Till being interrupted by my friends,
Suscepi that *provinciam* as they term it.
And to conclude, I am Protector now!
Now is all sure. The Queen and Mortimer
Shall rule the realm, the King; and none rule us.
Mine enemies will I plague, my friends advance.
And what I list command who dare control?
Major sum quam cui possit fortuna nocere.
And that this be the coronation-day,   **70**
It pleaseth me, and Isabel the Queen. [*Trumpets within.*]
The trumpets sound. I must go take my place.

Enter the young King [*Edward III*], [*Arch*]*bishop, Champion,
nobles, Queen.*

 A. of Cant. Long live King Edward, by the grace of God,
King of England and Lord of Ireland!
 Cham. If any Christian, Heathen, Turk, or Jew,
Dare but affirm that Edward's not true King,
And will avouch his saying with the sword,

I am the Champion that will combat him.

Y. Mor. None comes. Sound trumpets!

[*Trumpets sound.*]

K. Edw. Third. Champion, here's to thee. 80

[*Gives purse.*]

Q. Isab. Lord Mortimer, now take him to your charge.

Enter soldiers with the Earl of Kent prisoner.

Y. Mor. What traitor have we there with blades and bills?

Sol. Edmund, the Earl of Kent.

K. Edw. Third. What hath he done?

Sol. A would have taken the King away perforce
As we were bringing him to Killingworth.

Y. Mor. Did you attempt his rescue, Edmund? Speak.

Kent. Mortimer, I did. He is our King!
And thou compell'st this Prince to wear the crown!

Y. Mor. Strike off his head! He shall have martial law! 90

[*To soldiers.*]

Kent. Strike off my head! Base traitor, I defy thee!

K. Edw. Third. My lord, he is my uncle, and shall live.

Y. Mor. My lord, he is your enemy, and shall die.

Kent. Stay, villains! [*To soldiers who are trying to take
him away.*]

K. Edw. Third. Sweet mother, If I cannot pardon him,
Entreat my Lord Protector for his life.

Q. Isab. Son, be content. I dare not speak a word.

K. Edward. Third. Nor I. And yet methinks I should com-
mand. . . .
But seeing I cannot, I'll entreat for him—
My lord, if you will let my uncle live, 100
I will requite it when I come to age.

Y. Mor. 'Tis for Your Highness' good, and for the realm's.
—How often shall I bid you bear him hence? [*To soldiers.*]

Kent. Art thou King? Must I die at thy command?

Y. Mor. At *our* command.—Once more away with him!

Kent. Let me but stay and speak. I will not go! [*Struggles.*]
Either my brother or his son is King,
And none of both then thirst for Edmund's blood!
And therefore, soldiers, whither will you hale me?

*They hale Edmund away, and
carry him to be beheaded.*

K. Edw. Third. What safety may I look for at his hands 110

[*Points to Mortimer.*]

If that my uncle shall be murder'd thus?

Q. Isab. Fear not, sweet boy, I'll guard thee from thy
foes.

Had Edmund liv'd, he would have sought thy death.
Come, son, we'll ride a-hunting in the park.
  K. Edw. Third. And shall my uncle Edmund ride with us?
  Q. Isab. He is a traitor, think not on him, come.

Exeunt omnes.

[5.5]   *Enter Matrevis and Gurney. [Torches.]*

  Mat. Gurney, I wonder the King dies not,
Being in a vault up to the knees in water,
To which the channels of the castle run,
From whence a damp continually ariseth
That were enough to poison any man,
Much more a king brought up so tenderly.
  Gur. And so do I, Matrevis. Yesternight
I open'd but the door to throw him meat
And I was almost stifl'd with the savor!
  Mat. He hath a body able to endure   10
More than we can inflict. And therefore now
Let us assail his mind another while.
  Gur. Send for him out thence, and I will anger him.
  Mat. But stay, who's this?

Enter Lightborn.

  Light. My Lord Protector greets you.   *[Gives letter.]*
  Gur. What's here? I know not how to conster it.
  Mat. Gurney, it was left unpointed for the nonce,
Edwardum occidere nolite timere,
That's his meaning.
  Light. Know ye this token? I must have the King.   20
  Mat. Ay, stay awhile, thou shalt have answer straight.
(This villain's sent to make away the King.)   *[Aside.]*
  Gur. (I thought as much.)   *[Aside.]*
  Mat. (And when the murder's done,
See how he must be handled for his labor:
Pereat iste!) Let him have the King.   *[Aside.]*
What else? Here is the key, this is the lake: *[Points to*
Do as you are commanded by my lord.   *curtained*
  Light. I know what I must do. Get you away.   *back stage.]*
Yet be not far off, I shall need your help.   30
See that in the next room I have a fire,
And get me a spit and let it be red-hot.
  Mat. Very well.
  Gur. Need you anything besides?
  Light. What else, a table and a feather-bed.
  Gur. That's all?
  Light. Ay, ay. So, when I call you, bring it in.

Mat. Fear not thou that.

Gur. Here's a light, to go into the dungeon.

                  [Gives a torch and then exit with Matrevis.]

Light. So now   40

Must I about this gear. Ne'er was there any

So finely handled as this king shall be!   *[Opens curtains.]*

Foh, here's a place indeed with all my heart!

    K. Edw. Who's there? what light is that? wherefore com'st
        thou?

    Light. To comfort you, and bring you joyful news.

    K. Edw. Small comfort finds poor Edward in thy looks.

Villain, I know thou com'st to murder me!

    Light. To murder you, my most gracious lord?

Far is it from my heart to do you harm.

The Queen sent me to see how you were us'd,   50

For she relents at this your misery:

And what eyes can refrain from shedding tears

To see a king in this most piteous state?

    K. Edw. Weep'st thou already? List awhile to me,

And then thy heart, were it as Gurney's is,

Or as Matrevis', hewn from the Caucasus,

Yet will it melt, ere I have done my tale.

This dungeon where they keep me is the sink

Wherein the filth of all the castle falls.

    Light. O villains!   60

    K. Edw. And there in mire and puddle have I stood

This ten days' space, and lest that I should sleep,

One plays continually upon a drum.

They give me bread and water, being a king!

So that for want of sleep and sustenance

My mind's distemper'd, and my body's numb'd,

And whether I have limbs or no I know not.

O, would my blood dropp'd out from every vein

As doth this water from my tatter'd robes!

Tell Isabel the Queen I looked not thus   70

When for her sake I ran at tilt in France

And there unhors'd the Duke of Cleremont!

    Light. O speak no more, my lord, this breaks my heart!

        [Claps hands, and a servant brings in a feather-bed.]

Lie on this bed and rest yourself awhile.

    K. Edw. These looks of thine can harbor nought but death:

I see my tragedy written in thy brows.

Yet stay a while, forbear thy bloody hand,

And let me see the stroke before it comes,

That, and even then, when I shall lose my life,

My mind may be more steadfast on my God!   80

Light. What means Your Highness to mistrust me thus?

K. Edw. What mean'st thou to dissemble with me thus?

Light. These hands were never stain'd with innocent
      blood—

Nor shall they now be tainted with a king's.

K. Edw. Forgive my thought for having such a thought.

One jewel have I left. Receive thou this.   [*Gives jewel.*]

Still fear I, and I know not what's the cause,

But every joint shakes as I give it thee.

O, if thou harbor'st murder in thy heart,

Let this gift change thy mind, and save thy soul!   90

Know that I am a King! O, at that name

I feel a Hell of grief! Where is my crown?

Gone, gone, and do I remain alive?

Light. You're overwatch'd, my lord, lie down and rest.

K. Edw. But that grief keeps me waking, I should sleep,

For not these ten days have these eye-lids clos'd.

Now as I speak they fall, and yet with fear

Open again. O wherefore sits thou here?   [*Lies on bed.*]

Light. If you mistrust me, I'll be gone, my lord.

K. Edw. No, no, for if thou mean'st to murder me   100

Thou wilt return again, and therefore stay.   [*Sleeps.*]

Light. He sleeps.

K. Edw. [*wakes.*] O let me not die, yet stay, O stay a while!

Light. How now, my lord?

K. Edw. Something still buzzeth in mine ears

And tells me if I sleep I never wake,

This fear is that which makes me tremble thus,

And therefore tell me, wherefore art thou come?

Light. To rid thee of thy life!—Matrevis, come!

[*Enter Matrevis and Gurney.*]

K. Edw. I am too weak and feeble to resist. . . .   110

Assist me, sweet God, and receive my soul!

Light. Run for the table.

K. Edw. O spare me, or despatch me in a trice!

                    [*Matrevis brings in a table.*]

Light. So lay the table down, and stamp on it. [*Put table*

But not too hard, lest that you bruise his body.   *on King.*]

                [*The King calls out and then dies.*]

Mat. I fear me that this cry will raise the town,

And therefore, let us take horse and away.

Light. Tell me, sirs, was it not bravely done?

Gur. Excellent well! Take this for thy reward!

                  Then Gurney stabs Lightborn.

Come, let us cast the body in the moat,   120
And bear the King's to Mortimer our lord.
Away!   *Exeunt* [*with the bodies.*]

[5.6]   *Enter Mortimer and Matrevis.*

  Y. Mor. Is't done, Matrevis, and the murderer dead?
  Mat. Ay, my good lord! I would it were undone!
  Y. Mor. Matrevis, if thou now grow'st penitent
I'll be thy ghostly father! Therefore choose
Whether thou wilt be secret in this,
Or else die by the hand of Mortimer?
  Mat. Gurney, my lord, is fled, and will, I fear,
Betray us both. Therefore let me fly.
  Y. Mor. Fly to the savages!
  Mat. I humbly thank your honor.   [*Exit.*]   10
  Y. Mor. As for myself, I stand as Jove's huge tree,
And others are but shrubs compar'd to me!
All tremble at my name! And I fear none.
Let's see who dare impeach me for his death?

Enter the Queen.

  Q. Isab. Ah, Mortimer, the King my son hath news
His father's dead, and we have murder'd him!
  Y. Mor. What if he have? The King is yet a child.
  Q. Isab. Ay, ay, but he tears his hair and wrings his hands
And vows to be reveng'd upon us both!
Into the council-chamber he is gone   20
To crave the aid and succor of his peers:
Ay me, see where he comes, and they with him!
Now, Mortimer, begins our tragedy.

Enter the King with the lords [*and attendants*].

  [1] *Lord.* Fear not, my lord. Know that you are a king!
  K. Edw. Third. Villain!
  Y. Mor. How now, my lord?
  K. Edw. Third. Think not that I am frighted with thy words:
My father's murder'd through thy treachery!
And thou shalt die! And on his mournful hearse
Thy hateful and accursed head shall lie   30
To witness to the world that by thy means
His kingly body was too soon interr'd.
  Q. Isab. Weep not, sweet son.
  K. Edw. Third. Forbid me not to weep, he was my father;
And had you lov'd him half so well as I,
You could not bear his death thus patiently,
But you, I fear, conspir'd with Mortimer.

[1] *Lord.* Why speak you not unto my lord the King?

Y. Mor. Because I think scorn to be accus'd!
Who is the man dares say I murder'd him?   40

K. Edw. Third. Traitor in me my loving father speaks
And plainly saith, 'twas thou that murd'rest him.

Y. Mor. But hath Your Grace no other proof than this?

K. Edw. Third. Yes, if this be the hand of Mortimer.
                              [*Shows letter.*]

Y. Mor. (False Gurney hath betray'd me and himself.)
                              [*Aside to Queen.*]

Q. Isab. (I fear'd as much. Murder cannot be hid!)
                              [*Aside to Mortimer.*]

Y. Mor. 'Tis my hand. What gather you by this?

K. Edw. Third. That thither thou didst send a murderer.

Y. Mor. What murderer? Bring forth the man I sent!

K. Edw. Third. Ah, Mortimer, thou knowest that he is
      slain—   50
And so shalt thou be too! Why stays he here?
Bring him unto a hurdle, drag him forth;
Hang him, I say, and set his quarters up:
But bring his head back presently to me.

Q. Isab. For my sake, sweet son, pity Mortimer!

Y. Mor. Madam, entreat not, I will rather die
Than sue for life unto a paltry boy.

K. Edw. Third. Hence with the traitor, with the murderer!

Y. Mor. Base Fortune, now I see, that in thy wheel
There is a point, to which when men aspire,   60
They tumble headlong down. That point I touch'd,
And seeing there was no place to mount up higher,
Why should I grieve at my declining fall?
Farewell, fair Queen, weep not for Mortimer,
That scorns the world, and as a traveller
Goes to discover countries yet unknown.

K. Edw. Third. What, suffer you the traitor to delay?
      [*Mortimer is taken away by 1 Lord and attendants.*]

Q. Isab. As thou received'st thy life from me,
Spill not the blood of gentle Mortimer!

K. Edw. Third. This argues that you spilt my father's
      blood,   70
Else would you not entreat for Mortimer.

Q. Isab. I spill his blood? No!

K. Edw. Third. Ay, madam, you, for so the rumor runs.

Q. Isab. That rumor is untrue. For loving thee
Is this report rais'd on poor Isabel.

K. Edw. Third. I do not think her so unnatural.

[2] *Lord.* My lord, I fear me it will prove too true.

K. Edw. Third. Mother, you are suspected for his death
And therefore we commit you to the Tower
Till farther trial may be made thereof.   80
If you be guilty, though I be your son,
Think not to find me slack or pitiful.

Q. Isab. Nay, to my death, for too long have I liv'd
Whenas my son thinks to abridge my days.

K. Edw. Third. Away with her! Her words enforce these
tears.
And I shall pity her if she speak again.

Q. Isab. Shall I not mourn for my beloved lord?
And with the rest accompany him to his grave?

[2] Lord. Thus, madam, 'tis the King's will you shall hence.

Q. Isab. He hath forgotten me. Stay, I am his mother.   90

[2] Lord. That boots not. Therefore, gentle madam, go.

Q. Isab. Then come, sweet death, and rid me of this grief!
                                                    [*Exit.*]

[*Re-enter 1 Lord with Mortimer's head.*]

[1] Lord. My lord, here is the head of Mortimer.

K. Edw. Third. Go fetch my father's hearse, where it shall lie.
And bring my funeral robes.   [*Exeunt attendants.*]
                        Accursed head,
Could I have rul'd thee then, as I do now,
Thou had'st not hatch'd this monstrous treachery!
Here comes the hearse. Help me to mourn, my lords.

[*Re-enter attendants with Edward II lying in the hearse and
with funeral robes, which Edward III dons.*]

Sweet father, here unto thy murder'd ghost
I offer up this wicked traitor's head.   100
                        [*Puts it on father's body.*]
And let these tears, distilling from mine eyes,
Be witness of my grief and innocency.   [*Exeunt.*]

THE
TRAGICAL HISTORY OF
THE LIFE AND DEATH
OF DOCTOR FAUSTUS

[*Speaking Characters*

CHORUS
DOCTOR FAUSTUS
WAGNER, *his servant*
GOOD ANGEL
BAD ANGEL
VALDES ⎫
CORNELIUS ⎬ *magicians*
THREE SCHOLARS
LUCIFER
MEPHOSTOPHILIS
ROBIN, *called the Clown*
BELZEBUB
PRIDE ⎫
COVETOUSNESS │
ENVY │
WRATH ⎬ *the Seven Deadly Sins*
GLUTTONY │
SLOTH │
LECHERY ⎭
DICK, *a clown, hostler at an inn*
POPE ADRIAN
RAYMOND, *King of Hungary*
BRUNO, *rival Pope appointed by the Emperor*
TWO CARDINALS
ARCHBISHOP OF RHEIMS
FRIARS
VINTNER'S BOY
MARTINO ⎫
FREDERICK ⎬ *gentlemen at the Emperor's court*
BENVOLIO ⎭
THE GERMAN EMPEROR, CHARLES THE FIFTH
DUKE OF SAXONY
TWO SOLDIERS
HORSE-COURSER, *a clown*
CARTER, *a clown*
HOSTESS OF TAVERN
DUKE OF VANHOLT
DUCHESS OF VANHOLT
SERVANT
OLD MAN

Mute Characters

DARIUS, ALEXANDER THE GREAT, HIS PARAMOUR, HELEN OF TROY,
DEVILS, PIPER, CARDINALS, MONKS, FRIARS, ATTENDANTS, SOL-
DIERS, SERVANTS, TWO CUPIDS]

Enter Chorus.

Not marching in the fields of Trasimene
Where Mars did mate the warlike Carthagens,
Nor sporting in the dalliance of love
In courts of kings where state is overturn'd,
Nor in the pomp of proud audacious deeds
Intends our muse to vaunt his heavenly verse.
Only this, gentles: We must now perform
The form of Faustus' fortunes, good or bad,
And now to patient judgments we appeal
And speak for Faustus in his infancy.   10
Now is he born of parents base of stock
In Germany within a town call'd Rhode;
At riper years to Wittenberg he went
Whereas his kinsmen chiefly brought him up.
So much he profits in divinity
That shortly he was grac'd with doctor's name,
Excelling all, and sweetly can dispute
In th' heavenly matters of theology—
Till swoll'n with cunning, of a self-conceit,
His waxen wings did mount above his reach   20
And melting, Heavens conspir'd his overthrow!
For falling to a devilish exercise
And glutted now with learning's golden gifts
He surfeits upon cursed necromancy:
Nothing so sweet as magic is to him
Which he prefers before his chiefest bliss . . .
And this the man that in his study sits.

[1.1] [*Chorus points to curtains in back of stage. They are drawn to discover*] *Faustus in his study.* [*Chorus exit.*]

Fau. Settle thy studies Faustus, and begin
To sound the depth of that thou wilt profess.
Having commenc'd, be a Divine in show—
Yet level at the end of every art
And live and die in Aristotle's works.
Sweet Analytics, 'tis thou hast ravish'd me. . . .

[*Opens a book and turns over pages.*]

Bene disserere est finis logices.
Is to dispute well logic's chiefest end?
Affords this art no greater miracle?
Then read no more, thou hast attain'd that end.   10
A greater subject fitteth Faustus' wit:
Bid *on kai me on* farewell, and Galen come:

[*Opens another book.*]

Be a physician Faustus, heap up gold,
And be eterniz'd for some wondrous cure.
Summum bonum medicinae sanitas,
The end of physic is our body's health.
Why Faustus, hast thou not attain'd that end?
Are not thy bills hung up as monuments
Whereby whole cities have escap'd the plague
And thousand desperate maladies been cur'd?   20
Yet art thou still but Faustus and a man.
Could'st thou make men to live eternally
Or being dead raise them to life again,
Then this profession were to be esteem'd.
Physic farewell! Where is Justinian?   [*Opens another book.*]
*Si una eademque res legatur duobus, alter rem, alter valorem
rei, et cetera.*
A petty case of paltry legacies. . . .
Exhereditare filium non potest pater, nisi—
Such is the subject of the Institute   30
And universal body of the law!
This study fits a mercenary drudge
Who aims at nothing but external trash,
Too servile and illiberal for me.
When all is done, Divinity is best.
Jerome's Bible, Faustus, view it well.   [*Opens another book.*]
Stipendium peccati mors est. Ha! *Stipendium et cetera* . . .
The reward of sin is death? That's hard: *Si peccasse negamus,
fallimur, et nulla est in nobis veritas.* If we say that we have no
sin, we deceive ourselves, and there is no truth in us. Why,   40

then belike, we must sin, and so consequently die.
Ay, we must die an everlasting death.
What doctrine call you this? *Che serà, serà:*
What will be, shall be! Divinity, adieu!
These metaphysics of magicians   [*Opens another book raptly.*]
And necromantic books are heavenly;
Lines, circles, letters, characters—
Ay, these are those that Faustus most desires!
O, what a world of profit and delight,
Of power, of honor, and omnipotence   50
Is promis'd to the studious artisan!
All things that move between the quiet poles
Shall be at my command. Emperors and kings
Are but obey'd in their several provinces
But his dominion that exceeds in this
Stretcheth as far as doth the mind of man—
A sound magician is a demi-god!
Here tire my brains to get a deity! [*Reads awhile with delight.*]
Wagner, commend me to my dearest friends, *Enter Wagner.*
The German Valdes and Cornelius.   60
Request them earnestly to visit me.
    Wag. I will, sir.   *Exit.*
    Fau. Their conference will be a greater help to me
Than all my labors, plod I ne'er so fast.   [*He reads.*]

    Enter the [*Good*] *Angel and Spirit* [*i.e., Bad Angel*].

Good Ang. O Faustus, lay that damned book aside
And gaze not on it lest it tempt thy soul
And heap God's heavy wrath upon thy head!
Read, read the Scriptures—that is blasphemy!
    Bad Ang. Go forward Faustus, in that famous art
Wherein all nature's treasure is contain'd.   70
Be thou on earth as Jove is in the sky,
Lord and commander of these elements!   *Exeunt.*
    Fau. How am I glutted with conceit of this!
                              [*Raises head from book.*]
Shall I make spirits fetch me what I please?
Resolve me of all ambiguities?
Perform what desperate enterprise I will?
I'll have them fly to India for gold,
Ransack the ocean for orient pearl,
And search all corners of the new-found world
For pleasant fruits and princely delicates;   80
I'll have them read me strange philosophy
And tell the secrets of all foreign kings;
I'll have them wall all Germany with brass

And make swift Rhine circle fair Wittenberg;
I'll have them fill the public schools with [silk]
Wherewith the students shall be bravely clad.
I'll levy soldiers with the coin they bring
And chase the Prince of Parma from our land
And reign sole king of all our provinces!
Yea, stranger engines for the brunt of war   90
Than was the fiery keel at Antwerp's bridge
I'll make my servile spirits to invent.

Enter Valdes and Cornelius [with books].

Come German Valdes and Cornelius
And make me blest with your sage conference.
Valdes, sweet Valdes, and Cornelius,
Know that your words have won me at the last
To practice magic and concealed arts.
Philosophy is odious and obscure,
Both law and physic are for petty wits,
⟨Divinity is basest of the three—   100
Unpleasant, harsh, contemptible, and vilde.⟩
'Tis magic, magic, that hath ravish'd me!
Then, gentle friends, aid me in this attempt
And I, that have with subtle syllogisms
Gravell'd the pastors of the German church
And made the flow'ring pride of Wittenberg
⟨Swarm⟩ to my problems as th' infernal spirits
On sweet Musaeus when he came to Hell,
Will be as cunning as Agrippa was,
Whose shadows made all Europe honor him.   110
     Val. Faustus, these books, thy wit, and our experience
Shall make all nations to canonize us.
As Indian Moors obey their Spanish lords,
So shall the spirits of every element
Be always serviceable to us three:
Like lions shall they guard us when we please,
Like Almain rutters with their horsemen's staves
Or Lapland giants trotting by our sides;
Sometimes like women or unwedded maids
Shadowing more beauty in their airy brows   120
Than has the white breasts of the queen of love;
From Venice shall they drag huge argosies
And from America the golden fleece
That yearly stuff⟨s⟩ old Philip's treasury—
If learned Faustus will be resolute.
     Fau. Valdes, as resolute am I in this

As thou to live; therefore object it not.

Cor. The miracles that magic will perform
Will make thee vow to study nothing else.
He that is grounded in astrology,   130
Enrich'd with tongues, well seen in minerals,
Hath all the principles magic doth require.
Then doubt not Faustus but to be renown'd
And more frequented for this mystery
Than heretofore the Delphian oracle.
The spirits tell me they can dry the sea
And fetch the treasure of all foreign wracks,
Yea, all the wealth that our forefathers hid
Within the massy entrails of the earth.
Then tell me Faustus, what shall we three want?   140

Fau. Nothing, Cornelius! O, this cheers my soul!
Come, show me some demonstrations magical
That I may conjure in some bushy grove
And have these joys in full possession.

Val. Then haste thee to some solitary grove,
And bear wise Bacon's and [Albertus'] works,
The Hebrew Psalter, and New Testament;
And whatsoever else is requisite
We will inform thee ere our conference cease.

Cor. Valdes, first let him know the words of art,   150
And then, all other ceremonies learn'd,
Faustus may try his cunning by himself.

Val. First I'll instruct thee in the rudiments,
And then wilt thou be perfecter than I.

Fau. Then come and dine with me, and after meat
We'll canvass every quiddity thereof—
For ere I sleep I'll try what I can do.
This night I'll conjure though I die therefor!

                                              Exeunt omnes.

[1.2]   *Enter two scholars.*

1 Sch. I wonder what's become of Faustus that was wont
to make our schools ring with *sic probo*.

                Enter Wagner [*with a bottle*].

2 Sch. That shall we presently know. Here comes his boy.
1 Sch. How now sirrah, where's thy master?
Wag. God in Heaven knows.
2 Sch. Why, dost not thou know then?
Wag. Yes, I know, but that follows not.
1 Sch. Go to sirrah, leave your jesting and tell us where he is.

Wag. That follows not by force of argument, which you, being licentiates, should stand upon; therefore acknowledge   10
your error and be attentive.

2 Sch. Then you will not tell us?

Wag. You are deceiv'd, for I will tell you. Yet if you were
not dunces, you would never ask me such a question. For is
he not *corpus naturale?* And is not that *mobile?* Then wherefore should you ask me such a question? But that I am by
nature phlegmatic, slow to wrath, and prone to lechery—to
love, I would say—it were not for you to come within forty
foot of the place of execution—although I do not doubt but to
see you both hang'd the next sessions. Thus, having tri-   20
umphed over you, I will set my countenance like a precisian
and begin to speak thus: Truly, my dear brethren, my master is
within at dinner, with Valdes and Cornelius, as this wine, if
it could speak, would inform your worships; and so, the Lord
bless you, preserve you, and keep you, my dear brethren.

Exit.

1 Sch. O Faustus, then I fear that which I have long
    suspected,
That thou art fall'n into that damned art
For which they two are infamous through the world.

2 Sch. Were he a stranger, not allied to me,
The danger of his soul would make me mourn.   30
But come, let us go and inform the Rector.
It may be his grave counsel may reclaim him.

1 Sch. I fear me nothing will reclaim him now.

2 Sch. Yet let us see what we can do.   *Exeunt.*

[1.3] *Thunder. Enter Lucifer and four devils [above]:*
    Faustus [in magician's robe] to them with this speech:

Fau. Now that the gloomy shadow of the night,
Longing to view Orion's drizzling look,
Leaps from th' antarctic world unto the sky
And dims the welkin with her pitchy breath,
Faustus, begin thine incantations
And try if devils will obey thy hest,
Seeing thou hast pray'd and sacrific'd to them.
Within this circle is Jehovah's name
Forward and backward anagrammatiz'd,
Th' abbreviated names of holy saints,   10
Figures of every adjunct to the heavens,
And characters of signs and ⟨erring⟩ stars,
By which the spirits are enforc'd to rise:
Then fear not, Faustus, to be resolute
And try the uttermost magic can perform.   *Thunder.*

Sint mihi dei Acherontis propitii! Valeat numen triplex Ie-
hovae! Ignei, aerii, aquatici, spiritus, salvete! Orientis prin-
ceps, Belzebub inferni ardentis monarcha, et Demogorgon,
propitiamus vos ut appareat et surgat Mephostophilis! Quid
tu moraris? Per Iehovam, Gehennam, et consecratam 20
aquam quam nunc spargo, signumque crucis quod nunc facio, et
per vota nostra, ipse nunc surgat nobis dicatus Mephostophilis!

Enter a devil [i.e., a dragon-head rises from the open trap.
Faustus recoils].

I charge thee to return and change thy shape,
Thou art too ugly to attend on me.
Go, and return an old Franciscan friar:
That holy shape becomes a devil best.   *Exit devil [i.e., dragon-*
I see there's virtue in my heavenly words.   *head sinks].*
Who would not be proficient in this art?
How pliant is this Mephostophilis,
Full of obedience and humility,   30
Such is the force of magic and my spells!

Enter Mephostophilis [from the back as an elderly friar].

Meph. Now Faustus, what wouldst thou have me do?
Fau. I charge thee wait upon me whilst I live
To do whatever Faustus shall command,
Be it to make the moon drop from her sphere
Or the ocean to overwhelm the world.
Meph. I am a servant to great Lucifer
And may not follow thee without his leave.
No more than he commands must we perform.
Fau. Did not he charge thee to appear to me?   40
Meph. No, I came now hither of mine own accord.
Fau. Did not my conjuring raise thee? Speak.
Meph. That was the cause, but yet *per accidens:*
For when we hear one rack the name of God,
Abjure the Scriptures and his savior Christ,
We fly in hope to get his glorious soul.
Nor will we come unless he use such means
Whereby he is in danger to be damn'd.
Therefore the shortest cut for conjuring
Is stoutly to abjure all godliness   50
And pray devoutly to the Prince of Hell.
Fau. So Faustus hath already done, and holds this principle,
There is no chief but only Belzebub:
To whom Faustus doth dedicate himself.
This word *damnation* terrifies not me
For I confound Hell in Elysium:

My ghost be with the old philosophers!
But leaving these vain trifles of men's souls,
Tell me, what is that Lucifer thy lord?

    Meph. Arch-Regent and Commander of All Spirits.   60
    Fau. Was not that Lucifer an angel once?
    Meph. Yes Faustus, and most dearly lov'd of God.
    Fau. How comes it then that he is Prince of Devils?
    Meph. O, by aspiring pride and insolence,
For which God threw him from the face of Heaven.
    Fau. And what are you that live with Lucifer?
    Meph. Unhappy spirits that (fell) with Lucifer,
Conspir'd against our God with Lucifer,
And are for ever damn'd with Lucifer.
    Fau. Where are you damn'd?   70
    Meph. In Hell.
    Fau. How comes it then that thou art out of Hell?
    Meph. Why this is Hell, nor am I out of it. . . .
Think'st thou that I who saw the face of God
And tasted the eternal joys of Heaven
Am not tormented with ten thousand Hells
In being depriv'd of everlasting bliss?
O Faustus, leave these frivolous demands
Which strike a terror to my fainting soul!
    Fau. What, is great Mephostophilis so passionate   80
For being deprived of the joys of Heaven?
Learn thou of Faustus manly fortitude
And scorn those joys thou never shalt possess.
Go bear these tidings to great Lucifer:
Seeing Faustus hath incurr'd eternal death
By desperate thoughts against Jove's deity,
Say he surrenders up to him his soul
So he will spare him four and twenty years,
Letting him live in all voluptuousness,
Having thee ever to attend on me,   90
To give me whatsoever I shall ask,
To tell me whatsoever I demand,
To slay mine enemies and to aid my friends
And always be obedient to my will.
Go and return to mighty Lucifer
And meet me in my study at midnight,
And then resolve me of thy master's mind.
    Meph. I will, Faustus.   *Exit.*
    Fau. Had I as many souls as there be stars
I'd give them all for Mephostophilis!   100
By him I'll be great emperor of the world

And make a bridge thorough the moving **air**
To pass the ocean with a band of men;
I'll join the hills that bind the Afric shore
And make that country continent to Spain,
And both contributary to my crown;
The Emperor shall not live but by my leave,
Nor any potentate of Germany.
Now that I have obtain'd what I desir'd
I'll live in speculation of this art   110
Till Mephostophilis return again.   *Exit.*

[1.4]   *Enter Wagner and [Robin] the Clown.*

Wag. Come hither, sirrah boy.

Rob. Boy! O, disgrace to my person! Zounds, boy in your
face! You have seen many boys with such ⟨pickadevants⟩, I
am sure.

Wag. Sirrah, hast thou no comings in?

Rob. Yes, and goings out too, you may see sir.

Wag. Alas, poor slave! See how poverty jests in his naked-
ness. I know the villain's out of service, and so hungry that I
know he would give his soul to the Devil for a shoulder of
mutton, though it were blood-raw.   10

Rob. Not so, neither! I had need to have it well roasted, and
good sauce to it, if I pay so dear, I can tell you.

Wag. Sirrah, wilt thou be my man and wait on me? And
I will make thee go like *Qui mihi discipulus.*

Rob. What, in verse?

Wag. No, slave, in beaten silk and stavesacre.

Rob. Stavesacre? That's good to kill vermin! Then, belike,
if I serve you I shall be lousy.

Wag. Why, so thou shalt be, whether thou dost it or no; for
sirrah, if thou dost not presently bind thyself to me for   20
seven years, I'll turn all the lice about thee into familiars and
make them tear thee in pieces.

Rob. Nay sir, you may save yourself a labor, for they are
as familiar with me as if they paid for their meat and drink,
I can tell you.

Wag. Well sirrah, leave your jesting and take these guilders.

Rob. Yes marry sir, and I thank you too.

Wag. So, now thou art to be at an hour's warning when-
soever and wheresoever the Devil shall fetch thee.   30

Rob. Here, take your guilders, I'll none of 'em!

Wag. Not I, thou art press'd. Prepare thyself, for I will
presently raise up two devils to carry thee away. Banio!
Belcher!   *[Makes magical gestures.]*

Rob. Belcher! And Belcher come here I'll belch him. I am not afraid of a devil!

    Enter two devils [and the Clown runs about].

Wag. How now sir, will you serve me now?

Rob. Ay, good Wagner, take away the Devil then.

Wag. Spirits, away! [*Exeunt.*] Now sirrah, follow me.

Rob. I will sir! But hark you master, will you teach me   40
this conjuring occupation?

Wag. Ay sirrah, I'll teach thee to turn thyself to a dog or
a cat or a mouse or a rat or anything.

Rob. A dog or a cat or a mouse or a rat? O brave Wagner!

Wag. Villain, call me Master Wagner. And see that you
walk attentively, and let your right eye be always diametrally
fixed upon my left heel, that thou mayst *quasi vestigiis nostris
insistere.*

Rob. Well sir, I warrant you.   *Exeunt.*

  [Perhaps a Chorus before the second act is lost.]

[2.1]   *Enter Faustus in his study.*

 Fau. Now, Faustus, must thou needs be damn'd, canst thou
    not be sav'd!
What boots it then to think on God or Heaven?
Away with such vain fancies, and despair—
Despair in God and trust in Belzebub!
Now go not backward. Faustus, be resolute!
Why waver'st thou? O something soundeth in mine ear,
"Abjure this magic, turn to God again. . . ."
Why, He loves thee not—
The god thou serv'st is thine own appetite
Wherein is fix'd the love of Belzebub!   10
To him I'll build an altar and a church
And offer lukewarm blood of newborn babes!

     Enter the two Angels.

 Bad Ang. Go forward, Faustus, in that famous art.

 Good Ang. Sweet Faustus, leave that execrable art.

 Fau. Contrition, prayer, repentance, what of these?

 Good. O, they are means to bring thee unto Heaven.

 Bad. Rather illusions, fruits of lunacy,
That make men foolish that do use them most.

 Good. Sweet Faustus, think of Heaven and heavenly things.

Bad. No Faustus, think of honor and of wealth.   20

Exeunt Angels.

Fau. Wealth!
Why, the signory of Emden shall be mine!
When Mephostophilis shall stand by me
What power can hurt me? Faustus, thou art safe.
Cast no more doubts! Mephostophilis, come,
And bring glad tidings from great Lucifer.
Is't not midnight? Come Mephostophilis,
Veni, veni, Mephostophilis!

Enter Mephostophilis.

Now tell me, what saith Lucifer thy lord?
⟨*Meph.*⟩ That I shall wait on Faustus whilst he lives,   30
So he will buy my service with his soul.
Fau. Already Faustus hath hazarded that for thee.
Meph. But now thou must bequeath it solemnly
And write a deed of gift with thine own blood,
For that security craves Lucifer.
If thou deny it I must back to Hell.
Fau. Stay Mephostophilis and tell me
What good my soul will do thy lord?
Meph. Enlarge his kingdom.
Fau. Is that the reason why he tempts us thus?   40
Meph. Solamen miseris socios habuisse doloris.
Fau. Why, have you any pain that torture other?
Meph. As great as have the human souls of men.
But tell me, Faustus, shall I have thy soul—
And I will be thy slave and wait on thee
And give thee more than thou hast wit to ask?
Fau. Ay Mephostophilis, I'll give it him.
Meph. Then, Faustus, stab thy arm courageously
And bind thy soul that at some certain day
Great Lucifer may claim it as his own.   50
And then be thou as great as Lucifer!
Fau. Lo, Mephostophilis, for love of thee
[*Faustus cuts his arm, dips a pen in his blood, and writes.*]
Faustus hath cut his arm and with his proper blood
Assures his soul to be great Lucifer's,
Chief lord and regent of perpetual night.
View here this blood that trickles from mine arm
And let it be propitious for my wish.
Meph. But Faustus,
Write it in manner of a deed of gift.
Fau. Ay so I do—But Mephostophilis,   60

My blood **congeals** and I can write no more!

    Meph. I'll fetch thee fire to dissolve it straight.   *Exit.*

    Fau. What might the staying of my blood portend?
Is it unwilling I should write this bill?
Why streams it not that I may write afresh:
"Faustus gives to thee his soul"? O there it stay'd. . . .
Why shouldst thou not? Is not thy soul thine own?
Then write again: "Faustus gives to thee his soul."

Enter Mephostophilis with the chafer of fire.

    Meph. See Faustus, here is fire. Set it on.

                    [*Faustus puts his arm over the fire.*]

    Fau. So, now the blood begins to clear again.   70
Now will I make an end immediately.

    Meph. [*aside.*] (What will not I do to obtain his soul!)

    Fau. Consummatum est! This bill is ended:
And Faustus hath bequeath'd his soul to Lucifer.
—But what is this inscription on mine arm?
Homo fuge! Whither should I fly?
If unto Heav'n, He'll throw me down to Hell.
—My senses are deceiv'd, here's nothing writ.
—O yes, I see it plain! Even here is writ
Homo fuge! Yet shall not Faustus fly!   80

    Meph. [*aside.*] (I'll fetch him somewhat to delight his mind.)

                              Exit.

*Enter devils giving crowns and rich apparel to Faustus.
They dance and then depart.*

Enter Mephostophilis.

    Fau. What means this show? Speak, Mephostophilis.

    Meph. Nothing Faustus, but to delight thy mind
And let thee see what magic can perform.

    Fau. But may I raise such spirits when I please?

    Meph. Ay Faustus, and do greater things than these.

    Fau. Then, Mephostophilis, receive this scroll,
A deed of gift of body and of soul—
But yet conditionally that thou perform
All covenants and articles between us both.   90

    Meph. Faustus, I swear by Hell and Lucifer
To effect all promises between us both.

    Fau. Then hear me read it, Mephostophilis:

*On these conditions following—First, that Faustus may be a
spirit in form and substance. Secondly, that Mephostophilis
shall be his servant and be by him commanded. Thirdly, that
Mephostophilis shall do for him and bring him whatsoever.*

Fourthly, that he shall be in his chamber or house invisible.
Lastly, that he shall appear to the said John Faustus at all
times in what form or shape soever he please: 100
I, John Faustus of Wittenberg, Doctor, by these presents, do
give both body and soul to Lucifer, Prince of the East, and his
minister Mephostophilis, and furthermore grant unto them that,
four and twenty years being expired, and these articles above
written being inviolate, full power to fetch or carry the said
John Faustus, body and soul, flesh, blood, into their habitation
wheresoever.

By me, John Faustus.

Meph. Speak Faustus, do you deliver this as your deed?
Fau. Ay, take it, and the Devil give thee good of it!   110
Meph. So now Faustus, ask me what thou wilt.
Fau. First will I question with thee about Hell.
Tell me, where is the place that men call Hell?
Meph. Under the heavens.
Fau. Ay, so are all things else, but whereabouts?
Meph. Within the bowels of these elements
Where we are tortur'd and remain forever.
Hell hath no limits nor is circumscrib'd
In one self place, but where we are is Hell,
And where Hell is there must we ever be.   120
And to be short, when all the world dissolves
And every creature shall be purifi'd
All places shall be Hell that is not Heaven!
Fau. I think Hell's a fable.
Meph. Ay, think so still—till experience change thy mind!
Fau. Why, dost thou think that Faustus shall be damn'd?
Meph. Ay, of necessity, for here's the scroll
In which thou hast given thy soul to Lucifer.
Fau. Ay, and body too—but what of that?
Think'st thou that Faustus is so fond to imagine   130
That after this life there is any pain?
No, these are trifles and mere old wives' tales.
Meph. But I am an instance to prove the contrary,
For I tell thee I am damn'd and now in Hell!
Fau. Nay, and this be Hell, I'll willingly be damn'd—
What, sleeping, eating, walking, and disputing? But leaving
this, let me have a wife, the fairest maid in Germany, for I am
wanton and lascivious and cannot live without a wife.
Meph. Well Faustus, thou shalt have a wife.

He fetches in a woman devil.
Fau. What sight is this?   140
Meph. Now Faustus, wilt thou have a wife?
Fau. Here's a hot whore indeed! No, I'll no wife.

Meph. Marriage is but a ceremonial toy,   [*She-devil exit.*]
And if thou lovest me, think no more of it.
I'll cull thee out the fairest courtesans
And bring them every morning to thy bed.
She whom thine eye shall like thy heart shall have,
Were she as chaste as was Penelope,
As wise as Saba, or as beautiful
As was bright Lucifer before his fall.   150
Here, take this book, peruse it well.
The iterating of these lines brings gold;   [*Points to certain*
The framing of this circle on the ground   *pages.*]
Brings thunder, whirlwinds, storm, and lightning;
Pronounce this thrice devoutly to thyself,
And men in harness shall appear to thee,
Ready to execute what thou command'st.

[*He gives Faustus the book.*]

Fau. Thanks Mephostophilis for this sweet book.
This will I keep as chary as my life.

                            Exeunt.

[Apparently at this point there occurred a comic scene, which
is now lost.]

[2.2]   *Enter Faustus in his study and Mephostophilis.*

Fau. When I behold the heavens, then I repent—
And curse thee, wicked Mephostophilis,
Because thou hast depriv'd me of those joys.
Meph. 'Twas thine own seeking Faustus, thank thyself.
But think'st thou Heaven is such a glorious thing?
I tell thee, Faustus, it is not half so fair
As thou or any man that breathe on earth.
Fau. How prov'st thou that?
Meph. 'Twas made for man: then he's more excellent.
Fau. If Heaven was made for man, 'twas made for me!   10
I will renounce this magic and repent.

Enter the two Angels.

Good Ang. Faustus, repent: yet God will pity thee!
Bad Ang. Thou art a spirit: God cannot pity thee!
Fau. Who buzzeth in mine ears I am a spirit?
Be I a devil, yet God may pity me—
Yea, God will pity me if I repent.
   Bad. Ay, but Faustus never shall repent.   *Exeunt Angels.*
   Fau. My heart is harden'd, I cannot repent.
Scarce can I name salvation, faith, or Heaven,

Swords, poison, halters, and envenom'd steel   20
Are laid before me to dispatch myself.
And long ere this I should have done the deed
Had not sweet pleasure conquer'd deep despair.
Have not I made blind Homer sing to me
Of Alexander's love and Oenon's death?
And hath not he that built the walls of Thebes
With ravishing sound of his melodious harp
Made music with my Mephostophilis?
Why should I die then or basely despair?—
I am resolv'd Faustus shall not repent!—   30
Come Mephostophilis, let us dispute again
And reason of divine astrology.
Speak, are there many spheres above the moon?
Are all celestial bodies but one globe
As is the substance of this centric earth?
    Meph. As are the elements, such are the heavens,
Even from the moon unto the empyreal orb
Mutually folded in each others' spheres—
And jointly move upon one axle-tree,
Whose termine is termed the world's wide pole.   40
Nor are the names of Saturn, Mars, or Jupiter
Feign'd but are (erring) stars.
    Fau. But have they all one motion, both *situ et tempore?*
    Meph. All move from east to west in four and twenty hours
upon the poles of the world but differ in their motions upon
the poles of the zodiac.
    Fau. These slender questions Wagner can decide. Hath
Mephostophilis no greater skill? Who knows not the double
motion of the planets?—That the first is finish'd in a natural
day. The second thus: Saturn in thirty years; Jupiter in   50
twelve; Mars in four; the sun, Venus, and Mercury in a year;
the moon in twenty-eight days. These are freshmen's supposi-
tions. But tell me, hath every sphere a dominion or *intelligentia?*
    Meph. Ay.
    Fau. How many heavens or spheres are there?
    Meph. Nine: the seven planets, the firmament, and the
empyreal heaven.
    Fau. But is there not *coelum igneum* and *crystallinum?*
    Meph. No Faustus, they be but fables.
    Fau. Resolve me then in this one question. Why are not   60
conjunctions, oppositions, aspects, eclipses all at one time, but
in some years we have more, in some less?
    Meph. Per inaqualem motum respectu totius.
    Fau. Well, I am answer'd. Now tell me, who made the world?
    Meph. I will not.

Fau. Sweet Mephostophilis, tell me.

Meph. Move me not, Faustus!

Fau. Villain, have not I bound thee to tell me anything?

Meph. Ay, that is not against our kingdom. This is. Thou
art damn'd. Think thou of Hell!   70

Fau. Think, Faustus, upon God, that made the world.

Meph. Remember this!   *Exit.*

Fau. Ay, go accursed spirit to ugly Hell!
'Tis thou hast damn'd distressed Faustus' soul.—
Is't not too late?

Enter the two Angels.

Bad Ang. Too late.

Good Ang. Never too late, if Faustus will repent.

Bad. If thou repent, devils will tear thee in pieces.

Good. Repent, and they shall never raze thy skin.

Exeunt Angels.

Fau. O Christ, my savior, my savior! Help to save dis-   80
tressed Faustus' soul.

Enter Lucifer, Belzebub, and Mephostophilis [from trap. Lucifer menaces Faustus].

Luc. Christ cannot save thy soul, for He is just.
There's none but I have interest in the same.

Fau. [*retreating.*] O, what art thou that look'st so terribly?

Luc. I am Lucifer
And this is my companion prince in Hell.

Fau. [*wildly.*] O Faustus, they are come to fetch thy soul!

Bel. We are come to tell thee thou dost injure us.

Luc. Thou call'st on Christ contrary to thy promise.

Bel. Thou should'st not think on God.   90

Luc. Think on the Devil.

Bel. And his dam too.

Fau. Nor will Faustus henceforth. Pardon him for this,
And Faustus vows never to look to Heaven!

Luc. So shalt thou show thyself an obedient servant, and
we will highly gratify thee for it.

Bel. Faustus, we are come from Hell in person to show thee
some pastime. Sit down and thou shalt behold the Seven
Deadly Sins appear to thee in their own proper shapes and
likeness.   100

Fau. That sight will be as pleasant to me as Paradise was to
Adam the first day of his creation.

Luc. Talk not of Paradise or creation but mark the show.
Go Mephostophilis, fetch them in.

[*Mephostophilis goes to one of the entrances and beckons.*]

Enter the Seven Deady Sins [led by a piper].

Bel. Now Faustus, question them of their names and dispositions.

Fau. That shall I soon. What art thou, the first?

Pride. I am Pride. I disdain to have any parents. I am like to Ovid's flea, I can creep into every corner of a wench: sometimes, like a periwig I sit upon her brow; next, like a necklace   110 I hang about her neck; then, like a fan of feathers I kiss her; and then, turning myself to a wrought smock, do what I list. . . . But fie, what a smell is here! I'll not speak a word more for a king's ransom unless the ground be perfum'd and cover'd with cloth of arras.

Fau. Thou art a proud knave indeed. What art thou, the second?

Covetousness. I am Covetousness, begotten of an old churl in a leather bag.—And might I now obtain my wish, this house, you and all, should turn to gold that I might lock you   120 safe into my chest. O my sweet gold!

Fau. And what art thou, the third?

Envy. I am Envy, begotten of a chimney-sweeper and an oyster-wife. I cannot read and therefore wish all books burn'd. I am lean with seeing others eat. O, that there would come a famine over all the world that all might die and I live alone! Then thou shouldst see how fat I'd be. But must thou sit and I stand? Come down, with a vengeance!

Fau. Out, envious wretch! But what art thou, the fourth?

Wrath. I am Wrath. I had neither father nor mother. I   130 leapt out of a lion's mouth when I was scarce an hour old and ever since have run up and down the world with these case of rapiers, wounding myself when I could get none to fight withal. I was born in Hell! And [*to audience*] look to it, for some of you shall be my father.

Fau. And what art thou, the fifth?

Gluttony. I am Gluttony. My parents are all dead, and the devil a penny they have left me, but a small pension: and that buys me thirty meals a day and ten bevers, a small trifle to suffice nature. I come of a royal pedigree. My father   140 was a gammon of bacon, and my mother was a hogshead of claret wine. My godfathers were these: Peter Pickl'd-Herring and Martin Martlemas-Beef. But my godmother, O, she was an ancient gentlewoman: her name was Mistress Margery March-Beer. Now Faustus, thou hast heard all my progeny, wilt thou bid me to supper?

Fau. Not I.

Glut. Then the Devil choke thee!

Fau. Choke thyself, glutton! What art thou, the sixth?

Sloth. Heigh-ho! I am Sloth. I was begotten on a sunny 150
bank. Heigh-ho, I'll not speak a word more for a king's ransom.

Fau. And what are you, Mistress Minx, the seventh and last?

Lechery. Who, I, I sir? I am one that loves an inch of raw
mutton better than an ell of fried stockfish. . . . And the
first letter of my name begins with Lechery.

Luc. Away to Hell, away! On, piper!

                                          Exeunt the Seven Sins.

Fau. O, how this sight doth delight my soul!

Luc. But Faustus, in Hell is all manner of delight.

Fau. O, might I see Hell and return again safe, how happy
were I then!   160

Luc. Faustus, thou shalt. At midnight I will send for thee.
Meanwhile peruse this book and view it thoroughly, and thou
shalt turn thyself into what shape thou wilt.

Fau. Thanks mighty Lucifer. This will I keep as chary as
my life.

Luc. Now Faustus, farewell.

Fau. Farewell great Lucifer. Come Mephostophilis.

                                      Exeunt omnes several ways.

[2.3]   *Enter the Clown [Robin, with a book].*

Rob. [*to off-stage*] What, Dick, look to the horses there till
I come again! [*to audience*] I have gotten one of Doctor
Faustus' conjuring books, and now we'll have such knavery
as't passes.

                    Enter Dick.

Dick. What, Robin, you must come away and walk the horses.

Rob. I walk the horses? I scorn't, 'faith. I have other matters in hand. Let the horses walk themselves an they will.

                    [*Chants, making a circle.*]

A per se—a; t, h, e—the; o per se—o; deny orgon—gorgon.
Keep further from me, O thou illiterate and unlearned hostler!

Dick. 'Snails, what hast thou got there? A book! Why, 10
thou canst not tell ne'er a word on't.

Rob. That thou shalt see presently. Keep out of the circle,
I say, lest I send you into the hostry with a vengeance.

Dick. That's like, 'faith! You had best leave your foolery,
for an my master come, he'll conjure you, 'faith.

Rob. My master conjure me? I'll tell thee what. An my
master come here, I'll clap as fair a pair of horns on's head
as e'er thou sawest in thy life.

Dick. Thou need'st not do that, for my mistress hath done it.

Rob. Ay, there be of us here have waded as deep into   20
matters as other men—if they were disposed to talk.

Dick. A plague take you! I thought you did not sneak up
and down after her for nothing. But I prithee tell me in good
sadness Robin, is that a conjuring book?

Rob. Do but speak what thou't have me to do, and I'll do't.
If thou't dance naked, put off thy clothes, and I'll conjure
thee about presently. Or if thou't go but to the tavern with
me, I'll give thee white wine, red wine, claret wine, sack,
muscadine, malmesey, and whippincrust—hold-belly-hold. And
we'll not pay one penny for it!   30

> [*Pats his stomach at "hold-belly-hold."*]

Dick. O brave! Prithee let's to it presently, for I am as dry
as a dog.

Rob. Come then, let's away.   *Exeunt.*

Enter the Chorus.

Learned Faustus,
To find the secrets of astronomy
Graven in the book of Jove's high firmament,
Did mount him up to scale Olympus' top:
Where, sitting in a chariot burning bright
Drawn by the strength of yoked dragons' necks,
He views the clouds, the planets, and the stars,
The tropic[s], zones, and quarters of the sky,
From the bright circle of the horned moon
Even to the height of *primum mobile:*   10
And whirling round with this circumference
Within the concave compass of the pole,
From east to west his dragons swiftly glide
And in eight days did bring him home again.
Not long he stay'd within his quiet house
To rest his bones after his weary toil
But new exploits do hale him out again.
And mounted then upon a dragon's back,
That with his wings did part the subtle air,
He now is gone to prove cosmography,   20
That measures coasts and kingdoms of the earth,
And as I guess will first arrive in Rome
To see the Pope and manner of his court
And take some part of holy Peter's feast,
The which this day is highly solemniz'd.   *Exit.*

[3.1]   *Enter Faustus and Mephostophilis.*

  Fau. Having now, my good Mephostophilis,
Pass'd with delight the stately town of Trier,
Environ'd round with airy mountain tops,
With walls of flint, and deep-entrenched lakes,
Not to be won by any conquering prince:
From Paris next, coasting the realm of France,
We saw the river Main fall into Rhine,
Whose banks are set with groves of fruitful vines:
Then up to Naples, rich Campania,
Whose buildings fair and gorgeous to the eye,   10
The streets straight forth and pav'd with finest brick,
⟨Quarters the town in four equivalents.⟩
There saw we learned Maro's golden tomb,
The way he cut an English mile in length
Th⟨o⟩rough a rock of stone in one night's space.
From thence to Venice, Padua, and the ⟨rest⟩,
In one of which a sumptuous temple stands
That threats the stars with her aspiring top,
Whose frame is pav'd with sundry color'd stones
And roof'd aloft with curious work in gold.   20
Thus hitherto hath Faustus spent his time.
But tell me now, what resting-place is this?
Hast thou, as erst I did command,
Conducted me within the walls of Rome?
  Meph. I have, my Faustus, and for proof thereof
This is the goodly palace of the Pope,
And 'cause we are no common guests
I choose his privy chamber for our use.
  Fau. I hope His Holiness will bid us welcome.
  Meph. All's one, for we'll be bold with his venison.   30
But now my Faustus, that thou may'st perceive
What Rome contains for to delight thine eyes,
Know that this city stands upon seven hills
That underprop the groundwork of the same:
Just through the midst runs flowing Tiber's stream
With winding banks that cut it in two parts,
Over the which four stately bridges lean
That make safe passage to each part of Rome.
Upon the bridge call'd Ponte Angelo
Erected is a castle passing strong   40
Where thou shalt see such store of ordinance
As that the double cannons forg'd of brass
Do ⟨match⟩ the number of the days contain'd
Within the compass of one complete year,

Beside the gates and high pyramides
That Julius Caesar brought from Africa.

    Fau. Now, by the kingdoms of infernal rule,
Of Styx, of Acheron, and the fiery lake
Of ever-burning Phlegethon, I swear
That I do long to see the monuments   50
And situation of bright-splendent Rome.
Come therefore, let's away!

    Meph. Nay stay my Faustus. I know you'd see the Pope
And take some part of holy Peter's feast,
The which this day with high solemnity,
This day, is held through Rome and Italy
In honor of the Pope's triumphant victory.

    Fau. Sweet Mephostophilis, thou pleasest me.
Whilst I am here on earth let me be cloy'd
With all things that delight the heart of man.   60
My four and twenty years of liberty
I'll spend in pleasure and in dalliance,
That Faustus' name, whilst this bright frame doth stand,
May be admired through the furthest land.

    Meph. 'Tis well said, Faustus, come then, stand by me
And thou shalt see them come immediately.

    Fau. Nay stay, my gentle Mephostophilis,
And grant me my request, and then I go.
Thou know'st, within the compass of eight days
We view'd the face of Heaven, of Earth, and Hell—   70
So high our dragons soar'd into the air
That looking down the earth appear'd to me
No bigger than my hand in quantity—
There did we view the kingdoms of the world,
And what might please mine eye I there beheld.
Then in this show let me an actor be
That this proud Pope may Faustus' [cunning] see!

    Meph. Let it be so, my Faustus, but first stay
And view their triumphs as they pass this way.
And then devise what best contents thy mind   80
By [cunning] in thine art to cross the Pope
Or dash the pride of this solemnity—
To make his monks and abbots stand like apes
And point like antics at his triple crown,
To beat the beads about the friars' pates,
Or clap huge horns upon the cardinals' heads,
Or any villainy thou canst devise—
And I'll perform it, Faustus. Hark, they come!
This day shall make thee be admir'd in Rome!   *[They stand
aside.]*

*Enter the cardinals and bishops, some bearing crosiers, some
the pillars; monks and friars singing their procession; then the
Pope and Raymond King of Hungary, with Bruno led in chains.*

    Pope. Cast down our footstool.   90
    Ray. Saxon Bruno, stoop,
Whilst on thy back His Holiness ascends
Saint Peter's chair and state pontifical.
    Bru. Proud Lucifer, that state belongs to me—
But thus I fall to Peter, not to thee!   [*He lies flat.*]
    Pope. To me and Peter shalt thou grov'lling lie
And crouch before the papal dignity!
Sound trumpets then, for thus Saint Peter's heir
From Bruno's back ascends Saint Peter's chair!
        A flourish while he ascends [*stepping on Bruno*].
Thus as the gods creep on with feet of wool   100
Long ere with iron hands they punish men,
So shall our sleeping vengeance now arise
And smite with death thy hated enterprise.   [*Bruno rises.*]
Lord Cardinals of France and Padua,
Go forthwith to our holy consistory
And read amongst the Statutes Decretal
What by the holy council held at Trent
The sacred synod hath decreed for him
That doth assume the papal government
Without election and a true consent.   110
Away, and bring us word with speed!
    1 Card. We go my lord.   *Exeunt* [*two*] *cardinals.*
    Pope. Lord Raymond. . . . [*Talks to him in pantomime.*]
    Fau. [*coming forward.*] Go haste thee, gentle Mephostophilis
Follow the cardinals to the consistory
And as they turn their superstitious books
Strike them with sloth and drowsy idleness
And make them sleep so sound that in their shapes
Thyself and I may parley with this Pope,
This proud confronter of the Emperor!   120
—And in despite of all his holiness
Restore this Bruno to his liberty
And bear him to the states of Germany!
    Meph. Faustus, I go.
    Fau. Dispatch it soon.
The Pope shall curse that Faustus came to Rome.
             Exeunt Faustus and Mephostophilis.
    Bru. Pope Adrian, let me have some right of law:
I was elected by the Emperor.
    Pope. We will depose the Emperor for that deed

And curse the people that submit to him.   130
Both he and thou shalt stand excommunicate
And interdict from church's privilege
And all society of holy men.
He grows too proud in his authority,
Lifting his lofty head above the clouds,
And like a steeple overpeers the church.
But we'll pull down his haughty insolence.
And as Pope Alexander, our progenitor,
Trod on the neck of German Frederick,
Adding this golden sentence to our praise: 140
That Peter's heirs should tread on emperors
And walk upon the dreadful adder's back,
Treading the lion and the dragon down,
And fearless spurn the killing basilisk—
So will we quell that haughty schismatic
And by authority apostolical
Depose him from his regal government.
 Bru. Pope Julius swore to princely Sigismond,
For him and the succeeding Popes of Rome,
To hold the Emperors their lawful lords.   150
 Pope. Pope Julius did abuse the church's rites
And therefore none of his decrees can stand.
Is not all power on earth bestowed on us?
And therefore though we would, we cannot err.
Behold this silver belt whereto is fix'd
Seven golden [keys] fast seal'd with seven seals
In token of our sevenfold power from Heaven
To bind or loose, lock fast, condemn, or judge,
Resign or seal, or whatso pleaseth us.
Then he and thou and all the world shall stoop—   160
Or be assured of our dreadful curse
To light as heavy as the pains of Hell.

Enter Faustus and Mephostophilis like the [two] cardinals.

 Meph. [*aside.*] (Now tell me Faustus, are we not fitted well?)
 Fau. [*aside.*] (Yes Mephostophilis, and tow such cardinals
Ne'er serv'd a holy Pope as we shall do.
But whilst they sleep within the consistory
Let us salute his reverend Fatherhood.)
 Ray. Behold my lord, the cardinals are return'd.
 Pope. Welcome grave fathers, answer presently,
What have our holy council there decreed   170
Concerning Bruno and the Emperor
In quittance of their late conspiracy
Against our state and papal dignity?

Fau. Most sacred patron of the church of Rome,
By full consent of all the synod
Of priests and prelates it is thus decreed:
That Bruno and the German Emperor
Be held as lollards and bold schismatics
And proud disturbers of the church's peace.
And if that Bruno by his own assent,   180
Without enforcement of the German peers,
Did seek to wear the triple diadem
And by your death to climb Saint Peter's chair,
The Statutes Decretal have thus decreed:
He shall be straight condemn'd of heresy
And on a pile of fagots burnt to death.

Pope. It is enough. Here, take him to your charge
And bear him straight to Ponte Angelo
And in the strongest tower enclose him fast.
Tomorrow, sitting in our consistory   190
With all our college of grave cardinals
We will determine of his life or death.
Here, take his triple crown along with you   [*Removes tiara*
And leave it in the church's treasury.   *from Bruno and gives*
Make haste again, my good lord cardinals,   *it to Faustus.*]
And take our blessing apostolical.

Meph. [*aside.*] (So, so! Was never devil thus bless'd before.)
Fau. [*aside.*] (Away sweet Mephostophilis, be gone!
The cardinals will be plagu'd for this anon.)

        Exeunt Faustus and Mephostophilis [*with Bruno*].
Pope. Go presently and bring a banquet forth,   200
That we may solemnize Saint Peter's feast
And with Lord Raymond, King of Hungary,
Drink to our late and happy victory.   *Exeunt.*

[3.2] *A sennet while the banquet is brought in, and then enter*
    Faustus and Mephostophilis in their own shapes.

Meph. Now Faustus, come prepare thyself for mirth.
The sleepy cardinals are hard at hand
To censure Bruno, that is posted hence,
And on a proud-pac'd steed as swift as thought
Flies o'er the Alps to fruitful Germany,
There to salute the woeful Emperor.
Fau. The Pope will curse them for their sloth today
That slept both Bruno and his crown away!
But now, that Faustus may delight his mind
And by their folly make some merriment,   10
Sweet Mephostophilis, so charm me here
That I may walk invisible to all

And do whate'er I please unseen of any.

    Meph. [*takes a wand and a girdle from beneath his robe.*]
Faustus, thou shalt. Then kneel down presently,
> *Whilst on thy head I lay my hand*
> *And charm thee with this magic wand.*
> *First wear this girdle, then appear*
> *Invisible to all are here:*
> *The planets seven, the gloomy air,*
> *Hell, and the furies' forked hair,*   20
> *Pluto's blue fire, and Hecat's tree*
> *With magic spells so compass thee*
> *That no eye may thy body see.*

So Faustus, now for all their holiness,
Do what thou wilt, thou shalt not be discern'd.

    Fau. Thanks Mephostophilis. Now friars, take heed [*Puts on*
Lest Faustus make your shaven crowns to bleed.   *girdle.*]

    Meph. Faustus, no more. See where the cardinals come.

Enter Pope [*and friars*] *and all the lords* [*with King Raymond
and the Archbishop of Rheims*]. *Enter the* [*two*] *cardinals with
a book.*

    Pope. Welcome lord cardinals. Come, sit down.
Lord Raymond, take your seat. Friars, attend,   30
And see that all things be in readiness
As best beseems this solemn festival.

    1 Card. First may it please Your Sacred Holiness
To view the sentence of the reverend synod
Concerning Bruno and the Emperor.

    Pope. What needs this question? Did I not tell you
Tomorrow we would sit i' th' consistory
And there determine of his punishment?
You brought us word, even now, it was decreed
That Bruno and the cursed Emperor   40
Were by the holy council both condemn'd
For loathed lollards and base schismatics.
Then wherefore would you have me view that book?

    1 Card. Your Grace mistakes. You gave us no such charge.

    Ray. Deny it not. We all are witnesses
That Bruno here was late deliver'd you
With his rich triple crown to be reserv'd
And put into the church's treasury.

    Both Cards. By holy Paul we saw them not!

    Pope. By Peter you shall die   50
Unless you bring them forth immediately!
Hale them to prison, lade their limbs with gyves.
False prelates, for this hateful treachery

Curs'd be your souls to hellish misery.

[Two cardinals are removed.]

Fau. [*aside.*] (So, they are safe. Now Faustus, to the feast. The Pope had never such a frolic guest.)

Pope. Lord Archbishop of Rheims, sit down with us.

Arch. I thank Your Holiness.

Fau. Fall to, the Devil choke you an you spare!

Pope. Who's that spoke? Friars, look about. Lord Ray-   60
mond, pray fall to. I am beholding to the Bishop of Milan for this so rare a present.

Fau. [*aside.*] (I thank you, sir!)   [*Snatches the dish.*]

Pope. How now! Who snatch'd the meat from me? Villains, why speak you not?—My good Lord Archbishop, here's a most dainty dish was sent me from a cardinal in France.

Fau. [*aside.*] (I'll have that too!)   [*Snatches the dish.*]

Pope. What lollards do attend our Holiness that we receive such great indignity! Fetch me some wine.

Fau. [*aside.*] (Ay, pray do, for Faustus is adry.)   [*Wine*   70

Pope. Lord Raymond, I drink unto Your Grace.   *is served.*]

Fau. [*aside.*] (I pledge Your Grace!)   [*Snatches the goblet.*]

Pope. My wine gone too? Ye lubbers, look about and find the man that doth this villainy, or by our sanctitude you all shall die.—I pray, my lords, have patience at this troublesome banquet.

Arch. Please it Your Holiness, I think it be some ghost crept out of purgatory, and now is come unto Your Holiness for his pardon.

Pope. It may be so. Go then, command our priests to   80
sing a dirge to lay the fury of this same troublesome ghost.

[One of the servitors exit.]

[The Pope crosses himself before beginning to eat. He takes a bite and then crosses himself again.]

Fau. How now! Must every bit be spiced with a cross? Nay then take that!   [*Faustus strikes the Pope.*]

Pope. O, I am slain! Help me my lords! O come and help to bear my body hence. Damn'd be this soul for ever for this deed!   *Exeunt the Pope [supported] and his train.*

Meph. Now Faustus, what will you do now? For I can tell you, you'll be curs'd with bell, book, and candle.

Fau. Bell, book, and candle. Candle, book, and bell.

Forward and backward, to curse Faustus to Hell!   90

Enter the friars, with bell, book, and candle for the dirge.

1 Friar. Come brethren, let's about our business with good devotion.

Cursed be he that stole away His Holiness' meat from the table.
   Maledicat Dominus!
Cursed be he that struck His Holiness a blow ⟨on⟩ the face.
   Maledicat Dominus!

[*Faustus strikes a friar and moves among them, disturbing them.*]

Cursed be he that took Friar Sandelo a blow on the pate.
   Maledicat Dominus!
Cursed be he that disturbeth our holy dirge.
   Maledicat Dominus!   100
Cursed be he that took away His Holiness' wine.
   Maledicat Dominus!

[*Faustus and Mephostophilis*] *beat the friars, fling fireworks among them and exeunt.*

[3.3]   *Enter Clown* [*Robin*] *and Dick with a cup.*

Dick. Sirrah Robin, we were best look that your Devil can answer the stealing of this same cup, for the vintner's boy follows us at the hard heels.

Rob. 'Tis no matter, let him come! An he follow us I'll so conjure him as he was never conjur'd in his life, I warrant him. Let me see the cup.

Enter Vintner[*'s Boy*].

Dick. Here 'tis. Yonder he comes. Now Robin, now or never show thy cunning.

[*Boy.*] O, are you here? I am glad I have found you. You are a couple of fine companions! Pray, where's the cup you 10 stole from the tavern?

Rob. How, how! We steal a cup? Take heed what you say. We look not like cup-stealers, I can tell you.

[*Boy.*] Never deny't, for I know you have it, and I'll search you.

Rob. Search me? Ay, and spare not! [*Aside*] (Hold the cup, Dick!) [*To Boy*] Come, come. Search me, search me. [*Robin behind his back gives cup to Dick. Boy searches Robin.*]

[*Boy.*] Come on sirrah, let me search you now.

Dick. Ay ay, do do. [*Aside*] (Hold the cup, Robin!) [*To Boy*] I fear not your searching. We scorn to steal your 20 cups, I can tell you. [*Dick behind his back gives cup to Robin. Boy searches Dick*]

[*Boy.*] Never outface me for the matter, for sure the cup is between you two.

Rob. Nay, there you lie! 'Tis beyond us both. [*Behind his back Robin flings cup away.*]

[*Boy.*] A plague take you. I thought 'twas your knavery to take it away. Come, give it me again.

Rob. Ay, much! When, can you tell? [*Aside*] (Dick, make me a circle and stand close at my back and stir not for thy life.) [*Dick makes a circle enclosing him and Robin. Robin addresses Boy.*] Vintner, you shall have your cup anon.   30
[*Aside*] (Say nothing, Dick!) *O per se, o; Demogorgon, Belcher, and Mephostophilis!*

Enter Mephostophilis [*from trap. Boy rushes off frightened*].

Meph. You princely legions of infernal rule,
How am I vexed by these villains' charms!
From Constantinople have they brought me now
Only for pleasure of these damned slaves.

Rob. By lady sir, you have had a shrewd journey of it. Will it please you to take a shoulder of mutton to supper and a tester in your purse and go back again?

Dick. Ay, I pray you heartily, sir. For we called you but in jest, I promise you.   40

Meph. To purge the rashness of this cursed deed, [*Turns to
First be thou turned to this ugly shape,   Dick.*]
For apish deeds transformed to an ape.   [*Dick grimaces, acts
                                                    like a monkey.*]

Rob. O brave! An ape! I pray sir, let me have the carrying of him about to show some tricks.

Meph. And so thou shalt. Be thou transform'd to a dog. [*Turns to Robin, who gets down on all fours, acts like a dog.*] and carry him upon thy back. Away, be gone!

Rob. A dog! That's excellent. Let the maids look well to their porridge-pots, for I'll into the kitchen presently. Come Dick, come.   *Exeunt the two Clowns* [*, Dick on Robin's back*].   50

Meph. Now with the flames of ever-burning fire
I'll wing myself and forthwith fly amain
Unto my Faustus, to the Great Turk's court.   *Exit.*

⟨*Enter Chorus.*

When Faustus had with pleasure ta'en the view
Of rarest things and royal courts of kings,
He stay'd his course and so returned home,
Where such as bare his absence but with grief,
I mean his friends and nearest companions,
Did gratulate his safety with kind words.
And in their conference of what befell
Touching his journey through the world and air

They put forth questions of astrology
Which Faustus answer'd with such learned skill   10
As they admir'd and wond'red at his wit.
Now is his fame spread forth in every land.
Amongst the rest the Emperor is one,
Carolus the Fifth, at whose palace now
Faustus is feasted 'mongst his noblemen.
What there he did in trial of his art
I leave untold, your eyes shall see perform'd.   *Exit.*⟩

[4.1]   *Enter Martino and Frederick at several doors.*

    Mar. What ho, officers, gentlemen!
Hie to the presence to attend the Emperor.
Good Frederick, see the rooms be voided straight,
His Majesty is coming to the hall.
Go back and see the state in readiness.   [*Frederick opens,*
    Fre. But where is Bruno, our elected Pope, *curtains at back,*
That on a fury's back came post from Rome? *revealing throne.*]
Will not His Grace consort the Emperor?
    Mar. O yes, and with him comes the German conjurer,
The learned Faustus, fame of Wittenberg,   10
The wonder of the world for magic art:
And he intends to show great Carolus
The race of all his stout progenitors
And bring in presence of His Majesty
The royal shapes and warlike semblances
Of Alexander and his beauteous paramour.
    Fre. Where is Benvolio?
    Mar. Fast asleep, I warrant you.
He took his rouse with stoups of Rhenish wine
So kindly yesternight to Bruno's health   20
That all this day the sluggard keeps his bed.
    Fre. See, see, his window's ope. We'll call to him.
    Mar. What ho, Benvolio!

Enter Benvolio above at a window, in his night-cap, buttoning.

    Ben. What a devil ail you two?
    Mar. Speak softly sir, lest the Devil hear you,
For Faustus at the court is late arriv'd
And at his heels a thousand furies wait
To accomplish whatsoever the doctor please.
    Ben. What of this?
    Mar. Come, leave thy chamber first, and thou shalt see 30
This conjurer perform such rare exploits

Before the Pope and royal Emperor
As never yet was seen in Germany.
    Ben. Has not the Pope enough of conjuring yet?
He was upon the Devil's back late enough!
An if he be so far in love with him
I would he would post with him to Rome again.
    Fre. Speak, wilt thou come and see this sport?
    Ben. Not I.
    Mar. Wilt thou stand in thy window and see it then?   40
    Ben. Ay, an I fall not asleep i' th' meantime.
    Mar. The Emperor is at hand, who comes to see
What wonders by black spells may compass'd be.
    Ben. Well, go you attend the Emperor. I am content for
this once to thrust my head out at a window, for they say if a
man be drunk overnight the Devil cannot hurt him in the
morning. If that be true, I have a charm in my head shall
control him as well as the conjurer, I warrant you.
                          Exit [Martino and Frederick. Benvolio
                                   remains above at window].

*A sennet. Charles the German Emperor, Bruno [wearing
tiara], [the Duke of] Saxony, Faustus, Mephostophilis [in-
visible], Frederick, Martino, and attendants. [Emperor seats
                          himself.]*

    Emp. Wonder of men, renown'd magician,
Thrice-learned Faustus, welcome to our court.   50
This deed of thine in setting Bruno free
From his and our professed enemy,
Shall add more excellence unto thine art
Than if by powerful necromantic spells
Thou could'st command the world's obedience.
For ever be belov'd of Carolus!
And if this Bruno thou hast late redeem'd
In peace possess the triple diadem
And sit in Peter's chair despite of chance,
Thou shalt be famous through all Italy   60
And honor'd of the German Emperor.
    Fau. These gracious words, most royal Carolus,
Shall make poor Faustus to his utmost power
Both love and serve the German Emperor
And lay his life at holy Bruno's feet.
For proof whereof, if so Your Grace be pleas'd,
The doctor stands prepar'd by power of art
To cast his magic charms that shall pierce through
The ebon gates of ever-burning Hell,

And hale the stubborn furies from their caves   70
To compass whatsoe'er Your Grace commands.

   Ben. Blood! He speaks terribly! But for all that I do not
greatly believe him. He looks as like [a] conjurer as the Pope
to a costermonger.

   Emp. Then Faustus, as thou late didst promise us,
We would behold that famous conqueror
Great Alexander and his paramour
In their true shapes and state majestical,
That we may wonder at their excellence.

   Fau. Your Majesty shall see them presently.   80
[Aside] (Mephostophilis away,
And with a solemn noise of trumpets' sound
Present before this royal Emperor
Great Alexander and his beauteous paramour.)

   Meph. [*aside.*] (Faustus, I will.)   [*Exit.*]

   Ben. Well master doctor, an your devils come not away
quickly, you shall have me asleep presently. Zounds, I could
eat myself for anger to think I have been such an ass all this
while to stand gaping after the devils' governor and can see
nothing.   90

   Fau. [*aside, looking up.*] (I'll make you feel something anon
if my art fail me not!)
My lord, I must forewarn Your Majesty
That when my spirits present the royal shapes
Of Alexander and his paramour,
Your Grace demand no questions of the King
But in dumb silence let them come and go.

   Emp. Be it as Faustus please. We are content.

   Ben. Ay ay, and I am content too. An thou bring Alexander
and his paramour before the Emperor, I'll be Actaeon and   100
turn myself to a stag.

   Fau. [*aside.*] (And I'll play Diana and send you the horns
presently.)

*[During ensuing dumb-show, Benvolio puts his head on his
arms and falls asleep. Mephostophilis fastens horns on Benvolio's head.]*
*Sennet. Enter at one [door] the Emperor Alexander, at the
other Darius. They meet. Darius is thrown down. Alexander
kills him, takes off his crown, and offering to go out, his Paramour meets him. He embraceth her and sets Darius' crown
upon her head, and coming back both salute the Emperor; who
leaving his state [i.e., throne] offers to embrace them, which
Faustus seeing suddenly stays him. Then trumpets cease and
music sounds.*

My gracious lord, you do forget yourself.
These are but shadows, not substantial.

Emp. O pardon me, my thoughts are so ravish'd
With sight of this renowned Emperor,
That in mine arms I would have compass'd him.
But Faustus, since I may not speak to them,
To satisfy my longing thoughts at full,
Let me this tell thee: I have heard it said   110
That this fair lady whilst she liv'd on earth,
Had on her neck a little wart or mole.
How may I prove that saying to be true?

Fau. Your Majesty may boldly go and see.

Emp. Faustus, I see it plain!
And in this sight thou better pleasest me
Than if I gain'd another monarchy.

Fau. Away, be gone!   *Exit show.*
See, see, my gracious lord, what strange beast is yon that
thrusts his head out at [the] window!   120

Emp. O wondrous sight! See, Duke of Saxony, two spreading horns most strangely fasten'd upon the head of young Benvolio.

Sax. What, is he asleep or dead?

Fau. He sleeps my lord, but dreams not of his horns.

Emp. This sport is excellent. We'll call and wake him.
What ho, Benvolio!

Ben. A plague upon you! Let me sleep awhile.

Emp. I blame thee not to sleep much, having such a head
of thine own.   130

Sax. Look up Benvolio! 'Tis the Emperor calls.

Ben. The Emperor! Where? O zounds, my head!
[*He tries to pull his head in but width of horns
prevents him. Puts hand to head in pain.*]

Emp. Nay, an thy horns hold, 'tis no matter for thy head,
for that's arm'd sufficiently.

Fau. Why, how now Sir Knight? What, hang'd by the horns?
This [is] most horrible! Fie fie, pull in your head for shame!
Let not all the world wonder at you.

Ben. Zounds doctor, is this your villainy?

Fau. Oh, say not so sir: The doctor has no skill,
No art, no cunning to present these lords   140
Or bring before this royal Emperor
The mighty monarch, warlike Alexander.
If Faustus do it, you are straight resolv'd
In bold Actaeon's shape to turn a stag.
And therefore my lord, so please Your Majesty,
I'll raise a kennel of hounds shall hunt him so

As all his footmanship shall scarce prevail
To keep his carcass from their bloody fangs.
Ho, Belimote, Argiron, Asterote!

Ben. Hold, hold! Zounds, he'll raise up a kennel of devils 150
I think, anon. Good my lord, entreat for me. 'Sblood, I am
never able to endure these torments. [*Tries to pull off horns.*]

Emp. Then good master doctor,
Let me entreat you to remove his horns.
He has done penance now sufficiently!

Fau. My gracious lord, not so much for injury done to me,
as to delight Your Majesty with some mirth, hath Faustus
justly requited this injurious knight—which being all I desire,
I am content to remove his horns. [*Aside to Mephostophilis,
who appears behind Benvolio*] (Mephostophilis, transform
him.) [*Mephostophilis removes horns and exit.*] And hereafter
sir, look you speak well of scholars. 160

Ben. [*aside.*] (Speak well of ye! 'Sblood, an scholars be such
cuckold-makers to clap horns of honest men's heads o' this
order, I'll ne'er trust smooth faces and small ruffs more. But
an I be not reveng'd for this, would I might be turned to a
gaping oyster and drink nothing but salt water.) [*Exit from*
Emp. Come Faustus, while the Emperor lives, *window.*]
In recompense of this thy high desert,
Thou shalt command the state of Germany
And live belov'd of mighty Carolus. *Exeunt omnes.*

[4.2] *Enter Benvolio, Martino, Frederick, and soldiers. [Trees*
at the back.]

Mar. Nay, sweet Benvolio, let us sway thy thoughts
From this attempt against the conjurer.

Ben. Away! You love me not to urge me thus.
Shall I let slip so great an injury
When every servile groom jests at my wrongs
And in their rustic gambols proudly say,
"Benvolio's head was grac'd with horns today"?
O, may these eyelids never close again
Till with my sword I have that conjurer slain!
If you will aid me in this enterprise, 10
Then draw your weapons and be resolute;
If not, depart. Here will Benvolio die
But Faustus' death shall quit my infamy.

Fre. Nay, we will stay with thee, betide what may,
And kill that doctor if he come this way.

Ben. Then, gentle Frederick, hie thee to the grove
And place our servants and our followers
Close in an ambush there behind the trees.

By this, I know, the conjurer is near.
I saw him kneel and kiss the Emperor's hand   20
And take his leave laden with rich rewards.
Then soldiers, boldly fight. If Faustus die,
Take you the wealth, leave us the victory.
    Fre. Come soldiers, follow me unto the grove.
Who kills him shall have gold and endless love.
                              Exit Frederick with the soldiers.
    Ben. My head is lighter than it was by th' horns—
But yet my heart more ponderous than my head,
And pants until I see that conjurer dead.
    Mar. Where shall we place ourselves, Benvolio?
    Ben. Here will we stay to bide the first assault.   30
O, were that damned hell-hound but in place
Thou soon should'st see me quit my foul disgrace.

                    Enter Frederick.

    Fre. Close, close! The conjurer is at hand
And all alone comes walking in his gown.
Be ready then and strike the peasant down!
    Ben. Mine be that honor then! Now sword, strike home!
                              [*Draws his sword.*]
For horns he gave I'll have his head anon.

            Enter Faustus with the false head.

    Mar. See see, he comes.
    Ben. No words. This blow ends all!
        [*Strikes Faustus with sword. Faustus falls to his knees.*]
Hell take his soul, his body thus must fall.   40
    Fau. O!
    Fre. Groan you, master doctor?
    Ben. Break may his heart with groans! Dear Frederick, see,
Thus will I end his griefs immediately.
            [*Cuts Faustus' false head off. Faustus falls flat.*]
    Mar. Strike with a willing hand! His head is off.
    Ben. The devil's dead, the furies now may laugh.
    Fre. Was this that stern aspect, that awful frown,
Made the grim monarch of infernal spirits
Tremble and quake at his commanding charms?
    Mar. Was this that damned head whose [art] conspir'd   50
Benvolio's shame before the Emperor?
    Ben. Ay, that's the head, and here the body lies
Justly rewarded for his villainies.
    Fre. Come let's devise how we may add more shame
To the black scandal of his hated name.

Ben. First, on his head in quittance of my wrongs
                    [*Benvolio lifts false head by hair.*]
I'll nail huge forked horns and let them hang
Within the window where he yok'd me first
That all the world may see my just revenge.

Mar. What use shall we put his beard to?   60

Ben. We'll sell it to a chimney-sweeper. It will wear out ten
birchen brooms, I warrant you.

Fre. What shall eyes do?

Ben. We'll put out his eyes, and they shall serve for buttons
to his lips to keep his tongue from catching cold.

Mar. An excellent policy! And now sirs, having divided him,
what shall the body do?   [*Faustus rises without a head.*]

Ben. Zounds, the devil's alive again!

Fre. Give him his head for God's sake!

Fau. Nay keep it. Faustus will have heads and hands,   70
Ay, [all] your hearts, to recompense this deed.
Knew you not, traitors, I was limited   [*Faustus shows his*
For four and twenty years to breathe on earth?   *own head.*]
And had you cut my body with your swords
Or hew'd this flesh and bones as small as sand,
Yet in a minute had my spirit return'd
And I had breath'd a man made free from harm.
But wherefore do I dally my revenge?
Asteroth, Belimoth, Mephostophilis!

Enter Mephostophilis and other devils [from trap].

Go horse these traitors on your fiery backs   80
And mount aloft with them as high as Heaven,
Thence pitch them headlong to the lowest Hell.
Yet stay, the world shall see their misery,
And Hell shall after plague their treachery.
Go Belimoth, and take this caitiff hence
And hurl him in some lake of mud and dirt: [*Belimoth grasps*
Take thou this other, drag him through the woods   *Frederick.*]
Amongst the pricking thorns and sharpest briars: [*Asteroth*
Whilst with my gentle Mephostophilis   *grasps Martino.*]
This traitor flies unto some steepy rock   90
That rolling down may break the villain's bones
As he intended to dismember me.   [*Mephostophilis grasps*
Fly hence, dispatch my charge immediately!   *Benvolio.*]

Fre. Pity us, gentle Faustus, save our lives!

Fau. Away!

Fre. He must needs go that the Devil drives.
                    Exeunt spirits with the knights.

Enter the ambushed soldiers.

1 Sold. Come sirs, prepare yourselves in readiness.
Make haste to help these noble gentlemen.
I heard them parley with the conjurer.
   2 Sold. See where he comes. Dispatch, and kill the slave!   100
   Fau. What's here, an ambush to betray my life?
Then Faustus, try thy skill. Base peasants, stand!
For lo, these trees remove at my command   *[Motions with*
And stand as bulwarks 'twixt yourselves and me   *hands.]*
To shield me from your hated treachery!
            [Trees move between Faustus and soldiers.]
Yet to encounter this your weak attempt
Behold an army comes incontinent.

*Faustus strikes the door, and enter a devil playing on a drum,
after him another bearing an ensign, and divers with weapons:
Mephostophilis with fireworks: they set upon the soldiers and
drive them out. [Exeunt all.]*

*Enter at several doors Benvolio, Frederick, and Martino, their
heads and faces bloody and besmeared with mud and dirt, all
having horns on their heads.*

   Mar. What ho, Benvolio!
   Ben. Here! What, Frederick, ho!
   Fre. O, help me gentle friend. Where is Martino?   110
   Mar. Dear Frederick, here,
Half smother'd in a lake of mud and dirt,
Through which the furies dragg'd me by the heels.
   Fre. Martino, see, Benvolio's horns again.
   Mar. O misery! How now Benvolio?
   Ben. Defend me, Heaven! Shall I be haunted still?
   Mar. Nay fear not man, we have no power to kill.
   Ben. My friends transformed thus! O hellish spite,
Your heads are all set with horns.
   Fre. You hit it right: 120
It is your own you mean. Feel on your head.
   Ben. Zounds, horns again!   *[Benvolio feels horns.]*
   Mar. Nay chafe not man, we all are sped.
   Ben. What devil attends this damn'd magician,
That spite of spite our wrongs are doubled?
   Fre. What may we do that we may hide our shames?
   Ben. If we should follow him to work revenge
He'd join long asses' ears to these huge horns
And make us laughing-stocks to all the world.
   Mar. What shall we then do, dear Benvolio?   130

Ben. I have a castle joining near these woods,
And thither we'll repair and live obscure
Till time shall alter this our brutish shapes.
Sith black disgrace hath thus eclips'd our fame,
We'll rather die with grief than live with shame.

Exeunt omnes.

[4.3] *Enter Faustus and the Horse-Courser [with money in his hand].*

Hor. I beseech your worship, accept of these forty dollars.

Fau. Friend, thou canst not buy so good a horse for so small a price. I have no great need to sell him, but if thou likest him for ten dollars more, take him, because I see thou hast a good mind to him.

Hor. I beseech you sir, accept of this. I am a very poor man and have lost very much of late by horse-flesh, and this bargain will set me up again.

Fau. Well, I will not stand with thee. Give me the money.

[Takes money.]

Now sirrah, I must tell you that you may ride him o'er   10
hedge and ditch and spare him not. But, do you hear, in any case ride him not into the water.

Hor. How sir, not into the water! Why, will he not drink of all waters?

Fau. Yes, he will drink of all waters, but ride him not into the water: o'er hedge and ditch or where thou wilt, but not into the water. Go bid the hostler deliver him unto you, and remember what I say.

Hor. I warrant you sir. O joyful day! Now am I a made man forever.   *Exit.*   20

Fau. What art thou, Faustus, but a man condemn'd to die? Thy fatal time draws to a final end . . .
Despair doth drive distrust into my thoughts.
Confound these passions with a quiet sleep.
Tush, Christ did call the thief upon the cross!
Then rest thee Faustus, quiet in conceit.

He sits to sleep.

Enter the Horse-Courser wet.

Hor. O what a cozening doctor was this! I riding my horse into the water, thinking some hidden mystery had been in the horse—I had nothing under me but a little straw and had much ado to escape drowning! Well, I'll go rouse him and   30
make him give me my forty dollars again. Ho, sirrah doctor, you cozening scab! Master doctor, awake and rise, and give me my money again, for your horse is turned to a bottle of hay.

Master doctor—.   *He pulls off his leg.*
Alas, I am undone! What shall I do? I have pull'd off his leg.

Fau. O help, help! The villain hath murder'd me!

Hor. Murder or not murder, now he has but one leg I'll outrun him, and cast this leg into some ditch or other.

                                        [*Exit with the leg.*]

Fau. Stop him, stop him, stop him!—Ha, ha, ha! Faustus
hath his leg again, and the horse-courser a bundle of hay   40
for his forty dollars.

Enter Wagner.

How now, Wagner? What news with thee?

Wag. If it please you, the Duke of Vanholt doth earnestly
entreat your company, and hath sent some of his men to attend
you with provision fit for your journey.

Fau. The Duke of Vanholt's an honorable gentleman, and
one to whom I must be no niggard of my cunning. Come, away!

                                                Exeunt.

[4.4] *Enter Clown [Robin], Dick, Horse-Courser, and a Carter.*

Cart. Come my masters, I'll bring you to the best beer in
Europe. What ho, hostess! Where be these whores?

Enter Hostess.

Host. How now? What lack you? What, my old guests,
welcome.

Rob. [*aside.*] (Sirrah Dick, dost thou know why I stand so
mute?)

Dick. [*aside.*] (No Robin, why is't?)

Rob. [*aside.*] I am eighteen pence on the score. But say
nothing. See if she have forgotten me.)

Host. Who's this that stands so solemnly by himself?   10
What, my old guest!

Rob. O, hostess, how do you? I hope my score stands still.

Host. Ay, there's no doubt of that, for methinks you make
no haste to wipe it out.

Dick. Why hostess, I say, fetch us some beer!

Host. You shall, presently.—Look up into th' hall, there, ho!
                              [*To someone off-stage.*] *Exit.*

Dick. Come sirs, what shall we do now till mine hostess
comes?

Cart. Marry sir, I'll tell you the bravest tale how a conjurer
served me. You know Doctor Fauster?   20

Hor. Ay, a plague take him! Here's some on's have cause
to know him. Did he conjure thee too?

Cart. I'll tell you how he serv'd me. As I was going to Witten-

berg t'other day with a load of hay, he met me and asked
me what he should give me for as much hay as he could
eat. Now sir, I thinking that a little would serve his turn, bad
him take as much as he would for three farthings. So he presently gave me my money and fell to eating; and as I am a
cursen man, he never left eating till he had eat up all my load
of hay.   30
   All. O monstrous, eat a whole load of hay!
   Rob. Yes yes, that may be, for I have heard of one that has
eat a load of logs.
                     [*Hostess enters and serves drinks, then exit.*]
   Hor. Now sirs, you shall hear how villainously he served
me. I went to him yesterday to buy a horse of him, and he
would by no means sell him under forty dollars. So sir, because I knew him to be such a horse as would run over hedge
and ditch and never tire, I gave him his money. So, when I
had my horse, Doctor Fauster bad me ride him night and
day and spare him no time. "But," quoth he, "in any   40
case ride him not into the water." Now sir, I thinking the horse
had had some quality that he would not have me know of,
what did I but rid him into a great river—and when I came
just in the midst, my horse vanish'd away and I sate straddling
upon a bottle of hay!
   All. O brave doctor!
   Hor. But you shall hear how bravely I serv'd him for it.
I went me home to his house, and there I found him asleep.
I kept ahallowing and whooping in his ears, but all could not
wake him. I seeing that, took him by the leg and never   50
rested pulling till I had pull'd me his leg quite off, and now
'tis at home in mine hostry.
   [*Dick.*] And has the doctor but one leg then? That's excellent, for one of his devils turned me into the likeness of an
ape's face.
   Cart. Some more drink, hostess!
   Rob. Hark you, we'll into another room and drink awhile,
and then we'll go seek out the doctor.   *Exeunt omnes.*

[4.5] *Enter the Duke of Vanholt, his [pregnant] Duchess,
     Faustus, and Mephostophilis [invisible, and servants].*

   Duke. Thanks master doctor, for these pleasant sights. Nor
know I how sufficiently to recompense your great deserts in
erecting that enchanted castle in the air, the sight whereof
so delighted me, as nothing in the world could please me more.
   Fau. I do think myself, my good lord, highly recompens'd
in that it pleaseth Your Grace to think but well of that which
Faustus hath perform'd.—But gracious lady, it may be that
you have taken no pleasure in those sights. Therefore I pray

you tell me what is the thing you most desire to have: be it in
the world it shall be yours. I have heard that great-bellied   10
women do long for things are rare and dainty.

    Duch. True master doctor, and since I find you so kind, I
will make known unto you what my heart desires to have: and
were it now summer, as it is January, a dead time of the winter,
I would request no better meat than a dish of ripe grapes.

    Fau. This is but a small matter.—[*Aside*] (Go Mephosto-
philis, away!)   *Exit Mephostophilis.*
Madam, I will do more than this for your content.

*Enter Mephostophilis [invisible] again with the grapes [,hands
them to Faustus, who gives them to Duchess].*

Here, now taste ye these. They should be good, for they come
from a far country, I can tell you.   20

    Duke. This makes me wonder more than all the rest, that
at this time of the year when every tree is barren of his fruit,
from whence you had these ripe grapes.

    Fau. Please it Your Grace, the year is divided into two
circles over the whole world, so that when it is winter with us,
in the contrary circle it is likewise summer with them, as in
India, Saba, and such countries that lie far east, where they
have fruit twice a year. From whence, by means of a swift
spirit that I have, I had these grapes brought as you see.

    Duch. And trust me, they are the sweetest grapes that   30
e'er I tasted.

*The Clown[s—Robin, Dick, Carter, and Horse-Courser who are
all drunk—] bounce [i.e., thump] at the gate within.*

    Duke. What rude disturbers have we at the gate?
Go pacify their fury, set it ope,
And then demand of them what they would have.

*They knock again and call out [off-stage] to talk with Faustus.
[They ad-lib in calling out.]*

    A Servant. [*at back of stage.*] Why, how now masters, what a
      coil is there!
What is the reason you disturb the Duke?

    Dick. [*off-stage.*] We have no reason for it, therefore a fig for
him!

    Ser. Why saucy varlets, dare you be so bold!

    Hor. [*off-stage.*] I hope sir, we have wit enough to be   40
more bold than welcome.

    Ser. [*at back of stage.*] It appears so. Pray be bold elsewhere
and trouble not the Duke.

    Duke. What would they have?

Ser. They all cry out to speak with Doctor Faustus.

Cart. [*off-stage.*] Ay, and we will speak with him.

Duke. Will you sir? Commit the rascals.

Dick. [*off-stage.*] Commit with us! He were as good commit with his father as commit with us!

Fau. I do beseech Your Grace, let them come in.   50
They are good subject for a merriment.

Duke. Do as thou wilt, Faustus. I give thee leave.

Fau. I thank Your Grace.

Enter the Clown [*Robin*], *Dick, Carter, and Horse-Courser.*

Why, how now my good friends? 'Faith, you are too outrageous.
But come near, I have procur'd your pardons. Welcome all!

Rob. Nay sir, we will be welcome for our money, and we will pay for what we take. What ho, give's half a dozen of beer here, and be hang'd!

Fau. Nay, hark you, can you tell me where you are?

Cart. Ay, marry can I, we are under Heaven.   60

Ser. Ay, but Sir Sauce-Box, know you in what place?

Hor. Ay ay, the house is good enough to drink in. Zounds, fill us some beer, or we'll break all the barrels in the house and dash out all your brains with your bottles.

Fau. Be not so furious. Come, you shall have beer.—My lord, beseech you give me leave awhile; I'll gage my credit 'twill content Your Grace.

Duke. With all my heart, kind doctor, please thyself. Our servants and our court's at thy command.

Fau. I humbly thank Your Grace.—Then fetch some beer.   70

> [*To servants, some of whom exeunt.*
> *Mephostophilis also exit.*]

Hor. Ay marry, there spake a doctor indeed! And 'faith, I'll drink a health to thy wooden leg for that word.

Fau. My wooden leg? What dost thou mean by that?

Cart. Ha, ha, ha, dost hear him Dick? He has forgot his leg.

Hor. Ay ay, he does not stand much upon that.

Fau. No, 'faith, not much upon a wooden leg.

Cart. Good lord, that flesh and blood should be so frail with your worship! Do not you remember a horse-courser you sold a horse to?   80

Fau. Yes, I remember I sold one a horse.

Cart. And do you remember you bid he should not ride into the water?

Fau. Yes, I do very well remember that.

Cart. And do you remember nothing of your leg?

Fau. No, in good sooth.

Cart. Then I pray remember your curtsy.

Fau. I thank you sir [*bows*].

Cart. 'Tis not so much worth. I pray you tell me one thing. 90

Fau. What's that?

Cart. Be both your legs bedfellows every night together?

Fau. Would'st thou make a colossus of me that thou askest me such questions?

Cart. No, truly sir, I would make nothing of you, but I would fain know that.

Enter [Mephostophilis invisible leading astonished] Hostess with drink.

Fau. Then I assure thee certainly they are.

Cart. I thank you, I am fully satisfied.

Fau. But wherefore dost thou ask?

Cart. For nothing, sir, but methinks you should have a 100 wooden bedfellow of one of 'em.

Hor. Why, do you hear sir, did not I pull off one of your legs when you were asleep?

Fau. But I have it again now I am awake. [*Opens robe*] Look you here sir.

All. O horrible! Had the doctor three legs?

Cart. Do you remember sir, how you cozened me and eat up my load of—

Faustus charms him dumb.

Dick. Do you remember how you made me wear an ape's— [*Same.*] 110

Hor. You whoreson conjuring scab! Do you remember how you cozened me of a ho— [*Same.*]

Rob. Ha' you forgotten me? You think to carry it away with your *hey-pass* and *re-pass?* Do you remember the dog's fa— [*Same.*]

Exeunt Clowns [rigidly, like automata].

Host. Who pays for the ale? Hear you master doctor, now you have sent away my guests, I pray who shall pay me for my a— [*Faustus charms her.*] *Exit Hostess.*

Duch. My lord,
We are much beholding to this learned man. 120

Duke. So are we madam, which we will recompense
With all the love and kindness that we may:
His artful sport drives all sad thoughts away. *Exeunt.*

[Perhaps a Chorus before the fifth act is lost.]

[5.1] *Thunder and lightning. Enter devils with covered dishes:*
Mephostophilis leads them into Faustus' study. Then enter
Wagner.

Wag. I think my master means to die shortly. He has made
his will and given me his wealth: his house, his goods, and
store of golden plate—besides two thousand ducats ready
coin'd. I wonder what he means. If death were nigh, he would
not frolic thus. He's now at supper with the scholars, where
there's such belly-cheer as Wagner in his life ne'er saw the like!
And see where they come. Belike the feast is done.

Exit.

Enter Faustus, Mephostophilis [invisible], and two or three
scholars.

1 Sch. Master Doctor Faustus, since our conference about
fair ladies, which was the beautifulest in all the world, we
have determin'd with ourselves that Helen of Greece was   10
the admirablest lady that ever liv'd. Therefore master doctor, if
you will do us so much favor as to let us see that peerless dame
of Greece, whom all the world admires for majesty, we should
think ourselves much beholding unto you.

Fau. Gentlemen,
For that I know your friendship is unfeign'd,
It is not Faustus' custom to deny
The just request of those that wish him well:
You shall behold that peerless dame of Greece
No otherwise for pomp and majesty   20
Than when Sir Paris cross'd the seas with her
And brought the spoils to rich Dardania.
Be silent then, for danger is in words.

[*He motions to Mephostophilis.*]

Music sounds. Mephostophilis brings in Helen: she passeth
over the stage.

2 Sch. Was this fair Helen, whose admir'd worth
Made Greece with ten years' wars afflict poor Troy?
3 Sch. Too simple is my wit to tell her worth,
Whom all the world admires for majesty.
1 Sch. Now we have seen the pride of nature's work,
We'll take our leaves, and for this blessed sight
Happy and blest be Faustus evermore!   30
Fau. Gentlemen, farewell! The same I wish to you.

Exeunt scholars.

Enter an Old Man.

Old. O gentle Faustus, leave this damned **art,**
This magic that will charm thy soul to Hell
And quite bereave thee of salvation.
Though thou hast now offended like a man,
Do not persever in it like a devil.
Yet, yet, thou hast an amiable soul
If sin by custom grow not into nature.
Then, Faustus, will repentance come too late!
Then, thou art banish'd from the sight of Heaven!   40
No mortal can express the pains of Hell!
It may be this my exhortation
Seems harsh and all unpleasant. Let it not.
For gentle son, I speak it not in wrath
Or envy of thee but in tender love
And pity of thy future misery:
And so have hope that this my kind rebuke,
Checking thy body, may amend thy soul.

    Fau. Where art thou, Faustus? Wretch, what hast thou
        done!

                              Mephostophilis gives him a dagger
                              [which Faustus seems about to use].
Hell claims his right and with a roaring voice   50
Says "Faustus, come, thine hour is almost come!"
And Faustus now will come to do thee right!

    Old. O stay, good Faustus, stay thy desperate steps!
                        [Holds out hand to stop him.]
I see an angel hover o'er thy head,
And with a vial full of precious grace
Offers to pour the same into thy soul:
Then call for mercy and avoid despair.

    Fau. O friend, I feel
Thy words to comfort my distressed soul:
Leave me awhile to ponder on my sins.   60

    Old. Faustus, I leave thee, but with grief of heart,
Fearing the enemy of thy hapless soul.   *Exit.*

    Fau. Accursed Faustus! Wretch, what hast thou done!
I do repent, and yet I do despair:
Hell strives with grace for conquest in my breast!
What shall I do to shun the snares of death?
                          [Stares at dagger in his hand.]

    Meph. Thou traitor Faustus, I arrest thy soul   *[Advances.]*
For disobedience to my sovereign lord.
Revolt, or I'll in piecemeal tear thy flesh.

Fau. I do repent I e'er offended him.   70
                                        [*Retreats, frightened.*]
Sweet Mephostophilis, entreat thy lord
To pardon my unjust presumption,
And with my blood again I will confirm
The former vow I made to Lucifer.
⟨*Meph.*⟩ Do it then, Faustus, with unfeigned heart
Lest greater dangers do attend thy drift.
⟨*Fau.*⟩ Torment, sweet friend, that base and aged man
That durst dissuade me from thy Lucifer,
With greatest torment that our Hell affords.
   Meph. His faith is great. I cannot touch his soul.   80
But what I may afflict his body with
I will attempt, which is but little worth.
   Fau. One thing, good servant, let me crave of thee
To glut the longing of my heart's desire:
That I may have unto my paramour
That heavenly Helen which I saw of late,
Whose sweet embraces may extinguish clear
Those thoughts that do dissuade me from my vow,
And keep [the] ⟨oath⟩ I made to Lucifer.
   Meph. This or what else my Faustus shall desire   90
Shall be perform'd in twinkling of an eye.

Enter Helen again, passing over between two Cupids.

   Fau. Was this the face that launch'd a thousand ships
And burnt the topless towers of Ilium?
Sweet Helen, make me immortal with a kiss.
Her lips suck forth my soul. See where it flies!   [*Kisses her.*]
Come Helen, come, give me my soul again.   [*Kisses again.*]
Here will I dwell, for Heaven is in these lips   [*Embraces her.*]
And all is dross that is not Helena.
I will be Paris, and for love of thee
Instead of Troy shall Wittenberg be sack'd;   100
And I will combat with weak Menelaus
And wear thy colors on my plumed crest.—
Yea, I will wound Achilles in the heel
And then return to Helen for a kiss!
O, thou art fairer than the evening's air
Clad in the beauty of a thousand stars,
Brighter art thou than flaming Jupiter
When he appear'd to hapless Semele,
More lovely than the monarch of the sky
In wanton Arethusa's azure arms,   110
And none but thou shalt be my paramour.   *Exeunt.*

[5.2] *Thunder. Enter Lucifer, Belzebub, and Mephostophilis
[from trap and then go above, where they watch all this scene].*

   Luc. Thus from infernal Dis do we ascend
To view the subjects of our monarchy,
Those souls which sin seals the black sons of Hell.
'Mong which as chief, Faustus, we come to thee,
Bringing with us lasting damnation
To wait upon thy soul. The time is come
Which makes it forfeit.
   Meph. And this gloomy night
Here in this room will wretched Faustus be.
   Bel. And here we'll stay   10
To mark him how he doth demean himself.
   Meph. How should he but in desperate lunacy?
Fond wordling, now his heart blood dries with grief,
His conscience kills it, and his laboring brain
Begets a world of idle fantasies
To overreach the Devil—but all in vain:
His store of pleasures must be sauc'd with pain!
He and his servant Wagner are at hand.
Both come from drawing Faustus' latest will.
See where they come!   20

Enter Faustus and Wagner.

   Fau. Say Wagner, thou hast perus'd my will;
How dost thou like it?
   Wag. Sir, so wondrous well
As in all humble duty I do yield
My life and lasting service for your love.

Enter the scholars.

   Fau. Gramercies, Wagner.—Welcome gentlemen.
                             [Exit Wagner.]
   1 Sch. Now worthy Faustus, methinks your looks are
     chang'd.
   Fau. O gentlemen!
   2 Sch. What ails Faustus?
   Fau. Ah my sweet chamber-fellow, had I liv'd with thee,   30
then had I liv'd still!—But now must die eternally. Look sirs,
comes he not, comes he not?   *[Points at trap.]*
   1 Sch. O my dear Faustus, what imports this fear?
   2 Sch. Is all our pleasure turned to melancholy?
   3 Sch. He is not well with being over-solitary.

2 Sch. If it be so, we'll have physicians and Faustus shall be cur'd.

3 Sch. 'Tis but a surfeit sir, fear nothing.

Fau. A surfeit of deadly sin that hath damn'd both body and soul! 40

2 Sch. Yet Faustus, look up to Heaven and remember mercy is infinite.

Fau. But Faustus' offense can ne'er be pardoned. The serpent that tempted Eve may be saved, but not Faustus! O gentlemen, hear with patience and tremble not at my speeches. Though my heart pant and quiver to remember that I have been a student here these thirty years, O, would I had never seen Wittenberg, never read book.—And what wonders I have done all Germany can witness, yea all the world!—For which Faustus hath lost both Germany and the world, yea 50 Heaven itself—Heaven, the seat of God, the throne of the blessed, the kingdom of joy—and must remain in Hell forever! Hell, O Hell forever! Sweet friends, what shall become of Faustus being in Hell forever?

2 Sch. Yet Faustus, call on God.

Fau. On God, whom Faustus hath abjur'd? On God, whom Faustus hath blasphem'd? O my God, I would weep, but the Devil draws in my tears! Gush forth blood instead of tears, yea life and soul! O, he stays my tongue! I would lift up my hands, but see, they hold 'em, they hold 'em! 60

All. Who, Faustus?

Fau. Why, Lucifer and Mephostophilis. O gentlemen, I gave them my soul for my cunning.

All. O, God forbid!

Fau. God forbade it indeed, but Faustus hath done it. For the vain pleasure of four and twenty years hath Faustus lost eternal joy and felicity. I writ them a bill with mine own blood. The date is expired. This is the time. And he will fetch me.

1 Sch. Why did not Faustus tell us of this before, that Divines might have pray'd for thee? 70

Fau. Oft have I thought to have done so, but the Devil threaten'd to tear me in pieces if I nam'd God—to fetch me body and soul if I once gave ear to Divinity. And now 'tis too late! Gentlemen, away, lest you perish with me.

2 Sch. O, what may we do to save Faustus?

Fau. Talk not of me but save yourselves and depart.

3 Sch. God will strengthen me! I will stay with Faustus.

1 Sch. Tempt not God, sweet friend, but let us into the next room and pray for him.

Fau. Ay, pray for me, pray for me. And what noise 80

soever you hear, come not unto me, for nothing can rescue me.

2 Sch. Pray thou, and we will pray, that God may have
mercy upon thee.

Fau. Gentlemen, farewell! If I live till morning, I'll visit
you. If not, Faustus is gone to Hell.

All. Faustus, farewell.

     Exeunt scholars. [*Mephostophilis descends to stage.*]

Meph. Ay, Faustus, now hast thou no hope of Heaven.
Therefore, despair! Think only upon Hell,
For that must be thy mansion, there to dwell.

Fau. O thou bewitching fiend, 'twas thy temptation   90
Hath robb'd me of eternal happiness.

Meph. I do confess it Faustus, and rejoice.
'Twas I, that when thou wert i' the way to Heaven
Damm'd up thy passage. When thou took'st the book
To view the Scriptures, then I turn'd the leaves
And led thine eye.
What, weep'st thou! 'Tis too late, despair, farewell!
Fools that will laugh on earth, most weep in Hell. *Exit.*

Enter the Good Angel and the Bad Angel at several doors.

Good. O Faustus, if thou hadst given ear to me
Innumerable joys had followed thee.   100
But thou did'st love the world.

Bad.—Gave ear to me,
And now must taste Hell's pains perpetually.

Good. O, what will all thy riches, pleasures, pomps
Avail thee now?

Bad.—Nothing but vex thee more,
To want in Hell, that had on earth such store.

        Music while the throne descends.

Good. O, thou hast lost celestial happiness,
Pleasures unspeakable, bliss without end.
Had'st thou affected sweet Divinity,   110
Hell or the Devil had had no power on thee.
Had'st thou kept on that way, Faustus behold
In what resplendent glory thou had'st sat
In yonder throne, like those bright shining saints,
And triumphed over Hell! That hast thou lost. [*Throne*
And now, poor soul, must thy good angel leave thee, *ascends.*]
The jaws of Hell are open to receive thee.   *Exit.*

    Hell is discovered. [*Trap opens: fire and smoke
     come out as Bad Angel points down in it.*]

Bad. Now Faustus, let thine eyes with horror stare [*Faustus*
Into that vast perpetual torture-house. *stares into trap.*]

There are the furies, tossing damned souls   120
On burning forks. Their bodies [boil] in lead.
There are live quarters broiling on the coals,
That ne'er can die. This ever-burning chair
Is for o'er-tortur'd souls to rest them in.
These that are fed with sops of flaming fire
Were gluttons and lov'd only delicates
And laughed to see the poor starve at their gates.
But yet all these are nothing. Thou shalt see
Ten thousand tortures that more horrid be.
    Fau. O, I have seen enough to torture me.   130
    Bad. Nay, thou must feel them, taste the smart of all—
He that loves pleasure must for pleasure fall.
And so I leave thee Faustus, till anon:
Then wilt thou tumble in confusion.   *Exit.*
                          The clock strikes eleven.

    Fau. O Faustus!
Now hast thou but one bare hour to live
And then thou must be damn'd perpetually!
Stand still, you ever-moving spheres of Heaven
That time may cease and midnight never come:
Fair nature's eye, rise, rise again and make   140
Perpetual day, or let this hour be but a year,
A month, a week, a natural day—
That Faustus may repent and save his soul!
O lente lente currite noctis equi!
The stars move still, time runs, the clock will strike:
The Devil will come, and Faustus must be damn'd!
O, I'll leap up to Heaven! Who pulls me down?
⟨See, see where Christ's blood streams in the firmament!⟩
One drop of blood will save me. O, my Christ!
—Rend not my heart for naming of my Christ!   150
Yet will I call on Him! O spare me, Lucifer!
Where is it now? 'Tis gone!
And see a threat'ning arm, an angry brow!
Mountains and hills, come, come and fall on me
And hide me from the heavy wrath of Heaven!
No?
Then will I headlong run into the earth.
Gape earth! O no, it will not harbor me.
You stars that reign'd at my nativity,
Whose influence hath allotted death and Hell,   160
Now draw up Faustus like a foggy mist
Into the entrails of yon laboring cloud
That when you vomit forth into the air,

My limbs may issue from your smoky mouths—
But let my soul mount and ascend to Heaven!

The watch strikes.

O half the hour is pass'd! 'Twill all be pass'd anon!
O if my soul must suffer for my sin,
Impose some end to my incessant pain!
Let Faustus live in Hell a thousand years,
A hundred thousand, and at last be sav'd!   170
No end is limited to damned souls!
Why wert thou not a creature wanting soul?
Or why is this immortal that thou hast?
O, Pythagoras' metempsychosis, were that true
This soul should fly from me and I be chang'd
Unto some brutish beast.—All beasts are happy
For when they die
Their souls are soon dissolv'd in elements.
But mine must live still to be plagu'd in Hell!
Curs'd be the parents that engender'd me!   180
No Faustus, curse thyself, curse Lucifer
That hath depriv'd thee of the joys of Heaven. . . .

The clock strikes twelve.

It strikes, it strikes! Now body, turn to air,
Or Lucifer will bear thee quick to Hell!
O soul, be changed into small water-drops
And fall into the ocean, ne'er be found.

Thunder, and enter the devils.

O mercy, Heaven! Look not so fierce on me!
Adders and serpents! Let me breathe awhile!
Ugly Hell, gape not! Come not Lucifer!
I'll burn my books!—O Mephostophilis. . . .   190
*Exeunt [devils with Faustus into the trap. He is heard shriek-
ing. Then his limbs are thrown up. Devils above exeunt].*

[5.3]   *Enter the scholars.*

 1 Sch. Come gentlemen, let us go visit Faustus,
For such a dreadful night was never seen
Since first the world's creation did begin!
Such fearful shrieks and cries were never heard!
Pray Heaven, the doctor have escaped the danger.
 2 Sch. O, help us Heaven, see, here are Faustus' limbs
All torn asunder by the hand of death!
 3 Sch. The devils whom Faustus serv'd have torn him thus:
For 'twixt the hours of twelve and one, methought
I heard him shriek and call aloud for help,   10
At which self time the house seem'd all on fire

With dreadful horror of these damned fiends.
  2 Sch. Well gentlemen, though Faustus' end be such
As every Christian heart laments to think on,
Yet for he was a scholar once admir'd
For wondrous knowledge in our German schools,
We'll give his mangled limbs due burial;
And all the students, cloth'd in mourning black,
Shall wait upon his heavy funeral.   *Exeunt [with limbs]*.

                    Enter Chorus.

Cut is the branch that might have grown full straight
And burned is Apollo's laurel bough
That sometime grew within this learned man.
Faustus is gone. Regard his hellish fall!
—Whose fiendful fortune may exhort the wise
Only to wonder at unlawful things
Whose deepness doth entice such forward wits
To practice more than heavenly power permits.   *[Exit.]*

THE
FAMOUS TRAGEDY OF
THE RICH JEW
OF MALTA

[*Speaking Characters*

MACHIAVEL
BARABAS
1 MERCHANT
2 MERCHANT
1 JEW
2 JEW
3 JEW
FERNEZE, *Governor of Malta*
CALYMATH
1 BASSO
1 KNIGHT
2 KNIGHT
1 OFFICER
2 OFFICER
ABIGAIL
FRIAR JACOMO
FRIAR BARNARDINE
ABBESS
LODOWICK, *Ferneze's son*
MATHIAS
MARTIN DEL BOSCO
SLAVE
ITHAMORE
KATHERINE, *Mathias' mother*
BELLAMIRA
PILIA-BORZA
MESSENGER
CARPENTER

Mute Characters

3 OFFICER, KNIGHTS, BASSOES, OTHER TURKS, FRIAR, TWO NUNS, SLAVES, CARPENTERS]

[Enter] Machiavel [as Prologue].

Machiavel. Albeit the world thinks Machiavel is dead—
Yet was his soul but flown beyond the Alps—
And, now the Guise is dead, is come from France
To view this land and frolic with his friends!
To some perhaps my name is odious. . . .   *[Smiles.]*
(But such as love me guard me from their tongues!)
And let them know that I am Machiavel,
And weigh not men, and therefore not men's words.
Admir'd I am of those that hate me most.
Though some speak openly against my books,   10
Yet they will read me, and thereby attain
To Peter's chair—and when they cast me off
Are poison'd by my climbing followers!
I count religion but a childish toy,   *[Snaps his fingers.]*
And hold there is no sin but ignorance.
Birds of the air will tell of murders past?
I am asham'd to hear such fooleries!
Many will talk of title to a crown:
What right had Cæsar to the empire?
Might first made kings, and laws were then most sure   20
When like the [Draco's] they were writ in blood.
Hence comes it that a strong-built citadel
Commands much more than letters can import—
Which maxim had Phalaris observed,
H'ad never bellow'd in a brazen bull
Of great ones' envy! O' the poor petty wights
Let me be envi'd and not pitied!
But whither am I bound? I come not, I,
To read a lecture here in Britain,
But to present the tragedy of a Jew,   30
Who smiles to see how full his bags are cramm'd—
Which money was not got without my means. . . .
I crave but this: Grace him as he deserves!
And let him not be entertain'd the worse
Because he favors me.   *[Exit.]*

[ACTUS PRIMUS.]

[1.1] [*The curtains at the back of the stage open. Barabas is discovered*] *in his counting-house, with heaps of gold* [*and bags*] *before him.*

Bar.—So that of thus much that return was made:
And of the third part of the Persian ships,
There was the venture summ'd and satisfi'd. . . .
As for those [Saenites], and the men of Uz,
That bought my Spanish oils and wines of Greece,
Here have I purs'd their paltry silverlings.
Fie, what a trouble 'tis to count this trash!
Well fare the Arabians, who so richly pay
The things they traffic for with wedge of gold,
Whereof a man may easily in a day   10
Tell that which may maintain him all his life.
The needy groom that never finger'd groat
Would make a miracle of thus much coin—
But he whose steel-barr'd coffers are cramm'd full,
And all his lifetime hath been tired
Wearying his fingers' ends with telling it,
Would in his age be loth to labor so
And for a pound to sweat himself to death.   [*Barabas closes*
Give me the merchants of the Indian mines   *the curtains and*
That trade in metal of the purest mold;   *comes forward.*] 20
The wealthy Moor that in the eastern rocks
Without control can pick his riches up,
And in his house heap pearls like pebble-stones,
Receive them free, and sell them by the weight:
Bags of fiery opals, sapphires, amethysts,
Jacinths, hard topaz, grass-green emeralds,
Beauteous rubies, sparkling diamonds,
And seld-seen costly stones of so great price,
As one of them indifferently rated
And of a carat of this quantity   [*Points to ring* 30
May serve in peril of calamity   *on finger.*]
To ransom great kings from captivity!
This is the ware wherein consists my wealth!
And thus methinks should men of judgment frame
Their means of traffic from the vulgar trade,
And as their wealth increaseth, so inclose
Infinite riches in a little room.
But now how stands the wind?   [*Holds up hand.*]
Into what corner peers my halcyon's bill?

Ha, to the east? Yes. See how stands the vanes?   40
East and by south. Why then I hope my ships
I sent for Egypt and the bordering isles
Are gotten up by Nilus' winding banks:
Mine argosy from Alexandria,
Loaden with spice and silks, now under sail,
Are smoothly gliding down by Candy shore
To Malta, through our Mediterranean Sea.
But who comes here?

Enter [1] *Merchant.*

How now?
[1] *Merch.* Barabas, thy ships are safe,
Riding in Malta-road. And all the merchants   50
With other merchandise are safe arriv'd
And have sent me to know whether yourself
Will come and custom them.
   Bar. The ships are safe thou say'st, and richly fraught?
   [1] *Merch.* They are.
   Bar. Why then go bid them come ashore.
And bring with them their bills of entry.
I hope our credit in the Custom-House
Will serve as well as I were present there.
Go send 'em threescore camels, thirty mules,   60
And twenty wagons to bring up the ware.
But art thou master in a ship of mine,
And is thy credit not enough for that?
   [1] *Merch.* The very custom barely comes to more
Than many merchants of the town are worth,
And therefore far exceeds my credit, sir.
   Bar. Go tell 'em the Jew of Malta sent thee, man!
Tush, who amongst 'em knows not Barabas?
   [1] *Merch.* I go.
   Bar. So then, there's somewhat come.   70
Sirrah, which of my ships art thou master of?
   [1] *Merch.* Of the Speranza, sir.
   Bar. And saw'st thou not mine argosy at Alexandria?
Thou could'st not come from Egypt or by Caire
But at the entry there into the sea
Where Nilus pays his tribute to the main,
Thou needs must sail by Alexandria.
   [1] *Merch.* I neither saw them nor inquir'd of them:
But this we heard some of our seamen say,
They wonder'd how you durst with so much wealth   80
Trust such a crazed vessel, and so far.
   Bar. Tush, they are wise! I know her and her strength.

But go, go thou thy ways, discharge thy ship,
And bid my factor bring his loading in.   [*Exit* 1 *Merch.*]
And yet I wonder at this argosy.

Enter a second Merchant.

2 *Merch.* Thine argosy from Alexandria,
Know, Barabas, doth ride in Malta-road,
Laden with riches and exceeding store
Of Persian silks, of gold, and orient pearl.
   Bar. How chance you came not with those other ships   90
That sail'd by Egypt?
   2 *Merch.* Sir, we saw 'em not.
   Bar. Belike they coasted round by Candy shore
About their oils, or other businesses.
But 'twas ill done of you to come so far
Without the aid or conduct of their ships.
   2 *Merch.* Sir, we were wafted by a Spanish fleet
That never left us till within a league,
That had the galleys of the Turk in chase.
   Bar. O, they were going up to Sicily. Well, go   100
And bid the merchants and my men despatch
And come ashore, and see the fraught discharg'd.
   [2] *Merch.* I go.   *Exit.*
   Bar. Thus trowls our fortune in by land and sea,
And thus are we on every side enrich'd:
These are the blessings promis'd to the Jews,
And herein was old Abram's happiness!
What more may Heaven do for earthly man
Than thus to pour out plenty in their laps,
Ripping the bowels of the earth for them,   110
Making the seas their servants, and the winds
To drive their substance with successful blasts?
Who hateth me but for my happiness?
Or who is honor'd now but for his wealth?
Rather had I a Jew be hated thus,
Than pitied in a Christian poverty:
For I can see no fruits in all their faith
But malice, falsehood, and excessive pride,
Which methinks fits not their profession.
Haply some hapless man hath conscience—   120
And for his conscience lives in beggary!
They say we are a scatter'd nation—
I cannot tell—but we have scambled up
More wealth by far than those that brag of faith.
There's Kirriah Jairim, the great Jew of Greece,
Obed in Bairseth, Nones in Portugal,

Myself in Malta, some in Italy,
Many in France, and wealthy every one—
Ay, wealthier far than any Christian.
I must confess we come not to be kings: 130
That's not our fault: alas, our number's few,
And crowns come either by succession,
Or urg'd by force; and nothing violent,
Oft have I heard tell, can be permanent.
Give us a peaceful rule, make Christians kings,
That thirst so much for principality.
I have no charge, nor many children,
But one sole daughter, whom I hold as dear
As Agamemnon did his Iphigen:
And all I have is hers. But who comes here?   140

Enter three Jews.

1. Tush, tell not me 'twas done of policy.
2. Come, therefore, let us go to Barabas,
For he can counsel best in these affairs.
—And here he comes.
   Bar. Why, how now, countrymen!
Why flock you thus to me in multitudes?
What accident's betided to the Jews?
   1. A fleet of warlike galleys, Barabas,
Are come from Turkey and lie in our road.
And they this day sit in the Council-House   150
To entertain them and their embassy.
   Bar. Why, let 'em come, so they come not to war;
Or let 'em war so we be conquerors.
(—Nay, let 'em combat, conquer, and kill all,
So they spare me, my daughter, and my wealth!)   *Aside.*
   1. Were it for confirmation of a league,
They would not come in warlike manner thus.
   2. I fear their coming will afflict us all.
   Bar. Fond men, what dream you of their multitudes?
What need they treat of peace that are in league?   160
The Turks and those of Malta are in league.
Tut, tut, there is some other matter in't.
   1. Why, Barabas, they come for peace or war.
   Bar. Happily for neither, but to pass along
Towards Venice by the Adriatic Sea,
With whom they have attempted many times
But never could effect their stratagem.
   3. And very wisely said. It may be so.
   2. But there's a meeting in the Senate-House,
And all the Jews in Malta must be there.   170

Bar. Hum, all the Jews in Malta must be there?
Ay, like enough, why then let every man
Provide him, and be there for fashion-sake.
If anything shall there concern our state,
Assure yourselves I'll look (—unto myself.)   *Aside.*
   1. I know you will. Well, brethren, let us go.
   2. Let's take our leaves. Farewell, good Barabas.
   Bar. Do so. Farewell, Zaareth; farewell, Temainte.
                              [*Exeunt Jews.*]

And, Barabas, now search this secret out.
Summon thy senses, call thy wits together.   180
These silly men mistake the matter clean.
Long to the Turk did Malta contribute,
Which tribute, all in policy I fear,
The Turks have let increase to such a sum
As all the wealth of Malta cannot pay:
And now by that advantage thinks, belike,
To seize upon the town. Ay, that he seeks.
Howe'er the world go, I'll make sure for one,
And seek in time to intercept the worst,
Warily guarding that which I ha' got.   190
Ego mihimet sum semper proximus.
Why, let 'em enter, let 'em take the town.   [*Exit.*]

[1.2] *Enter [Ferneze,] Governors of Malta (Knights), [and*
     Officers]; met by Bassoes of the Turk, Calymath.

   [*Fern.*] Now, Bassoes, what demand you at our hands?
   [1] *Bass.* Know, Knights of Malta, that we came from
     Rhodes,
From Cyprus, Candy, and those other isles
That lie betwixt the Mediterranean seas.
   [*Fern.*] What's Cyprus, Candy, and those other isles
To us, or Malta? What at our hands demand ye?
   Caly. The ten years' tribute that remains unpaid.
   [*Fern.*] Alas, my lord, the sum is over-great!
I hope Your Highness will consider us.
   Caly. I wish, grave governors, 'twere in my power   10
To favor you! But 'tis my father's cause—
Wherein I may not, nay, I dare not dally.
   [*Fern.*] Then give us leave, great Selim Calymath.
               [*Consults apart with Knights.*]
   Caly. Stand all aside, and let the Knights determine,
And send to keep our galleys under sail,
For happily we shall not tarry here.
Now, governors, how are you resolv'd?

[*Fern.*] Thus: since your hard conditions are such
That you will needs have ten years' tribute past,
We may have time to make collection   20
Amongst the inhabitants of Malta for't.
  [1] *Bass.* That's more than is in our commission.
  Caly. What, Callipine, a little courtesy!
Let's know their time, perhaps it is not long:
And 'tis more kingly to obtain by peace
Than to enforce conditions by constraint.
What respite ask you, governors?
  [*Fern.*] But a month.
  Caly. We grant a month—but see you keep your promise!
Now launch our galleys back again to sea,   30
Where we'll attend the respite you have ta'en,
And for the money send our messenger.
Farewell, great governors and brave Knights of Malta.
  [*Fern.*] And all good fortune wait on Calymath!   *Exeunt.*
Go one and call those Jews of Malta hither.
Were they not summon'd to appear today?
  Off. They were, my lord, and here they come.

Enter Barabas and three Jews.

  1 *Knight.* Have you determined what to say to them?
  [*Fern.*] Yes, give me leave.—And, Hebrews, now come near.
From the Emperor of Turkey is arriv'd   40
Great Selim Calymath, His Highness' son,
To levy of us ten years' tribute past.
Now then, here know that it concerneth us—.
  Bar. Then, good my lord, to keep your quiet still,
Your lordship shall do well to let them have it!
  [*Fern.*] Soft, Barabas, there's more 'longs to 't than so.
To what this ten years' tribute will amount
That we have cast, but cannot compass it
By reason of the wars that robb'd our store:
And therefore are we to request your aid.   50
  Bar. Alas, my lord, we are no soldiers!
And what's our aid against so great a Prince?
  1 *Knight.* Tut, Jew, we know thou art no soldier.
Thou art a merchant and a money'd man—
And 'tis thy money, Barabas, we seek.
  Bar. How, my lord, my money?
  [*Fern.*]—Thine and the rest.
For, to be short, amongst you 't must be had.
  [1] *Jew.* Alas, my lord, the most of us are poor!
  [*Fern.*] Then let the rich increase your portions.   60

Bar. Are strangers with your tribute to be tax'd?

2 *Knight.* Have strangers leave with us to get their
    wealth?

Then let them with us contribute.

Bar. How, equally?

[*Fern.*] No, Jew, like infidels.

For through our sufferance of your hateful lives,

Who stand accursed in the sight of Heaven,

These taxes and afflictions are befall'n!

And therefore thus we are determined:

Read there the articles of our decrees.   70

[1 *Officer reads*]. "First, the tribute-money of the Turks shall
all be levied amongst the Jews, and each of them to pay one
half of his estate."

Bar. How, half his estate? I hope you mean not mine.

[*Fern.*] Read on.

[1 *Off. reads*]. "Secondly, he that denies to pay shall straight
become a Christian."

Bar. How, a Christian? Hum, what's here to do?

[1 *Off. reads.*] "Lastly, he that denies this shall absolutely lose
all he has."   80

All three Jews. O my lord, we will give half!

Bar. O earth-mettl'd villains, and no Hebrews born!

And will you basely thus submit yourselves

To leave your goods to their arbitrament?

[*Fern.*] Why, Barabas, wilt thou be christ'ned?

Bar. No, Governor, I will be no convertite.

[*Fern.*] Then pay thy half.

Bar. Why, know you what you [do] by this device?

Half of my substance is a city's wealth.

Governor, it was not got so easily,   90

Nor will I part so slightly therewithal.

[*Fern.*] Sir, half is the penalty of our decree:

Either pay that, or we will seize on all.

Bar. Corpo di Dio! Stay! You shall have half!

Let me be us'd but as my brethren are.

[*Fern.*] No, Jew, thou hast denied the articles, [*Makes sign*

And now it cannot be recall'd.   *to Officers who*

Bar. Will you then steal my goods?   *exeunt.*]

Is theft the ground of your religion?

[*Fern.*] No, Jew, we take particularly thine   100

To save the ruin of a multitude:

And better one want for the common good

Than many perish for a private man!

Yet, Barabas, we will not banish thee,

But here in Malta, where thou gott'st thy wealth,

Live still; and if thou canst, get more.

Bar. Christians, what or how can I multiply?
Of naught is nothing made.

1 *Knight.* From naught at first thou cam'st to little wealth,
From little unto more, from more to most.   110
If your first curse fall heavy on thy head
And make thee poor and scorn'd of all the world,
'Tis not our fault but thy inherent sin!

Bar. What, bring you Scripture to confirm your wrongs?
Preach me not out of my possessions.
Some Jews are wicked, as all Christians are!
But say the tribe that I descended of
Were all in general cast away for sin,
Shall *I* be tried by their transgression?
The man that dealeth righteously shall live   120
And which of you can charge me otherwise?

[Fern.] Out, wretched Barabas!
Sham'st thou not thus to justify thyself,
As if we knew not thy profession?
If thou rely upon thy righteousness,
Be patient and thy riches will increase.
Excess of wealth is cause of covetousness:
And covetousness, O, 'tis a monstrous sin!

Bar. Ay, but theft is worse! Tush, take not from me then,
For that is theft! And if you rob me thus,   130
I must be forc'd to steal and compass more.

1 *Knight.* Grave governors, list not to his exclaims!
Convert his mansion to a nunnery:
His house will harbor many holy nuns.

[Fern.] It shall be so.

Enter Officers.

              Now, officers have you done?

[1] *Off.* Ay, my lord, we have seiz'd upon the goods
And wares of Barabas, which being valued,
Amount to more than all the wealth in Malta.
And of the other we have seized half.

⟨*Fern.*⟩ Then we'll take order for the residue.   140

Bar. Well then, my lord, say, are you satisfied?
You have my goods, my money, and my wealth,
My ships, my store, and all that I enjoy'd—
And, having all, you can request no more—
Unless your unrelenting flinty hearts
Suppress all pity in your stony breasts
And now shall move you to bereave my life!

[Fern.] No, Barabas, to stain our hands with blood

Is far from us and our profession.

    Bar. Why, I esteem the injury far less   150
To take the lives of miserable men
Than be the causers of their misery.
You have my wealth, the labor of my life,
The comfort of mine age, my children's hope,
And therefore ne'er distinguish of the wrong.

    [*Fern.*] Content thee, Barabas, thou hast naught but right.

    Bar. Your extreme right does me exceeding wrong:
But take it to you, i' th' Devil's name!

    [*Fern.*] Come, let us in, and gather of these goods
The money for this tribute of the Turk.   160

    1 *Knight.* 'Tis necessary that be looked unto:
For if we break our day, we break the league,
And that will prove but simple policy.

                Exeunt [all except Barabas and the Jews].

    Bar. Ay, *policy*, that's their profession!
—And not simplicity, as they suggest.
The plagues of Egypt, and the curse of Heaven,
Earth's barrenness, and all men's hatred
Inflict upon them, thou great *Primus Motor!*
And here upon my knees, striking the earth,   [*Kneels, looks
I ban their souls to everlasting pains   up, strikes* 170
And extreme tortures of the fiery deep   *floor.*]
That thus have dealt with me in my distress!

    1 *Jew.* O yet be patient, gentle Barabas.

    Bar. O silly brethren, born to see this day!
Why stand you thus unmov'd with my laments?
Why weep you not to think upon my wrongs?
Why pine not I and die in this distress?

    1 *Jew.* Why, Barabas, as hardly can we brook
The cruel handling of ourselves in this:
Thou seest they have taken half our goods.   180

    Bar. Why did you yield to their extortion?
You were a multitude, and I but one:
And of me only have they taken all.

    1 *Jew.* Yet, brother Barabas, remember Job.

    Bar. What tell you me of Job? I wot his wealth
Was written thus: he had seven thousand sheep,
Three thousand camels, and two hundred yoke
Of laboring oxen, and five hundred
She asses. But for every one of those,
Had they been valued at indifferent rate,   190
I had at home, and in mine argosy
And other ships that come from Egypt last,
As much as would have bought his beasts and him,

And yet have kept enough to live upon!
So that not he, but I, may curse the day,
Thy fatal birthday, forlorn Barabas,
And henceforth wish for an eternal night,
That clouds of darkness may inclose my flesh
And hide these extreme sorrows from mine eyes!
For only I have toil'd to inherit here   200
The months of vanity and loss of time
And painful nights have been appointed me.
    2 Jew. Good Barabas, be patient.
    Bar. Ay, ay! Pray, leave me in my patience! You that
Were ne'er possess'd of wealth are pleas'd with want.
But give him liberty at least to mourn
That in a field amidst his enemies
Doth see his soldiers slain, himself disarm'd,
And knows no means of his recovery—.
Ay, let me sorrow for this sudden chance.   210
'Tis in the trouble of my spirit I speak.
Great injuries are not so soon forgot.
    1 Jew. Come, let us leave him in his ireful mood.
Our words will but increase his ecstasy.
    2 Jew. On, then. But trust me 'tis a misery
To see a man in such affliction.—
Farewell, Barabas!   *Exeunt [the three Jews].*
    Bar. Ay, fare you well.
See the simplicity of these base slaves,
Who, for the villains have no wit themselves,   220
Think me to be a senseless lump of clay
That will with every water wash to dirt.
No, Barabas is born to better chance
And fram'd of finer mold than common men
That measure naught but by the present time!
A reaching thought will search his deepest wits
And cast with cunning for the time to come:
For evils are apt to happen every day.—

       Enter Abigail, the Jew's daughter.

But whither wends my beauteous Abigail?
O, what has made my lovely daughter sad?   230
What, woman, moan not for a little loss.
Thy father hath enough in store for thee.
    Abig. Not for myself, but aged Barabas,
Father, for thee, lamenteth Abigail!
But I will learn to leave these fruitless tears
And, urg'd thereto with my afflictions,
With fierce exclaims run to the Senate-House

And in the Senate reprehend them all—
And rent their hearts with tearing of my hair—
Till they reduce the wrongs done to my father! 240
   Bar. No, Abigail, things past recovery
Are hardly cur'd with exclamations.
Be silent, daughter, sufferance breeds ease,
And time may yield us an occasion
Which on the sudden cannot serve the turn.
Besides, my girl, think me not all so fond
As negligently to forgo so much
Without provision for thyself and me:
Ten thousand portagues, besides great pearls,
Rich costly jewels, and stones infinite, 250
Fearing the worst of this before it fell,
I closely hid.
   Abig. Where, father?
   Bar. In my house, my girl.
   Abig. Then shall they ne'er be seen of Barabas
For they have seiz'd upon thy house and wares.
   Bar. But they will give me leave once more, I trow,
To go into my house?
   Abig. That may they not.
For there I left the Governor placing nuns, 260
Displacing me. And of thy house they mean
To make a nunnery, where none but their own sect
Must enter in, men generally barr'd.
   Bar. My gold, my gold, and all my wealth is gone!
You partial heavens, have I deserv'd this plague?
What, will you thus oppose me, luckless stars,
To make me desperate in my poverty?
And knowing me impatient in distress
Think me so mad as I will hang myself
That I may vanish o'er the earth in air 270
And leave no memory that e'er I was?
No, I will live! Nor loathe I this my life!
And since you leave me in the ocean thus
To sink or swim, and put me to my shifts,
I'll rouse my senses and awake myself.—
Daughter, I have it. Thou perceiv'st the plight
Wherein these Christians have oppressed me.
Be rul'd by me, for in extremity
We ought to make bar of no policy.
   Abig. Father, whate'er it be to injure them 280
That have so manifestly wronged us,
What will not Abigail attempt?
   Bar. Why, so.

Then thus: thou told'st me they have turn'd my house
Into a nunnery, and some nuns are there?
  Abig. I did.
  Bar. Then, Abigail, there must my girl
Entreat the Abbess to be entertain'd.
  Abig. How, as a nun?
  Bar. Ay, daughter, for religion   290
Hides many mischiefs from suspicion.
  Abig. Ay, but, father, they will suspect me there.
  Bar. Let 'em suspect, but be thou so precise
As they may think it done of holiness.
Entreat 'em fair, and give them friendly speech,
And seem to them as if thy sins were great,
Till thou has gotten to be entertain'd.
  Abig. Thus, father, shall I much dissemble.
  Bar. Tush!
As good dissemble that thou never mean'st   300
As first mean truth and then dissemble it—
A counterfeit profession is better
Than unseen hypocrisy.
  Abig. Well, father, say I be entertain'd,
What then shall follow?
  Bar. This shall follow then:
There have I hid, close underneath the plank
That runs along the upper chamber floor,
The gold and jewels which I kept for thee.
But here they come. Be cunning, Abigail!   310
  Abig. Then, father, go with me.
  Bar. No, Abigail, in this
It is not necessary I be seen:
For I will seem offended with thee for't:
Be close, my girl, for this must fetch my gold.

    [They retire as] enter three friars and two nuns.

  [F. Jac.] Sisters,
We now are almost at the new-made nunnery.
  [Abb.] The better, for we love not to be seen.
'Tis thirty winters long since some of us
Did stray so far among the multitude.   320
  [F. Jac.] But, madam, this house
And waters of this new-made nunnery
Will much delight you.
  [Abb.] It may be so. But who comes here?

      [Abigail comes forward.]

  Abig. Grave Abbess, and you, happy virgins' guide,

Pity the state of a distressed maid.

    Abb. What art thou, daughter?

    Abig. The hopeless daughter of a hapless Jew,
The Jew of Malta, wretched Barabas—
Sometimes the owner of a goodly house,   330
Which they have now turn'd to a nunnery.

    Abb. Well, daughter, say, what is thy suit with us?

    Abig. Fearing the afflictions which my father feels
Proceed from sin, or want of faith in us,
I'd pass away my life in penitence
And be a novice in your nunnery
To make atonement for my laboring soul.

    [*F. Jac.*] No doubt, brother, but this proceedeth of the spirit.

    [*F. Barn.*] Ay, and of a moving spirit too, brother. But come,
Let us entreat she may be entertain'd.   340

    Abb. Well, daughter, we admit you for a nun.

    Abig. First let me as a novice learn to frame
My solitary life to your strait laws,
And let me lodge where I was wont to lie:
I do not doubt, by your divine precepts
And mine own industry, but to profit much.

    Bar. (As much, I hope, as all I hid is worth.)   *Aside.*

    Abb. Come, daughter, follow us.

    Bar. [*coming forward.*] Why, how now, Abigail,
What mak'st thou amongst these hateful Christians?   350

    [*F. Jac.*] Hinder her not, thou man of little faith,
For she has mortified herself.

    Bar. How, mortified?

    [*F. Jac.*] And is admitted to the sisterhood.

    Bar. Child of perdition, and thy father's shame,
What wilt thou do among these hateful fiends?
I charge thee on my blessing that thou leave
These devils and their damned heresy!

    Abig. Father, give me—.

    Bar. (Nay, back, Abigail,   *Whispers to her.* 360
And think upon the jewels and the gold.
The board is marked thus that covers it.)   [*Makes cross.*]
Away, accursed, from thy father's sight!

    [*F. Jac.*] Barabas, although thou art in misbelief,
And wilt not see thine own afflictions,
Yet let thy daughter be no longer blind.

    Bar. Blind friar, I reck not thy persuasions,
(The board is marked thus that covers it.)   [*Aside to her,*
For I had rather die than see her thus.   *makes cross.*]
Wilt thou forsake me too in my distress,   370
Seduced daughter? (Go, forget not.)   *Aside to her.*

Becomes it Jews to be so credulous?
(Tomorrow early I'll be at the door.)   *Aside to her.*
No, come not at me! If thou wilt be damn'd,
Forget me, see me not, and so be gone!
(Farewell, remember tomorrow morning.)   *Aside.*
Out, out, thou wretch!

>   [*As all exeunt,*] *enter Mathias.*

Math. Who's this? Fair Abigail, the rich Jew's daughter,
Become a nun! Her father's sudden fall
Has humbled her and brought her down to this.   380
Tut, she were fitter for a tale of love
Than to be tired out with orisons:
And better would she far become a bed,
Embraced in a friendly lover's arms,
Than rise at midnight to a solemn mass.

>   *Enter Lodowick.*

Lod. Why, how now, Don Mathias, in a dump?
Math. Believe me, noble Lodowick, I have seen
The strangest sight, in my opinion,
That ever I beheld.
Lod. What wa't, I prithee?   390
Math. A fair young maid, scarce fourteen years of age,
The sweetest flower in Cytherea's field,
Cropt from the pleasures of the fruitful earth,
And strangely metamorphis'd nun.
Lod. But say, what was she?
Math. Why, the rich Jew's daughter.
Lod. What, Barabas, whose goods were lately seiz'd?
Is she so fair?
Math. And matchless beautiful!
—As, had you seen her, 'twould have moved your heart,   400
Though countermin'd with walls of brass, to love,
Or at the least to pity.
Lod. And if she be so fair as you report,
'Twere time well spent to go and visit her.
How say you, shall we?
Math. I must and will, sir, there's no remedy.
Lod. And so will I too, or it shall go hard.
Farewell, Mathias.
Math. Farewell, Lodowick.   *Exeunt.*

ACTUS SECUNDUS.

[2.1]   *Enter Barabas with a light.*

Bar. Thus, like the sad presaging raven that tolls
The sick man's passport in her hollow beak
And in the shadow of the silent night
Doth shake contagion from her sable wings,
Vex'd and tormented runs poor Barbas
With fatal curses towards these Christians.
The incertain pleasures of swift-footed time
Have ta'en their flight—and left me in despair!
And of my former riches rests no more
But bare remembrance—like a soldier's scar   10
That has no further comfort for his maim.
O Thou that with a fiery pillar led'st
The sons of Israel through the dismal shades,
Light Abraham's offspring: and direct the hand
Of Abigail this night: or let the day
Turn to eternal darkness after this!
No sleep can fasten on my watchful eyes,
Nor quiet enter my distemper'd thoughts,
Till I have answer of my Abigail!

                Enter Abigail above [carrying bags].

Abig. Now have I happily espied a time   20
To search the plank my father did appoint
And here behold, unseen, where I have found
The gold, the pearls, and jewels which he hid.
Bar. Now I remember those old women's words   [*Sits
Who in my wealth would tell me winter's tales   *facing*
And speak of spirits and ghosts that glide by night   *audience.*]
About the place where treasure hath been hid:
And now methinks that I am one of those:
For whilst I live, here lives my soul's sole hope,
And when I die, here shall my spirit walk.   30
Abig. Now that my father's fortune were so good   [*Peers
As but to be about this happy place.   *about.*]
'Tis not so happy. Yet when we parted last,
He said he would attend me in the morn.
Then, gentle sleep, where'er his body rests,
Give charge to Morpheus that he may dream
A golden dream, and of the sudden walk,
Come and receive the treasure I have found!

Bar. [*Bueno para todos mi ganado no era.*]
As good go on as sit so sadly thus.   40
But stay, what star shines yonder in the east?   [*Turns around*
The lodestar of my life, if Abigail.   *and looks up.*]
Who's there?
    Abig. Who's that?
    Bar. Peace, Abigail, 'tis I.
    Abig. Then, father, here receive thy happiness.
    Bar. Hast thou't?
    Abig. Here, hast thou't?   *Throws down bags.*
There's more, and more, and more.
    Bar. O my girl,   50
My gold, my fortune, my felicity!
Strength to my soul! Death to mine enemy!
Welcome the first beginner of my bliss!
O Abigail, Abigail, that I had thee here too!
Then my desires were fully satisfied!
But I will practice thy enlargement thence—
O girl! O gold! O beauty! O my bliss!   *Hugs his bags.*
    Abig. Father, it draweth towards midnight now,
And 'bout this time the nuns begin to wake:
To shun suspicion, therefore, let us part.   60
    Bar. Farewell, my joy, and by my fingers take
A kiss from him that sends it from his soul.   [*Blows a kiss.*
                                                  Exit Abigail above.]
Now Phœbus ope the eyelids of the day,
And for the raven wake the morning lark,
That I may hover with her in the air—
Singing o'er these, as she does o'er her young!
[*Hermoso placer de los dineros.*]   *Exit.*

[2.2] *Enter Governor, Martin del Bosco, the Knights, [and Officers].*

[*Fern.*] Now, captain, tell us whither thou art bound?
Whence is thy ship that anchors in our road?
And why thou cam'st ashore without our leave?
    Bosc. Governor of Malta, hither am I bound:
My ship, the *Flying Dragon,* is of Spain,
And so am I, Del Bosco is my name,
Vice-Admiral unto the Catholic King.
    1 *Knight.* 'Tis true, my lord, therefore entreat him well.
    Bosc. Our fraught is Grecians, Turks, and Afric Moors.
For late up on the coast of Corsica,   10
Because we vail'd not to the [Turkish] fleet,
Their creeping galleys had us in the chase:
But suddenly the wind began to rise,

And then we [luff'd and tack'd] and fought at ease:
Some have we fir'd, and many have we sunk;
But one amongst the rest became our prize:
The captain's slain, the rest remain our slaves,
Of whom we would make sale in Malta here.
    [*Fern.*] Martin del Bosco, I have heard of thee.
Welcome to Malta, and to all of us!   20
But to admit a sale of these thy Turks
We may not, nay, we dare not give consent
By reason of a tributary league.
    1 *Knight.* Del Bosco, as thou lov'st and honor'st us,
Persuade our Governor against the Turk.
This truce we have is but in hope of gold.
And with that sum he craves might we wage war.
    Bosc. Will Knights of Malta be in league with Turks?
And buy it basely too for sums of gold?
My lord, remember that to Europe's shame,   30
The Christian Isle of Rhodes, from whence you came,
Was lately lost, and you were stated here
To be at deadly enmity with Turks.
    [*Fern.*] Captain, we know it, but our force is small.
    Bosc. What is the sum that Calymath requires?
    [*Fern.*] A hundred thousand crowns.
    Bosc. My lord and king hath title to this isle,
And he means quickly to expel [them] hence.
Therefore be rul'd by me and keep the gold:
I'll write unto His Majesty for aid,   40
And not depart until I see you free.
    [*Fern.*] On this condition shall thy Turks be sold:
Go, officers, and set them straight in show.

                                                 [*Exeunt Officers.*]

Bosco, thou shalt be Malta's general:
We and our warlike Knights will follow thee
Against these barbarous misbelieving Turks.
    Bosc. So shall you imitate those you succeed:
For when their hideous force environ'd Rhodes,
Small though the number was that kept the town,
They fought it out, and not a man surviv'd   50
To bring the hapless news to Christendom.
    [*Fern.*] So will we fight it out. Come, let's away!
Proud-daring Calymath, instead of gold,
We'll send thee bullets wrapt in smoke and fire!
Claim tribute where thou wilt, we are resolv'd,
Honor is bought with blood and not with gold!   *Exeunt.*

[2.3] *Enter Officers with [Ithamore and other] Slaves.*

1 *Off*. This is the market-place. Here let 'em stand.
Fear not their sale, for they'll be quickly bought.
2 *Off*. Every one's price is written on his back,
And so much must they yield or not be sold.
1 *Off*. Here comes the Jew. Had not his goods been seiz'd,
He'd give us present money for them all.

Enter Barabas.

Bar. In spite of these swine-eating Christians—
Unchosen nation, never circumcis'd,
Such as (poor villains) were ne'er thought upon
Till Titus and Vespasian conquer'd us—   10
Am I become as wealthy as I was.
They hop'd my daughter would ha' been a nun,
But she's at home. And I have bought a house
As great and fair as is the Governor's:
And there in spite of Malta will I dwell—
Having Ferneze's hand—whose heart I'll have—
Ay, and his son's too, or it shall go hard!
I am not of the tribe of Levi, I,
That can so soon forget an injury.
We Jews can fawn like spaniels when we please: 20
And when we grin we bite: yet are our looks
As innocent and harmless as a lamb's . . .
I learn'd in Florence how to kiss my hand,
Heave up my shoulders when they call me dog,
And duck as low as any barefoot friar—
Hoping to see them starve upon a stall;
Or else be gather'd for in our synagogue
That when the offering-basin comes to me
Even for charity I may spit into't!
Here comes Don Lodowick, the Governor's son,   30
One that I love for his good father's sake.

Enter Lodowick.

Lod. I hear the wealthy Jew walked this way:
I'll seek him out and so insinuate
That I may have a sight of Abigail
For Don Mathias tells me she is fair.
Bar. (Now will I show myself
To have more of the serpent than the dove:
That is, more knave than fool!)   [*Aside*.]
Lod. Yond walks the Jew, now for fair Abigail.

 Bar. (Ay, ay, no doubt but she's at your command.) 40
                      [*Aside.*]
 Lod. Barabas, thou know'st I am the Governor's son.
 Bar. I would you were his father, too, sir.
—That's all the harm I wish you. (The slave looks
Like a hog's cheek new sing'd.)   [*Aside.*]
 Lod. Whither walk'st thou, Barabas? [*Barabas walks a few*
 Bar. No further. 'Tis a custom held with us, *steps away.*]
That when we speak with Gentiles like to you,
We turn into the air to purge ourselves—
For unto us the promise doth belong.
 Lod. Well, Barabas, canst help me to a diamond? 50
 Bar. O, sir, your father had my diamonds.
Yet I have one left that will serve your turn.
(I mean my daughter, but ere he shall have her
I'll sacrifice her on a pile of wood.
I ha' the poison of the city for him,
And the llhite leprosy.)   *Aside.*
 Lod. What sparkle does it give without a foil?
 Bar. The diamond that I talk of ne'er was foil'd.
(But when he touches it, it will be foil'd!) [*Aside.*]
Lord Lodowick, it sparkles bright and fair.   60
 Lod. Is it square or pointed, pray let me know.
 Bar. Pointed it is, good sir—(but not for you!) *Aside.*
 Lod. I like it much the better.
 Bar. So do I too.
 Lod. How shows it by night?
 Bar. Outshines Cynthia's rays.
(You'll like it better far a-nights than days.) *Aside.*
 Lod. And what's the price?
 Bar. (Your life an if you have it!) [*Aside.*] O my lord,
We will not jar about the price; come to my house 70
And I will give't your honor—(with a vengeance!) *Aside.*
 Lod. No, Barabas, I will deserve it first.
 Bar. Good sir,
Your father has deserv'd it at my hands
Who of mere charity and Christian ruth
To bring me to religious purity,
And as it were in catechising sort
To make me mindful of my mortal sins,
Against my will, and whether I would or no,
Seiz'd all I had and thrust me out o' doors   80
And made my house a place for nuns most chaste.
 Lod. No doubt your soul shall reap the fruit of it.
 Bar. Ay, but, my lord, the harvest is far off.
And yet I know the prayers of those nuns
And holy friars (having money for their pains) [*Aside.*]

Are wondrous. (—And indeed do no man good!)   *Aside.*
And seeing they are not idle but still doing,
'Tis likely they in time may reap some fruit,
I mean in fulness of perfection.

    Lod. Good Barabas, glance not at our holy nuns.   90

    Bar. No, but I do it through a burning zeal—
(Hoping ere long to set the house afire;
For though they do a while increase and multiply,
I'll have a saying to that nunnery.)   *Aside.*
As for the diamond, sir, I told you of,
Come home and there's no price shall make us part,
Even for your honorable father's sake.
(It shall go hard but I will see your death.)   *Aside.*
But now I must be gone to buy a slave.

    Lod. And, Barabas, I'll bear thee company.   100

    Bar. Come then—here's the market-place.
What's the price of this slave? Two hundred crowns?
Do the Turks weigh so much?

    [2] *Off.* Sir, that's his price.

    Bar. What, can he steal that you demand so much?
Belike he has some new trick for a purse:
And if he has, he is worth three hundred plates,
So that, being bought, the town-seal might be got
To keep him for his lifetime from the gallows.
The sessions day is critical to thieves,   110
And few or none 'scape but by being purg'd.

    Lod. Ratest thou this Moor but at two hundred plates?

    1 *Off.* No more, my lord.

    Bar. Why should this Turk be dearer than that Moor?

    [2] *Off.* Because he is young and has more qualities.

    Bar. What, hast the philosopher's stone? An thou hast, break
my head with it, I'll forgive thee.

    ⟨*Slave.*⟩ No, sir, I can cut and shave.

    Bar. Let me see, sirrah, are you not an old shaver?

    ⟨*Slave.*⟩ Alas, sir, I am a very youth.   120

    Bar. A youth? I'll buy you, and marry you to Lady Vanity
if you do well.

    ⟨*Slave.*⟩ I will serve you, sir.

    Bar.—Some wicked trick or other! It may be, under color
of shaving, thou'lt cut my throat for my goods. Tell me, hast
thou thy health well?

    ⟨*Slave.*⟩ Ay, passing well.

    Bar. So much the worse! I must have one that's sickly, and
be but for sparing victuals: 'tis not a stone of beef a day will
maintain you in these chops! Let me see one that's some-   130
what leaner.

    1 *Off.* Here's a leaner. How like you him?

Bar. Where wast thou born?

Itha. In Thrace, brought up in Arabia.

Bar.—So much the better. Thou art for my turn.
An hundred crowns? I'll have him. There's the coin.

                                     [Gives money.]

1 *Off.* Then mark him, sir, and take him hence.

Bar. (Ay, mark him, you were best, for this is he
That by my help shall do much villainy.)   *[Aside.]*
My lord, farewell. Come, sirrah, you are mine.   140
As for the diamond, it shall be yours.
I pray, sir, be no stranger at my house:
All that I have shall be at your command.

Enter Mathias, Mater.

Math. (What makes the Jew and Lodowick so private?
I fear me 'tis about fair Abigail.)   *[Aside.]*

Bar. Yonder comes Don Mathias, let us stay.
He loves my daughter, and she holds him dear:
But I have sworn to frustrate both their hopes. *[Exit Lodowick.]*
And be reveng'd upon the—Governor!

    [Kath.] This Moor is comeliest, is he not? Speak, son.   150

Math. No, this is the better, mother: view this well.

                       [While Katherine examines the slaves,
                       Barabas and Mathias whisper together.]

Bar. Seem not to know me here before your mother
Lest she mistrust the match that is in hand
When you have brought her home, come to my house.
Think of me as thy father. Son, farewell.

Math. But wherefore talk'd Don Lodowick with you?

Bar. Tush, man, we talk'd of diamonds, not of Abigail.

        [Katherine approaches with a slave she has chosen.]

    [Kath.] Tell me, Mathias, is not that the Jew?

Bar. As for the comment on the *Maccabees,*
I have it, sir, and 'tis at your command.   160

Math. Yes, madam, and my talk with him was
About the borrowing of a book or two.

    [Kath.] Converse not with him, he is cast off from Heaven.
Thou hast thy crowns, fellow.   *[Pays 2 Officer.]*
Come, let's away.

Math. Sirrah Jew, remember the book.

Bar. Marry will I, sir.

              [Exeunt Mathias, his mother, and Slave.]

    [2] *Off.* Come, I have made reasonable market. Let's away.

                       [Exeunt Officers with Slaves.]

Bar. Now let me know thy name, and therewithal
Thy birth, condition, and profession.   170
    Itha. Faith, sir, my birth is but mean, my name's Ithamore,
my profession what you please.
    Bar. Hast thou no trade? Then listen to my words,
And I will teach that shall stick by thee:
First, be thou void of these affections—
Compassion, love, vain hope, and heartless fear.
Be mov'd at nothing. See thou pity none.
But to thyself smile when the Christians moan.
    Itha. O brave master, I worship your nose for this!
    Bar. As for myself, I walk abroad a-nights   180
And kill sick people groaning under walls:
Sometimes I go about and poison wells:
And now and then, to cherish Christian thieves,
I am content to lose some of my crowns,
That I may, walking in my gallery,
See 'em go pinion'd along by my door:
Being young, I studied physic and began
To practice first upon the Italian:
There I enriched the priests with burials,
And always kept the sextons' arms in ure   190
With digging graves and ringing dead men's knells:
And after that was I an engineer,
And in the wars 'twixt France and Germany,
Under pretense of helping Charles the Fifth,
Slew friend and enemy with my stratagems:
Then after that was I an usurer,
And with extorting, cozening, forfeiting,
And tricks belonging unto brokery,
I fill'd the jails with bankrouts in a year,
And with young orphans planted hospitals,   200
And every moon made some or other mad,
And now and then one hang himself for grief,
Pinning upon his breast a long great scroll
How I with interest tormented him.—
But mark how I am blest for plaguing them!
I have as much coin as will buy the town!
But tell me now, how hast thou spent thy time?
    Itha. Faith, master,
In setting Christian villages on fire,
Chaining of eunuchs, binding galley-slaves: 210
One time I was an ostler in an inn,
And in the nighttime secretly would I steal
To travellers' chambers and there cut their throats:

Once at Jerusalem where the pilgrims kneel'd
I strowed powder on the marble stones
And therewithal their knees would rankle so
That I have laugh'd a-good to see the cripples
Go limping home to Christendom on stilts!

Bar. Why this is something! Make account of me
As of thy fellow! We are villains both!   220
—Both circumcised, we hate Christians both!
Be true and secret, thou shalt want no gold.
But stand aside, here comes Don Lodowick.

Enter Lodowick.

Lod. O Barabas, well met.
Where is the diamond you told me of?
Bar. I have it for you, sir. Please you walk in with me.
What ho, Abigail! Open the door, I say.

Enter Abigail [with letters].

Abig.—In good time, father. Here are letters come
From Ormus, and the post stays here within.
Bar. Give me the letters. Daughter, do you hear,   230
Entertain Lodowick the Governor's son
With all the courtesy you can afford
Provided that you keep your maidenhead.
Use him as if he were a—(Philistine!
Dissemble, swear, protest, vow to love him,
He is not of the seed of Abraham.)   *Aside.*
I am a little busy, sir, pray pardon me.
Abigail, bid him welcome for my sake.
Abig. For your sake and his own he's welcome hither.
Bar. Daughter, a word more. (Kiss him. Speak him fair, 240
And like a cunning Jew so cast about   *[Barabas and Abigail*
That ye be both made sure ere you come out.)   *whisper*
Abig. (O father, Don Mathias is my love!)   *together.]*
Bar. (I know it. Yet I say, make love to *him*.
Do, it is requisite it should be so!)
Nay, on my life, it is my factor's hand—
But go you in, I'll think upon the account.
                              [Exeunt Abigail and Lodowick.]
The account is made, for Lodowick dies!
My factor sends me word a merchant's fled
That owes me for a hundred tun of wine.   250
I weigh it thus much [*snaps his fingers*]. I have wealth enough.
—For now by this has he kiss'd Abigail
And she vows love to him, and he to her.
As sure as Heaven rain'd manna for the Jews,

So sure shall he and Don Mathias die!
—His father was my chiefest enemy.

Enter Mathias.

Whither goes Don Mathias? Stay awhile.
  Math. Whither, but to my fair love, Abigail?
  Bar. Thou know'st, and Heaven can witness it is true,
That I intend my daughter shall be thine.   260
  Math. Ay, Barabas, or else thou wrong'st me much.
  Bar. O, Heaven forbid I should have such a thought!
—Pardon me though I weep. The Governor's son
Will, whether I will or no, have Abigail.
He sends her letters, bracelets, jewels, rings.
  Math. Does she receive them?
  Bar. She? No, Mathias, no, but sends them back,
And when he comes, she locks herself up fast—
Yet through the keyhole will he talk to her,
While she runs to the window looking out   270
When you should come and hale him from the door.
  Math. O treacherous Lodowick!
  Bar. Even now as I came home, he slipt me in,
And I am sure he is with Abigail.
  Math. I'll rouse him thence!   [*Draws sword.*]
  Bar. Not for all Malta, therefore sheathe your sword.
If you love me, no quarrels in my house;
But steal you in, and seem to see him not.
I'll give him such a warning ere he goes
As he shall have small hopes of Abigail!   280
Away, for here they come.

Enter Lodowick, Abigail.

  Math. What, hand in hand? I cannot suffer this.
  Bar. Mathias, as thou lov'st me, not a word.
  Math. Well, let it pass, another time shall serve.   *Exit.*
  Lod. Barabas, is not that the widow's son?
  Bar. Ay, and take heed, for he hath sworn your death.
  Lod. My death? What, is the base-born peasant mad?
  Bar. No, no, but happily he stands in fear
Of that which you, I think, ne'er dream upon,
My daughter here, a paltry silly girl.   290
  Lod. Why, loves she Don Mathias?
  Bar. Doth she not with her smiling answer you?
  Abig. (*He* has my heart: I smile against my will.)   [*Aside.*]
  Lod. Barabas, thou know'st I have lov'd thy daughter long.
  Bar. And so has she done you, even from a child.
  Lod. And now I can no longer hold my mind.

Bar. Nor I the affection that I bear to you.

Lod. This is thy diamond. Tell me, shall I have it?

Bar. Win it, and wear it, it is yet unsoil'd.

O, but I know your lordship would disdain   300

To marry with the daughter of a Jew!

And yet I'll give her many a golden cross

With Christian posies round about the ring.

Lod. 'Tis not thy wealth, but her that I esteem.

Yet crave I thy consent.

Bar. And mine you have, yet let me talk to her.

(This offspring of Cain, this Jebusite,   [*Aside to Abigail.*]

That never tasted of the Passover,

Nor e'er shall see the land of Canaan,

Nor our Messias that is yet to come: 310

This gentle maggot—Lodowick, I mean,

Must be deluded. Let him have thy hand,

But keep thy heart till Don Mathias comes.)

    Abig. (What, shall I be betroth'd to Lodowick?)   [*Aside to

    Bar. (It's no sin to deceive a Christian   *Barabas.*]

For they themselves hold it a principle:

Faith is not to be held with heretics.

But all are heretics that are not Jews—

This follows well, and therefore, daughter, fear not.)

                                       [*Aside to Abigail.*]

I have entreated her, and she will grant.   320

    Lod. Then, gentle Abigail, plight thy faith to me.

    Abig. I cannot choose, seeing my father bids.—

(Nothing but death shall part my love and me.)   [*Aside.*]

    Lod. Now have I that for which my soul hath long'd!

    Bar. (So have not I, but yet I hope I shall.)   *Aside.*

    Abig. (O wretched Abigail, what hast [thou] done?)

                                           [*Aside.*]

    Lod. Why on the sudden is your color chang'd?

    Abig. I know not, but farewell, I must be gone.

    Bar. Stay her, but let her not speak one word more.

    Lod. Mute o' the sudden! Here's a sudden change. [*Abigail* 330

    Bar. O, muse not at it, 'tis the Hebrews' guise   *weeps.*]

That maidens new betroth'd should weep awhile.

Trouble her not, sweet Lodowick; depart:

She is thy wife, and thou shalt be mine heir.

    Lod. O, is't the custom? Then I am resolv'd.

But rather let the brightsome heavens be dim,

And nature's beauty choke with stifling clouds,

Than my fair Abigail should frown on me.

—There comes the villain, now I'll be reveng'd.

Enter Mathias.

Bar. Be quiet, Lodowick, it is enough   340
That I have made thee sure to Abigail.
Lod. Well, let him go.   *Exit.*
Bar. Well, but for me, as you went in at doors
You had been stabb'd—but not a word on't now:
Here must no speeches pass, nor swords be drawn.
Math. Suffer me, Barabas, but to follow him.
Bar. No! So shall I, if any hurt be done,
Be made an accessory of your deeds.
Revenge it on him when you meet him next.
Math. For this I'll have his heart!   350
Bar. Do so. Lo, here I give thee Abigail!
Math. What greater gift can poor Mathias have?
Shall Lodowick rob me of so fair a love?
My life is not so dear as Abigail.
Bar. —My heart misgives me that to cross your love
He's with your mother! Therefore after him!
Math. What, is he gone unto my mother?
Bar. Nay, if you will, stay till she comes herself.
Math. I cannot stay, for if my mother come
She'll die with grief.   *Exit.*   360
Abig. I cannot take my leave of him for tears.
Father, why have you thus incens'd them both?
Bar. What's that to thee?
Abig. I'll make 'em friends again.
Bar. You'll make 'em friends?
Are there not Jews enow in Malta,
But thou must dote upon a Christian!
Abig. I will have Don Mathias—he is my love!
Bar. Yes, you shall have him!—Go put her in.   [*To Itha-*
                                                          more.]
Itha. Ay, I'll put her in.   [*Exits with Abigail, then*   370
Bar. Now tell me, Ithamore, how lik'st thou this?   *returns.*]
Itha. Faith, master, I think by this
You purchase both their lives. Is it not so?
Bar. True, and it shall be cunningly perform'd.
Itha. O master, that I might have a hand in this!
Bar. Ay, so [thou] shalt, 'tis thou must do the deed:
Take this, and bear it to Mathias straight

                                           [*Gives a letter.*]
And tell him that it comes from Lodowick.
Itha. 'Tis poison'd, is it not?
Bar. No, no—and yet it might be done that way—   380
It is a challenge feign'd from Lodowick.

Itha. Fear not, I will so set his heart afire
That he shall verily think it comes from him.
    Bar. I cannot choose but like thy readiness.
Yet be not rash, but do it cunningly.
    Itha. As I behave myself in this, employ me hereafter.
    Bar. Away then.   *Exit.*
So, now will I go in to Lodowick,
And like a cunning spirit feign some lie
Till I have set 'em both at enmity!   *Exit.*   390

ACTUS TERTIUS.

[3.1]   *Enter [Bellamira,] a Courtesan.*

    [*Bell.*] Since this town was besieg'd, my gain grows cold.
The time has been that but for one bare night
A hundred ducats have been freely given.
But now against my will I must be chaste.
And yet I know my beauty doth not fail:
From Venice merchants, and from Padua
Were wont to come rare-witted gentlemen,
Scholars I mean, learned and liberal.
And now, save Pilia-Borza, comes there none,
And he is very seldom from my house—.   10
And here he comes.

Enter Pilia-Borza.

    Pilia. Hold thee, wench, there's something for thee to spend.
                    [*Gives her a bag, which she opens.*]
    [*Bell.*] 'Tis silver. I disdain it.
    Pilia. Ay, but the Jew has gold,
And I will have it or it shall go hard!
    [*Bell.*] Tell me, how cam'st thou by this?
    Pilia. Faith, walking the back-lanes, through the gardens,
I chanc'd to cast mine eye up to the Jew's counting-house,
where I saw some bags of money, and in the night I clamber'd
up with my hooks, and, as I was taking my choice, I heard   20
a rumbling in the house; so I took only this, and run my way.
But here's the Jew's man.
    [*Bell.*] Hide the bag.

Enter Ithamore.

    Pilia. Look not towards him, let's away. Zoons, what a
looking thou keep'st. Thou'lt betray 's anon.
                  [*Exeunt Bellamira and Pilia-Borza.*]

Itha. O the sweetest face that ever I beheld! I know she is a courtesan by her attire. Now would I give a hundred of the Jew's crowns that I had such a concubine.
Well, I have deliver'd the challenge in such sort,
As meet they will, and fighting die. Brave sport!   *Exit.*   30

[3.2]   *Enter Mathias [holding a letter].*

Math. This is the place. Now Abigail shall see
Whether Mathias holds her dear or no!
What, dares the villain write in such base terms?

Enter Lodowick reading [a letter].

Lod. I did it, and revenge it if thou dar'st!

Fight: Enter Barabas above.

Bar. O bravely fought, and yet they thrust not home.
Now, Lodowick! Now, Mathias! So——.   [*Both fall.*]
So now they have show'd themselves to be tall fellows.
Within. Part 'em, part 'em.
Bar. Ay, part 'em now they are dead. Farewell, farewell.
                                                    Exit.

Enter Governor, Mater, [and attendants.]

[*Fern.*] What sight is this?—My Lodowick slain!   10
These arms of mine shall be thy sepulcher.
[*Kath.*] Who is this? My son Mathias slain!
[*Fern.*] O Lodowick! Had'st thou perish'd by the Turk,
Wretched Ferneze might have veng'd thy death.
[*Kath.*] Thy son slew mine, and I'll revenge his death.
[*Fern.*] Look, Katherine, look, thy son gave mine these
           wounds.
[*Kath.*] O leave to grieve me, I am griev'd enough.
[*Fern.*] O that my sighs could turn to lively breath,
And these my tears to blood, that he might live.
[*Kath.*] Who made them enemies?   20
[*Fern.*] I know not. And that grieves me most of all!
[*Kath.*] My son lov'd thine.
[*Fern.*] And so did Lodowick him.
[*Kath.*] Lend me that weapon that did kill my son,
And it shall murder me.
[*Fern.*] Nay, madam, stay, that weapon was my son's,
And on that rather should Ferneze die.
[*Kath.*] Hold, let's inquire the causers of their deaths,
That we may venge their blood upon their heads.
[*Fern.*] Then take them up, and let them be interr'd   30
Within one sacred monument of stone:

Upon which altar I will offer up
My daily sacrifice of sighs and tears,
And with my prayers pierce impartial heavens
Till they [reveal] the causers of our smarts,
Which forc'd their hands divide united hearts:
Come, Katherine, our losses equal are,
Then of true grief let us take equal share.

Exeunt [with the bodies].

[3.3]   *Enter Ithamore [laughing].*

Itha. Why, was there ever seen such villainy?
So neatly plotted, and so well perform'd?
Both held in hand, and flatly both beguil'd!   [*Roars.*]

Enter Abigail.

Abig. Why, how now, Ithamore, why laugh'st thou so?
Itha. O mistress, ha ha ha!
Abig. Why, what ail'st thou?
Itha. O my master . . .   [*Laughs so much he can't*
Abig. Ha?   *continue.*]
Itha. O mistress! I have the bravest, gravest, secret, subtle, bottle-nos'd knave to my master that ever gentle-   10
man had.
Abig. Say, knave, why rail'st upon my father thus?
Itha. O, my master has the bravest policy.
Abig. Wherein?
Itha. Why, know you not?
Abig. Why, no.
Itha. Know you not of Mathias' and Don Lodowick['s] disaster?
Abig. No, what was it?
Itha. Why, the Devil invented a challenge, my master   20
writ it, and I carried it, first to Lodowick, and *imprimis* to Mathias.
And then they met, as the story says:
In doleful wise they ended both their days.
Abig. And was my father furtherer of their deaths?
Itha. Am I Ithamore?
Abig. Yes.
Itha. So sure did your father write and I carry the challenge.
Abig. [*after a pause.*] Well, Ithamore, let me request thee
this: 30
Go to the new-made nunnery, and inquire
For any of the friars of Saint [Jaques]
And say, I pray them come and speak with me.
Itha. I pray, mistress, will you answer me to one question?

Abig. Well, sirrah, what is't?

Itha. A very feeling one! Have not the nuns fine sport with the friars now and then?

Abig. Go to, Sirrah Sauce! Is this your question? Get ye gone!

Itha. I will, forsooth, mistress.   *Exit.*   40

Abig. Hard-hearted father, unkind Barabas!
Was this the pursuit of thy policy?
—To make me show them favor severally
That by my favor they should both be slain!
Admit thou lov'dst not Lodowick for his [sire],
Yet Don Mathias ne'er offended thee!
But thou wert set upon extreme revenge
Because the [sire] dispossess'd thee once—
And could'st not venge it but upon his son!
—Nor on his son but by Mathias' means!   50
—Nor on Mathias but by murdering me!
But I perceive there is no love on earth,
Pity in Jews, nor piety in Turks.
But here comes cursed Ithamore with the friar.

Enter Ithamore [and] Friar [Jacomo].

F. [*Jac.*] Virgo, salve!   [*Continues to bow.*]
Itha. When? Duck you?
Abig. Welcome, grave friar. Ithamore, begone.

        Exit [Ithamore].

Know, holy sir, I am bold to solicit thee.

F. [*Jac.*] Wherein?

Abig. To get me be admitted for a nun.   60

F. [*Jac.*] Why, Abigail, it is not yet long since
That I did labor thy admission,
And then thou did'st not like that holy life.

Abig. Then were my thoughts so frail and unconfirm'd,
And I was chain'd to follies of the world.
But now experience, purchased with grief,
Has made me see the difference of things.
My sinful soul, alas, hath pac'd too long
The fatal labyrinth of misbelief,
Far from the Son that gives eternal life.   70

F. [*Jac.*] Who taught thee this?

Abig. The Abbess of the house,
Whose zealous admonition I embrace.
O, therefore, Jacomo, let me be one,
Although unworthy, of that sisterhood!

F. [*Jac.*] Abigail, I will. But see thou change no more,
For that will be most heavy to thy soul.

Abig. That was my father's fault.

F. [*Jac.*] Thy father's? How!

Abig. Nay, you shall pardon me. (O Barabas,   80
Though thou deservest hardly at my hands,
Yet never shall these lips bewray thy life!)   [*Aside.*]

F. [*Jac.*] Come, shall we go?

Abig. My duty waits on you.   *Exeunt.*

[3.4]   *Enter Barabas, reading a letter.*

Bar. What, Abigail become a nun again?
False and unkind! What, hast thou lost thy father?
—And all unknown and unconstrain'd of me,
Art thou again got to the nunnery?
Now here she writes, and wills me to repent.
Repentance! *Spurca!* What pretendeth this?
I fear she knows ('tis so!) of my device
In Don Mathias' and Lodovico's deaths.
If so, 'tis time that it be seen into!
For she that varies from me in belief   10
Gives great presumption that she loves me not;
Or loving, doth dislike of something done.
—But who comes here?

[*Enter Ithamore.*]

    O Ithamore, come near:
Come near, my love: come near, thy master's life,
My trusty servant, nay, my second [self]:
For I have now no hope but even in thee,
And on that hope my happiness is built.
When saw'st thou Abigail?

Itha. Today.

Bar. With whom?   20

Itha. A friar.

Bar. A friar! False villain, *he* hath done the deed!

Itha. How, sir?

Bar. Why, made mine Abigail a nun.

Itha. That's no lie, for she sent me for him.

Bar. O unhappy day!
False, credulous, inconstant Abigail!
—But let 'em go! And, Ithamore, from hence
Ne'er shall she grieve me more with her disgrace;
Ne'er shall she live to inherit aught of mine,   30
Be blest of me, nor come within my gates,
But perish underneath my bitter curse,
Like Cain by Adam for his brother's death!

Itha. O master!

Bar. Ithamore, entreat not for her, I am mov'd,
And she is hateful to my soul and me:
And ['less] thou yield to this that I entreat,
I cannot think but that thou hat'st my life.

Itha. Who, I, master? Why, I'll run to some rock, and
throw myself headlong into the sea! Why, I'll do anything   40
for your sweet sake!

Bar. O trusty Ithamore, no servant, but my friend!
I here adopt thee for mine only heir!
All that I have is thine when I am dead!
And whilst I live use half! Spend as myself!
Here take my keys—I'll give 'em thee anon.
Go buy thee garments—but thou shalt not want.
Only know this, that thus thou art to do—
But first go fetch me in the pot of rice
That for our supper stands upon the fire.   50

Itha. (I hold my head my master's hungry.) [*Aside to audience.*] I go, sir.   *Exit.*

Bar. Thus every villain ambles after wealth,
Although he ne'er be richer than in hope.
But husht!

Enter Ithamore with the pot [and a ladle].

Itha. Here 'tis, master.

Bar. Well said, Ithamore. What, hast thou brought the ladle
with thee too?

Itha. Yes, sir, the proverb says he that eats with the Devil
had need of a long spoon. I have brought you a ladle.   60

Bar. Very well, Ithamore, then now be secret:
And for thy sake, whom I so dearly love,
Now shalt thou see the death of Abigail,
That thou may'st freely live to be my heir.

Itha. Why, master, will you poison her with a mess of
rice porridge? That will preserve life, make her round and
plump, and batten more than you are aware.

Bar. Ay, but Ithamore, seest thou this?   [*Shows packet of*
It is a precious powder that I bought   *powder.*]
Of an Italian in Ancona once,   70
Whose operation is to bind, infect,
And poison deeply, yet not appear
In forty hours after it is ta'en.

Itha. How, master?

Bar. Thus, Ithamore.
This even they use in Malta here ('tis call'd
Saint Jacques' Even) and then I say they use
To send their alms unto the nunneries.

Among the rest bear this, and set it there;
There's a dark entry where they take it in,   80
Where they must neither see the messenger
Nor make inquiry who hath sent it them.

 Itha. How so?

 Bar. Belike there is some ceremony in't.
There, Ithamore, must thou go place this pot.
Stay, let me spice it first.   [*About to pour poison in.*]

 Itha. Pray do, and let me help you, master. Pray let me
taste first.

 Bar. Prithee do! [*Ithamore tastes*]: What say'st thou now?

 Itha. Troth, master, I'm loth such a pot of pottage   90
should be spoil'd.

 Bar. Peace, Ithamore, 'tis better so than spar'd.   [*Puts
Assure thyself thou shalt have broth by the eye! poison in.*]
My purse, my coffer, and myself is thine!

 Itha. Well, master, I go.

 Bar. Stay, first let me stir it, Ithamore.   [*Stirs with ladle.*]
As fatal be it to her as the draught
Of which great Alexander drunk and died:
And with her let it work like Borgia's wine,
Whereof his sire, the Pope, was poison'd.   100
In few, the blood of Hydra, Lerna's bane:
The juice of hebon, and Cocytus' breath,
And all the poisons of the Stygian pool
Break from the fiery kingdom and in this
Vomit your venom and envenom her
That like a fiend hath left her father thus!

 Itha. What a blessing has he given't! Was **ever** pot of rice
porridge so sauc'd! What shall I do with it?

 Bar. O, my sweet Ithamore, go set it down,
And come again so soon as thou hast done,   110
For I have other business for thee.

 Itha. Here's a drench to poison a whole stable of Flanders
mares. I'll carry 't to the nuns with a powder!

 Bar. And the horse pestilence to boot! Away!

 Itha. I am gone.
Pay me my wages, for my work is done!   *Exit.*

 Bar. I'll pay thee with a vengeance, Ithamore!   *Exit.*

[3.5]   *Enter Governor, Del Bosco, Knights, Basso.*

 [*Fern.*] Welcome, great bassoes. How fares Calymath?
What wind drives you thus into Malta road?

 [1] *Bass.* The wind that bloweth all the world besides:
Desire of gold.

 [*Fern.*] Desire of gold, great sir?

That's to be gotten in the Western Inde.
In Malta are no golden minerals.

   [1] *Bass*. To you of Malta thus saith Calymath—
The time you took for respite is at hand
For the performance of your promise pass'd: 　　　　10
And for the tribute-money I am sent.

   [*Fern.*] Basso, in brief, shalt have no tribute here;
Nor shall the heathens live upon our spoil!
First will we race the city walls ourselves,
Lay waste the island, hew the temples down,
And, shipping off our goods to Sicily,
Open an entrance for the wasteful sea,
Whose billows beating the resistless banks,
Shall overflow it with their refluence.

   [1] *Bass*. Well, Governor, since thou hast broke the league 20
By flat denial of the promis'd tribute,
Talk not of racing down your city walls:
You shall not need trouble yourselves so far,
For Selim Calymath shall come himself
And with brass bullets batter down your towers
And turn proud Malta to a wilderness
For these intolerable wrongs of yours . . .
And so farewell!

   [*Fern.*] Farewell! 　　　　　　　　　　　[*Exit Basso.*]
And now, you men of Malta, look about, 　　　　30
And let's provide to welcome Calymath:
Close your portcullis, charge your basilisks,
And as you profitably take up arms,
So now courageously encounter them!
—For by this answer, broken is the league,
And naught is to be look'd for now but wars,
And naught to us more welcome is than wars. 　　*Exeunt.*

[3.6] 　　　*Enter two friars, [Jacomo and Barnardine].*

   [*F. Jac.*] O, brother, brother, all the nuns are sick,
And physic will not help them: they must die.

   [*F. Barn.*] The Abbess sent for me to be confess'd:
O, what a sad confession will there be!

   [*F. Jac.*] And so did fair Maria send for me:
I'll to her lodging. Hereabouts she lies. 　　　　　*Exit.*

Enter Abigail.

   [*F. Barn.*] What, all dead save only Abigail?
   Abig. And I shall die too, for I feel death coming.
Where is the friar that convers'd with me?

   [*F. Barn.*] O, he is gone to see the other nuns. 　　　10

Abig. I sent for him, but seeing you are come,
Be you my ghostly father: and first know,
That in this house I liv'd religiously,
Chaste, and devout, much sorrowing for my sins.
But ere I came——.

[*F. Barn.*] What then?

Abig. I did offend high Heaven so grievously
As I am almost desperate for my sins!
And one offense torments me more than all.
You knew Mathias and Don Lodowick? 20

[*F. Barn.*] Yes, what of them?

Abig. My father did contract me to 'em both:
First to Don Lodowick—him I never lov'd.
Mathias was the man that I held dear,
And for his sake did I become a nun.

[*F. Barn.*] So, say how was their end?

Abig. Both jealous of my love, envied each other,
And by my father's practice, which is there
Set down at large, the gallants were both slain.

[*Gives writing.*]

[*F. Barn.*] O monstrous villainy! 30

Abig. To work my peace, this I confess to thee.
Reveal it not, for then my father dies.

[*F. Barn.*] Know that confession must not be reveal'd,
The canon law forbids it; and the priest
That makes it known, being degraded first,
Shall be condemn'd, and then sent to the fire.

Abig. So I have heard. Pray, therefore keep it close.
Death seizeth on my heart. Ah, gentle friar,
Convert my father that he may be sav'd.
And witness that I die a Christian! [*Dies.*] 40

[*F. Barn.*] Ay, and a virgin too; that grieves me
most.
But I must to the Jew, and exclaim on him,
And make him stand in fear of me.

Enter 1 *Friar* [*Jacomo*].

[*F. Jac.*] O brother, all the nuns are dead! Let's bury
them.

[*F. Barn.*] First help to bury this, then go with me
And help me to exclaim against the Jew.

[*F. Jac.*] Why? What has he done?

[*F. Barn.*] A thing that makes me tremble to unfold.

[*F. Jac.*] What, has he crucified a child?

[*F. Barn.*] No, but a worse thing. 'Twas told me in shrift: 50

Thou know'st 'tis death an if it be reveal'd.
Come, let's away.   *Exeunt.*

ACTUS QUARTUS.

[4.1]   *Enter Barabas, Ithamore. Bells within.*

Bar. There is no music to a Christian's knell . . .
How sweet the bells ring now the nuns are dead,
That sound at other times like tinker's pans!
I was afraid the poison had not wrought;
Or though it wrought, it would have done no good—
For every year they swell, and yet they live!
Now all are dead, not one remains alive.

Itha. That's brave, master, but think you it will not be
known?

Bar. How can it if we two be secret?   10

Itha. For my part fear you not.

Bar. I'd cut thy throat if I did.

Itha. And reason too.
But here's a royal monastery hard by.
Good master, let me poison all the monks?

Bar. Thou shalt not need, for now the nuns are dead
They'll die with grief.

Itha. Do you not sorrow for your daughter's death?

Bar. No, but I grieve because she liv'd so long:
An Hebrew born, and would become a Christian—   20
Cazzo! Diabolo!

          Enter the two friars [, *Jacomo and Barnardine*].

Itha. Look, look, master, here come two religious caterpillars.

Bar. I smelt 'em ere they came.

Itha. God-a-mercy, nose! Come, let's begone.

[*F. Barn.*] Stay, wicked Jew, repent, I say, and stay.

[*F. Jac.*] Thou hast offended, therefore must be damn'd.

Bar. (I fear they know we sent the poison'd broth.)   [*Whis-*
Itha. (And so do I, master: therefore speak 'em fair.)   *per.*]

[*F. Barn.*] Barabas, thou hast——.   30

[*F. Jac.*] Ay, that thou hast——.

Bar. True, I have money, what though I have?

[*F. Barn.*] Thou art a——.

[*F. Jac.*] Ay, that thou art, a——.

Bar. What needs all this? I know I am a Jew.

[*F. Barn.*] Thy daughter——.

[F. Jac.] Ay, thy daughter——.
Bar. O speak not of her: then I die with grief!
[F. Barn.] Remember that——.
[F. Jac.] Ay, remember that——.   40
Bar. I must needs say that I have been a great usurer.
[F. Barn.] Thou hast committed——.
Bar. Fornication? But that was in another country:
And besides, the wench is dead.
[F. Barn.] Ay, but, Barabas,
Remember Mathias and Don Lodowick.
Bar. Why, what of them?
[F. Barn.] I will not say that by a forged challenge they
    met.
Bar. (She has confess'd: and we are both undone,
My bosom [intimates]! But I must dissemble——.)   50
                                        Aside [to Ithamore].
O holy friars, the burden of my sins
Lie heavy on my soul! Then pray you tell me,
Is't not too late now to turn Christian?
I have been zealous in the Jewish faith:
Hard-hearted to the poor, a covetous wretch,
That would for lucre's sake have sold my soul:
A hundred for a hundred I have ta'en!
And now for store of wealth may I compare
With all the Jews of Malta—But what is wealth?
I am a Jew, and therefore am I lost. . . .   60
Would penance serve for this my sin,
I could afford to whip myself to death!
    Itha. And so could I, but penance will not serve!
    Bar.—To fast, to pray, and wear a shirt of hair,
And on my knees creep to Jerusalem!
Cellars of wine, and sollars full of wheat,
Warehouses stuff'd with spices and with drugs,
Whole chests of gold, in [bullion] and in coin,
Besides I know not how much weight in pearl
Orient and round, have I within my house: 70
At Alexandria, merchandise unsold:
But yesterday two ships went from this town,
Their voyage will be worth ten thousand crowns:
In Florence, Venice, Antwerp, London, Seville,
Frankfort, Lubeck, Moscow, and where not,
Have I debts owing: and in most of these,
Great sums of money lying in the banco:
All this I'll give to some religious house.
So I may be baptiz'd and live therein!
    [F. Jac.] O good Barabas, come to our house!   80

[*F. Barn.*] O no, good Barabas, come to our house!
And, Barabas, you know——.
   Bar. I know that I have highly sinn'd.
You shall convert me, *you* shall have all my wealth.   [*To Barn.*]
   [*F. Jac.*] O Barabas, their laws are strict.
   Bar. I know they are, and I will be with *you*.   [*To Jacomo.*]
   ⟨*F. Barn.*⟩ They wear no shirts, and they go barefoot too.
   Bar. Then 'tis not for me; and I am resolv'd
You shall confess me, and have all my goods!   [*To Barnardine.*]
   [*F. Jac.*] Good Barabas, come to me.   90
   Bar. You see I answer him, and yet he stays!
Rid him away, and go you home with me.   [*To Jacomo.*]
   ⟨*F. Jac.*⟩ (I'll be with you tonight.)   [*Aside.*]
   Bar. (Come to my house at one o'clock this night.)   [*Aside.*]
   [*F. Jac.*] You hear your answer, and you may be gone.
   [*F. Barn.*] Why, go get you away.
   [*F. Jac.*] I will not go for thee.
   [*F. Barn.*] Not! Then I'll make thee go.
   [*F. Jac.*] How, dost call me rogue?   *Fight.*
   Itha. Part 'em, master, part 'em!   100
   Bar. This is mere frailty, brethren, be content.
Friar Barnardine, go you with Ithamore:
(*You* know my mind, let me alone with him.)

                              [*Aside to Barnardine.*]
   ⟨*F. Jac.*⟩ Why does he go to thy house? Let him be
      gone!
   Bar. I'll give him something and so stop his mouth.   [*To
                                          Jacomo.*]
                    Exit [*Ithamore with Barnardine*].
I never heard of any man but he
Malign'd the order of the Jacobins.
But do you think that I believe his words?
Why, brother, you converted Abigail!
And I am bound in charity to requite it,   110
And so I will. O Jacomo, fail not, but come!
   [*F. Jac.*] But, Barabas, who shall be your godfathers?
For presently you shall be shriv'd.
   Bar. Marry, the Turk shall be one of my godfathers—
But not a word to any of your covent.
   [*F. Jac.*] I warrant thee, Barabas!   *Exit.*
   Bar. So, now the fear is past, and I am safe:
For he that shriv'd her is within my house.
What if I murder'd him ere Jacomo comes?
Now I have such a plot for both their lives   120
As never Jew nor Christian knew the like!
One turn'd my daughter, therefore he shall die:

The other knows enough to have my life,
Therefore 'tis not requisite he should live.
But are not both these wise men to suppose
That I will leave my house, my goods, and all,
To fast and be well whipp'd? I'll none of that!
Now Friar Barnardine I come to you,
I'll feast you, lodge you, give you fair words,
And after that, I and my trusty Turk— 130
No more, but so: it must and shall be done!

[*Curtains at back of stage open. Barnardine is asleep in a chair.
Ithamore comes forward.*]

Bar. Ithamore, tell me, is the friar asleep?
Itha. Yes, and I know not what the reason is.
Do what I can he will not strip himself,
Nor go to bed, but sleeps in his own clothes:
I fear me he mistrusts what we intend.
Bar. No, 'tis an order which the friars use:
Yet, if he knew our meanings, could he 'scape?
Itha. No, none can hear him, cry he ne'er so loud.
Bar. Why, true, therefore did I place him there. 140
The other chambers open towards the street.
Itha. You loiter, master, wherefore stay we thus?
O how I long to see him shake his heels.
Bar. Come on, sirrah.
Off with your girdle, make a handsome noose.

[*Barabas takes off Barnardine's girdle,
Ithamore ties a noose in it.*

Friar, awake! [*They put the noose around Barnardine's neck.*]
[*F. Barn.*] What, do you mean to strangle me?
Itha. Yes, 'cause you use to confess.
Bar. Blame not us but the proverb, "Confess and be
hang'd!" Pull hard! 150
[*F. Barn.*] What, will you [have] my life?
Bar. Pull hard, I say! You would have had my goods.
Itha. Ay, and our lives too, therefore pull amain!

[*Barnardine dies.*]

'Tis neatly done, sir, here's no print at all.
Bar. Then is it as it should be. Take him up.
Itha. Nay, master, be rul'd by me a little. [*Stands the body
upright against the wall and puts a staff in its hand. Closes
curtains.*] So, let him lean upon his staff. Excellent! He stands
as if he were begging of bacon.
Bar. Who would not think but that this friar liv'd?
What time o'night is't now, sweet Ithamore? 160
Itha. Towards one.

Bar. Then will not Jacomo be long from hence.

> [*Exit. Ithamore hides himself.*]

Enter Jacomo.

F. Jac. This is the hour wherein I shall proceed,
O happy hour, wherein I shall convert
An infidel and bring his gold into our treasury!
But soft, is not this Barnardine? It is!
And understanding I should come this way,
Stands here a purpose, meaning me some wrong,
And intercept my going to the Jew!
Barnardine!   170
Wilt thou not speak? Thou think'st I see thee not!
Away, I'd wish thee, and let me go by!
No, wilt thou not? Nay, then, I'll force my way.
And see, a staff stands ready for the purpose.
As thou lik'st that, stop me another time!

Strike him, he falls. Enter Barabas.

Bar. Why, how now, Jacomo, what hast thou done?
F. Jac. Why, stricken him that would have struck at me.
Bar. Who is it? Barnardine? Now out, alas, he is slain!
Itha. Ay, master, he's slain. Look how his brains drop out
on's nose!   180
F. Jac. Good sirs, I have done't, but nobody knows it but
you two—I may escape.
Bar. So might my man and I hang with you for com-
pany.
Itha. No, let us bear him to the magistrates.
F. Jac. Good Barabas, let me go!
Bar. No, pardon me, the law must have its course.
I must be forc'd to give in evidence
That being importun'd by this Barnardine
To be a Christian, I shut him out,   190
And there he sat. Now I, to keep my word,
And give my goods and substance to your house,
Was up thus early, with intent to go
Unto your friary because you stay'd.
Itha. Fie upon 'em, master! Will you turn Christian when
holy friars turn devils and murder one another?
Bar. No, for this example I'll remain a Jew.
Heaven bless me! What, a friar a murderer?
When shall you see a Jew commit the like?
Itha. Why, a Turk could ha' done no more.   200
Bar. Tomorrow is the sessions. You shall to it.
Come, Ithamore, let's help to take him hence.

[*They grasp him on each side.*]

F. Jac. Villains, I am a sacred person. Touch me not.

Bar. The law shall touch you, we'll but lead you, we
'Las, I could weep at your calamity!
Take in the staff too, for that must be shown:
Law wills that each particular be known.   *Exeunt.*

[4.2]   *Enter   Courtesan   and   Pilia-Borza.*

[*Bell.*] Pilia-Borza, did'st thou meet with Ithamore?

Pilia. I did.

[*Bell.*] And did'st thou deliver my letter?

Pilia. I did.

[*Bell.*] And what think'st thou? Will he come?

Pilia. I think so, and yet I cannot tell, for at the reading of
the letter he look'd like a man of another world.

[*Bell.*] Why so?

Pilia. That such a base slave as he should be saluted by such
a tall man as I am, from such a beautiful dame as you.   10

[*Bell.*] And what said he?

Pilia. Not a wise word, only gave me a nod, as who should
say: " Is it even so?" and so I left him, being driven to a *non-plus*
at the critical aspect of my terrible countenance.

[*Bell.*] And where did'st meet him?

Pilia. Upon mine own freehold, within forty foot of the
gallows, conning his neck-verse I take it, looking of a friar's
execution, whom I saluted with an old hempen proverb: *Hodie
tibi, cras mihi,* and so I left him to the mercy of the hangman.
But the exercise being done, see where he comes.   20

Enter Ithamore.

Itha. [*to audience.*] I never knew a man take his death so
patiently as this friar; he was ready to leap off ere the halter
was about his neck; and when the hangman had put on his
hempen tippet, he made such haste to his prayers as if he had
had another cure to serve. Well, go whither he will, I'll be none
of his followers in haste. And now I think on't, going to the
execution, a fellow met me with a muschatoes like a raven's
wing, and a dagger with a hilt like a warming-pan, and he gave
me a letter from one Madam Bellamira, saluting me in such
sort as if he had meant to make clean my boots with his   30
lips: the effect was, that I should come to her house. I wonder
what the reason is. It may be she sees more in me than I can find
in myself: for she writes further that she loves me ever since
she saw me! And who would not requite such love? Here's her
house—and here she comes—and now would I were gone—I am
not worthy to look upon her.

Pilia. This is the gentleman you writ to.

Itha. Gentleman! He flouts me! What gentry can be in a poor Turk of tenpence? I'll be gone.   [*To audience.*]

[*Bell.*] Is't not a sweet-faced youth, Pilia?   40

Itha. Again, "sweet youth!" [*To audience.*]—Did not you, sir, bring the sweet youth a letter?

Pilia. I did, sir, and from this gentlewoman, who, as myself and the rest of the family, stand or fall at your service.

[*Bell.*] Though woman's modesty should hale me back, I can withhold no longer: Welcome, sweet love!

Itha. Now am I clean, or rather foully, out of the way!
                                        [*To audience.*]

[*Bell.*] [*As Ithamore attempts to slip away.*] Whither so
    soon?

Itha. [*to audience.*] I'll go steal some money from my   50 master to make me handsome.—Pray pardon me, I must go and see a ship discharg'd.

[*Bell.*] Canst thou be so unkind to leave me thus?

Pilia. An ye did but know how she loves you, sir!

Itha. Nay, I care not how much she loves me——. Sweet Allamira, would I had my master's wealth for thy sake!

Pilia. And you *can* have it, sir, an if you please.

Itha. If 'twere above ground, I could and would have it: but he hides and buries it up as partridges do their eggs, under the earth.

Pilia. And is't not possible to find it out?   60

Itha. By no means possible.

[*Bell.*] (What shall we do with this base villain then?)
                                        [*Aside to Pilia-Borza.*]

Pilia. (Let me alone, do you but speak him fair.)
                                        [*Aside to her.*]
But you know some secrets of the Jew
Which if they were reveal'd would do him harm?

Itha. Ay, and such as——. Go to, no more! I'll make him send me half he has, and glad he 'scapes so too. Pen and ink! I'll write unto him. We'll have money straight!

Pilia. Send for a hundred crowns at least.

Itha. Ten hundred thousand crowns! "Master   70 Barabas."   *He writes.*

Pilia. Write not so submissively, but threat'ning him.

Itha. [*writing.*] "Sirrah, Barabas, send me a hundred crowns!"

Pilia. Put in two hundred at least.

Itha. [*writing.*] "I charge thee send me three hundred by this bearer, and this shall be your warrant. If you do not, no more, but so——."

Pilia. Tell him you will confess.

Itha. [*writing.*] "Otherwise I'll confess all."—Vanish, 80
and return in a twinkle.

Pilia. Let me alone, I'll use him in his kind.

[*Exit Pilia-Borza with the letter.*]

Itha. Hang him, Jew!

[*Bell.*] Now, gentle Ithamore, lie in my lap.

[*Curtains open to reveal bed, etc.*]

Where are my maids? Provide a running banquet!
Send to the merchant, bid him bring me silks!
Shall Ithamore, my love, go in such rags?

Itha. And bid the jeweller come hither too.

[*Bell.*] I have no husband, sweet, I'll marry thee!

Itha. Content: but we will leave this paltry land,   90
And sail from hence to Greece, to lovely Greece!
I'll be thy Jason, thou my golden fleece!
Where painted carpets o'er the meads are hurl'd,
And Bacchus' vineyards o'erspread the world,
Where woods and forests go in goodly green,
I'll be Adonis, thou shalt be Love's Queen!
The meads, the orchards, and the primrose-lanes,
Instead of sedge and reed, bear sugar-canes.
Thou in those groves, by Dis above,
Shalt live with me and be my love!   100

[*Bell.*] Whither will I not go with gentle Ithamore?

[*Caresses him.*]

Enter Pilia-Borza.

Itha. How now? Hast thou the gold?

Pilia. Yes.

Itha. But came it freely? Did the cow give down her milk
freely?

Pilia. At reading of the letter, he star'd and stamp'd and
turn'd aside. I took him by the [beard] and look'd upon him
thus. [*Looks fierce.*] Told him he were best to send it. Then
he hugg'd and embrac'd me.

Itha. Rather for fear than love.   110

Pilia. Then, like a Jew, he laugh'd and jeer'd, and told me
he lov'd me for your sake, and said what a faithful servant
you had been.

Itha. The more villain he to keep me thus! Here's goodly
'parel, is there not?

Pilia. To conclude, he gave me ten crowns.

[*Puts the money down.*]

Itha. But ten? I'll not leave him worth a gray groat. Give me
a ream of paper. We'll have a kingdom of gold for 't.

Pilia. Write for five hundred crowns.

Itha. [*writing.*] "Sirrah, Jew, as you love your life send   120
me five hundred crowns, and give the bearer one hundred." Tell
him I must have 't.

Pilia. I warrant your worship shall have 't.

Itha. And if he ask why I demand so much, tell him I scorn
to write a line under a hundred crowns.

Pilia. You'd make a rich poet, sir. I am gone.   *Exit.*

Itha. Take thou the money. Spend it for my sake.

[*Bell.*] 'Tis not thy money, but thyself I weigh;
Thus Bellamira esteems of gold.   [*Throws it aside.*]
But thus of thee.   *Kiss him.*   130

Itha. That kiss again! She runs division of my lips.
What an eye she casts on me! It twinkles like a star.

[*Bell.*] Come, my dear love, let's in and sleep together.

Itha. O, that ten thousand nights were put in one, that we
might sleep seven years together afore we wake!

[*Bell.*] Come, amorous wag, first banquet, and then sleep.

[*Exeunt into enclosure. Curtains close.*]

[4.3]   *Enter Barabas, reading a letter.*

Bar. "Barabas, send me three hundred crowns."
—Plain Barabas! O, that wicked courtesan!
He was not wont to call me Barabas.
"Or else I will confess." Ay, there it goes!
But, if I get him, *coupe de gorge* for that! [*Makes gesture of
He sent a shaggy totter'd staring slave,   *cutting throat.*]
That when he speaks draws out his grisly beard
And winds it twice or thrice about his ear;
Whose face has been a grindstone for men's swords;
His hands are hack'd, some fingers cut quite off;   10
Who, when he speaks, grunts like a hog and looks
Like one that is employ'd in catzerie
And crossbiting—such a rogue
As is the husband to a hundred whores—
And I by him must send three hundred crowns!
Well, my hope is, he will not stay there still.
And when he comes—O, that he were but here!

Enter Pilia-Borza.

Pilia. Jew, I must ha' more gold.

Bar. Why, want'st thou any of thy tale?

Pilia. No, but three hundred will not serve his turn.   20

Bar. Not serve his turn, sir?

Pilia. No, sir! And therefore I must have five hundred more.

Bar. I'll rather——.

Pilia. O good words, sir, and send it you were best! See, there's his letter.   [*Gives letter.*]

Bar. Might he not as well come as send? Pray bid him come and fetch it. What he writes for you, ye shall have straight.

Pilia. Ay, and the rest too, or else——.

Bar. (I must make this villain away.)   [*Aside.*]
Please you dine with me, sir? (And you shall be most   30
heartily poison'd!)   *Aside.*

Pilia. No, God-a-mercy. Shall I have these crowns?

Bar. I cannot do it, I have lost my keys.

Pilia. O, if that be all, I can pick ope your locks.

Bar. Or climb up to my counting-house window? You know my meaning?

Pilia. I know enough, and therefore talk not to me of your counting-house. The gold! Or know, Jew, it is in my power to hang thee.

Bar. (I am betray'd!—)   [*Aside.*]   40
'Tis not five hundred crowns that I esteem:
I am not moved at *that*. This angers me—
That he who knows I love him as myself
Should write in this imperious vein! Why, sir,
You know I have no child, and unto whom
Should I leave all but unto Ithamore?

Pilia. Here's many words, but no crowns—the crowns!

Bar. Commend me to him, sir, most humbly,
And unto your good mistress, as unknown.

Pilia. Speak, shall I have 'em, sir?   50
Bar. Sir, here they are.—   [*Gives bag.*]
(O, that I should part with so much gold!)   [*Aside.*]
Here, take 'em, fellow, with as good a will——
(As I would see thee hang'd!) [*Aside.*] O, love stops my breath.
Never lov'd man servant as I do Ithamore!

Pilia. I know it, sir.

Bar. Pray, when, sir, shall I see you at my house?

Pilia. Soon enough, to your cost, sir. Fare you well.   *Exit.*

Bar. Nay, to thine own cost, villain, if thou com'st!
Was ever Jew tormented as I am?   60
To have a shag-rag knave to come—
Three hundred crowns!—And then five hundred crowns!—
Well, I must seek a means to rid 'em all,
And presently: for in his villainy
He will tell all he knows, and I shall die for't.
I have it!
I will in some disguise go see the slave,
An how the villain revels with my gold.   *Exit.*

[4.4] Enter: [the curtains at the back open revealing] Courte-
san, Ithamore [who is drunk], and Pilia-Borza. [Bellamira con-
stantly refills Ithamore's goblet.]

[*Bell.*] I'll pledge thee, love, and therefore drink it off.
Itha. Say'st thou me so? Have at it! And do you hear?
                                                        [*Whispers.*]
[*Bell.*] Go to, it shall be so.
Itha. Of that condition I will drink it up.
Here's to thee!
⟨*Bell.*⟩ Nay, I'll have all or none.
Itha. There! If thou lov'st me do not leave a drop.
[*Bell.*] Love thee? Fill me three glasses!
Itha. Three and fifty dozen, I'll pledge thee.
Pilia. Knavely spoke, and like a knight-at-arms.   10
Itha. Hey, *Rivo Castiliano*, a man's a man!
[*Bell.*] Now to the Jew.
Itha. Ha! To the Jew. And send me money you were best!
Pilia. What would'st thou do if he should send thee none?
Itha. Do? Nothing . . . But I know what I know. He's a
murderer.
[*Bell.*] I had not thought he had been so brave a man.
Itha. You knew Mathias and the Governor's son? He and I
killed 'em both, and yet never touched 'em!
Pilia. O, bravely done!   20
Itha. I carried the broth that poison'd the nuns! And he
and I, snicle hand too fast, strangled a friar!
[*Bell.*] You two alone?
Itha. We two, and 'twas never known, nor never shall be
for me. . . .
Pilia. (This shall with me unto the Governor.)
                                           [*Aside to Bellamira.*]
Bell. (And fit it should! But first let's ha' more gold.—)
                                           [*Aside to Pilia-Borza.*]
Come, gentle Ithamore, lie in my lap.
Itha. Love me little, love me long, let music rumble—
Whilst I in thy incony lap do tumble.   30

Enter Barabas with a lute, disguised.

[*Bell.*] A French musician! Come, let's hear your skill.
Bar. Must tuna my lute for sound, twang-twang
first.
Itha. Wilt drink, Frenchman? Here's to thee with a——Pox
on this drunken hiccup!

Bar. Gramercy, monsieur.

[*Bell.*] Prithee, Pilia-Borza, bid the fiddler give me the posy in his hat there.

Pilia. Sirrah, you must give my mistress your posy.

Bar. A votre commandement, madame.   40

[*All smell the posy.*]

[*Bell.*] How sweet, my Ithamore, the flowers smell!

Itha. Like thy breath, sweetheart. No violet like 'em.

Pilia. Foh! methinks they stink like a hollyhock.

Bar. (So, now I am reveng'd upon 'em all!
The scent thereof was death. I poison'd it.)   [*Aside.*]

Itha. Play, fiddler, or I'll cut your cat's guts into chitterlings.

Bar. Pardonnez moi, be no in tune yet. So now, now all be in.

Itha. Give him a crown, and fill me out more wine.

Pilia. There's two crowns for thee. Play!   50

Bar. (How liberally the villain gives me mine own
gold!   *Aside.* [*Barabas plays lute.*]

Pilia. Methinks he fingers very well.

Bar. (So did you when you stole my gold!)   *Aside.*

Pilia. How swift he runs!

Bar. (You run swifter when you threw my gold out of my
window!)   *Aside.*

[*Bell.*] Musician, hast been in Malta long?

Bar. Two, three, four month, madame.

Itha. Dost not know a Jew, one Barabas?   60

Bar. Very much. Monsieur, you no be his man?

Pilia. His man.

Itha. I scorn the peasant! Tell him so.

Bar. (He knows it already!)   [*Aside.*]

Itha. 'Tis a strange thing of that Jew, he lives upon pickled grasshoppers and sauc'd mushrooms.

Bar. (What a slave's this! The Governor feeds not as I
do.)   *Aside.*

Itha. He never put on clean shirt since he was circumcis'd.   70

Bar. (O rascal! I change myself twice a day.)   *Aside.*

Itha. The hat he wears, Judas left under the elder when he hang'd himself.

Bar. ('Twas sent me for a present from the great
Cham.)   *Aside.*

Pilia. A [nasty] slave he is. Whither now, fiddler?

Bar. Pardonnez moi, monsièur, me be no well.   *Exit.*

Pilia. Farewell, fiddler! One letter more to the Jew.

[*Bell.*] Prithee, sweet love, one more, and write it sharp.

ACT 5   SCENE 1

Itha. No, I'll send by word of mouth now. Bid him de-   80
liver thee a thousand crowns by the same token that the nuns
lov'd rice, that Friar Barnardine slept in his own clothes: Any
of 'em will do it!

Pilia. Let me alone to urge it now I know the meaning.

Itha. The meaning has a meaning. Come let's in:
To undo a Jew is charity, and not sin!   *Exeunt.*

ACTUS QUINTUS.

[5.1] *Enter Governor, Knights, Martin del Bosco, [and*
Officers].

[*Fern.*] Now, gentlemen, betake you to your arms.
And see that Malta be well fortifi'd.
—And it behooves you to be resolute:
For Calymath having hover'd here so long
Will win the town, or die before the walls.
Knight. And die he shall, for we will never yield.

Enter Courtesan, Pilia-Borza [dying].

[*Bell.*] O, bring us to the Governor!
[*Fern.*] Away with her! She is a courtesan.
[*Bell.*] Whate'er I am, yet, Governor, hear me speak:
I bring thee news by whom thy son was slain: 10
Mathias did it not: it was the Jew.
Pilia.—Who, besides the slaughter of these gentlemen,
Poison'd his own daughter and the nuns,
Strangl'd a friar, and I know not what
Mischief besides.
[*Fern.*] Had we but proof of this?—
[*Bell.*]—Strong proof, my lord! His man's now at my
lodging
That was his agent: he'll confess it all.
[*Fern.*] Go fetch him straight [*Exeunt Officers*]. I always
fear'd that Jew.

Enter [Officers with] Jew, [dying] Ithamore.

Bar. I'll go alone. Dogs, do not hale me thus!   20
Itha. Nor me neither! I cannot outrun you, constable—
O my belly!
Bar. (One dram of powder more had made all sure.
What a damn'd slave was I!)   [*Aside.*]
[*Fern.*] Make fires, heat irons, let the rack be fetch'd.

Knight. Nay stay, my lord, 't may be he will confess.

Bar. Confess! What mean you, lords? Who should confess?

[Fern.] Thou and thy Turk. 'Twas you that slew my son!

Itha. Guilty, my lord, I confess. Your son and Mathias were both contracted unto Abigail—forg'd a counterfeit 30 challenge.   *[Pointing to Barabas.]*

Bar. Who carried that challenge?

Itha. I carried it, I confess. But who writ it? Marry, even he that strangled Barnardine, poison'd the nuns, and his own daughter.

[Fern.] Away with him! His sight is death to me!

Bar. For what, you men of Malta? Hear me speak.
She is a courtesan, and he a thief,
And he my bondman. Let me have law,
For none of this can prejudice my life.   40

Fern. Once more, away with him! You shall have law!

Bar. Devils, do your worst! I live in spite of you!
As these have spoke, so be it to their souls!
(—I hope the poison'd flowers will work anon.)   *[Aside.]*
            Exeunt [Officers with Barabas, Ithamore,
                        Bellamira, and Pilia-Borza.]

Enter Mater.

[Kath.] Was my Mathias murder'd by the Jew?
Ferneze, 'twas thy son that murder'd him.

[Fern.] Be patient, gentle madam, it was he.
He forg'd the daring challenge made them fight.

[Kath.] Where is the Jew? Where is that murderer?

[Fern.] In prison till the law has pass'd on him.   50

Enter Officer.

Off. My lord, the courtesan and her man are dead;
So is the Turk and Barabas the Jew.

[Fern.] Dead?

Off. Dead, my lord, and here they bring his body.

Bosco. This sudden death of his is very strange.

[Enter Officers carrying Barabas as dead.]

[Fern.] Wonder not at it, sir, the heavens are just:
Their deaths were like their lives, then think not of 'em.
Since they are dead, let them be buried.
For the Jew's body, throw that o'er the walls
To be a prey for vultures and wild beasts.   60

So now away, and fortify the town.

[*Officers fling Barabas down.*] *Exeunt* [*all except Barabas.
He rises*].

Bar. What, all alone? Well fare, sleepy drink!
I'll be reveng'd on this accursed town
For by my means Calymath shall enter in:
I'll help to slay their children and their wives!
To fire the churches! pull their houses down!
Take my goods too, and seize upon my lands!
I hope to see the Governor a slave,
And rowing in a galley whipp'd to death!

Enter Calymath, Bassoes, Turks.

Caly. Whom have we here, a spy?   **70**
Bar. Yes, my good lord, one that can spy a place
Where you may enter and surprise the town.
My name is Barabas; I am a Jew.
Caly. Art thou that Jew whose goods we heard were sold
For tribute-money?
Bar. The very same, my lord.
And since that time they have hir'd a slave (my man)
To accuse me of a thousand villanies.
I was imprison'd but 'scap'd their hands.
Caly. Did'st break prison?   **80**
Bar. No, no!
I drank of poppy and cold mandrake juice:
And being asleep, belike they thought me dead
And threw me o'er the walls. So, or how else,
The Jew is here, and rests at your command.
Caly. 'Twas bravely done! But tell me, Barabas,
Canst thou, as thou reportest, make Malta ours?
Bar. Fear not, my lord, for here against the [sluice]
The rock is hollow, and of purpose digg'd
To make a passage for the running streams   **90**
And common channels of the city.
Now whilst you give assault unto the walls,
I'll lead five hundred soldiers through the vault
And rise with them i' the middle of the town,
Open the gates for you to enter in:
And by this means the city is your own.
Caly. If this be true, I'll make thee Governor.
Bar. And if it be not true, then let me die.
Caly. Thou'st doom'd thyself. Assault it presently.
                                        Exeunt.

[5.2] *Alarms. Enter Turks, Barabas—Governor and Knights prisoners.*

    Caly. Now vail your pride, you captive Christians,
And kneel for mercy to your conquering foe.
Now where's the hope you had of haughty Spain?
Ferneze, speak, had it not been much better
To['ve] kept thy promise than be thus surpris'd?
    [*Fern.*] What should I say? We are captives and must yield.
    Caly. Ay, villains, you must yield, and under Turkish yokes
Shall groaning bear the burthen of our ire.
And, Barabas, as erst we promis'd thee,
For thy desert we make thee Governor.   10
Use them at thy discretion.
    Bar. Thanks, my lord.
    [*Fern.*] O fatal day, to fall into the hands
Of such a traitor and unhallow'd Jew!
What greater misery could Heaven inflict?
    Caly. 'Tis our command. And, Barabas, we give
To guard thy person these our Janizaries:
Intreat them well, as we have used thee.
And now, brave bassoes, come, we'll walk about
The ruin'd town, and see the wrack we made.   20
Farewell, brave Jew! Farewell, great Barabas!   *Exeunt.*
    Bar. May all good fortune follow Calymath!
And now, as entrance to our safety—
To prison with the Governor and these
Captains, his consorts and confederates!
    Fern. O villain! Heaven will be reveng'd on thee.   *Exeunt.*
    Bar. Away! No more! Let him not trouble me.
—Thus hast thou gotten by thy policy
No simple place, no small authority.
I now am Governor of Malta. True—   30
But Malta hates me, and in hating me
My life's in danger. And what boots it thee,
Poor Barabas, to be the Governor
Whenas thy life shall be at their command?
No, Barabas, this must be look'd into.
And since by wrong thou got'st authority,
Maintain it bravely by firm policy—
At least unprofitably lose it not:
For he that liveth in authority,
And neither gets him friends nor fills his bags,   40
Lives like the ass that Æsop speaketh of,
That labors with a load of bread and wine—

And leaves it off to snap on thistle-tops!
But Barabas will be more circumspect.
Begin betimes: occasion's bald behind:
Slip not thine opportunity, for fear too late
Thou seek'st for much but canst not compass it.
—Within here!

Enter Governor with a guard.

  [*Fern.*] My lord?
    Bar. Ay, "lord," thus slaves will learn.   50
Now, Governor—. Stand by there, wait within.
                             [Exeunt guard.]
This is the reason that I sent for thee:
Thou seest thy life and Malta's happiness
Are at my arbitrament; and Barabas
At his discretion may dispose of both.
Now tell me, Governor, and plainly too,
What think'st thou shall become of it and thee?
  [*Fern.*] This, Barabas: since things are in thy power,
I see no reason but of Malta's wrack,
Nor hope of thee but extreme cruelty.   60
Nor fear I death, nor will I flatter thee.
    Bar. Governor, good words, be not so furious.
'Tis not thy life which can avail me aught.
Yet you do live, and live for me you shall.
And as for Malta's ruin, think you not
'Twere slender policy for Barabas
To dispossess himself of such a place?
For sith, as once you said, within this isle,
In Malta here, that I have got my goods,
And in this city still have had success,   70
And now at length am grown your Governor,
Yourselves shall see it shall not be forgot:
For as a friend not known but in distress,
I'll rear up Malta now remediless.
  [*Fern.*] Will Barabas recover Malta's loss?
Will Barabas be good to Christians?
    Bar. What wilt thou give me, Governor, to procure
A dissolution of the slavish bands
Wherein the Turk hath yok'd your land and you?
What will you give me if I render you   80
The life of Calymath, surprise his men,
And in an outhouse of the city shut
His soldiers, till I have consum'd 'em all with fire?
What will you give him that procureth this?
  [*Fern.*] Do but bring this to pass which thou pretendest,

Deal truly with us as thou intimatest,
And I will send amongst the citizens
And by my letters privately procure
Great sums of money for thy recompense.
Nay more! Do this, and live thou Governor still!   90
    Bar. Nay, do thou this, Ferneze, and be free!
Governor, I enlarge thee. Live with me.
Go walk about the city, see thy friends.
—Tush, send not letters to 'em, go thyself,
And let me see what money thou canst make.
Here is my hand that I'll set Malta free.   [*They clasp hands.*]
And thus we cast it: To a solemn feast
I will invite young Selim Calymath
Where be thou present only to perform
One stratagem that I'll impart to thee,   100
Wherein no danger shall betide thy life:
And I will warrant Malta free for ever.
    [*Fern.*] Here is my hand! Believe me, Barabas,   [*They clasp
I will be there and do as thou desirest.   *hands again.*]
When is the time?
    Bar. Governor, presently:
For Calymath, when he hath view'd the town,
Will take his leave and sail towards Ottoman.
    [*Fern.*] Then will I, Barabas, about this coin,
And bring it with me to thee in the evening.   110
    Bar. Do so, but fail not. Now farewell, Ferneze!
                        [*Exit Ferneze.*]
And thus far roundly goes the business:
Thus loving neither, will I live with both,
Making a profit of my policy:
And he from whom my most advantage comes
Shall be my friend.
This is the life we Jews are us'd to lead—
And reason too, for Christians do the like.
Well, now about effecting this device:
First to surprise great Selim's soldiers,   120
And then to make provision for the feast,
That at one instant all things may be done:
My policy detests prevention:
To what event my secret purpose drives,
I know. And they shall witness with their lives!   *Exit.*
[5.3]   *Enter Calymath, Bassoes.*
    Caly. Thus have we view'd the city, seen the sack,
And caus'd the ruins to be new-repair'd
Which with our bombards' shot and basilisk

We rent in sunder at our entry.
And now I see the situation,
And how secure this conquer'd island stands—
Environ'd with the Mediterranean Sea;
Strong [countermur'd] with other petty isles;
And, toward Calabria, back'd by Sicily
([Where] Syracusian Dionysius reign'd)   10
Two lofty turrets that command the town—*
I wonder how it could be conquer'd thus.

Enter a Messenger.

Mess. From Barabas, Malta's Governor, I bring
A message unto mighty Calymath.
Hearing his Sovereign was bound for sea,
To sail to Turkey, to great Ottoman,
He humbly would entreat Your Majesty
To come and see his homely citadel,
And banquet with him ere thou leav'st the isle.
Caly. To banquet with him in his citadel . . .   20
I fear me, messenger, to feast my train
Within a town of war so lately pillag'd
Will be too costly and too troublesome:
Yet would I gladly visit Barabas,
For well has Barabas deserv'd of us.
Mess. Selim, for that, thus saith the Governor,
That he hath in store a pearl so big,
So precious, and withal so orient,
As, be it valued but indifferently,
The price thereof will serve to entertain   30
Selim and all his soldiers for a month.
Therefore he humbly would entreat Your Highness
Not to depart till he has feasted you.
Caly. I cannot feast my men in Malta walls,
Except he place his tables in the streets.
Mess. Know, Selim, that there is a monastery
Which standeth as an outhouse to the town:
There will he banquet them; but thee at home,
With all thy bassoes and brave followers.
Caly. Well, tell the Governor we grant his suit: 40
We'll in this summer evening feast with him.
Mess. I shall, my lord.   *Exit.*
Caly. And now, bold bassoes, let us to our tents,
And meditate how we may grace us best
To solemnize our Governor's great feast.   *Exeunt.*

---

* Lines 10-11 are transposed in Q.

[5.4]   *Enter Governor, Knights, Del Bosco.*

[*Fern.*] In this, my countrymen, be rul'd by me:
Have special care that no man sally forth
Till you shall hear a culverin discharg'd
By him that bears the linstock, kindled thus;   [*Pantomimes*
Then issue out and come to rescue me,   *careful lighting*
For happily I shall be in distress,   *of cannon.*]
Or you released of this servitude.
1 *Knight.* Rather than thus to live as Turkish thralls,
What will we not adventure?
[*Fern.*] On then, begone!   10
Knights. Farewell, grave Governor!   [*Exeunt.*]

[5.5] *Enter with a hammer above, very busy* [*Barabas. Carpenters enter below. There is a taut rope from the tarras to the platform*].

Bar. How stand the cords? How hang these hinges?
        Fast?
Are all the cranes and pulleys sure?
⟨*Carp.*⟩ All fast.
Bar. Leave nothing loose, all levell'd to my mind.
Why now I see that you have art indeed.
There, carpenters, divide that gold amongst you:
                                [*Throws money down.*]
Go swill in bowls of sack and muscadine!
Down to the cellar, taste of all my wines.
Carp. We shall, my lord, and thank you.
                        Exeunt [*Carpenters*].
Bar. And, if you like them, drink your fill and die—   10
For so I live, perish may all the world!
Now Selim Calymath return me word
That thou wilt come, and I am satisfied.

                Enter Messenger [*below*].

Now, sirrah, what, will he come?
Mess. He will; and has commanded all his men
To come ashore, and march through Malta streets,
That thou mayest feast them in thy citadel.   [*Exit.*]
Bar. Then now are all things as my wish would have
        'em.
There wanteth nothing but the Governor's pelf—
And see, he brings it.   20

Enter Governor [below, with a bag of money].

Now, Governor, the sum?

    [*Fern.*] With free consent, a hundred thousand pounds.

    Bar. Pounds say'st thou, Governor? Well, since it is no
      more,

I'll satisfy myself with that. Nay, keep it still,

For if I keep not promise, trust not me.

And, Governor, now partake my policy.

First, for his army: they are sent before,

Enter'd the monastery, and underneath

In several places are field-pieces pitch'd,

Bombards, whole barrels full of gunpowder,   30

That on the sudden shall dissever it

And batter all the stones about their ears,

Whence none can possibly escape alive.

Now as for Calymath and his consorts:

Here have I made a dainty gallery,

The floor whereof, this cable being cut,

Doth fall asunder; so that it doth sink

Into a deep pit past recovery.

Here, hold that knife [*throws down a knife*] and when thou
    seest he comes

And with his bassoes shall be blithely set,   40

A warning-piece shall be shot off from the tower

To give thee knowledge when to cut the cord

And fire the house. Say, will not this be brave?

    [*Fern.*] O excellent! Here, hold thee, Barabas,   [*Holds up*
I trust thy word, take what I promis'd thee.   *bag.*]

    Bar. No, Governor, I'll satisfy thee first.

Thou shalt not live in doubt of anything.

Stand close, for here they come. [*Ferneze retires.*] Why, is
    not this

A kingly kind of trade to purchase towns

By treachery and sell 'em by deceit?   50

Now tell me, worldlings, underneath the [sun]   [*To audience.*]

If greater falsehood ever has been done?

Enter Calymath and Bassoes.

    Caly. Come, my companion bassoes. See, I pray,

How busy Barabas is there above

To entertain us in his gallery.

Let us salute him. Save thee, Barabas!

    Bar. Welcome, great Calymath!

    [*Fern.*] (How the slave jeers at him.)   [*Aside.*]

Bar. Will 't please thee, mighty Selim Calymath,
To ascend our homely stairs?   60
    Caly. Ay, Barabas.
Come, bassoes, ascend.
    [*Fern.*] [*coming forward.*] Stay Calymath!
For I will show thee greater courtesy
Than Barabas would have afforded thee.
    Knight [*within.*] Sound a charge there!

[*Trumpet sounds. A cannon is shot off within. The curtains at
back open to disclose a cauldron. Ferneze cuts rope, and Barabas
    falls through tarras trap into cauldron.*]*

[*Enter Martin del Bosco and Knights.*]

    Caly. How now! What means this?
    Bar. Help, help me! Christians, help!
    [*Fern.*] See, Calymath, this was devis'd for thee.
    Caly. Treason! Treason! Bassoes, fly!   70
    [*Fern.*] No, Selim, do not fly.
See his end first, and fly then if thou canst.
    Bar. O help me, Selim! Help me, Christians!
Governor, why stand you all so pitiless?
    [*Fern.*] Should I in pity of thy plaints or thee,
Accursed Barabas, base Jew, relent?
No! Thus I'll see thy treachery repaid,
But wish thou hadst behav'd thee otherwise.
    Bar. You will not help me, then?
    [*Fern.*] No, villain, no!   80
    Bar. And, villains, know you cannot help me now.
Then, Barabas, breathe forth thy latest fate,
And in the fury of thy torments strive
To end thy life with resolution.
Know, Governor, 'twas I that slew thy son;
I fram'd the challenge that did make them meet.
Know, Calymath, I aim'd thy overthrow,
And had I but escap'd this stratagem,
I would have brought confusion on you all—
Damn'd Christians, dogs, and Turkish infidels!   90
But now begins the extremity of heat
To pinch me with intolerable pangs.
Die, life! fly, soul! tongue, curse thy fill, and die!   [*Dies.*]
    Caly. Tell me, you Christians, what doth this por-
        tend?
    [*Fern.*] This train he laid to have entrapp'd thy life.
Now, Selim, note the unhallowed deeds of Jews!

---

* Original s.d.: *A charge, the cable cut. A Caldron discovered.*

Thus he determin'd to have handled thee,
But I have rather chose to save thy life.
   Caly. Was this the banquet he prepar'd for us?
Let's hence, lest further mischief be pretended.   100
   [*Fern.*] Nay, Selim, stay; for since we have thee   [*Knights*
    here,   *surround Calymath.*]
We will not let thee part so suddenly:
Besides, if we should let thee go, all's one,
For with thy galleys could'st thou not get hence,
Without fresh men to rig and furnish them.
   Caly. Tush, Governor, take thou no care for that,
My men are all aboard,
And do attend my coming there by this.
   [*Fern.*] Why, heard'st thou not the trumpet sound a
    charge?
   Caly. Yes, what of that?   110
   [*Fern.*] Why then the house was fir'd,
Blown up, and all thy soldiers massacred.
   Caly. O monstrous treason!
   [*Fern.*] A Jew's courtesy:
For he that did by treason work our fall,
By treason hath delivered thee to us:
Know, therefore, till thy father hath made good
The ruins done to Malta and to us,
Thou canst not part: for Malta shall be freed,
Or Selim ne'er return to Ottoman.   120
   Caly. Nay, rather, Christians, let me go to Turkey,
In person there to meditate your peace.
To keep me here will not advantage you.
   [*Fern.*]Content thee, Calymath, here thou must stay,
And live in Malta prisoner. For come call the world
To rescue thee, so will we guard us now,
As sooner shall they drink the ocean dry
Than conquer Malta, or endanger us.
So march away, and let due praise be given
Neither to Fate nor Fortune, but to Heaven.   [*Exeunt.*]   130

TEXTUAL NOTES
AND ACT-SCENE COMPARISONS
WITH THE CASE AND GREG EDITIONS

1 AND 2 TAMBURLAINE

The disintegration of 1 and 2 *Tamburlaine*—that is, the refusal
to grant to Marlowe's hand the comic prose scenes—goes directly
back to the prefatory epistle which Richard Jones, the printer-
publisher of the first edition in 1590, put before the plays, "To
the Gentlemen Readers and Others That Take Pleasure in
Reading Histories":

> Gentlemen and courteous readers whosoever: I have here
> published in print for your sakes the two tragical discourses of
> the Scythian shepherd Tamburlaine, that became so great a
> conqueror and so mighty a monarch. My hope is that they will
> be now no less acceptable unto you to read after your serious
> affairs and studies than they have been lately delightful for
> many of you to see when the same were showed in London upon
> stages. I have purposely omitted and left out some fond and
> frivolous gestures, digressing, and in my poor opinion, far
> unmeet for the matter, which I thought might seem more tedious
> unto the wise than any way else to be regarded, though, haply,
> they have been of some vain, conceited fondlings greatly gaped
> at, what times they were showed upon the stage in their graced
> deformities. Nevertheless now to be mixtured in print with
> such matter of worth, it would prove a great disgrace to so
> honorable and stately a history. Great folly were it in me to
> commend unto your wisdoms either the eloquence of the author
> that writ them or the worthiness of the matter itself. I
> therefore leave unto your learned censures both the one and
> the other—and myself the poor printer of them unto your most

courteous and favorable protection, which if you vouchsafe to accept, you shall evermore bind me to employ what travail and service I can to the advancing and pleasuring of your excellent degree.

Yours, most humble at commandment,
R. J., Printer

Now, actually, Jones does *not* supply a foundation for the disintegrators. He says he has "omitted" the "fond and frivolous gestures" which, presumably, he found in the manuscript behind the octavo. Perhaps, he was speaking of Kempe-like or Tarleton-like (i.e., low comedy) intrusions, such as jigs (song-dance-dialogues) between the acts. I do not know. But can Jones' prefatory matter be initially trusted? Probably not. His credibility is severely attacked by Professor Hyder Rollins in the latter's edition (Harvard University Press, 1924) of Jones' *A Handful of Pleasant Delights* (1584):

> The title-page of the *Handful* . . . announces that the book contains "sundrie *new* Sonets. . . . *Newly* devised to the *newest* tunes. . . . With *new additions* of certain Songs, to *verie late* devised Notes, not commonly knowen, nor *vsed here-tofore.*" But this is false from beginning to end. Like the typical dishonest stationer whose character George Wither was later to portray so vividly, Richard Jones provided this new title-page to delude customers into buying old wares. Most of the ballads had been printed before 1566, and the tunes were old. . . .

So today's Marlowe scholars and editors have decided that the comic prose sections in the two parts of *Tamburlaine* cannot be by the same hand as writes the mighty line of verse. An entirely gratuitous assumption, to begin with. In Ellis-Fermor's General Index in her edition of the plays, we read: "Prose passages in *Tamburlaine*, almost invariably suggest corruption," but we find this editor being illogical, I think. Surely, if the prose is closely integrated with the blank verse portions, it is reasonable that both were written by the same hand. We remember that in 2.3, *1 Tamburlaine*, the simple-minded Mycetes, King of Persia, and the Scythian hero have a prose comic interplay—just before which Mycetes *in verse* attempts to hide his crown. Now in 3.4 of the Second Part, in a scene that is primarily verse, Tamburlaine refers to this incident while commenting in prose on the semi-comic Almeda's becoming a king: "Look to him, Theridamas, when we are fighting, lest he hide his crown as the foolish King of Persia did." Verse and prose are thus closely related not merely in the same scenes but between the two parts. Yet Miss Ellis-Fermor in a note to the second passage writes (p. 241): "This reference . . . reads like actor's gag—a happy reference to a popular episode in the earlier play. That fact, combined with its prose form, throws suspicion on this speech and, no less, on parts of the episode alluded to." This is not legitimate textual criticism: it is irresponsible subjectivism.

And even when common sense enters in seeing Marlowe as a
possible comic dramatist, the traditional view that deprives him
of such necessary dramatic variety sometimes enters by the
back door. For example, in Paul H. Kocher, *Christopher Marlowe: A Study of His Thought, Learning, and Character* (University of North Carolina Press, 1946), pp. 270 ff., the author, in
perceptive criticism, sees the Mycetes and Calyphas scenes as
comic and integrated *and* Marlovian—but ends by writing (p.
277): "Even if, as seems probable, the prose scenes in which most
of this kind of thing occurs were written by someone other than
Marlowe. . . ."

Typical of what students and general readers get in anthologies
are the footnotes in Hazelton Spencer's *Elizabethan Plays* (Boston,
1940). Here is one on p. 14 on the Tamburlaine-Mycetes scene we
have just discussed:

> This departure from blank verse looks suspicious. We may
> have here a fragment of a longer comic scene, perhaps not
> composed by Marlowe; or perhaps we have merely actors' gags
> here. The publisher of [the first edition] states that he has "left
> out some fond and frivolous gestures" which "were showed upon
> the stage in their graced deformities."

I might add that reference to "actors' gags" is the recourse
of critics of Elizabethan drama who find elements in the plays
they, the critics, do not personally like. Such excuses go back to
Pope's edition of Shakespeare, and are still very much alive in
Coleridge's dicta.

THIS EDITION	1 TAMBURLAINE	CASE
	Act 1	
1.1		1.1
1.2		1.2
	Act 2	
2.1		2.1
2.2		2.2
2.3		{ 2.3 { 2.4
2.4		2.5
2.5		{ 2.6 { 2.7
	Act 3	
3.1		3.1
3.2		3.2
3.3		3.3
	Act 4	
4.1		4.1
4.2		4.2
4.3		4.3
4.4		4.4

Act 5

5.1 $\left\{ \begin{array}{l} 5.1 \\ 5.2 \end{array} \right.$

THIS EDITION	2 TAMBURLAINE	CASE

Act 1

1.1 $\left\{ \begin{array}{l} 1.1 \\ 1.2 \end{array} \right.$

1.2   1.3

1.3 $\left\{ \begin{array}{l} 1.4 \\ 1.5 \\ 1.6 \end{array} \right.$

Act 2

2.1   2.1

2.2 $\left\{ \begin{array}{l} 2.2 \\ 2.3 \end{array} \right.$

2.3   2.4

Act 3

3.1   3.1

3.2   3.2

3.3 $\left\{ \begin{array}{l} 3.3 \\ 3.4 \end{array} \right.$

3.4   3.5

Act 4

4.1   4.1

4.2   4.2

4.3   4.3

Act 5

5.1   5.1

5.2   5.2

5.3   5.3

EDWARD II

Although there may have been a 1593 edition, now lost, the earliest extant edition of *Edward II* is that of 1594, octavo, of which two copies exist. All variants in my text from the octavo—except for Edmund—will be found in square brackets, even where I put *Niece* for *Lady.* I have used pointed brackets to insert *Arundel* for *Matrevis,* where this error begins at 3.2.89. In one important matter I have departed widely from past texts. In 4.3 Spencer is supposed to read the names of the executed rebels, but the play supplies no list. I have gone to Holinshed (1587), 231 b, and given the names the chronicler puts down. This seems the best way out of an insurmountable difficulty.

THIS EDITION	CASE
Act 1	
1.1	1.1
1.2	1.2
1.3	1.3
1.4	1.4
Act 2	
2.1	2.1
2.2	2.2
2.3	2.3
2.4	2.4
2.5	2.5
Act 3	
3.1	3.1
3.2	{ 3.2
	3.3
Act 4	
4.1	4.1
4.2	4.2
4.3	4.3
4.4	4.4
4.5	4.5
4.6	4.6
Act 5	
5.1	5.1
5.2	5.2
5.3	5.3
5.4	5.4
5.5	5.5
5.6	5.6

DOCTOR FAUSTUS

"Where there is great or complicated divergence between the editions, as in the case of Marlowe's *Faustus,* the production of a resultant text which may be relied upon to represent the ultimate intentions of the author is well-nigh impossible." J. P. Postgate, *Encyclopaedia Britannica,* 14th ed. (1941), p. 7. Such probably was the viewpoint shared by the late F. S. Boas in his edition of the play. Boas conflates usually, but sometimes gives each scene twice, that is, as it appears in each version.

There are two chief texts of the play, the 1604 or A text and the 1616 or B text. The one always copied in college and high school anthologies of Elizabethan drama is the A text. In the March 1946 issue of *The Library,* pp. 272-93, I showed that the A text is a memorial corruption of the B text (i.e., that the 1604 is a bad quarto of the B version with constant restatement, omission, and misplacing *and that it is more or less completely untrust-worthy in regard to what Marlowe actually wrote:* to regard it as possessing independent authority, except where we are *forced* to employ it, is bad theory and practice). I also showed that the B version was already in existence by 1594.

In his monumental *Marlowe's "Doctor Faustus," 1604-1616: Parallel Texts* (Oxford, 1950), the late Sir Walter Greg concurred in my relation of the texts but argued multiple authorship, revision, variant substantive passages, etc., in B. Despite apparent general acceptance of his disintegration of the 1616 version, I have found Greg's case neither proved nor convincing. He categorically assumed the ability to distinguish between Marlowe and not Marlowe—and, of course, the comic portions were by Samuel Rowley! (How presumptive Greg was is shown by his allocation to Rowley of lines that end in *majestical* or words with the same suffix. Yet glance at four lines of *1 Tamburlaine,* 1.2.209-12!

> *Ther.* Not Hermes, prolocutor to the gods,
> Could use persuasions more pathetical.
> *Tamb.* Nor are Apollo's oracles more true
> Than thou shalt find my vaunts substantial.)

This semimagical power to select absolutely the truly Marlovian cannot be granted Sir Walter or anyone else. Let me show the difficulties that disintegrators refuse to recognize: *"The Faithful Shepherdess,* which we have every external reason to take as wholly Fletcher's, is notably at odds with the accepted notion of Fletcher's characteristic versification, being indeed strangely closer to the accepted notion of Beaumont's."* Clifford Leech, "The Dramatic Style of John Fletcher," *English Studies Today,* Lectures and Papers Read at the Fourth Conference of the International Association of University Professors of English Held at Lausanne and Berne, August 1959 (Berne, 1961), p. 143. And I would challenge the Shakespeare student who doesn't know the play from which it comes to place chronologically the following rhymed soliloquy:

> Most sweet voices!
> Better it is to die, better to starve,
> Than crave the hire which first we do deserve.
> Why in this [woolless toge] should I stand here
> To beg of Hob and Dick, that [do] appear,
> Their needless vouches? Custom calls me to't.
> What custom wills, in all things should we do't,
> The dust on antique time would lie unswept,
> And mountainous error be too highly heapt
> For truth to o'er-peer. Rather than fool it so,
> Let the high office and the honor go
> To one that would do thus.—I am half through;
> The one part suffer'd, th' other I will do.

This rhymed passage is not from an early play but from a very late one, *Coriolanus*, 2.3.119-31. Yet the versification studies of Shakespeare's final tragedies hardly prepare one to find such a passage as this in them. Still, Greg confidently divided what was surely Marlowe's from what was not! Out of a total of 2109 lines in B he gave only 805 to Marlowe's authorship!

Furthermore, Greg seems never to have grasped that a typical bad quarto, like the A text of *Doctor Faustus*, is so corrupt that to postulate cutting or revision accounts for the differences between it and the good text is wholly inadmissible.

My text of *Doctor Faustus* utilizes only 21 lines from A (in pointed brackets). Everything else is B. As such it differs radically from the still composite: W. W. Greg (ed.), *The Tragical History of the Life and Death of Doctor Faustus, by Christopher Marlowe, A Conjectural Reconstruction* (Oxford, 1950). Since mine is a new text, it is quite impossible to compare its scene and line numbering with earlier editions. I give its correspondence to the numbering in Greg's parallel text edition.

THIS EDITION		GREG
	Act 1	
Chorus		B2-28
1.1		B30-188+A141-2
1.2		B190-224
1.3		B227-339
1.4		B341-388
	Act 2	
2.1		B390-556
2.2		B570-741
2.3		B744-775
	Act 3	
Chorus		B778-801+A833
3.1		B803-1011
3.2		B1015-1126
3.3		B1129-1180
	Act 4	
Chorus		A931-947
4.1		B1182-1370
4.2		B1373-1521
4.3		B1526-1576
4.4		B1578-1635
4.5		B1639-1773
	Act 5	
5.1		B1777-1893
5.2		B1895-2092+A1463
5.3		B2094-2112
Chorus		B2114-2121

In "Mephostophilis and the Lost 'Dragon,'" *RES,* XVIII (1942), 312-15, I indicated that on the basis of the strayed word "dragon" in Faustus' invocation in the 1616 text (this word really being a marginal *warning* for the use of the particular property), the illustration on the 1624 title page, and the listing of a dragon for the play in one of Henslowe's inventories that Mephostophilis first appeared to the magician from a trap door in the shape of a dragon.

THE JEW OF MALTA

Despite all the vague generalizations written about it, the 1633 quarto of *The Jew of Malta* is fundamentally a good one, with very few cruxes. See J. C. Maxwell, "How Bad Is the Text of *The Jew of Malta?*" *MLR,* XLVIII (1953), 435-8. A long line of scholar-critics have asserted that Marlowe did not finish the play and/or that Heywood or someone else reworked it. The latter part has been most suspect, yet in "Some Light on *The Jew of Malta,*" *MLQ,* VII (1946), 53-6, I showed (a) that the final scene is postulated by Henslowe's entry in March 1598 of "j cauderm for the Jewe" and (b) that the friar scenes are probably "echoed" in *Titus Andronicus* (in or before 1592), where Aaron, palpably imitating Barabas' catalogue of crimes: "As for myself, I walk abroad a-nights, etc.," says: "Oft have I digd vp dead men from their graues/And set them vpright at their deare friends dore." It is categorical that aesthetic objection to the depiction of the Jew, a purely subjective reaction, is the sole foundation of the disintegration of this play. There is not a shred of real evidence, however, for not taking it, as it is, as Marlowe's total creation And a very fine piece of stagecraft, too, if one allows the playwright the scope of change and development, and if one refuses to get unnecessarily Arnoldian about effective theater. Need I add that some critics have rejected certain comic portions as not by Marlowe?

The probability is that the manuscript behind the 1633 quarto was an author's draft. I avoid the phrase *foul papers,* which is usually used, because it seems to postulate only a single draft prior to the author's handing the manuscript to the theater. At any rate, in directions and speech prefixes Ferneze is *Governor,* Katherine is *Mater,* and Bellamira is *Courtesan.* In the prefixes Jacomo and Barnardine are *1 Fry.* and *2 Fry.,* and sometimes just *Fry.* when one is present; however, Jacomo is *Ioco* in 4.1 when he re-enters to strike Barnardine's body. The Abbess is *1 Nun, Nun,* and *Abb.* in sequence in 1.2. Most interesting of all, Barabas in the prefixes is both *Iew* and *Bar.* Generic prefixes and variation in prefixes are accepted today as auctorial stigmata. Thus, I would not hesitate to declare that *The Jew of Malta* as we have it must be very close to Marlowe's own hand.

The 1633 quarto is ushered in by an epistle of Thomas Heywood and two prologues and epilogues by the same dramatist. I append them here:

TO MY WORTHY FRIEND, MASTER THOMAS HAMMON, OF GRAY'S INN, ETC.

This play, composed by so worthy an author as Mr. Marlowe, and the part of the Jew presented by so unimitable an actor as Master Alleyn, being in this later age commended to the stage: as I usher'd it unto the Court and presented it to the Cock-pit, with these Prologues and Epilogues here inserted, so now being newly brought to the press, I was loath it should be published without the ornament of an Epistle; making choice of you unto whom to devote it; than whom (of all those gentlemen and acquaintance, within the compass of my long knowledge) there is none more able to tax ignorance or attribute right to merit. Sir, you have been pleased to grace some of mine own works with your courteous patronage. I hope this will not be the worse accepted because commended by me, over whom none can claim more power or privilege than yourself. I had no better a New Year's gift to present you with; receive it therefore as a continuance of that inviolable obligement by which he rests still engaged: who, as he ever hath, shall always remain,

Tuissimus,
Tho. Heywood

THE PROLOGUE TO THE STAGE
At the Cock-pit

We know not how our play may pass this stage,
But by the best of poets* in that age
The Malta-Jew had being and was made;
And he, then by the best of actors† play'd.
In *Hero and Leander*, one did gain
A lasting memory; in *Tamburlaine*,
This *Jew*, with others many: th' other wan
The attribute of peerless, being a man
Whom we may rank with (doing no one wrong)
Proteus for shapes and Roscius for a tongue,
So could he speak, so vary. Nor is't hate
To merit in him‡ who doth personate
Our *Jew* this day; nor is it his ambition
To exceed or equal, being of condition
More modest: this is all that he intends
(And that, too, at the urgence of some friends)
To prove his best, and, if none here gainsay it,
The part he hath studied, and intends to play it.

---

* Marlowe.
† Alleyn.
‡ Perkins.

EPILOGUE TO THE STAGE
At the Cock-pit

In graving, with Pygmalion to contend;
Or painting, with Apelles, doubtless the end
Must be disgrace: our actor did not so—
He only aim'd to go but not out-go.
Nor think that this day any prize was play'd;
Here were no bets at all, no wagers laid:
All the ambition that his mind doth swell
Is but to hear from you (by me) 'twas well.

THE PROLOGUE SPOKEN AT COURT

Gracious and great, that we so boldly dare
('Mongst other plays that now in fashion are)
To present this, writ many years agone,
And in that age thought second unto none,
We humbly crave your pardon: We pursue
The story of a rich and famous Jew
Who liv'd in Malta: you shall find him still,
In all his projects, a sound Machevill;
And that's his character. He that hath past
So many censures, is now come at last
To have your princely ears: grace you him; then
You crown the action, and renown the pen.

EPILOGUE SPOKEN AT COURT

It is our fear (dread sovereign) we have bin
Too tedious. Neither can 't be less than sin
To wrong your princely patience. If we have
(Thus low dejected) we your pardon crave.
And if aught here offend your ear or sight,
We only act and speak what others write.

THIS EDITION	CASE
Prologue	Prologue
Act 1	
1.1	1.1
1.2	1.2
Act 2	
2.1	2.1
2.2	2.2
2.3	2.3
Act 3	
3.1	3.1
3.2	3.2
3.3	3.3
3.4	3.4
3.5	3.5
3.6	3.6

Act 4

4.1		⎧ 4.1
		⎨ 4.2
		⎩ 4.3
4.2		4.4
4.3		4.5
4.4		4.6

Act 5

5.1	5.1
5.2	5.2
5.3	5.3
5.4	5.4
5.5	5.5

I add as a pleasant postscript that Ithamore's several references to Barabas' tremendous proboscis, put on during make-up, is confirmed by W. Rowley in 1609: "the artificial Jewe of Maltaes nose" (Bennett's ed., p. 88).

GLOSSARY

a: dialectal for "he"

abate: lessen

abject (v.) humiliate

abjection: degradation

abridge: shorten

abroad: out of the house or place where one resides

abstracts: summaries

aby: pay for

Acantha: Acanta, southeast Asia Minor

accidental heat: excessive heat (accidental means nonsubstantive)

accidents: events

accomplishments: fulfillments of obligations

Actaeon: turned by Diana into a stag and torn to pieces by his own dogs

adamant: magnet

address (v.): direct

adjunct to the heavens: heavenly body

adjuncts: those which are joined to

admire: wonder at

admired: wondrous

admonition: advice, counsel

Adonis: beloved by Aphrodite (Venus)

advance: raise (as of a banner or flag); give offices to

advance your standard: fight under your flag

adventure: chance

advocate: pleader

Aeacus: one of the judges of the underworld

Aegyptia: Egypt

Aeque tandem: equally at length

Aeneas: the hero of Virgil's *Aeneid*

affected: attached oneself to

affections: emotions, feelings

afflictions: sins

afore: before

against: till the time when

Agamemnon: leader of the Greeks in the Trojan War

a-good: heartily

Agrippa: the German magician Cornelius Agrippa was believed to have the power to call up the dead

ail'st thou: is the matter with you

aim'd: plotted

air: breath

alarm, alarum: call to arms

Albania: the district lying along the west coast of the Caspian Sea

albeit: although

Albertus: Albertus Magnus,

medieval philosopher, reputed
a magician

Alcibiades: Greek leader known
for his charm and bravery

Alcides: Hercules

Alcides' post: entrance to the
temple of Hercules

Alcoran: the Mohammedan
holy book (the Koran)

Aldeboran: star in the constellation Taurus

Aleppo: a city in northwest
Syria

Aleppo, Soldino, Tripoli: Syria,
on the seacoast near Cyprus

Alexander: Paris of Troy as
well as the Macedonian emperor; the latter overcame
Babylonia 331 B.C.—he is supposed to have drunk much
wine before his death

allied: related to noble families

all's one: it comes to the same
thing

along (v.): come along

Almain rutters: German cav-
alrymen

amain: with full force; speedily

Amasia: on northern seaboard
of Asia Minor

Amazonia: country of the Am-
azons, warlike women, in
Africa

amiable: worthy of divine love

an, and: if

analytics: logic

Ancona: a seaport in East Italy

annagrammatize: make a
word's letters into another
word (for magical purposes)

annoy: molest

anon: soon

answer: pay for (a crime or
misdemeanor)

antic: grotesque

antics: grotesque human figures

Antioch: city on the border of
Syria and Turkey

Antipodes: the southernmost
and northernmost regions of
the world

Aonian: the Aonian Plain in
Greece extends from Mt.
Hypatus to Thebes (Strabo)

apace: quickly

A per se: by itself

appointed: equipped

Apollo: one of his functions
was god of medicine

Apollo's laurel bough: a great
man of learning

Apollo's oracles: prophecies inspired by Apollo

appoint: designate

approve: prove

a purpose: on purpose

Araris: Ararus, the Aluta, a
Hungarian river (Ortelius)

arbitrament: absolute decision

Archipelago: islands of the
Mediterranean

Arethusa: as Jove's mistress,
one of Marlowe's inventions

Argier: Algeria

argin: earthwork

argosy: large ship or ships

argument: subject; plot

argument of arms: the meaning of military life

argument of art: medical diag-
nosis

Ariadan: town in northeastern
Africa

Aristarchus: severe classical
teacher

armadoes: armadas, large war
vessels

armor of proof: tested armor

arms: armor

arms: heraldry (i.e., noble
ancestry), coat of arms

arras: fine cloth used for tapes-
try hangings

art: a particular branch of
learning; a skill (cf. artisan);
professional skill

artier: artery

as: as yet

Asant: Zante, a large island off
the west coast of southern
Greece

Ascalon: a town in Palestine
(Ortelius)

Asphaltis: bituminous lake near
Babylon

aspire: mount to

assay: try

asseiz'd: taken possession of
(legal term)

assuage: get milder

Assyria: ancient empire in
southwest Asia; Marlowe
makes it equivalent to Babylonia

astonied: astonished

astracism: asterism, a group of stars, a constellation

Atlas: the Titan who upheld the heavens and stars (Marlowe has him upholding the world)

attend: await

Aurora: the dawn

Auster and Aquilon: southwest and north winds

Austric: Austrian

Avernus: the entrance to the underworld

axle-tree: pole around which something rotates

axle-tree of heaven: the pole upon which the earth and spheres supposedly turn

aye: ever

Azamor: coast town of Morocco

Babylonians: Babylonia had been a Persian province since Cyrus subdued it 538 B.C.

Bacchus: the god of wine (Dionysius)

back: support

Bacon: Roger Bacon, the medieval philosopher, had the popular reputation of being a magician

Bad Angel: devil, demon, evil spirit

Bagdeth: Bagdad

baited: attacked (with a sense of bear-baiting, in which dogs attacked the chained animal)

ballads: not the traditional oral ballads, but poems printed on cheap paper and sold in the streets: broadside ballads

balsamum: gum of trees

Balsera: probably Passera, on the frontier of Natolia

ban: curse

banco: bank

bankrout: bankrupt

band: cloth collar

bands: bonds

bandy: exchange hits (tennis, but frequently used metaphorically in Elizabethan literature)

bane: deadly poison

baneful: painful, hateful; death-dealing, poisonous

bann'd: execrable

Barbarian steeds: Barbary horses

Barbary: the northwest African coast

base, bid a: challenge (prisoner's base is a game in which one challenges another to run after him: if the former is caught, he is made prisoner)

basilisk: a mythical creature whose glance killed (cockatrice)

basilisks: large cannon

basso, bashaw: title of a high Turkish dignitary (pasha)

bastones: cudgels (cf. bastinado)

batten: fatten

bawd: procurer of prostitutes

bay, at a: forced to fight

beads: prayer beads

bear it out: act openly

bear thee: accompany you

beard (v.): defy

beards: elderly statesmen (a beard was a sign of age and respectability)

beat on his conceits: affect his ideas

beaten silk: metal-embroidered silk

behest (n.): command, order

beholding: obliged, in debt to

behoof: profit, benefit

behoves you: concerns you

Belgasar: Beglasar, in Natolia

belike: perhaps, probably

Belimote, Argiron, Asterote: names of devils: Greg suggests that Belimote is from Behemoth, Argiron from Acheron, and Asterote from Astaroth (Astarte)

bell, book, and candle: "At the close of the office of excommunication the bell is tolled, the book closed, and the candle extinguished" (Boas)

belly-cheer: food and drink

Belus: the legendary founder of Babylon

bend . . . steps: walk, go

bereave: take away

beseem: fit, be suitable for

beseeming: proper to, seemly

bespeak: speak to

betake: resort

betide: befall, happen to

betimes: soon, in time, before it is too late

bevers: light meals, snacks

bewitching: acting like a witch

bewray: betray (a secret), expose

bickering: dispute

bide: await

bid him arms: challenge to battle

Biledull: Biledulgerid, the land of dates, south of the Barbary states

bill: a long-shafted weapon

bill: medical prescription; contract

bind: encircle, enclose

bind: make helpless?

Bithynia: in northwest Asia Minor

black coat: traditional dress of student as scholar

blink-ey'd: dim-eyed (hence, shirking?)

block: wooden block where executioner chopped off heads

blood: blood relationship

bloods: lives

blots: blemishes

blubbered: covered with tears (serious word in Elizabethan literature)

Boheme: Bohemia

Bohemia: what is now western Czechoslovakia

bolstered up: supported

bombards: cannon

bondman: slave

bonnet: hat (of a male)

Boötes: Arcturus, the Bear constellation

bootless: unavailing

boots: avails, profits

Boreas: the north wind

Borgias: Pope Alexander VI was believed to have died of poison; the Borgias were reputed to use this means of getting rid of their enemies

Borno: Bornu, chief town of Nubia, central-east Africa

boss: a gross woman

bottle of hay: bunch of hay

bottle-nos'd: with a very large nose

brats: children (this word was not quite as colloquial in Elizabethan English as it is in ours)

brave: wonderful, splendid, fine; presumptuous

brave (v.): affront; oppose; insult

bravely: splendidly, richly, efficiently

brawns: muscles (i.e., flesh)

breeching: spanking

brent: burned

brigandines: two-masted vessels

bright-splendent: brilliantly magnificent

brisk: overdressed

broad seal to gather: authority to collect special alms

broils: wars, argument

broken-winded: of a horse suffering from an asthmatic disease

brokery: relating to broker, a middleman in a business transaction

brook: endure

brunt: attack

buckler (v.): protect, shield

Buda: city on the Danube

Bueno para todos mi granado no era: my wealth is not for everybody (freely translated)

bugs: bugbears, things to frighten

bullion: uncoined gold

bulwarks: defensive mounds

burghers: town or city dwellers

buzzeth: whispers

Byather: province in Africa (Biafar)

Byron: near Babylon

Caesarea: city in northwest Palestine

Caire: Cairo

caitiff: base fellow

calling: office (profession)

Canarea: Canaria, the Canary Islands

Candy: Candia or Crete

canon law: the laws of the Roman Catholic Church

caper: dance

carbonadoes: meat which has been sliced into thin strips

Carmonia: Caramania, a province of the Persian empire, on the Gulf of Oman

Carnon: elevation near Constantinople? (Seaton)

carry it away: come off best

casemate: a room with openings for shot

cassia, ambergris, and myrhh: fragrant grain, perfume, and resin—all sweet-smelling

cast: anticipate; think; plan, arrange

cast: computed

cast about: arrange matters

cast away: damned

cast up caps: be joyful

cast up hills: the Titans threw mountains at Jove

catechising: religious teaching

caterpillars: a term of contempt, indicating that those so designated depend on others for their sustenance

cates: food

Catiline: Roman politician—standing for any villainous conspirator

catzerie: roguery

cavalieros: mounds on which cannon were placed

Cazates: the region of the woman-warriors, the Amazonians

Cazzo!: an exclamation of contempt

censure (v.): judge

censures: judgments

Cephalus: According to Bk. VII of Ovid's *Metamorphoses,* Cephalus hunted a monstrous beast in the country around Thebes, with his hound Laelaps—but suddenly both beast and dog were changed to marble

ceremony: conventional observance

Ceres: earth-goddess (Demeter)

certify: report, inform reliably

chafe: fuss

chafer: portable grate

Cham: Emperor of the Mongols, or any Asian sovereign

chamber-fellow: roommate

champion: at a coronation one who formally defends the King's right to the sovereignty

champion: level country land

chance: ill fortune; occurrence

chanc'd: happened to

channel: gutter, ditch

channel: collarbone

chaplet: crown

characters: facial characteristics by which one's disposition can be read (the Elizabethan science of metoscopy)

characters of signs and erring stars: symbols of the zodiac and planets

charge (v.): command; discharge

charge (n.): order, command; appointed task; responsibility

charge: trumpet call

Charon: the ferryman who took souls in his boat to the land of the dead

chary: careful

checking: reproving

check the ground: stamp on the ground (of horses)

chitterlings: animal intestines

choler: anger

chops: cheeks

churl: low fellow; miser

Cimmerian: black

Circes: the enchantress in the Odyssey who changed men into animals (Circe)

circle: the conjurer drew a circle around him both to protect himself from the spirits and to practice his art in

circle: orbit (of the moon)

circuit: particular territory

circumspect: careful

citadel: fortress

civil: civilized; central

clap: when a business deal was settled, the merchants would strike their hands together; enter intimately

clean (adv.): completely

clift: cliff

clime: region

clog: a heavy block of wood to impede a prisoner

close (v.): encircle, embrace

close (adj.): secret; concealed

close (adv.): secretly

closet of my heart: breast

clout: the center of a target

Clymene's brain-sick son: Phaeton, who drove his father, Apollo's, chariot of the sun to destruction

cockerel: young cock (i.e., one who is both boasting and probably ineffectual)

Cocytus: a river surrounding the underworld

Codemia: northeast of Stoko

coelum igneum and crystal-linum: fiery and crystal sphere (Ptolemaic)

coil: row, disturbance, stir

Colchos: the golden fleece was in Colchis

cold: shrunken, small

college: assembly, council

color: pretext; reason; guise

colors: flags

colossus: statue of great height

comeliest: best looking (in the sense of suitable)

comets: these were considered to foretell misfortune, e.g., the fall or death of kings

comings in: earnings

command (n.) : control, disposal

commenc'd: taken a university degree

comments volumes: writes reflections

commit: put in prison

commit with: have sexual intercourse with

common: not necessarily pejorative, often refers to the people as an estate of the realm (i.e., commons)

companions: disreputable fellows

company: accompany

compass: encompass, achieve, accomplish; embrace

competitor: mate, companion

'complices: accomplices

conceit: conception, idea, thought; imagination

conceit of foil: idea of defeat

conceits as clownage keeps in pay: the farcical figures in popular drama before Marlowe were allowed great leeway in inventing business to get an audience to laugh

concocted: digested

concubine: female slave

conduct, with my: under my control

conference: discourse

confines: borders

confound: confuse; overcome

conclude: decide

conge: bow

conjunctions, oppositions, aspects: "A *conjunction* is the apparent proximity of two heavenly bodies; an *opposition* is their extreme divergence; any other relative position for these two is termed an *aspect*" (Wheeler)

conning his neck-verse: studying the verse (in the Latin Bible) which would save him from execution because of "benefit of clergy"

consistory: "the meeting-place of the papal consistory or senate, where naturally the decrees of canon law would be kept" (Greg)

consort (v.) : be with

consort: a group of musicians

consorts: fellows

conspire: plot

conster: construe, interpret

consuls: rulers

consummate (adj.) : fulfilled

Consummatum est: it is finished (John 19:30), the last words of Jesus

consumption: wasting disease

consumption: destruction, at *2 Tamb.,* 4.1.198

contagion: sickness

contemn: scorn

continent: land

continent (adj.) : chaste

continent (adj.) : next to, bordering

continent to: continuous with

contract: formally promise

convertite: convert

convey: steal like a thief

convoys: at *2 Tamb.,* 3.3.39 it probably means "military aid"

cope with: fight with

Corpo di Dio!: Body of God!

corpus naturale . . . mobile: natural body . . . moving (physics)

Corinna: Ovid's love in his poetry

costermonger: street-seller, hawker of fruit, etc.

council held at Trent: the real council was held 1545-63

countenance (n.): authority

countenance (v.): give a good name to, authorize, support

counterbuff: struck hard enough to cause a recoil

countermand: command, control; deny; revoke; make ineffective

countermin'd: enclosed?

countermines (v.): tunnels

countermur'd: surrounded as with walls

counterscarps: walls of ditch facing fort

countervail: equal

counting-house: room set aside for bookkeeping

County Palatine: ruler of the Palatinate, southwest Germany

coupe de gorge: cut the throat

course: journey

courtesan . . . attire: Elizabethan prostitutes wore distinctive loose gowns

cousin: indicating a variety of blood relationships

covent: convent, religious house

cozening: cheating

crazed: dilapidated, broken, ruined

crest: helmet or decoration atop the helmet—feathers, etc.

critical: crucial; dangerous (sometimes in an astrological sense)

crosier: shepherd's staff borne by ecclesiastics

cross: interfere with; disagree with

crossbiting: cheating

crouch: bend

crown: coin bearing a crown

crucified a child: this was a crime of which Jews were often accused

Cubar: Guber, the land of the Negroes

cullion: base fellow

culverin: cannon

cunning (n.): ability, learning

cunningly: deceptively

curate: vicar's assistant

curb: check, control

cure: parish

curse: excommunicate

cursen: corruption of "Christian"

curstly: harshly, bitterly

curtains of the fort: walls joining two fortress towers

curtesy: making a leg, bowing (curtsy)

curtle-axe: short curved sword

curvet (v.): make a horse leap so that all four legs are off the ground

custom: custom fees

custom (v.): see through the Custom-House

Cutheia . . . and Orminius mount: in Caucasia (between Black and Caspian Seas)

Cyclopians: the Titans who fought Jove (according to Marlowe)

Cyclops: the giant assistants of the blacksmith god, Vulcan (according to Marlowe)

Cymbrian: Danish

Cynthia: the moon; astrologically the moon stands for giddiness (because it changed so often); the Elizabethans made much of the moon's causing tides to flow and ebb

Cyrus: the great Persian king, who subdued Asia Minor—but it was Darius who invaded Greece

Cytherea: Aphrodite, Venus

dainty: exquisitely beautiful

dalliance: dallying

dam: mate (n.)

Damon: the beloved friend of Pythias

Danae: her father locked her in a brazen tower, but Jupiter came to her in the form of a golden shower

dangereth: endangers

Danubius: the Danube River

dapper Jack: overdressed fellow

Dardania: Troy

Darote: a town on the Nile

dash (v.): ruin

dated: limited, transitory

dead: cold

dear: expensive; beloved

decay: death

declin'd: turned away from

Decretal: see *Statutes Decretal*

degraded: unfrocked, deprived of priesthood

delicates: delicacies

demean himself: act

Demogorgon: master of the Fates in Hell

desert of holiness: that which deserves religious worship

despair: one of the cardinal sins, giving up hope of God's love and aid

desperate: hopelessly reckless

despite: spite

Deucalion: after a deluge which destroyed the inhabitants of the world, he threw stones over his shoulder which became men

device: plan, plot, stratagem, trick

device: picture plus motto on a shield

devoir: duty

Diablo: devil

diadem: crown

diametrally: in a straight line

Dian: Diana

die: in Elizabethan English this sometimes means a sexual orgasm

digest: reduce to words

digested: mentally digested

dirge: prayer for the dead

Dis: Pluto, god of the underworld; the underworld itself

discharg'd: unloaded (of a ship)

disdainful: to be disdained

dismal: dark

dispatch: finish a task; kill; hurry

dispens'd with: given up

dispensive faith: loyalty from which the church can excuse us

dispossess'd: overcame in a business deal?

dispute: discuss

distain: stain

distemper'd: emotionally disturbed or overwrought; de-

ranged; physically ill

distinguish: discriminate

divers: many, various

divines: priests

do: sometimes in Elizabethan English equivocally in the sense of copulate

do for him: serve him

doleful: sad

dominion or intelligentia: ruling spirit or angel

doom (n.): opinion, judgment

doom (v.): judge, sentence

Draco: Athenian legislator who promulgated very severe laws

dragons, teeth of: after Cadmus sowed dragon's teeth in the earth, armed men arose who fought one another

dram: small quantity

drave: drove

drench: a draft of medicine for animals

dress: prepare food

drift: plan, plot; purpose

drink: absorb

drink of all waters: probably, "go anywhere" (Greg)

drizzle: drop (of tears)

droop: be depressed, despondent

drudge: one who performs servile, distasteful tasks

drugs: ingredients used in dyeing, etc.

ducat: gold coin

duck: bow

dump: melancholy or musing mood

dunces: discredited followers of the medieval theologian, Duns Scotus

earns: grieves

earth-mettl'd: the Elizabethans made little difference between *metal* and *mettle* (spirit, courage)

East India and the late discovered isles: India and the West Indies

eat . . . logs: be insulted without retaliating (?). I think this is a proverb: Cf. *Oxford Dictionary of English Proverbs:* "Gnaw the bone which is fallen to thy lot. 1678 Ray

Adag. Hebr. 411 . . . that is, He that hath an ill wife must patiently bear with her: it may also be applied to other things"

Ebena: untraceable

ebon: black

ecstasy: distraction

Ego mihimet sum semper proximus: I always think of myself first

egregious: eminent

elegy: long poem (not necessarily on a death)

element: sky

ell: forty-five inches

Elysium: the classical heaven

embassage: mission

emboss'd: decorated

embrace: joyfully accept

Emden, signiory of: domain of chief town of East Friesland, commercially important

empale: encircle

Emperor: the Holy Roman Emperor

Emperor, the: Charles V, 1519-56

empery: empire

empyreal orb: the Primum Mobile in Ptolemaic astronomy

enchas'd: decorated

encompass: surround

encounter: meet in battle

enforce: force

engineer: one who makes engins (weapons of warfare)

engines: instruments

enjoy: often, sexually enjoy

enlarge: free from prison or retention

enow: enough

ensign: flag

entertain: take care of; employ; receive in a friendly fashion; receive a guest

entertainment: treatment

entrance: beginning

entreat: treat, act towards, deal with

envied: hated

envy (n.): in Elizabethan English frequently hatred or violent dislike

epigram: short poem

equinoctial line: equator

Erebus: Hades

erring: wandering (frequently used of certain planets the paths of which early astronomers could not plot)

erst: formerly, before the present time

Erycina: one of Venus' names

essential form: fundamental quality (alchemy)

esteem: consider; consider important

Ethiopian sea: in Ortelius, the ocean between Africa and South America

Europe: Europa, mounted on Jove in the shape of a bull

Euxine Sea: Black Sea

even: evening

exasperate (adj.): exasperated

exclaim against: accuse, speak roughly of

exclaim on: accuse

exclaims: exclamations

excommunicate and interdict: expelled from the church, unable to receive the sacraments

excruciate: torture

execution: pun for eating and hanging

exequies: funeral services

exercise: religious ceremony

Ex hereditare filium non potest pater, nisi: "a father cannot disinherit his son unless" (Dean)

exigent: emergency

expedition: speed; carrying on

expert (adj.): proved

expressless: inexpressible

exquisite: keen (of pain)

extreme: most violent

extremes: extreme feelings

eye, by the: abundantly

fac'd: insulted

factious lord: one of a group of noblemen who opppose the King

factor: agent

facts: deeds

fail: decrease in numbers

fain: gladly

faint (adj.): cowardly

faintness: weakness

fair (adv.): agreeably

'faith: in faith (a common ejaculation)

fall to: begin eating

false (v.) : betray

familiars: demons, bad spirits

fare: food

fares (v.) : goes

farthing: quarter-penny coin

fashion-sake, for: as a formality

Fatal Sisters: the three goddesses of destiny—Clotho, Lachesis, Atropos (the Fates)

favors (v.) : resembles

favors, women's: parts of female costume, such as loose sleeve, handkerchief, etc. given as tokens of esteem or love and worn by knights

fear: frighten

fearful: full of fear

fear not: do not be worried about

fear'st: be fearful for

feather-bed: heavy quilt

feathered steel: arrow

feeling (adj.) : indicating emotion

fell: fierce, destructive

fen: swamp

fetch'd about: gone around

Fez, Morocco, and Argier: the area of Barbary, the coastal region of northwest Africa

field-pieces: light cannon

fiery keel at Antwerp's bridge: fireship with which the Dutch made a breach in the Spanish bridge built to blockade Antwerp, 1585

fig: fico (a mild curse)

fig: insignificant something

figure (v.) : prefigure, prophesy

figures: facial characteristics prefiguring one's destiny (metoscopy)

fill me out: pour out for me

fingers: plays (a musical instrument)

first curse: the Jews were believed to be cursed because of the Crucifixion

fit: an acute attack of disease

Flanders (adj.) : Belgian

flatly: positively

fleer: jeer

fleet: float

Fleet: prison

Flora: goddess of flowers

flout: make fun of, laugh at

fly: at *Ed. II,* 2.2.195 it means "be sold"

foil: defeat

foil: thin piece of metal placed behind a gem to set it off

foil'd: defiled

follows: follows logically

fond: foolish

fondly: foolishly

fool: not always pejorative in Elizabethan usage—e.g., applied to a child or dear one

for being seen: for fear of being seen

foreslow: waste

forfeiting: confiscation or forcing to pay a fine or financially ruining (O.E.D.)

form: document

form a verb: conjugate (i.e., copulate)

forward: ready, prompt, eager; overly bright

for why: because

frame: organize, plan, arrange, guide

fraught: freight; freighted

fray'd: frightened

freehold: one's own particular territory

frolic: in *Ed. II* frequently in a sexual or disreputable sense

front: face; affront

fruition: result

furniture: dress, accouterments

fury: hideous winged creature, usually connected with vengeance

gabions: large baskets filled with earth

gage: pledge

Galen: the great classical and medieval medical authority

gall: bitterness of spirit

gallery: balcony on upper, outside part of house

galley: a large vessel propelled by oars and sail

gammon: chunk of bacon

Ganymede: the lad whom Jupiter loved sexually, cupbearer to the gods

gape: stare (hungrily)

gat: got

gather'd for: in reference to alms

gather head: collect soldiers

gear: affair, business, matter

gentle: gentile

gentry: respectable ancestry

Georgia: a province on the west of the Black Sea

ghostly father: priest

Gihon: sometimes identified with the Oxus, whose shores possessed gold

glaive: sword, broadsword, lance

glance: allude (ironically or satirically)

glass: mirror

glorious: boastful

glozing: lying; flattering

glutted: satiated

god of arms: Mars, who had a love affair with Aphrodite-Venus

goings out: expenses, but also a pun for exposure of body because of holes in clothing

golden cross: money with a cross on it

goodly: fine

goods: possessions

gore: pierce

Gorgon: shortened form of Demogorgon, potentate of Hell

Go to: a rather meaningless exclamation

governor: controller

grace: God's aid; prayer before meal

grace (v.): act pleasingly

Graecia: Greece

Gramercies: Thank you!

gratify: repay

gratulate: express joy at

gravell'd: defeated, confounded

Grecian dame: Helen of Troy

greedy spoils: greedy for spoils

Greekish strumpet: Helen of Troy

gripe: grip

groat: coin of small value

groom: low fellow, servant

gross: thick

ground: basis

grounded argument: argument with a sure foundation

Gruntland: Greenland

Guallatia: Galatia, a province in central Asia Minor

guard: protect; ward, keep off

guardian: guard

guilders: Dutch coins worth two shillings

guise: fashion, custom

Guise: the Machiavellian Henri of Lorraine, third Duke of Guise, enemy of the French Protestants; assassinated 1588

Guyron: Guiron, a town near the upper Euphrates, hence not far from the Natolian border

gyves: chains

Hades: the underworld, hell

hags: furies, witches

halberd: a shafted weapon with hook and sharp cutting blade at end

halcyon's bill: a dead kingfisher was hung by the bill to show in what direction the wind was blowing

hale: drag

Halla: town in Syria

halter: hangman's rope

hand: signature

hand, in: in process

handsome: used by Elizabethans in regard to apparel

hap (n.): occurrence

hap (v.): happen

hapless: unfortunate, unlucky

haply: perhaps

happily: perhaps

harbor (v.): entertain in the mind

hard (adv.): with difficulty (it shall go hard = there will be trouble)

hard at hand: near by

hard heels: very heels

hardy: daring

harness: armor

harps upon: talks unceasingly of

harpy: mythical creature, woman-headed and winged, known for its voracity

hart: deer

haught, haughty: high, important

haunted (v.): followed

have a saying to: have something to say or do about

have at him: begin against him

hay: country dance

hazard: expose to risk

headed: beheaded

hearse: coffin

heaven, heavens, Heaven: it is very difficult to determine on occasion whether Marlowe is referring to the Christian seat of God (Heaven) or to the abode of the classical deities (heaven, heavens). Sometimes he merely uses the word for the upper region or sky

heavenly words: quotations from the Bible

heavy: sinful, grave; sad, dreary

hebon: the poisonous yew?

Hebrew Psalter: the Psalms of the Old Testament in the original tongue

Hecate: a goddess of the underworld

Hector: Trojan hero (it was not he but Hercules who loved Hylas); according to versions of the Trojan war later than Homer, he visited the Greek camp to issue a challenge and there saw his great rival, Achilles

held in hand: kept in expectation

Hell, hell: in Marlowe it is difficult, if not impossible, to distinguish between the classical underworld (hell) and the Christian region of the damned (Hell)

hempen: rope (for hanging)

hempen tippet: noose of the hangman's rope (a tippet is a cloth worn around the neck)

Hephestion: friend of Emperor Alexander

Hercules: Greek demigod, who strangled snakes in his cradle; he is also known as Alcides

Hermes: Mercury, messenger of Jove and the god of eloquence

Hermoso placer de los dineros: the beautiful pleasure of money

hest: command

hey-pass: juggler's jargon

Hippolytus: Theseus' son was dragged by his chariot horses over rocks to his death

his: very often in Elizabethan England = its

Hodie tibi, cras mihi: you today, me tomorrow

hogshead: cask or barrel

hold: fortress

hold (v.): wager, bet

homage: payment of feudal requirements

hold thee: hold out your hand

home: to the heart

Homo fuge!: Fly, man!

horns: what the cuckold (i.e., the husband of an unchaste wife) wears on his forehead

horse-courser: horse-dealer. "Horse-coursers had a reputation for knavery, and the groundlings would relish a conjurer's trick at their expense" (Boas)

horsed on: carried by

hospital: in Elizabethan times a refuge for destitute soldiers; a charitable institution for the housing and care of the needy or young

hostler: one who takes care of horses, especially at an inn

hostry: hostelry, inn

hover'd: waited

hoy: small ship

hugy: huge

humidum and calor: the sanguine humor, made up of wet and hot

humors: vital internal fluids and substances

hundred: a hundred per cent interest

hurdle: cart on which criminals were dragged to execution

Hyades: stars which supposedly bring rain

Hydra, Lerna's bane: this many-headed monster, whose heads grew back as soon as they were struck off, inhabited the region of Lerna; its bite was poisonous

Hylas: beloved of Hercules, who mourned his disappearance deeply

Hymen: god of marriage
hypostasis: the sediment in a urine examination

Ibis: sacred bird of the Egyptians, related to stork and heron
Ida: mountain near Troy
ill-entreated: badly treated
Ilium: Troy
illustrate: beautify
imbecility: feebleness
immure: enclose, close in
impartial: partial, i.e., unfair, unkind
impeach: accuse
import (n.): importance; consequence; significance
import (v.): signify, mean; *imports us:* concerns us greatly dicate
importune: plead with, strongly request
imprecations: prayers
imprimis: in the first place
in (v.): come in
incens'd: made angry
incense: make hot; set on fire, at *2 Tamb.,* 4.1.197
incivil: barbaric
in compass of: together with
in conduct of: under the direction of
incontinent: immediately
incony: sexually attractive
Inde: India
India: used of the new-found world, America, as well as of the Orient
indifferent: impartial
indifferently: impartially
infernal hag: fury
infernal Jove: Pluto
in few: in short
influence: astrological influence affecting man
in good time: right away
injurious: insulting
in keep: in custody ("keep" is a prison)
in place: here
insinuate: ingratiate one's self
Institutes: see *Justinian*
insufficient: unable
intelligentia: see *dominion*
interdict: prohibited
interr'd: buried

intreat: deal with, act toward (treat)
intrench: dig
invest: metaphorical for "place in a high office"
invested: dressed in regal robes
investion: investiture
Io: Jove's beloved, she was metamorphosed by Juno into a white heifer
Iphigen: Iphigenia was sacrificed by her father, Agamemnon, in order to appease Artemis' wrath and so get the Greek ships moving again toward Troy
Iris: messenger of Juno
issue: son, successor
Italian: in Elizabethan English almost always pejorative, whether in regard to dress, politics, art, or religion
I wis: I know

Jacob's staff: a mathematical instrument for measuring height and distance
Jaertis: the Jaxartes River, runs from Tartary to Caspian Sea
Janizaries: soldiers guarding the Sultan
Janus: the doors of this god's temple were open in time of war, closed in peace
jar: quarrel
Jason: chief of the Argonauts, who sailed for the golden fleece in Colchis
jealous: faithful
jealousy: zeal; suspicion
Jebusite: a non-Jewish, Canaanite tribe
Jehovah's name: the tetragrammaton, the holy name of God (Jahveh)
Jerome's Bible: the Latin Vulgate (used by Roman Catholics)
jesses: straps attached to the trained hawk's legs
jets it: shows off, struts
jetty feathers: black feathers on helmet's crest
jig: popular poem or song; sometimes a dance-dialogue given on the stage

jigging veins of rhyming mother wits: the coarse versification of popular drama before Kyd and Marlowe employed the fourteener couplet, seven-beat iambic lines, hardly suitable for serious address

Jove: frequently used in Renaissance to stand for God; Marlowe rarely uses "Jupiter"

Jove, black: Pluto

Jove's huge tree: oak

Jove, infernal: Pluto

Jubalter: Gibraltar

Judas: it was believed that Judas hanged himself on an elder-tree

judge: at *1 Tamb.*, 1.2.162 it means "correctly indicates"

Jupiter: astrologically the planet stands for magnificence

Justinian: famous code of laws going back to late classical times: the Justinian *Institutes*

keep: keep in this condition

keep courts: maintain courts

kept: continued a route on or through

kern: Irish foot soldier

kicking colts: metaphorical for tongues at *2 Tamb.*, 4.3.49

Killingsworth: Kenilworth

kind: satisfactory; natural

kind, in his: according to what he is

knell: sound of death bell

Knights of Malta: Knights of St. John of Jerusalem, whose headquarters was Malta 1530 on

knit: joined

knot: cluster of persons

labels: "slips of paper or parchment for affixing a seal to a document" (Charlton and Waller)

labor thy admission: work hard for your admission

Lachryma Christi: a very sweet Italian wine

lade: load

Lady Vanity: a figure in the old morality plays

lake: pit, den, or dungeon (Briggs)

lanceres: lancers, mounted soldiers armed with lances

lanch: lance

Lantchidol: a part of the Indian Ocean

lapt: wrapped (bodies were formerly wrapped in a lead sheet before burial)

larded: covered

largess: gift of money

Larissa: a sea-coast town, south of Gaza

Latona's daughter: Artemis or Diana, virgin huntress, goddess of chastity

lavish (adj.): extravagant (lavish tongues = free-speaking mouths)

lavish (n.): great destruction

lawn: thin cloth

lay: dwelt

lay hands on: arrest; grasp

lays: songs

league: about three miles

leaguer, lain in: stayed in a camp that was engaged in a siege

Leander: Hero's lover, who swam the Hellespont to come to her

leave (v.): cease

leave (n.): permission

legate: papal representative; envoy

leg: curtsy

lemans: lovers

lenity: gentle treatment

Lerna: see *Hydra*

Lesbia: Catullus' beloved in his poetry

let: hinder

letters: documents (letters of conduct = documents for safe passage)

level at: aim at

levell'd: arranged, disposed; purposed

levy arms: raise troops

liberal: free-handed

licentiates: holders of a lower university degree

liege: feudal superior

lies: dwells

lift: lifted
light on: happen to
lightsome: lighted
light upon: fall upon
like: please (e.g., this likes me)
Limnasphaltis: see *Asphaltis*
linstock: forked staff holding match used to light cannon
list: be pleasing (I list = is pleasing to me); incline
list to: care to, want to
live: live eternally
lively (adj.): living
liveries: costumes worn by a nobleman's retinue
lodestar: guiding star (Polaris)
lodge: dwell
lodging: dwelling place
logs: see *eat . . . logs*
lollards: heretics
'long of: concerning
'longs: belongs
looseness: careless behavior, with connotation of immorality
lots are cast: fortunes are decreed
lown: low fellow
lubbers: louts, clumsy fellows
Lubeck: a seaport in East Germany, formerly commercially important
luff'd and tack'd: brought the ship into the wind and thus changed its course
lusty: brave, strong

Maccabees: last two books of the Apocrypha of the Bible, recounting a Jewish revolt against Rome
Macedonians: Alexander (of Macedonia) defeated Darius, King of Persia, in 333 B.C.
Machda: an Abyssian town on the Nile, where Prester John, a mythical Christian potentate, lived
made sure: betrothed
magnanimity: honor, nobleness of mind
mails: bags
maim: injury, wound
main: sea
mainly: with strength
Major sum quam cui possit fortuna nocere: I am too great for fortune to injure (Hazelton Spencer)
make account of: consider
Maledicat Dominus!: May God curse!
malgrado: in spite of
malice: evil
malice (v.): dislike, hate, threaten
malmesey: a strong sweet wine of distinctive flavor
man: servant
manage arms: fight, battle
manage words with her: engage in a flyting (or insulting) match
mandrake: mandragora, a narcotic
Manico: Manicongo, a province in northern Africa
manna: miraculous food supplied Israelites fleeing from Egypt
mantle: covering garment
mantled: covered
March-Beer: choice ale
Mare Majore: the Black Sea
Mare Roso: the Red Sea
mark (v.): pay attention to; put a mark on
mark: target
Maro: Virgil, in the Middle Ages known as a great magician
marry: a meaningless oath
marshal: lead (marshal us the way = show us the way)
martial feast: victory banquet
Martlemas-Beef: "It was common to slaughter cattle at Martinmass [November 11] to be salted for winter provision" (O.E.D.)
martyred: tortured
mask (v.): dress, disguise oneself
masks: performances with rich costumes, poetry, splendid sets, and music
masters: friends; gentlemen (as a salutation)
match: encounter; love or marriage arrangement
mate: companion
mate (v.): cope with?
mated and amaz'd: rendered mentally shocked

Mauritanian: of northwest Africa

Mausolus: who built a magnificent tomb for his wife (mausoleum)

meads: meadows

mean (adj.): small; poor

meat: food in general

Median: of the country Media, south of the Caspian Sea

meed (n.): reward, recompense

meet: proper, suitable; necessary

Meleager . . . Argolian knights . . . Calydonian boar: Meleager with many Greek heroes hunted the savage boar which Artemis had sent

Memphis: ancient capital of Egypt

Menelaus: Helen of Troy's husband

merchants: merchantmen (ships)

Mercury: see *Hermes*

Mercury: astrologically, giver of quickness of wit

meridian: noon

Mesopotamia: country lying between Tigris and Euphrates rivers (modern Iraq)

Messias: variant of Messiah

metaphysical: magical

meteor: any atmospheric phenomenon

methinks: it seems to me

mew'd: enclosed

mickle: much

Midas: legendary figure whose touch turned all to gold

Minerva: Roman name for Athena

Minerva . . . Poseidon: Athena and Poseidon strove for the rulership of Athens: he produced the horse, she the olive tree; the victory was awarded to her

minion: male favorite, often with a sexual suggestion

minions, falc'nets, and sakers: small pieces of ordnance

miscreants: those who hold a false religious belief

miss: probably means "loss" at *2 Tamb.,* 4.1.189

mithdridate: poison

minx: prostitute

misgives: is apprehensive

mobile: able to move

Moors: sometimes used of the dark-skinned inhabitants of the New World

Moors . . . whose coal-black faces: the Elizabethans considered the Moors to be black; cf. Othello

Morpheus: the god of sleep

mortal sins: those that lead to damnation

Mort Dieu!: the equivalent of "To Hell!"

mortified: become dead to the world (in a religious sense)

mortified lineaments: afflicted bodily organs

motion: suggestion, idea

moved: emotionally moved, excited

multiply: get wealth

Musaeus: poet who dwelt in the Elysian fields of the underworld; see Book VI of *Aeneid*

muscadine: a strong sweet wine made from muscat grapes (muscatel)

muschatoes: mustache

musketers: soldiers armed with muskets

muster: gather (of soldiers)

napkin: handkerchief

nasty: filthy

nativity: what the stars prognosticate at one's birth, a horoscope

Natolia: the peninsula of Asia Minor (modern Turkey)

nearer: used in expressing human relationships (e.g., nearer in blood)

necessity: that which must occur

nectar and ambrosia: the food and drink of the gods

needs (adv.): of necessity

Neptune: Roman god of the sea (Poseidon)

niggard: cheap fellow

nightly bird: owl

Nigra Silva: black forest near Odessa

Nilus: the Nile river

Ninus: the founder of Nineveh, whose queen, Semiramis, built Babylon

non-plus: perplexity

nosegay: bunch of flowers

nourish'd: encouraged

novel: new

novelty: something new and attractive

Oblia: Olbia, near Nigra Silva, in Scythia

obloquy: disgrace

observations: ceremonies, rites

Octavius: heir of Julius Caesar, later became Augustus, first Roman emperor

Oenon: Paris' wife, who killed herself when he left her for Helen of Troy

of: at; on; concerning

offering: showing purpose

offering-basin: receptacle for collecting alms or other offerings

O lente lente currite noctis equi: O slowly, slowly run, you horses of the night (Ovid)

Olympus: the mountain of the gods

on: concerning

on kai me on: Aristotle's "being and not being"

on's: of his; of us

onset: sudden attack

onus quam gravissimum: a very heavy load

Ops: mother of Jove and wife of Saturn

or: before

Orcus gulf: the mouth of the underworld

ordinance: ordnance, artillery

organons: means

orient: precious or shining

orifex: orifice, opening

Orion: constellation south of Gemini and Taurus

orisons: prayers

Ormus: city on the shores of the Persian gulf, famous for its trade in spices, pearls, etc.

ostler: horse-keeper

o' this order: in this way

out, alas: an exclamation of grief or horror

outface: defy

outhouse: house outside walls of city

out of the way: bewildered

outlandish: foreign

out of doubt: confident

outrageous: violent, fierce

overmatch (n.): at *2 Tamb.,* 3.4.76 it probably, because Tamburlaine is so huge, means "unfair match"

over-peer'd: looked down on (with a pun on peer, i.e., nobleman)

overstretched: drained of money

overwatch'd: wearied by watching

overweighing: overruling

Ovid's flea: "The lascivious *Carmen de pulice,* formerly supposed to be by Ovid" is a production of the late Middle Ages (Greg)

oyster-wife: smelly sea-food seller

pac'd: walked

Padolia: Podalia, Russian province on the Black Sea

pageants: spectacles

pains: labors

painted: bedecked with flowers

pale, English: the territory around Dublin

paramour: beloved one

parbreak: vomit

parcel: necessary part

park-pale: park wall or fence

parle (v.): parley; speak, talk

parley (n.): truce between opposing armies during which a discussion occurs

parliament: theoretically the English parliament contained the three estates: commons, nobles, and clergy; any kind of general meeting

Parma, Prince of: he was Spanish governor-general in the Netherlands 1579-92

Parthia: country southeast of Caspian Sea

partial: biased, prejudiced

pash: smash

pass: occur

pass'd on: judged

passengers: travelers

passes: surpasses, beats anything

passing (adv.): quite

pass . . . not: care not

pass not for: don't take seriously

passionate: emotional

Passover: during it Jews eat unleavened bread

passport: document giving admission

pate: head

pathetical: emotionally moving

Patroclus: dear friend of Achilles

pay . . . home: punish

peers: noblemen

peal of ordinance: shot of artillery

peevish: brainless

Pegasus: mythical winged horse

pelf: money

Penelope: faithful and beautiful wife of Odysseus (Ulysses)

pensions: money

pent: confined

per accidens: a scholastic formula, roughly "indirectly"

Pereat iste: Let him perish

peremptory: finally imperative

pericranium: skull, brain

Per inaequalem motum respectu totius: "because of their unequal motion relative to the whole" (Dean)

period: complete piece or section of writing; end

periwig: peruke, formal wig

perpendicular: line drawn from the zero point or meridian

Persepolis: ancient capital of Persia

personage: appearance

persuasions: arguments

Peter's chair: the papal throne

Phaeton: Apollo's son who was unable to control the horses of the chariot of the sun when he attempted to drive them

Phalaris: Sicilian tyrant who died in the brazen bull in which he had roasted alive his victims

Pharsalia: scene of battle between Julius Caesar and Pompey

Philistine: someone to despise

philosopher's stone: a substance, sought by alchemists, to turn base metals into precious ones

philosophy: learning, sometimes with connotation of magic

Phoebus: the sun (Apollo)

Phrygia: in central and northwest Asia Minor

physic: medical profession; medicine

Phyteus: Pythius, one of Apollo's names

pickadevants: pointed beards

Pierides: the daughters of Pierus contested with the Muses and were transformed to birds after their defeat

pike: long-shafted weapon with a metal head

pill: plunder

pillars: portable pillars used by Wolsey in processions, 3½ to 4 ft. long (O.E.D.)

pin: the peg which fastened the clout to the target

pinch (v.): pain sharply

pinch (n.): a sudden, important occasion; emergency

pinion'd: bound, shackled

pioners: those who dig underground in military operations; trench diggers

pitch: shoulder

pitiful: pitying

plac'd: put in a high place

plage: region, district

plague (v.): treat badly

plain: complain

plainer: complainer

plaint: complaint

plates: silver money

Plato's wondrous year: Cicero computed it as 15,000 years ahead

pleasure: will, inclination

pledge: drink a person's health

plight thy faith: pledge your honor to marry me (a solemn promise in Elizabethan times)

Pluto: god of the underworld or Hades

pointed: appointed

pole: axis of the universe

poles: criminals' heads were

frequently mounted on pikes

policy: Machiavellian underhand or hypocritical procedure; statesmanship

poll: cut off a head

Polypheme: Polyphemus, the huge Cyclops who held Ulysses and his men prisoners

poniard: dagger

Pope Alexander . . . German Frederick: Pope Alexander III (1159-81) excommunicated Barbarossa, Emperor Frederick I, in 1160 and compelled him to acknowledge papal supremacy

Pope Julius swore to princely Sigismond etc.: not historical; Julius I was pope in 4th century, Julius III in 16th, Sigismund reigned 1368-1438

poppy: opium

porpentine: porcupine, which was thought to be able to shoot its quills

port: gate, door

portague: a Portuguese gold coin

portcullis: descending iron gate

Portingale: Portugal

portly: stately

posies: mottoes (the words on a coin)

post: letter-carrier, messenger

post (v.): ride quickly

potion: medicinal drink (e.g., to cause sleep)

pottage: thick soup

powder, with a: quickly

pox: syphilis, used often as a disparaging exclamation

practice: sly stratagem

practise: act (in Elizabethan English often in a pejorative sense)

prates: talks loosely, carelessly, wildly

pray them: beg them, ask them

preachments: sermons

precinct: province

precise: puritanical; religiously strict

precisian: Puritan

prefer: advance in rank

preferr'd: preferentially treated

prejudice (v.): be prejudicial to

prelate: officer of the church

presaging: forecasting, prophesying

presence: throne room (properly, *presence* is the sovereign himself; *in presence* means with the king)

present: immediate

present money: immediate payment

presently: immediately

president: governor

press'd: enlisted (because of money paid)

prest: ready

presumption: supposition

pretend: intend; mean; offer

prevail: avail

prevented of: kept from

preventeth: anticipates

prevention: forestalling, anticipation

primum mobile: in Ptolemaic astronomy the outermost of the ten concentric spheres of the universe; as it moved it caused the other spheres to move

Primus Motor: First Mover (God)

principality: supreme power, i.e., a crown

print: mark

prithee: corruption of "pray thee"

privy (adj.): hidden; private

privy seal: the seal affixed to important documents (cf. *great seal,* the principal seal)

privy signet: the sovereign's own seal

prize: an enemy ship with its contents captured in war

prize: treasure, riches

prize was play'd: test of proficiency in fencing

proceed: do well, prosper

profess: make a particular study of

profession: creed; trade

profession: the act of entering a religious order

progenitor: predecessor; ancestor

progeny: lineage

Progne: she had her husband, Tereus, eat his own child after he had seduced her sister, Philomela

prolocutor: spokesman, advocate

promise: God's promise of finally redeeming the Jews

proof, to the: irrefutably

proper: own (their proper = their own)

proper rooms: rightful places

propterea quod: because

prorex: viceroy

Proserpina: Pluto while in Sicily stole Proserpina (daughter of Ceres, Roman Demeter) and brought her to the underworld

protest: vow

Proteus: marine god who could take various shapes

proud: expensive

Provinces: the United Provinces of the Netherlands

publish'd: announced

puissant: powerful

pull my plumes: metaphorical for "deprive me of my office or dignity"

purchase: win; obtain

purchase (n.): undertaking

purge: evacuate, cleanse (at 2.3.47 of *The Jew of Malta* it means, "to expel contaminated breath")

purg'd: at 2.3.107 the *Jew of Malta* it is a pun, "being declared innocent + being hung"

purifi'd: "no longer mixed, but of one essence, either wholly good or wholly evil" after the Day of Judgment (Greg)

pursuit: end, purpose

put me to my shifts: place me in an intolerable situation

Pygmalion's ivory girl: Galatea, the statue that came alive

Pylades and Orestes: classical close friends

Pyramides: pyramids; obelisk (sg.)

Pythagoras' metempsychosis: the transmigration of souls into other bodies

Quam male conveniunt!: How ill they agree! (Hazelton Spencer)

quandoquidem: since (the first syllable probably conceals a sexual pun)

quarrel: conflict

quarters: pieces of flesh; traitors were hung, drawn, and quartered

quasi vestgiis nostris insistere: as if to tread in our tracks (Dean)

Queen of Heaven: Juno

quell: put down

Quem dies vidit etc.: Whom the morning saw high, the evening sees thrown down

question: talk with

quick: alive

quicksilver: mercury

quiddity: essence

Qui mihi discipulus: "It may seem surprising the author should expect his Clown (or his audience) to recognize in *Qui mihi discipulus* the beginning of a didactic poem, but Lily's *Carmen de moribus* would be as familiar to every grammar-school boy as to Wagner" (Greg)

quinque-angle: five-pointed star

quit: clear (as of a crime)

quit: requite, pay for

quittance: requital

Rabbi: man of great learning (not necessarily Jewish)

race: raze, destroy

rack: machine on which prisoners were tortured by stretching the body

rack: twist, torture, abuse

racking clouds: clouds scudding before the wind

rail: deride loudly

rampiers: ramparts, earthworks

ran at tilt: charged in a joust or tournament

rankle: fester

rape (n.): seizure

rapine: stealing

rapt: deeply engrossed

rate (v.): price

raven: bird of ill-omen, signifying death or misfortune

raw mutton: flesh (i.e., the male member)

Raymond King of Hungary:

unknown to history
raze: scratch; destroy
rebated: blunted
record: recall
recreant: traitor
Rector: head of the university
recure my pain: recover me from my pain
redeem: free
redoubted: dreaded; renowned
re-edified: rebuilt
reflex (v.): turn; reflect
reflexing: reflecting
refluence: ebbing
regent: ruler, governor
regiment: rule
remits: gives up, abandons
remorse: pity
remorseful: pitying
remove: move, change place
remov'd the walls: removed from the walls
renied: renegade (referring to Christians who had given up their faith)
rent: rend; torn
repair: come, go; "camp," at *2 Tamb.,* 2.1.14
repeal: recall
repeal'd: called back
repos'd: placed, put
repute: reckon, consider
requite: pay back
resign: unseal (resignare)
resolve: dissolve
resolve: satisfy; determine; decide upon; relieve of anxiety
resolve me: let me know
respect: particular circumstance
respect (v.): pay attention to
retorqued: twisted inward
reverend: worthy of reverence
Rhadamanth: one of the judges of the underworld
Rhamnis: the temple of Nemesis was at Rhamnus in Attica
Rhode: Roda, in the Duchy of Saxe-Altenburg
Rhodope: Thracian mountain, containing silver mines
ride: lie at anchor
rifle: take away spoils from, plunder
rig: to put a ship in order
riven: broken

Rivo Castiliano!: an inexplicable drinker's cry
road: harbor, haven, roadstead
road: raid
roes: deer
rombelow: meaningless refrain in sailor songs
Rome: at *2 Tamb.,* 2.1.9 it may mean Constantinople
Roscius: a famous Roman actor
round: dance
roundly: successfully
rouse: drive a beast from his lair
rouse (n.): heavy drinking bout
royal monastery: possessing a charter from the king
rude: barbarous; uncivilized
rue: suffer for; repent; pity
ruffs, small: narrow stiff flat collars worn by academics
runagates: renegades; apostates
running banquet: quickly prepared repast
runs: plays music
runs division: rapidly divides long notes into short ones
ruthful: pitiful

Saba: Sheba; a city in Ethiopia
sack: wine, particularly sherry
sack'd: ruined, destroyed
sad: serious, sober
sadness: seriousness
Saenites: nomads
St. Jaques, friars of: Dominicans
sally: rush
salutation: greeting
salute: greet
salve: cure (i.e., pay for)
Samarcanda: Samarkand, north of modern Afghanistan
sarell: seraglio, harem
Saturn: Jove took the rulership from his father, Saturn; astrologically, its influence was saturnine, moody, melancholy
Saturnia: one of Juno's names
satyrs: half-human, half-goat creatures
Sauce-Box: saucy fellow
sauc'd: paid for
saving your reverence: often used before a nasty or dirty remark
savor: smell

Saxon: sometimes means German

'Sblood: corruption of "God's blood"

scab: scurvy fellow

scald (adj.): mean, contemptible

scale: climb

Scalonian: of Ascalon

scambled: scrambled

scathe: injury

science metaphysical: magic

Sclavonians: Slavs

score: account book, tavern reckoning

scour: range over

scutcheon: shield; coat of arms

Scythia: an undefined region in southeast Europe, northeast of the Black Sea

seal: at *Ed. II*, 5.1.89 it probably means "pay for"

seat: cushion; arse

sect: sex

security: defense

securities: safeties

sedge: grasslike plant growing in wet places

see: ecclesiastical seat or region

seld-seen: seldom-seen

Selinus: a Sicilian town

Semele: one of Jupiter's loves, she wanted to see him in his glory and so was destroyed by lightning

Semiramis: Assyrian queen who rebuilt Babylon

sennet: fanfare of trumpets

serge: cheap, homely cloth

serve the turn: be of use; suffice for one's needs

sessions: times when law courts were in session

severally: separately

sexton: church officer in charge of burials, ringing bells, etc.

shadow: image by means of reflection

shadowing: sheltering

shadows: shades of the dead; ghosts, spirits

shag-rag: ragged

shake . . . heels: be hanged

shake off: cast off

shape: direct

shaver: a term of disrepute, from the shaven crowns of monks

shortest northern parallel: the most northerly regions of the globe

shrewd: hard, difficult

shrift: confession

shriv'd: confessed by a priest

shroud: cover; hide from view

sib: relative, relation, wife

sic probo: thus, I prove it—scholastic terminology

silk: silk would be much too sumptuous for scholars' garb —most of the schools had regulations concerning dress

silly: innocent; helpless; inexperienced

silverlings: silver coins

simplest extracts: elemental forms (alchemy)

simplicity: simple-mindedness

sinewy: strong

sing'd: to have the hair burned off

single: solitary, alone

sink: cesspool

Sint mihi dei Acherontis, etc.: "May the Gods of Acheron be favorable to me! Away with the triple deity of Jehovah [i.e., the Trinity]! Spirits of fire, air, water, hail! Prince of the East [Lucifer], Beelzebub monarch of burning hell, and Demogorgon, we ask your grace that Mephostophilis may appear and rise. Why do you linger? By Jehovah, hell, and the holy water which I now sprinkle, and the sign of the cross I now make, and by our vows, may Mephostophilis now rise to do us service" (Boas)

Sinus Arabicus: Arabia

sire: father

Sir Paris: Paris of the Trojan war

sirrah: usually used in Elizabethan times for social inferiors

Sirrah Sauce: saucy fellow

sith: since

situ et tempore: place and time

Si una eademque res legatur duobus, alter rem, alter va-

lorem rei, et cetera: "If one
and the same thing is willed
to two persons, let one take
the thing and the other its
value" (Dean)

slip: pass over without notice

slip: lose

sluice: drainage canal

smart: pain

smock: female undergarment

smoldering: smoking

smooth faces and small ruffs:
"beardless scholars in aca-
demical garb" (Boas)

'Snails: corruption of "By God's
nails" (which wounded Him)

snicle hand too fast: unex-
plained; *snicle* is a dialect
word = to catch in a noose

soft: quiet (an exclamation)

Sol: the sun; astrologically,
giver of richness in a mental
sense

*Solamen miseris socios habuisse
doloris:* misery loves company

soldan: sultan, sovereign of a
Mohammedan country

solemnize: perform appropriate
ceremonies

solicit: intreat

sollars: upper storage rooms

something quail: somewhat
lessened

sophister: wily employer of
false logic

sorer: more strongly

Soria: Syria

sort: arrange

sounds the main: casts anchor

sovereignty: high ability

speculation: study

sped: so treated

speed: prosper, succeed

spheres: eyes, at *2 Tamb.*,
2.3.81

spials: spies

spite of spite: despite opposition

spoil: plunder (i.e., tribute
money)

spoil: rewards to the victor in
battle

spoils: pillage; at *Ed. II,*
2.2.166 probably means "cattle"

sport: frequently in a sexual
sense in Elizabethan usage

Spurca!: Base!

spurn: kick

spy: see, discover

stablish: establish

stall: shop; bench on which
things are set for sale

stamp'd: impressed (as of the
image on a coin)

standard: flag (often on a pole)

standings: positions

stand . . . upon: give importance to

stand with thee: dispute, hag-
gle with you

start: force to move (in hunt-
ing to make an animal come
out of its den or hole)

starting holes: places of refuge

stars: The Elizabethans, on the
whole, were still believers in
astrology, the influence of the
planets and stars on one's
destiny, at birth and afterward

stars have promis'd: astrologically

state: throne; condition; estate; position

states: people of high estate

Statutes Decretal: the body of
ecclesiastical law

stavesacre: larkspur, to kill lice

stay: stop temporarily; await;
cease a conversation

steel (v.): hit; use steel

stem: prow, stern (of a ship)

stifled: choked

still: distill

stilts: crutches

stockfish: dried, salted fish

Stoka: Stoko, in Podalia, a
Russian province on Black
Sea

stole: robe

stomach: hunger

stomach (v.): be angry at, endure with reluctance, dislike

stone: fourteen pounds

store: storage

stoups: brimming measures of
liquor

stout: bold

straight: immediately

strait: strict, severe

Straits: the Strait of Gibraltar

strake: struck

strange: unfriendly

strangers: noncitizens, aliens

stratagem: surprise attack

stricken: struck

strong enough to break a staff: fight with a spear (metaphorical for "be of age")

strumpet: whore, prostitute

stuffed: supported (with money)

Stygian: of the underworld river Styx, whose waters were reputed to be poisonous

Styx, Acheron, Phlegethon: rivers of the underworld

suborn: bribe someone to do an evil act

subscribe: sign one's name

subscribe to: agree with (metaphorically)

substantial: possessing substance

success: result (bad success = ill fortune)

sue: beg (frequently with "to")

suffer: allow

sufferance: patience, endurance; suffering

suit (n.): request

sun and moon as dark . . . winding train: in an eclipse

sunder camps: break camp

superficies: surface

surcharg'd: burdened

surmounts: mounts above

surprise (v.): suddenly attack, without any warning

suscepi . . . provinciam: undertook the task

suspect: suspicion

swain: country person

swell: grow large; get pregnant

sylvan: of a wood, forest

synod: general church council

tackling: rigging of a ship

taint: touch (a technical term of the tiltyard)

take exceptions at: express objections against; dislike

take order: arrange for

tale: full number or amount

tall: brave, robust

Tanais: the Don River

Tanti: so much for that

taratantaras: bugle calls

target: small shield

targeteers: foot soldiers with shields

tartar: dregs

Tartar: Scythian

Tartarean: referring to Tartarus, the underworld

Tartarian: Scythian (adj.)

tax: censure

tell: read; measure; count

temporal: of this world

tend: attend

tender: care for

Tenedos: a small island in the Aegean Sea

termine: end, extremity

terms: appellations, words describing offices

Terrene Sea: Mediterranean Sea

Tesella: a village in Morocco

tester: sixpence

Thebes: Greek city, its walls were supposedly raised by the music of Amphion

theoria: contemplative studies?

Thessalian drugs: Thessaly was considered to be a region of magic and strange potions

Thetis: sea-goddess

thraldom: slavery; imprisonment

thralls: slaves

thrust: thirst?

tice: entice

tickle: excite

tilt (v.): fight

tilt (n.): knightly tournament

timeless: unending; untimely

tinker: a mender of pots and pans

Tisiphon: one of the furies whose heads were covered with snakes

Titus and Vespasian: Roman emperors who conquered Judea in the first century A.D.

to: compared to; for

topless: immeasurably high

torpedo: electric ray (fish)

totter'd: tattered

town-seal: document officially sealed by officers of town

toy: a thing of no importance

trace: travel over

traffic: business

traffic for: bargain for

tragic: in Elizabethan English

= serious, worthy of attention—not necessarily tragic in our sense

train: plot, stratagem, trick

train: procession; group of retainers, retinue

train'd: decoyed, enticed

trance: passage from life to death

trapped: caparisoned, dressed

Trasimene: Lake Trasimene, site of one of Hannibal's victories over the Romans, 217 B.C.

treat: deal with in speech or writing

Trebizon: a medieval empire in northeast Asia Minor, also a city on the Black Sea

Trebizon, Famastro, and Amasia . . . Riso, Sancina: all on the northern seaboard of Asia Minor

trencher: a wooden board holding food

trial: experiment

tributary league: alliance with money payments from one side

trick for a purse: purse-stealing

triple diadem: Pope's tiara

triple-headed dog: Cerberus, at the entrance of the underworld

triple region of the air: lower, middle, and upper parts of the air

triple region of the world: America, Africa, Europe-Asia

triumph: spectacular show or display; victory procession

triumphant: as in a military triumph, a procession to celebrate a victory

troops, in: in great numbers

trophies: signs of victory

tropics, zones, and quarters of the sky: "the tropics (of Cancer and Capricorn) and the five zones in which they (and the polar circles) divide or 'quarter' the heavens" (Greg)

Troth: in truth (an exclamation)

trow: believe, trust

trowls: flows in abundantly

trull: common woman, prostitute

Tully: Cicero

tun: large cask

Turk of tenpence: an unimportant infidel

Turks and Tartars: inhabitants of the Near East and Asia. Tartars=Scythians

turn: requirement, need

turns up: churns

Turnus . . . Aeneas: Turnus warred on Aeneas because the latter married Lavinia, formerly betrothed to Turnus (*Aeneid*)

turtles: turtledoves

Typhon: Typhaon, the father of the winds, whose children were Cerberus, the Hydra, etc.

tyrannies: unrestrained exercises of power

Tyras: Tyros, the Dniester river

unbowel: open with a knife

unconfirm'd: unsteady

uncouth: savage, uncivilized

undermine: the Elizabethans were familiar with setting explosives below the enemy

underwrit: subscribed

Undique mors est: death is everywhere

undo: ruin

unhallow'd: unholy

unkind: unnatural

unnatural: cruel

unpointed: unpunctuated

unrigg'd: without sails and other necessary equipment

unspotted: with unspotted reputations

unvalued: invaluable

ure: use

us'd: accustomed

use: treat; treat roughly; be accustomed to

use: possess for a length of time

usurer: one who charges a very high interest on loans

usury: high repayment

Uz: country in the Near East

vagrant: unattached to any particular country

vail: bend, bow; lower a ship's topsails in token of respect

vailing: lowering, taking off (a hat)

Valdes and Cornelius: German magicians invented by Marlowe

valurous: valuable

vanes: weather vanes

varlet: villain

vassal: serf, slave

vault: underground chamber or passage

venison: in Elizabethan English any kind of meat

venge: revenge

Verna: Varna, seaport in northeast Bulgaria, on Black Sea

vilde: vile

villain: evil person; base fellow (villein)

villeiness: female servant of low condition

vintner: wineseller

Virgo, salve!: Greetings, virgin!

virtue: strength, power, ability (virtú)

virtuous: powerful

voided: emptied

Volga, fifty-headed: Volga, with fifty issues at its mouth

vouchsafe: favor; graciously permit

wafted: carried along

wag: funny fellow

wait on: attend

walled garrisons: soldiers in forts

wan: won

want: are wanting

wanton: loose in behavior, clothes, money, etc.; unrestrained; free

ward: knock aside

warders: guards

ware: merchandise

warning-piece: signal gun

watches of the element: planets (watches = guards)

Water and air, being symbolized in one etc.: "the moist and cold qualities of water (corresponding to the phlegmatic humour) and the moist and hot qualities of air (corresponding to the sanguine humour) argue ill for the temperament which is overbalanced in these directions and lacks the firmness and fierceness due to a just admixture of the bile and choler (earth and fire)" (Ellis-Fermor)

weal: well-being

wean: cause to develop

wear ourselves: strive

wedge: ingot

weeds: clothing (feigned weeds = disguise)

weeneth: thinks

weigh: esteem; consider

welkin: sky

well fare: farewell

well said: well done

Welsh hook: a sharp, hooked instrument with a cross-piece below the blade

Western Isles: China, Japan, etc.

wheel: torture instrument on which victim was stretched while his limbs were broken with an iron bar

when: an exclamation of impatience

whenas: when

whereas: where

while: until

whilom: formerly

whippincrusts: "appears to be a humorous perversion of 'hippocras' (i.e., *vinum Hippocraticum*), a concoction of wine and spices . . .) with a suggestion of 'whipping-cheer'" (Greg)

whit: bit

white leprosy: scaly skin of the leper

why so: an exclamation of agreement

wields: controls

wight: person, individual

Wigmore: Young Mortimer's castle and estate

wild-fire: Greek fire, a military weapon

wilful: perversely obstinate

winter's tale: a fairy tale

wise (n.): manner, way

wist: known

wit: intelligence, mental ability, mental agility

withal: besides, also

Wittenberg: German university, which Luther and Hamlet attended

wonted: accustomed

work: bring about; work for

working: effective, moving (of words)

worldlings: those who follow the things of this world

wot: think, know

wrack: wreckage, ruin

wrack'd: wrecked

wreak it: take vengeance

wreath: circlet for the head

writ: holy book

wroth: angry

wrought: embroidered

Xerxes: Persian king

yoke (v.): hold tightly

youngling: young person

ysprung: sprung (the *y* is a meaningless archaic prefix

Zanzibar: in Ortelius, the western part of Africa

zenith: the point immediately above one

Zoacum: ezecum—Marlowe's account is ultimately from the Koran

Zona Mundi: a mountain range in Tartary

Zounds, Zoons: corruption of "By God's wounds"

Zula: north of the Danube

MERIDIAN BOOKS

published by The World Publishing Company
2231 West 110 Street, Cleveland 2, Ohio

M1 ABINGER HARVEST *by E. M. Forster*
M3 ROUSSEAU AND ROMANTICISM *by Irving Babbitt*
M4 IMPERIALISM AND SOCIAL CLASSES *by Joseph Schumpeter*
M5 WAYWARD YOUTH *by August Aichhorn*
M6 THE PLAYWRIGHT AS THINKER *by Eric Bentley*
M7 THE PHILOSOPHY OF MODERN ART *by Herbert Read*
M8 CREATIVE INTUITION IN ART AND POETRY *by Jacques Maritain*
M9 OUTLINES OF THE HISTORY OF GREEK PHILOSOPHY *by Eduard Zeller*
M10 LANGUAGE AND THOUGHT OF THE CHILD *by Jean Piaget*
M11 SEVEN TYPES OF AMBIGUITY *by William Empson*
M12 ESSAYS ON FREEDOM AND POWER *by Lord Acton*
M13 THE MAN OF LETTERS IN THE MODERN WORLD *by Allen Tate*
M14 THE ORDEAL OF MARK TWAIN *by Van Wyck Brooks*
M15 SEX AND REPRESSION IN SAVAGE SOCIETY *by Branslaw Malinowski*
M16 PRAGMATISM *by William James*
M17 HISTORY AS THE STORY OF LIBERTY *by Benedetto Croce*
M18 NEW DIRECTIONS 15: INTERNATIONAL ISSUE
M19 MATTHEW ARNOLD *by Lionel Trilling*
M20 SHAKESPEAREAN TRAGEDY *by A. C. Bradley*
M21 THE DEVIL'S SHARE *by Denis de Rougemont*
M22 THE HERO WITH A THOUSAND FACES *by Joseph Campbell*
M23 BYZANTINE CIVILIZATION *by Steven Runciman*
M24 ESSAYS AND SKETCHES IN BIOGRAPHY *by John Maynard Keynes*
M25 NIETZSCHE *by Walter Kaufmann*
M26 THE MIND AND HEART OF LOVE *by M. C. D'Arcy*
M27 CONGRESSIONAL GOVERNMENT *by Woodrow Wilson*
M28 TWO ESSAYS ON ANALYTICAL PSYCHOLOGY *by C. G. Jung*
M29 THE WRITINGS OF MARTIN BUBER *edited by Will Herberg*
M30 BERLIOZ AND HIS CENTURY *by Jacques Barzun*
M31 FREEDOM, EDUCATION, AND THE FUND *by Robert M. Hutchins*
M32 A PREFACE TO LOGIC *by Morris R. Cohen*
M33 VISION AND DESIGN *by Roger Fry*
M34 FREUD OR JUNG? *by Edward Glover*
M35 THE MAKING OF EUROPE *by Christopher Dawson*
M36 THE FORMS OF MUSIC *by Donald Francis Tovey*
M37 THE VARIETIES OF HISTORY *edited by Fritz Stern*
M38 THE ESSENCE OF LAUGHTER *by Charles Baudelaire*
M39 EXISTENTIALISM FROM DOSTOEVSKY TO SARTRE *edited by Walter Kaufmann*
M40 ITALIAN PAINTERS OF THE RENAISSANCE *by Bernard Berenson*
M41 SIGHTS AND SPECTACLES *by Mary McCarthy*
M42 MOHAMMED AND CHARLEMAGNE *by Henri Pirenne*

M43 THE WHEEL OF FIRE *by G. Wilson Knight*
M44 GOTHIC ARCHITECTURE AND SCHOLASTICISM *by Erwin Panofsky*
M45 FREUD AND THE 20TH CENTURY *edited by Benjamin Nelson*
M46 POLITICS AND THE NOVEL *by Irving Howe*
M47 A SHORTER HISTORY OF SCIENCE *by William Cecil Dampier*
M48 A GUIDE TO CONTEMPORARY FRENCH LITERATURE *by Wallace Fowlie*
M49 THE RENAISSANCE OF THE 12TH CENTURY *by C. H. Haskins*
M50 NEW POETS OF ENGLAND AND AMERICA *selected by Hall, Pack, and Simpson*
M51 ST. AUGUSTINE: HIS AGE, LIFE, AND THOUGHT
M52 CIVILIZATION ON TRIAL *and* THE WORLD AND THE WEST *by Arnold Toynbee*
M53 RELIGION AND CULTURE *by Christopher Dawson*
M54 PROUST: A BIOGRAPHY *by André Maurois*
M55 ST. THOMAS AQUINAS *by Jacques Maritain*
M56 MEMOIRS OF A REVOLUTIONIST *by Dwight Macdonald*
M57 DEBATES WITH HISTORIANS *by Pieter Geyl*
M58 POLITICS: WHO GETS WHAT, WHEN, HOW *by Harold Lasswell*
M59 GODS AND HEROES OF THE GREEKS *by H. J. Rose*
M60 RELIGION IN AMERICA *edited by John Cogley*
M61 MEN AND IDEAS *by Johan Huizinga*
M62 WITCHCRAFT *by Charles Williams*
M63 SCENES FROM THE DRAMA OF EUROPEAN LITERATURE *by Erich Auerbach*
M64 THE HUMAN MEANING OF THE SOCIAL SCIENCES *edited by Daniel Lerner*
M65 ARISTOTLE *by W. D. Ross*
M66 THE DISINHERITED MIND *by Erich Heller*
M67 THE BOOK OF JAZZ *by Leonard Feather*
M68 THE WORLD OF ODYSSEUS *by M. I. Finley*
M69 THE SCROLLS FROM THE DEAD SEA *by Edmund Wilson*
M70 GREY EMINENCE *by Aldous Huxley*
M71 THE LOGIC OF THE SCIENCES AND THE HUMANITIES *by F. S. C. Northrop*
M72 HISTORY 1
M73 ON MODERN POETS *by Yvor Winters*
M74 THE MAIN STREAM OF MUSIC AND OTHER ESSAYS *by Donald Francis Tovey*
M75 JONATHAN EDWARDS *by Perry Miller*
M76 THE CONFEDERACY *edited by Albert D. Kirwan*
M77 TALENTS AND GENIUSES *by Gilbert Highet*
M78 APES, ANGELS, AND VICTORIANS *by William Irvine*
M79 PAINTING AND REALITY *by Etienne Gilson*
M80 MOZART'S LIBRETTOS *translated by Robert Pack and Marjorie Lelash*
M81 PHILOSOPHY IN THE MIDDLE AGES *by Paul Vignaux*
M82 THE RECOLLECTIONS OF ALEXIS DE TOCQUEVILLE *edited by J. P. Mayer*

M83 HISTORY 2
M84 ON LOVE *by José Ortega y Gasset*
M85 THE ROMANTIC ENLIGHTENMENT *by Geoffrey Clive*
M86 ANSWER TO JOB *by C. G. Jung*
M87 NEWMAN *by Louis Bouyer*
M88 THE NOBLE SAVAGE 1 *edited by Saul Bellow, Keith Botsford, and Jack Ludwig*
M89 AMERICA AND THE IMAGE OF EUROPE *by Daniel J. Boorstin*
M90 PHILOSOPHY OF SCIENCE *edited by Arthur Danto and Sidney Morgenbesser*
M91 AMERICAN FOREIGN POLICY *edited by Robert A. Divine*
M92 DIONYSUS IN PARIS: A GUIDE TO CONTEMPORARY FRENCH THEATER *by Wallace Fowlie*
M93 THE KING AND THE CORPSE *by Heinrich Zimmer*
M94 THE BEDBUG AND SELECTED POETRY *by Vladimir Mayakovsky*
M95 HISTORY 3
M96 GOD AND THE WAYS OF KNOWING *by Jean Daniélou*
M97 AN OUTLINE OF PHILOSOPHY *by Bertrand Russell*
M98 SENATOR JOE MC CARTHY *by Richard H. Rovere*
M99 ON ART AND ARTISTS *by Aldous Huxley*
M100 I REMEMBER *by Boris Pasternak*
M101 A HISTORY OF THE UNITED STATES: FROM THE AGE OF EXPLORATION TO 1865 *edited by Hugh T. Lefler*
M102 THE NOBLE SAVAGE 2 *edited by Saul Bellow, Keith Botsford, and Jack Ludwig*
M103 THE IDEAL READER *by Jacques Rivière*
M104 THE PERSIAN LETTERS *by Montesquieu*
M105 THE AMERICAN PRAGMATISTS *edited by Milton R. Konvitz and Gail Kennedy*
M106 JERUSALEM AND ROME: THE WRITINGS OF JOSEPHUS *edited by Nahum N. Glatzer*
M107 LORD WEARY'S CASTLE *and* THE MILLS OF THE KAVANAUGHS *by Robert Lowell*
M108 THE GRASS ROOTS OF ART *by Herbert Read*
M109 LECTURES ON MODERN HISTORY *by Lord Acton*
M110 THE MEANING AND MATTTER OF HISTORY *by M. C. D'Arcy*
M111 THE AUTOBIOGRAPHY OF EDWARD GIBBON *edited by Dero A. Saunders*
M112 AESTHETICS TODAY *edited by Morris Philipson*
M113 THE NOBLE SAVAGE 3 *edited by Saul Bellow and Keith Botsford*
M114 ENCOUNTERS IN HISTORY *by Pieter Geyl*
M115 A HISTORY OF THE UNITED STATES: FROM 1865 TO THE PRESENT *edited by Frank W. Klingberg*
M116 THE NAZIS: A DOCUMENTARY HISTORY *edited by Walther Hofer*
M117 HISTORY 4
M118 THOMAS MANN: THE IRONIC GERMAN *by Erich Heller*
M119 OUTLINES OF CLASSICAL LITERATURE *by H. J. Rose*

M120 GOD AND THE UNCONSCIOUS *by Victor White*

M121 HELLENISTIC CIVILIZATION *by W. W. Tarn*

M122 A GUIDE TO CONTEMPORARY ITALIAN LITERATURE *by Sergio Pacifici*

M123 THE SUPREME COURT OF THE UNITED STATES *by Paul A. Freund*

M124 THE RENAISSANCE *by Walter Pater*

M125 THE NOBLE SAVAGE 4 *edited by Saul Bellow and Keith Botsford*

M126 THE MERIDIAN COMPACT ATLAS OF THE WORLD

M127 AMERICA IN THE WORLD *edited by Oscar Theodore Barck, Jr.*

M128 THE DECLINE OF THE INTELLECTUAL *by Thomas Molnar*

M129 YEARS OF CONSCIENCE: THE MUCKRAKERS *edited by Harvey Swados*

M130 ESSAYS ON FAITH AND MORALS *by William James*

M131 STEPHEN CRANE *by John Berryman*

M132 THE ROMANTICS *edited by Geoffrey Grigson*

M133 ANARCHISM: A HISTORY OF LIBERTARIAN IDEAS AND MOVEMENTS *by George Woodcock*

M134 HEREDITARY GENIUS *by Francis Galton*

M135 NEW POETS OF ENGLAND AND AMERICA: SECOND SELECTION *edited by Donald Hall and Robert Pack*

M136 THE NOBLE SAVAGE 5 *edited by Saul Bellow and Keith Botsford*

M137 IN PRAISE OF ENLIGHTENMENT *by Albert Salomon*

M138 THE DEATH OF SOCRATES *by Romano Guardini*

MERIDIAN BOOKS

published by The World Publishing Company
2231 West 110 Street, Cleveland 2, Ohio

MERIDIAN GIANTS

MG1   MYSTICISM *by Evelyn Underhill*
MG2   MEDIEVAL PANORAMA *by G. G. Coulton*
MG3   PROLEGOMENA TO THE STUDY OF GREEK RELIGION *by Jane Harrison*
MG4   MY LIFE IN ART *by Constantin Stanislavski*
MG5   THE ROMANTIC AGONY *by Mario Praz*
MG6   PHILOSOPHIES OF INDIA *by Heinrich Zimmer*
MG7   PLATO: THE MAN AND HIS WORK *by A. E. Taylor*
MG8   FRANCE AGAINST HERSELF *by Herbert Luethy*
MG9   THE LITERATURE OF THE SPANISH PEOPLE *by Gerald Brenan*
MG10 FILM FORM *and* THE FILM SENSE *by Sergei Eisenstein*
MG11 LITERATURE IN AMERICA *edited by Philip Rahv*
MG12 THE DISSOCIATION OF A PERSONALITY *by Morton Prince*
MG13 A TREASURY OF YIDDISH STORIES *edited by Irving Howe and Eliezer Greenberg*
MG14 CHINESE CIVILIZATION *by Marcel Granet*
MG15 THE ORIGINS OF TOTALITARIANISM *by Hannah Arendt*
MG16 THE PHILOSOPHY OF SPINOZA *by Harry Austryn Wolfson*
MG17 THE MAN OF THE RENAISSANCE *by Ralph Roeder*
MG18R NEW YORK PLACES & PLEASURES: REVISED EDITION *by Kate Simon*
MG19 THE PLACE OF VALUE IN A WORLD OF FACTS *by Wolfgang Köhler*
MG20 FROM THE N.R.F. *edited by Justin O'Brien*
MG21 JAIL KEYS MADE HERE AND OTHER SIGNS *photographs by Lee Boltin*
MG22 FRANK LLOYD WRIGHT: WRITINGS AND BUILDINGS *selected by Edgar Kaufmann and Ben Raeburn*
MG23 THE CHILDHOOD OF MAN *by Leo Frobenius*
MG24 THE MYSTIC ROSE *by Ernest Crawley*
MG25 WEBSTER'S NEW WORLD DICTIONARY OF THE AMERICAN LANGUAGE (CONCISE EDITION)
MG26A A HISTORY OF THE EARLY CHURCH, Vol. I *by Hans Lietzmann*
MG26B A HISTORY OF THE EARLY CHURCH, Vol. II *by Hans Lietzmann*
MG27 FOLKSONGS AND FOOTNOTES: AN INTERNATIONAL SONGBOOK *by Theodore Bikel*

MG28 THE SOUL AFIRE *edited by H. A. Reinhold*

MG29 AN INTRODUCTION TO THE LITERATURE OF THE OLD TESTA-MENT *by S. R. Driver*

MG30 EARLY GREEK PHILOSOPHY *by John Burnet*

MG31 ROMAN SOCIETY IN THE LAST CENTURY OF THE WESTERN EMPIRE *by Samuel Dill*

MG32 THE HISTORY OF ROME *by Theodor Mommsen*

MG33 THE NEW ARCHITECTURE OF EUROPE: AN ILLUSTRATED GUIDE-BOOK AND APPRAISAL *by G. E. Kidder Smith*

MG34 A DICTIONARY OF CLASSICAL ANTIQUITIES *by Oscar Seyffert*

MG35 PROLEGOMENA TO THE HISTORY OF ANCIENT ISRAEL *by Julius Wellhausen*

MG36 A HISTORY OF AESTHETIC *by Bernard Bosanquet*

MG37 AN ENCYCLOPEDIA OF RELIGION AND RELIGIONS *by E. Royston Pike*

MG38 CLEAR WRITING *by Leo Kirschbaum*

MG39 THE FEDERALIST *edited by Jacob E. Cooke*

MG40 FRENCH PHILOSOPHERS FROM DESCARTES TO SARTRE *edited by Leonard M. Marsak*

MG41 SCIENCE & TECHNOLOGY STOCKS: A GUIDE FOR INVESTORS *by Grant Jeffery*

MG42 THE PLAYS OF CHRISTOPHER MARLOWE *edited by Leo Kirschbaum*

MG43 LOVE AND DEATH IN THE AMERICAN NOVEL *by Leslie A. Fiedler*

MG44 THE ESSENE WRITINGS FROM QUMRAN *by A. Dupont-Sommer*

MG45 A HISTORY OF GERMAN LITERATURE *by Fritz Martini*

MG46A
MG46B } THE VARIETIES OF ECONOMICS *edited by Robert Lekachman*

MG47 THE EVERYDAY AMERICAN SATIRICON *by Samuel Milton Elam*

MERIDIAN BOOKS

published by The World Publishing Company
2231 West 110 Street, Cleveland 2, Ohio

LIVING AGE BOOKS

LA1   AN INTERPRETATION OF CHRISTIAN ETHICS *by Reinhold Niebuhr*

LA2   THE MIND OF THE MAKER *by Dorothy L. Sayers*

LA3   CHRISTIAN MYSTICISM *by W. R. Inge*

LA4   PRIMITIVE CHRISTIANITY IN ITS CONTEMPORARY SETTING *by Rudolf Bultmann*

LA5   THE DESCENT OF THE DOVE *by Charles Williams*

LA6   THE RELIGIOUS SITUATION *by Paul Tillich*

LA7   WHAT MEAN THESE STONES? *by Millar Burrows*

LA8   THE MEANING OF PAUL FOR TODAY *by C. H. Dodd*

LA9   MARTIN LUTHER: ROAD TO REFORMATION *by Heinrich Boehmer*

LA10   RELIGIOUS DRAMA 1: FIVE PLAYS *selected and introduced by Marvin Halverson*

LA11   THE SOCIAL SOURCES OF DENOMINATIONALISM *by H. Richard Niebuhr*

LA12   CHRISTIAN THOUGHT *by Ernest Troeltsch*

LA13   LEAVES FROM THE NOTEBOOKS OF A TAMED CYNIC *by Reinhold Niebuhr*

LA14   MYSTICISM EAST AND WEST *by Rudolf Otto*

LA15   DOSTOEVSKY *by Nicholas Berdyaev*

LA16   THE UNITY OF THE BIBLE *by H. H. Rowley*

LA17   THE SERMONS OF JOHN DONNE *selected and introduced by Theodore Gill*

LA18   A HANDBOOK OF CHRISTIAN THEOLOGY

LA19   ETHICS AND UNITED STATES FOREIGN POLICY *by Ernest Lefever; introduced by Hans Morgenthau*

LA20   RELIGIOUS DRAMA 2: MYSTERY AND MORALITY PLAYS *selected and introduced by E. Martin Browne*

LA21   PETER: DISCIPLE, APOSTLE, MARTYR *by Oscar Cullmann*

LA22   THE FAITH OF THE CHURCH *by Karl Barth*

LA23   AN INTRODUCTION TO THE BOOKS OF THE OLD TESTAMENT *by W. O. E. Oesterley and Theodore H. Robinson*

LA24   A SHORT HISTORY OF CHRISTIANITY *by Martin E. Marty*

LA25   THE CULTURAL SIGNIFICANCE OF THE REFORMATION *by Karl Holl*

LA26   ESSAYS IN APPLIED CHRISTIANITY *by Reinhold Niebuhr*

LA27   RELIGIOUS DRAMA 3 *selected and introduced by Marvin Halverson*

LA28 RELIGION IN THE MAKING *by Alfred North Whitehead*

LA29 EXISTENCE AND FAITH: SHORTER WRITINGS OF RUDOLF BULT-MANN *edited by Schubert M. Ogden*

LA30 REMBRANDT AND THE GOSPEL *by W. A. Visser 't Hooft*

LA31 GOD'S KNOTTY LOG: SELECTED WRITINGS OF JOHN BUNYAN *edited by Henri A. Talon*

LA32 THE PRIVATE DEVOTIONS OF LANCELOT ANDREWES *edited by F. E. Brightman*

LA33 HOW MY MIND HAS CHANGED *edited by Harold E. Fey*

LA34 THE INFIDEL: FREETHOUGHT AND AMERICAN RELIGION *by Martin E. Marty*

LA35 LITURGIES OF THE WESTERN CHURCH *edited by Bard Thompson*

LA36 THE MEANING OF HISTORY *by Nicholas Berdyaev*

LA37 SELECTED WRITINGS OF ST. AUGUSTINE *edited by Roger Hazelton*

MERIDIAN BOOKS

published by The World Publishing Company
2231 West 110 Street, Cleveland 2, Ohio

JEWISH PUBLICATION SOCIETY SERIES

JP1 FOR THE SAKE OF HEAVEN *by Martin Buber*

JP2 STUDENTS, SCHOLARS AND SAINTS *by Louis Ginzberg*

JP3 A HISTORY OF MEDIAEVAL JEWISH PHILOSOPHY *by Isaac Husik*

JP4 JEWISH LIFE IN THE MIDDLE AGES *by Israel Abrahams*

JP5 STUDIES IN JUDAISM *by Solomon Schechter*

JP6 HISTORY OF THE JEWISH PEOPLE *by Max Margolis and Alexander Marx*

JP7 GOD IN SEARCH OF MAN *by Abraham Joshua Heschel*

JP8 INTRODUCTION TO THE TALMUD AND MIDRASH *by Hermann L. Strack*

JP9 KIDDUSH HA-SHEM *and* SABBATAI ZEVI *by Sholem Asch*

JP10 JUDAISM AND MODERN MAN *by Will Herberg*

JP11 PRINCE OF THE GHETTO *by Maurice Samuel*

JP12 A HISTORY OF THE MARRANOS *by Cecil Roth*

JP13 THREE JEWISH PHILOSOPHERS *edited by Hans Lewy, Alexder Altmann, and Isaak Heinemann*

JP14 THE JEW IN THE MEDIEVAL WORLD *by Jacob R. Marcus*

JP15 THE JEW IN THE LITERATURE OF ENGLAND *by Montagu Frank Modder*

JP16 A HISTORY OF THE CONTEMPORARY JEWS *by Solomon Grayzel*

JP17 THE ZIONIST IDEA *edited by Arthur Hertzberg*

JP18 MODERN NATIONALISM AND RELIGION *by Salo W. Baron*

JP19 GERMANY'S STEPCHILDREN *by Solomon Liptzin*

JP20 NATIONALISM AND HISTORY: ESSAYS ON OLD AND NEW JUDAISM *by Simon Dubnow*

JP21 THE CONFLICT OF THE CHURCH AND THE SYNAGOGUE *by James Parkes*

JP22 THE DEVIL AND THE JEWS *by Joshua Trachtenberg*

JP23 JUDAISM AND CHRISTIANITY *by Leo Baeck*

JP24 AMERICAN JEWRY AND THE CIVIL WAR *by Bertram W. Korn*

JP25 AKIBA: SCHOLAR, SAINT AND MARTYR *by Louis Finkelstein*

JP26 ON JEWISH LAW AND LORE *by Louis Ginzberg*

JP27 HEBREW REBORN *by Shalom Spiegel*

MERIDIAN BOOKS

published by The World Publishing Company
2231 West 110 Street, Cleveland 2, Ohio

MERIDIAN FICTION

MF1   THE MANDARINS *by Simone de Beauvoir*
MF2   PICTURES FROM AN INSTITUTION *by Randall Jarrell*
MF3   THE COLLECTED STORIES *by Isaac Babel*
MF4   A LEGACY *by Sybille Bedford*
MF5   GOODBYE, COLUMBUS *by Philip Roth*
MF6   THE MIDDLE AGE OF MRS. ELIOT *by Angus Wilson*
MF7   A LONG DAY'S DYING *by Frederick Buechner*
MF8   THE TOWERS OF TREBIZOND *by Rose Macaulay*
MF9   DANGLING MAN *by Saul Bellow*
MF10 BEASTS AND MEN *and* THE SEED *by Pierre Gascar*
MF11 THE ACCEPTANCE WORLD *by Anthony Powell*
MF12 MEMENTO MORI *by Muriel Spark*
MF13 CARDS OF IDENTITY *by Nigel Dennis*
MF14 THE LITTLE DISTURBANCES OF MAN *by Grace Paley*
MF15 TEMPO DI ROMA *by Alexis Curvers*
MF16 LOVE AND LIKE *by Herbert Gold*
MF17 GOLK *by Richard G. Stern*
MF18 PASSAGE FROM HOME *by Isaac Rosenfeld*
MF19 THE CHARIOTEER *by Mary Renault*
MF20 THE RECOGNITIONS *by William Gaddis*